Microbiology—1982

Microbiology—1982

EDITED BY
DAVID SCHLESSINGER

American Society for Microbiology
Washington, D.C.

1982

LIBRARY OF CONGRESS CATALOG CARD NUMBER 75-331066

ISBN 0-914826-42-5

CONTENTS

Transformation, Transduction, and Bacteriophage

Drug Resistance

Genetics and Physiology

Metabolic and Bacteriocin-Related Plasmids

Development and Use of Recombinant DNA Technology

III. BACTERIAL ADHESION IN PATHOGENESIS

IV. THE MACROPHAGE IN HOST DEFENSE

V. CELL SURFACE RECEPTORS INVOLVED IN THE IMMUNE SYSTEM

Introductory Note

Microbiologists all know that no other organism is known as well as *Escherichia coli* (though few would have predicted that much of our information about molecular biology would come from studies of the intimate details of this minor component of human excrement). Yet, again and again during the last 30 years of triumphs, studies of additional systems have held their own, for at least three reasons. First, organisms have special features of particular interest—the capacity to fix nitrogen or cause disease, for example. Second, the study of additional organisms has repeatedly uncovered new phenomena. Third, comparative studies help to reveal variant and invariant features of cellular processes during evolution.

These three sources of interest are not exclusive. For example, *Bacillus subtilis* is traditionally considered important as the model for bacterial sporulation (see H. S. Levinson, A. L. Sonenshein, and D. J. Tipper, ed., *Sporulation and Germination*, American Society for Microbiology, 1981). But the enclosed Proceedings of the U.S.-Japan Cooperative Science Project on "The *Bacillus subtilis* Chromosome: Structure, Replication, Modification, and Molecular Cloning" also clarify and explore intriguing alternatives to the *E. coli* paradigm for every level of gene organization and expression. Examples are the possible function of chromosome association with the membrane; the metabolism of transforming DNA in cells; the sequence classes of promoters, and the modified promoter selection by RNA polymerase in the presence of different cellular or phage polypeptides; the distinctive organization of rRNA genes; the factors required for initiation of protein synthesis—and so on.

The accounts of the ASM International Conference on Streptococcal Genetics provide examples just as striking. These organisms were originally studied because of their disease-causing potential. But the early work also gave rise to molecular genetics, and the latest work has produced discoveries of pheromone-mediated plasmid transfer and the function of virulence factors.

As for the power of comparative studies, a notable example is provided by the proceedings of the ASM Conference on Bacterial Adhesion in Pathogenesis. The problem addressed is the basis of tropisms. The current notion is that tropism results from "adhesion," based on special cell surface interactions. These interactions are now being analyzed, tested, and compared in detail (see the contribution by S. C. Holt for a partial summary).

Cell surface interactions are also the topic of two fascinating seminars which conclude this volume. They relate to the interaction of pathogens and the immune system ("The Macrophage in Host Defense") and to the intricate interactions in the immune system itself ("Cell Surface Receptors Involved in the Immune System").

David Schlessinger

I. THE *BACILLUS SUBTILIS* CHROMOSOME: STRUCTURE, REPLICATION, MODIFICATION, AND MOLECULAR CLONING

(U.S./Japan Cooperative Science Project, 23–25 March 1981, Department of Cellular Biology, Research Institute of Scripps Clinic, La Jolla, California. Submitted to the Japan Society for the Promotion of Science.)

Isolation of *Bacillus subtilis* Genes from Charon Libraries

EUGENIO FERRARI, FRANCO FERRARI, DENNIS LANG, DENNIS HENNER, AND JAMES A. HOCH

Department of Cellular Biology, Research Institute of Scripps Clinic, Scripps Clinic and Research Foundation, La Jolla, California 92037

Several attempts have been made to prepare a plasmid library representative of the *Bacillus subtilis* genome by cloning restriction fragments or sheared fragments of *B. subtilis* DNA in *Escherichia coli* plasmids (5, 7; unpublished data from this laboratory). A number of problems have been encountered with this approach that lead to a less than random assortment of relatively small genomic fragments in the final library (5; unpublished data from this laboratory). Our goal was to prepare a cloned library of high-molecular-weight *B. subtilis* DNA that contained a close to random assortment of genomic fragments which would allow rapid identification and isolation of desired areas of the chromosome. To meet these requirements, we turned to the λ system. The cloning vector used was the modified λ phage Charon 4A and Charon 30 (2, 8).

The method of preparation of the *B. subtilis* DNA inserts to be cloned turned out to be crucial to obtain a close to random representation. Charon 4A libraries prepared from inserts generated by partial *Eco*RI digestion were found to contain only about 30% of the chromosomal regions tested (unpublished data). We believe this results from preferential cleavage by the *Eco*RI endonuclease at nonrandom sites on the chromosome (9). To overcome this problem, our strategy was to treat the chromosomal DNA with limiting *Eco*RI methylase followed by complete *Eco*RI endonuclease digestion, under the premise that *Eco*RI methylase would methylate *Eco*RI sites at random. High-molecular-weight *B. subtilis* 168 DNA was partially methylated for different times with *Eco*RI methylase, digested to completion with *Eco*RI endonuclease, and fractionated on a sucrose gradient. The fractions containing fragments from 13 to 20 kilobases were pooled and ligated with the purified arms of the vector (4). The Charon 30 library was prepared by partial digestion of high-molecular-weight chromosomal DNA with *Sau*3A, separation of the 13- to 20-kilobase fragments on a sodium chloride gradient, and ligation of this fraction to purified arms of Charon 30 (manuscript in preparation).

To test the library prepared by the partial methylation method, we picked and replated 1,710 individual plaques. The plaques were stored on 19 master plates of about 90 individual plaques. Replicates of these master plates were then used for subsequent manipulations. The 19 master plates were replated to confluent lysis on several plates, the phage were collected, and DNA was extracted. This method allows an entire pool of 90 plaques to be checked by transformation (1) for a desired marker and rapidly locates the marker of interest to a master plate. The DNA extracted from the plate lysate of the 19 individual pools was used to transform competent *B. subtilis* cells for 21 auxotrophic and sporulation markers scattered around the chromosome. Among the 1,710 plaques we were able to find the following loci: *spo0A*, *spo0B*, *aroI*, *dal*, *glnA*, *leuA*, *lys-1*, *metB*, *metC*, *pheA*, *purA*, *purB*, *pyrD*, *tms-26*, *sacB*, *gut*, and *aroD*.

rRNA genes, screened by hybridization to labeled rRNA, were found in 6 of 1,710 plaques or approximately 1 in 300 plaques. On the basis of their size and number, one would expect about 1 rRNA operon in 100 plaques (3), but since they are clustered (6), a reduced frequency might be expected. We were successful in detecting the presence of about 70% of the loci we screened. It is possible we were unable to detect the presence of some of the markers because of the poor transformability of the marker tested. The absence of some markers and the varying numbers of others in the sample tested suggest that this library is not completely random.

A number of areas of the *B. subtilis* chromosome have now been extensively mapped by use of restriction endonucleases and cloned fragments from the Charon 4A and Charon 30 libraries (J. A. Hoch et al., manuscripts in preparation). Several conclusions about the nature of *B. subtilis* libraries in Charon phage have resulted from these studies. Transformation of *B. subtilis* with cloned DNA is highly efficient when insert-containing Charon phage is used. The intact phage particle seems to be as efficient in trans-

[1] Present address: Istituto di Genetica, 27100 Pavia, Italy.

formation as extracted DNA, and transformation by the intact particle is insensitive to DNase (4). Neither the Charon 4A nor the Charon 30 library is a random collection of chromosomal fragments. This nonrandomness appears to result from regions of the chromosome that cannot be cloned. This may be caused by strong promoters or lethal genes on these regions that prevent a productive lytic cycle of the phage.

ACKNOWLEDGMENTS

This research was supported in part by Public Health Service grants GM19416 and GM25891 from the National Institute of General Medical Sciences. D.J.H. was the recipient of National Research Service Award GM07576, awarded by the National Institute of General Medical Sciences.

Shu Mie H. Chen provided excellent technical assistance.

LITERATURE CITED

1. **Anagnostopoulos, C., and J. Spizizen.** 1961. Requirements for transformation in *Bacillus subtilis*. J. Bacteriol. **81:**741–746.
2. **Blattner, F. R., B. G. Williams, A. E. Bleehl, K. D. Thompson, H. E. Faber, L. A. Furlong, D. J. Grunwald, D. O. Kiefer, D. D. Moore, J. W. Schumm, E. L. Sheldon, and O. Smithies.** 1977. Charon phage: safer derivatives of bacteriophage lambda for DNA cloning. Science **196:**161–169.
3. **Clarke, L., and J. Carbon.** 1976. A colony bank containing synthetic Col E1 hybrid plasmids representative of the entire *E. coli* genome. Cell **99:**91–99.
4. **Ferrari, E., D. Henner, and J. A. Hoch.** 1981. Isolation of *Bacillus subtilis* genes from a Charon 4A library. J. Bacteriol. **146:**430–432.
5. **Hutchison, K. W., and H. O. Halvorson.** 1980. Cloning of randomly sheared DNA fragments from a φ105 lysogen of *Bacillus subtilis*: identification of prophage-containing clones. Gene **8:**267–278.
6. **Moran, C. P., and K. F. Bott.** 1979. Restriction enzyme analysis of *Bacillus subtilis* ribosomal ribonucleic acid genes. J. Bacteriol. **140:**99–105.
7. **Rapoport, G., A. Klier, A. Billault, F. Fargette, and R. Dedonder.** 1979. Construction of a colony bank of *E. coli* containing hybrid plasmids representative of the *Bacillus subtilis* 168 genome. Expression of functions harbored by the recombinant plasmid in *B. subtilis*. Mol. Gen. Genet. **176:**239–246.
8. **Rimm, D. L., D. Horness, J. Kucera, and F. R. Blattner.** 1980. Construction of caliphage lambda Charon vectors with *Bam*HI cloning sites. Gene **12:**301–309.
9. **Thomas, M., and R. W. Davis.** 1975. Studies on the cleavage of bacteriophage lambda DNA with *Eco*RI restriction endonucleases. J. Mol. Biol. **91:**315–328.

Recombination Between Phage and Plasmid Vectors in *Bacillus subtilis*

HIUGA SAITO, HIROYUKI ANZAI, TOURU MIZUKAMI, HIDENORI SHIMOTSU, AND FUJIO KAWAMURA

Institute of Applied Microbiology, The University of Tokyo, Bunkyo-ku, Tokyo 113, Japan

The *Bacillus subtilis* bacteriophages PBS1 and AR9 have been known to transduce certain plasmids, although the frequency is low (1), and many temperate bacteriophages are incapable of such transduction. Recently, Marrero and Lovett (6) reported that cloning DNA fragments of φ105 or SP02 genome into plasmids rendered the chimeric derivatives susceptible to transduction specifically by the phage whose DNA was present in the chimera.

We have constructed derivatives of a temperate phage ρ11 and a plasmid pUB110, both of which have inserted homologous DNA of *B. subtilis* chromosomal fragments generated by restriction endonuclease cleavage. We find that the chimeric plasmid can be transduced by the ρ11 derivative. Examination of the pattern of endonuclease restriction sites on the transducing phage genome suggests that the entire plasmid is inserted in the phage chromosome by means of a Campbell-like recombination event.

The temperate phage ρ11*phisA1⁻* was derived from the specialized transducing phage ρ11*phisA⁺*, which had been constructed by the prophage transformation method (4, 5). *B. subtilis* PS9-24 (*purB6 metB5 hisA1 leuA8 trpC2*) previously lysogenized with ρ11*phisA⁺* was transformed to Ade⁺ by using a saturation amount of DNA from *B. subtilis* PS9-16 (*metB5 hisA1 leuA8 trpC2*). About 1,000 Ade⁺ transformants were examined for the His⁻ character, and one His⁻ strain was obtained by transformation of the prophage *hisA⁺* site. The addition of

mitomycin C to induce the prophage of this strain yielded ρ11*phisA1⁻* with the *hisA1⁻* gene on the 3.3-megadalton (Md) *Eco*RI fragment. The size of this fragment equaled that of the *Eco*RI fragment in the parental ρ11*phisA⁺* genome.

A derivative of plasmid pUB110 was constructed as follows. *Eco*RI fragments with the *hisA⁺* gene from ρ11*phisA⁺* were ligated with *Eco*RI-cleaved pUB110 DNA to form 6.3-Md pUBHA81. When a *B. subtilis* strain (*hisA1*) was transformed to kanamycin resistance (Km^r) by pUBHA81 DNA, one of the transformants, which became His⁻, was found to contain 4.1-Md pUBHA31. The new plasmid, pUBHA31, had lost a part of its *hisA* gene by a 2.2-Md deletion but retained its wild-type DNA sequence corresponding to the *hisA1⁻* mutation site (termed *hisA1⁺*).

We then constructed a strain containing pUBHA31, designated as UOT0459 [*hisA1 metB5* (pUBHA31)], and lysogenized this strain with ρ11*phisA1⁻* or with wild-type ρ11. Transduction of the plasmid was then tested with the

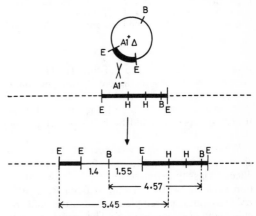

FIG. 1. Expected integration model. Thin line, pUB110; thick line, *B. subtilis* chromosomal DNA with the *hisA* gene; dashed line, phage ρ11 genome; E, *Eco*RI; B, *Bgl*II; H, *Hin*dIII. Numbers indicate molecular weights in millions.

TABLE 1. Transfer of plasmid pUBHA31 into a Rec⁺, *recE4*, or *Bsu*B recipient

Phage or recipient	Transduction of Km^r per PFU
Phage	(into Rec⁺)
ρ11 wild type	6.0×10^{-8}
ρ11*phisA1⁻*	8.0×10^{-5}
Recipient	(with ρ11*phisA1⁻*)
Rec⁺	6.0×10^{-5}
recE4	2.6×10^{-6}
*Bsu*B	6.0×10^{-6}

5

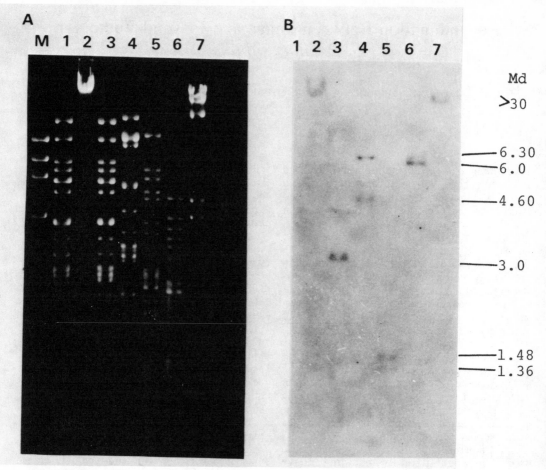

FIG. 2. Analysis of DNA from the transducing phages by (A) agarose gel electrophoresis and (B) hybridization with nick-translated pUB110. Lane M: φ105 DNA EcoRI digest used as a reference. Lane 1: ρ11phisA⁺-EcoRI digest (control). Lane 2: Undigested transducing phage DNA. Lanes 3–7 are digests of transducing phage DNA: 3, EcoRI digest; 4, BglII digest; 5, EcoRI and BglII double digest; 6, HindIII digest; 7, SalI digest. Numbers indicate calculated molecular weights in millions.

lysates of these lysogens (Table 1). The wild-type ρ11 was almost incapable of transduction of the plasmid, but ρ11phisA1⁻ performed transduction at a relatively high frequency. All these transductants contained both the prophage and the plasmid.

When the recipient was recombination deficient (recE4), transduction efficiency was reduced to less than one-tenth (Table 1). A restriction system, BsuB, introduced from B. subtilis IAM1247 into the recipient (3) also reduced the efficiency of transduction. The cause of this reduction may be the sensitivity of ρ11 DNA to the endonuclease BsuB; however, the resulting transductant did not have the prophage ρ11phisA1⁻. All the plasmids thus transduced

were equal in size to the parental pUBHA31.

Since the wild-type ρ11 did not transduce the plasmid, we cloned segments of the host chromosome and inserted them into phage and plasmid, rendering the derivatives susceptible to transduction. The properties of this transduction system indicate that the process should be recombinational insertion of plasmids into the phage genomes (Fig. 1). As a direct demonstration of insertion, we subjected phage DNA from the plasmid-containing lysogen to restriction and hybridization analyses. Fragments of the phage genome, generated by cleavage with restriction endonucleases, were separated electrophoretically and transferred to nitrocellulose. To visualize fragments containing the original plasmid pUB110, we exposed the nitrocellulose strips to the pUB110 probe, which had been nick-translated with [α-^{32}P]dATP (Fig. 2).

The insertion event of Fig. 1 predicts that, in transducing phage DNA, the EcoRI fragment of 2.95 Md, the BglII fragments of 4.57 Md and another fragment determined by a ρ11 BglII site, and the HindIII fragment determined by a ρ11 HindIII site (larger than 5.45 Md) should contain the pUB110 sequence. Double digestion with EcoRI and BglII should generate the 1.4- and 1.55-Md fragments containing the pUB110 sequence. The results of hybridization shown in Fig. 2 fit all these predictions and thus indicate that pUBHA31 is being inserted by means of a Campbell-like recombination event into the ρ11phisA1$^-$ genome. The similar recombination event between a B. subtilis chromosome and a nonreplicating plasmid containing a host chromosome fragment was reported by Haldenwang et al. (2).

The recombinant shown in Fig. 1 can be classified into two categories in terms of the hisA1 site: one is dhisA1$^-$–hisA$^+$, and the other is dhisA1$^+$–hisA1$^-$ (dhisA1$^+$ means the presence of a wild-type sequence for the hisA1$^-$ mutation site, accompanied by partial deletion of the hisA$^+$ gene). When a lysate from the lysogen UOT0459 (pUBHA31) was used to transduce the Km^r marker into a hisA1$^-$ (Rec$^+$) strain used as the recipient, about 13% of the Km^r transductants were His$^-$. The plasmids contained in these transductants were equal in size to pUBHA31, but the hisA1$^+$ sites changed to hisA1$^-$. These results suggest that, during multiplication, the two types of phage genomes (namely, dhisA1$^-$–hisA$^+$ and dhisA1$^+$–hisA1$^-$) were subjected to recombination generating a new type of phage genome with the dhisA1$^-$–hisA1$^-$ fragments. Insertion of plasmids into the ρ11phisA1$^-$ genome also seemed to occur after induction of the prophage. Thus, formed recombinant phages of a certain class can transduce the Km^r trait, but the transduced plasmid has a hisA1$^-$ site instead of hisA1$^+$.

These processes may be available for exchanging markers between phages and plasmids. This technique would be particularly useful for transferring a recessive deficiency trait into multicopy plasmids.

ACKNOWLEDGMENTS

Part of this study was supported by the Science and Technology Agency in Japan by contract with a special fund for multi-ministerial projects.

LITERATURE CITED

1. **Gryczan, T. J., S. Contente, and D. Dubnau.** 1978. Characterization of *Staphylococcus aureus* plasmids introduced by transformation into *Bacillus subtilis*. J. Bacteriol. **134:**318–329.

2. **Haldenwang, W. G., C. D. B. Banner, J. F. Ollington, R. Losick, J. A. Hoch, M. B. O'Connor, and A. L. Sonenshein.** 1980. Mapping a cloned gene under sporulation control by insertion of a drug resistance marker into the *Bacillus subtilis* chromosome. J. Bacteriol. **142:**90–98.

3. **Ikawa, S., T. Shibata, T. Ando, and H. Saito.** 1980. Genetic studies on site-specific endodeoxyribonucleases in *Bacillus subtilis*: multiple modification and restriction systems in transformants of *Bacillus subtilis* 168. Mol. Gen. Genet. **177:**359–368.

4. **Kawamura, F., H. Saito, H. Hirochika, and Y. Kobayashi.** 1980. Cloning of sporulation gene, *spo0F*, in *Bacillus subtilis* with ρ11 phage vector. J. Gen. Appl. Microbiol. **26:**345–355.

5. **Kawamura, F., H. Saito, and Y. Ikeda.** 1979. A method for construction of specialized transducing phage ρ11 of *Bacillus subtilis*. Gene **5:**87–91.

6. **Marrero, R., and P. S. Lovett.** 1980. Transductional selection of cloned bacteriophage φ105 and SP02 deoxyribonucleic acids in *Bacillus subtilis*. J. Bacteriol. **143:**879–886.

Bacillus subtilis α-Amylases: Regulation of Production and Molecular Cloning

KUNIO YAMANE AND SHOJI SHINOMIYA

Institute of Biological Sciences, The University of Tsukuba, Sakura, Ibaraki 305, and Institute of Applied Microbiology, The University of Tokyo, Bunkyo-ku, Tokyo 113, Japan

REGULATION OF α-AMYLASE PRODUCTION AND GENETIC CONSTRUCTION OF EXTRAHYPERPRODUCERS OF α-AMYLASE

α-Amylase is one of the major extracellular enzymes of *Bacillus subtilis*. This enzyme's structural gene (*amyE*) maps near the *aroI* locus on the chromosome according to genetic analysis of α-amylase–defective mutants (5, 8, 9). The gene order around *amyE* is *lin-2–tmrA7–amyR–amyE–tmrB8–aroI906*, as shown in Fig. 1.

The process by which α-amylase accumulates in the surrounding medium involves two essential steps: first, formation of the enzyme proteins or precursor peptides inside the cells or at some sites in the cell membrane, and second, excretion of the enzyme molecules from cells into the medium (including the maturation process of the enzyme proteins). Possibly, the production of extracellular enzymes may involve specific processes that are not required for the production of intracellular enzymes. This consideration suggests that more kinds of gene products participate in the production of extracellular enzymes than in that of intracellular enzymes.

Genes causing hyperproduction of α-amylase may be regulatory genes, and mutations in these genes have been obtained either by selection under different conditions after treatment of the bacterial cells with mutagenic agents or by transformation of cells with DNA extracted from naturally occurring strains with hyperproduction of α-amylase. These regulatory genes were separated into two groups. One group involves the regulatory genes *amyR*, *tmrA7*, and others that are specific for α-amylase production. These mapped near *amyE* (Fig. 1). *tmrA7* is a tunicamycin-resistant mutant that simultaneously expresses hyperproduction of α-amylase. The other group of genes stimulates production of α-amylase and protease at the same time. One of the latter regulatory genes, *pap-9*, mapped near the *hisA* locus (7) and showed a pleiotropic phenotype (hyperproduction of extracellular α-amylase, neutral protease, alkaline protease,

and levansucrase; lack of flagella and transformability) by a single-point mutation.

To study relationships among these regulatory genes, we combined them in one cell by DNA-mediated transformation. They showed a clear synergistic effect on the production of α-amylase. For example, *amyR2* and *pap-9* individuals produced only 4 to 5 times and 2 to 3 times more α-amylase, respectively, than the recipient strain of 6160, but transformants with the two regulatory genes produced 12 to 15 times more α-amylase. Based on this consideration, it appears likely that at least six regulatory genes for α-amylase production accumulated in one cell during the stepwise, DNA-mediated transformation and mutation shown diagrammatically in Fig. 2. Enzyme production by these bacterial cells increased at each step and reached, at the stage of T2N26 formation, more than 1,500 times as much α-amylase as the original strain, 6160. An individual gene or genes, or the absence of one or more of the regulatory genes in T2N26, could not bring about such enzyme-producing power. Thus, it seems likely that these six regulatory genes worked coordinately in different steps throughout the enzyme's formation and secretion process (2).

MOLECULAR CLONING OF THE *B. SUBTILIS* α-AMYLASE STRUCTURAL GENE (*amyE*) IN PHAGE ρ11

amyE+ maps between *tmrA7* and *tmrB8* (Fig. 1). The transformation relationships in *tmrA7-amyE+* and *amyE+-tmrB8* were completely lost when *B. subtilis* chromosomal DNA was digested with a restriction endonuclease, *Eco*RI. On the other hand, 3 to 5% of the cotransformation frequency of AroI+ with AmyE+ and 20 to 25% of that of TmrA with AmyE+ remained when the DNA was digested with *Bam*HI and *Sal*I, respectively. *aroI+* was used as the direct selection marker because, like other α-amylase-defective strains, AmyE− could grow on starch as the sole carbon source and so was ineffective in this experiment. A DNA fragment containing *aroI+* and *amyE+* was integrated into *B. subtilis*

8

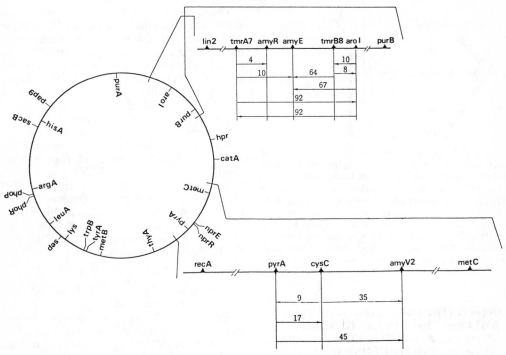

FIG. 1. Genetic map of structural genes for B. subtilis α-amylase ($amyE^+$) and for thermostable α-amylase ($amyV2^+$). Genes outside the circle are structural genes for extracellular enzymes and regulatory genes related to the production of extracellular enzymes. Genes inside the circle are genetic markers based on the B. subtilis map of Henner and Hoch (1). Numbers are expressed distances determined by DNA-mediated transformation. Arrows point from selected to unselected markers.

temperate phage ρ11 DNA through two steps. In the first step, an EcoRI-cleaved DNA fragment (molecular weight, 6×10^6 to 7×10^6) that contained $tmrB8\text{-}aroI^+$ was cloned in ρ11 DNA by the method of Kawamura et al. (3). In the second step, $aroI^-$ derivatives of the ρ11 were isolated by DNA-mediated transformation, and the $amyE^+\text{-}aroI^+$ DNA fragment (molecular weight, 10×10^6 to 20×10^6) digested with BamHI was cloned in the phage DNA.

The transducing activities of $AroI^+$ and $AmyE^+$ by the isolated phage $ρ11damyE^+aroI^+$ are shown in Table 1. More than 90% of the $AroI^+$ transductants are $AmyE^+$. Another specialized transducing phage strain, $ρ11lys^+$, and wild-type phage, ρ11, transduced only Lys^+ and Thy^+ traits, respectively. The transducing phages were purified by CsCl equilibrium centrifugation, after which DNAs were extracted from them and transferred into $aroI^-$ $amyE^-$ strain 207-21. The cotransformation frequency of $AroI^+$ with $AmyE^+$ was approximately 40%, which corresponds to the frequency determined by chromosomal DNA. These results indicate that $amyE^+$ and $aroI^+$ were actually cloned in the specialized transducing phage strain (4).

The strain lysogenic for $ρ11damyE^+aroI^+$ produced amounts of α-amylase similar to those produced by the parental strain, more than 90% of which was secreted into the surrounding medium.

Partial diploids in the α-amylase structural gene were constructed by the transfer of a different type of B. subtilis α-amylase into the chromosome of a strain lysogenic for $ρ11damyE^+aroI^+$, in which α-amylases coded by chromosomal $amyEn^+$ and the phage $amyEm^+$ were distinguished in 7.5% polyacrylamide disc gel electrophoresis at pH 8.3. At the same time, regulatory genes were introduced into the chromosome of the partial diploids, and their effect on the production of each α-amylase was studied. Regulatory genes, $tmrA7$ and $amyR$, did not stimulate α-amylase production by the phage $amyEm^+$. This result suggests that $amyR$ and $tmrA7$ are promoter- or operator-like for the α-amylase structural gene. On the other hand, the $pap\text{-}9$ mutation enhanced the production of both types of α-amylase (K. Yamane et al., unpublished data).

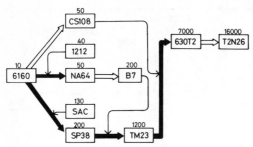

FIG. 2. Diagram showing the stepwise increase of α-amylase production in *B. subtilis* through mutation (white thick arrows) and by DNA-mediated transformation (black thick arrows) during construction of the T2N26 strain, an extrahyperproducer of α-amylase. The names of strains are given in rectangles, and the numbers above them represent the production of α-amylase. The thin arrows leading to black thick arrows imply that DNAs obtained from donor strains were transferred into the recipient strains.

INTEGRATION OF A THERMOSTABLE α-AMYLASE STRUCTURAL GENE (*amyV2*⁺) INTO THE *B. SUBTILIS* CHROMOSOME AND ITS CLONING

By using a donor DNA from a thermophilic bacterium, Thermophile V2, and a DNA recipient strain of the mesophilic bacterium *B. subtilis* 207-21 that had lost its modification and restriction system, a *B. subtilis* transformant, 207-SV1, producing thermostable α-amylase was isolated (6). The α-amylase did not cross-react with rabbit antiserum against *B. subtilis* α-amylase, and its enzymatic properties were different from those of *B. subtilis* α-amylase. The structural gene for the thermostable α-amylase was named *amyV2*⁺ and mapped near the *pyrA* region, but did not cotransform with *aroI*⁺. The chromosomal gene order around *amyV2*⁺ was *recA-pyrA-cysC-amyV2*⁺-*metC* (Fig. 1).

The growth rate of 207-SV1 was not thermostable. The strain did not grow at 55°C or higher temperatures as did *B. subtilis*. Furthermore, extracellular proteases, cell-bound alkaline phosphatase, and phosphodiesterase of 207-SV1 were not thermostable. These results indicated that the thermostability found in the α-amylase of 207-SV1 was encoded in the *amyV2*⁺ gene.

The cotransformation frequency of *cysC*⁺ with *amyV2*⁺ was approximately 65%. The transformation relationships between the two genes were lost after the DNA from a *cysC*⁺ *amyV2*⁺ derivative of 207-SV1 was digested with *Eco*RI, *Bam*HI, and *Bgl*II. However, 25% and 15% of the relationships remained after the DNA was digested with *Sal*I and *Hin*dIII, respectively. A specialized transducing phage, ρ11p*cysC*⁺, was isolated by using DNA fragments digested completely with *Hin*dIII; a ρ11p*cysC*⁻ derivative was prepared, and then ρ11d*cysC*⁺*amyV2*⁺ was constructed by using DNA fragments digested partially with *Hin*dIII.

The lysates prepared in the presence of helper phages exhibited CysC⁺ transducing activity; moreover, more than 95% of CysC⁺ transductants were AmyV2⁺ (Table 1). After *cysC*⁺ and *amyV2*⁺ transducing phage particles were purified by CsCl equilibrium centrifugation, DNA was extracted from the preparation and transferred into a *cysC*⁻ *amyV2*⁻ strain. The cotransformation frequency of CysC⁺ with AmyV2⁺ was approximately 65%. These results indicate that *cysC*⁺ and *amyV2*⁺ were cloned in the transducing phage ρ11d*cysC*⁺*amyV2*⁺ (5a).

Since α-amylase is a typical extracellular enzyme, it is quite possible that the structural gene for this enzyme contains a DNA sequence for a signal to excrete the enzyme into the surrounding medium. We might use regulatory genes and a suitable DNA sequence for the signal in *amyE*⁺ and *amyV2*⁺ to direct the synthesis and secretion of various hybrid proteins in *B. subtilis*.

TABLE 1. Transducing activity of specialized transducing phage strains and wild-type ρ11

Phage strain	Recipient strain[a]	No. of transductants per ml of lysates			Score for Amy⁺ transductants		
		AroI⁺	CysC⁺	Lys⁺	AmyE⁺/AroI⁺	AmyV2⁺/CysC⁺	Amy⁺/Lys⁺
ρ11d*aroI*⁺*amyE*⁺	207-21	4 × 10⁶	—[b]	0	37/40	—	—
ρ11d*cysC*⁺*amyV2*⁺	M07-S1C	—	4 × 10⁴	—	—	65/67	—
ρ11*lys*⁺	207-21	2	—	6 × 10⁷	—	—	0/100
ρ11 wild type	207-21	0	—	0	—	—	—
None	207-21	0	—	0	—	—	—

[a] *B. subtilis* 207-21 (*lys-21, leuA8, metB5, aroI906, amyE07, r₁₆₈⁻ m₁₆₈⁻*). *B. subtilis* M07-S1C (*pyrA, cysC, amyE07*).

[b] —, Not determined.

ACKNOWLEDGMENTS

This work was supported in part by Grants-in-Aid for Scientific Research from the Ministry of Education, Science and Culture, Japan.

LITERATURE CITED

1. **Henner, D. J., and J. A. Hoch.** 1980. The *Bacillus subtilis* chromosome. Microbiol. Rev. **44:**57–82.
2. **Hitotsuyanagi, K., K. Yamane, and B. Maruo.** 1979. Stepwise introduction of regulatory genes stimulating production of α-amylase into *Bacillus subtilis*: construction of α-amylase over-producing strains. Agric. Biol. Chem. **43:**2343–2349.
3. **Kawamura, F., H. Saito, and Y. Ikeda.** 1979. A method for construction of specialized transducing phage ρ11 of *Bacillus subtilis*. Gene **5:**87–91.
4. **Nomura, S., K. Yamane, T. Masuda, F. Kawamura, T. Mizukami, H. Saito, A. Takatsuki, M. Yamasaki, G. Tamura, and B. Maruo.** 1979. Construction of transducing phage ρ11 containing α-amylase structural gene of *Bacillus subtilis*. Agric. Biol. Chem. **43:**2637–2638.
5. **Nomura, S., K. Yamane, T. Sasaki, M. Yamasaki, G. Tamura, and B. Maruo.** 1978. Tunicamycin-resistant mutants and chromosomal locations of mutational sites in *Bacillus subtilis*. J. Bacteriol. **136:**818–821.
5a.**Shinomiya, S., K. Yamane, T. Mizukami, F. Kawamura, and H. Saito.** 1981. Cloning of thermostable α-amylase gene using *Bacillus subtilis* phage ρ11 as a vector. Agric. Biol. Chem. **45:**1733–1735.
6. **Shinomiya, S., K. Yamane, and T. Oshima.** 1980. Isolation of a *Bacillus subtilis* transformant producing thermostable α-amylase by DNA from a thermophilic bacterium. Biochem. Biophys. Res. Commun. **96:**175–179.
7. **Steinmetz, M., F. Kunst, and R. Dedonder.** 1976. Mapping of mutations affecting synthesis of exocellular enzymes in *Bacillus subtilis*. Mol. Gen. Genet. **148:**281–285.
8. **Yamaguchi, K., Y. Nagata, and B. Maruo.** 1974. Isolation of mutants defective in α-amylase from *Bacillus subtilis*: genetic analysis. J. Bacteriol. **119:**416–424.
9. **Yamane, K., K. Yamaguchi, and B. Maruo.** 1973. Purification and properties of a cross-reacting material related to α-amylase and biochemical comparison with the parental α-amylase. Biochim. Biophys. Acta. **295:**323–340.

Virulent Phage $\phi 1E1metB^+$-Mediated Transduction Dependent on Transformation Competence in *Bacillus subtilis*

FUJIO KAWAMURA AND HIUGA SAITO

Institute of Applied Microbiology, University of Tokyo, Bunkyo-ku, Tokyo 113, Japan

Processes of DNA-mediated transformation comprise two steps: DNA penetration through the bacterial surface and DNA integration with the bacterial chromosome. Our intent was to resolve these two steps by using a bacteriophage vector harboring a fragment of bacterial DNA.

We recently showed that the virulent *Bacillus subtilis* phage $\phi 1$, isolated by Reilly (9), can be used as a gene-cloning vector (8). We then analyzed this $\phi 1$ genome by agarose gel electrophoresis using 21 restriction endonucleases and constructed its cleavage site map for EcoRI, ThaI, BglII, SalI, and Bsu1247I, as shown in Fig. 1 (6). Meanwhile, a 2.6×10^6-dalton EcoRI fragment carrying a $metB^+$ gene of *B. subtilis* 168 was cloned in temperate phage $\phi 105$ by a "prophage transformation" method (4, 7). We inserted the 2.6×10^6-dalton EcoRI fragment into an EcoRI cleavage site on the $\phi 1E1$ genome by in vitro recombination (H. Shimotsu, F. Kawamura, and H. Saito, in preparation) (Fig. 1) and used this recombinant phage $\phi 1E1metB^+$ to introduce the $metB^+$ gene into $metB$ *B. subtilis*, which had been cultured to become competent for transformation.

Figure 2 shows the results of $\phi 1E1metB^+$-mediated transduction compared with DNA-mediated transformation during the course of "competency" development. To avoid the killing effect of $\phi 1E1metB^+$, we used as a recipient *B. subtilis* ISB8 (*leuA8 metB5 nonB1* r_{12471}^+ m_{12471}^+). ISB8 produces restriction endonuclease $Bsu1247I$, which cleaved the $\phi 1E1metB^+$ genome once in the $\phi 1E1$ DNA portion of the molecule (6) (Fig. 1). It is evident from Fig. 2 that the shift of Met$^+$ transduction frequency mediated by $\phi 1E1metB^+$ was parallel with that of DNA-mediated transformation frequency throughout the culture period. This indicates that the transduction mediated by $\phi 1E1metB^+$ is dependent upon "competency" for transformation of recipient cells. Furthermore, transduction frequencies were always more or less higher than transformation frequencies by *B. subtilis* DNA. This may reflect more efficient injection of DNA by $\phi 1E1metB^+$ than uptake of *B. subtilis* $metB^+$ DNA.

We next compared $\phi 1E1metB^+$-mediated transduction frequencies between competent cells and noncompetent cells, with or without

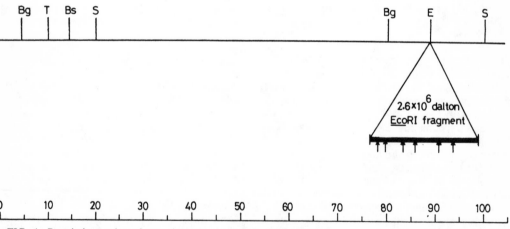

FIG. 1. Restriction endonuclease cleavage site maps of the $\phi 1E1$ genome and a 2.6×10^6-dalton EcoRI fragment carrying the $metB^+$ gene of *B. subtilis*. The vertical lines are sites of restriction endonucleases BglII (Bg), ThaI (T), Bsu1247I (Bs), SalI (S), and EcoRI (E). The restriction sites of the 2.6×10^6-dalton EcoRI fragment for HaeIII (BsuR) are indicated by arrows. Numbers represent molecular weights in millions.

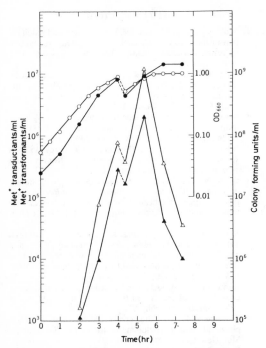

FIG. 2. Comparison between $\phi1metB^+$-mediated transduction and *B. subtilis* DNA-mediated transformation during "competency" development. *B. subtilis* ISB8 (*leuA8 metB5 nonB1* r_{1247I}^+ m_{1247I}^+ was grown on a TBAB (Difco) plate containing 0.5% glucose overnight at 37°C and inoculated into C1 medium (11) supplemented with 50 μg of required amino acids per ml (zero time). After 4 h, cells were collected by low-speed centrifugation and suspended in 2 volumes of C2 (11) medium. At indicated time intervals, *B. subtilis* 168 DNA (0.5 μg) or $\phi1E1metB^+$ (4 × 10⁸ PFU) was mixed with 0.1 ml of the culture. After incubation at 37°C for 20 min, Met⁺ transformants (▲) and transductants (△) were determined by plating on selective media. Optical density (○) and colony-forming units (●) were also followed.

the restriction-modification system of *Bsu*1247I (5, 10) or *Bsu*R (1, 2) (Fig. 3). The phage $\phi1$ genome has no recognition nucleotide sequence for *Bsu*R, whereas six *Bsu*R recognition sequences exist on the 2.6 × 10⁶-dalton *Eco*RI fragment of the $\phi1E1metB^+$ genome (Fig. 1). Phage $\phi1E1metB^+$ is thus restricted by *B. subtilis* ISR11 (*leuA8 metB5 nonB1* r_R^+ m_R^+), which produces restriction endonuclease *Bsu*R. A high level of Met⁺ transduction frequency was observed when competent cells were used as recipients, regardless of the restriction system's absence (Fig. 3). On the other hand, the transduction frequency was considerably lower when noncompetent cells growing exponentially in L-broth were used as recipients. These results

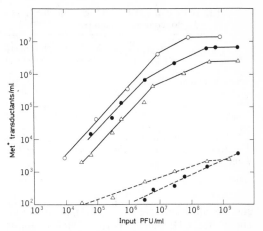

FIG. 3. $\phi1E1metB^+$-mediated transduction in competent and noncompetent cells of *B. subtilis* 1012, ISB8, and ISR11. Cells of *B. subtilis* 1012 (—○—), ISB8 (—●—), and ISR11 (—△—) incubated for 60 min in C2 medium were used as competent cells. Incompetent cells of ISB8 (--●--) and ISR11 (--△--) were grown to a density of about 10⁸ cells per ml in L-broth, collected, resuspended in 0.5 volume of phage dilution buffer (20 mM Tris-hydrochloride, pH 7.5, 0.1 M NaCl, and 10 mM MgSO₄), and mixed with $\phi1E1metB^+$. Met⁺ transductants were determined as described in Fig. 2.

again indicate that $\phi1E1metB^+$-mediated transduction depends on the "competency" of recipient cells and also strongly suggest that the ability of cells to take up transforming DNA would be accompanied with induction of some factor(s) required for recombination between the exogenous DNA and the resident chromosome. It is probable that the recombination enzyme(s) may be induced at a very low level in noncompetent cells, or that the enzyme(s) expressed in noncompetent cells, if any, is essentially inert for recombination between double-stranded, linear DNA and the resident chromosome.

Ganesan (3) reported that a restriction-modification enzyme system appears to be expressed in competent cells. We also found that $\phi1E1metB^+$ is somehow restricted by competent cells of *B. subtilis* 1012 (*leuA8 metB5 nonB1*) but retains high transducing activity. No transductant was observed when noncompetent cells of *B. subtilis* 1012 were used as recipients (data are not shown in Fig. 2). These results strongly suggest that some enzyme(s) responsible at least for the restriction of $\phi1E1metB^+$ is induced in the competent cells of *B. subtilis*. In addition, it is clear from Table 1, which shows the numbers of transductants and infectious centers after $\phi1E1metB^+$ infection of competent

TABLE 1. Fate of ϕ1E1*metB*$^+$ in competent and noncompetent cultures[a]

Recipient	Input ϕ1E1*metB*$^+$ (PFU/ml)	Met$^+$ transductants/ml	Infectious centers/ml
1012 competent cells	8.8×10^4	2.4×10^4	5.6×10^4
	8.8×10^3	2.2×10^3	5.2×10^4
1012 noncompetent cells	8.8×10^4	<10	8.7×10^4
	8.8×10^3	<10	9.0×10^3

[a] Competent and noncompetent cells of *B. subtilis* 1012 were prepared as described in the legends of Fig. 2 and 3.

and noncompetent cells of *B. subtilis* 1012, that one phage ϕ1E1*metB*$^+$ particle yields almost one Met$^+$ transductant, indicating that one incoming DNA molecule of ϕ1E1*metB*$^+$ unfailingly takes part in integrative recombination. To summarize, a restriction enzyme system as well as a recombination enzyme system, other than those expressed in noncompetent cells, were induced in competent cells of *B. subtilis*.

ACKNOWLEDGMENTS

We are grateful to T. Ando, T. Shibata, and S. Ikawa for providing *B. subtilis* ISB8 and ISR11. We also thank H. Anzai and H. Shimotsu for their help in construction of ϕ1E1*metB*$^+$ phage.

This research was supported in part by a Grant-in-Aid for Special Project Research from the Ministry of Education, Science and Culture of Japan.

LITERATURE CITED

1. **Bron, S., and K. Murray.** 1975. Restriction and modification in *Bacillus subtilis*, nucleotide sequence recognized by restriction endonuclease R.BsuR from strain R. Mol. Gen. Genet. **143**:25–33.
2. **Bron, S., K. Murray, and T. A. Trautner.** 1975. Restriction and modification in *B. subtilis*, purification and general properties of a restriction endonuclease from strain R. Mol. Gen. Genet. **143**:13–23.
3. **Ganesan, A. T.** 1979. Genetic recombination during transformation in *Bacillus subtilis*: appearance of a deoxyribonucleic acid methylase. J. Bacteriol. **139**:270–279.
4. **Iijima, T., F. Kawamura, H. Saito, and Y. Ikeda.** 1980. A specialized transducing phage constructed from *Bacillus subtilis* phage ϕ105. Gene **9**:115–126.
5. **Ikawa, S., T. Shibata, and T. Ando.** 1980. Genetic studies on a site-specific endodeoxyribonucleases in *Bacillus subtilis*: multiple modification and restriction systems in transformants of *Bacillus subtilis* 168. Mol. Gen. Genet. **177**:359–368.
6. **Kawamura, F., T. Mizukami, H. Shimotsu, H. Anzai, H. Takahashi, and H. Saito.** 1981. Unusually infrequent cleavage with several endonucleases and physical map construction of *Bacillus subtilis* bacteriophage ϕ1 DNA. J. Virol. **37**:1099–1102.
7. **Kawamura, F., H. Saito, and Y. Ikeda.** 1979. A method for construction of specialized transducing phage ρ11 of *Bacillus subtilis*. Gene **5**:87–91.
8. **Kawamura, F., H. Saito, and Y. Ikeda.** 1980. Bacteriophage ϕ1 as a gene-cloning vector in *Bacillus subtilis*. Mol. Gen. Genet. **180**:259–266.
9. **Reilly, B. E., and J. Spizizen.** 1965. Bacteriophage deoxyribonucleate infection of competent *Bacillus subtilis*. J. Bacteriol. **89**:782–790.
10. **Shibata, T., S. Ikawa, C. Kim, and T. Ando.** 1976. Site-specific deoxyribonucleases in *Bacillus subtilis* and other *Bacillus* strains. J. Bacteriol. **128**:473–476.
11. **Shibata, T., and H. Saito.** 1973. Repair of ultraviolet-induced DNA damage in the subcellular systems of *Bacillus subtilis*. Mutat. Res. **20**:159–173.

Construction of a *Bacillus subtilis* Plasmid and Molecular Cloning in *B. subtilis*

TERUO TANAKA

Mitsubishi-Kasei Institute of Life Sciences, 11 Minamiooya, Machida-shi, Tokyo, Japan

Molecular cloning with *Bacillus subtilis* cells as the host has been carried out mainly by using *Staphylococcus aureus* drug-resistant factors (3, 5, 8), bacteriophages (6), and *B. subtilis* plasmids (14). The cloning system in *B. subtilis* has several merits (4, 13), among which is the practical use of this organism for fermentation by industry. In producing certain gene products, for example, α-amylase and proteases, the plasmid cloning system may be advantageous because *B. subtilis* or *S. aureus* plasmids are usually present in a cell as multicopy plasmids (8, 13). However, in terms of practical use, *S. aureus* plasmids would be dangerous to humans because of possible insertion of drug resistance. Therefore, described here is a cloning vehicle consisting of the replicator and two selective markers, all of which are derived from *B. subtilis*.

CONSTRUCTION OF pTL12-CARRYING GENES FOR *leuB* AND TRIMETHOPRIM-RESISTANT (Tmp^r) DIHYDROFOLATE REDUCTASE

My associates and I have isolated seven classes of plasmids from 37 *B. subtilis* strains, including the *B. natto* strains used for fermentation of soybeans (12, 13). For basic research as well as for practical use, we chose one of the *B. natto* plasmids. First, we added *leu* genes derived from *B. subtilis* to this plasmid (Fig. 1). The plasmid pLS103 so constructed was further treated with *Eco*RI* to remove one of the *Eco*RI sites; thus, pLL10 was constructed. pLS103 has intact *leuB* and *leuC* genes (shown by a complementation test), whereas pLL10 has only the *leuC* gene (Fig. 2). Originally, we reported that the intact *leuA* gene was included in pLS103, since pLS103 complemented *B. subtilis* MI112 (14), which is a *recE4* mutant of *B. subtilis* RM125 *leuA8 arg-15 r⁻ m⁻* (15). However, subsequent studies revealed that both strains had the intact *leuA* gene product and that *B. subtilis* MI112 was a *leuB* mutant. To pLL10, a Tmp^r (16) DNA fragment was added that had been cloned into pBR322, and pTL12 was constructed after two restriction and ligation steps (Fig. 1).

CLONING OF DNA FRAGMENTS INTO RESTRICTION SITES OF pTL12

When DNA fragments are inserted into the *Bam*HI site of pTL12, the phenotype of pTL12

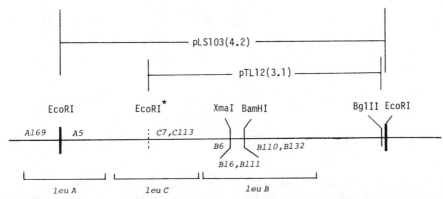

FIG. 1. Structure of the *B. subtilis* 168 *leu* gene region carried in pLS103 and pTL12. The symbols (A5, C7, and so on) represent *leu* mutants obtained from S. Zahler (17). The order of the markers in each DNA fragment surrounded by two neighboring restriction enzymes has not been determined. The sizes of the genes represented by *leuA*, *leuB*, and *leuC* are arbitrary. Numbers in parentheses indicate the molecular weight of the DNA fragment (in millions).

15

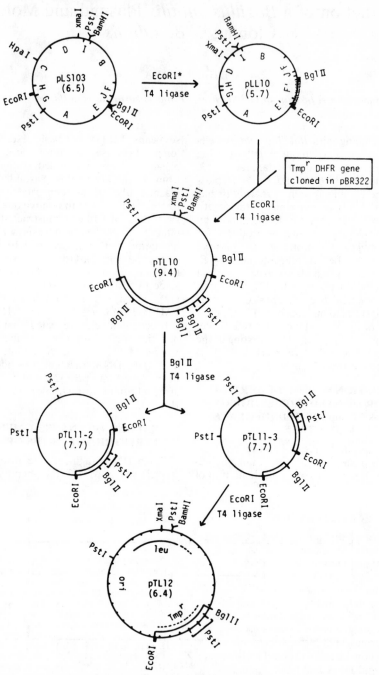

FIG. 2. Construction of *leu*⁺ *tmp*ʳ plasmids. Numbers in parentheses are the molecular weights (in millions) of the plasmids. The *Hind*III restriction sites are shown in inner circles of pLS103 and pLL10. The hatched area in pLL10 depicts an *Eco*RI* fragment inserted at the *Eco*RI site. The relative positions of the *Hind*III sites in pLL10 were preserved in pTL10, and the *Eco*RI fragment carrying *tmp*ʳ (depicted by the internal arcs) did not contain *Hind*III sites (data not shown). The broken lines in pTL12 show that the boundaries of the genes (*leu* and *tmp*ʳ) have not been localized. The map of pTL12 is divided into units of 2 × 10⁵ daltons (from 11).

TABLE 1. Frequency of transformation with plasmids obtained from restricting and nonrestricting strains[a]

No. of Leu⁺ transformants with MT120 (r^- m^- $recE4$) as recipient			
pSL102 and pLS103·MT120		pLS102 and pLS103·MT128	
Large colonies	Small colonies	Large colonies	Small colonies
41,500 (1)	166,000 (1)	9,300 (1)	36,000 (1)
25 (6×10^{-4})	220 (1.3×10^{-3})	8,800 (9.5×10^{-1})	36,000 (1)

[a] pLS102 and pLS103·X refer to the plasmids pLS102 and pLS103 obtained from strain X. The cells carrying pLS102 also harbor another plasmid, pLS103. Both plasmids have the B. subtilis leu DNA region, and when transformed into B. subtilis recE4 cells, pLS102 and pLS103 give rise to large and small colonies, respectively (14). The parentheses indicate relative transformation efficiency. DNA concentration was 1 μg/ml (from 10).

converts from Leu⁺ Tmpʳ to Leu⁻ Tmpʳ. Leu⁻ Tmpʳ cells grow as thin, flat colonies on minimal plates supplemented with various amino acids except leucine, but transformants carrying intact pTL12 form thick colonies (11), presumably because the rich medium used for phenotypic expression of Tmpʳ before plating carries over to the selective plates, enabling the Leu⁻ Tmpʳ transformants to replicate to a certain extent. A similar phenomenon was observed when DNA fragments were inserted into the XmaI site.

The Leu⁺ Tmpʳ phenotype of pTL12 did not change when DNA was inserted into either the EcoRI or BglII sites. However, the trimethoprim resistance level was affected when DNA fragments were inserted at the BglII site, as shown by the colony size (data not shown). The resistance level of cells carrying pTL12 or pTL11-3 is higher than that of cells carrying pTL11-2 or pTL10.

pTL12 was shown to be used for protoplast transformation (1) by using Tmpʳ as a selective marker (data not shown). In our hands, at least 10^6 transformants were obtained with 1 μg of pTL12 DNA.

B. SUBTILIS AS HOST

Host strains used for cloning must meet several general criteria, for example, safety, lack of restriction, recombination deficiency, etc. We examined B. subtilis MI112 arg-15 leuB thr-5 r^- m^- recE4, which we used as a host, to determine whether deficiencies in restriction and modification (r^- m^-) and recombination (recE4) would be advantageous for cloning. A rec^+ B. subtilis 168 strain (MT128) restricted incoming plasmid DNA considerably (Table 1). However, once the plasmid DNA had been maintained in r^+ m^+ cells, the DNA isolated from these cells was no longer restricted upon introduction into the r^+ m^+ strains (Table 1). This result may be an exceptional case, since B. subtilis 168 cells do not have a strong restriction ability as exemplified by the interaction of B. subtilis 168 and a phage, φ105 (15). Previously, trp genes from

other bacterial sources were successfully cloned into B. subtilis 168 (8). However, one should keep in mind that, although the restricting ability of B. subtilis 168 is weak, some DNA molecules are severely restricted, as shown in this paper. Therefore, higher transformation efficiency would be obtained in general with an r^- m^- strain.

Recombination or deletion of the plasmid DNA is unfavorable for cloning. One candidate strain without this problem seemed to be the recE4 mutant. This mutant strain does not allow incoming transforming DNA to incorporate into the homologous DNA region of the host chromosome (2). We observed that, when a plasmid contained a tandem repetition of the leu DNA region, a plasmid with one leu DNA region was also present at a high frequency (9). The possibility was ruled out that an insertion sequence-like structure was present at both ends of the one repeating unit (9). It should be noted here that the recombination frequency decreases to an undetectable level if two homologous DNA sequences are present in two separate replicons in the same recE4 mutant cell (7). A B. subtilis strain with a mutation equivalent to Escherichia coli recA would be desirable for cloning.

LITERATURE CITED

1. Chang, S., and S. N. Cohen. 1979. High frequency transformation of Bacillus subtilis protoplasts by plasmid DNA. Mol. Gen. Genet. 168:111–115.
2. Dubnau, D., R. Davidoff-Abelson, B. Scher, and C. Cirigliano. 1973. Fate of transforming deoxyribonucleic acid after uptake by competent Bacillus subtilis: phenotypic characterization of radiation-sensitive recombination-deficient mutant. J. Bacteriol. 114:273–286.
3. Ehrlich, S. D. 1978. DNA cloning in Bacillus subtilis. Proc. Natl. Acad. Sci. U.S.A. 74:1680–1682.
4. Gryczan, T. J., S. Contente, and D. Dubnau. 1978. Characterization of Staphylococcus aureus plasmids introduced by transformation into Bacillus subtilis. J. Bacteriol. 134:318–329.
5. Gryczan, T. J., and D. Dubnau. 1978. Construction and properties of chimeric plasmids in Bacillus subtilis. Proc. Natl. Acad. Sci. U.S.A. 75:1428–1432.
6. Kawamura, F., H. Saito, and Y. Ikeda. 1979. A method for construction of specialized transducing phage ρ11 of Bacillus subtilis. Gene 5:87–91.

7. **Keggins, K. M., E. J. Duvall, and P. S. Lovett.** 1978. Recombination between compatible plasmids containing homologous segments requires the *Bacillus subtilis recE* gene product. J. Bacteriol. **134**:514–520.

8. **Keggins, K. M., P. S. Lovett, and E. J. Duvall.** 1978. Molecular cloning of genetically active fragments of *Bacillus* DNA in *Bacillus subtilis* and properties of the vector plasmid pUB110. Proc. Natl. Acad. Sci. U.S.A. **75**:1423–1427.

9. **Tanaka, T.** 1979. *recE4*-independent recombination between homologous deoxyribonucleic acid segment of *Bacillus subtilis* plasmids. J. Bacteriol. **139**:775–782.

10. **Tanaka, T.** 1979. Restriction of plasmid-mediated transformation in *Bacillus subtilis* 168. Mol. Gen. Genet. **175**:235–237.

11. **Tanaka, T., and H. Kawano.** 1980. Cloning vehicles for the homologous *Bacillus subtilis* host-vector system. Gene **10**:131–136.

12. **Tanaka, T., and T. Koshikawa.** 1977. Isolation and characterization of four types of plasmids from *Bacillus subtilis (natto)*. J. Bacteriol. **131**:699–701.

13. **Tanaka, T., M. Kuroda, and K. Sakaguchi.** 1977. Isolation and characterization of four plasmids from *Bacillus subtilis*. J. Bacteriol. **129**:1487–1494.

14. **Tanaka, T., and K. Sakaguchi.** 1978. Construction of a recombinant plasmid composed of *B. subtilis* leucine genes and a *B. subtilis (natto)* plasmid: its use as cloning vehicle in *B. subtilis* 168. Mol. Gen. Genet. **165**:269–276.

15. **Uozumi, T., T. Hoshino, K. Miwa, S. Horinouchi, T. Beppu, and K. Arima.** 1977. Restriction and modification of *Bacillus* species. Genetic transformation of bacteria with DNA from different species. Part I. Mol. Gen. Genet. **116**:719–726.

16. **Wainscott, V. J., and J. F. Kane.** 1976. Dihydrofolate reductase in *Bacillus subtilis*, p. 208–213. *In* D. Schlessinger (ed.), Microbiology—1976. American Society for Microbiology, Washington, D.C.

17. **Ward, J. B., and S. A. Zahler.** 1976. Genetic studies of leucine biosynthesis in *Bacillus subtilis*. J. Bacteriol. **116**:719–726.

Ribosomal Genes in *Bacillus subtilis*: Comparison with *Escherichia coli*

SYOZO OSAWA[1]

Department of Biochemistry and Biophysics, Research Institute for Nuclear Medicine and Biology, Hiroshima University, Hiroshima, 734, Japan

Molecular and genetic studies of ribosomes have been done mainly with *Escherichia coli*, a gram-negative bacterium, and also to a considerable extent with *Bacillus subtilis*, a gram-positive bacterium. *B. subtilis* diverged from *E. coli* very early in the history of evolution. The phylogenic tree of their 5S RNAs revealed that the separation occurred about 1.2 billion years ago, which is just about the time of separation between yeast and human (5). It is interesting then to see the evolutionary changes of ribosomal components and their genes by comparing the results of various studies with *B. subtilis* and *E. coli*.

The organization of ribosomal protein genes in *E. coli* has been worked out almost completely by many investigators, including my colleagues and me. One of the most striking features of this organization is that many ribosomal protein genes together with the genes for α subunit of RNA polymerase and for elongation factors G and Tu are clustered at one region, i.e, the so-called streptomycin (*str*) region (4). There is a middle-sized cluster at the rifampin (*rif*) region that includes genes for the four 50S ribosomal proteins L1, L7, L10, and L11 together with genes for Tu, β, and β' (4). The other genes exist either in a small cluster or are scattered at different places on the chromosome (3).

Considerable progress has also been made in defining the genetics of *B. subtilis* ribosomal proteins in recent years. It is known that many genes involved in antibiotic resistance are clustered in one region near *cysA-str-spc* loci on the *B. subtilis* chromosome (see 2). Since the antibiotics examined are all related to ribosome function or RNA polymerase activity in *E. coli*, it is reasonable to assume that the resistant mutants of *B. subtilis* have alterations in ribosomal proteins or RNA polymerase. Several workers, including us, have analyzed the ribosomal proteins of these antibiotic-resistant mutants by

carboxymethyl cellulose chromatography or two-dimension electrophoresis and have frequently found protein alterations. Many of the genes coding the altered proteins have been successfully mapped on the *B. subtilis* strain 168 chromosome (see 2). However, most of the protein names adopted there have no relation to those given to the *E. coli* proteins, because the naming was simply based on the position of the protein peak or spot on carboxymethyl cellulose chromatographic profile or two-dimension electrophoretogram. Therefore, some results obtained with *B. subtilis* were not comparable to those obtained with *E. coli*. Before I proceed further in describing genetic work, it is necessary to establish nomenclature by which *B. subtilis* protein can be directly correlated to *E. coli* protein. To this end, we have purified most of the former's 30S and 50S ribosomal proteins by carboxymethyl cellulose chromatography and other techniques (E. Otaka et al., unpublished data). The N-terminal amino acid sequences, amino acid compositions, and molecular weights for many of these proteins were then determined to deduce the structural correspondence to *E. coli* proteins (K. Higo and T. Kumazaki, unpublished data). In this way, we have correlated most of the 30S ribosomal proteins and many of the 50S ribosomal proteins of *B. subtilis* to the *E. coli* proteins. In Table 1 the standard, i.e., *E. coli*-equivalent, nomenclature of ribosomal proteins and their gene symbols is used to localize several ribosomal protein genes for antibiotic resistance.

The use of antibiotic-resistance mutants to map ribosomal protein genes clearly has limitations and is also inefficient. Another way is to use genetic hybrids. Some *Bacillus* species can be used as donors for intra- or interspecies transformation experiments with *B. subtilis* strain 168 as recipient, using markers such as *str, spc*, and *cysA*. Therefore, several years ago we began this type of analysis in collaboration with H. Saito of the University of Tokyo (6). Systematic two-dimension electrophoretic analyses of ribosomal proteins from a number of

[1] Present address: Laboratory of Molecular Genetics, Department of Biology, Faculty of Science, Nagoya University, Nagoya, 464, Japan.

donor *Bacillus* species indicated that altogether 11 30S and 16 50S ribosomal proteins are distinguishable from those of the recipient strain 168. Thus, we can show by transformation whether the genes for these proteins are present in the *str* region on the strain 168 chromosome.

We have obtained the strain 168 transformants by various species of DNAs using *cysA, str*, or *spc* as selective markers. Altogether, 46 transformants were examined for ribosomal proteins. We analyzed predominantly the transformants by *B. licheniformis* DNA, since in this species the protein differs maximally from that in strain 168 compared with the other donor species examined. Table 1 shows a list of the genes for *B. subtilis* ribosomal and related proteins whose loci have so far been localized in the *str* region by using the hybrid bacteria mentioned above as well as the antibiotic resistance criterion. The genes found in the *str* region of *B. subtilis* also generally exist in *E. coli* in the *str* region. The exceptions are the genes for L1, L11, β, and β', which are in the *str* region in *B. subtilis* (see also 8) but are not in this region in *E. coli*. It should be stressed here that, in *E. coli*, all of these genes belong to the *rif* cluster (4). One explanation for this would be that the chromosomal segment corresponding to the *E. coli rif* region exists near the *str* region in *B. subtilis*. In this connection, it will be of interest to see whether genes for the other proteins, i.e., L7 and L10, that are known to exist in the *rif* region in *E. coli* can be localized in the *str* region in *B. subtilis*.

In Table 2 are listed the ribosomal protein genes that could not be mapped in the *str* region by transformation. Except for the S4 gene, none of the corresponding genes is located in the *str* region of *E. coli*. Therefore, it is probable that the organization of *B. subtilis* ribosomal and related protein genes in many ways resembles that of *E. coli*, but is not exactly the same, as seen in at least some of the genes belonging to the *rif* cluster.

In *E. coli*, the existence of seven rRNA operons has been established, each containing generally one copy of genes for 5S, 23S, and 16S rRNAs, and some tRNA genes (4). The operon *rrnD* contains two sets of 5S rRNA genes besides one copy each of 16S and 23S rRNA genes (1). These operons are distributed on the left half of the chromosome (4). In *B. subtilis* about comparable numbers of rRNA gene sets have been reported to exist (see 2), and most, if not all, of them were located just after the *str* region (see also G. C. Steward, F. E. Wilson, and K. F. Bott, this volume). We have recently estimated the copy number of rRNA genes in *B. subtilis* strain 168 (H. Kobayashi et al., unpub-

TABLE 1. Ribosomal and related protein genes mapped in the *str* region in *B. subtilis* strain 168

Gene for protein	Gene symbol	Mapped by[a]	Map position (min) of corresponding gene in *E. coli* (3, 4)
S3	*rpsC*	SL	74 (*strA* region)
S5	*rpsE*	*spc*, CK, SL	74
S8	*rpsH*	CK	74
S10	*rpsJ*	*tet*[b]	74
S12	*rpsL*	*str*	74
S17	*rpsQ*	CK	74
S19	*rpsS*	SL	74
L1	*rplA*	*cmlA*	89 (*rif* region)
L2	*rplB*	ASP, NSP	74
L4	*rplD*	CK, SL	74
L5	*rplE*	SL	74
L6	*rplF*	SL, ASP	74
L11	*rplK*	*tsp*[b]	89
L13	*rplM*	*cmlE*, SL	Unknown
L17	*rplQ*	*cmlB*, SL	74
L22	*rplV*	*ery*, SL	74
L23	*rplW*	SL	74
L24	*rplX*	SL	74
L29	*rpmC*	SL	74
β	*rpoB*	*rif*[b]	89
β'	*rpoC*	*std*[b]	89
EFTu	*tuf*	*tuf* (Ts)[b]	74
EFG	*fus*	*fus*[b]; *fus* (Ts)	74

[a] CK and SK, *B. subtilis* strain 168 transformants by *B. amyloliquefaciens* DNA; SL, by *B. licheniformis* DNA; ASP, by *B. subtilis* ATCC 6633 DNA; NSP, by *B. niger* DNA. Italic letters indicate mutants with protein alterations that cause resistance to the following antibiotics: *spc*, spectinomycin; *tet*, tetracycline; *str*, streptomycin; *cml*, chloramphenicol; *tsp*, thiostrepton; *ery*, erythromycin; *rif*, rifampin; *std*, streptolydigin; *fus*, fusidic acid.

[b] Determined by other workers (for references, see 2).

lished data). We applied the Southern hybridization technique (9) to the total restriction digests of DNA, using $[3'-^{32}P]$rRNAs as probes. The *Eco*RI digest gave 10 bands after hybridization to 5S $[3'-^{32}P]$rRNA, whereas *Sma*I and *Bam*HI gave 8 and 9 bands, respectively. However, double digestion of the DNA with *Sma*I or *Bam*HI plus *Eco*RI gave 10 bands when hybridized to 5S rRNA. Preliminary Southern hybridizations of the *Eco*RI digests to 23S $[3'-^{32}P]$rRNAs also gave 10 bands. From these results we suggest that the copy number of *B. subtilis* rRNA genes is 10, at minimum.

It has been reported that the rRNA gene copy number is only one in *Mycoplasma* according to hybridization-saturation experiments between DNA and rRNA (7). We have recently investigated this by Southern hybridization using

TABLE 2. Ribosomal protein genes not mapped in
the *str* region in *B. subtilis* strain 168

Gene for protein	Gene symbol	Mapped by[a]	Map position (min) of corresponding gene in *E. coli* (3, 4)
S4[b]	*rpsD*	SL	74 (*strA* region)
S6	*rpsF*	SL	97
S16	*rpsP*	CK, SK	56
S20	*rpsO*	SL	0
L19	*rplS*	SL	56
L21	*rplU*	CK	67
L32	*rpmF*	SL	31
L27	*rpmA*	SL	68

[a] See legend for Table 1.
[b] The electrophoretic difference between the donor
and recipient S4 is slight, and therefore the result is not
definite.

[3′-^{32}P]rRNAs as probes and have shown that
the number of genes for 5S, 16S, and 23S rRNAs
of *Mycoplasma* is two, at least (7a). Compared
with procaryotes, eucaryotes contain many
more rRNA genes, but even in procaryotes the
multiplicity of rRNA genes is variable in different bacteria, as discussed above. Such variation
probably relates to the size of chromosomes or
the potential protein-synthesizing activity in
each bacterial species, or both.

ACKNOWLEDGMENTS

This work was supported by grants from the Ministry of
Education of Japan (no. 511212 and 538027).
I am grateful for unpublished data supplied by my col-
leagues.

LITERATURE CITED

1. **Duester, G. L., and W. M. Holmes.** 1980. The distal end of the ribosomal RNA operon *rrnD* of *Escherichia coli* contains a tRNA^{thr} gene, two 5S rRNA genes and a transcription terminator. Nucleic Acids Res. **8:**3793–3807.
2. **Henner, D. J., and J. A. Hoch.** 1980. The *Bacillus subtilis* chromosome. Microbiol. Rev. **44:**57–82.
3. **Isono, K., A. G. Cumberlidge, S. Isono, M. Kitakawa, J. Schnier, and Y. Hirota.** 1980. Genetic studies of mutants of *Escherichia coli* with altered ribosomal proteins, p. 329–340. *In* S. Osawa, H. Ozeki, H. Uchida, and T. Yura (ed.), Genetics and evolution of RNA polymerase, tRNA and ribosomes. University of Tokyo Press, Tokyo.
4. **Nomura, M., and L. E. Post.** 1979. Organization of ribosomal genes and regulation of their expression in *Escherichia coli*, p. 671–691. *In* G. Chambliss, G. R. Craven, J. Davies, K. Davis, L. Kahan, and M. Nomura (ed.), Ribosomes—structure, function and genetics. University Park Press, Baltimore.
5. **Osawa, S., and H. Hori.** 1979. Molecular evolution of ribosomal components, p. 335–355. *In* G. Chambliss, G. R. Craven, J. Davies, K. Davis, L. Kahan, and M. Nomura (ed.), Ribosomes—structure, function and genetics. University Park Press, Baltimore.
6. **Osawa, S., A. Tokui, and H. Saito.** 1978. Mapping by interspecies transformation experiments of several ribosomal protein genes near the replication origin of *Bacillus subtilis* chromosome. Mol. Gen. Genet. **164:**113–129.
7. **Ryan, J. L., and H. J. Morowitz.** 1969. Partial purification of native rRNA and tRNA cistrons from *Mycoplasma* sp.(KID). Proc. Natl. Acad. Sci. U.S.A. **63:**1282–1289.
7a. **Sawada, M., S. Osawa, H. Kobayashi, H. Hori, and A. Muto.** 1981. The number of ribosomal RNA genes in *Mycoplasma capricolum*. Mol. Gen. Genet. **182:**502–504.
8. **Smith, I., E. Dubnau, G. Williams, K. Cabane, and P. Paress.** 1980. Genetics of the translational apparatus in *Bacillus subtilis*, p. 379–405. *In* S. Osawa, H. Ozeki, H. Uchida, and T. Yura (ed.), Genetics and evolution of RNA polymerase, tRNA and ribosomes. University of Tokyo Press, Tokyo.
9. **Southern, E. M.** 1975. Detection of specific sequences among DNA fragments by gel electrophoresis. J. Mol. Biol. **98:**503–517.

Heterospecific Gene Expression

JANE R. McLAUGHLIN, CHERYL L. MURRAY, AND JESSE C. RABINOWITZ

Department of Biochemistry, University of California, Berkeley, California 94720

We offer a very short explanation of how we began work on the *Bacillus* chromosome. About 10 years ago, we became interested in synthesizing a small-molecular-weight iron-sulfur protein, ferredoxin. The protein occurs in all *Clostridium* species and is composed of only 55 amino acids (2). Our attempts to prepare a protein-synthesizing system from clostridial cells analogous to the system used for *Escherichia coli* were unsuccessful in that the usual mRNA preparations that stimulated the *E. coli* system, such as f2 RNA or T4 early mRNA, did not stimulate amino acid incorporation by the system derived from the clostridial cells.

We finally demonstrated that the protein-synthesizing system of the clostridial cells could be stimulated to form protein when it was presented with mRNA from clostridial cells or from other gram-positive cells, but not with mRNA from gram-negative cells (7–10). This behavior was in marked contrast to that observed in protein-synthesizing systems from *E. coli* or other gram-negative cells. Such systems responded to mRNA derived from either gram-negative or gram-positive cells.

To determine the molecular basis for this specificity, we decided to examine the system in *B. subtilis* because of the difficulty in working with the clostridial cells, for which genetic tools and phages are not available. The in vitro translation system that we were using included four relatively crude fractions: the ribosomes; a high-salt wash of the ribosomes that contained initiation factors; a high-speed supernatant fraction that contained aminoacyl synthetases, elongation factors, and termination factors; and the mRNA (5). Assays with ribosomes from gram-positive organisms and *E. coli* RNA phage mRNAs showed that neither the ribosome salt wash nor the high-speed supernatant fraction from *E. coli* enabled ribosomes from gram-positive organisms to translate the mRNA derived from gram-negative sources. It therefore appeared that the basis for this translational specificity was a function of the difference in mRNA/ribosome interactions between components from the gram-positive and gram-negative organisms. This interaction occurs at the initiation step and is based on the following determinants:

(i) The first interaction recognized as important in the binding of a ribosome to an initiation site is that of the anticodon of tRNA^{fMet} with the initiator codon of the mRNA. Of the 123 known *E. coli* initiator regions (4), 119 have AUG (Met) and 4 have GUG (Val) as initiator codons.

(ii) The second type of RNA-RNA interaction in initiation site selection involves the Shine-Dalgarno site, named after the investigators who first recognized this factor in initiation site selection (6). It involves base pairing between a pyrimidine-rich sequence at the 3′ end of the 16S rRNA and a purine-rich region located 3 to 11 nucleotides 5′ to the initiation codon. Strong support for the importance of this feature in initiation site selection comes from analysis of the 123 *E. coli* initiation sites. All but one contain a purine-rich sequence that satisfies the requirement for complementarity to the rRNA. The pyrimidine-rich region at the 3′ end of *E. coli* to which the complementarity in the message is most frequently directed is the CUCC sequence.

Discovery of the role of Shine-Dalgarno pairing in initiation site selection suggested that perhaps the 3′ ends of 16S rRNA from gram-positive organisms were different from those of *E. coli* and that this was responsible for the translational specificity observed. The 3′ ends of 16S rRNA have been determined for about 100 different true bacteria by C. Woese (personal communication). The 3′ ends of the 16S rRNA from three *Bacillus* species that have been determined are very similar to those of *E. coli*, with the exception that they contain a small number of additional bases 3′ to the CCUCC sequence that appears to be conserved in all the 16S rRNA sequences examined.

(iii) An additional determinant that has been considered in initiation site selection by the *E. coli* ribosome is the distance between the Shine-Dalgarno site and the initiation codon. This is sometimes referred to as the "window." The variation observed in this distance is from 3 to 11 bases, but most fall within the range of 5 to 9 bases. Spacings smaller than 5 and larger than 11

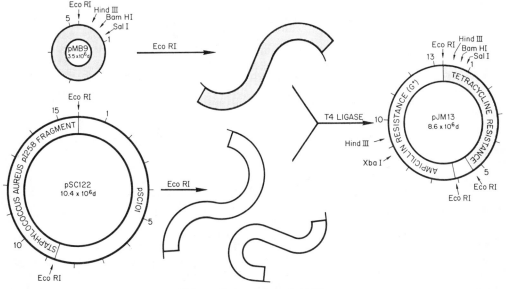

FIG. 1. Construction of pJM13.

do result in reduced translation.

(iv) Finally, one must recognize the possible role of initiation factors and various ribosomal proteins in this determination of specificity, since these factors have been shown to affect RNA-RNA interactions involved in initiation. When the RNA-RNA interactions are very strong, there appears to be less dependence upon the protein initiation factors to stabilize the initiation complex. This was shown in experiments involving the three initiation sites of R17 RNA phage (11). When *E. coli* ribosomes are washed in high salt, the initiation factors are removed, and the ribosomes retain the ability to recognize these three initiator sites correctly, but at low efficiency. Addition of crude salt wash stimulates initiation at the three sites, but not equally. The stronger the Shine-Dalgarno pairing, the weaker the response to the addition of salt wash is.

Having considered the factors that are thought to be of importance in the interaction of the mRNA and the rRNA in the formation of the initiation complex, we attempted to determine any differences in these factors as they occurred in the components derived from gram-positive organisms that might account for translational specificity. The first difference noted was the extent to which productive initiation occurred with mRNA from gram-positive organisms in the absence of salt wash, relative to that observed with components derived from gram-negative sources. This phenomenon was first observed in

the formation of undefined products from general cellular mRNA (7, 9), but is even more striking in more recent experiments. Addition of S1 does not permit translation of mRNAs derived from gram-negative sources by ribosomes from gram-positive sources.

If this reduced dependence on initiation factors is related to a stronger RNA-RNA complementarity with resulting decreased reliance on proteins for stabilization of the initiation complex, analysis of the primary sequence of a gram-positive mRNA might reveal such features. Until now, however, no sequences of ribosome binding sites of gram-positive sources have been published. We decided to characterize the ribosome binding site of the β-lactamase of the gram-positive organism *Staphylococcus aureus*. The amino acid sequence of the secreted protein is known, and its hydrolysis of the β-lactam bond found in penicillin is easily assayed.

The procedure used to clone the gram-positive *S. aureus* β-lactamase gene into a suitable plasmid is shown in Fig. 1. The pSC101 derivative carrying the *S. aureus* β-lactamase fragment was given to us by S. Cohen of Stanford University. The fragment confers penicillin resistance on both *E. coli* and *B. subtilis*. To facilitate isolation of the β-lactamase DNA, we chose to transfer the gene to another *E. coli* plasmid, pMB9, whose replication is under relaxed control. This was done by cutting both plasmids with *Eco*RI, mixing them, ligating them, and selecting transformants resistant to both tetracycline and ampi-

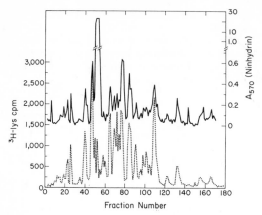

FIG. 2. Identification of 32,000-molecular-weight protein as β-lactamase.

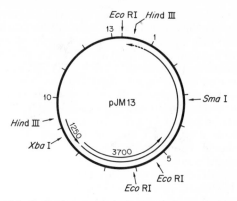

FIG. 3. In vitro transcription map of pJM13 DNA.

cillin. Restriction analysis of these transformants allowed identification of the pMB9/*S. aureus* hybrid, designated pJM13. From other work, it was known that the single *Xba*I site mapped in the vicinity of the gram-positive β-lactamase gene that was of interest to us.

The protein products synthesized from supercoiled pJM13 by the *B. subtilis* system include a major protein with a molecular weight of 32,000. The secreted form of β-lactamase has a molecular weight of 28,823. The additional 3,100 in this protein indicates that it might be the β-lactamase still possessing a leader of 20 to 25 amino acids. It is not unexpected that the β-lactamase synthesized by the in vitro system would have a leader, since many secreted proteins are synthesized with additional amino acids at the amino-terminal end. This heavily labeled band was cut out of the gel for tryptic peptide mapping of the protein in an attempt to determine whether it was related to the *S. aureus* β-lactamase.

The in vitro product, labeled with [³H]lysine,

was mixed with purified *S. aureus* β-lactamase. The mixture was digested with trypsin, and the resulting peptide mixture was chromatographed on Aminex A-5. The ninhydrin reaction and radioactivity of the fractions are shown in Fig. 2. The major radioactive peaks conform exactly to the peptide peaks. The large peak with no associated ³H is NH₃. This proves that the 32,000-molecular-weight protein synthesized by both *E. coli* and *B. subtilis* ribosomes directed by pJM13 is *S. aureus* β-lactamase complete with its leader peptide. In other experiments, it could be demonstrated, by measuring the appearance of a small amount of enzymatic activity, that β-lactamase activity formed in the translation assay mixture under the direction of pJM13. We believe that this is a rigorous demonstration of the competence of the *B. subtilis* in vitro translation system.

To determine which region of the plasmid DNA should be sequenced to obtain the β-lactamase ribosome binding site, we mapped the in vitro RNA transcripts directed by pJM13. A summary of the results is shown in Fig. 3. The

5′ AGCTTACTATGCCATTATTAATAACTTAGCCATTTCAACACCTTCTTTC

AAATATTTATAATAAACTA<u>TTGACA</u>CCGAT<u>ATTACA</u>ATTGTAA<u>TATTA</u>

<u>TT</u>GATTT<u>A</u>TAAAAATTACAACTGTAATATC<u>GGAGG</u>GTTTATT<u>TT</u>GAAA
                                                       Met Lys

AAGT<u>T</u>AATATTTTT<u>T</u>AATTGTAATTGCTTTAGTTTT<u>T</u>AAGTGCATGTAAT
Lys Leu Ile Phe Leu Ile Val Ile Ala Leu Val Leu Ser Ala Cys Asn

TCAAAC<u>A</u>GTTCACATGCCAAAGAGTTAAATGATTTAGAAAAAAAAT<u>A</u>T
Ser Asn Ser Ser His Ala Lys Glu Leu Asn Asp Leu Glu Lys Lys Tyr

AATGCTCATATTGGTGTTTATGCTTTAGATACTAAAAGT... 3′
Asn Ala His Ile Gly Val Tyr Ala Leu Asp Thr Lys Ser ...

FIG. 4. DNA sequence of the initiation region of *S. aureus* β-lactamase gene.

technique used to derive this map involved cutting the plasmid with either *Eco*RI or *Hin*dIII and then treating it for various lengths of time with exonuclease III and nuclease S1 to produce increasingly shortened duplex DNA. There was reason to believe that the 1,250-base RNA encoded β-lactamase. If the transcript initiates near this *Hin*dIII site and runs toward the *Xba*I site, digestion with *Hin*dIII should leave 1,250-base RNA intact and subsequent translation should result in β-lactamase synthesis. A short exonuclease III-nuclease S1 treatment of *Hin*dIII-digested pJM13 should result in a loss of 1,250-base RNA, since the promoter is removed, and subsequent loss of β-lactamase synthesis should occur. These expectations were fulfilled by experimental results.

The region between the *Hin*dIII and *Xba*I sites, a fragment of 840 base pairs, was isolated and then sequenced from the *Xba*I site in hopes of aligning the known amino acid sequence of mature β-lactamase. The *Xba*I site turned out to be at amino acid 210; 80% of the protein was encoded on this fragment. Thus, the region containing the ribosome binding site was about 700 base pairs away. The fragments and directions that were sequenced to give a DNA base sequence equivalent to the message are shown in Fig. 4. We were able to align the codons corresponding to the amino terminus of mature β-lactamase as determined by Ambler (1), starting with Lys-Glu-Leu. We knew that a leader of 20 to 25 amino acids should be encoded, but we did not know its sequence. The only region that displayed Shine-Dalgarno complementarity was the sequence GGAGG, but there was no typical initiation codon in the vicinity. Therefore, we guessed that perhaps TTG was the initiation codon even though the only example of its use in *E. coli* is as a reinitiation codon in the *lac* repressor synthesis. If, in fact, protein synthesis begins here at UUG, then the leader amino acid sequence is that shown by the amino acids that are underscored. Based on the observation that, at least in one known case, the initiation codon is GUG, normally the codon of valine but in this instance coding for methionine, we thought it possible that the UUG leucine codon could direct initiation with methionine, or perhaps leucine. We synthesized β-lactamase in vitro in the presence of [^{35}S]methionine and [^{3}H]leucine in one reaction and in the presence of [^{35}S]methionine and [^{3}H]lysine in another. If the UUG is indeed the initiation codon, then methionine or leucine should be in position 1, leucine in positions 4, 7, 12, and, 14, and lysine in positions 2 and 3. Using the sequenator to analyze the amino acid sequence gave rise to the data shown

in Fig. 5, confirming the predicted amino acid sequence.

Not only do we have a novel initiator tRNA-initiation codon interaction with the potential of forming four base pairs, because the 5'U and the

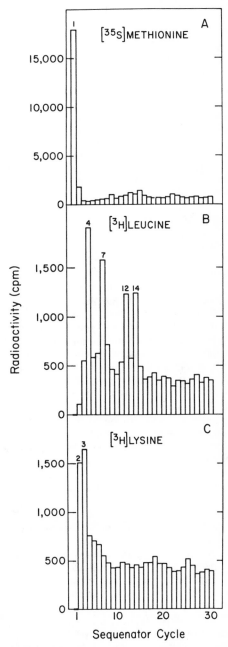

FIG. 5. Sequential Edman degradation of β-lactamase formed in the cell-free system.

GRAM-POSITIVE

(a) *S. aureus* β-lactamase   5′ ...UACAACUGUAAUAUC<u>GGAGG</u>GUUUAUU<u>UUG</u>AAAAAGUUAAUAUUUUUAAUUGUAAUUGCUU... 3′

(b) *B. licheniformis* β-lactamase   ...AUAUUCAAAC<u>GGAGG</u>GAGACGAUUUU<u>U</u>G<u>AUG</u>AAAUUAUGGUUCAGUACUUUAAAACUGAAAA...

(c) Phage φ29 22.4K protein   ...GACAACCAAUCAU<u>AGGAGG</u>AAUUACAC<u>AUG</u>AAUAACUAUCAAUUAACUAUCAAUGAGGUAA...

(d) Phage φ29 13.9K protein   ...AAAUAUAAAU<u>AGAAAG</u>U<u>GGG</u>ACGAAGAAA<u>AUG</u>GCAAAAAUGAUGCAGAGAGAAAUCACAAA...

(e) *S. aureus* Er^R peptide   pppAUUUUAU<u>AA</u><u>GGAGG</u>AAAAAA<u>U</u><u>AUG</u>GGCAUUUUUUAGUAUUUUUUGUAAUCAGCACAG...

(f) *S. aureus* Er^R 29K protein   ...UCAUAUAACCAAAUUAAA<u>GAGG</u>GUUAUA<u>AUG</u>AACGAGAAAAAUAUAAAACACAGUCAAAA...

(g) SP01 middle gene   ...AAA<u>GGAGG</u>AGAGGUUA<u>UUG</u>AGCACACU...

(h) SP01 middle gene   ...GAAUGG<u>AA</u><u>GGAGG</u>U<u>A</u>AACAAA<u>AUG</u>ACCAA...

GRAM-NEGATIVE

(i) T7 1.3 gene (ligase)   pCAUUUAACCAAU<u>AGGAG</u>AUAAACAUU<u>AUG</u>AUGAACAUUAAGACUAACCCGUUUAAAGCCGUGUC...

(j) R17 A protein   AUUCCU<u>AGGAGG</u>UUUGACC<u>U</u><u>AUG</u>CGAGCUUUUAGUACUCUC...

EUKARYOTIC

(k) SV40 12K small t antigen   ...CCUGAU<u>AAAGGAGG</u>AGAUGAAGAAAAA<u>AUG</u>AAGAAAAUGAAUACUCUGUACAAGAAAAUG...

(l)   16S rRNA 3′ _{OH}UCUUUC<u>CUCC</u>ACUAG... 5

FIG. 6. Initiation sites recognized by *B. subtilis* ribosomes.

3′A are both complementary to the anticodon loop of the initiator tRNA, but the Shine-Dalgarno sequence is the perfect complement to the CCUCC at the 3′ end of *B. subtilis* 16S rRNA. This message to ribosome pairing is expected to be quite strong because adjacent G·C/G·C pairs vastly increase the stability of a double helical region relative to the contribution of A·U/A·U or A·U/G·C stacks. Again, it is true that this strong message to rRNA pairing allowed *S. aureus* β-lactamase to be made in significant amounts in the absence of initiation factors, just as was the case for φ29 proteins and perhaps all proteins encoded by mRNAs from gram-positive sources.

The transcriptional start site, indicated by the arrow, was determined by the Donis-Keller (3) enzymatic method of RNA sequencing. A likely Pribnow box sequence and −35 region are underscored. These sequences are typical of those recognized by the gram-negative *E. coli* RNA polymerase as well. It is difficult to generalize about the structure of gram-positive ribosome binding sites from a single sequence, but it is hard to resist the temptation.

Figure 6 shows other gram-positive DNA sequences that may be bound by *B. subtilis* ribosomes. We obtained several of these through personal communication. The sequence of *S. aureus* β-lactamase appears first, followed by the *B. licheniformis* β-lactamase. There are no N-terminal amino acid sequences available to substantiate the position of the initiation codon.

The outstanding feature of all these sites is the perfect Shine-Dalgarno complementarity of GGAGG that can form four GC pairs with the CCUCC of the 16S rRNA. Another feature is the use of UUG as an initiation codon. This has not been observed in gram-negative systems. Furthermore, most initiation codons are followed by the nucleotide A, which has been shown to increase *E. coli* ribosome binding to Qβ mutant 3x, presumably by stabilizing the initiator tRNA/mRNA pairing. In some cases, there is an additional complementary U 5′ to the initiation codon. This would increase base pairing potential with the anticodon loop of the initiator tRNA.

The two gram-negative sites bound by *B. subtilis* have been shown to be bound by *E. coli* ribosomes with less dependence upon protein factors than most gram-negative initiation sites. As predicted by this observation, there is potential for strong RNA-RNA pairing both at the initiation codon to initiator RNA and at the Shine-Dalgarno sequence in the message to the 3′ end of *B. subtilis* 16S rRNA shown here. Among 123 available gram-negative sites, only about 10% show this extensive complementarity. Note the presence of both the 5′U and 3′A in the T7 ligase site which might compensate for the lack of a fourth GC pair in the Shine-Dalgarno region.

Finally, we have an example of a plasmid carrying simian virus 40 small t-antigen (12), kindly given to us by R. Tjian of this department, which directed a small amount of synthesis by *B. subtilis* ribosomes of internally initiated small t. This small t, lacking an amino-terminal peptide of the real 17,000-dalton small t, is also synthesized by *E. coli*, both in vivo and in vitro. There is a very strong RNA-RNA complementarity here, so it is not surprising that this site is recognized. The distance between the Shine-Dalgarno region and the initiation codon varies from 6 to 13 nucleotides in these initiator regions. This seems consistent with the tolerance of variation within limits that is observed for *E. coli* ribosomes.

How strong are the Shine-Dalgarno complementarities of these sites relative to those bound by *E. coli*? The average value for the free energies of formation of the Shine-Dalgarno pairs of the gram-negative binding sites is -8 kcal/mol, whereas a few available gram-positive initiation sites appear to center about -17 kcal/mol. This weaker Shine-Dalgarno pairing of the predominant population of gram-negative initiation sites is consistent with the strict dependence on initiation factors for initiation. The stronger RNA-RNA pairing of gram-positive sites may not only be a requirement for efficient initiation by gram-positive ribosomes, but may also be the feature of gram-positive mRNAs that renders them factor independent. Thus, analysis of the ribosome binding site of gram-positive *S. aureus* β-lactamase suggests some differences in the gram-positive ribosome-mRNA interaction and gives us a clue to the basis of species-specific translation.

LITERATURE CITED

1. **Ambler, R. P.** 1975. The amino acid sequence of *Staphylococcus aureus* penicillinase. Biochem. J. **151:**197–218.
2. **Brodrick, J. W., and J. C. Rabinowitz.** 1977. Biosynthesis of iron-sulfur proteins, p. 101–119. *In* W. Lovenberg (ed.), Iron-sulfur proteins. Academic Press, Inc., New York.
3. **Donis-Keller, H., A. M. Maxam, and W. Gilbert.** 1977. Mapping adenines, guanines, and pyrimidines in RNA. Nucleic Acids Res. **4:**2527–2538.
4. **Gold, L., D. Pribnow, T. Schneider, S. Shinedling, B. S. Singer, and G. Stormo.** 1981. Translational initiation in prokaryotes. Annu. Rev. Microbiol., in press.
5. **Sharrock, W. J., and J. C. Rabinowitz.** 1979. Protein synthesis in *Bacillus subtilis*. I. Hydrodynamics and in vitro functional properties of ribosomes from *B. subtlis* W.168. J. Mol. Biol. **135:**611–626.
6. **Shine, J., and L. Dalgarno.** 1974. The 3′-terminal sequence of *Escherichia coli* 16S ribosomal RNA: complementarity to nonsense triplets and ribosome binding sites. Proc. Natl. Acad. Sci. U.S.A. **71:**1342–1346.
7. **Stallcup, M. R., and J. C. Rabinowitz.** 1973. Specificity in the translation of natural messenger ribonucleic acids. J. Biol. Chem. **248:**3209–3215.
8. **Stallcup, M. R., and J. C. Rabinowitz.** 1973. The roles of initiation factors and salt-washed ribosomes in determining specificity in the translation of natural messenger ribonucleic acids. J. Biol. Chem. **248:**3216–3219.
9. **Stallcup, M. R., W. J. Sharrock, and J. C. Rabinowitz.** 1974. Ribosome and messenger specificity in protein synthesis by bacteria. Biochem. Biophys. Res. Commun. **58:**92–98.
10. **Stallcup, M. R., W. J. Sharrock, and J. C. Rabinowitz.** 1976. Specificity of bacterial ribosomes and messenger ribonucleic acids in protein synthesis reactions. J. Biol. Chem. **251:**2499–2510.
11. **Steitz, J. A., A. J. Wahba, M. Laughrea, and P. B. Moore.** 1977. Differential requirements for polypeptide chain initiation complex formation at the three bacteriophage R17 initiator regions. Nucleic Acids Res. **4:**1–15.
12. **Thummel, C. S., T. L. Burgess, and R. Tjian.** 1981. Properties of simian virus 40 small t antigen overproduced in bacteria. J. Virol. **37:**683–697.

Physical Map of the rRNA Genes of *Bacillus subtilis*

GEORGE C. STEWART, FRANCES E. WILSON, AND KENNETH F. BOTT

Department of Bacteriology, University of North Carolina School of Medicine, Chapel Hill, North Carolina 27514

Genes that encode rRNA in bacteria occur in multiple, noncontiguous copies about the chromosome. The multiple copies are presumably necessary to provide sufficient rRNA for rapidly growing cells. In *Escherichia coli*, which contains seven rRNA operons per haploid chromosome (13), the 16S, 23S, and 5S rRNA species are transcribed as a single precursor RNA and processed through several steps to yield the mature rRNAs (5, 6). The rRNA genes of the gram-positive, endospore-forming bacterium *Bacillus subtilis* have also been demonstrated to undergo a 16S, 23S, 5S transcriptional order (4, 19), but since the direct products of gene transcription have not been characterized, it is not yet accurate to refer to them as "operons." On the basis of density transfer analysis, these rRNA determinants have been localized to positions in the early replicating regions of the chromosome (17). The heteroduplex analysis by Chow and Davidson (3) suggested that there are 7 to 10 copies of the ribosomal genes on the chromosome and that each is homologous and separated from the others by heterologous spacer DNA sequences. One of the gene sets is located 6.2 kilobases (kb) from the attachment site for the lysogenic phage SP02, and a second gene set is separated from the first by less than 0.6 kb. Thus one finds a clustering of the rRNA gene sets in *B. subtilis* that contrasts to the situation in *E. coli* (14). In this study we describe a physical map of the *B. subtilis* rRNA gene sets. These gene sets differ from their *E. coli* counterparts with regard to chromosomal arrangement, relationship to tRNA determinants, and multiplicity of copies.

PATTERNS OF rRNA HOMOLOGY IN RESTRICTION ENDONUCLEASE DIGESTS OF CHROMOSOMAL DNA

Shown in Table 1 are the patterns of hybridization obtained when *Eco*RI, *Bam*HI, *Sma*I, or *Bgl*I restriction endonuclease digests of *B. subtilis* strain 168 chromosomal DNA are probed with ³²P-labeled rRNA. The multiple copies of rRNA gene sets present on the chromosome result in a unique multiple-band hybridization pattern for each enzyme. Increased hybridization intensity in several of the bands presumably represents internal fragments common to all of the rRNA gene sets or fortuitous comigration of two or more hybridizing species. The fewest bands in any digest seen to date is seven, resolved when the *Bgl*I digest was electrophoresed in a 0.35% agarose gel. The chromosomal patterns, aside from their usefulness in constructing a physical map of the rRNA gene sets and contributing information regarding their chromosomal organization, provide controls in the examination of cloned ribosomal sequences to ensure that the cloned DNA is representative of the true chromosomal arrangement of the ribosomal DNA (rDNA).

ANALYSIS OF CLONED rDNA SEQUENCES

E. coli plasmid and Charon 4A phage clones containing rRNA sequences were identified by using either ³²P-labeled rRNA or nick-translated DNA from clones previously obtained with the labeled RNA (7, 11). Figure 1 illustrates some of the cloned isolates characterized to date.

The plasmids p14B1 and p14B8, obtained from P. Zuber and W. Steinberg (University of Virginia), contain complete but noncontiguous gene sets. Each is comprised of fragments from two gene sets separated by short spacer sequences (approximately 0.5 and 0.1 kb, respectively). The plasmid p21C4 was obtained from K. Hutchison (7). The insert of this plasmid contains sequences from the middle of a 16S rRNA determinant including the single *Eco*RI site of this gene (see below). The phage clones D2, G4, and P11 were isolated from the library of *B. subtilis* DNA cloned into a Charon 4A vector (E. Ferrari, D. Henner, and J. A. Hoch, personal communication). Phage G4 carries three *Eco*RI-derived insert fragments: a 1.1-kb fragment with 16S + 23S rRNA homology, a 0.76-kb fragment that hybridizes to 23S rRNA and a 4.5-kb fragment, the 0.76-kb fragment-proximal portion of which has 23S + 5S rRNA homology.

The plasmid p12E2 contains a *Bam*HI-generated DNA insert homologous to 23S and 5S rDNA and 3.5 kb of DNA that is distal to the 5S determinant and lacks rDNA homology. The

TABLE 1. Molecular size and number of chromosomal restriction fragments that hybridize to rRNA[a]

EcoRI		BamHI		SmaI		BglI	
16S RNA	23S RNA	16S RNA	23S RNA	16S RNA	23S RNA	16S RNA	23S RNA
10		27		30		42	42
	9.2		25	18[b]	18[b]	19	19
	8.0	23	23	14	14	18	18
	6.3		14		7.3	15	15
	4.5		11		5.4	14.5	14.5
	4.3	8.0		3.3		13.5	13.5
4.0	4.0	6.4		3.0[b]	3.0	10	10
3.4	3.4		6.3[b]	2.6	2.6		
2.9	2.9	6.2[b]			2.2[b]		
	2.2	5.4	5.4	2.1	2.1		
2.0		4.9	4.9	2.0			
1.8		4.4		0.5[b]	0.5[b]		
1.3			3.5				
1.1[b]	1.1[b]						
	0.8[b]						

[a] B. subtilis 168 DNA was digested with the indicated restriction endonuclease, electrophoresed in 0.8% agarose gels (0.35% agarose gel required for resolution of BglI digests), and transferred to nitrocellulose filters (11). rRNA probes were isolated from cells grown for four to six generations in the presence of P32 as described (11, 16). Hybridization with purified species of 16S or 23S rRNA in the presence of a 10-fold excess of the other unlabeled RNA species was as described (11). Alternatively, rDNA probes prepared from previously characterized plasmid and phage clones (2) by nick translation (10) were utilized. Sizes of the bands obtained by autoradiography are given in kilobases.

[b] Intensity on the autoradiographs suggests multiple copies present (internal fragments common to the rRNA gene sets or comigration of nonidentical fragments).

rRNA gene set represented by this plasmid has been mapped genetically to a location between recG and abrB on the chromosome of B. subtilis and has been designated rrnA (F. E. Wilson, J. A. Hoch, and K. F. Bott, submitted for publication). The 2.1- and 1.1-kb HindIII fragments distal to the 5S determinant from p12E2 were used to probe the Charon 4A bank and resulted in the isolation of phage D2. This phage contains, in addition to the 23S + 5S rDNA homology, 7.1 kb of "spacer" DNA adjacent to the gene set.

Phage P11 contains five EcoRI-generated insert fragments. In sequence order these are (i) a 2.9-kb fragment containing the terminal 2.2 kb of one rRNA gene set and the initial 0.7 kb of a second gene set, the two being separated by less than 0.1 kb of spacer DNA; (ii) a 1.1-kb fragment with 16S + 23S rRNA homology; (iii) a 0.76-kb fragment homologous to 23S rRNA; (iv) a 2.2-kb fragment with homology to 23S and 5S rRNA; and (v) a 4.6-kb fragment lacking rRNA homology. The insert of P11 thus contains a complete ribosomal gene set. The insert of the plasmid p14B8 is essentially a subset of the P11 insert. The intact gene set on this phage has allowed verification of a physical map constructed for the rRNA gene sets of B. subtilis.

All of the rRNA-homologous DNA fragments correspond in size to the hybridizing fragments found in the chromosome of B. subtilis 168. Thus, there is no evidence that the DNA sequences have been rearranged during cloning.

The ribosomal gene sets of the clones p12E2 and p14B8 (phage P11) have been shown by hybridization analysis to be located on the 15-kb and 42-kb BglI chromosomal fragments, respectively (Table 1).

PHYSICAL MAP OF AN rRNA GENE SET

A physical map of the ribosomal gene sets of B. subtilis is presented in Fig. 2. All evidence to date indicates that the different gene sets are homologous with regard to the restriction endonuclease sites indicated. The rDNA lacks cleavage sites for the enzymes SalI, BglI, and BglII. There is a single BamHI site (within the 23S rDNA) and a single internal HindIII site (also within the 23S rRNA encoding sequence). The only restriction site that was found to be variable is the HindIII site distal to the 5S rRNA determinant. A precursor for 5S rRNA of B. subtilis has been sequenced (18), and analysis of this sequence indicates that a HindIII site is located one base outside the coding sequence for mature 5S rRNA. Of the distinct precursors of 5S rRNA reported for this organism (15), our analysis indicates that only one possesses the 5S distal HindIII site.

The rRNA gene sets of B. subtilis differ funda-

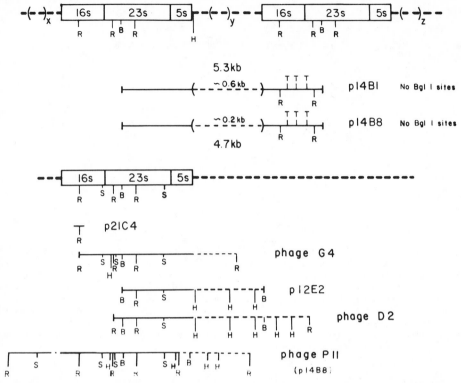

FIG. 1. Plasmid and Charon 4A clones containing rDNA sequences from *B. subtilis*. Dashed lines represent "spacer" DNA sequences that have no homology to rRNA; solid lines represent sequences corresponding to an rRNA gene set. Figures are not drawn to scale. Clones were identified and physical characterizations were performed with rRNA and rDNA probes used as described (1, 2, 11). The conditions for restriction enzyme digestions were as given in the 1980 catalog of Bethesda Research Laboratories, Inc. Abbreviations used for the restriction endonucleases are as follows: B, *Bam*HI; H, *Hind*III; R, *Eco*RI; S, *Sma*I; and T, *Taq*I.

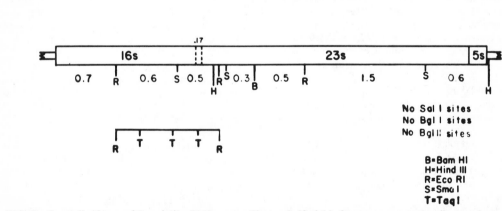

FIG. 2. Generalized map of *B. subtilis* rRNA genes. The top half of this figure represents the ribosomal gene sets located adjacent to the attachment site for the lysogenic phage SP02 as identified by Chow and Davidson (3). The bottom half represents the physical map of an rRNA gene set. Sizes are given in kilobases. The vertical dashed lines represent the abutment of the 16S and 23S rRNA genes. The coding sequences for mature 16S and 23S are separated by approximately 0.17 kb of DNA.

mentally in organization from their *E. coli* counterparts. Preliminary evidence indicates that 4S RNA genes are linked to the 5S rRNA determinants of most, if not all, of the rRNA gene sets, but 4S RNA does not hybridize to the 16S to 23S abutment region of the gene set (12; C. P. Moran and K. F. Bott, unpublished data). The plasmid p12E2 (Fig. 1), which has sequences from *rrnA*, has been shown to contain a 4S RNA determinant closely linked to the 5S rRNA-encoding region.

Because it is well documented that there are seven rRNA operons per haploid chromosome in *E. coli* (8, 9, 14), determining the number of gene sets present on the chromosome of *B. subtilis* was of interest. We noted that the rRNA gene sets lack *Bgl*I cleavage sites, and when *Bgl*I-digested chromosomal DNA is resolved on 0.35% agarose gels, seven distinct ribosomal hybridizing bands result. The plasmids p14B1 and p14B8 contain short spacer sequences separating ribosomal gene sets. These two spacer regions are seen to lack *Bgl*I sites and, therefore, the two rRNA gene sets represented on each plasmid would reside on a single chromosomal *Bgl*I fragment. The seven hybridizing fragments thus represent at least nine rRNA gene sets. An estimate of 9 is also consistent with the finding of 11 *Eco*RI chromosomal fragments hybridizing to 23S rRNA (Table 1). Two of these represent internal fragments (0.76 kb and 1.1 kb) common to all of the gene sets, so the remainder must represent the terminal sequences from nine 23S rRNA determinants.

The genetic organization of the rRNA gene sets in this gram-positive bacterium differs considerably from that of its gram-negative counterpart, and the number of ribosomal gene sets is increased. Whether this increased multiplicity is related to the biosynthetic shift that occurs during the process of endospore formation is unclear at this time.

ACKNOWLEDGMENTS

We thank L. M. Anderson, M. F. Lampe, and M. A. Hollis for valuable discussion, technical assistance, and enthusiastic criticism during this study. P. Zuber generously exchanged plasmid clones and unpublished data from his dissertation.

This project was supported by grant PCM78-09814 from the National Science Foundation and by grant GM26399 from the National Institute of General Medical Sciences to K.B. G.S. is supported by National Institutes of Health postdoctoral fellowship GM12345.

LITERATURE CITED

1. **Benton, W. D., and R. W. Davis.** 1977. Screening λgt recombinant clones by hybridization to single plaques in situ. Science **196**:180–182.

2. **Bott, K. F., F. E. Wilson, and G. C. Stewart.** 1980. Characterization of *Bacillus subtilis* rRNA genes, p. 119–122. *In* H. S. Levinson, A. L. Sonenshein, and D. J. Tipper (ed.), Sporulation and germination. Proceedings of the 8th International Spores Conference. American Society for Microbiology, Washington, D.C.

3. **Chow, L. T., and N. Davidson.** 1973. Electron microscope mapping of the distribution of ribosomal genes of the *Bacillus subtilis* chromosome. J. Mol. Biol. **75**:265–279.

4. **Colli, W., I. Smith, and M. Oishi.** 1971. Physical linkage between 5s, 16s, and 23s ribosomal RNA genes in *Bacillus subtilis*. J. Mol. Biol. **56**:117–127.

5. **Dunn, J. J., and F. W. Studier.** 1973. T7 early RNAs and *Escherichia coli* ribosomal RNAs are cut from large precursor RNAs in vivo by ribonuclease III. Proc. Natl. Acad. Sci. U.S.A. **70**:3296–3300.

6. **Gegenheimer, P., and D. Apirion.** 1980. Precursors to 16s and 23s ribosomal RNA from a ribonuclease III⁻ strain of *Escherichia coli* contain intact ribonuclease III processing sites. Nucleic Acids Res. **8**:1873–1891.

7. **Hutchison, K. W., and H. O. Halvorson.** 1980. Cloning of randomly sheared DNA fragments from a φ105 lysogen of *Bacillus subtilis*: identification of prophage containing clones. Gene **8**:267–278.

8. **Kenerley, M. E., E. A. Morgan, L. E. Post, L. Lindahl, and M. Nomura.** 1977. Characterization of hybrid plasmids carrying individual ribosomal ribonucleic acid transcription units of *Escherichia coli*. J. Bacteriol. **132**:931–949.

9. **Kiss, A., B. Sain, and P. Venetianer.** 1977. The number of rRNA genes in *Escherichia coli*. FEBS Lett. **79**:77–79.

10. **Maniatis, T., A. Jeffrey, and D. G. Kleid.** 1975. Nucleotide sequence of the rightward operator of phage lambda. Proc. Natl. Acad. Sci. U.S.A. **72**:1184–1188.

11. **Moran, C. P., and K. F. Bott.** 1979. Restriction enzyme analysis of the ribosomal RNA genes of *Bacillus subtilis*. J. Bacteriol. **140**:99–105.

12. **Moran, C. P., and K. F. Bott.** 1979. Organization of transfer RNA genes and ribosomal RNA genes in *Bacillus subtilis*. J. Bacteriol. **140**:742–744.

13. **Nomura, M., E. A. Morgan, and S. R. Jaskunas.** 1977. Genetics of bacterial ribosomes. Annu. Rev. Genet. **11**:297–347.

14. **Nomura, M., and L. E. Post.** 1980. Organization of ribosomal genes and regulation of their expression in *E. coli*, p. 671–691. *In* G. Chambliss, G. R. Craven, J. Davies, K. Davis, L. Kahan, and M. Nomura (ed.), Ribosomes: structure, function, and genetics. University Park Press, Baltimore.

15. **Pace, N. R., M. L. Pato, J. McKibbin, and C. W. Radcliffe.** 1973. Precursors of 5s ribosomal RNA in *Bacillus subtilis*. J. Mol. Biol. **75**:619–631.

16. **Potter, S. S., K. F. Bott, and J. E. Newbold.** 1977. Two dimensional restriction analysis of the *Bacillus subtilis* genome: gene purification and ribosomal ribonucleic acid gene organization. J. Bacteriol. **129**:492–500.

17. **Smith, I., D. Dubnau, P. Morell, and J. Marmur.** 1968. Chromosomal location of DNA base sequences complementary to transfer RNA and to 5s, 16s, and 23s ribosomal RNA in *Bacillus subtilis*. J. Mol. Biol. **33**:123–140.

18. **Sogin, M. L., N. R. Pace, M. Rosenberg, and S. M. Weissman.** 1976. Nucleotide sequence of a 5s precursor from *Bacillus subtilis*. J. Biol. Chem. **251**:3480–3488.

19. **Zingales, B., and W. Colli.** 1977. Ribosomal RNA genes in *Bacillus subtilis*. Evidence for a cotranscription mechanism. Biochim. Biophys. Acta **474**:562–577.

RNA Processing in *Bacillus subtilis*

NORMAN R. PACE, KATHELEEN GARDINER, BERND MEYHACK, BERNADETTE PACE,
MITCHELL L. SOGIN, AND DAVID A. STAHL

Department of Molecular and Cellular Biology, National Jewish Hospital and Research Center, and Department of Biochemistry, Biophysics, and Genetics, University of Colorado Medical Center, Denver, Colorado 80206

Most RNA molecules, both in procaryotes and in eucaryotes, undergo more or less extensive posttranscriptional processing. Precursor RNAs are reduced to the sizes of their mature, functional forms by endonucleolytic and exonucleolytic tailoring. Specific residues in some RNA species (e.g., tRNA, rRNA) are modified by methylation or other chemical changes. Also, some RNA molecules undergo specific degradation during normal cellular growth. This paper reviews information currently available on the enzymes that specifically cleave RNA during its metabolism in *Bacillus subtilis*. This organism turns out to be convenient for the investigation of some of the RNA-processing nucleases, although studies are hardly begun. *Escherichia coli* has received the most attention with regard to working out the details of RNA processing and identifying the enzymes and genes involved. RNA metabolism in *B. subtilis* seems to parallel that of *E. coli* closely, but interesting and useful differences in detail are emerging. Abelson (1) has provided a useful review of RNA processing in general; Apirion et al. (4) and Mazarra and McClain (12) have concisely reviewed rRNA and tRNA processing in *E. coli*.

Because of the dearth of information available on RNA processing in *B. subtilis*, it is instructive to compare what is known to the counterpart events in *E. coli*. Table 1 lists the RNA-processing enzymes that have been characterized or are known to be required by *E. coli* and *B. subtilis*, together with their functions. Table 1 is not exhaustive for enzymes reported in the literature, but it includes those whose characterization has been adequate to identify them as unique in action and to ascribe to them some function. Some candidate processing enzymes (e.g., RNases BN, P2, and F) that are apparently distinct from those listed have been identified in mutant *E. coli* strains or have been partially purified, or both, but their roles in the cell remain obscure.

Each of the tabulated endonucleases acts on the product of the rRNA transcriptional unit, which in *E. coli* contains some tRNA genes in addition to the 16S, 23S, and 5S rRNA genes, so their activities are conveniently summarized in Fig. 1. There seem to be no tRNA genes between the 16S and 23S rRNA genes in the case of *B. subtilis* (17), but some may lie downstream from the 5S rRNA cistron.

Newly synthesized RNA chains often are acted upon by multiple enzymes (e.g., Fig. 1), so the processing events fall loosely into two classes. "Primary" processing is upon the initial RNA transcript; "secondary" processing generates mature RNA termini. In normally growing cells, primary processing generally precedes secondary cleavages, but cleavage pathways do not seem to be very rigid. For example, *E. coli* mutants defective in RNase III, the key primary processing enzyme, are viable. Thus, the secondary processing enzymes are capable of independent function, but the collection of precursor forms differs from that seen in normal cells. Apirion et al. (4) have summarized such results. Therefore, pathways of RNA processing probably should be viewed as following the kinetic availability of optimal substrate sites in the RNA. Primary cleavages mostly occur rapidly, on nascent RNA chains, soon after the passage of the RNA polymerase. Some secondary cleavages also may occur on nascent RNA, but other cleavage enzymes require ribonucleoprotein substrates (e.g., ribosome precursors), whose assembly probably is rate limiting in the kinetic flow of processing. Additionally, the products of primary cleavages generally seem to be the best substrates for the secondary processing enzymes, probably because of conformational hindrances in the bulkier primary transcript. Substrate preference will be commented upon as the various specific enzymes are discussed.

RNase III

It is remarkable that *E. coli* mutants defective in RNase III function are viable, because this enzyme seems central to RNA metabolism. It effects the primary scissions in the product of the rRNA transcriptional unit (Fig. 1); it cleaves polycistronic mRNAs to shorter forms, which

TABLE 1. RNA-processing enzymes of *E. coli* and *B. subtilis*

Enzyme	Function	*E. coli*	*B. subtilis*
RNase III	Endonuclease; cleaves primary rRNA transcript and mRNA	Yes	Must exist
RNase "M16"	Endonuclease; cleaves precursor segments from 5' and 3' ends of 16S rRNA	Identified in extracts; may be two activities	Must exist
RNase "M23"	Probably endonuclease; cleaves precursor segments from 5' and 3' ends of 23S rRNA	Must exist; may be two activities	Must exist
RNase M5	Cleaves precursor segments from 5' and 3' ends of 5S rRNA in *B. subtilis*, only 5' end in *E. coli*	Must exist; may be exonuclease	Yes; endonuclease
RNase E	Endonuclease; produces mature 3' end of 5S rRNA but cuts inaccurately at 5'	Yes	Probably does not exist
RNase P	Endonuclease; cleaves 5' precursor segment from tRNA	Yes, contains RNA element	Yes, contains RNA element
RNase D	3' Exonuclease; removes 3' precursor segments from tRNA	Yes	Probably
RNase II	3' Exonuclease; degrades unstable RNA	Yes	Probably

are more active in protein synthesis; and it may be involved in polymeric tRNA transcript scission. The enzyme has been purified to homogeneity and has received substantial attention from a number of laboratories. An important aspect of the *E. coli* RNase III that has facilitated its study is its low substrate specificity under certain assay conditions. Although in the cell, and in vitro at relatively high ionic strength (>0.1 M NH_4Cl), RNase III cleavages are restricted to very specific substrate sites, at low ionic strength (<0.05 M NH_4Cl) specificity is relaxed so that many duplex RNAs are extensively digested (6). Poly r(AU), for example, is an excellent substrate for RNase III under low salt conditions; 10 to 20 base pair fragments containing 5'-phosphoryl and 3'-hydroxyl termini result. Thus, there is available a convenient assay (formation of acid-soluble material) that does not depend on cellular precursor RNAs and gel electrophoretic analysis for specific cleavage products. Several natural cleavage sites for RNase III have been sequenced (24) and also are located in regions of high duplex content, as hinted in Fig. 1. There are no real nucleotide sequence homologies between the various RNase III substrate sites, so it is probably the local folding of the RNA chain, and the consequent matrix of hydrogen bond and ionic contacts, that defines the substrate site rather than the nucleotide sequence per se.

No homolog of the *E. coli* RNase III has been isolated from *B. subtilis*, but one must exist. The rRNA genes in *B. subtilis* are transcriptionally linked (18), although a tandem transcript from the rRNA genes does not appear even in cells treated with inhibitors of protein synthesis, which also inhibit the secondary processing enzymes. In *B. cereus* (a close relative of *B. subtilis*), however, the tandem transcript does accumulate in cells poisoned with nucleoside analogs (18), so the tandem rRNA precursor must be cut by an RNase III homolog. Additionally, certain *B. subtilis* phage mRNAs are cleaved soon after transcription (5). By analogy with *E. coli*, these cleavages possibly are effected by the same enzyme.

Study of the *B. subtilis* RNase III probably will not be as easy as with *E. coli*, because the *B. subtilis* enzyme does not seem to relax its specificity under low salt reaction conditions in vitro. Members of our laboratory made a brief, by no means exhaustive, search for RNase III-like activity, using as assay substrates a few duplex homo- and heteropolymers of RNA, in various ionic conditions, but observed no acid solubilization of the test substrates. Although further convenient substrates and other reaction environments (e.g., with solvents) should be sought, it may be necessary to turn to natural substrates such as phage mRNAs from pulse-labeled cells. Such an undertaking would be difficult with *E. coli*, because of the high nonspecific nuclease content of crude cellular extracts, but *B. subtilis* offers a happier aspect. Our general experience is that *B. subtilis* extracts are remarkably low in nonspecific nuclease activities, so it should be possible to see specific cleavage products on gels. This is one advantage of the organism for studies of RNA processing.

RNases "M16" AND "M23"

Even with *E. coli*, there is little information on RNases "M16" and "M23," which are responsible for trimming the large rRNA precursors to their mature lengths. Both certainly exist; their substrates, discrete precursors of the mature 16S and 23S rRNAs, accumulate in the absence of protein synthesis (18). These substrates contain 5'- and 3'-terminal precursor-specific segments (ca. 100 to 150 nucleotides on each molecule) and are derived from cleavage of the tandem transcript of the ribosomal DNA by RNase III (and other enzymes—see below). Since inhibition of protein synthesis abolishes their action, RNases "M16" and "M23" must recognize only ribonucleoprotein particles (ribosome precursors). This contrasts with most of the known RNA-processing enzymes, which are capable of handling naked RNA, and occurs because the naked rRNA precursors never exist in growing cells. The ribosomal (and probably other) proteins normally collect on the nascent transcript.

Both termini of the 16S and 23S sequences must be present before cleavage can occur. As alluded to in Fig. 1, the substrate sites are formed by complementary pairing of the precursor sequences immediately adjacent to the mature termini (24). It is not known for sure whether RNase "M16" is different from RNase "M23"; perhaps more than two enzymes are involved. The fact that the 5'- and 3'-terminal substrate sites are drawn into juxtaposition suggests, however, that one enzyme is involved in the maturation of both termini, following a single binding event. The concomitant release of both precursor segments from 16S rRNA in pulse-labeled preribosomal particles has been demonstrated by using crude extracts of *E. coli* (11, 13), but difficulties in dealing with the complex substrate, a cumbersome assay (polyacrylamide gels), and nonspecific nucleases seem to have discouraged pursuit of the maturation enzyme.

In the absence of RNase III, RNases "M16" and "M23" are capable of producing mature 16S and 23S rRNA; however, they probably mainly operate on growing RNA chains (4). Consider-

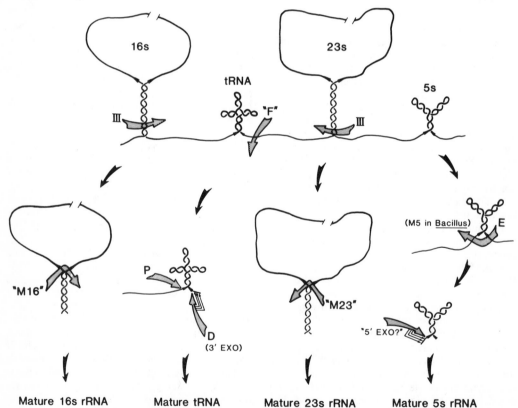

FIG. 1. RNA processing in *E. coli*. Bold lines diagram the mature domains. The arrows indicate cleavages by the various enzymes listed in Table 1. The enzymes in quotations are not well characterized.

able tandem ribosomal DNA transcript accumulates in RNase III mutants, but it seems mostly to be destroyed, rather than serving as a substrate pool for terminal maturation. Probably the completed tandem transcript is so cluttered with excess RNA and proteins that it is hardly recognizable by the RNases "M16" and "M23" (and other secondary processing enzymes that normally act on RNase III products). Thus, RNase III, although important in much posttranscriptional processing, offers a kinetic rather than an absolute advantage to cells, by providing substrates that are handled with facility by other and perhaps more discriminating enzymes, such as the RNases "M16" and "M23."

Nothing is known of the RNases "M16" and "M23" of *B. subtilis* except that, as in *E. coli*, they must exist; in the absence of protein synthesis, their substrates accumulate. Again, because of the relatively low nonspecific nuclease activity in extracts of *B. subtilis*, the organism may be more fruitful than *E. coli* as a system for exploring these interesting enzymes.

RNases M5 AND E

The *B. subtilis* RNase M5, which catalyzes the terminal maturation of 5S rRNA, is one of the best-characterized RNA-processing enzymes (19). We discovered the enzyme several years ago, while searching for an RNA-processing scheme sufficiently simple to analyze in chemical detail. We chose 5S rRNA because of its small size (ca. 120 nucleotides), lack of modified bases, and unique structure. Additionally, precursors of 5S rRNA were known to accumulate upon inhibition of protein synthesis. The precursor seen in chloramphenicol-treated *E. coli* was not attractive, however. It is maximally only three nucleotides larger than the mature form, and we thought such limited precursor-specific length would be insignificant, functionally. We therefore scanned a variety of organisms for a more complex 5S rRNA precursor; *B. subtilis*, among other members of that genus, offered such.

Three precursors of 5S rRNA, having lengths about 150, 180, and 240 nucleotides, and deriving from different genes, appear in chloramphenicol-treated *B. subtilis*. The endonuclease RNase M5, which we have purified substantially, cleaves 5'- and 3'-terminal sequences from each precursor (22). Figure 2 shows the reaction catalyzed by RNase M5 with one of the precursors. The 3' segment of this precursor has the structure of a strong transcription termination site, so the 5S gene is the last one in that rRNA transcriptional unit. The 240-nucleotide precursor also contains the transcription step, but the

150-nucleotide class (three to four species) does not. Possibly, the transcriptional units for these latter have other genes, perhaps for tRNA, distal to the 5S gene. The enzyme(s) that cleaves the 5S precursors from the tandem transcript of the ribosomal DNA is not yet known.

The *B. subtilis* RNase M5 consists of two readily separable components, α and β (22). The β component is capable of binding the precursor (and other RNAs) to a membrane filter, but no scission of the RNA occurs until α, the presumed catalytic component, is added; β, the binding component, promises to be interesting. Substantially more of it is present in cells than would be anticipated if it were merely catalytic, and it binds many types of RNA. The β component does not correspond in size and properties to any of the ribosomal proteins or protein synthesis factors, but we have obtained from *E. coli* a β equivalent that complements the *B. subtilis* α component in the RNase M5 reaction. These observations suggest that β may play other roles in the cell besides being involved in 5S rRNA metabolism (D. Stahl, unpublished data).

We have explored in some detail the features of the 5S precursors that are required by RNase M5 for recognition and cleavage. The precursor-specific segments do not convey significant information to the enzyme. Rather, a considerable portion of the mature domain is involved; only residues ca. 90 to 120 in the 179-nucleotide precursor in Fig. 2 are exempt from requirement by the enzyme (14). As with RNase III, which must recognize many substrates, RNase M5 does not recognize the substrate site simply on the basis of the local nucleotide sequence (15, 23). We envisage that the tertiary structure of the mature domain offers multiple specific ionic and hydrogen bond contacts to the enzyme (α or β, or both) surface, and that these cooperatively provide the requisite specificity of the interaction. An analogous picture is emerging for the interaction between the aminoacyl tRNA synthetases and their cognate substrates (20) and between RNase P (see below) and its multiple substrates.

When it became clear that the most significant RNase M5 recognition elements are in the mature domain of the precursor RNA, we were able to develop a processing assay that is more convenient than gel electrophoresis of reaction products (15). Phage T4 RNA ligase was used to append an oligoribonucleotide (normally U_3G) to the 5' end of mature 5S rRNA. The construct then was labeled at the 5' end by using [γ-^{32}P]ATP and polynucleotide kinase. The release of [5'-^{32}P]U_3G_{OH} from the labeled construct by

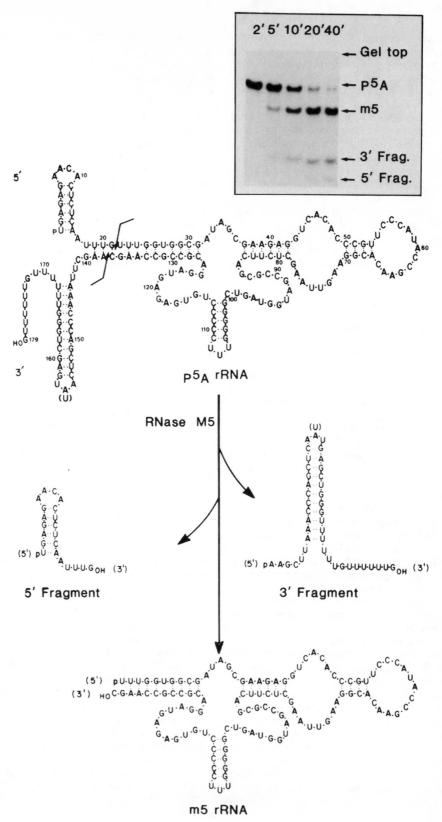

P5A rRNA

RNase M5

5' Fragment

3' Fragment

m5 rRNA

RNase M5 is readily followed by acid-soluble radioactivity or by thin-layer chromatography (23).

The nature of the enzyme, which in *E. coli* trims the 5'-terminal few nucleotides from the immediate precursor of 5S rRNA, remains unexamined. There are suggestions that it may be a 5' exonuclease (7), which would be unique among processing enzymes so far examined, but this is not certain. If it is an exonuclease, then the *E. coli* equivalent to the *B. subtilis* RNase M5 would be RNase E. This enzyme was identified during screening for temperature-sensitive mutants by Apirion and his colleagues (4); so-called *rne* mutants were found to accumulate a ca. 400-nucleotide (9S) precursor of 5S RNA. By using this as an assay substrate, RNase E was partially purified from normal *E. coli* and shown to trim precursor segments endonucleolytically from both ends of the 9S RNA to yield the 5S precursor, which is slightly larger than the mature molecule (16). It is obscure why *E. coli* would require two discrete steps for mature 5S rRNA, whereas *B. subtilis* requires only one. It may be that RNase E is involved in more than 5S rRNA processing and so must contain a versatile substrate binding site. The 9S RNA fit to the enzyme surface may not precisely align the mature 5' terminus to the catalytic site, so subsequent trimming is required.

RNase P

All procaryotic tRNAs known are cleaved from longer precursors (12). Some tRNAs in *E. coli* are part of the rRNA transcriptional unit; others occur as poly-tRNA transcriptional units. The transcriptional organization of most tRNA genes is unknown, however. In all cases examined, the 5' terminus of mature tRNA molecules is produced by the endonuclease RNase P (2, 10). RNase P does not act at the 3' end of the tRNA, although it is influenced by the presence or absence of residues at the 3' terminus, depending on the tRNA precursor species. From studies with a temperature-sensitive mutant of RNase P, it is known that the enzyme also is involved in the processing of other cellular and viral RNAs, of unknown function (2).

The RNase P of *E. coli* has been extensively purified and characterized (2, 10). Remarkably, RNase P contains both RNA and protein components. The RNA moiety is about 300 nucleotides long and constitutes about 75% of the enzyme's mass; its removal destroys RNase P activity.

Because of the novelty offered by an RNA element in a processing enzyme, we considered it important to test its occurrence in an organism phylogenetically disparate from *E. coli*. If an intrinsic RNA is, in general, essential for the processing of tRNA by RNase P, then interesting questions are posed regarding the mechanisms of many protein-polynucleotide interactions. Using a $tRNA^{Gln}$-$tRNA^{Leu}$ dimer precursor from phage T4-infected *E. coli* as a test substrate, we have identified and partially purified the RNase P of *B. subtilis* (8). This enzyme also contains an essential RNA element, but it has features that promise to be usefully different from those of the *E. coli* RNase P.

The search for enzymes containing RNA elements, in principle, is straightforward; the RNA confers upon the RNA-protein aggregate a higher bouyant density than that of the bulk cellular protein. The *E. coli* RNase P has a density of about 1.7 to 1.8 g/cm^3 in CsCl equilibrium gradients, whereas most of the cellular proteins, including nonspecific nucleases that may obscure specific cleavages in gel electrophoresis assays, band at about 1.2 to 1.3 g/cm^3. Fortunately, extracts from *B. subtilis* are low in nonspecific nucleases because, as shown in Fig. 3, when fractionated in a CsCl gradient, the recovery of RNase P activity required the recombination of fractions of high (1.7 to 1.8 g/cm^3) and low (<1.4 g/cm^3) density. The "heavy" component, in turn, can be reversibly dissociated into protein and RNA components. The *B. subtilis* RNase P thus consists of at least three elements—two proteins and one RNA. This promises to be a useful aspect of the *B. subtilis* RNase P, because the "heavy" RNA-protein component is capable of binding the substrate to a membrane filter, with the addition of the "light" component required for substrate cleavage (K. Gardiner, unpublished data). Thus, we should be able to study the substrate recognition/binding aspects of the enzyme in the absence of catalysis.

For the continued examination of the *B. subtilis* RNase P, we have devised a more convenient assay system, modeled after the synthetic substrates used in the RNase M5 studies. The RNase P substrate consists of the oligonucleotide A_3C appended to the 5' end of *E. coli* $tRNA^{Fmet}$ by the action of RNA ligase. RNase P specifically releases $[5'-^{32}P]A_3C_{OH}$ from the 5'-terminally labeled construct (K. Gardiner, unpublished data).

FIG. 2. *B. subtilis* RNase M5 reaction. The inset is an autoradiogram representing polyacrylamide gel analysis of the reaction time course, as detailed previously (22).

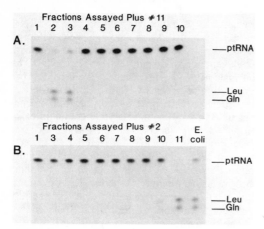

FIG. 3. Separation of *B. subtilis* RNase P components in a CsCl gradient. RNase P from *B. subtilis* was resolved by CsCl equilibrium buoyant density centrifugation. Fractions were assayed by gel electrophoresis for their ability to cleave a Gln-Leu tRNA dimer in the presence of gradient fraction 11 (top of gradient, panel A) or fraction 2 (1.7 g/ml, panel B), all as detailed previously (8).

The fact that RNase P readily and specifically cleaves substrates such as the A_3C-tRNA^{Fmet} synthetic "precursor" means that the substrate recognition elements are in the mature domain of the tRNA. This same conclusion derives from the studies of McClain and his colleagues (12), who have mapped mutations in a tRNA molecule that render it unsusceptible to the *E. coli* RNase P. To identify such mutations, they used phage T4 strains that produce a suppressor form of tRNA^{Ser} and also carry an essential, suppressible nonsense mutation. Thus, growth of the mutant phage in a wide-type host requires the production of mature phage tRNA^{Ser}. Numerous T4 mutants were identified that did not produce the mature suppressor tRNA, but instead accumulated a variety of tRNA^{Ser}-containing precursors, many of which were defective as RNase P substrates. In each case, the mutations were scattered throughout the tRNA mature domain at positions strategic to the secondary and tertiary structures of the molecule. RNase P, as with other processing enzymes examined, seems to use a matrix of substrate contacts, distributed widely over the tRNA mature domain and arranged by its tertiary structure. The mature domains of all tRNAs, of course, have similar conformations. The nucleotide sequence in the vicinity of the cut site in the RNA evidently is not important; the enzyme is capable of handling many tRNA precursors, with quite different sequences.

The fact that RNase P must manipulate so many substrates with similar but not identical structures may explain why it needs an RNA element. The RNA component might mold the precursor tRNAs, which must vary subtly in their geometries, to fit precisely both binding and catalytic elements on the enzyme surface.

RNase D

The immediate precursors of mature tRNAs in *E. coli* commonly have a few extra residues beyond their 3'-terminal C-C-A sequences. RNase D seems to be responsible for trimming these. Deutscher and his colleagues (9) have purified the enzyme substantially and shown it to be a 3' exonuclease that releases 5'-mononucleotides. There are other 3' exonucleases in the cell, but only RNase D abruptly reduces action upon reaching the mature C-C-A end. Nothing is known of the events resulting in mature 3' tRNA termini in *B. subtilis*.

Although all of the *E. coli* tRNA 3'-terminal C-C-A sequences seem to be defined by their genes, some phage (T4, T2) tRNA precursors have sequences replacing the C-C-A. These and any extra residues are removed by RNase BN (12); the correct C-C-A 3' sequence then is added by nucleotidyl transferase. It is not completely clear that RNase BN and RNase D are different enzymes, but they probably are. An *E. coli* mutant defective in RNase BN produces normal tRNAs if their 3' C-C-A sequences are defined by the DNA, whereas phage tRNAs with replacements for C-C-A sequences are not acted upon.

The terminal maturation of the tRNA molecule is quite involved, then. In addition to all the cleavages and appendages, many nucleotide residues in the tRNAs are subject to modifications such as methylation, thiolation, etc. The modifications accumulate as the precursors are reduced in size, probably in preferred pathways. The modifying enzymes are little studied, but many must exist. As with RNase P or RNase D, enzymes responsible for a particular modification seem to be capable of handling many different tRNAs. It would be interesting to see whether any of the modifying enzymes contain RNA elements.

RNase II

All of the enzymes so far discussed are involved in the synthesis of mature RNAs. Some additional enzyme(s) must exist that selectively degrades unstable RNAs, such as mRNA or precursor-specific RNA segments released during endonucleolytic processing. From mutant and other studies in *E. coli*, it seems that the most likely candidate for the scavenging enzyme is RNase II (3). This is a 3' exonuclease which generates 5'-mononucleotides and acts processively; it does not release and rebind the substrate between cleavages. This contrasts with RNase D, which removes residues in successive bindings. Another 3' exonuclease that may participate in RNA turnover, particularly in RNase II mutants, is polynucleotide phosphorylase. This is a phosphorylytic 3' exonuclease; inorganic phosphate is required in the reaction, and 5'-mononucleoside diphosphates result. Unstable RNA in *E. coli* seems to decay via 5'-mononucleotides, however, so the hydrolytic mode of RNase II is attractive as the operating mechanism. There is evidence that endonucleolytic cleavages in mRNA may be a prelude to exonucleolytic terminal degradation, but there are no clues to the enzyme(s) responsible. It (they) may be a processing enzyme that already is known (e.g., RNase III) or that shares elements (e.g., the RNase M5 β component) with known enzymes.

Little information is available regarding RNA scavenging in *B. subtilis*, but it probably is effected by an RNase II-like enzyme. This suggestion stems from an analysis of the selective degradation products of the precursor-specific fragments released during 5S rRNA maturation (21). As shown in Fig. 4, the mature 5S rRNA cleaved from a labeled precursor (the reaction shown in Fig. 2) in crude extracts from *B. subtilis* is stable to degradation, but the precursor-specific fragments are rapidly destroyed. Analysis of the degradation products showed clearly that the process is 3' exonucleolytic, and that 5'-mononucleotides result exclusively.

The *B. subtilis* fragment degradation system may be a good one for examining the nature of substrate selection by the scavenging enzyme. Our feeling is that the scavenging enzyme probably does not distinguish "stable" (nonsubstrate) from "unstable" (substrate) RNA by specific recognition; it needs only to degrade all available RNA 3' termini. Selectivity in degradation could result because the stable RNAs are never free from a protein complex for a significant length of time. The rRNAs are well-protected in the ribosomes, and tRNAs are almost always associated with elongation factor Tu or other elements of the translation apparatus. The tRNA 3' termini are occasionally attacked, but they are repaired by nucleotidyl transferase. The 3' (growing) termini of mRNAs are protected until their transcription is complete, and they do not survive long after that. The mature 5S rRNA generated in crude extracts from *B. subtilis* probably is protected by continued association with the β component of the RNase M5. Thus, the scavenging exonuclease may not be very interesting in terms of protein-polynucleotide recognition.

WHY RNA PROCESSING?

The question of course arises: why RNA processing? Or, more specifically: what do the precursor sequences do? Several roles may be envisaged. Some of the precursor elements clearly are remnants of transcription, for example, initiation and termination sites such as the 3' end of the *B. subtilis* 5S rRNA precursor (Fig. 2). Others are residual information used by processing enzymes that separate polycistronic RNAs. A more interesting role for precursor RNA sequences might be to assist in the folding of the mature domain or in its association with other molecules, for example, ribosomal proteins. Precursor segments in the procaryotic rRNA precursors are small, only a few hundred residues collectively, and thus probably do not engage extensively in RNA or protein assembly. The eucaryotic rRNA precursors, on the other hand, have many thousands (ca. 7 kilobases in humans) of evolutionarily conserved, precursor-specific residues, some of which may be involved in scaffolding. The general complexity of eucaryotic RNA precursor segments, not only those associated with rRNA, suggests that they are of use to the cell. For example, some ele-

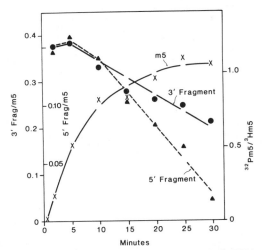

FIG. 4. Selective degradation of released 5S rRNA precursor-specific fragments. The fragments released from ^{32}P-labeled p5$_A$ rRNA precursor (Fig. 2) in a crude extract prepared from *B. subtilis* were scored by gel electrophoresis as detailed previously (21). Recoveries of reaction products were normalized by including a constant amount of ^{3}H-labeled 5S rRNA.

ments associated with mRNA precursors may direct transcripts into alternative conformations, displaying alternative splicing sites. Other precursor sequences may be involved in transport or contain regulatory information dictating the fate of a molecule in the heterogeneous nuclear RNA pool. The processing enzymes that manipulate these large RNA precursors promise to be interesting indeed.

ACKNOWLEDGMENTS

Research from this laboratory was supported by a National Institutes of Health grant and a Research Career Development Award to N.R.P.

LITERATURE CITED

1. **Abelson, J.** 1979. RNA processing and the intervening sequence problem. Annu. Rev. Biochem. **48:**1035–1065.
2. **Altman, S., E. J. Brown, R. L. Garber, R. Kole, R. A. Koski, and B. C. Stark.** 1980. Aspects of RNase P structure and function, p. 71–82. *In* D. Soll, J. Abelson, and P. R. Schimmel (ed.), Transfer RNA: biological aspects. Cold Spring Harbor Laboratory, Cold Spring Harbor, N.Y.
3. **Apirion, D.** 1974. The fate of mRNA and rRNA in *Escherichia coli*. Brookhaven Symp. Biol. **26:**286–306.
4. **Apirion, D., B. K. Ghora, G. Plautz, T. K. Misra, and P. Gegenheimer.** 1980. Processing of rRNA and tRNA in *Escherichia coli*: cooperation between processing enzymes, p. 139–154. *In* D. Soll, J. Abelson, and P. R. Schimmel (ed.), Transfer RNA: biological aspects. Cold Spring Harbor Laboratory, Cold Spring Harbor, N.Y.
5. **Downard, J. S., and H. R. Whiteley.** 1980. Early RNAs in SP82- and SP01-infected *Bacillus subtilis* may be processed. J. Virol. **37:**1075–1078.
6. **Dunn, J. J.** 1976. RNase III cleavage of single-stranded RNA. J. Biol. Chem. **251:**3807–3814.
7. **Galibert, F., P. Tiollais, F. Sanfourche, and M. Boiron.** 1971. Coordination de la transcription des RNA 5S et 23S et coordination de la maturation du RNA 5S et de la sousunité ribosonique 50S chez *Escherichia coli*. Eur. J. Biochem. **20:**381–391.
8. **Gardiner, K., and N. R. Pace.** 1980. RNase P of *Bacillus subtilis* has a RNA component. J. Biol. Chem. **255:**7507–7509.
9. **Ghosh, R. K., and M. P. Deutscher.** 1980. The purification of 3′ processing nuclease using synthetic tRNA precursors, p. 59–69. *In* D. Soll, J. Abelson, and P. R. Schimmel (ed.), Transfer RNA: biological aspects. Cold Spring Harbor Laboratory, Cold Spring Harbor, N.Y.
10. **Guthrie, C., and R. Atchison.** 1980. Biochemical characterization of RNase P: a tRNA processing activity with

protein and RNA components, p. 83–97. *In* D. Soll, J. Abelson, and P. R. Schimmel (ed.), Transfer RNA: biological aspects. Cold Spring Harbor Laboratory, Cold Spring Harbor, N.Y.
11. **Hayes, F., and M. Vasseur.** 1976. Processing of 17S *Escherichia coli* precursor RNA in the 27S pre-ribosomal particle. Eur. J. Biochem. **61:**433–438.
12. **Mazarra, G. P., and W. H. McClain.** 1980. tRNA synthesis, p. 3–27. *In* D. Soll, J. Abelson, and P. R. Schimmel (ed.), Transfer RNA: biological aspects. Cold Spring Harbor Laboratory, Cold Spring Harbor, N.Y.
13. **Meyhack, B., I. Meyhack, and D. Apirion.** 1974. Processing of precursor particles containing 17S rRNA in a cell free system. FEBS Lett. **49:**215–219.
14. **Meyhack, B., and N. R. Pace.** 1978. Involvement of the mature domain in the *in vitro* maturation of *Bacillus subtilis* precursor 5S ribosomal RNA. Biochemistry **17:**5804–5810.
15. **Meyhack, B., B. Pace, O. Uhlenbeck, and N. R. Pace.** 1978. Use of T$_4$ RNA ligase to construct model substrates for a ribosomal RNA maturation endonuclease. Proc. Natl. Acad. Sci. U.S.A. **75:**3045–3049.
16. **Misra, T. K., and D. Apirion.** 1979. RNase E, an RNA processing enzyme from *Escherichia coli*. J. Biol. Chem. **254:**11154–11159.
17. **Moran, C. P., Jr., and K. F. Bott.** 1979. Organization of transfer and ribosomal ribonucleic acid genes in *Bacillus subtilis*. J. Bacteriol. **140:**742–744.
18. **Pace, N. R.** 1973. Structure and synthesis of the ribosomal RNA of prokaryotes. Bacteriol. Rev. **37:**562–603.
19. **Pace, N. R., B. Meyhack, B. Pace, and M. L. Sogin.** 1980. The interaction of RNase M5 with 5S rRNA precursor, p. 155–171. *In* D. Soll, J. Abelson, and P. R. Schimmel (ed.), Transfer RNA: biological aspects. Cold Spring Harbor Laboratory, Cold Spring Harbor, N.Y.
20. **Schimmel, P. R., and D. Soll.** 1979. Aminoacyl-tRNA synthetases: general features and recognition of transfer RNAs. Annu. Rev. Biochem. **48:**601–648.
21. **Schroeder, E., J. McKibbin, M. L. Sogin, and N. R. Pace.** 1977. Mode of degradation of precursor-specific ribonucleic acid fragments by *Bacillus subtilis*. J. Bacteriol. **130:**1000–1009.
22. **Sogin, M. L., B. Pace, and N. R. Pace.** 1977. Partial purification and properties of a ribosomal RNA maturation endonuclease from *Bacillus subtilis*. J. Biol. Chem. **252:**1350–1357.
23. **Stahl, D. A., B. Meyhack, and N. R. Pace.** 1980. Recognition of local nucleotide conformation in contrast to sequence by a rRNA processing endonuclease. Proc. Natl. Acad. Sci. U.S.A. **77:**5644–5648.
24. **Young, R. A., R. J. Bram, and J. A. Steitz.** 1980. rRNA and tRNA processing signals in the rRNA operons of *Escherichia coli* p. 99–106. *In* D. Soll, J. Abelson, and P. R. Schimmel (ed.), Transfer RNA: biological aspects. Cold Spring Harbor Laboratory, Cold Spring Harbor, N.Y.

Structure and Function of the Region of Replication Origin in the *Bacillus subtilis* Chromosome

HIROSHI YOSHIKAWA, MOTOHARU SEIKI, NAOTAKE OGASAWARA, AND MARI SHIMOYACHI

Cancer Research Institute, Kanazawa University, 13-1, Takaramachi, Kanazawa 920, Japan

The chromosome of *Bacillus subtilis* is a circular molecule of 2×10^9 daltons and replicates bidirectionally from a genetically fixed origin. Initiation of its replication is a highly regulated process. Although little is known about the mechanism of initiation, we have identified at least three *dna* genes involved in this process (5, 18). Taking advantage of the fact that the *din* gene (9) product (*dnaB* by other groups [5]) is reversibly inactivated in *din* temperature-sensitive (*ts*) mutants at nonpermissive temperatures, we demonstrated a direct involvement of RNA or RNA synthesis at the last step in sequential events leading to initiation (8). Recently, we found that the DNA gyrase and the superhelical structure of DNA are also involved in initiation (11).

Structurally, the origin region is closely associated with the cell membrane (14, 15). Our extensive study of the chromosome's organization near the site of origin revealed two structurally distinct domains in this region. One is a segment of some 3×10^7 daltons that forms a specific DNA-RNA-protein complex (S complex) (16). Formation of the complex correlates closely with formation of the initiation potential (cell's ability to initiate one round of replication without new synthesis of protein and RNA) (19). The other is a region of some 2×10^7 daltons that is replicated in the presence of an overdose of novobiocin once replication has been initiated. Elongation of DNA strands in this domain is completely insensitive to inhibition by DNA gyrase, whereas further elongation is drastically inhibited by novobiocin (10). Replication origin is located between these two domains (13). As illustrated in Fig. 1, the unique organizational features near this site suggest the important roles played by these two domains in the initiation of replication.

MAP OF THE RESTRICTION ENZYME CLEAVAGE SITES NEAR THE SITE OF ORIGIN

To analyze the structure and function of these domains, our first attempt was to construct a map of restriction enzyme cleavage sites near

the area of origin. Following the experiment by Marsh and Worcel (7) in *Escherichia coli*, we labeled the origin region of the chromosome preferentially with [^{3}H]thymidine during synchronous initiations of replication by germinating spores or by *din ts* mutant cells. Analysis of the labeled origin DNA with three enzymes, *Bam*HI, *Eco*RI, and *Sma*I, permitted us to construct a physical map encompassing a region of some 2×10^7 daltons near the origin region (13) (Fig. 2). Replication order among the fragments was determined by pulse labeling the origin region for various periods of time. Addition of novobiocin or initiation of replication at 20°C enabled us to determine the order of early replicating fragments, because the rate of elongation was markedly reduced. By this method, either a *Bam*HI fragment B7 or an *Eco*RI fragment E19, which is located within the B7 fragment, was identified as the first replicating fragment. Accordingly, the origin of replication should reside in the E19 fragment (10).

DETERMINATION OF THE PROTEIN-BINDING SITES IN THE S COMPLEX

In addition to the fragments mapped above, *Eco*RI fragments derived from the neighboring region were identified, and·their relative locations were roughly deduced from the replication order. In this way locations of the DNA segments forming the S complex were determined in the region contiguous to and at one side of the E19 fragment (19) (Fig. 2).

Next, we questioned whether proteins in the complex bind to DNA at specific or random sites. To determine this, the intact S complex was digested with *Eco*RI or *Hin*dIII, and the resultant fragments were passed through a membrane filter. Several protein-binding fragments trapped on the filter were recovered by extraction with sodium dodecyl sulfate-pronase. Then common sequences were identified between these protein-binding fragments produced by *Eco*RI and *Hin*dIII. Relative locations of these fragments indicate that the protein-binding sites were dispersed within the 3×10^7-dalton region. Interaction between these proteins or with the

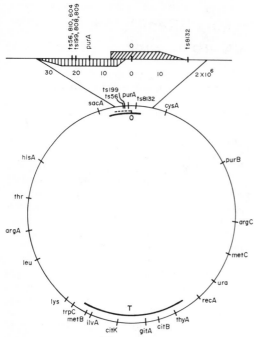

FIG. 1. Map of the *B. subtilis* chromosome, membrane binding sites, and organization of the chromosome near the replication origin. A circular map with various genetic markers is illustrated. Replication starts from O and proceeds toward T bidirectionally. Solid lines in the circle represent regions tightly associated with the cell membrane. The dashed line shows the region of S complex formation. The region near the replication origin is magnified above the map. The shaded area at the left side is the region that forms the S complex; that at the right is the segment replicated in the presence of novobiocin.

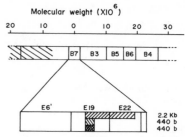

FIG. 2. Map of the restriction enzyme cleavage sites near the site of origin and the locations of the sequences responsible for adverse effects attributable to the B7 fragment. *Bam*HI cleavage sites near the replication origin are shown. Zero in the molecular-weight scale corresponds to the approximate position of replication origin. B3–B7 represent fragments produced by *Bam*HI. *Eco*RI cleavage sites within the B7 fragment are shown in an expanded scale. E6′ represents a portion of the E6 fragment cleaved by *Bam*HI. Within the expanded picture of the B7 fragment, locations of the sequences responsible for three adverse properties of the B7 fragment are illustrated. From the top: (i) stickiness of *E. coli* cells (2.2 kbp), (ii) instability of the plasmid in *E. coli* (440 bp), (iii) inhibition of plasmid transformation of *B. subtilis* (440 bp).

membrane, aided by DNA gyrase, may form several DNA loops with a superhelical conformation.

CLONING THE FIRST REPLICATING FRAGMENT B7 CONTAINING THE REPLICATION ORIGIN

To clone a DNA segment from the replication origin region of the *B. subtilis* chromosome, we constructed a shuttle vector plasmid pMS102 composed of *Eco*RI fragments of pUB110 (6) and pBR322 (1). The plasmid can replicate in *E. coli* by using the pBR replicator system and in *B. subtilis* by using the pUB replicator. Both kanamycin-resistant (Km^r) and ampicillin-resistant (Am^r) genes are expressed in *E. coli*, but only Km^r is functional in *B. subtilis*. A derivative of pMS102 in which the pUB replicator region is deleted was constructed to isolate an autonomously replicating sequence from the *B. subtilis*

chromosome. All attempts to isolate such a sequence by using B7 as well as a mixture of restriction enzyme fragments derived from the chromosomal region of replication origin have failed. Therefore, we have constructed a shuttle plasmid containing the B7 fragment and have examined the effects of B7 on plasmid replication in *E. coli* and *B. subtilis*.

ADVERSE EFFECTS OF THE B7 FRAGMENT AND THEIR LOCATIONS

Plasmids containing the B7 fragment caused various adverse effects in *E. coli* and *B. subtilis*, among which the following three are particularly interesting. (i) *E. coli* cells transformed by the plasmid to Km^r and Am^r, and grown in the presence of kanamycin or ampicillin, rapidly stuck to each other and to glass walls. (ii) When these transformed *E. coli* cells were grown in the absence of the drugs, segregants lacking the plasmid appeared frequently. In other words, the B7 fragment caused instability of the plasmid within the cells. (iii) Transformation of *B. subtilis* cells by the B7-containing plasmid was only about 1/1,000 as efficient as that by the parental plasmid. Properties ii and iii are caused by the failure of replication by B7 and coexisting plasmids that have the same compatibility but have no B7, and are not affected by the B7-containing plasmid in the same cell. No other fragments obtained from the origin region showed these effects.

To examine such effects in molecular terms, we determined the size and location of the DNA sequence responsible for these properties. For this purpose, we developed a new and widely applicable method that deletes various length segments sequentially from either end of a DNA fragment which is of fairly large size (such as the B7 with 5.7 kilobase pairs [kbp]) and is inserted into plasmids. A set of 27 plasmids was isolated with various length deletions in B7 from either end. Assaying these plasmids for the three adverse effects revealed that property i occupied a 2.2-kbp segment, whereas ii and iii were located within the identical 440-bp segment. The locations of these essential regions are illustrated in Fig. 2. The 440-bp segment is located at the terminal portion of the 2.2-kbp segment, suggesting that they compose one unit of a genetic element. Preliminary determination of the base sequence of the 440-bp segment revealed that a large inverted repeat of 34 bp, resembling termination signals for transcription in *E. coli* (12), and many small repeats are clustered within the terminal 150-bp region distal to the 2.2-kbp segment.

CHARACTERISTIC SEQUENCE IN B7 IS MULTIPLY DISTRIBUTED IN THE *B SUBTILIS* CHROMOSOME

Hybridization experiments, with cloned *Eco*RI fragments in B7 used as probes, showed that the segment corresponding to the 2.2-kbp segment identified at least seven homologous sequences in the *B. subtilis* chromosome. On the basis of the pattern of the *Eco*RI digest, the sequence seemed to be well conserved after multiplication of the original copy.

ORGANIZATION OF THE CHROMOSOME IN THE ORIGIN REGION AND ITS ROLE IN THE REGULATION OF INITIATION

Analysis of the function attributable to a DNA segment near the replication origin of the *B. subtilis* chromosome led to the discovery of the characteristic sequence that strongly inhibits self-replication. The fact that this sequence is located so close to the replication origin may be the reason for our failure to isolate an autonomously replicating sequence from *B. subtilis*. This result is in sharp contrast to that with *E. coli*, whose replicator was isolated fairly easily by a shotgun-type cloning experiment (4, 17).

The *cis*-acting repressible sequence at the origin region of the chromosome favors the regulation of initiation by providing the means to shut off replication autonomously and, thereby,

to prevent premature reinitiation. The 440-bp segment alone may act as a stop signal; alternatively, a protein coded by the 2.2-kbp segment may act on the 440-bp segment and prevent initiation from taking place.

The initiation of replication, in turn, requires the release of inhibition by this sequence. Activation may be achieved by altering the secondary or tertiary structures of the sequence. Formation of the DNA-RNA-protein complex may directly affect the structure of the contiguous DNA sequence.

Multiple distribution of the sequence homologous to the repressive origin sequence is an unexpected finding. Although the function of these sequences is unknown, we propose that they function as weak termination-initiation signals. It has been reported that replication of the *B. subtilis* chromosome stopped at several sites during amino acid starvation and resumed from the same sites when amino acids were restored (2, 3).

LITERATURE CITED

1. Bolivar, F., R. L. Rodriguez, P. J. Greene, M. C. Betlach, H. L. Heyneker, H. W. Boyer, J. H. Cross, and S. Falkaw. 1977. Construction and characterization of new cloning vehicles. II. A multipurpose cloning system. Gène 2:95–113.
2. Copeland, J. C. 1970. Regulation of chromosome replication in *Bacillus subtilis*. Effects of amino acid starvation in strain W23. J. Bacteriol. 105:595–603.
3. Copeland, J. C. 1971. Regulation of chromosome replication in *Bacillus subtilis*. Marker frequency analysis after amino acid starvation. Science 172:159–161.
4. Hiraga, S. 1976. Novel F prime factors able to replicate in *Escherichia coli* Hfr strains. Proc. Natl. Acad. Sci. U.S.A. 73:198–202.
5. Karamata, D., and J. D. Gross. 1970. Isolation and genetic analysis of temperature-sensitive mutants of *B. subtilis* defective in DNA synthesis. Mol. Gen. Genet. 108:277–287.
6. Keggins, K. M., P. S. Lovett, and E. J. Duvall. 1978. Molecular cloning of genetically active fragments of *Bacillus* DNA in *Bacillus subtilis* and properties of vector plasmid pUB110. Proc. Natl. Acad. Sci. U.S.A. 75:1423–1427.
7. Marsh, R. C., and A. Worcel. 1977. DNA fragment containing origin of replication of *Escherichia coli* chromosome. Proc. Natl. Acad. Sci. U.S.A. 74:2720–2724.
8. Murakami, S., N. Inuzuka, M. Yamaguchi, K. Yamaguchi, and H. Yoshikawa. 1976. Initiation of DNA replication in *Bacillus subtilis*. III. Analysis of molecular events involved in the initiation using a temperature-sensitive *dna* mutant. J. Mol. Biol. 108:683–704.
9. Murakami, S., S. Murakami, and H. Yoshikawa. 1976. Gene that controls initiation of chromosomal replication and prophage induction in *Bacillus subtilis*. Nature (London) 259:215–218.
10. Ogasawara, N., M. Seiki, and H. Yoshikawa. 1979. Effect of novobiocin on initiation of DNA replication in *Bacillus subtilis*. Nature (London) 281:702–704.
11. Ogasawara, N., M. Seiki, and H. Yoshikawa. 1981. Initiation of DNA replication in *Bacillus subtilis*. V. Role of DNA gyrase and superhelical structure in initiation. Mol. Gen. Genet., in press.
12. Rosenberg, M., and D. Court. 1979. Regulatory sequences

involved in the promotion and termination of RNA transcription. Annu. Rev. Genet. **13**:319–353.

13. **Seiki, M., N. Ogasawara, and H. Yoshikawa.** 1979. Structure of the region of the replication origin of the *Bacillus subtilis* chromosome. Nature (London) **281**:699–701.

14. **Sueoka, N., and W. G. Quinn.** 1968. Membrane attachment of the chromosome replication origin in *Bacillus subtilis*.

15. **Yamaguchi, K., and H. Yoshikawa.** 1973. Topography of chromosome membrane junction in *Bacillus subtilis*. Nature (London) **244**:204–206.

16. **Yamaguchi, K., and H. Yoshikawa.** 1977. Chromosome-membrane association in *Bacillus subtilis*. III. Isolation and characterization of a DNA-protein complex carrying

replication origin markers. J. Mol. Biol. **110**:219–253.

17. **Yasuda, S., and Y. Hirota.** 1977. Cloning and mapping of the replication origin of *Escherichia coli*. Proc. Natl. Acad. Sci. U.S.A. **74**:5458–5462.

18. **Yoshikawa, H., S. Murakami, K. Yamaguchi, N. Inuzuka, and S. Murakami.** 1977. DNA replication cycle in bacteria, with emphasis on regulation of initiation, p. 37–58. *In* T. Ishikawa, Y. Maruyama, and H. Matsumiya (ed.), NRI Symposia on Modern Biology, Growth and differentiation in microorganisms. University of Tokyo Press, Tokyo.

19. **Yoshikawa, H., K. Yamaguchi, M. Seiki, N. Ogasawara, and H. Toyoda.** 1978. Organization of the replication origin region of the *Bacillus subtilis* chromosome. Cold Spring Harbor Symp. Quant. Biol. **43**:569–576.

Replication of *Bacillus* Small Phage DNA

HIDEO HIROKAWA, KOUJI MATSUMOTO, and MOCHIHIKO OHASHI

Life Science Institute, Sophia University, 7-Kioicho, Chiyoda-ku, Tokyo 102, and Department of Biochemistry, Tokyo Metropolitan Institute of Gerontology, 35-2 Sakaecho, Itabashi-ku, Tokyo 173, Japan

Several studies on the DNA synthesis of *Bacillus* phage φ29 have indicated displacement replication in which a protein bound at the 5′ termini of its DNA provides an important function, most likely the initiation of DNA synthesis (1, 4, 5). Displacement replication was also suggested in the synthesis of adenovirus DNA (6), which, like φ29 DNA, is known to have a protein bound at the 5′ termini of its DNA molecules.

In recent years, much information about the mechanism of DNA replication in eucaryotic cells has accumulated and been compared with information about procaryotic replication. During such investigations, aphidicolin, tetracyclic diterpenoid, was rediscovered in Japan as a useful agent for studying DNA replication in eucaryotic cells (3, 7, 8). The drug also inhibits the replication of viruses such as herpes simplex virus and adenovirus. Synthesis of DNA from adenovirus type 2 was established in vitro and found to be sensitive to this drug (2), indicating that DNA polymerase α of the host cells is required for the synthesis.

We have examined the effect of aphidicolin on the multiplication of *Bacillus* small phages containing protein-bound DNA, although the drug is known to affect only eucaryotic cells. However, in the present paper we report that the drug inhibited replication of small phages such as M2 and φ29, but not SP50, SP01, or SPP1.

B. subtilis SR22 cells were infected with these small phages. After phage adsorption for 5 min, different concentrations of aphidicolin were added to the culture at 37°C (Fig. 1). At a high concentration (80 μg/ml) of the drug, cells infected with M2 were not lysed even though control cells cultured without the drug were lysed completely. However, aphidicolin did not prevent the growth of *Bacillus* cells at any dose. Titers of phages were measured in the cultures at 120 min after infection. The multiplication of such other phages as SP50, SP01, and SPP1, which were not sensitive to protease during transfection, was determined by measuring the titers of infection in the presence of the drug. Multiplication of the latter three phages was not affected by aphidicolin (Fig. 2). However, essentially no multiplication of phages M2 and φ29 was observed in the presence of the drug (Table 1). Thus, aphidicolin inhibited the multiplication of these two small phages.

DNA synthesis was analyzed by measuring the incorporation of [3H]thymidine into 10% cold trichloroacetic acid-insoluble fractions in the presence of 6-*p*-hydroxyphenylazouracil, which completely inhibited host cell DNA synthesis but not that of M2 and φ29. The results clearly indicated that aphidicolin prevented the incorporation. When a high concentration of the drug was added to the culture 20 min after the infection of M2, [3H]thymidine incorporation stopped almost immediately.

The effects of rifamycin and chloramphenicol on the DNA synthesis of M2 were then compared with that of aphidicolin. With aphidicolin the sensitivity for [3H]thymidine incorporation

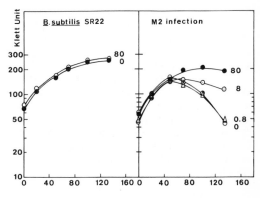

FIG. 1. Growth of *B. subtilis* SR22 cells with or without phage M2 in the presence of aphidicolin. Left: Uninfected *B. subtilis* SR22 in TY medium (10 g of tryptone, 5 g of yeast extract, 5 g of NaCl, 0.1 mM MnCl₂, 10 mM MgSO₄, and 0.2% glucose per liter). Right: SR22 cells infected with phage M2 and containing different concentrations of aphidicolin. Aphidicolin was dissolved in dimethyl sulfoxide at a concentration of 4,000 μg/ml and diluted with TY medium to give the different concentrations (μg/ml) shown by numbers at the right. Aphidicolin was added to the culture 5 min after the infection. The multiplicity of infection was about 5.

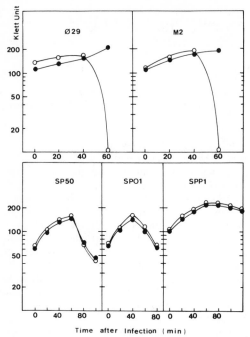

FIG. 2. Growth of *B. subtilis* SR22 cells infected with different *Bacillus* phages. Conditions for the culture were the same as in Fig. 1. Multiplicity of infection for each phage was about 10. Symbols: ○, without aphidicolin; ●, with 80 μg of aphidicolin per ml.

was extended to the late stage of the infection, whereas with rifamycin and chloramphenicol the insensitivity appeared in pre-early and early stages, respectively.

The products made by pulse label for 2 min and chase at 25°C were analyzed by using both neutral and alkaline sucrose density gradient centrifugation. Patterns of the fractions after alkaline centrifugation revealed that small DNA fragments remained in relatively large amounts after the addition of aphidicolin to both M2 and φ29 phages.

TABLE 1. Effect of aphidicolin on phage M2 multiplication

Addition of aphidicolin, 80 μg/ml	No. of infective centers/ml		Ratio, input/output
	Input	Output	
+	10^8	3.1×10^{9a}	31
−	10^8	1.1×10^{11}	1,100

[a] Several drops of chloroform were added to the culture at 140 min.

The drug's effects can be summarized as follows. (i) Aphidicolin inhibited the multiplication of phage M2 and φ29, but not that of SP50, SP01, or SPP1. (ii) Incorporation of [^{3}H]thymidine during infection of M2 and φ29 was prevented by the drug. (iii) The drug seems to affect extensive DNA replication concomitant with elongation of newly synthesized DNA strands.

LITERATURE CITED

1. **Harding, N. E., and J. Ito.** 1980. DNA replication of bacteriophage φ29: characterization of the intermediates and location of the termini of replication. Virology **104**:323–338.
2. **Ikeda, J.-E., T. Enomoto, and J. Hurwitz.** 1981. Replication of adenovirus DNA-protein complex with purified proteins. Proc. Natl. Acad. Sci. U.S.A. **78**:884–888.
3. **Ikegami, S., T. Taguchi, M. Ohashi, M. Oguro, H. Nagano, and Y. Mano.** 1978. Aphidicolin prevents mitotic cell division by interfering with the activity of DNA polymerase-α. Nature (London) **275**:458–460.
4. **Inciarte, M. R., M. Salas, and J. M. Sogo.** 1980. Structure of replicating DNA molecules of *Bacillus subtilis* bacteriophage φ29. J. Virol. **34**:187–199.
5. **Ito, J., N. E. Harding, and K. Saigo.** 1978. φ29 DNA-protein complex and the structure of replicating DNA molecules. Cold Spring Harbor Symp. Quant. Biol. **43**:525–536.
6. **Lechner, R. L., and T. J. Kelly, Jr.** 1977. The structure of replicating adenovirus 2 DNA molecules. Cell **12**:1007–1020.
7. **Oguro, M., C. Suzuki-Hori, H. Nagano, Y. Mano, and S. Ikegami.** 1979. The mode of inhibitory action by aphidicolin on eukaryotic DNA polymerase-α. Eur. J. Biochem. **97**:603–607.
8. **Ohashi, M., T. Taguchi, and S. Ikegami.** 1978. Aphidicolin: a specific inhibitor of DNA polymerase in the cytosol of rat liver. Biochem. Biophys. Res. Commun. **83**:1084–1090.

Is Membrane Association Necessary for the Initiation of Chromosome Replication?

NOBORU SUEOKA, SCOTT WINSTON, RON KORN, TIM McKENZIE, AND STEPHANIE DANIELS

Department of Molecular, Cellular, and Developmental Biology, University of Colorado, Boulder, Colorado 80309

The regulation of initiation of chromosome replication is the key to the understanding of cell proliferation, in which cell division and chromosome replication proceed coordinately. We have been studying the nature of chromosome-membrane association and its role in the regulatory aspect of chromosome and plasmid replication in *Bacillus subtilis* (4, 10, 13, 14). Our studies indicate that the origin of replication or its vicinity for the *B. subtilis* chromosome and some plasmids is associated with the cell membrane and that in temperature-sensitive initiation mutants both the membrane association and initiation are inhibited at the nonpermissive temperature.

We (18) have shown that two initiation genes, *dnaBI* and *dnaBII*, act differently in inhibiting replication initiation of the host chromosome and the two plasmids pSL103 and pUB110, which share the same replication origin (7). At the nonpermissive temperature, the *dnaBI* gene inhibits the initiation of both the host chromosome and the plasmids (18), whereas *dnaBII* inhibits only the initiation of host chromosome replication (11). The formation of the gene product of the *dnaBI* locus, therefore, is necessary for the initiation process of both replicons. On the other hand, the product of the *dnaBII* locus apparently is required only for the host chromosome initiation. It is, therefore, an interesting possibility that the *dnaBII* gene product may be involved in the regulatory aspect of the initiation of the host chromosome replication.

Recently, we observed in *B. subtilis* that the DNA-membrane association at the origin of replication is specifically reduced in these initiation-defective mutants at the nonpermissive temperature (18). Thus, at 45°C the membrane binding of both the origin area of the host chromosome and the origin area of pSL103 was drastically reduced in the *dnaBI* mutant. On the other hand, in the *dnaBII* mutant, the origin area of the host chromosome but not that of pSL103 was decreased (18). These results indicate that the inhibition of initiation is strictly correlated with the decrease of membrane association of the replication origin area of the chromosome.

INITIATION GENES, *dnaBI* AND *dnaBII*

Two groups of temperature-sensitive *dna* mutations reported in *B. subtilis* have been clearly characterized as initiation defective at the nonpermissive temperature. The mutations in the first group are reported to be linked to *argA*, *leuA*, or *pheA* (6, 8, 9, 15, 16). The second group is mapped between *purA* and *sacA* (3). Recently, we have made a detailed genetic analysis of the first group of mutations by using transformation (4). Our results show that all mutations analyzed can be located betwen *polA* and *citK* (Fig. 1). Whereas most mutations are clustered within a recombination frequency of less than 0.03, one, *dnaB19* (6), is distant from the other mutation sites by 0.13 to 0.25. Thus, we have designated the first group as *dnaBI* and the second as *dnaBII*. The *dnaBI* locus includes *dna-1*, *dna-20*, *dna-27*, and *dna-134*, which have been studied in detail (1, 9, 16), and its function is reported to be involved in the priming of the initiation (9). The *dnaBII* locus is currently represented only by *dnaB19*, which has been confirmed as an initiation mutation by a synchro-density transfer experiment (18).

A functional distinction between *dnaBI* and *dnaBII* has been revealed by their different abilities to support plasmid replication. Thus, *dna-1* (16), a *dnaBI* mutant, stops the replication of pUB110, isolated by Ehrlich (2), and its derivative pSL103 (7) at the nonpermissive temperature (18). The gene *dnaB19* (6) allows the replication of these plasmids (11, 18). This distinction is particularly interesting, since unlike the host chromosome, these plasmids are of high copy number (30 to 40 per cell) (2) and replicate randomly throughout the cell cycle (17). Thus, the function of the gene *dnaB19* is exclusive to the host initiation.

IN VIVO AND IN VITRO EFFECT OF HIGH TEMPERATURE IN *dnaBI* AND *dnaBII*

Earlier work with *B. subtilis* has shown that the chromosomal areas close to the replication origin and the terminus are enriched in membrane fraction (10, 12–14, 19). Recently, we

47

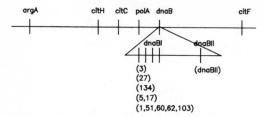

FIG. 1. Map positions of *dnaBI* and *dnaBII* (5).

showed that the membrane association of host origin area and plasmid pSL103 significantly decreases at the nonpermissive temperature, both in vivo and in vitro (18). When the DNA-membrane complex is isolated at various times after the temperature of a *dnaBI* culture is raised to 45°C, both a host marker *purA16* (near the origin) and a plasmid marker Nm^r decrease in the complex (Fig. 2A). In *dnaBII*, however, only the host marker, and not the plasmid marker, shows a decrease from the complex (Fig. 2C). It is also clear that in *dnaBI* cells initiation of both the host chromosome (judged by *purA16* replication) and the plasmid (judged by Nm^r replication) are inhibited at 45°C (Fig. 2B), whereas in *dnaBII* cells only initiation of the host chromo-

some and not that of pSL103 is inhibited (Fig. 2D) (18). Control experiments with a wild type (*dna$^+$*) did not show any of these effects on membrane association. Essentially the same results were obtained in vitro by incubating the DNA-membrane complex isolated from these mutants at 45°C (18).

The isolated plasmid was able to bind to the membrane fraction when the mixture of *dnaBI* DNA-membrane complex and pSL103 was incubated in vitro at 45°C and then the temperature was lowered to 32°C. This binding is specific to the replication origin-carrying fragment (pUB110) of pSL103 but not to the remaining portion of pSL103 (*trpC$^+$*-carrying fragment from *B. pumilus*). The above conclusion was obtained from the results of in vitro competition experiments between radioactive pSL103 and the two unlabeled fragments of pSL103. Only the origin-carrying fragment effectively competed with pSL103 in membrane binding (Fig. 3). ColE1 DNA did not compete with pSL103. These results strongly support the notion that the binding of the replication origin (or its vicinity) is necessary to the initiation of pSL103 and pUB110, and most likely to that of the host chromosome.

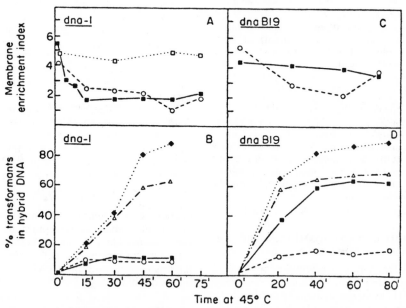

FIG. 2. Effect of nonpermissive temperature on chromosomal and pSL103 replication and membrane association in *dna-1* (*dnaBI*) and *dnaB19* (*dnaBII*) cells (18). Membrane enrichment indices were calculated by using the *leuA8* marker as the standard (14). Percentage values for transformants for each marker were calculated from the number of transformants in the hybrid DNA fraction obtained from cell lysates prepared from cells incubated for various times at 45°C with [³H]thymine and bromouracil by CsCl density gradient centrifugation. Symbols: ■, Nm^r (pSL103); ○, *purA16* (a host marker near the origin); ◆, *metB5* (a host marker near the terminus); △, *leuA8* (a host marker); □, Nm^r in *dna$^+$* cells.

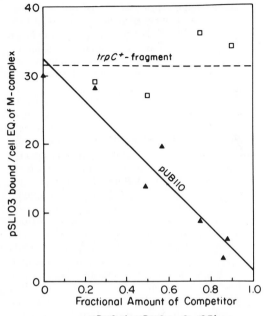

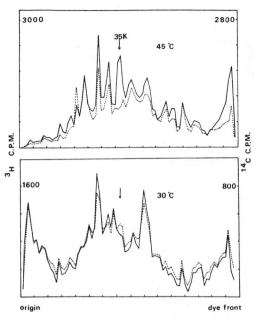

FIG. 3. Competition binding studies of radioactive pSL103 with pUB110 and *trpC*⁺ fragment. The plasmid pSL103 consists of pUB110 and a *trpC*⁺-carrying fragment from *B. pumilus*. The membrane complex (M complex) was prepared as previously described (18). The M complex was then added to tubes containing either various amounts of covalently closed supercoiled pUB110 and ³H-labeled pSL103 of a high specific activity (145,000 cpm/μg) or the linear *Eco*RI fragment coding for the *trpC*⁺ gene from *B. pumilus* and supercoiled ³H-labeled pSL103. The reaction was incubated at 45°C for an additional 5 min. The samples were then shifted to 32°C for 30 min and diluted 1:10 at 0°C. The samples were assayed and analyzed as described previously. In the figure, the fractional number of pSL103 molecules added (abscissa) is calculated as (number of pUBL10 or number of *trpC*⁺ fragments)/ (number of pUB110 or *trpC*⁺ fragments plus number of pSL103) (R. Korn, S. Winston, and N. Sueoka, unpublished data).

FIG. 4. Polyacrylamide gel electrophoresis of M2. Membane proteins of *dna-1* (*dnaBI*) and *dna*⁺ cells grown at 30°C and 45°C (4). Proteins of the two strains were labeled separately with [¹⁴C]leucine and [³H]leucine. The two M2 fractions were mixed and electrophoresed in a polyacrylamide gel. Solid line, *dna*⁺ cells; dotted line, *dna-1* cells.

DNA-MEMBRANE COMPLEX IN *B. SUBTILIS*

Salt-resistant DNA-membrane complex (M2) can be separated from the bulk of membrane fraction (M1) by centrifugation of cell lysates in a CsCl-sucrose gradient (13). Membrane proteins were compared between *dna-1* (*dnaBI*) and wild-type (*dna*⁺) cells grown at 30°C and 45°C (Fig. 4) (4). The M2 fraction of *dna-1* cells labeled with [¹⁴C]leucine 5 min after the temperature shift from 30°C to 45°C for 1 h was compared with the M2 fraction of *dna*⁺ cells

labeled with [³H]leucine under the same condition (Fig. 4, upper panel). A similar comparison was made between the M2 fractions of *dna-1* and *dna*⁺ cells by labeling them at 30°C (Fig. 4, lower panel). A 35,000-dalton protein is missing from the M2 fraction of *dna-1* cells labeled at 45°C. This protein, therefore, is a candidate for *dnaBI* gene product. The unequivocal proof of this should be the analysis of the translation product of cloned DNA of this locus.

CONCLUSION

The results summarized in this article strongly support the notion that membrane association of the origin area may be critical to the initiation of replicon replication and to its regulation. It is interesting to note that the products of the *dnaBI* and *dnaBII* genes are necessary for the host chromosome initiation and only the product of *dnaBI* gene is necessary for the initiation of the two plasmids. If the *dnaBI* product binds to the specific region near the origins of the host chromosome and pUB110, the two replicons should have a homologous sequence.

Some of the immediate problems to be investigated are (i) isolation and sequencing of the initiation fragments of the host chromosome and pUB110, (ii) isolation and characterization of the gene products of *dnaBI* and *dnaBII* genes, and their locations in the membrane, (iii) determination of DNA binding sites of these product proteins, and (iv) functional analysis of these two initiation genes.

ACKNOWLEDGMENTS

This work was supported by grant PCM-8011549 from the National Science Foundation and by Public Health Service grant GM28133 from the National Institute of General Medical Sciences.

LITERATURE CITED

1. **Burnett, L., and R. G. Wake.** 1977. Initiation and termination of chromosome replication at 45°C in a temperature-sensitive deoxyribonucleic acid initiation mutant of *Bacillus subtilis* 168, tsB134. J. Bacteriol. **130:**538–539.
2. **Ehrlich, S. D.** 1977. Replication and expression of plasmids from *Staphylococcus aureus* in *Bacillus subtilis*. Proc. Natl. Acad. Sci. U.S.A. **74:**1680–1682.
3. **Hara, H., and H. Yoshikawa.** 1973. Asymmetric bidirectional replication of *Bacillus subtilis* chromosome. Nature (London) New Biol. **244:**200–203.
4. **Imada, S., L. E. Carroll, and N. Sueoka.** 1976. Membrane DNA complex in *Bacillus subtilis*, p. 116–122. *In* D. Schlessinger (ed.), Microbiology—1976. American Society for Microbiology, Washington, D.C.
5. **Imada, S., L. E. Carroll, and N. Sueoka.** 1980. Genetic mapping of a group of temperature-sensitive *dna* initiation mutants. Genetics **94:**809–823.
6. **Karamata, D., and J. D. Gross.** 1970. Isolation and genetic analysis of temperature sensitive mutants in *B. subtilis* defective in DNA synthesis. Mol. Gen. Genet. **108:**277–287.
7. **Keggins, K., P. Lovett, and E. J. Duvall.** 1978. Molecular cloning of genetically active fragments of *Bacillus* DNA in *Bacillus subtilis* and properties of the vector plasmid pUB110. Proc. Natl. Acad. Sci. U.S.A. **75:**1423–1427.
8. **Laurent, S.** 1973. Initiation of DNA replication in a temperature-sensitive mutant of *B. subtilis*. Evidence for a transcriptional step. J. Bacteriol. **116:**141–145.
9. **Murakami, S., N. Inuzuka, M. Yamaguchi, K. Yamaguchi, and H. Yoshikawa.** 1976. Initiation of DNA replication in *B. subtilis*. III. Analysis of molecular events involved in the initiation using a temperature sensitive *dna* mutant. J. Mol. Biol. **108:**683–701.
10. **O'Sullivan, A., and N. Sueoka.** 1972. Membrane attachment of the replication origins of a multifork (dichotomous) chromosome in *Bacillus subtilis*. J. Mol. Biol. **69:**237–248.
11. **Shivakumar, A. G., and D. Dubnau.** 1978. Plasmid replication in *dna*TS mutants of *B. subtilis*. Plasmid **1:**405–416.
12. **Snyder, R., and F. Young.** 1969. Association between the chromosome and cytoplasmic membrane in *B. subtilis*. Biochem. Biophys. Res. Commun. **35:**354–362.
13. **Sueoka, N., and J. Hammers.** 1974. Isolation of DNA-membrane complex in *Bacillus subtilis*. Proc. Natl. Acad. Sci. U.S.A. **71:**4787–4791.
14. **Sueoka, N., and W. Quinn.** 1968. Membrane attachment of the chromosome replication origin in *B. subtilis*. Cold Spring Harbor Symp. Quant. Biol. **33:**695–705.
15. **Upcroft, P., H. J. Dyson, and R. G. Wake.** 1975. Characteristics of a *Bacillus subtilis* W23 mutant temperature sensitive for initiation of a chromosome replication. J. Bacteriol. **121:**121–127.
16. **White, K., and N. Sueoka.** 1973. Temperature sensitive DNA synthesis mutants of *Bacillus subtilis*. Genetics **73:**185–214.
17. **Winston, S., R. Korn, and N. Sueoka.** 1980. DNA-membrane association and initiation of DNA replication of *Bacillus subtilis*, p. 207–219. *In* B. Alberts (ed.), Mechanistic studies of DNA replication and genetic recombination. ICN-UCLA Symposia on Molecular and Cellular Biology, vol. 19. Academic Press, Inc., New York.
18. **Winston, S., and N. Sueoka.** 1980. DNA-membrane association is necessary for initiation of chromosomal and plasmid replication in *Bacillus subtilis*. Proc. Natl. Acad. Sci. U.S.A. **77:**2834–2838.
19. **Yamaguchi, K., S. Murakami, and H. Yoshikawa.** 1971. Chromosome-membrane association in *Bacillus subtilis*. I. DNA release from membrane fraction. Biochem. Biophys. Res. Commun. **44:**1559–1565.

Novel Promoters on the *Bacillus subtilis* Chromosome

RICHARD LOSICK, CHARLES P. MORAN, JR., AND NAOMI LANG

The Biological Laboratories, Harvard University, Cambridge, Massachusetts 02138

The recognition of promoters in bacteria is largely determined by hexanucleotide sequences centered approximately 35 and 10 base pairs upstream from the starting point of transcription (10). These are known as the −35 or recognition sequence (TTGACA) and the −10 or Pribnow box sequence (TATAAT). Among eubacteria these sites are highly conserved in evolution; promoters from distantly related bacteria are homologous to each other in their −35 and −10 regions (4, 10, 12). Moreover, RNA polymerases from a variety of eubacteria recognize and initiate transcription from identical promoters on well-defined phage DNA templates (5, 13). An important exception to the conservation of bacterial promoters occurs, however, in *Bacillus subtilis*. In uninfected cells and in cells infected with *B. subtilis* phage SP01 (or the related phage SP82), a variety of modified RNA polymerases are observed that differ strikingly in their promoter recognition specificities from the unmodified form of the bacterial RNA polymerase (6). In these modified RNA polymerases the usual sigma subunit of 55,000 daltons (σ^{55}), which dictates promoter selection, has been replaced by a variety of bacterium- and phage-coded sigma factors, which dictate novel promoter specificities. One such modified RNA polymerase containing on SP01-coded sigma factor (the product of gene *28* or σ^{gp28}) recognizes phage promoters that differ substantially at both the −10 and −35 regions from the conserved eubacterial promoters (4, 12). Here we report on the nucleotide sequence of two chromosomal promoters (*veg* and *tms*) (9), whose recognition is dictated by σ^{55}, and a novel chromosomal promoter (*spoVC*) (3, 9), whose recognition is controlled by a *B. subtilis* sigma factor of 37,000 daltons (σ^{37}).

Table 1 shows that the rules for promoter recognition by *B. subtilis* RNA polymerase containing σ^{55} appear to conform closely to those established for *Escherichia coli* RNA polymerase. The *veg* and *tms* promoters, as well as two previously reported σ^{55}-controlled promoters of phage SP01 (4, 5), differ at no more than one position in their −35 and −10 hexamers from the corresponding *E. coli* consensus sequences. Moreover, from a comparison with other *B. subtilis* promoters for which starting points have not been firmly established, bases at eight positions are nearly invariant. These are the first four bases in the −35 regions (*TTGACA*) and the second, third, fourth, and sixth bases in the −10 regions (T*ATAA*T). Moreover, in accordance with the rules for *E. coli* promoters, the spacer between the −35 and −10 regions was 17 or 18 base pairs. Indeed, *B. subtilis* promoters appear to conform more closely to the canonical structure for *E. coli* promoters than do *E. coli* promoters.

The *spoVC* promoter (8), in contrast, appears to differ significantly from the conserved features of σ^{55}-controlled promoters. The *spoVC* −10 (GTATTGTTT) and −35 (AGGTTTAAA) regions each differ at least at two positions from the corresponding σ^{55} canonical sequences, lacking, in particular, the invariant A at position 4 of the Pribnow box and the invariant G at position 3 of the recognition sequence (see Table 1). As reported elsewhere (7), another σ^{37}-controlled promoter (*spoVG*) also differs significantly from the canonical structure for σ^{55} promoters.

This pattern of distinctive nucleotide sequences in the −10 and −35 regions is emerging as a general feature of promoters whose recognition is controlled by one of a variety of sigma factors. Pero and her co-workers (4, 12) previously observed that the promoters for five *B. subtilis* phage SP01 middle genes, which are transcribed by RNA polymerase containing a phage-coded sigma factor (σ^{gp28}) in place of σ^{55}, exhibit the canonical sequences AGGAGA and TTT-TTT in the −35 and −10 positions, respectively. Recently, Gilman et al. (2) have shown that two *B. subtilis* promoters whose recognition is controlled by the *B. subtilis* sigma factor σ^{28} share identical pentamers (CTAAA) and heptamers (CCGATAT) in the −35 and −10 positions, respectively. Thus, the promoters controlled by four species of *B. subtilis* sigma factor (σ^{55}, σ^{37}, σ^{28}, and the SP01 factor σ^{gp28}) exhibit distinctive nucleotide sequences in homologous positions.

These observations strongly imply that sigma factors are sequence-specific DNA-binding proteins that work by recognizing specific bases in

TABLE 1. Nucleotide sequences

	"−35"	"−10" 5′
veg	AAATTTAT<u>TTGACA</u>AAAAT	GGGCTCGTGTTG<u>TACAAT</u>AAATGT<u>A</u>GT
tms	AAGTCTCC<u>TTGA</u>AATCAGA	AGATATTTAGGATATATTTTTCTATGG
SP01 #15	AAAAGGTA<u>TTGACT</u>TTCCC	TACAGGGTGTGT<u>AATAAT</u>TTAATT<u>A</u>CA
SP01 #26	AAAAGTTG<u>TTGACT</u>TTATC	TACAAGGTGTGGC<u>ATAAT</u>AATCTTAAC
spoVC	TTTTTCGA<u>GGTTT</u>AAATCCTTATCGTTATGGG<u>TATTGTTT</u>GTAAT<u>A</u>G

the −35 and −10 regions of promoters during the process of transcription initiation. Indeed, by means of cross-linking experiments, Simpson (11) and Chenchick et al. (1) have shown that *E. coli* sigma contacts bases at or near the −10 and −35 regions of the *lacUV5* promoter.

In summary, the *B. subtilis* chromosome displays multiple classes of promoters whose recognition is controlled by a variety of RNA polymerase sigma factors. It will be of interest to determine whether multiple promoter classes will emerge as a general feature of the chromosome of other gram-positive bacteria such as the closely related clostridia and the more distantly related actinomycetes.

LITERATURE CITED

1. **Chenchick, A., R. Beabcalashvilli, and A. Mirzabekov.** 1981. Topography of the interaction of *Escherichia coli* polymerase subunits with *lac*UV5 promoter. FEBS Lett. **128**:46–50.
2. **Gilman, M. Z., J. L. Wiggs, and M. J. Chamberlin.** 1981. Nucleotide sequences of two *Bacillus subtilis* promoters used by *Bacillus subtilis* sigma-28 RNA polymerase. Nucleic Acids Res. **9**:5991–6000.
3. **Haldenwang, W. G., and R. Losick.** 1980. Novel RNA polymerase σ factor from *Bacillus subtilis*. Proc. Natl. Acad. Sci. U.S.A. **77**:7000–7004.
4. **Lee, G., and J. Pero.** 1981. Conserved nucleotide sequences in temporally-controlled phage promoters. J. Mol. Biol. **152**:247–265.
5. **Lee, G., C. Talkington, and J. Pero.** 1980. Nucleotide sequences of a promoter recognized by *Bacillus subtilis* RNA polymerase. Mol. Gen. Genet. **180**:57–65.
6. **Losick, R., and J. Pero.** 1981. Cascades of sigma factors. Cell **25**:582–584.
7. **Moran, C. P., Jr., N. Lang, C. D. B. Banner, W. G. Haldenwang, and R. Losick.** 1981. Promoter for a developmentally-regulated gene in *Bacillus subtilis*. Cell **25**:783–791.
8. **Moran, C. P., Jr., N. Lang, and R. Losick.** 1981. Nucleotide sequence of a *Bacillus subtilis* promoter recognized by *Bacillus subtilis* RNA polymerase containing σ^{37}. Nucleic Acids Res. **9**:5979–5990.
9. **Ollington, J. F., W. G. Haldenwang, T. V. Huynh, and R. Losick.** 1981. Developmentally regulated transcription in a cloned segment of the *Bacillus subtilis* chromosome. J. Bacteriol. **147**:432–442.
10. **Rosenberg, M., and D. Court.** 1979. Regulatory sequences involved in the promotion and termination of transcription. Annu. Rev. Genet. **13**:319–353.
11. **Simpson, R. B.** 1979. The molecular topography of RNA polymerase-promoter interaction. Cell **18**:277–285.
12. **Talkington, C., and J. Pero.** 1979. Distinctive nucleotide sequence of promoters recognized by RNA polymerase containing a phage-coded "sigma-like" protein. Proc. Natl. Acad. Sci. U.S.A. **76**:5465–5469.
13. **Wiggs, J. L., J. W. Bush, and M. J. Chamberlin.** 1979. Utilization of promoter and terminator sites on bacteriophage T7 DNA by RNA polymerases from a variety of bacterial orders. Cell **16**:97–109.

Mapping Bacteriophage SP01 Transcription

SEAN M. BRENNAN, BARRY K. CHELM, JOSEPH M. ROMEO, AND E. PETER GEIDUSCHEK

Department of Biology, University of California, San Diego, La Jolla, California 92093

The hydroxymethyl uracil-containing lytic viruses of *Bacillus subtilis* have large genomes consisting of approximately 145 kilobase pairs (kbp) of double-stranded DNA with large (12 to 13 kbp) direct repeats at the termini. The genetic complexity is thus approximately 130 kbp. This DNA is encapsidated in virions with icosahedral heads attached to tails with elaborate base plates. The closely related SP01 and SP82 phages are the most studied examples of this group (for reviews, see 7, 8, 15). Our own work having been done with SP01, we shall emphasize this phage in the following pages.

It is useful to distinguish three phases of gene expression—early, middle, and late—in the development of these viruses, but some genes are transcribed during the early and middle stages and some during the middle and late stages of viral gene expression. The control that generates this temporal sequence is predominantly (and possibly exclusively) exerted at the transcriptional level. Four SP01 genes are associated with transcriptional regulation. Mutants in one gene (gene 28) are pleiotropically defective in middle and late gene expression and lack various enzymes that are essential for DNA replication. In the nonpermissive host, gene 28 *sus* mutants can synthesize only early viral RNA. Mutants in three other genes (genes 27, 33, and 34) are defective in late transcription. The gene 28, 33, and 34 proteins are RNA polymerase-binding proteins. *B. subtilis* RNA polymerase bearing SP01 gp28 in place of σ selectively transcribes SP01 middle genes; *B. subtilis* RNA polymerase bearing SP01 gp33 and 34 in place of σ selectively transcribes SP01 late genes. The role of gene 27 in regulating viral late transcription has only recently been identified (7a, 7b), and its mechanism of action is not yet known.

A physical map of the SP01 genome has been constructed, and several viral genes have been mapped to restriction fragments. Both Southern blot hybridization with RNA synthesized in phage-infected bacteria and filter retention experiments (19) with RNA polymerase and DNA restriction fragments have been used to identify the genomic regions associated with early, middle, and late transcription (14, 18).

TRANSCRIPTIONAL MAPPING

The experiments reported here deal with transcriptional mapping of two segments of the genome in which the viral early genes are located. Our experiments combine the use of several analytical methods: R-loop hybridization (21) with in vivo RNA to map the most active sites of early transcription in vivo; gel electrophoretic analysis of ternary transcription complexes (2) to identify DNA segments that are transcriptionally active in vitro; electron microscopic mapping of RNA polymerase-DNA complexes (22) to identify promoters and directions of transcription; and transcriptional mapping by various hybridization methods and by RNA size analysis to identify sites at which purified RNA polymerase terminates transcription.

Ternary complex gels (2) identify the terminally redundant ends of the SP01 genome as bearing the strong early promoters. With limiting quantities of bacterial RNA polymerase (E.σ), transcription is primarily confined to the termini. When more E.σ polymerase is used for in vitro transcription, or if the dominating terminal segments of the genome are removed, subsidiary early transcriptional activity can be detected in the region extending from about 90 to 115 kbp on the SP01 genome (Fig. 1). Early in vivo RNA also hybridizes to this region of the genome (although relatively weakly; 18), and the essential early gene 28 is located there.

Detailed mapping of the early transcription units in the terminal redundancy exposes a quite remarkable pattern (1, 17). Thirteen early promoters are distributed over approximately 10 kbp of DNA in a convergent array of overlapping transcription units (Fig. 2). Eleven of these promoters are very strong, although not equally so; P_E1 is weaker, and its neighbor, P_E1', is quite weak. Transcription from these promoters converges on strong termination signals located near 8 kbp. Subsidiary partial termination sites generate a complex set of overlapping in vitro transcripts, some of which are as large as 7 kb. In vivo transcripts of comparable length have never been found (16; Imamoto, unpublished data). This obviously implies one or both of the

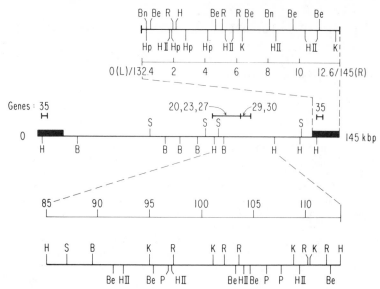

FIG. 1. Restriction map of the SP01 genome. The locations of *Hae*III (H), *Sal*I (S), *Bgl*II (B), and *Eco*RI (R) sites are consistent with those found by Pero et al. (14) with a redetermination of the sizes of certain large fragments, based on further mapping. Data for other enzymes, including *Kpn*I (K), *Hae*II (HII), *Bst*EII (Be), *Pvu*II (P), and *Hpa*II (Hp), are from our work. The existence of the terminal redundancy was experimentally established by Cregg and Stewart (5), and its length was determined by Pero et al. (14). Genes 20, 23, 27, 29, and 30 (12) have been physically mapped by Cregg and Stewart (4). Genes 23, 29, and 30 code for replication functions; gene 20 codes for a phage tail/tailplate-associated function; gene 35 codes for an as yet unspecified phage morphogenetic function (reviewed in 7). Gene 27 is referred to in the text.

following: first, that mRNA is post-transcriptionally processed (the processing of SP82 RNA has recently been suggested [6]), and second, that termination of transcription is more efficient in vivo than it is in vitro, possibly utilizing additional sites that are not detected with pure RNA polymerase holoenzyme.

What might be the function of such a high promoter density in the terminal redundancy? Both termini of the hydroxymethyl uracil phage genomes probably become available for transcription very soon after infection (10). The high density of early promoters would immediately allow the incoming phage genome to compete effectively for transcriptional activity in the newly infected cell. Since transcription of the host genome is not irreversibly shut off after infection, such competition is probably an essential element of the phage's developmental strategy. If it can become fully loaded with enzyme along its entire terminal redundancy, a single SP01 genome can capture 250 to 500 RNA polymerase molecules. A very high promoter density also allows the conjugate set of genes to come to their transcriptional steady state very rapidly, and this may be significant since the early phase of phage development only lasts approximately 4 min at 37°C.

Two of the partial transcription terminators, T_H2 and T_L3 (the nomenclature is explained in the legend of Fig. 2), have interesting properties: no termination occurs at these sites by pure *B. subtilis* RNA polymerase holoenzyme at high concentrations of all four ribonucleoside triphosphates. These sites may resemble the phage T3 early terminator at which low nucleotide concentrations have recently been shown to favor RNA chain termination (11). T_H2 and T_L3 differ from pause sites (9) at which RNA chain elongation is only temporarily blocked, but they share some features with attenuator sites (13), most notably in that they are partial terminators and that the products of termination are relatively short transcripts.

REGION OF EARLY AND MIDDLE TRANSCRIPTION

SP01 gene 28 is necessarily an early gene, since it regulates middle transcription. Yet it is far removed from the major early transcription units in the terminally redundant ends of the genome. We have mapped early transcription in the relatively weakly active large region of the genome extending from about 85 to 115 kbp (3, 14, 18). Gene 28 has been more precisely located, between 89.5 and 91.5 kbp, by DNA-depen-

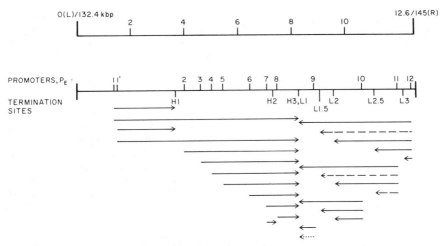

FIG. 2. In vitro mapping of the major early transcription units. These units are located in the terminally redundant region of the genome. The scale shows the coordinates for the left end (L), but the coordinates for the right end (R) are also given. The early promoters are numbered from left to right along the genome, with locations indicated above the line and sites at which transcription is terminated in vitro shown below the line. T_H terminators are sites at which rightward transcription terminates; T_L are terminators of leftward transcription. Termination at sites H1, L1.5, L2, and L2.5 is only partly effective. Termination at H2 and L3 is discussed in the text. The collection of transcripts generated by these signals is shown in the lower part of the figure. Dashed lines designate minor transcripts whose existence is inferred but which have not been directly identified. The dotted line indicates a transcript whose termini are not precisely mapped. At least one relatively strong but unmapped early promoter is located in the nonredundant segment of the genome located between a *Sal*I site near 128 kbp and the terminal redundancy (1).

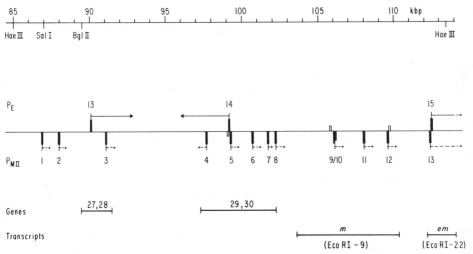

FIG. 3. In vitro mapping of early and middle transcription in the 85- to 114-kbp region of the SP01 genome ("middle region II"). Sites at which *B. subtilis* RNA polymerase holoenzyme (E.σ) binds to SP01 DNA are shown above the line. Initiation of RNA synthesis occurs at sites indicated with closed boxes. E.σ also binds at two sites (open boxes) near 106 and 110 kbp, but does not initiate RNA synthesis efficiently. Sites at which the SP01-modified middle enzyme, E.gp28, binds to SP01 DNA are shown below the line. At a site near 99 kbp (open box), this enzyme binds to SP01 DNA but does not initiate RNA synthesis effectively. Polarities of transcription are indicated by arrows. The continuous lines indicate two transcripts whose termination sites have been mapped. The RNA polymerases that yield this transcriptional map do not contain δ. The locations of genes 29 and 30 are taken from Fig. 1. Gene 28 is referred to in the text. Hybridization-competition experiments referred to in the text and in Fig. 4 show that the genome segments lying at 112 to 114 kbp and 104 to 110 kbp yield *em* and *m* class transcripts, respectively, in vivo.

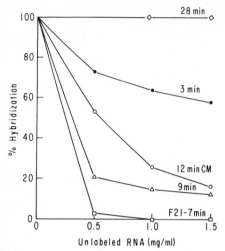

FIG. 4. Hybridization-competition analysis of in vitro and in vivo RNA. The labeled RNA was synthesized in vitro with E.σ on the *Eco*RI restriction fragment spanning 112 to 114 kbp. Unlabeled in vivo RNA, which was used as the competitor, was isolated from *B. subtilis* 3 min (●), 9 min (△), or 28 min (◇) after infection at 37°C with wild-type SP01 phage, 7 min (□) after infection with *susF21* (gene 28) mutant phage, or 12 min (○) after infection with wild-type SP01 in the presence of chloramphenicol (CM). Nine minutes after infection represents approximately the end of the middle phase of viral gene expression, and 28 min represents the late phase. Thus, *susF21* and chloramphenicol RNAs contain no middle or late transcripts. Each hybridization sample contained, in 100 μl, approximately 0.2 ng of ^{32}P-labeled RNA synthesized in vitro, 1.0 μg of denatured total SP01 DNA, and the concentration of total in vivo RNA shown on the abscissa. Hybridization and analysis were done by traditional methods (3).

dent protein synthesis in vitro with restriction fragments (3). A relatively weak early promoter is located nearby, at 90.1 kbp (Fig. 3). If this is the true in vivo gene 28 early promoter, then gene 28 must be located within about 1.2 kbp to its right. (Gene 27, which is tightly linked to gene 28 [12], has also been located within the 89.5- to 91.5-kbp segment.) Expression of gene 28 from a *weak* early promoter might provide the means for delaying its expression during infection and preventing a premature transition from early to middle transcription. Two additional early promoters have been found in this large region of the SP01 genome, at 99.2 and 112.5 kbp. Their functions are unknown. P_E13 and 14 generate convergent transcription. Two sites have been identified at which *B. subtilis* RNA polymerase (E.σ) binds to SP01 DNA but does not initiate transcription (or, at least, does not do so effi-

ciently under the conditions that have been used thus far). One of these binding sites, near 110 kbp, is so located that it could interact with transcription from a middle promoter (see below).

SP01 middle transcription comes predominantly from two regions of the genome. One of these (designated as middle region I) extends from approximately 12 to 40 kbp and contains middle as well as late transcription units (14, 18). Several middle promoters in this region have been sequenced (20). The other, middle region II, extending approximately from 85 to 115 kbp, contains middle and early transcription units. Although there are, as we have already seen, only a few relatively weak early promoters in middle region II, Fig. 3 shows a large number of relatively active middle transcription units (3). Thirteen promoters for E.gp28 (designated P_{MII} 1–13) have so far been mapped: 12 of these generate rightward transcription, as the genetic map of Fig. 1 is drawn (the rightward transcripts are complementary to the SP01 DNA strand designated as H). There is one site at 99 kbp, near P_E14, at which E.gp28 binds to SP01 DNA without readily initiating RNA synthesis. Here, as at the site near $P_{MII}12$, interactions between the RNA polymerases that execute early and middle transcription might generate regulatory effects. Without specific analysis it is not, however, certain what those regulatory effects might be. Early transcription (by E.σ) at P_E14 might conceivably activate E.gp28 initiation at the 99-kbp binding site. Alternatively, bound, uninitiated E.gp28 might block transcription by E.σ.

Given the organization of promoters in middle region II, one would predict that certain SP01 genes must be transcribed from early *and* from middle promoters. The class of SP01 RNA that is transcribed at early and middle times after infection is designated as *em*. Using hybridization competition analysis, we have directly tested whether a genome segment containing early and middle promoters (P_E15 and $P_{MII}13$) yields *em* class RNA in vivo. RNA was synthesized from this segment with E.σ, purified, and hybridized to total SP01 DNA in the presence of increasing amounts of unlabeled RNA isolated from bacteria infected with phage SP01 wild type or mutants. The results are shown in Fig. 4. The RNA synthesized in vitro behaves as expected for an *em* transcript. It starts to accumulate early (3 min after infection) and can be made under conditions that forbid middle transcription, but it does not become really abundant until the middle phase of infection. Its synthesis is eventually repressed and it disappears from the infected cell. Similar experiments show that the in vivo RNA coming from the DNA segment that extends from 104 to 110 kbp (covering $P_{MII}9$ to 12) is middle RNA of class m; it is under gene 28 positive control and is repressed during the late phase of the viral development. One should stress that this model for em transcription need not be exclusive; other control mechanisms might generate em transcripts that map elsewhere on the genome. By analogy, expression of the so-called m_1l class of SP01 RNA might be generated from overlapping transcription units served by middle and late promoters.

ACKNOWLEDGMENTS

S.M.B. and J.M.R. acknowledge postdoctoral traineeships of a Cell and Molecular Biology training grant from the National Institute of General Medical Sciences. B.K.C. acknowledges a postdoctoral fellowship from the same Institute. Our research has been supported by grants from the National Science Foundation and the American Cancer Society.

LITERATURE CITED

1. Brennan, S. M., B. K. Chelm, J. M. Romeo, and E. P. Geiduschek. 1981. A transcriptional map of the bacteriophage SP01 genome. II. The major early transcription units. Virology 111:604–628.
2. Chelm, B. K., and E. P. Geiduschek. 1979. Gel electrophoretic separation of transcription complexes: an assay for RNA polymerase selectivity and a method for promoter mapping. Nucleic Acids. Res. 7:1851–1867.
3. Chelm, B. K., J. M. Romeo, S. M. Brennan, and E. P. Geiduschek. 1981. A transcriptional map of the bacteriophage SP01 genome. III. A region of early and middle promoters (the gene 28 region). Virology 112:572–588.
4. Cregg, J. M., and C. R. Stewart. 1978. EcoRI cleavage of DNA from Bacillus subtilis phage SP01. Virology 85:601–605.
5. Cregg, J. M., and C. R. Stewart. 1978. Terminal redundancy for "high frequency of recombination" markers of Bacillus subtilis phage SP01. Virology 86:530–541.
6. Downard, J. S., and H. R. Whiteley. 1981. Early RNAs in SP82- and SP01-infected Bacillus subtilis may be processed. J. Virol. 37:1075–1077.
7. Geiduschek, E. P., and J. Ito. 1982. Regulatory mechanisms in the development of lytic bacteriophage in Bacillus subtilis, p. 203–245. In D. Dubnau (ed.), The molecular biology of the bacilli. Academic Press, Inc., New York.
7a.Green, J. R., B. K. Chelm, and E. P. Geiduschek. 1982. SP01 gene 27 is required for viral late transcription. J. Virol. 41:715–720.
7b.Heintz, N., and D. A. Shub. 1982. Transcriptional regula-
tion of bacteriophage SP01 protein synthesis in vivo and in vitro. J. Virol. 42:951–962.
8. Losick, R., and J. Pero. 1976. Regulatory subunits of RNA polymerase, p. 227–246. In R. Losick and M. Chamberlin (ed.), RNA polymerase. Cold Spring Harbor Laboratory, Cold Spring Harbor, N.Y.
9. Maizels, N. 1973. The nucleotide sequence of the lactose messenger ribonucleic acid transcribed from the UV5 promoter mutant of Escherichia coli. Proc. Natl. Acad. Sci. U.S.A. 70:3585–3589.
10. McAllister, W. T. 1970. Bacteriophage infection: which end of the SP82G genome goes in first? J. Virol. 5:194–198.
11. Neff, N., and M. Chamberlin. 1980. Termination of transcription by Escherichia coli ribonucleic acid polymerase in vitro. Effect of altered reaction conditions and mutations in the enzyme protein on termination with T7 and T3 deoxyribonucleic acids. Biochemistry 19:3005–3015.
12. Okubo, S., T. Yanagida, D. J. Fujita, and B. M. Ohlsson-Wilhelm. 1972. The genetics of bacteriophage SP01. Biken J. 15:81–97.
13. Oxender, D., G. Zurawski, and C. Yanofsky. 1979. Attenuation in the Escherichia coli tryptophan operon: role of RNA secondary structure involving the tryptophan codon region. Proc. Natl. Acad. Sci. U.S.A. 76:5524–5528.
14. Pero, J., N. Hannett, and C. Talkington. 1979. Restriction cleavage map of SP01 DNA: general location of early, middle, and late genes. J. Virol. 31:156–171.
15. Rabussay, D. P., and E. P. Geiduschek. 1977. Regulation of gene action in the development of lytic bacteriophages, p. 1–196. In H. Fraenkel-Conrat and R. Wagner (ed.), Comprehensive virology 8. Plenum Press, New York.
16. Reeve, J., G. Mertens, and E. Amann. 1978. Early development of bacteriophages SP01 and SP82G in minicells of Bacillus subtilis. J. Mol. Biol. 120:183–207.
17. Romeo, J. M., S. M. Brennan, B. K. Chelm, and E. P. Geiduschek. 1981. A transcriptional map of the bacteriophage SP01 genome. I. The major early promoters. Virology 111:588–603.
18. Talkington, C., and J. Pero. 1977. Restriction fragment analysis of the temporal program of bacteriophage SP01 transcription and its control by phage-modified RNA polymerases. Virology 83:365–379.
19. Talkington, C., and J. Pero. 1978. Promoter recognition by phage SP01-modified RNA polymerase. Proc. Natl. Acad. Sci. U.S.A. 75:1185–1189.
20. Talkington, C., and J. Pero. 1979. Distinctive nucleotide sequences of promoters recognized by RNA polymerase containing a phage-coded "σ-like" protein. Proc. Natl. Acad. Sci. U.S.A. 76:5465–5469.
21. Thomas, M., R. L. White, and R. W. Davis. 1976. Hybridization of RNA to double stranded DNA: formation of R-loops. Proc. Natl. Acad. Sci. U.S.A. 73:2294–2298.
22. Williams, R. C. 1977. Use of polylysine for adsorption of nucleic acids and enzymes to electron microscope specimen films. Proc. Natl. Acad. Sci. U.S.A. 74:2311–2315.

Functions of *Bacillus subtilis* RNA Polymerase Core-Associated Polypeptides

ROY H. DOI, TOSHIAKI KUDO, CYNTHIA D. DICKEL, MARY SHARPE-HAYES, AND SHING CHANG

Department of Biochemistry and Biophysics, University of California, Davis, California 95616, and Cetus Corporation, Berkeley, California 94710

Recent analyses of *Bacillus subtilis* RNA polymerase have revealed the increasingly complex nature of this enzyme (6). The development of suitable protease inhibition techniques (17) and enzyme purification methods (2, 10, 12) has facilitated the identification of several native forms of the enzyme. These different forms consist of the RNA polymerase core enzyme (E) with the subunit composition $\alpha_2\beta\beta'$ in association with a diverse number of polypeptides (Table 1). The functions of these polypeptides have been the subject of intense investigation during the past few years, particularly in terms of determining whether they play a role in gene selection (5).

We have identified three forms of RNA polymerase that are present in vegetative cells with the composition $E\sigma^{55}$, $E\sigma^{37}$, and $E\delta^{21}$ (E stands for the core, and the superior numerals stand for the molecular weight [$\times 10^3$] of the associated polypeptide) (6). In cells grown in rich medium, the relative amounts of $E\sigma^{55}$, $E\sigma^{37}$, and $E\delta^{21}$ are about 75, 5, and 20%, respectively. The relative affinities of the three polypeptides to the core appear to be $\sigma^{37} > \delta^{21} > \sigma^{55}$. This is based on competition studies between σ^{55} and δ^{21} for the core (27) and the fact that σ^{37} cannot be dissociated from the core during passage through a phosphocellulose column, a treatment that readily removes σ^{55} and δ^{21} from the core (25, 27). Both $E\sigma^{55}$ and $E\sigma^{37}$ have high enzymatic activity, whereas $E\delta^{21}$ has little or no enzymatic activity on synthetic and natural DNA templates.

The function of σ^{55}, which is the major core-associated polypeptide in vegetative cells, has been shown to be similar to that of the *Escherichia coli* σ factor described earlier, i.e., it is essential for specific initiation of transcription at a promoter site (21). Since *E. coli* does not have polypeptides comparable to σ^{37} and δ^{21}, we have been interested in determining the roles of these two polypeptides during transcription. In addition, we report a new function for the σ^{55} that suggests a role for the factor during initiation of transcription.

CAN FREE σ^{55} FACTOR BIND TO DNA?

In earlier studies with *E. coli* σ factor, it had been reported that free σ factor could not bind to DNA, but that only free β' subunit formed a complex with DNA in vitro (28). These results suggested that β' subunit was the major subunit used in binding the enzyme to the template. We have now obtained evidence by use of nondenaturing polyacrylamide gel electrophoresis methods that free *B. subtilis* σ^{55} factor can form a complex with DNA (15). Complex formation is most efficient with supercoiled DNA and much less efficient with linear double- or single-stranded DNA. About one σ^{55} molecule bound to 140 base pairs of supercoiled pGR-1 DNA, whereas with linear double-stranded *B. subtilis* DNA, one σ^{55} molecule bound per 1,000 base pairs. Furthermore, we have been able to trap σ^{55}-DNA complexes on nitrocellulose filters (Table 2). Again, the supercoiled form of the DNA was more efficient in forming these complexes. Since negative supercoils of DNA thermodynamically favor the binding of proteins that cause local denaturation of DNA (26), these results suggest that, as the $E\sigma^{55}$ settles on the promoter site, σ^{55} denatures the DNA locally near the Pribnow box (23) to form the open complex (13) required for initiation of RNA synthesis. The free δ^{21} factor did not form a complex with supercoiled DNA (15), and we have not been able to obtain enough free σ^{37} factor to test its affinity to DNA.

WHAT IS THE ROLE OF δ^{21} FACTOR?

The δ^{21} factor was first described by Pero and her colleagues (19), who showed that its presence favored transcription of phage SP01 middle genes by the phage-modified RNA polymerase. We have investigated the role of δ^{21} by examining its effect on general transcription and by testing its effect on ternary complex formation during initiation of RNA synthesis. When δ^{21} was added to a reaction mixture containing $E\sigma^{55}$ and a variety of DNA templates, it was observed that δ^{21} inhibited the activity of the enzyme severely with some templates but hardly affect-

TABLE 1. Forms of RNA polymerase in vegetative and sporulating cells of *B. subtilis*

Type of cell	Forms of enzymes[a]	References
Vegetative cell	$E\sigma^{55}$	1, 16, 22
	$E\sigma^{37}$	6, 10, 11
	$E\delta^{21}$ or EP^{21}	12, 19, 20, 27
Sporulating cell	$E\sigma^{55}$	7, 8, 18
	$E\sigma^{37}$	10
	$E\sigma^{29}$	7, 8, 9, 17
	EP^{20}	7, 8

[a] E = core enzyme = $\alpha_2\beta\beta'$; only polypeptides that confer promoter specificity on the core have been designated as sigma factors; other proteins associated with the core, but whose functions are still unclear, are designated as P; the superior numerals indicate the molecular weights ($\times10^3$) of the polypeptides.

ed the enzyme activity with other templates (4). The overall effect indicated that the δ^{21} factor promoted the transcription of efficient promoters or increased the specificity of $E\sigma^{55}$, or both. The results of ternary complex formation between $E\sigma^{55}$ oligonucleotides and DNA templates in the presence and absence of δ^{21} factor are shown in Fig. 1. In these experiments, *Hin*dIII-restricted fragments of ϕ29 phage DNA were mixed with $E\sigma^{55}$, three of the usual ribonucleoside triphosphates, and δ^{21}. The resulting complexes were trapped on nitrocellulose filters; DNA was removed from the filters by treatment with sodium dodecyl sulfate, and the resulting DNA was analyzed by agarose gel electrophoresis. The results showed that, in the absence of δ^{21}, all fragments formed a ternary complex with $E\sigma^{55}$ (Fig. 1, lane 1). However, in the presence of δ^{21} factor, only those fragments with known promoters (3, 4, 14, 24) formed ternary complexes with $E\sigma^{55}$ (Fig. 1, lane 2). Thus, these results also indicate that the role of δ^{21} is to promote specific interaction between $E\sigma^{55}$ and promoters in DNA. The fact that RNA synthesis can be initiated from nonpromoter-containing DNA fragments suggests that care must be taken in the interpretation of various in vitro transcription studies.

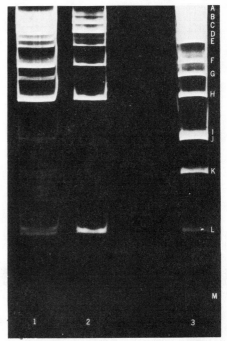

FIG. 1. Ternary complex formation between $E\sigma^{55}$ and *Hin*dIII-restricted phage ϕ29 DNA. See reference 4 and text for methods. Lane 1, contained no δ factor; lane 2, contained δ factor; lane 3, control lane with *Hin*dIII-restricted phage ϕ29 DNA.

WHAT IS THE ROLE OF $E\sigma^{37}$?

Since core enzyme has little or no activity on natural templates and $E\sigma^{37}$ itself has high activity, is σ^{37} acting analogously to σ^{55}? To test this hypothesis, the activities of both $E\sigma^{55}$ and $E\sigma^{37}$ were examined on a number of DNA templates. Both enzymes had comparably high activities on several natural DNA templates. The specificities of the two forms of enzymes were then tested by using two different templates. Earlier studies had shown that $E\sigma^{55}$ could use the early promoters of phage ϕ29 DNA (3, 4, 14, 24). A *B. licheniformis* β-lactamase gene has been characterized by S. Chang (unpublished data), and its

TABLE 2. Sigma-DNA complex binding to nitrocellulose filters

Tube	σ^{55} (μg)	$E\sigma^{55}$ (μg)	pBRH4 DNA (μg)	Molar ratio (protein/DNA)	Avg cpm[a]	Net cpm
1	0.74		12	3	694	247
2		5.8	12	3	2,138	1,691
3			12		447	0
4	0.74		12 (linear)	3	83	10
5			12 (linear)		73	0

[a] Average values for triplicate experiments. The 12 μg of supercoiled ^{3}H-labeled pBRH4 contained 5,357 cpm. In tubes 4 and 5 *Eco*RI-restricted linear DNA was used. The method of Hinkle and Chamberlin (13) was used.

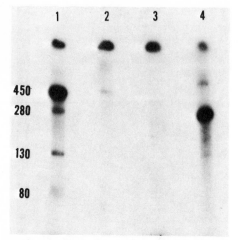

FIG. 2. Differential transcription of phage φ29 DNA and the Pen P (β-lactamase) gene from *B. licheniformis* by Eσ⁵⁵ and Eσ³⁷. The reaction mixtures in lanes 1 and 2 contained φ29 DNA and in lanes 3 and 4 contained Pen P DNA. Eσ⁵⁵ was present in the reaction mixtures of lanes 1 and 3, and Eσ³⁷ was present in the reaction mixtures for lanes 2 and 4. The ³²P-labeled RNA from the reaction mixtures was analyzed by 6 M urea–polyacrylamide gel electrophoresis. The numbers stand for the length of the RNA products in bases.

promoter base sequence was found to be quite different from the canonical promoter sequences used by Eσ⁵⁵. This sequence was similar to the *spoVC* promoter sequence found by C. P. Moran, Jr., and R. Losick (unpublished data). When the two forms of enzymes were tested for activity on the two templates, and the resulting transcripts were analyzed, Eσ⁵⁵, but not Eσ³⁷, could transcribe from the early promoters of φ29 DNA (Fig. 2, lanes 1 and 2). On the other hand, Eσ³⁷ used the β-lactamase gene promoter of *B. licheniformis*, whereas the Eσ⁵⁵ could not use this promoter at all (Fig. 2, lanes 3 and 4). Thus, these data indicate that σ³⁷ is acting like the canonical σ factor and conferring promoter specificity to the core. Previous results from Losick and his colleagues (10, 11) also support this idea. Furthermore, evidence is increasing that core-associated small polypeptides, first observed by Fukuda et al. (8) with sporulating cell enzyme, may also be involved in the recognition of spore-specific genes (9, 18).

Thus, a major regulatory mechanism for transcription in *B. subtilis* appears to be a family of sigma factors that confer promoter specificity to the RNA polymerase core. This hypothesis also requires that different spectra of promoters exist and that a particular enzyme form could recog-

nize a specific spectrum or partially overlapping promoter spectra. Although this model of transcription apparently does not apply to *E. coli*, it suggests a possible regulatory mode for other gram-positive procaryotes and eucaryotic organisms.

ACKNOWLEDGMENTS

This research was partially supported by National Science Foundation grant PCM 7924872 and Public Health Service grant GM 19673 from the National Institute of General Medical Sciences to R.H.D.

LITERATURE CITED

1. **Avila, J., J. M. Hermoso, E. Vinuela, and M. Salas.** 1970. Subunit of *B. subtilis* RNA polymerase. Nature (London) **226**:1244–1245.
2. **Davison, B. L., T. Leighton, and J. C. Rabinowitz.** 1979. Purification of *Bacillus subtilis* RNA polymerase with heparin-agarose. *In vitro* transcription of φ29 DNA. J. Biol. Chem. **254**:9220–9226.
3. **Davison, B. L., C. L. Murray, and J. C. Rabinowitz.** 1980. Specificity of promoter site utilization *in vitro* by bacterial RNA polymerases on *Bacillus* phage φ29 DNA. J. Biol. Chem. **255**:8819–8830.
4. **Dickel, C. D., K. C. Burtis, and R. H. Doi.** 1980. Delta factor increases promoter selectivity by *Bacillus subtilis* vegetative cell RNA polymerase. Biochem. Biophys. Res. Commun. **95**:1789–1795.
5. **Doi, R. H.** 1977. Role of ribonucleic acid polymerase in gene selection in procaryotes. Bacteriol. Rev. **41**:568–594.
6. **Doi, R. H., S. M. Halling, V. M. Williamson, and K. C. Burtis.** 1980. The transcriptional apparatus of *Bacillus subtilis*: a model for Gram-positive prokaryotes. p. 117–136. *In* S. Osawa, H. Ozeki, H. Uchida, and T. Yura (ed.), Genetics and evolution of RNA polymerase, tRNA and ribosomes. University of Tokyo Press, Tokyo.
7. **Fukuda, R., and R. H. Doi.** 1977. Two polypeptides associated with ribonucleic acid polymerase core of *Bacillus subtilis* during sporulation. J. Bacteriol. **129**:422–432.
8. **Fukuda, R., G. Keilman, E. McVey, and R. H. Doi.** 1975. RNA polymerase pattern of sporulating *Bacillus subtilis*. p. 213–220. *In* P. Gerhardt, R. N. Costilow, and H. L. Sadoff (ed.), Spores VI. American Society for Microbiology, Washington, D.C.
9. **Haldenwang, W. G., N. Lang, and R. Losick.** 1981. A sporulation-induced sigma-like regulatory protein from *B. subtilis*. Cell **23**:615–624.
10. **Haldenwang, W. G., and R. Losick.** 1979. A modified RNA polymerase transcribes a cloned gene under sporulation control in *Bacillus subtilis*. Nature (London) **282**:256–260.
11. **Haldenwang, W. G., and R. Losick.** 1980. A novel of RNA polymerase σ factor from *Bacillus subtilis*. Proc. Natl. Acad. Sci. U.S.A. **77**:7000–7004.
12. **Halling, S. M., K. C. Burtis, and R. H. Doi.** 1977. Reconstitution studies show that rifampicin resistance is determined by largest polypeptide of *Bacillus subtilis* RNA polymerase. J. Biol. Chem. **252**:9024–9031.
13. **Hinkle, D. C., and M. J. Chamberlin.** 1972. Studies of the binding of *Escherichia coli* RNA polymerase to DNA. I. The role of sigma subunit in site selection. J. Mol. Biol. **70**:157–185.
14. **Kawamura, F., and J. Ito.** 1977. Transcription of the genome of bacteriophage φ29: isolation and mapping of the major early mRNA synthesized in vivo and in vitro. J. Virol. **23**:562–577.
15. **Kudo, T., D. Jaffe, and R. H. Doi.** 1981. Sigma factor of *Bacillus subtilis* RNA polymerase binds to DNA. Mol. Gen. Genet. **181**:63–68.

16. **Maia, J. C. C., P. Kerjan, and J. Szulmajster.** 1971. DNA-dependent RNA polymerase from vegetative cells and from spores of *Bacillus subtilis*. IV. Subunit composition. FEBS Lett. **13:**269–274.

17. **Nakayama, T., L. Munoz, and R. H. Doi.** 1977. Procedure to remove protease activities from *Bacillus subtilis* sporulating cells and their crude extracts. Anal. Biochem. **78:**165–170.

18. **Nakayama, T., V. Williamson, K. Burtis, and R. H. Doi.** 1978. Purification and properties of two RNA polymerases from sporulating cells of *Bacillus subtilis*. Eur. J. Biochem. **88:**155–164.

19. **Pero, J., J. Nelson, and T. D. Fox.** 1975. Highly asymmetric transcription by RNA polymerase containing phage SP01-induced polypeptides and a new host protein. Proc. Natl. Acad. Sci. U.S.A. **72:**1589–1593.

20. **Plevani, P., A. M. Albertini, A. Galizzi, A. Adamole, G. Mastromei, S. Riva, and G. Cassani.** 1977. RNA polymerase from *Bacillus subtilis*—isolation of core and holoenzyme by DNA-cellulose chromatography. Nucleic Acids Res. **4:**603–623.

21. **Shorenstein, R. G., and R. Losick.** 1973. Comparative size and properties of the sigma subunits of RNA polymerase from *B. subtilis* and *E. coli*. J. Biol. Chem. **248:**6170–6173.

22. **Shorenstein, R. G., and R. Losick.** 1973. Purification and properties of the sigma subunit of RNA polymerase from vegetative cells of *B. subtilis*. J. Biol. Chem. **248:**6163–6169.

23. **Siebenlist, U.** 1979. RNA polymerase unwinds an 11-base pair segment of a phage T7 promoter. Nature (London) **279:**651–652.

24. **Sogo, J. M., M. R. Inciarte, J. Corral, E. Vinuela, and M. Salas.** 1979. RNA polymerase binding sites and transcription map of the DNA of *Bacillus subtilis* phage φ29. J. Mol. Biol. **127:**411–436.

25. **Tjian, R., R. Losick, J. Pero, and A. Hinnebush.** 1977. Purification and comparative properties of the delta and sigma subunits of RNA polymerase from *Bacillus subtilis*. Eur. J. Biochem. **74:**149–154.

26. **Wang, J. C.** 1978. Some aspects of DNA strand separation, p. 49–70. *In* I. Molineux and M. Kohiyama (ed.), DNA synthesis, present and future, NATO Advance Study Institute Series, vol. 17. Plenum Press, New York.

27. **Williamson, V. M., and R. H. Doi.** 1978. Delta factor can displace sigma factor from *Bacillus subtilis* RNA polymerase holoenzyme and regulate its initiation activity. Mol. Gen. Genet. **161:**135–141.

28. **Zillig, W., P. Palm, and A. Heil.** 1976. Function and reassembly of subunits of DNA-dependent RNA polymerase, p. 101–125. *In* R. Losick and M. Chamberlin (ed.), RNA polymerase. Cold Spring Harbor Laboratory, Cold Spring Harbor, N.Y.

Molecular Events During Transformation in *Bacillus subtilis*

J. S. FEITELSON AND A. T. GANESAN

Lt. J. P. Kennedy Laboratories, Department of Genetics, Stanford Medical School, Stanford, California 94305

Earlier studies on the uptake of DNA by *Bacillus subtilis* suggested the conversion of donor double-stranded DNA (ds DNA) to single-stranded DNA (ss DNA) and its complementary strand into deoxyribomononucleotides. The ss DNA eventually took part in recombination after synapsis with the resident chromosome (1, 3). We analyzed some of the steps in this system, using sensitive methods that include cloned homogenous donor DNA molecules, specific labeling of their termini, and identification of the intracellular state of added DNA by autoradiography after agarose gel electrophoresis. The results indicate the presence of donor ds DNA inside the cell, which is subjected to restriction in appropriate recipient strains. No donor ss DNA forms were detected. A summary of the results is given below.

The donor DNA molecules were from a *B. subtilis* DNA segment carrying genes that control leucine biosynthesis (*leu* DNA), cloned originally in *Escherichia coli* by using phage lambda vectors (2), and have a molecular weight of 4.5 $\times 10^6$. The DNA segment has been subcloned in plasmid pBR322, referred here as *pleu 16*. This segment was used as donor DNA for transformation of *B. subtilis* leucine auxotrophs. At appropriate time intervals, cells were removed and their DNA was analyzed by agarose gel electrophoresis to detect the intracellular forms of donor DNA.

In using the protocol of the *Haemophilus* system (5), i.e., labeling the 5′ ends of donor DNA with ^{32}P, we found that the end label was very rapidly removed by extracellular phosphatases and 5′ exonuclease, a reaction not crucial for transformation. Reisolated DNAs, after incubation with cellular supernatant, retained their biological activity, even though their 5′ end label was eliminated.

Since the above method was ineffective for identifying the donor DNA in cells by direct autoradiography (5), we labeled the 3′ ends of the molecule by degrading the ends to a limited extent with exonuclease III and then repairing the DNA with avian myeloblastosis virus reverse transcriptase, using alpha [^{32}P]dATP and other deoxynucleotide triphosphates. The label-

ing was largely confined to terminal segments of 160 and 190 base pairs in length or 2.3% of the molecular length. Using this DNA donor for cells, we made the following observation. The 3′-labeled DNA is present in the cell as a duplex in increasing amounts with time. There is *no* label migrating in the chromosomal position, suggesting that greater than 190 bases from each 3′ terminus could have been removed intracellularly in a step possibly crucial to recombination. Nevertheless, this labeling protocol could not also be used for effectively studying certain intracellular forms of donor DNA.

The final approach was to treat the competent cells with purified *leu* DNA. The cellular DNA was analyzed at different time intervals by agarose gel electrophoresis. The presence of donor DNA on the gels was detected by hybridization with highly labeled probes made from *leu* DNA templates, followed by autoradiography. Typically, one would expect hybridization to the probes at a position where high-molecular-weight cellular DNA is present and at positions where donor ss and ds DNA molecules migrate.

The autoradiogram shown in Fig. 1 presents two regions that hybridize with the specific probe. These are chromosomal DNA and a band that corresponds to *leu* DNA, i.e., molecular weight of 4.5 $\times 10^6$, which is also resistant to S1 nuclease. Although this DNA is mainly present in 2- and 5-min points, its presence is noted in other experiments at later time points also. Quantitation of the donor DNA in this experiment indicated disappearance of 90% of the molecules between 5 and 15 min. More strikingly, there was no detectable hybridization of the probe at positions corresponding to ss DNA in the gel. The inset in Fig. 1 shows that transformation continues linearly with time after a lag of 2 min. Electron microscopic analysis of the DNA molecules isolated from the gel revealed intact bihelical donor DNA, although single-stranded ends of 100 to 200 bases would not have been detected. Failure to detect ss DNA intermediates could be due to their binding with cellular DNA-binding proteins that could alter their mobility in the gels. This is ruled out since all the DNA purification regimens included rig-

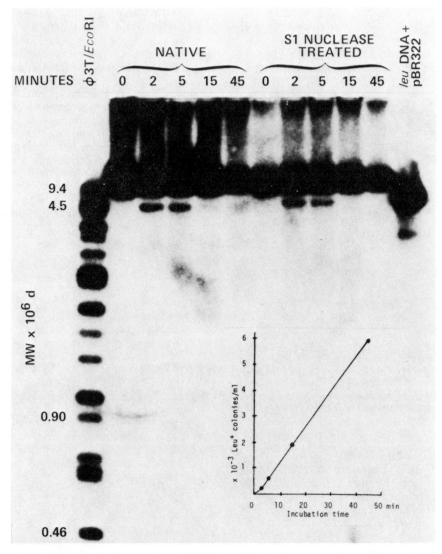

FIG. 1. Autoradiogram showing that donor DNA is in a bihelical form soon after uptake by *B. subtilis* cells. DNA molecules containing the three leucine genes were incubated with competent *leuC* cells. Samples were taken at the indicated times, and DNA was purified and analyzed by gel electrophoresis. The DNA was then transferred to nitrocellulose paper and hybridized with nick-translated ^{32}P-labeled DNA probe. The hybridized regions were then visualized by autoradiography. From the left, slot 1 shows the molecular weight standard, *Eco*RI digested, 5'-^{32}P-labeled phage ϕ3T DNA. Slot 12 is the donor *leu* and pBR322 DNA. Slots 7 to 11 are like 2 to 6, but the DNA was treated initially with S1 nuclease. The inset shows the kinetics of *leu*$^+$ transformants obtained for each time point.

orous deproteinization steps. Another possibility is that single strands are present but are degraded by nucleases or lost during isolation. A third possibility is that, as a result of complete homology, complementary donor single strands inside the cell renature during isolation to give the bihelical DNA forms.

To set a limit of detection of single strands and the proportion of renatured donor molecules, we performed reconstruction experiments. Denatured *leu* DNA was added to the cells immediately before lysis or directly to the lysate. DNA was purified and analyzed as in Fig. 1. Almost all of the hybridization occurred at the chromo-

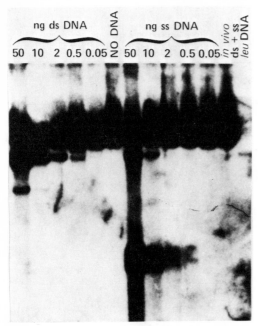

FIG. 2. Addition of *leu* DNA to cell lysates. The lysate of 10^8 *leuC* competent cells was mixed with the indicated quantity of ds or ss *leu* DNA. The left lane represents the lysate of competent cells after mixing with 50 ng of *leu* DNA for 45 min. The right-most lane is a mixture of 150 pg of ds and ss *leu* DNA only. Total DNA was purified and analyzed as described in Fig. 1.

somal and single-stranded regions of the gel (Fig. 2). No differences were observed in hybridization patterns whether the denatured DNA was added before or after lysis. We also saw that the added ss DNA remains in the same configuration in all steps of purification. Only at higher DNA concentrations was renaturation of 8 to 10% of the strands observed. The sensitivity of the techniques employed here could detect 50 pg of *leu* DNA with 24 h of autoradiographic exposure.

In our experiments, cells were transformed at a DNA concentration of 50 ng of donor DNA per 10^8 cells. About 0.6 ng of this DNA is taken up by the cells in bihelical forms. If there was total conversion of this DNA to free single strands, these would have been easily detected. The reconstruction experiment using donor DNA concentrations (Fig. 2, 2 to 0.5 ng of ss DNA) shows that less than 10% of the input ss DNA renatures, and that the purification conditions do not preferentially degrade the DNA. Thus, it is safe to conclude that over 90% of the intracellular donor DNA remains double stranded in the cell during the early stages of uptake, and that

less than 10% (60 pg) could have been rendered single stranded and escaped detection.

Although exogenously supplied ss DNA can be recovered from lysates, a possible artifactual reason for the absence of ss DNA in the autoradiogram is that it is bound up in the cell in a "complex" and lost during purification. The method used for deproteinization involved several organic extractions (5), as described. Piechowska and Fox (4) showed that treatment involving high salt, high temperature, and dialysis against EDTA was necessary to detect high-molecular-weight ss DNA from transformed cellular lysates.

It is clear (Fig. 3) that, even with the treatments designed to liberate ss DNA from a cellular complex, none of the *leu* DNA recovered from the cells was single stranded. No differ-

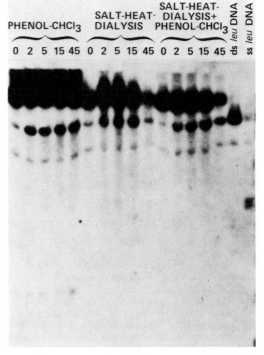

FIG. 3. Alternate purification protocols showing the presence of ds *leu* DNA. *B. subtilis* (*leuC*), 2×10^8 cells in a volume of 1 ml, was incubated with 0.1 µg of *leu* DNA for each of the time points. At 2, 5, 15, and 45 min (given as numbers in the figures), the cells were treated with DNase I and washed. DNA was then prepared by three methods: the first set with phenol-chloroform (5), the second set by the method described in reference 4, and the third by a combination of the first two. The purified DNA was analyzed as described in the legend of Fig. 1.

ences were seen between the alternative DNA purification schemes. The hybridization bands located between the DNA with a molecular weight of 4.5×10^6 and the ss *leu* DNA regions of the gel are due to marker pBR322 sequences. (There was some leakage between adjacent lanes prior to electrophoresis, causing artifactual hybridization at the ds *leu* DNA position in the control lanes [cells only].)

In conclusion, it is clear that intact bihelical donor DNA could be detected inside the cell. The cloned donor DNA appears to be processed by the cell-like plasmid DNA (6). This intracellular ds *leu* DNA is recognized and restricted in a strain that is constitutive for restriction and modification enzymes (r^+ m^+). The biochemical aspects of how different forms of DNA molecules are taken up by *B. subtilis* are not clear. Transfecting, unmodified viral DNA molecules are restricted in the r^+ m^+ cells. The same cells do not restrict unmodified transforming DNA (7).

ACKNOWLEDGMENT

This research was supported by Public Health Service grant GM-14108 from the National Institute of General Medical Sciences to A.T.G.

LITERATURE CITED

1. **Bodmer, W. F., and A. T. Ganesan.** 1964. Biochemical and genetic studies of integration and recombination in *Bacillus subtilis* transformation. Genetics **50**:717–738.
2. **Chi, Ning-Yen, W., S. D. Ehrlich, and J. Lederberg.** 1978. Functional expression of two *Bacillus subtilis* chromosomal genes in *Escherichia coli*. J. Bacteriol. **133**:816–821.
3. **Dubnau, D.** 1976. Genetic transformation of *Bacillus subtilis*: a review with emphasis on recombination mechanisms, p. 14–27. In D. Schlessinger (ed.), Microbiology—1976. American Society for Microbiology, Washington, D.C.
4. **Piechowska, M., and M. S. Fox.** 1971. Fate of transforming deoxyribonucleate in *Bacillus subtilis*. J. Bacteriol. **108**:681–689.
5. **Sisco, K. L., and H. O. Smith.** 1979. Sequence specific DNA uptake in *Haemophilus* transformation. Proc. Natl. Acad. Sci. U.S.A. **76**:972–976.
6. **Tanaka, T.** 1979. Restriction of plasmid mediated transformation in *B. subtilis* 168. Mol. Gen. Genet. **175**:235–237.
7. **Trautner, T. A., B. Pawlek, S. Bron, and C. Anagnostopoulous.** 1974. Restriction and modification in *B. subtilis*: biological aspects. Mol. Gen. Genet. **131**:181–191.

Site-Specific Restriction Endodeoxyribonucleases in Bacilli

TADAHIKO ANDO, EIJI HAYASE,[1] SHUKUKO IKAWA, AND TAKEHIKO SHIBATA

Department of Microbiology, The Institute of Physical and Chemical Research, Wako-shi, Saitama 351, Japan

Biochemical studies on the biological phenomena of restriction and modification of phages have resulted in the discovery of site-specific endonucleases (type II restriction endonucleases) that cleave double-stranded DNA at

[1] Deceased 26 March 1980.

or near nucleotide sequences specific to each enzyme. Site-specific endonucleases have been widely used as tools for research in molecular biology, particularly that on recombinant DNA.

During restriction and modification of phage ϕ105C (6), we previously observed that *Bacillus subtilis* (including *B. amyloliquefaciens*) had

TABLE 1. Site-specific restriction endonucleases of bacilli

Bacillus strain	Endodeoxyribonucleases	Sequence recognized (5′–3′)[a]	No. of cleavage sites		
			ϕ105C	λ	ϕX174
B. subtilis					
168	*Bsu*M(II)	(a)	+	+	
ATCC6633	R·*Bsu*A	(b)	+	+	
IAM 1076	R·*Bsu*1076	(c) GGCC	+	+	11
IAM 1145	R·*Bsu*1145	(c) GGCC	+	+	11
IAM 1192	R·*Bsu*D	(b)	+	+	
	R·*Bsu*G	(d)	+	+	
IAM 1193	R·*Bsu*1193	(b)	+	+	
IAM 1231	R·*Bsu*E	(b)	+	+	
	R·*Bsu*F	(d)	+	+	
IAM 1247	R·*Bsu*B	(e) CTGCAG	+	18	1
	R·*Bsu*C		+		
IAM 1259	R·*Bsu*1259	(f) GGATCC	0	5	0
B. amyloliquefaciens (*B. subtilis*)					
F	R·*Bam*F1	(f) GGATCC	0	5	0
K	R·*Bam*K1	(f) GGATCC	0	5	0
N	R·*Bam*N1	(f) GGATCC	0	5	0
	R·*Bam*Nx	(g) GG(^A_T)CC	16	15	1
B. cereus					
ATCC14579	R·*Bce*14579		+	+	
Rf sm st	R·*Bce*R	(h) CGCG	+	+	14
IAM 1229	R·*Bce*1229		+	+	
Bacillus sp. 170	R·*Bce*170	(e) CTGCAG	+	18	1
B. megaterium					
899	R·*Bme*899		+	+	
IAM 1111	R·*Bme*205		+	+	
B. pumilus					
AHU 1387	R·*Bpu*1387		+	+	
B. sphaericus					
IAM 1286	R·*Bsp*1286		+	+	

[a] (a) This endonuclease is different from restriction enzyme (R·*Bsu*MI) controlled by the *hsrM* gene, since this was as active on ϕ105C DNA replicated in this strain as on ϕ105C DNA replicated in other strains. (b) The corresponding modification methylase modifies all sites for endo R·*Mlu*I, which recognizes 5′ACGCGT3′. (c) Isoschizomer of endo R·*Hae*III or endo R·*Bsu*R. (d) The enzymes recognize a common sequence which is not known. (e) Isoschizomer of endo R·*Pst*I. (f) Isoschizomer of endo R·*Bam*HI. (g) Isoschizomer of endo R·*Ava*II. (h) Isoschizomer of endo R·*Tha*I.

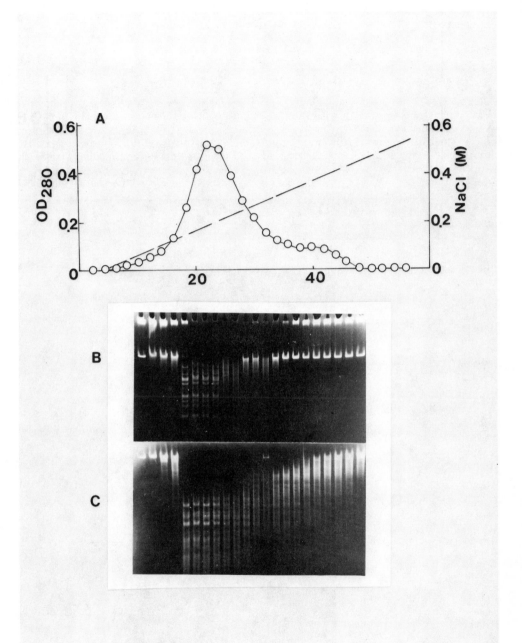

FIG. 1. DEAE-cellulose column chromatography of an Ultragel AcA 34 fraction from ISMRBE 17. Active fraction of Ultragel AcA 34 was loaded onto a DEAE-cellulose (Whatman DE 52) column (2.5 by 9 cm). Proteins were eluted by using a linear gradient of NaCl. (A) Proteins (absorbancy at 280 nm) and gradient. (B) Activity of endo R·*Bsu*B. Phage ф105C DNA carrying modifications specific for *Bsu*E and *Bsu*M was treated with 10 μl of each fraction at 37°C (see text), and samples of treated DNA were analyzed by electrophoresis on agarose. (C) Activity of *Bsu*E. Phage ф105C DNA carrying modifications specific for *Bsu*B and *Bsu*M was used as the substrate.

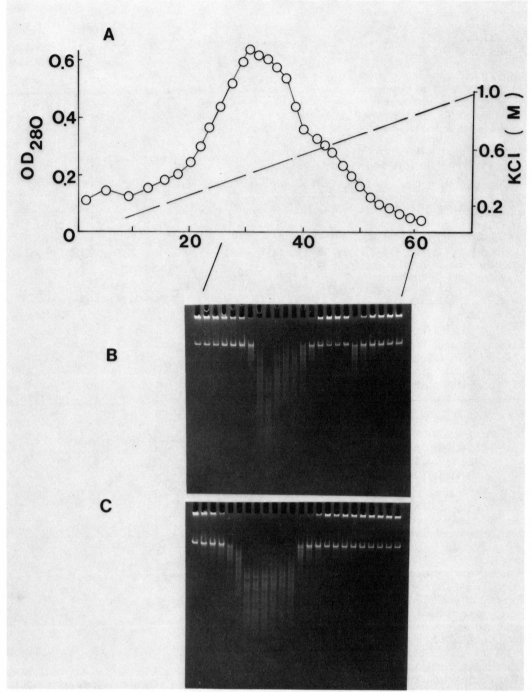

FIG. 2. Phosphocellulose column chromatography of the ammonium sulfate fraction from *B. subtilis* IAM 1231. The ammonium sulfate fraction from *B. subtilis* IAM 1231 was loaded onto a phosphocellulose column (8 by 1.1 cm) and eluted by using a linear gradient of KCl. (A) Proteins (absorbance at 280 nm) and gradient of KCl. (B) Activity of endo R·*Bsu*E. Phage φ105C DNA carrying a modification specific for *Bsu*F was used as the substrate. (C) Activity of endo R·*Bsu*F. Phage φ105C DNA carrying a modification specific for *Bsu*E was used as the substrate.

site-specific restriction endonucleases *Bam*NI and *Bam*Nx, which recognize

$$\begin{array}{cc} \downarrow & \downarrow \\ 5'\overset{}{\text{GGATCC}}\ 3' & 5'\overset{}{\text{GGACC}}\ 3' \\ 3'\text{CCTAGG}\ 5' & 3'\text{CCTGG}\ 5'' \\ \uparrow & \uparrow \end{array} \quad \text{and}$$

respectively, and cut the phosphodiester bonds (4, 7, 8) as indicated by arrows. We have, since then, systematically screened strains of bacilli for site-specific endonucleases (3, 9). In this paper, we describe related biochemical studies.

SCREENING OF *BACILLUS* STRAINS THAT HAVE SITE-SPECIFIC ENDONUCLEASES

Systematic screening of site-specific endonuclease activities in cell-free extracts from strains of bacilli revealed that 21 of 66 strains tested contained such endonuclease. Strains tested include 37 strains of *B. subtilis*, 3 of *B. amyloliquefaciens*, 5 of *B. cereus*, 4 of *B. licheniformis*, 7 of *B. megaterium*, 2 of *B. polymyxa*, 7 of *B. pumilus*, and 1 strain of *B. sphaericus* (3, 7, 8, 9).

Endonuclease activity was assayed at 37°C for 50 min in a reaction mixture (30 µl) containing 0.1 µg of DNA, 50 mM Tris-hydrochloride (pH 7.5), 0.2 mM EDTA, 15 mM $MgCl_2$, 2 mM 2-mercaptoethanol, and the enzyme preparation. Treated DNA samples were analyzed by agarose gel electrophoresis as described previously (8). The properties of these site-specific endonucleases are summarized in Table 1.

SIMULTANEOUS PREPARATION OF SEVERAL RESTRICTION ENDONUCLEASES FROM A TRANSFORMANT THAT HAS MULTIPLE RESTRICTION AND MODIFICATION SYSTEMS

We constructed a transformant, ISMRBE 17, with four restriction and modification systems, *Bsu*M(I), *Bsu*R, *Bsu*B, and *Bsu*E, three of which were introduced during transformation by using DNA from the *B. subtilis* strains R, IAM 1247, and IAM 1231 (5). The cell-free extracts of these strains were prepared by disruption with glass beads. We detected no restriction endonuclease activity of the *Bsu*M(I) system. Subsequently, streptomycin added to the cell-free extracts precipitated endo R·*Bsu*R (1, 2). The protein fraction precipitated by ammonium sulfate at 40 to 80% saturation from the streptomycin sulfate supernatant contained endo R·*Bsu*B and endo R·*Bsu*E, free from endo R·*Bsu*R.

To detect endo R·*Bsu*B and endo R·*Bsu*E during the subsequent fractionations, we used DNA that lacked one of three modifications corresponding to endonucleases *Bsu*M(I), *Bsu*B, and *Bsu*E. Accordingly, endo R·*Bsu*B was assayed by using φ105C DNA carrying modifica-

tions specific for *Bsu*M(I) and *Bsu*E, and endo R·*Bsu*E was assayed by using φ105C DNA carrying modifications specific for *Bsu*M(I) and *Bsu*B.

The ammonium sulfate fraction was then chromatographed on an Ultragel AcA 34 column (LKB Instruments Inc.) and then chromatographed on a DEAE-cellulose column; endo R·*Bsu*B and endo R·*Bsu*E eluted from the column as a single peak (Fig. 1). In this way, endo R·*Bsu*R and a mixture of endo R·*Bsu*B and endo R·*Bsu*E were prepared from a single strain. This result shows that transformant ISMRBE 17 possesses at least three site-specific endonucleases correlating with the three newly introduced restriction and modification systems. Although we could not separate endo R·*Bsu*B and endo R·*Bsu*E (Fig. 1), such transformants are potentially useful for preparation of several endonucleases at one time.

GENETIC SEPARATION OF RESTRICTION ENDONUCLEASES THAT ARE DIFFICULT TO SEPARATE BY BIOCHEMICAL MEANS

Site-specific endonucleases are sometimes difficult to purify when a strain has more than two such components. For example, *B. subtilis* IAM 1231 has two site-specific endonucleases, endo R·*Bsu*E and endo R·*Bsu*F. These two endonucleases could not be separated by chromatography on a DEAE-cellulose column, phosphocellulose column (Fig. 2), or hydroxylapatite column, or by gel filtration. To solve this problem, we constructed transformants that acquired only one of the genes for endonucleases in the DNA donor strain. We first constructed transformants ISE 15 and ISF 18, each of which had one of the two genes for site-specific endonucleases of IAM 1231 (5). Then we easily purified endo R·*Bsu*E from ISE 15 and endo R·*Bsu*F from ISF 18. This method is generally applicable in other, similar situations.

ACKNOWLEDGMENTS

This work was supported by a grant for "Life-science" of the Institute of Physical and Chemical Research from the Science and Technology Agency of Japan, a grant from Ministry of Education, Science, and Culture of Japan, and a grant from Miles Laboratories, Inc. (U.S.A.).

LITERATURE CITED

1. **Bron, S., and K. Murray.** 1975. Restriction and modification in *B. subtilis*. Nucleotide sequence recognized by restriction endonuclease R·*Bsu*R from strain R. Mol. Gen. Genet. **143**:25–33.
2. **Bron, S., K. Murray, and T. A. Trautner.** 1975. Restriction and modification in *B. subtilis*. Purification and general properties of a restriction endonuclease from strain R. Mol. Gen. Genet. **143**:13–23.
3. **Ikawa, S., T. Shibata, and T. Ando.** 1976. The site-specific

deoxyribonuclease from *Bacillus pumilus* (endonuclease R·*Bpul*387). J. Biochem. **80:**1457–1460.

4. **Ikawa, S., T. Shibata, and T. Ando.** 1979. Recognition sequence of endonuclease R·*Bam*Nx from *Bacillus amyloliquefaciens* N. Agric. Biol. Chem. **43:**873–875.

5. **Ikawa, S., T. Shibata, T. Ando, and H. Saito.** 1980. Genetic studies on site-specific endodeoxyribonucleases in *Bacillus subtilis*: multiple modification and restriction systems in transformants of *Bacillus subtilis* 168. Mol. Gen. Genet. **177:**359–368.

6. **Shibata, T., and T. Ando.** 1974. Host controlled modifica-tion and restriction in *Bacillus subtilis*. Mol. Gen. Genet. **131:**275–280.

7. **Shibata, T., and T. Ando.** 1975. *In vitro* modification and restriction of phage φ105C DNA with *Bacillus subtilis* N cell-free extract. Mol. Gen. Genet. **138:**269–279.

8. **Shibata, T., and T. Ando.** 1976. The restriction endonucle-ases in *Bacillus amyloliquefaciens* N strain. Substrate specificities. Biochim. Biophys. Acta **442:**184–196.

9. **Shibata, T., S. Ikawa, C. Kim, and T. Ando.** 1976. Site-specific deoxyribonucleases in *Bacillus subtilis* and other *Bacillus* strains. J. Bacteriol. **128:**473–476.

Genetic Study of Restriction Endonucleases in *Bacillus subtilis*

TAKEHIKO SHIBATA, SHUKUKO IKAWA, AND TADAHIKO ANDO

Department of Microbiology, The Institute of Physical and Chemical Research, Wako-shi, Saitama 351, Japan

During this decade, research has revealed that various microorganisms have a type of intracellular endodeoxyribonuclease that recognizes specific nucleotide sequences in double-stranded DNA and introduces double-stranded scissions at or near the sequences (see 10 for review). These endonucleases are called site-specific endonucleases or type II restriction endonucleases, although only a few of them have been proven to be involved in restriction and modification of genetically foreign entities invading into a cell. Therefore, this type of endonuclease might have other biological roles in living cells, such as recombination.

In *Bacillus subtilis*, restriction and modification of phages were not known until 1974, when Trautner et al. (18) and we (12) found, independently, that strains of *B. subtilis*, including the 168 strain, exhibited restriction and modification of phages SPP1 or φ105C. We then found that 13 of 40 *B. subtilis* strains (including *B. amyloliquefaciens*) and 11 strains of other *Bacillus* species have site-specific endonucleases (7, 13–15). As an initial step in elucidating the biological roles

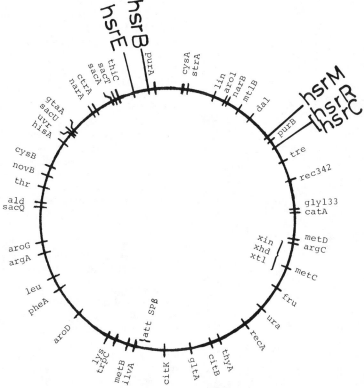

FIG. 1. Genetic loci of restriction enzymes on the chromosome of *B. subtilis* strain 168. This linkage map is based on that published by Kejzlarova-Lepesant et al. (9). Genes *xin*, *xhd*, and *xtl* are those of defective prophage PBSX (17), and *att* SPβ is the attachment site for temperate phage SPβ.

TABLE 1. Restriction and modification activities of transformants[a] of B. subtilis strain 168

| Indicator strain | Relative plating efficiency[a] phage φ105C grown on | | | | | | | | | | |
	101 ($m^+_{BsuM(I)}$)	ISR6 (m^+_{BsuR})	ISF23 (m^+_{BsuF})	ISC30 (m^+_{BsuC})	ISB43 (m^+_{BsuB})	ISE22 (m^+_{BsuE})	ISJ48 (m^+_{BsuJ})	ISL47 (m^+_{BsuL})	RM125 (m^-)	ISMRBEJ 50	ISMRBE 17
1 101 ($r^+_{BsuM(I)}$)	0.9	9×10^{-3}	9×10^{-2}	4×10^{-2}	3×10^{-2}	2×10^{-1}	6×10^{-2}	2×10^{-2}	1×10^{-2}	1.0	1.0
2A ISR6 (r^+_{BsuR})	2×10^{-5}	1.0	8×10^{-5}	5×10^{-6}	4×10^{-6}	1×10^{-6}	3×10^{-5}	1×10^{-5}	3×10^{-5}	1.1	1.2
2B ISF23 (r^+_{BsuF})	6×10^{-6}	1×10^{-6}	0.5	1×10^{-6}	3×10^{-6}	2×10^{-6}	1×10^{-6}	2×10^{-6}	3×10^{-6}	—	—
2C ISC30 (r^+_{BsuC})	3×10^{-3}	1×10^{-3}	3×10^{-3}	0.6	3×10^{-3}	3×10^{-4}	5×10^{-3}	5×10^{-3}	6×10^{-3}	—	—
3 ISB43 (r^+_{BsuB})	6×10^{-7}	3×10^{-7}	3×10^{-6}	9×10^{-7}	0.5	1×10^{-6}	2×10^{-6}	2×10^{-6}	5×10^{-6}	1.1	1.0
4 ISE22 (r^+_{BsuE})	5×10^{-5}	2×10^{-6}	4×10^{-6}	2×10^{-6}	4×10^{-6}	1.7	2×10^{-6}	2×10^{-6}	4×10^{-6}	1.7	1.2
5 ISJ48 (r^+_{BsuJ})	1×10^{-6}	1×10^{-5}	2×10^{-4}	2×10^{-4}	1×10^{-5}	1×10^{-5}	2.0	4×10^{-6}	1×10^{-6}	0.9	1×10^{-7}
6 ISL47 (r^+_{BsuL})	3×10^{-6}	2×10^{-6}	1×10^{-5}	1×10^{-5}	2×10^{-5}	1×10^{-6}	2×10^{-6}	0.7	1×10^{-5}	—	—
1012 (r^-)	1	1	1	1	1	1	1	1	1	1	1
ISMRBEJ50	—	—	—	—	—	—	—	—	$<10^{-7}$	0.6	1×10^{-7}

[a] Number of plaques appearing on 1012 (r^-) is defined as 1. Phages were assayed by a simplified method called dilution-spot. Observed efficiency of restriction was sometimes smaller than that in the classical assay; especially in the case of 101 ($r^+_{BsuM(I)}$), relative plating efficiency of the restricted phage was about 10-fold greater by the dilution-spot method than by the classical assay (7).

of site-specific endonucleases, we analyzed the genes for such endonucleases.

INTRODUCTION OF GENES FOR RESTRICTION AND MODIFICATION ACTIVITIES AND RESTRICTION ENDONUCLEASES INTO B. SUBTILIS 168 BY TRANSFORMATION

We isolated DNA from cells of B. subtilis strains in which site-specific endonucleases had been found. Using this DNA, we transformed B. subtilis 168 to add the capacity for restriction and modification of phage φ105C for the convenience of genetic study (6, 7, 16). B. subtilis 168 is known to be competent for transformation by free DNA, and its genetic structure has been extensively analyzed (see 4 and 9 for review). After preparing cell-free extacts (13, 15) of these transformants, we compared the specificities of the site-specific endonuclease activities in the extracts with those in DNA donor strains. In this way, we introduced genes for eight sets of restriction and modification systems and site-specific endonucleases from five strains of B. subtilis into B. subtilis 168: BsuA system from ATCC 6633, BsuB system and BsuC system from IAM 1247, BsuD system and BsuG system from IAM 1192, BsuE system and BsuF system from IAM 1231, and BsuR system from strain R (6, 7, 16, 18). The frequency of introducing these systems by transformation was about 0.01 to 0.1 that of transformation of auxotrophic markers such as purB or leuA (6, 7). During this study, we isolated two types of transformants that acquired new restriction and modification systems (BsuJ system and BsuL system), the origins of which were unknown (Table 1).

Restriction and modification systems introduced into the 168 strain and the original system of the 168 strain were classified into eight groups based on the specificity of restriction and modification of phage φ105C (Tables 1 and 2).

CONSTRUCTION OF TRANSFORMANTS THAT HAVE MULTIPLE RESTRICTION AND MODIFICATION SYSTEMS

To examine how many loci of genes for restriction and modification the cells of B. subtilis 168 contain, we tried to construct a series of transformants that acquired more than two restriction and modification systems. We constructed a transformant, ISMRBE 17, with the BsuB, BsuE, BsuM(I), and BsuR systems (7) and another transformant, ISMRBEJ 50, with the BsuB, BsuE, BsuJ, BsuM(I), and BsuR systems (Table 1). Therefore, genes for or activities of BsuB, BsuE, BsuJ, BsuM(I), and BsuR systems

TABLE 2. Specificities of restriction enzymes of transformants of *B. subtilis* strain 168

Group	Recognized sequence[a]	Systems introduced in strain 168 by transformation[b]	Restriction endonuclease
1	ND	*Bsu*M(I) [*Bsu*168][c]	Not detected
2A	5'GGCC 3' 3'CCGG 5'	*Bsu*R	Site-specific
2B	ND	*Bsu*F [*Bsu*1231(II)], *Bsu*G [*Bsu*1192(II)]	Site-specific
2C	ND	*Bsu*C [*Bsu*1247(II)]	Site-specific
3	5'CTGCAG 3' 3'GACGTC 5'	*Bsu*B [*Bsu*1247(I)]	Site-specific
4	ND[d]	*Bsu*E [*Bsu*1231(I)], *Bsu*A [*Bsu*6633], *Bsu*D [*Bsu*1192(I)]	Site-specific
5	ND	*Bsu*J	Not detected
6	ND	*Bsu*L	Not detected

[a] ND, Not determined.

[b] Names in brackets were used in our previous publications (6–8, 15, 16).

[c] The original restriction and modification system of strain 168.

[d] Modification enzyme of this system modified all sites for endonuclease R·*Mlu*I that recognized:

$$5'ACGCGT 3'$$
$$3'TGCGCA 5''$$

can coexist in the cell of a strain 168 transformant. On the other hand, we found that no two systems of the *Bsu*C system, *Bsu*F system, or *Bsu*R system can coexist in a cell (7). These observations indicate that *B. subtilis* 168 has at least five genetic loci for restriction and modification.

MAPPING OF GENES FOR RESTRICTION ON THE CHROMOSOME OF *B. SUBTILIS* 168

Next, we determined the genetic loci for restriction activities that had been introduced into *B. subtilis* 168. Genes were located by PBS1 transduction. A gene, *hsrM*, for the original restriction activity of strain 168 has been mapped between *dal* and *purB* on the chromosome (11; Fig. 1).

Genes *hsrE* and *hsrB* for restriction activities of the *Bsu*E system and *Bsu*B system, respectively, were cotransferred with the *purA* marker, and genes *hsrR* and *hsrC* for restriction activities of the *Bsu*R system and *Bsu*C system, respectively, were cotransferred with the *purB* marker. Further studies, including three-factor crosses, revealed that (i) *hsrE* was between *thiC* (or *sacA*) and *purA*, (ii) *hsrB* was between *hsrE* and *purA*, and (iii) *hsrR* and *hsrC* were between *purB* and *tre* (Fig. 1; 8). Therefore, *B. subtilis* 168 has at least four genetic loci for restriction enzymes on the chromosome.

The presence or absence of *hsrB*⁺ did not affect the linkage between *hsrE* and *purA* (8). However, the presence of *hsrR*⁺ or *hsrC*⁺ significantly influenced the linkage between *purB* and *tre* (8).

All loci for restriction are remote from the attachment site of a temperate phage SPβ (19)

and from the genes for defective prophage PBSX (3, 17). Unlike *Escherichia coli*, in which all the known genes for site-specific restriction endonucleases (*Eco*RI and *Eco*RII) were coded on plasmid DNA (1, 2), all the genes for site-specific endonucleases of *B. subtilis* so far mapped were located on the chromosome of strain 168.

We are now attempting to clone genes for site-specific endonucleases so as to study the structure of genes, mode of integrating information for restriction enzymes into the chromosome of strain 168, and possible allelism of *hsrC, hsrR,* and *hsrF* (8).

ACKNOWLEDGMENTS

We located genes for restriction activities by collaboration with Koji Matsumote (present address, Sophia University, Tokyo), Tadako Iijima (Tokyo University), and Hiuga Saito (Tokyo University).

This work was supported by a grant for "Life-science" of the Institute of Physical and Chemical Research (Saitama) from the Science and Technology Agency of Japan, a grant from Ministry of Education, Science, and Culture of Japan, and a grant from Miles Laboratories, Inc. (U.S.A.).

LITERATURE CITED

1. **Betlach, M., V. Hershfield, L. Chow, W. Brown, H. Goodman, and H. W. Boyer.** 1976. A restriction endonuclease analysis of the bacterial plasmid controlling the *Eco*RI restriction and modification of DNA. Fed. Proc. Fed. Am. Soc. Exp. Biol. **35:**2037–2043.

2. **Bigger, C. H., K. Murray, and N. E. Murray.** 1973. Recognition sequence of a restriction enzyme. Nature (London) New Biol. **244:**7–10.

3. **Garro, A. J., H. Leffert, and J. Marmur.** 1970. Genetic mapping of a defective bacteriophage on the chromosome of *Bacillus subtilis* 168. J. Virol. **6:**340–343.

4. **Henner, D. J., and J. A. Hoch.** 1980. The *Bacillus subtilis* chromosome. Microbiol. Rev. **44:**57–82.

5. **Ikawa, S., T. Shibata, and T. Ando.** 1976. The site-specific deoxyribonuclease form *Bacillus pumilus* (endonuclease R.*Bpu*1387). J. Biochem. **80:**1457–1460.

6. **Ikawa, S., T. Shibata, T. Ando, and H. Saito.** 1979. Host-controlled modification and restriction in *Bacillus subtilis*. *Bsu*168-system and *Bsu*R-system in *B. subtilis* 168. Mol. Gen. Genet. **170**:123–127.

7. **Ikawa, S., T. Shibata, T. Ando, and H. Saito.** 1980. Genetic studies on site-specific endodeoxyribonucleases in *Bacillus subtilis*: multiple modification and restriction systems in transformants of *Bacillus subtilis* 168. Mol. Gen. Genet. **177**:359–368.

8. **Ikawa, S., T. Shibata, K. Matsumoto, T. Iijima, H. Saito, and T. Ando.** 1981. Chromosomal loci of genes controlling site-specific restriction endonucleases of *Bacillus subtilis*. Mol. Gen. Genet. **183**:1–6.

9. **Kejzlarova-Lepesant, J., N. Harford, J. A. Lepesant, and R. Dedonder.** 1975. Revised genetic map for *Bacillus subtilis* 168, p. 592–595. *In* P. Gerhardt, R. N. Costilow, and H. L. Sadoff (ed.), Spores VI. American Society for Microbiology, Washington, D.C.

10. **Roberts, R. J.** 1980. Restriction and modification enzymes and their recognition sequences. Gene **8**:329–343.

11. **Saito, H., T. Shibata, and T. Ando.** 1979. Mapping of genes determining nonpermissiveness and host-specific restriction to bacteriophages in *Bacillus subtilis* Marburg. Mol. Gen. Genet. **170**:117–122.

12. **Shibata, T., and T. Ando.** 1974. Host controlled modification and restriction in *Bacillus subtilis*. Mol. Gen. Genet. **131**:275–280.

13. **Shibata, T., and T. Ando.** 1975. *In vitro* modification and restriction of phage φ105C DNA with *Bacillus subtilis* N cell-free extract. Mol. Gen. Genet. **138**:269–279.

14. **Shibata, T., and T. Ando.** 1976. The restriction endonucleases in *Bacillus subtilis*. Biochim. Biophys. Acta **442**:184–196.

15. **Shibata, T., S. Ikawa, C. Kim, and T. Ando.** 1976. Site-specific deoxyribonucleases in *Bacillus subtilis* and other *Bacillus* strains. J. Bacteriol. **128**:473–476.

16. **Shibata, T., S. Ikawa, Y. Komatsu, T. Ando, and H. Saito.** 1979. Introduction of host-controlled modification and restriction systems of *Bacillus subtilis* IAM 1247 into *Bacillus subtilis* 168. J. Bacteriol. **139**:308–310.

17. **Thurm, P., and A. J. Garro.** 1975. Isolation and characterization of prophage mutants of the defective *Bacillus subtilis* bacteriophage PBSX. J. Virol. **16**:184–191.

18. **Trautner, T. A., B. Pawlek, S. Bron, and C. Anagnostopoulos.** 1974. Restriction and modification in *B. subtilis*. Biological aspects. Mol. Gen. Genet. **131**:181–191.

19. **Zahler, S. A., R. Z. Korman, R. Rosenthal, and H. E. Hemphill.** 1977. *Bacillus subtilis* bacteriophage SPβ: localization of the prophage attachment site, and specialized transduction. J. Bacteriol. **129**:556–558.

High Frequency of Recombination at a Particular Site of the Phage M2 Genome[1]

HIDEO HIROKAWA, KOUJI MATSUMOTO, TAKAO MINEZAKI, MICHIYO HIRUTA, AND YUKIKO MIZUKAMI

Life Science Institute, Sophia University, 7-Kioicho, Chiyoda-ku, Tokyo 102, Japan

Such DNA structures as insertion sequences in enterobacteria (2) and the Chi structure of lambda phage (3) are interesting to investigate because they influence both gene rearrangement and recombination. During genetic studies of phage M2, an anomalous recombination was observed in a particular region of the genome. This recombination appeared to be related somehow to different-sized parental DNA molecules in which short deletions were located coincidentally in that particular region. We describe preliminary evidence of a high frequency of recombination between mutants mapped at sites flanking the short deletion in one of the parental DNAs.

RECOMBINATION MAP AND PHYSICAL LOCATION MAP

A recombination map of phage M2 mutants was constructed by the usual method of a two-factor cross between representative supressor-sensitive mutants of 13 cistrons. At the same time, physical locations of these mutations were determined by using the helper phage transfection system (1) with defined DNA fragments produced by treatment with several restriction endonucleases (4). These maps are compared in Fig. 1. The locations of all mutations in these fragments corresponded with those of the recombination map, except mutations in cistron F. Cistrons F and O were located on HindIII fragment B, according to the results of physical location analysis. However, the recombination frequency between these two was remarkably higher than values estimated from the physical distance between them. This fact suggests that an unknown structure exists between cistrons F and O.

SHORT DELETION AND HETEROGENEOUS POPULATION

M2 DNA was extracted from the stock population and was analyzed by treatments with

[1] A preliminary report was presented at the 5th European Meeting on Bacterial Transformation and Transfection, Florence, Italy, 1980.

several restriction endonucleases. HindIII produced 10 characteristic fragments. Among these fragments, HindIII-B was heterogeneous in size, whereas each of the other nine fragments was completely homogeneous. This evidence implies that the stock population of phage M2 is a mixture of heterogeneous sizes in this particular region of the genome. Subclones of M2 were reisolated at random, and their DNAs were analyzed with HindIII (Fig. 2). Each subclone fell into at least four classes. Incidentally, phage Nf DNA showed one additional HindIII site consisting of HindIII-B_1 and -B_2. All other fragments precisely resembled the M2 fragments. The size of each HindIII-B subclone remained stable for several passages of the culture under conditions in which agarose gel electrophoresis and ethidium bromide staining were used for detection.

Two *sus* mutants of cistron O exhibited the same size HindIII-B. The same was true for two *sus* mutants of cistron F. However, the former mutants were obviously larger than the latter. After these two mutants were crossed by infection, the 10 randomly selected recombinants that we examined were composed of the shorter HindIII-B that was similar in size to the F mutants.

Wild-type M2 DNA extracted from the original stock was heated, annealed, and treated with nuclease S1, after which this material was also subjected to agarose gel electrophoresis (Fig. 3). As expected, annealed DNAs of the original stock separated into two fragments. On the other hand, subclone M2H1 and φ29 were not sensitive to nuclease S1. Long and short fragments of the original stock were both extracted from the agarose gel, and the fragment carrying cistron O or F was determined by using the helper transfection system. As shown in Table 1, cistrons O and F existed, respectively, on long and short fragments. These results indicate that the deletion is located between these cistrons.

Although it is difficult to explain the anomalous recombination frequency, there are two

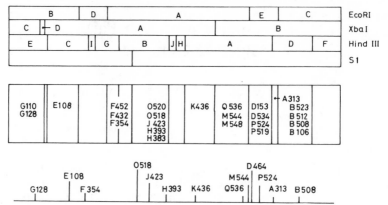

FIG. 1. Cleavage, physical localization, and recombination maps of M2 (from the top). Mutation sites of the recombination map are adjusted to the relative length of physical map. S1 site on the cleavage map was made by treatment with nuclease S1 of annealed DNA of the original stock of phage M2 (see Fig. 3).

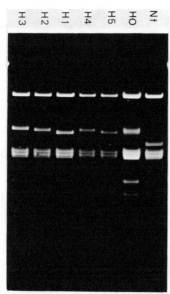

FIG. 2. HindIII digestion. Phage M2 DNA was digested with restriction nuclease HindIII, and the fragments were separated by electrophoresis in 0.7% agarose gel. The fragments were stained with ethidium bromide. HO, Our original stock of phage M2 that was heterogeneous in terms of the HindIII-B fragment's size; H1–H5, reisolated subclones; Nf, phage Nf.

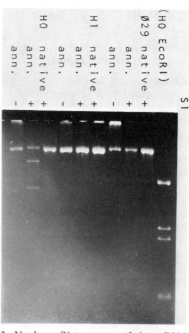

FIG. 3. Nuclease S1 treatment of phage DNA with or without annealing. DNA (20 μg/ml in Tris-hydro-chloride, pH 7.6) was heated to 100°C for 5 min and then cooled slowly (68°C for 120 min and kept over-night at 4°C). This DNA was treated with nuclease S1 (2 U/ml) for 15 min at 37°C and subjected to electro-phoresis in 0.7% agarose gel. φ29, DNA of phage φ29; H1, reisolated subclone of phage M2; HO, our original stock of phage M2; HO EcoRI, reference fragments of HO DNA digested with EcoRI; ann., annealed.

TABLE 1. Helper transfection with the fragments produced by nuclease S1-treated heteroduplex of phage M2 DNA[a]

Helper phage	No. of infective centers/plate			Ratio	
	Intact DNA[b]	Long-fragment DNA (a)	Short-fragment DNA (b)	b/a	a/b
F 354	6,212	110	289	2.60	—
F 432-2	3,177	15	82	5.47	—
O 520	6,553	104	16	—	6.50
O 518	6,986	141	47	—	3.00

[a] M2 DNA (heterogeneous), self-annealing. Nuclease S1 treatment. Separation of fragments DNAs. Helper transfection with *sus* mutant phages.
[b] Proteinase-treated DNA.

alternatives: (i) a heteroduplex DNA structure formed in the particular region during the processes of recombination could be responsible, or (ii) a specific base sequence, such as a tandem repeat, might be located in the region and influence both recombination and deletions there.

LITERATURE CITED

1. **Behrens, B., G. Lüder, M. Behncke, and T. A. Trautner.** 1979. The genome of *B. subtilis* phage SPP1: physical arrangement of phage genes. Mol. Gen Genet. **175:**351–357.

2. **Bukhari, A. I., J. A. Shapiro, and S. L. Adhya (ed.).** 1977. DNA insertion elements, plasmids, and episomes. Cold Spring Harbor Laboratory, Cold Spring Harbor, N.Y.

3. **Chattoraj, D. K., J. M., Creasemann, N. Dower, D. Faulds, P. Faulds, R. E. Malone, F. W. Stahl, and M. M. Stahl.** 1979. Chi. Cold Spring Harbor Symp. Quant. Biol. **43:**1063–1066.

4. **Matsumoto, K., and H. Hirokawa.** 1981. Physical arrangement of suppressor-sensitive mutations of *Bacillus* phage M2. Mol. Gen. Genet. **184:**180–182.

II. STREPTOCOCCAL GENETICS

(from the ASM International Conference on Streptococcal Genetics, held 9–12 November 1981 in Sarasota, Florida)

Introduction

DONALD J. LeBLANC AND DON B. CLEWELL

Laboratory of Molecular Biology, National Institute of Allergy and Infectious Diseases, Frederick, Maryland 21701, and Department of Oral Biology and Microbiology and The Dental Research Institute, Schools of Dentistry and Medicine, The University of Michigan, Ann Arbor, Michigan 48109

The following communications represent abbreviated accounts of the proceedings of the ASM International Conference on Streptoccocal Genetics held 9–12 November 1981 in Sarasota, Florida. This represented the first major conference to be held exclusively on this topic. Approximately 140 scientists from 14 different countries attended the symposium. Covering a wide range of topics, the conference offered an opportunity for many investigators to meet and interact for the first time. The intensity and enthusiasm with which the conferees participated in the 33 oral and 44 poster presentations reflected the rapidly growing interest in genetic aspects of streptococci.

The keynote speaker was Maclyn McCarty, who presented an historical account of "streptococci and the birth of molecular genetics," in which he summarized some of the early classical pneumococcal transformation work. The topics which followed dealt with the molecular biology of streptococcal plasmids, gene transfer, and drug resistance, as well as basic chromosomal genetics and physiology.

The first formal session, on conjugation, began with an overview of plasmid transfer systems in streptococci, with particular emphasis on the diversity of conjugation mechanisms in this genus (LeBlanc). Two presentations dealt with non-plasmid-mediated conjugative transfer in *Streptococcus pneumoniae* (Guild) and *S. faecalis* (Gawron-Burke). The session ended with an update on pheromone-mediated plasmid transfer systems of *S. faecalis* (Clewell). Discussion of genetic transfer systems continued through the second session, on transformation and transduction, which began with an excellent review of streptococcal phages and transduction (Wannamaker) and was followed by a talk on the role of phage in the expression of erythrogenic toxin in group A streptococci (Ferretti). The remainder of this session dealt with the nature of plasmid transfer by transformation in pneumococcus and various factors affecting such transfer (Guild, Barany, and Lacks).

A session on drug resistance began with presentations on the general problem of antibiotic-resistant streptococci in Canada (Dixon) and Japan (Mitsuhashi). Talks on the transmissibility of resistance in clinical isolates (Horodniceanu) and detailed analyses of streptococcal resistance to tetracyclines (Burdett), the MLS antibiotics (Weisblum), and aminoglycosides (Courvalin) rounded out this session.

The next session, on genetics and physiology, dealt with virulence factors of group A streptococci (Totolian and Cleary), the potential of mutagenesis in caries prevention (Freedman and Hillman), the application of antibiotic synergism in the treatment of enterococcal infections (Krogstad), and a genetic analysis of the reason for the need for synergy, i.e., penicillin resistance and tolerance in group D streptococci (Daneo-Moore).

The fifth session was devoted to genetic and molecular analyses of the industrially important group N, or dairy, streptococci and began with a review of plasmids and their transmissibility in these organisms (McKay). This was followed by discussion of phage restriction (Daly), plasmid-mediated lactose metabolism (Gasson), and production of antibiotics (Pearce) and bacteriocins (Dobrzanski) by various species of the lactic streptococci.

The final session, concerning the applicability of recombinant DNA methodology, testified to the growing rate at which these organisms are becoming amenable to analysis at the molecular level. Macrina discussed various strategies for cloning selectable and nonselectable traits in the *S. sanguis* host-vector system and described the development of a transgeneric shuttle vector for cloning in both *Escherichia coli* and *S. sanguis*. The cloning of antibiotic-resistance genes and the advantages of a helper plasmid system with *S. sanguis* were discussed by Behnke and by Malke, respectively. The use of recombinant DNA technology to study the transformation process in *S. pneumoniae* was discussed by Sicard. Finally, Curtiss described recent studies on *S. mutans* virulence genes, using an *E. coli* host-vector system.

The streptococci encompass a broad group of organisms with both medical and industrial importance. The collection of articles presented here represent an up-to-date summary of what is currently known about the genetics of these organisms.

CONJUGATION

Plasmid Transfer in Streptococci (an Overview)

DONALD J. LeBLANC, LINDA N. LEE, JACOB A. DONKERSLOOT, AND ROBERT J. HARR

Laboratory of Molecular Microbiology, National Institute of Allergy and Infectious Diseases, Frederick, Maryland 21701, and Laboratory of Microbiology and Immunology, National Institute for Dental Research, Bethesda, Maryland 20205

The presence of plasmids in streptococci, as in other bacterial genera, may influence the ecological, taxonomic, and pathogenic status of a number of species. Since the first report, in 1972, of plasmid-mediated antibiotic resistance in a strain of *Streptococcus faecalis* (5), plasmids have been isolated from nearly every species of *Streptococcus* examined. Although the vast majority of these extrachromosomal elements remain cryptic, a variety of antibiotic resistance traits, metabolic capabilities, and taxonomically significant phenotypes have been assigned to streptococcal plasmids (4). In addition to their association with these environmental determinants, a great deal has been learned about the plasmids themselves. Much of the progress in streptococcal plasmid biology in recent years can be attributed to the availability of genetic transfer systems. All three of the "natural" genetic transfer mechanisms associated with bacteria—transduction, transformation, and conjugation—have been employed in the study of streptococcal plasmids. In this article we briefly review the various plasmid-dependent, and in some cases apparent plasmid-independent, transfer systems that have been described among the streptococci. We also present some recent results from our laboratory, as they relate to streptococcal conjugation systems.

TRANSDUCTION

The use of transduction for the transfer and analysis of streptococcal plasmids has been limited primarily by a lack of appropriate transducing phages in several species, most notably among the group B and group D streptococci. Other factors, such as natural restrictions on viral host range and DNA packaging size, may have limited the use of this transfer mechanism as well. Historically, however, the first genetic transfer experiments in two areas of streptococcal plasmid biology were carried out by transduction.

The MLS plasmids, characterized by the expression of a genetic determinant(s) that mediates resistance to macrolides such as erythromycin, lincosamides such as lincomycin, and streptogramin type B antibiotics, have been the most thoroughly studied of the extrachromosomal elements found in streptococci to date. These plasmids generally share considerable DNA homology with one another and have been transferred, by one or more of the "natural" transfer mechanisms, to virtually every species of *Streptococcus*, as well as other genera of gram-positive bacteria (6). The first of these transfers, between strains of group A streptococci, was accomplished by transduction (12). The same MLS plasmid, ERL1, was also transduced from group A to group C and G (14), and back to group A (18) streptococci. These studies provided the first evidence that a plasmid originating in one streptococcal species could be transferred to, and stably maintained by, heterologous species.

Several metabolic traits of the group N streptococci are extremely important in the manufacture of a number of dairy products. Genetic evidence for plasmid mediation of one of these traits, the fermentation of lactose by strains of *S. lactis*, was first obtained by transduction (15). The role of plasmids in the metabolism of the group N streptococci is currently an area of intense research activity.

TRANSFORMATION

Although transformation was first described in an organism now classified in the genus *Streptococcus* (1), the introduction of plasmid DNA into streptococci by this mechanism was not reported until recently. In 1976, we reported the transformation of the Challis strain of *S. sanguis* by the MLS plasmid pAMβ1, isolated from a strain of *S. faecalis* (18). In 1978, the same plasmid was introduced into a group F strain (17). More recently, isolates from two additional streptococcal species have been transformed by plasmid DNA, *S. pneumoniae* (2, 16) and *S. mutans* (H. K. Kuramitsu and C. M. Long, this volume). All of the transformable strains of streptococci described thus far exhibit a natural competence, occurring early in the growth cycle of the host. Until recently, all attempts to transform noncompetent streptococci by artificial induction of competence, using such methods as CaCl$_2$ treatment or protoplast regeneration, had been unsuccessful. Preliminary results now suggest that it may be possible to introduce plasmid DNA into protoplasts of *S. faecalis* (D. B. Clewell, personal communication) and *S. lactis* (L. L. McKay, personal communication).

The Challis strain of *S. sanguis* has been the most popular for transformation with streptococcal plasmids. Numerous antibiotic resistance plasmids (4), a lactose plasmid from a strain of *S. lactis* (E. J. St. Martin, L. N. Lee, and D. J. LeBlanc, this volume), and cryptic plasmids from *S. ferus* (11) have all been transferred to the Challis strain. More recently, *S. pneumoniae* has received considerable attention for plasmid transformation studies (4).

The value of streptococcal plasmid transformation systems lies not only in the ability to transfer different plasmids to new host strains, but also in the potential for studying individual chromosomal, as well as plasmid, functions directly in streptococci by the application of recombinant DNA technology. Appropriate host-vector systems using the Challis strain of *S. sanguis* and *S. pneumoniae*, and streptococcal replicons, have been developed (4). Thus far, it has been possible to clone only genes mediating directly selectable phenotypic traits. This shortcoming is very likely due to the two-hit kinetics observed in the transformation of streptococci by plasmid DNA (10, 17). It should be possible, however, to clone nonselectable streptococcal genes in *Escherichia coli* and subsequently transfer the recombinant molecules to streptococci for expression, by using a trans-generic plasmid shuttle vector (F. L. Macrina et al., this volume).

CONJUGATION

One of the most intriguing aspects of streptococcal plasmid biology to emerge over the past few years is the apparent diversity of conjugation-like systems observed among these organisms. In the most thoroughly studied system to date, certain relatively large plasmids (35 to 46 megadaltons), thus far confined to strains of *S. faecalis*, transfer at very high frequencies during mixed incubation in broth culture. The system is characterized by a novel signaling mechanism whereby recipient strains excrete small peptides, or sex pheromones, which induce donors to mate (D. B. Clewell et al., this volume).

Among the group N streptococci certain metabolic plasmids transfer at very low frequencies, and only if donor and recipient cells have been forced together on an agar surface or membrane filter. Some *S. lactis* transconjugants that have received a lactose metabolic plasmid after this type of mating subsequently exhibit an unusual cell aggregation phenotype and can now donate the lactose plasmid at a high frequency in broth culture. The lactose plasmid in these high-frequency donors is approximately twice as large as the original plasmid found in the primary donor. The increase in size of the lactose plasmid is apparently not due to dimerization of the original molecule, but rather to the acquisition of heterologous DNA, either from the host chromosome or from a previously undetected plasmid (L. L. McKay and K. A. Baldwin, this volume).

The most common transmissible plasmids found in streptococci, and the only ones capable of mediating interspecies transfer, are those requiring forced cell-to-cell contact between donors and recipients before transfer can occur. Such contact is generally facilitated by collecting a mixture of donor and recipient cells on a membrane filter, which is then incubated on a solid medium. Most, but not all, of these transmissible plasmids mediate resistance to one or more antibiotics. The best studied are the transmissible MLS plasmids, which range in size from 15 to 20 megadaltons and are extremely promiscuous, having been transferred to virtually every species of streptococci. In addition, certain MLS plasmids have also been transferred from streptococci to strains of three other genera of gram-positive bacteria (6).

MOLECULAR ANALYSES OF MLS PLASMIDS

Streptococcal plasmids often undergo deletions or molecular rearrangements during or after transfer to new host species by either transformation or conjugation (4). Among the MLS plasmids such deletions have resulted in loss of transmissibility, failure to mediate resistance to MLS antibiotics, or alterations in plasmid copy number (3; V. Hershfield and F. Macrina, personal communications; D. J. LeBlanc and L. N. Lee, unpublished data). Several groups of investigators have begun to construct restriction endonuclease maps of parent and deleted plasmids to locate these genetic functions on the parent molecules (3, 9, 13; R. P. Evans, personal communication). We have chosen the 26.5-kilobase (kb) plasmid pAMβ1 for such a purpose. A detailed restriction endonuclease map of this plasmid is illustrated in Fig. 1. Four independent deletions have been located on this map so far. One of these derivatives, obtained from V. Burdett, had lost approximately 2.0 kb of DNA and no longer mediated resistance to MLS antibiotics. This deletion spanned the region between 12 and 1 o'clock on the map. Three other deleted plasmids, two from F. Macrina with sizes of 10.2 and 16.8 kb, and an 11.6-kb molecule isolated in our laboratory,

could no longer be transferred by conjugation. All three of these derivatives had lost a common region located between 6 and 9 o'clock on the map in Fig. 1.

Every deleted molecule of plasmid pAMβ1 examined thus far has retained the smaller EcoRI endonuclease fragment, and preliminary data suggest that the replication functions are totally contained in this fragment. Furthermore, a number of MLS plasmids contain a region of closely spaced HindIII, KpnI, and HpaI restriction sites (3, 13; R. P. Evans, personal commu-

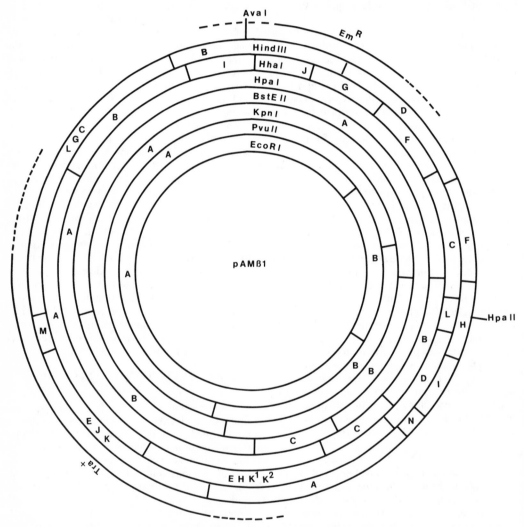

FIG. 1. Restriction endonuclease map of the transmissible MLS plasmid pAMβ1. Cleavage sites were determined by simultaneous and sequential, double and triple digests. Confirmation of the arrangement of HhaI and HindIII fragments was accomplished by blotting electrophoretically separated fragments from digests of each enzyme and hybridizing with purified, ^{32}P-labeled, BstEII and HpaI fragments. The locations of resistance (Em^R) and transfer (Tra$^+$) determinants were based on the absence of specific fragments in deleted pAMβ1 derivatives.

TABLE 1. Transmissibility of tetracycline resistance from *S. mutans* strain DL5

Donor strain	Recipient strain	Conjugation frequency per donor colony-forming unit
S. mutans DL5	*S. faecalis* JH2-2	2×10^{-6}
	S. faecalis UV202	1×10^{-6}
	S. mutans DR0001/1	1×10^{-8}
S. mutans DL43 (DL5 × DR0001/1 transconjugant)	*S. faecalis* JH2-2	1×10^{-8}
S. faecalis DL40 (DL5 × JH2-2 transconjugant)	*S. faecalis* JH201	$<1 \times 10^{-9}$
	S. faecalis JH203	$<1 \times 10^{-9}$
	S. mutans DL54	$<1 \times 10^{-9}$
	S. agalactiae MV759	$<1 \times 10^{-9}$

nication). This region, located just beyond 3 o'clock on the map of pAMβ1, appears to be involved in the regulation of copy number in at least one MLS plasmid (3).

The MLS resistance genes of these plasmids have already been isolated by recombinant DNA technology and, in fact, have been used in the construction of streptococcal plasmid vectors (4). We are currently attempting to clone those regions of plasmid pAMβ1 associated with replication, copy number control, and transmissibility. Since none of these functions is directly selectable, each will be cloned first in *E. coli* and then transferred to the Challis strain of *S. sanguis*, either by the use of separate *E. coli* and *S. sanguis* vectors, or with the trans-generic shuttle vector described by Macrina et al. (this volume). A major objective of this effort is to compare the cloned functions from pAMβ1 with their counterparts on other transmissible MLS plasmids.

"PLASMID-LESS" CONJUGATION

The transfer of antibiotic resistance determinants between species of streptococci, as well as other bacterial genera, in the absence of detectable plasmids has been reported by several laboratories (4). Confirmation of plasmid-less transfer requires evidence for a chromosomal location of the transferred genetic trait in either donor or transconjugant cells. Such evidence has been provided in only two instances among streptococci: the conjugative tetracycline (Tc) resistance transposon, Tn916, from a strain of *S. faecalis* (M. C. Gawron-Burke and D. B. Clewell, this volume) and the transmissible chloramphenicol-Tc resistance determinants of a strain of *S. pneumoniae* (W. R. Guild, M. D. Smith, and N. B. Shoemaker, this volume). A number of beta-hemolytic streptococci have been shown to transfer various antibiotic resist-ance traits in the absence of detectable plasmids in either donor or transconjugant strains (T. Horodniceanu et al., this volume), but no evidence for a chromosomal location of these determinants has been presented.

We have been working with a porcine isolate of *S. mutans*, strain DL5, that is highly resistant to streptomycin (>10 mg/ml), erythromycin (1 mg/ml), and Tc (100 μg/ml). This strain was mixed with a number of potential recipients and incubated on membrane filters, followed by selection for the transfer of each of the above antibiotic resistance traits. Transconjugants resistant to Tc, but not streptomycin or erythromycin, were readily obtained. Strain DL5 transferred Tc resistance to *S. faecalis* and *S. mutans* recipients at frequencies of 10^{-6} and 10^{-8}, respectively (Table 1). The *S. mutans*, but not *S. faecalis*, transconjugants could serve as secondary donors of the Tc resistance determinant in subsequent mating experiments.

Cultures of strain DL5 and the transconjugant isolates were subjected to a variety of standard plasmid isolation techniques, but no plasmid DNA could be detected. However, after applying multiple plasmid enrichment procedures to cell lysates obtained from 1-liter cultures, agar-ose gel electrophoresis revealed the presence of extrachromosomal DNA in three of the trans-conjugant strains, but not in strain DL5 or any of the original recipient strains (Table 2). The cova-lently closed circular (CCC) conformation of the extrachromosomal DNA was confirmed in dye buoyant density gradients, and by conversion of the CCC form to the open circular form by using superhelical DNA relaxing enzyme. The size of the plasmid, pJD2, which appeared to be the same in all three of the transconjugant strains, was approximately 8 megadaltons (12 kb). The *S. faecalis* transconjugants became sensitive to Tc at relatively high frequencies when grown in

TABLE 2. Properties of donors, recipients, and transconjugants after transfer of Tc resistance from *S. mutans* strain DL5

Strain	Derivation	Tc resistance (μg/ml)	Plasmid (megadaltons)	Curing frequency[a] (%)
DL5	*S. mutans* donor	100	ND[b]	<0.1
DR0001/1	*S. mutans* recipient	<1	ND	NA[b]
JH2-2	*S. faecalis* recipient	<1	ND	NA
UV202	*S. faecalis* recipient	1	ND	NA
DL43	DL5 × DR0001/1 (*S. mutans* × *S. mutans*)	100	8	<0.1
DL40	DL5 × JH2-2 (*S. mutans* × *S. faecalis*)	150	8	4.5
DL178	DL5 × UV202 (*S. mutans* × *S. faecalis*)	100	8	13.5

[a] Curing frequencies determined after 40 to 50 generations in the absence of Tc.
[b] ND, Not detected; NA, not applicable.

the absence of antibiotic (Table 2). Loss of Tc resistance was accompanied by the loss of plasmid pJD2. There was no detectable curing of Tc resistance from *S. mutans* strains DL5 or DL43.

The total yield of plasmid DNA from the *S. faecalis* transconjugant, strain DL40, varied between 0.2 and 0.5 μg per 5-liter culture, whether grown in the presence or absence of Tc. Similar yields were obtained from transconjugant strain DL178, isolated from a mating between strain DL5 and the recombination-deficient *S. faecalis* strain, UV202 (19). On the basis of typical plasmid yields from JH2-2 transconjugants carrying other, single-copy plasmids, we calculated that the amount of plasmid DNA obtained from strain DL40 corresponded to less than 0.01 copy per genome equivalent.

We have begun a series of experiments to determine whether plasmid pJD2 is present in resistant cells entirely as an autonomous plasmid that may be refractile to isolation, or if it may be integrated into the chromosome of the host. Preliminary results revealed that plasmid pJD2 contained one *Eco*RI and one *Hin*dIII restriction site. Total cellular DNA from strain DL40 and a Tc-sensitive derivative of this strain, DL40-A1, was digested by each of these enzymes. The DNA fragments were separated by agarose gel electrophoresis and transferred to a nitrocellulose blot, which was used in a hybridization reaction with ^{32}P-labeled pJD2. A 12-kb *Eco*RI fragment and a 12-kb *Hin*dIII fragment from strain DL40, but not DL40-A1, hybridized to the probe. There was no hybridization to the DNA from either strain corresponding to CCC or open circular pJD2. These results suggest that, at least in transconjugant strain DL40, DNA homologous to plasmid pJD2 is, for the most part, not integrated in the chromosome of the host.

CONCLUSIONS

The rapid progress in streptococcal plasmid biology in recent years has been due, in large measure, to the availability of genetic transfer systems. Future advances in this area, and in genetic and molecular analyses of total streptococcal genomes, will depend on efforts to expand the applicability of these transfer systems. Such efforts should include a systematic search for new transducing systems, studies on the mechanisms of plasmid-mediated and plasmid-independent conjugation, and development of new transformation systems for broader application of recombinant DNA technology.

LITERATURE CITED

1. **Avery, O., and M. McCarty.** 1944. Studies on the chemical nature of the substance inducing transformation of pneumococcal types. Induction of transformation by a DNA fraction isolated from pneumococcus type III. J. Exp. Med. **79:**147–168.
2. **Barany, F., and A. Tomasz.** 1980. Genetic transformation of *Streptococcus pneumoniae* by heterologous plasmid deoxyribonucleic acid. J. Bacteriol. **144:**698–709.
3. **Behnke, D., and M. S. Gilmore.** 1981. Location of antibiotic resistance determinants, copy control, and replication functions on the double-selective streptococcal cloning vector pGB301. Mol. Gen. Genet. **184:**115–120.
4. **Clewell, D. B.** 1981. Plasmids, drug resistance, and gene transfer in the genus *Streptococcus*. Microbiol. Rev. **45:**409–436.
5. **Courvalin, P. M., C. Carlier, and Y. A. Chabbert.** 1972. Plasmid linked tetracycline and erythromycin resistance in group D "*Streptococcus.*" Ann. Inst. Pasteur Paris **123:**755–759.
6. **LeBlanc, D. J.** 1981. Plasmids in streptococci: a review, p. 81–90. *In* S. B. Levy, R. C. Clowes, and E. L. Koenig (ed.), Molecular biology, pathogenicity, and ecology of bacterial plasmids. Plenum Publishing Corp., New York.
7. **LeBlanc, D. J., L. Cohen, and L. Jensen.** 1978. Transformation of group F streptococci by plasmid DNA. J. Gen. Microbiol. **106:**49–54.
8. **LeBlanc, D. J., and F. P. Hassell.** 1976. Transformation of *Streptococcus sanguis* Challis by plasmid deoxyribonu-

cleic acid from *Streptococcus faecalis*. J. Bacteriol. **128**:347–355.

9. **Macrina, F. L., C. L. Keeler, Jr., K. R. Jones, and P. H. Wood.** 1980. Molecular characterization of unique deletion mutants of the streptococcal plasmid, pAMβ1. Plasmid **4**:8–16.

10. **Macrina, F. L., J. A. Tobian, R. P. Evans, and K. R. Jones.** 1981. Molecular cloning in the streptococci, p. 195–210. *In* A. Hollaender (ed.), Genetic engineering of microorganisms for chemicals. Plenum Press, New York.

11. **Macrina, F. L., P. H. Wood, and K. R. Jones.** 1980. Genetic transformation of *Streptococcus sanguis* (Challis) with cryptic plasmids from *Streptococcus ferus*. Infect. Immun. **28**:692–699.

12. **Malke, H.** 1975. Transfer of a plasmid mediating antibiotic resistance between strains of *Streptococcus pyogenes* in mixed cultures. Z. Allg. Mikrobiol. **15**:645–649.

13. **Malke, H., L. G., Burman, and S. E. Holm.** 1981. Molecular cloning in streptococci: physical mapping of the vehicle plasmid pSM10 and demonstration of intergroup DNA transfer. Mol. Gen. Genet. **181**:259–267.

14. **Malke, H., R. Starke, W. Kohler, T. G. Kolesnichenko, and A. A. Totolian.** 1975. Bacteriophage P13234mo-mediated intra- and intergroup transduction of antibiotic resistance among streptococci. Zentralbl. Bakteriol. Parasitenkd. Infektionskr. Hyg. Abt. 1 Orig. Reihe A **233**:24–34.

15. **McKay, L. L., K. A. Baldwin, and J. D. Efstathiou.** 1976. Transductional evidence for plasmid linkage of lactose metabolism in *Streptococcus lactis* C2. Appl. Environ. Microbiol. **32**:45–52.

16. **Saunders, C. W., and W. R. Guild.** 1980. Properties and transforming activities of two plasmids in *Streptococcus pneumoniae*. Mol. Gen. Genet. **180**:573–578.

17. **Saunders, C. W., and W. R. Guild.** 1981. Monomer plasmid DNA transforms *Streptococcus pneumoniae*. Mol. Gen. Genet. **181**:57–62.

18. **Skjold, S. A., H. Malke, and L. W. Wannamaker.** 1979. Transduction of plasmid-mediated erythromycin resistance between group-A and G streptococci, p. 274–275. *In* M. T. Parker (ed.), Pathogenic streptococci. Reedbooks, Chertsey, England.

19. **Yagi, Y., and D. B. Clewell.** 1980. Recombination deficient mutant of *Streptococcus faecalis*. J. Bacteriol. **143**:966–970.

Conjugative Transfer of Chromosomal R Determinants in *Streptococcus pneumoniae*

WALTER R. GUILD, MICHAEL D. SMITH, AND NADJA B. SHOEMAKER[1]

Biochemistry Department, Duke University, Durham, North Carolina 27710

A novel form of conjugative transfer of drug resistance has been found for R determinants appearing in clinical isolates of pneumococci and other streptococci containing no detectable plasmid DNA. We used transformation to obtain direct evidence that *cat* and *tet* genes were in the chromosomes of pneumococcal strains BM6001 and N77 (12) and have extended this analysis to other strains (5; below). We then observed that *cat* and *tet* cotransferred during matings on membrane filters in the presence of sufficient DNase to eliminate transformation (13, 14). Buu-Hoi and Horodniceanu reported transfer from more pneumococcal strains (2), and similar transfers are being reported in other streptococci (4, 6). Both intra- and interspecies transfer occurs (2, 6; unpublished data). In all cases the R determinants that transfer are part of a large insertion (Ω) that carries a *tet* gene and presumably encodes transfer functions, inasmuch as transconjugants are able to retransfer the insertion. Most of the *tet* genes are homologous to each other but differ from plasmid-carried *tet* genes (15). Our results so far (15; below) suggest that the homology is more extensive and that other determinants insert within and delete from a basic conjugative Ωtet element. Transfer of these almost certainly accounts for the recent spread of resistance to and among pneumococci. An apparently plasmid-free transfer of ability to ferment lactose has been reported in *S. lactis* (18). Below, after a brief review, we will examine results that may bear on the mechanism of the transfer process.

CHROMOSOMAL INSERTION

For BM6001, N77, and derivatives, the primary evidence that *cat* and *tet* are in the chromosomes, as shown in Fig. 1, is twofold: (i) they are linked to each other and to the chromosomal *nov-1* gene as shown by cotransformation (12; S. Priebe, personal communication); (ii) *cat* transforming activity, which is relatively insensitive to shear of the donor DNA, cosediments with chromosomal DNA markers both in unsheared

[1] Present address: Department of Microbiology, University of Illinois, Urbana, IL 61801.

lysates and after shearing them to much smaller DNA sizes (12). Also, none of the transforming activity is found with covalently closed DNA in dye-buoyancy gradients (12). This behavior is very different from that of plasmids (11, 12).

The evidence that Ωtet is large is that its frequency of transforming a wild-type strain to resistance is low and very sensitive to shear of the donor lysate (12), a behavior like that seen when wild-type DNA transforms a recipient with an extended deletion. It implies that success requires entry of a DNA strand long enough to span the nonhomology and still have some flanking homology with which to pair (Fig. 1b). Finding *tet-3*, a point mutation to sensitivity, allowed us to show that DNAs from numerous tetracycline-resistant strains had sufficient homology to transform $\Omega tet-3$ recipients with the efficiency of point markers but that plasmid *tet* genes did not (15). More generally, recipients carrying Ωtet or $\Omega tet-3$ can be transformed readily by *erm* and *aphA* genes linked to *tet* in other donors (see below), suggesting homology to Ωtet on both sides of smaller insertions carrying *cat, erm*, and *aphA*.

CONJUGATION

Transfer of the insertions by filter mating is insensitive to the presence of DNase or to the cells being deficient in an endonuclease needed for entry of transforming DNA (13, 14). Transfer of other chromosomal genes is not detected unless the DNase is omitted. The specificity for the insertions excludes generalized transduction and cell fusion as well as transformation for the pathway of transfer. Although an ad hoc hypothesis about specialized transduction by an undetected prophage cannot be excluded, the process fits the formal definition of conjugation.

GENERALITY OF TRANSFER

Of 20 pneumococcal isolates, 7 transferred resistances to *S. faecalis* and 2 transferred to other pneumococci (2). We also saw transfer-deficient (Tra⁻) pneumococci (see below) and found that transformants which acquire only *cat* or *tet* from a Tra⁺ block are Tra⁻, whereas those

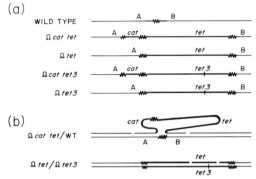

FIG. 1. $\Omega(cat\text{-}tet)$ region in the pneumococcal chromosome and transformation reactions involving it. (a) Schematic maps of $\Omega(cat\text{-}tet)$ or Ωtet inserted between A and B, a specific but unknown region linked to *nov* (12). Zigzags indicate sequences of unknown character that were invoked because crossover to the wild-type Rx chromosome occurs between *cat* and *tet* but at a frequency suggesting that homology is limited (12). (b) Intermediates in the transformation of wild-type (WT) or the *tet-3* recipient by DNAs carrying $\Omega(cat\text{-}tet)$ or Ωtet.

which acquire the entire block are Tra$^+$ (15). Horodniceanu et al. (6) found transfer among apparently plasmid-free streptococci of groups A, B, F, and G. Their group B strain B109 transfers a *cat-tet-erm* block to pneumococci at $>10^{-4}$ per donor, and we have confirmed that this block is in the chromosomes of B109 and the transconjugants by sedimentation analysis as above (not shown).

Franke and Clewell (4) described the *tet* transposon Tn916 in *S. faecalis* and showed that it both transposes within a cell and transfers to other *S. faecalis* recipients, both Rec$^+$ and Rec$^-$. We found that it also transfers *tet* to pneumococci but have yet to see retransfer. What appears to be a similar plasmid-free transfer of *tet* and *erm* in the gram-negative *Bacteroides fragilis* has been reported by two groups (9, 17). In *Haemophilus influenzae*, Stuy (16) reported that resistance transfers reflected rare excision of chromosomally integrated plasmids, which could often be detected in transconjugants and sometimes in the donors. We return below to whether this is what occurs in streptococci.

On homologies of *tet* genes, three further tests of transformation of *tet-3* recipients are interesting: (i) the *B. fragilis tet* DNAs (9, 17) gave negative results; (ii) *S. faecalis* JH-1 gave strongly positive results, presumably because of its chromosomal *tet* (8); and (iii) DNA from *Staphylococcus aureus* ISP92, carrying *tmn-*

3106, transformed *tet-3* cells to resistance at high efficiency. *tmn-3106* has been mapped in the *S. aureus* chromosome near the site of insertion of various plasmids and *attϕ11* (10).

RESULTS BEARING ON MECHANISMS

Sites of insertion. Some results relevant to the organization of genes in various strains and to the transfer process are indicated schematically in Fig. 2. BM4200 cotransfers the indicated block *cat-tet-erm-aphA* but does not transfer other resistances (2). We used a transconjugant as donor to a BM6001 derivative, selected for *erm*, and obtained DP1408. It transformed a *tet-3* strain as though it had two copies of *tet*, and by conjugation it transferred either $\Omega(cat\text{-}tet)$ or $\Omega(cat\text{-}tet\text{-}erm\text{-}aphA)$ at comparable frequencies. Sedimentation analysis of transforming activities in BM4200 showed that the genes are in the chromosome (5), and S. Priebe (personal communication) found linkage of this block to *nov-1*. Thus the insertions appear to be at different sites in the same region of the chromosome. A significant point is that the presence of one did not exclude the acquisition of another.

B381 has at least two *tet* insertions (perhaps three) and linked *str* and *sul* point mutations, as identified by transformation analysis, plus resistances to penicillins and trimethoprim that we have not analyzed. Nothing transfers by conjugation. When a transformant carrying the tightly linked *tet-erm* pair was the recipient for mating with a BM6001 derivative, transconjugant DP1306 had two copies of *tet* but transferred only $\Omega(cat\text{-}tet)$. In contrast, transformation of an $\Omega(cat\text{-}tet)$ strain by *tet-erm* DNA gave DP1434, which has only one copy of *tet* and cotransfers *erm* with *cat* and *tet*, much like B109. Thus it appears that in transformation the integration process used homology at *tet* to direct the integration but that in conjugation another signal was used. Because the presence of a Tra$^+$ element did not mobilize the Tra$^-$ *tet-erm* in DP1306, it lacked at least one site of action necessary for transfer.

On whether there are preferred sites for integration, 25 of 25 $\Omega(cat\text{-}tet)$ transconjugants showed linkage of *cat* and *tet* to *nov-1* similar to that in the donor, implying a regional preference at the very least (Priebe, personal communication).

Possible mechanisms. Two models for transfer (Fig. 3) are (I) an Hfr-like mobilization of the chromosome, or (II) excision and transfer of a plasmid, followed by reintegration, as implied by Stuy's results for *H. influenzae* (16) and as has been suggested by Clewell for Tn916 (3). These and one of various other models that can

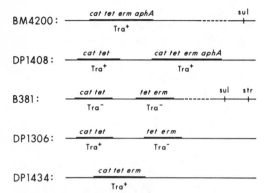

FIG. 2. Gene organizations and Tra phenotypes of clinical strains BM4200 (Paris; 2), B381 (South Africa), and some derivatives (see text). DNAs from DP1408 and DP1306 gave about twice as many tetracycline-resistant transformants of a *tet-3* recipient as did those of BM4200 and DP1434. DNA of B381 gave almost three times as many tetracycline-resistant transformants, suggesting that it probably has a third *tet*.

be postulated are indicated in Fig. 3. Two features of the results exclude the Hfr model in its simplest form, where transfer starts within the element: the transconjugants are all Tra$^+$, and we did not see detectable mobilization of the chromosome as a whole (although a short unmarked region would not have been detected). Model III postulates that transfer of a single strand starts at or beyond the end of the element. This version suggests that flanking homology might direct the integration, but see below for alternatives.

On whether there can be a plasmid intermediate as in II, we found that transfer of insertions is not inhibited by what appears to be an in vivo restriction system that strongly affects transfer of two plasmids (Table 1). Bernheimer's strain 8R1 has restriction nuclease *Dpn*II, which cuts Rx DNA in vitro (7), and she has shown a reciprocal restriction of phage infection between R6 (*Dpn*I) and 8R1 (1). Rx strains have neither enzyme (S. Hazum, unpublished data), a result of some interest in itself that has been confirmed by S. Lacks (personal communication) by the phage restriction test. We found that no form of transformation—for point markers, insertions, or plasmids—is restricted in vivo in 8R1 recipients (data not shown). However, conjugative transfer of pIP501 is restricted about 10^4-fold from Rx to 8R1, and the smaller pMV158, when mobilized by pIP501, is restricted 50-fold (Table 1). When present in 8R1, pIP501 transfers to 8R1 and to Rx with normal efficiency. These data suggest that a classical restriction-modification system acts on the plasmids as it does on phage,

without proving that it is due to *Dpn*II itself. The insertions are cut by *Dpn*II in vitro (not shown), and their presence in the recipient did not inhibit restriction of pIP501 in vivo (Table 1, experiment 4).

Whatever the cause of the apparent restriction, the significant result is that the insertions behaved differently from the plasmids. This makes it highly unlikely that transfer involved circularization into a typical plasmid that transferred, reestablished itself, and then integrated into the chromosome. Therefore the mode of transfer remains to be established, and other models, perhaps of the sort in III (Fig. 3), need consideration.

What about transposition? In the absence of evidence we have refrained from calling the pneumococcal insertions transposons. However, the term "conjugative transposon" clearly applies to Tn*916* (3, 4) and would be useful for identifying the phenomenon if other Tra$^+$ elements were found also to be transposons. We now find that the Tra$^+$ Ω(*cat-tet-erm*) of B109 appears to be a transposon (M. D. Smith and W. R. Guild, this volume), and it also transfers to and from pneumococci. This increases the probability that all Tra$^+$ elements are "conjugative transposons." Thus, although model III, as drawn in Fig. 3, suggests that legitimate pairing might direct integration, the data so far are also compatible with transposition functions being involved. The entire process might even be a concerted act of transposition through the walls

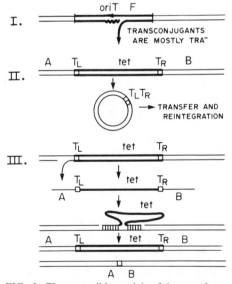

FIG. 3. Three possible models of the transfer process for an Ω*tet* element in streptococci. See text.

TABLE 1. Restriction in vivo in *Dpn*II-producing strain 8R1[a]

Expt	Donor element	Donor type	Recipient type	Transfer frequency	Ratio (Rx/8R1)
1	$\Omega(cat\text{-}tet)$[b]	Rx	Rx 8R1	6×10^{-5} 2×10^{-5}	3
2	$\Omega(cat\text{-}tet\text{-}erm)$[b]	Rx	Rx 8R1	2×10^{-5} 3×10^{-5}	0.7
3	pIP501	Rx	Rx 8R1	1×10^{-3} $<5 \times 10^{-7}$	$\sim 10^4$
	pMV158[c]		Rx 8R1	4×10^{-4} 2×10^{-6}	~ 50
4	pIP501	8R1 Rx	8R1[d]	4×10^{-3} 3×10^{-7}	$\sim 10^{-4}$
5	pIP501	Rx	Rx 8R1	1×10^{-3} $<4 \times 10^{-7}$	$\sim 10^4$
	$\Omega(cat\text{-}tet)$[b]		Rx 8R1	2×10^{-6} 1.3×10^{-6}	1.5

[a] Donors carried one or two transferable elements as indicated. Recipients were streptomycin-resistant derivatives of the indicated strain types.

[b] This $\Omega(cat\text{-}tet)$ is that from BM6001. $\Omega(cat\text{-}tet\text{-}erm)$ is that from B109 transferred into an Rx strain by conjugation.

[c] pMV158 was mobilized by pIP501.

[d] This 8R1 recipient carried $\Omega(cat\text{-}tet)$. Similar results were observed in 8R1 strains without the insertion.

and membranes of donor and recipient. Transposons show various degrees of target site specificity, and detailed mechanisms of transposition remain obscure. Tn916 transfers to Rec⁻ *S. faecalis* (4); tests with Rec⁻ pneumococci recently isolated by D. A. Morrison (personal communication) are to be done shortly and should be informative.

ACKNOWLEDGMENTS

We thank H. Bernheimer, T. Horodniceanu, P. Courvalin, P. Pattee, and D. Clewell for strains; S. Hazum, S. Priebe, and S. Lacks for personal communications; and V. Lee for technical assistance.

This work was supported by grants to W.R.G. from the National Institutes of Health and the Department of Energy. M.D.S. was a genetics trainee under a grant from the National Institutes of Health.

LITERATURE CITED

1. **Bernheimer, H. P.** 1979. Lysogenic pneumococci and their bacteriophages. J. Bacteriol. **138:**618–624.
2. **Buu-Hoi, A., and T. Horodniceanu.** 1980. Conjugative transfer of multiple antibiotic resistance markers in *Streptococcus pneumoniae.* J. Bacteriol. **143:**313–320.
3. **Clewell, D. B.** 1981. Plasmids, drug resistance, and gene transfer in the genus Streptococcus. Microbiol. Rev. **45:**409–436.
4. **Franke, A. E., and D. B. Clewell.** 1981. Evidence for a chromosome-borne resistance transposon (Tn916) in *Streptococcus faecalis* that is capable of "conjugal" transfer in the absence of a conjugative plasmid. J. Bacteriol. **145:**494–502.
5. **Guild, W. R., S. Hazum, and M. D. Smith.** 1981. Chromosomal location of conjugative R determinants in strain BM4200 of *Streptococcus pneumoniae,* p. 610. *In* S. B. Levy, R. C. Clowes, and E. L. Koenig (ed.), Molecular biology, pathogenicity, and ecology of bacterial plasmids. Plenum Publishing Corp., New York.
6. **Horodniceanu, T., L. Bougueleret, and G. Bieth.** 1981. Conjugative transfer of multiple-antibiotic resistance markers in beta-hemolytic group A, B, F, and G streptococci in the absence of extrachromosomal deoxyribonucleic acid. Plasmid **5:**127–137.
7. **Lacks, S., and B. Greenberg.** 1977. Complementary specificity of restriction endonucleases of *Diplococcus pneumoniae* with respect to DNA methylation. J. Mol. Biol. **114:**153–168.
8. **LeBlanc, D. J.** 1981. Plasmids in streptococci: a review, p. 81–90. *In* S. B. Levy, R. C. Clowes, and E. Koenig (ed.), Molecular biology, pathogenicity, and ecology of bacterial plasmids. Plenum Publishing Corp., New York.
9. **Mays, T. D., F. L. Macrina, R. A. Welch, and C. J. Smith.** 1981. Unusual conjugal transfer of antibiotic resistance in bacteroides: non-involvement of plasmids, p. 631. *In* S. B. Levy, R. C. Clowes, and E. Koenig (ed.), Molecular biology, pathogenicity, and ecology of bacterial plasmids. Plenum Publishing Corp., New York.
10. **Pattee, P. A., N. E. Thompson, D. Haubrich, and R. P. Novick.** 1977. Chromosomal map locations of integrated plasmids and related elements in *Staphylococcus aureus.* Plasmid **1:**31–38.
11. **Saunders, C. W., and W. R. Guild.** 1980. Properties and transforming activities of two plasmids in *Streptococcus pneumoniae.* Mol. Gen. Genet. **180:**573–578.
12. **Shoemaker, N. B., M. D. Smith, and W. R. Guild.** 1979. Organization and transfer of heterologous chloramphenicol and tetracycline resistance genes in pneumococcus. J. Bacteriol. **139:**432–441.
13. **Shoemaker, N. B., M. D. Smith, and W. R. Guild.** 1980. DNase-resistant transfer of chromosomal *cat* and *tet* insertions by filter mating in pneumococcus. Plasmid **3:**80–87.
14. **Smith, M. D., and W. R. Guild.** 1980. Improved method

for conjugative transfer by filter mating of *Streptococcus pneumoniae*. J. Bacteriol. **144**:457–459.

15. **Smith, M. D., S. Hazum, and W. R. Guild.** 1981. Homology among *tet* determinants in conjugative elements in streptococci. J. Bacteriol. **148**:232–240.

16. **Stuy, J. H.** 1980. Chromosomally integrated conjugative plasmids are common in antibiotic-resistant *Haemophilus influenzae*. J. Bacteriol. **142**:925–930.

17. **Tally, F. P., M. J. Shimell, G. R. Carson, and M. H. Malamy.** 1981. Chromosomal and plasmid-mediated transfer of clindamycin resistance in *Bacteroides fragilis*, p. 51–59. *In* S. B. Levy, R. C. Clowes, and E. Koenig (ed.), Molecular biology, pathogenicity, and ecology of bacterial plasmids. Plenum Publishing Corp., New York.

18. **Walsh, P. M., and L. L. McKay.** 1981. Recombinant plasmid associated with cell aggregation and high-frequency conjugation of *Streptococcus lactis* ML3. J. Bacteriol. **146**:937–944.

Tn*916* (Tc^r), a Transferable Nonplasmid Element in *Streptococcus faecalis*

M. CYNTHIA GAWRON-BURKE AND DON B. CLEWELL

Departments of Oral Biology and Microbiology, Schools of Dentistry and Medicine, and The Dental Research Institute, The University of Michigan, Ann Arbor, Michigan 48109

Streptococcus faecalis strain DS16 harbors a conjugative hemolysin-bacteriocin–determining plasmid pAD1 (35 megadaltons) and a nonconjugative multiple drug resistance plasmid pAD2 (16 megadaltons) (15). A chromosome-borne tetracycline resistance determinant is located on a 10-megadalton transposon designated Tn*916* and is capable of transposition to several different conjugative hemolysin plasmids (pAD1, pOB1, and pAMγ1) at a frequency of about 10^{-6} (3). Tn*916* is also able to transfer at low frequency (10^{-8}) from plasmid-free derivatives of DS16 to plasmid-free recipients (JH2-2) in filter matings by a conjugation-like event requiring direct contact between the donor and recipient. This phenomenon is Rec independent, and transfer of the mutational markers *str* and *spc* was not observed under these conditions (3).

Here we present data obtained from recent DNA filter hybridization experiments indicating that the transfer of Tn*916* from plasmid-free donors to plasmid-free recipients results in the insertion of the transposon into different sites on the recipient chromosome. In addition, we report the isolation of JH2-2 tetracycline-resistant (Tc^r) transconjugants which exhibit altered transfer frequencies of Tn*916* and address the question of whether transposition involves an excision from its original site.

Tn*916* TRANSFER

The transfer of Tn*916* in overnight filter matings from plasmid-free donors is shown in the data of Table 1. DS16C3 (a derivative of DS16 cured of both pAD1 and pAD2) is capable of transferring Tc^r at a frequency of about 10^{-8} to the plasmid-free recipient strain JH2-2. Transconjugants derived from this mating are capable of retransferring Tc^r to the isogenic recipient strain JH2SS (Table 1). To examine this transfer event more closely, chromosomal DNA was isolated from the donor and transconjugant strains listed in Table 1, digested with *Hind*III restriction endonuclease, resolved by agarose gel electrophoresis, and blotted to nitrocellulose by the Southern technique (12). These DNAs were then probed with a ^{32}P-labeled *Eco*RI

restriction fragment of pAD1::Tn*916* (pAM211) containing the entire transposon. Tn*916* is not cleaved by *Eco*RI, and about 85% of this fragment consists of Tn*916* sequences (3). Since Tn*916* contains a single *Hind*III site, two host-transposon junction fragments should be resolvable after hybridization. An autoradiogram of the Southern blot resulting after hybridization with the ^{32}P-labeled Tn*916* probe is shown in Fig. 1. Gel slot A contained chromosomal DNA from the DS16C3 donor, and the two host-transposon junction fragments (X and Y) are readily detected. Slots B through D contained chromosomal DNA from three different transconjugants derived from the DS16C3 × JH2-2 mating detailed in Table 1. In all three transconjugant strains, the hybridization profiles differed from those seen in the donor and, interestingly, also from each other. Strains such as CG140 (gel slot B) gave rise to two host-transposon junction fragments (X and Y), whereas other transconjugant strains, CG110 (gel slot C) and CG130 (gel slot D), gave rise to at least six and four bands, respectively. Gel slots E through G contained chromosomal DNA from three different transconjugants obtained from the secondary mating experiment shown in Table 1 that had used strain CG130 as the donor and JH2SS as the recipient strain. Again, the transconjugant patterns differed from the donor and also from each other. Two of the transconjugants (CG131 and CG133) exhibited the simpler banding pattern (fragments X and Y only), whereas the strain CG132 gave rise to multiple bands. Gel slot H contained *Hind*III-digested pAD1::Tn*916* from which the probe had been made.

These data indicate that Tn*916* can insert at different sites on the recipient chromosome, since the size of the fragments observed after hybridization varied greatly among different transconjugants that had been obtained from matings performed with the same recipient. (These results also argue against the possibility that Tn*916* exists on a plasmid which had escaped physical detection; if the latter were true, identical patterns would have been expected in the transconjugants.)

TABLE 1. Transfer of Tn916 from plasmid-free donors

Donor strain	Recipient strain (chromosomal markers)[a]	Frequency of Tc^r transconjugants per recipient[b]	Representative transconjugant
DS16C3	JH2-2 (Rif, Fa)	8.5×10^{-9}	CG110 CG130 CG140
CG130	JH2SS (Sm, Sp)	1.7×10^{-8}	CG131 CG132 CG133
CG110	JH2SS	4.2×10^{-6}	

[a] Tc, Rif, Fa, Sm, and Sp indicate tetracycline, rifampin, fusidic acid, streptomycin, and spectinomycin, respectively. JH2-2 and JH2SS strains are described in references 6 and 14.

[b] Frequency of spontaneous Tc^r mutation was $<10^{-10}$. Filter matings were carried out with an initial ratio of 1 donor per 10 recipients (0.5 ml of recipient, 0.05 ml of donor, 4.5 ml of AB3 medium). After incubation (18 to 20 h), the mixture was resuspended in 1.0 ml of medium and spread on appropriate selective plates (tetracycline, 10 μg/ml; rifampin and fusidic acid, 25 μg/ml; and streptomycin, 1,000 μg/ml). Frequencies are expressed as a function of recipient rather than donor concentration as a result of the low frequencies encountered and the variation in viable count between donors and recipients after overnight growth (see reference 3).

The multiple bands observed in the case of strains CG110, CG130, and CG132 are not the result of partial digestion products, since control digests that contained an equivalent amount of JH2-2 chromosomal DNA plus additional pAD1::Tn916 plasmid DNA gave rise to only fragments A and B (i.e., similar to those shown in Fig. 1, gel slot H, for pAD1::Tn916 plasmid DNA alone). Preliminary hybridization experiments involving EcoRI-digested DNAs probed with ^{32}P-labeled Tn916 indicate that there is more than one hybridizable fragment (greater than 10 megadaltons) in the chromosome of strains CG110, CG130, and CG132 (data not shown). Since there are no EcoRI sites in Tn916, the occurrence of multiple copies of the entire element is possible.

DERIVATIVES WITH ALTERED TRANSFER FREQUENCIES

Certain Tc^r transconjugants of JH2-2 exhibit altered transfer frequencies in secondary matings. Strain CG110 is able to donate tetracycline resistance at frequencies of about 10^{-6} (see Table 1). We were interested in determining the transposition frequency for Tn916 in a strain

such as CG110, and this was measured in the following way. The conjugative hemolysin plasmid pAD1 was introduced into strains CG110 and CG130, and the frequency of Tn916 transposition from the chromosome to pAD1 was measured by the frequency of Tc^r hyperhemolytic transconjugants obtained after filter mating these donor strains with JH2SS. The hyperhemolytic phenotype results from an insertion of Tn916 into or near the hemolysin determinant of pAD1 (3) and is readily detected by an increased diameter of zones of hemolysis on horse blood agar plates. Data presented in Table 2 indicate that the frequency of hyperhemolytic Tc^r transconjugants per recipient is more than 100-fold higher when CG110 is the donor strain than when CG130 is the donor strain. Thus, both Tn916 transfer and transposition are increased in strain CG110.

ON THE MECHANISM OF Tn916 TRANSFER AND TRANSPOSITION

The data indicating an increase in both the transfer and transposition frequencies of Tn916 in the CG110 strain suggest that these two events may have a common step(s). The notion that this common step may involve an excision of the transposon from the donor chromosome stems from observations made while studying DS16 derivatives with increased levels of tetracycline resistance. Since specially constructed strains which carry Tn916 on pAD1 as well as on the chromosome have been shown to have an approximate doubling of the minimal inhibitory concentration of tetracycline (i.e., 75 μg/ml versus 37 μg/ml) when compared to DS16, one would expect a twofold increase in tetracycline resistance if transposition resulted in a duplication of the transposon. Tn916 transposition from the DS16 chromosome to pAD1 has been estimated to occur at a frequency of 10^{-6}, yet DS16 cells with increased levels of tetracycline resistance appear at a much lower frequency of 10^{-8}. Furthermore, the derivatives that do appear on plates containing elevated concentrations of drug do not contain duplications of the transposon, as ascertained by Southern blot analysis (M. C. Gawron-Burke and D. B. Clewell, manuscript in preparation). This implies that if, indeed, Tn916 transposes spontaneously to pAD1 at 10^{-6}, there is not a net increase in transposon copy number. These observations are consistent with an excision-insertion mechanism.

If one supposes that Tn916 insertion into the recipient chromosome could be enhanced by a "zygotic induction" of an "integrase" (transposase?), one would predict that one might detect the excision of Tn916 from a donor replicon after

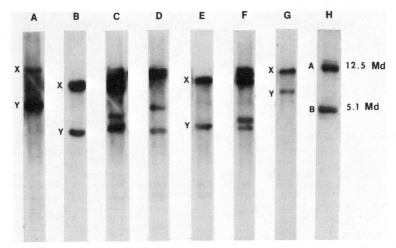

FIG. 1. Autoradiogram obtained from Southern blot of HindIII-digested chromosomal DNA after hybridization with ^{32}P-labeled Tn916 probe DNA. Gel slots B–D contain DNA (1 to 2 μg) from transconjugants CG140, CG110, and CG130, respectively, which were obtained by using DS16C3 (gel slot A) as donor (see Table 1). Gel slots E–G contain DNA from transconjugants CG131, CG132, and CG133, respectively, which were obtained by using CG130 as donor. Fragments marked X and Y denote presumed host-transposon junction fragments. Gel slot H contains HindIII-digested pAM211 plasmid DNA, and only those fragments containing Tn916 sequences (A and B) hybridized to probe DNA. (Isolation of DNA by CsCl-ethidium bromide equilibrium gradient centrifugation and agarose gel electrophoresis was as detailed elsewhere [3]. DNA transfer and hybridization were performed essentially by the Southern method [12], with the use of a BRL [Bethesda Research Laboratories] blot transfer system. Nick translation of probe DNA with either ^{32}P-labeled dATP or ^{32}P-labeled dCTP was accomplished with a BRL or NEN [New England Nuclear] nick-translation kit, respectively. Autoradiography employed Kodak X-Omat R film and a Dupont Cronex intensifying screen. Film was exposed for 1 to 4 days at −70°C.)

its transfer into a cell lacking Tn916. This was, in fact, seen in mating experiments which used strains containing the plasmid pAM81::Tn916 (pAM81 is a 17-megadalton erythromycin resistance plasmid). A high degree of segregation of the erythromycin and tetracycline resistance determinants was observed when transconjugants were selected on erythromycin. Interestingly, a varying number of those erythromycin-resistant (Em^r) transconjugants that remain Tc^r represent cells in which Tc^r and Em^r were no longer linked. HindIII-digested plasmid DNA from such Em^r Tc^r transconjugants gave a fragment pattern identical to that of pAM81 DNA when analyzed by agarose gel electrophoresis (M. C. Gawron-Burke and D. B. Clewell, Proceedings of the 3rd Tokyo Symposium on Microbial Drug Resistance, 1981, in press). Presumably, Tn916 transposed to the bacterial chromosome since these strains were Tc^r and capable of Tn916 transfer at low frequency. These data are again consistent with the notion of an excision step in Tn916 transfer and transposition, and in the case of pAM81::Tn916, the excision appears to be precise within the limits of detection by agarose gel electrophoresis. Thus, our current working

hypothesis for Tn916 transfer and transposition is one in which we envision the transposon to be capable of excision from the donor replicon, after which it may undergo one of three options: (i) reinsertion into the donor replicon, (ii) insertion into a resident plasmid, or (iii) conjugal transfer into another cell. After transfer into the recipient cell, the transposon could then insert into the recipient chromosome or perhaps into a plasmid in the recipient.

CONCLUSION

Southern blot hybridization experiments have shown that conjugal transfer of Tn916 results in the insertion of the transposon into different sites on the recipient chromosome. Certain Tc^r transconjugants of JH2-2 such as strain CG110 can donate Tc^r at elevated frequencies, and transposition of Tn916 from the chromosome to a newly introduced pAD1 is also increased. Although the basis for the elevation of transfer frequency remains obscure, it may be related to the apparent redundancy of Tn916. (Despite the suggestion of more than one copy of Tn916 in CG110, it is puzzling that the level of tetracycline resistance in the strain does not appear to

TABLE 2. Increased transposition frequency in *S. faecalis* CG110

Donor strain	Frequency of Tc^r transconjugants per recipient[a]	Frequency of hyperhemolytic Tc^r transconjugants per recipient
CG110(pAD1)	9.8×10^{-5}	4.9×10^{-6}
CG130(pAD1)	3.9×10^{-7}	1.8×10^{-8}

[a] Donor strains were filter mated with JH2SS as described in Table 1. Transconjugant frequencies are elevated in both matings as a result of the ability of pAD1 to mobilize chromosomal determinants (4). pAD1 transferred equally well from either host background in control mating experiments (data not shown).

be doubled [unpublished data].) Lastly, we obtained data consistent with an excision-insertion mechanism being involved in the transposition and transfer process.

Chromosome-borne resistance determinants which transfer in the absence of conjugative plasmids appear to be common in the streptococci (1–3, 5, 8, 9). It will be of interest to see to what extent these determinants will represent "conjugative transposons"; in this regard we note that Guild's group has recently demonstrated homology between Tn916 and the transferable tetracycline resistance element that they have studied in *S. pneumoniae* (11). We also note recent reports suggesting that transferable nonplasmid elements exist in *Clostridium difficile* (10) and *Bacteroides fragilis* (7, 13).

ACKNOWLEDGMENTS

This work was supported by Public Health Service grants DEO2731 and AIO318 from the National Institutes of Health. M.C.G. is the recipient of a Public Health Service postdoctoral fellowship.

We thank R. Craig, A. Franke, R. Hart, and Y. Yagi for helpful discussions.

LITERATURE CITED

1. **Buu-hoi, A., and T. Horodniceanu.** 1980. Conjugative transfer of multiple antibiotic resistance markers in *Streptococcus pneumoniae.* J. Bacteriol. **143:**313–320.
2. **Franke, A., and D. Clewell.** 1980. Evidence for conjugal transfer of a *Streptococcus faecalis* transposon (Tn916) from a chromosomal site in the absence of plasmid DNA. Cold Spring Harbor Symp. Quant. Biol. **45:**77–80.
3. **Franke, A., and D. B. Clewell.** 1981. Evidence for a chromosome-borne resistance transposon (Tn916) in *Streptococcus faecalis* that is capable of "conjugal" transfer in the absence of a conjugative plasmid. J. Bacteriol. **145:**494–502.
4. **Franke, A. E., G. M. Dunny, B. Brown, F. An, D. Oliver, S. P. Damle, and D. B. Clewell.** 1978. Gene transfer in *Streptococcus faecalis*: evidence for mobilization of chromosomal determinants by transmissable plasmids, p. 45–57. *In* D. Schlessinger (ed.), Microbiology—1978. American Society for Microbiology, Washington, D.C.
5. **Horodniceanu, T., L. Bougueleret, and G. Bieth.** 1981. Conjugative transfer of multiple antibiotic resistance markers in beta-hemolytic group A, B, F, and G streptococci in the absence of extrachromosomal deoxyribonucleic acid. Plasmid **5:**127–137.
6. **Jacob, A. E., and S. J. Hobbs.** 1974. Conjugal transfer of plasmid-borne multiple antibiotic resistance in *Streptococcus faecalis* var. *zymogenes.* J. Bacteriol. **117:**360–372.
7. **Mays, T. D., F. L. Macrina, R. A. Welch, and C. J. Smith.** 1981. Unusual conjugal transfer of antibiotic resistance in Bacteroides: non-involvement of plasmids, p. 631. *In* S. B. Levy, R. C. Clowes, and E. L. Koenig (ed.), Molecular biology, pathogenicity, and ecology of bacterial plasmids. Plenum Press, New York.
8. **Shoemaker, N. B., M. D. Smith, and W. R. Guild.** 1979. Organization and transfer of heterologous chloramphenicol and tetracycline resistance genes in pneumococcus. J. Bacteriol. **139:**432–441.
9. **Shoemaker, N. B., M. D. Smith, and W. R. Guild.** 1980. DNAse-resistant transfer of chromosomal *cat* and *tet* insertions by filter mating in pneumococcus. Plasmid **3:**80–87.
10. **Smith, C. J., S. M. Markowitz, and F. Macrina.** 1981. Transferable tetracycline resistance in *Clostridium difficile.* Antimicrob. Agents Chemother. **19:**997–1003.
11. **Smith, M. D., S. Hazum, and W. R. Guild.** 1981. Homology among *tet* determinants in conjugative elements of streptococci. J. Bacteriol. **148:**232–240.
12. **Southern, E. M.** 1975. Detection of specific sequences among DNA fragments separated by gel electrophoresis. J. Mol. Biol. **98:**503–517.
13. **Tally, F. P., M. J. Shimell, G. R. Carson, and M. H. Malamy.** 1981. Chromosomal and plasmid-mediated transfer of clindamycin resistance in *Bacteroides fragilis*, p. 51–59. *In* S. B. Levy, R. C. Clowes, and E. L. Koenig (ed.), Molecular biology, pathogenicity, and ecology of bacterial plasmids. Plenum Press, New York.
14. **Tomich, P. K., F. Y. An, and D. B. Clewell.** 1980. Properties of erythromycin-inducible transposon Tn917 in *Streptococcus faecalis.* J. Bacteriol. **141:**1366–1374.
15. **Tomich, P. K., F. Y. An, S. P. Damle, and D. B. Clewell.** 1979. Plasmid-related transmissibility and multiple drug resistance in *Streptococcus faecalis* subsp. *zymogenes* strain DS16. Antimicrob. Agents Chemother. **15:**828–830.

Sex Pheromones in *Streptococcus faecalis*: Multiple Pheromone Systems in Strain DS5, Similarities of pAD1 and pAMγ1, and Mutants of pAD1 Altered in Conjugative Properties

D. B. CLEWELL, Y. YAGI, Y. IKE, R. A. CRAIG, B. L. BROWN, AND F. AN

Department of Oral Biology and Department of Microbiology and Immunology, Schools of Dentistry and Medicine, and the Dental Research Institute, The University of Michigan, Ann Arbor, Michigan 48109

Streptococcus faecalis strains harboring certain conjugative plasmids exhibit a characteristic mating response upon exposure to specific sex pheromones excreted by recipients (1, 6, 8). Examples of such plasmids are pAD1, pAMγ1, pPD1, pOB1, and pJH2. Responding donor cells synthesize an adherent surface protein(s) that facilitates the formation of donor-recipient aggregates. Exposure of donor cells to recipient filtrates leads to self clumping, a phenomenon useful in the quantitation (by serial dilution) of pheromone (8). Aggregation requires phosphate and a divalent cation; these ions are not required, however, if induced cells are exposed to a pH of 2 to 3 (15; Y. Yagi et al., in preparation). In addition to aggregation, the pheromone induces at least one process related to the transfer of plasmid DNA (2).

Recipient strains excrete multiple pheromones, each specific for a particular class of plasmids (8). Upon acquisition of a given plasmid, transconjugants cease to excrete the related sex pheromone; they continue, however, to produce other pheromones.

The pheromones cPD1 and cAD1 (which relate to pPD1 and pAD1, respectively) have been partially purified and can be resolved on molecular sizing columns, as well as by high-performance liquid chromatography. Both have molecular weights of less than 1,500 and are heat stable (3; R. A. Craig and D. B. Clewell, in preparation). They are not affected by trypsin but are sensitive to chymotrypsin and other proteases, including leucine aminopeptidase and carboxypeptidases A and B. The pheromones probably represent small linear peptides.

MULTIPLE PHEROMONE SYSTEMS IN *S. FAECALIS* STRAIN DS5

Several years ago, we reported on the plasmid content of *S. faecalis* strain DS5 (4, 5, 7). On the basis of sucrose density gradient centrifugation and electron microscopy, molecules of three size classes were identified and designated pAMα1 (6 megadaltons), pAMβ1 (17 megadaltons), and pAMγ1 (35 megadaltons). From restriction enzyme analyses it subsequently became evident that the largest class actually consists of three different molecules very similar in size. These have been designated pAMγ1, pAMγ2, and pAMγ3. From mating experiments which took advantage of the ability to mobilize the nonconjugative tetracycline resistance plasmid pAMα1, it was possible to construct strains which separately harbor each of the large plasmids. In doing so, different phenotypes could be ascribed to three plasmids (Table 1). pAMγ1 determines hemolysin-bacteriocin, whereas pAMγ2 determines a second bacteriocin. pAMγ3 has the property of reducing the production of the pheromone cPD1 from a titer of 64 down to 4. All three plasmids are conjugative and can mobilize pAMα1 independently. Determination of the associated phenotypes of these plasmids clarifies earlier data (7) which had suggested that one plasmid, pAMγ1, determined two bacteriocins. Figure 1 shows the *Eco*RI restriction profile of each plasmid separately. Two fragments from pAMα1 (14) are also present in each case.

TABLE 1. Plasmids in *S. faecalis* strain DS5[a]

Plasmid	Mol wt	Related phenotype	Conjugative
pAMα1	6×10^6	Tc^r	No
pAMβ1	17×10^6	MLS^r	Yes
pAMγ1	$\sim$$35 \times 10^6$	Hly-Bac	Yes (PR)
pAMγ2	$\sim$$35 \times 10^6$	Bac	Yes (PR)
pAMγ3	$\sim$$35 \times 10^6$	cPD1 ↓	Yes (PR)

[a] The three large plasmids can be resolved by agarose gel electrophoresis and are of sizes ranging from about 33 to 36 megadaltons. PR, Pheromone response.

97

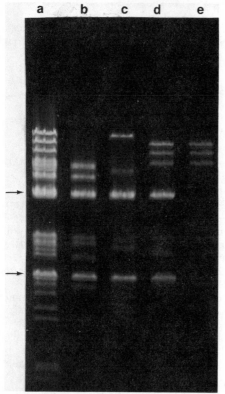

FIG. 1. Agarose gel electrophoresis of *Eco*RI restriction fragments. The analysis was as described elsewhere (9). (a) Plasmid DNA from *S. faecalis* strain DS5-C1 (i.e., a strain of DS5 cured of pAMβ1; 5). (b, c, and d) Plasmid DNA from strains YA103, YA102, and YA101, respectively (see Table 2). (e) Plasmid DNA from a JH2-2 strain harboring pAD1. The arrows point to the two fragments deriving from pAMα1 (14).

Interestingly, each of the three large plasmids maintains its own pheromone system. As shown in Table 2, strains harboring one of the plasmids undergo an aggregation response when exposed to filtrates of strains harboring the other plas-

mids. (We note that the presence of pAMγ2 prevented the detection of cAMγ1, whereas pAMγ1 did not prevent the production of cAMγ2.) Although pAMγ3 shuts off the production of its related pheromone cAMγ3, the basis of its partial reduction of cPD1 is not yet clear.

SIMILARITIES OF pAMγ1 AND pAD1

As shown in Fig. 1, pAMγ1 has an *Eco*RI restriction profile essentially identical to that of pAD1. The latter, a hemolysin-bacteriocin plasmid also with a molecular mass of 35 megadaltons, was originally identified in *S. faecalis* strain DS16 (13). Filtrates of a strain harboring one of these plasmids do not induce aggregation of a strain harboring the other, implying that both plasmids use the same pheromone system. In addition, derivatives of the two plasmids with distinguishable resistance markers, Tn*916* (9) and Tn*917* (11, 12), are incompatible with each other. As shown in Table 3, pAD1 and pAMγ1 both exhibit the interesting behavior of inhibiting the transfer of pAMβ1. (The latter plasmid is conjugative but does not make use of a pheromone system.) Since pAD1 and pAMγ1, themselves, transfer efficiently, the inhibition of pAMβ1 is different from the "fertility inhibition" phenomenon exhibited by some plasmids in gram-negative bacteria (10).

Strain DS5 (harboring pAMγ1) was originally isolated in 1963 at Jackson Memorial Hospital in Miami, Fla., whereas DS16 (harboring pAD1) was isolated in 1975 at St. Joseph's Mercy Hospital in Ann Arbor, Mich. The apparent identity of the two molecules implies a wide dissemination of this hemolysin-bacteriocin plasmid.

VARIANTS OF pAD1 WITH ALTERED CONJUGATION BEHAVIOR

Two transposons have been identified in *S. faecalis* strain DS16 (9, 11). Tn*916* (Tc) is located on the chromosome, whereas Tn*917* (Em) is

TABLE 2. Evidence for separate pheromone systems[a] for pAMγ1, pAMγ2, and pAMγ3

Responder strain	Filtrate			
	JH2-2	YA101	YA102	YA103
YA101 JH2-2(pAMγ1, pAMα1)	+	−	−	+
YA102 JH2-2(pAMγ2, pAMα1)	+	+	−	+
YA103 JH2SS(pAMγ3, pAMα1)	+	+	+	−

[a] Filtrates from log cultures in N2GT were prepared as previously described (6) and autoclaved. One milliliter of filtrate was mixed with 1 ml of a mid-log culture of responder cells and allowed to incubate for 90 min. Plus signs indicate a characteristic clumping response; minus signs indicate that no response was observed.

TABLE 3. Inhibition of pAMβ1 transfer by pAMγ1 and pAD1[a]

Donor used in mating (4-h broth) with JH2SS recipients	Frequency per donor of Em[r] transconjugants
BB101 JH2-2(β1, γ3)	1×10^{-4}
BB102 JH2-2(β1, γ3, γ1::Tn916)	5×10^{-7}
BB103 JH2-2(β1, γ3, γ2::Tn916)	2×10^{-4}
BB104 JH2-2(β1, γ3, pAD1::Tn916)	3×10^{-7}

[a] Matings were carried out in N2GT broth (8) as previously described (7). Generally, pAMβ1 does not transfer in broth (i.e., transfer usually requires that matings be carried out on filter membranes); however, the additional presence of a plasmid that responds to a pheromone facilitates generation of cell to cell contact which, in turn, results in pAMβ1 transfer. β1, pAMβ1; γ1::Tn916, pAMγ1::Tn916; γ2::Tn916, pAMγ2::Tn916; γ3, pAMγ3. The plasmids containing Tn916 insertions were derived as described elsewhere (9).

located on the resident multiple resistance plasmid pAD2. Derivatives of pAD1 with an insertion of either of these transposons are easily generated (9, 12), and the resulting derivatives in some cases exhibited an altered mating phenotype. Table 4 lists different groups of such pAD1::Tn917 derivatives. One class is characterized by a self-clumping behavior. These strains aggregate without exposure to pheromone and, in contrast to the parent plasmid, donate DNA quite efficiently in 10-min matings. (A normal response to pheromone generally requires about 30 min, and short [10 min] matings generally give rise to little or no transfer.)

The self-clumping derivatives fall into two subclasses exhibiting different colony morphologies. In one case the colonies appear normal, whereas the other type has a "dry" characteristic. Another class of mutants fails to respond at all to pheromone and also fails to transfer plasmid DNA, even in long (4 h) matings (Table 4).

A model suggesting how the plasmid-related pheromone response might be controlled has been published elsewhere (8). The generation of mutants resembling those listed in Table 4 is entirely consistent with this model. Self-clumping derivatives could be defective in the shutting off of endogenous cAD1 or in the control of expression of the surface "aggregation substance." Further analyses (mapping, etc.) of these and similar mutants should provide further insight into mechanisms controlling the mating response.

ON THE SIGNIFICANCE OF PHEROMONE PRODUCTION IN S. FAECALIS

Sex pheromones are widely known in yeast, fungi, and higher eucaryotes. Among bacteria, plasmid-related sex pheromones of the nature described here have still not been reported in species other than S. faecalis. There are conjugative plasmids in S. faecalis that do not use pheromones, an example of which is pAMβ1. (See reference 1 for a tabulation and review of these and other streptococcal plasmids.)

Analyses of 100 clinical isolates of S. faecalis showed that drug-resistant strains were significantly more likely to be both producers and responders to sex pheromones (8). A role of pheromones in the evolution of drug resistance would be predicted in that producers of multiple

TABLE 4. pAD1::Tn917 derivatives altered in pheromone response[a]

Plasmid derivative harbored by JH2SS	Colony morphology	Clumping		Frequency of transfer to FA2-2	
		No exposure to pheromone	Exposure to pheromone	10-min mating	4-h mating
pAM713	Normal	−	+	$<10^{-7}$	1×10^{-3}
pAM714	Normal	−	+	$<10^{-7}$	1×10^{-3}
pAM701	Normal	+	+	7×10^{-4}	2×10^{-3}
pAM702	Normal	+	+	1×10^{-3}	2×10^{-3}
pAM705	Normal	+	+	1×10^{-4}	1×10^{-3}
pAM706	Normal	+	+	4×10^{-4}	1×10^{-3}
pAM707	Dry	+	+	1×10^{-3}	5×10^{-3}
pAM715	Dry	+	+	1×10^{-4}	2×10^{-3}
pAM712	Normal	−	−	$<10^{-9}$	$<10^{-9}$
pAM717	Normal	−	−	$<10^{-9}$	$<10^{-9}$

[a] The pAD1::Tn917 derivatives were generated as described elsewhere (11, 12). The clumping response was determined as described in Table 2.

pheromones would seem prime targets for R plasmids which were pheromone inducible or capable of mobilization by such plasmids.

It is conceivable that bacterial production of the substances which donor strains recognize as sex pheromones could have preceded the evolution of the related conjugative systems. The latter may have evolved subsequently in such a way as to take advantage of these molecules as mating signals. If this were indeed the case, the question arises as to the nature of the original, perhaps continuing, function of these peptides.

ACKNOWLEDGMENTS

This work was supported by Public Health Service grants DE02731 and AI10318 from the National Institutes of Health.
We thank M. C. Gawron-Burke and A. Franke for helpful discussions.

LITERATURE CITED

1. **Clewell, D. B.** 1981. Plasmids, drug resistance, and gene transfer in the genus *Streptococcus*. Microbiol. Rev. **45**:409–436.
2. **Clewell, D., and B. Brown.** 1980. Sex pheromone cAD1 in *Streptococcus faecalis*: induction of a function related to plasmid transfer. J. Bacteriol. **143**:1063–1065.
3. **Clewell, D., G. Dunny, B. Brown, R. Craig, and Y. Yagi.** 1979. Sex pheromones in *Streptococcus faecalis*, p. 284–285. *In* M. T. Parker (ed.), Pathogenic streptococci. Reedbooks, Chertsey, England.
4. **Clewell, D., Y. Yagi, and B. Bauer.** 1975. Plasmid-determined tetracycline resistance in *Streptococcus faecalis*. Evidence for gene amplification during growth in the presence of tetracycline. Proc. Natl. Acad. Sci. U.S.A. **72**:1720–1724.
5. **Clewell, D., Y. Yagi, G. Dunny, and S. Schultz.** 1974. Characterization of three plasmid DNA molecules in a strain of *Streptococcus faecalis*. Identification of a plasmid determining erythromycin resistance. J. Bacteriol. **117**:283–289.
6. **Dunny, G., B. Brown, and D. B. Clewell.** 1978. Induced cell aggregation and mating in *Streptococcus faecalis*. Evidence for a bacterial sex pheromone. Proc. Natl. Acad. Sci. U.S.A. **75**:3479–3483.
7. **Dunny, G., and D. Clewell.** 1975. Transmissible toxin (hemolysin) plasmid in *Streptococcus faecalis* and its mobilization of a noninfectious drug resistance plasmid. J. Bacteriol. **124**:784–790.
8. **Dunny, G., R. Craig, R. Carron, and D. B. Clewell.** 1979. Plasmid transfer in *Streptococcus faecalis*. Production of multiple sex pheromones by recipients. Plasmid **2**:454–465.
9. **Franke, A., and D. B. Clewell.** 1981. Evidence for a chromosome-borne resistance transposon in *Streptococcus faecalis* capable of "conjugal" transfer in the absence of a conjugative plasmid. J. Bacteriol. **145**:494–502.
10. **Meynell, E., G. G. Meynell, and N. Datta.** 1968. Phylogenetic relationships of drug-resistance factors and other transmissible bacterial plasmids. Bacteriol. Rev. **32**:55–83.
11. **Tomich, P., F. An, and D. Clewell.** 1978. A transposon (Tn917) in *Streptococcus faecalis* which exhibits enhanced transposition during induction of drug resistance. Cold Spring Harbor Symp. Quant. Biol. **43**:1217–1221.
12. **Tomich, P., F. An, and D. B. Clewell.** 1980. Properties of erythromycin-inducible transposon Tn917 in *Streptococcus faecalis*. J. Bacteriol. **141**:1366–1374.
13. **Tomich, P., F. An, S. Damle, and D. B. Clewell.** 1979. Plasmid related transmissibility and multiple drug resistance in *Streptococcus faecalis* subsp. *zymogenes* strain DS16. Antimicrob. Agents Chemother. **15**:828–830.
14. **Yagi, Y., and D. Clewell.** 1976. Plasmid-determined tetracycline resistance in *Streptococcus faecalis*. Tandemly repeated resistance determinants in amplified forms of pAMα1 DNA. J. Mol. Biol. **102**:538–600.
15. **Yagi, Y., R. Kessler, B. Brown, D. Lopatin, and D. Clewell.** 1981. Pheromone-induced aggregation substance in *Streptococcus faecalis*, p. 674. *In* S. B. Levy, R. C. Clowes, and E. L. Koenig (ed.), Molecular biology, pathogenicity, and ecology of bacterial plasmids. Plenum Press, New York.

Identification and Partial Purification of a Surface Antigen of *Streptococcus faecalis* That Is Synthesized During Pheromone-Induced Aggregation

R. E. KESSLER, Y. YAGI, AND D. B. CLEWELL

The Dental Research Institute and Department of Oral Biology, School of Dentistry, The University of Michigan, Ann Arbor, Michigan 48109

Some strains of *Streptococcus faecalis*, including plasmid-free strains, excrete specific pheromones which induce other strains carrying certain conjugative plasmids to become adherent. Plasmid transfer takes place after the induced donors form aggregates with recipients. Exposure of donors to recipient filtrates containing sex pheromones induces self aggregation (2, 3). The aggregation response to pheromones appears to require RNA and protein synthesis but not DNA synthesis (2). Aggregation is sensitive to trypsin and pronase but not mixed glycosidases or nucleic acid hydrolases. Divalent cations and phosphate are required (Y. Yagi et al., manuscript in preparation). Our current understanding of pheromones and their relationships to the mating process is described elsewhere in this volume (D. B. Clewell et al.).

Immunofluorescence and immunoelectron microscopy studies have provided evidence for at least one unique immunodeterminant on the surface of induced cells (5). Antisera against pheromone-induced strain 39-5 containing the plasmid pPD1 were raised in rabbits and absorbed with uninduced 39-5 cells until no reaction with uninduced cells was observed by indirect immunofluorescence. These sera continued to react with induced 39-5 cells as well as other induced strains containing several different conjugative plasmids (pAD1, pOB1, pAMγ1, pAMγ2, and pAMγ3) (5). Immunoelectron micrographs of cells which were incubated sequentially with the same absorbed sera as in the immunofluorescence studies and then with horseradish peroxidase-conjugated goat anti-rabbit immunoglobulin G revealed a dense amorphous layer on the surface of induced cells but not uninduced cells (5; Yagi et al., in preparation). Presumably, this represents specific binding to the induced surface antigen; the latter has been referred to as aggregation substance (3).

On the basis of crossed immunoelectrophoresis of detergent extracts of induced and uninduced 39-5 cells versus antisera to induced and uninduced 39-5 cells, there appears to be only a single unique antigen associated with induced cells (Fig. 1). In addition, the immunoprecipitate containing this antigen was the only one visible after crossed immunoelectrophoresis of induced cell extracts versus absorbed serum. These tentative results suggest that there is indeed a new molecule synthesized during induction. That this molecule was involved in the aggregation process was supported by findings that the antigen contained within the immunoprecipitate was sensitive to trypsin and papain (aggregation also is sensitive to both of these proteases) and that synthesis of the antigen was blocked when chloramphenicol was added within 15 min after induction (as is aggregation). In addition, the point in time after induction that antigen could be detected in extracts coincided with the time of aggregation.

We also have evidence that Fab fragments of these absorbed sera will block aggregation. The immunoglobulin fraction of absorbed serum, which gave no reaction with uninduced cells and yielded only the single immunoprecipitate by crossed immunoelectrophoresis of whole cell extracts, was digested with papain, dialyzed, and chromatographed on Biogel P-60 to yield Fab fragments free from papain and Fc fragments. Since Fab fragments contain only a single combining site, they are incapable of giving rise to agglutination of the cells, which occurs with whole antibody molecules. Incorporation of these Fab fragments in the microtiter aggregation assay (3) inhibited aggregation. Inhibition was dependent upon concentration of both Fab fragments and pheromone. This provides, provisionally, direct evidence for the induced antigen being involved in the aggregation process as an adhesin. The dependence upon pheromone concentration also suggests that different proportions of the responder cell population are induced at different concentrations of pheromone.

Although detergent extracts of induced cells yield a single immunoprecipitate by conventional crossed immunoelectrophoresis, the same extracts yielded two immunoprecipitates when the

101

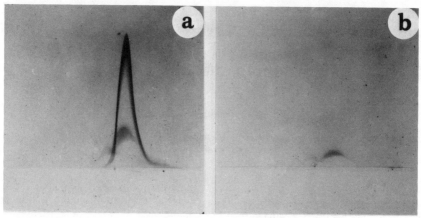

FIG. 1. Crossed immunoelectrophoresis of detergent extracts of pheromone-induced (a) and uninduced (b) *S. faecalis*. Pheromone (cPD1)-induced and uninduced cells of strain 39-5 were extracted with 0.2% Zwittergent 3-12 (Calbiochem, La Jolla, Calif.) in phosphate-buffered saline. Each extract was examined by crossed immunoelectrophoresis using a modification (1) of the Laurell technique (4). First-dimension electrophoresis of 5 μl of extract was carried out at 6 V/cm for 45 min. Second-dimension electrophoresis was at 2 V/cm for 16 h into agarose containing 75 μl/ml of a three times concentrated immunoglobulin fraction of sera from three rabbits previously immunized with glutaraldehyde-fixed, pheromone-induced strain 39-5. Anode to left and top.

first-dimension separation was carried out by sodium dodecyl sulfate-polyacrylamide gel electrophoresis. Thus, there may be two forms of the induced antigen, one of apparent molecular weight 78,000 to 82,000 and the other of approximately 65,000 to 67,000. The two forms have been partially separated and appear to be immunochemically identical as judged by tandem and crossed-line immunoelectrophoresis, but distinguishable in that the lower-molecular-weight form yields a much sharper immunoprecipitate on reaction with antibody in crossed immunoelectrophoresis. Partial purification of the lower-molecular-weight form has been achieved by chromatography on DEAE Sephacel followed by Sephacryl S-200 and hydroxylapatite chromatography. However, during purification there appears to be breakdown of this lower-molecular-weight form as evidenced by a broader less symmetrical immunoprecipitate on immunoplates on which sodium dodecyl sulfate-polyacrylamide gel electrophoresis was used for the first-dimension electrophoresis of samples from hydroxylapatite chromatography as compared with original extracts. Three polypeptides (molecular weights of 62,500, 65,000, and 67,000) remain after hydroxylapatite fractionation, all of which are included under the immunoprecipitate. Continued breakdown can be demonstrated on incubation at 4 or 37°C into five or six distinct polypeptides of apparent molecular weights between approximately 55,000 and 67,000. The relationships of the two forms of induced antigen and the apparent breakdown of the lower-molecular-weight form and their influence on aggregation are currently under investigation.

LITERATURE CITED

1. **Clarke, H. G. M., and T. A. Freeman.** 1967. A quantitative immunoelectrophoresis method, p. 503–509. *In* H. Peeters (ed.), Protides of the biological fluids, vol. 14. Elsevier, Amsterdam.
2. **Dunny, G. M., B. L. Brown, and D. B. Clewell.** 1978. Induced cell aggregation and mating in *Streptococcus faecalis*: evidence for a bacterial sex pheromone. Proc. Natl. Acad. Sci. U.S.A. **75:**3479–3483.
3. **Dunny, G. M., R. A. Craig, R. L. Carron, and D. B. Clewell.** 1979. Plasmid transfer in *Streptococcus faecalis*: production of multiple sex pheromones by recipients. Plasmid **2:**454–465.
4. **Laurell, C.** 1965. Antigen-antibody crossed immunoelectrophoresis. Anal. Biochem. **10:**358–361.
5. **Yagi, Y., R. Kessler, B. Brown, D. Lopatin, and D. Clewell.** 1981. Pheromone-induced aggregation substance in *Streptococcus faecalis*, p. 674. *In* S. B. Levy, R. C. Clowes, and E. L. Koenig (ed.), Molecular biology, pathogenicity, and ecology of bacterial plasmids. Plenum Press, New York.

Genetic and Physiological Parameters Affecting the Conjugal Transfer of a Sex Pheromone-Dependent Streptococcal R Plasmid

GARY DUNNY, MICHAEL YUHASZ, AND ELIZABETH EHRENFELD

Department of Microbiology, New York State College of Veterinary Medicine, Cornell University, Ithaca, New York 14853

With regard to transfer properties, two types of conjugative streptococcal plasmids have been described (for a recent review of streptococcal plasmids, see reference 1). One class transfers to a wide variety of streptococcal and other gram-positive species, but often the frequencies of transfer are fairly low. A second class of hemolysin and bacteriocin plasmids, found in *Streptococcus faecalis*, transfers very efficiently, but its host range, based on available data, is limited to *S. faecalis*. High-frequency transfer of these plasmids is induced by recipient-produced sex pheromones, designated clumping-inducing agents, or CIAs (3, 4). We recently reported the isolation of R plasmids whose transfer is stimulated by CIA (5), and we have initiated a detailed analysis of streptococcal conjugation, using a CIA-dependent tetracycline resistance plasmid called pCF-10. In this report we present a brief description of this system, along with a summary of the results we have obtained thus far.

pCF-10 is a 35-megadalton plasmid which was first identified in a strain of *S. faecalis* isolated from a urinary tract infection. The plasmid determines tetracycline resistance and transfers at frequencies of 10^{-1} to 10^{-3} per donor in 2-h broth matings. Exposure of cells carrying pCF-10 to CIA preparations from recipients causes the cells to clump and also increases the frequency of transfer in a 10-min mating by three to four orders of magnitude. Thus, the transfer properties of this plasmid resemble those of previously described hemolysin and bacteriocin plasmids in *S. faecalis* (3, 4). Since pCF-10 carries a readily selectable marker as well as genetic determinants for conjugal transfer and cell surface properties which can be turned on and off, we believe that it is an attractive model system for the study of streptococcal conjugation.

Thus far, we have isolated two types of pCF-10 mutants. We recently described (6) the isolation of derivatives of the plasmid that are defective in donor functions. By carrying out experiments originally designed to enrich for strains cured of the plasmid (5), we found that the tetracycline determinant appears to be linked to the transfer genes. Selection for tetracycline-sensitive derivatives often results in formation of plasmids deleted in genetic regions involved in CIA response, as well as tetracycline resistance. Current efforts are directed to utilizing these findings in a physical and genetic analysis of the plasmid.

A mutant derivative of pCF-10 which transfers at high frequencies in the absence of CIA has also been isolated. This was accomplished

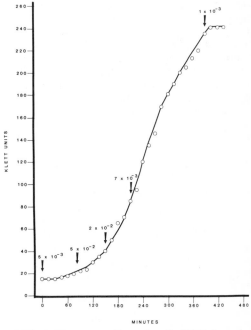

FIG. 1. Frequency of transfer of pCF-11 from donors in various phases of growth. At each time point indicated by an arrow, a sample from a culture of *S. faecalis* donor cells was removed, diluted to a standardized concentration, and mated for 10 min with a plasmid-free recipient strain. The numbers adjacent to each arrow indicate the frequency per donor of plasmid transfer.

by screening rare transconjugants, obtained from short matings using wild-type donors, for increased donor potential in a second round of transfer. Cells carrying this mutant plasmid (termed pCF-11) appear to constitutively produce the aggregation substance (4) responsible for cell clumping, since in addition to their elevated transfer properties, they spontaneously clump when grown in liquid culture.

Mating experiments utilizing both pCF-11 and pCF-10 indicate that at least two genetic functions, in addition to clumping, are involved in plasmid transfer. In a series of experiments carried out to define optimal conditions for plasmid transfer, we have observed that the donor potential of cells carrying either pCF-10 or pCF-11 is enhanced at the time they begin to grow exponentially after being diluted from a stationary culture. This effect is illustrated in Fig. 1. This peak of transfer activity resembles the peak of competence for DNA uptake exhibited by transformable streptococci (7). Since a similar peak in transferability is observed with cells carrying either pCF-10 (and not exposed to CIA) or pCF-11, it is probably unrelated to cell aggregation. It is not known whether the effect is mediated by plasmid or chromosomal genes. We have also found that exposure of donor cells carrying pCF-11 to exogenous CIA prior to a short mating causes a reproducible three- to fourfold increase in transfer frequency. This finding is in agreement with previous data (2) indicating that CIA induces, in addition to clumping, specific functions related directly to plasmid transfer.

By carrying out a relatively simple series of physiological and genetic experiments with the plasmid pCF-10, we have identified some of the genetic functions involved in conjugal DNA transfer. We hope that, by following up on these observations with a more in-depth biochemical and genetic analysis, we can gain a better understanding of this phenomenon and perhaps shed some light on other biological problems related to cell-hormone interactions and expression of cell surface components.

LITERATURE CITED

1. **Clewell, D. B.** 1981. Plasmids, drug resistance, and gene transfer in the genus *Streptococcus*. Microbiol. Rev. **45:**409–436.

2. **Clewell, D., and B. Brown.** 1980. Sex pheromone cADI in *Streptococcus faecalis*: induction of a function related to plasmid transfer. J. Bacteriol. **143:**1063–1065.

3. **Dunny, G., B. Brown, and D. Clewell.** 1978. Induced cell aggregation and mating in *Streptococcus faecalis*. Evidence for a bacterial sex pheromone. Proc. Natl. Acad. Sci. U.S.A. **75:**3479–3483.

4. **Dunny, G., R. Craig, R. Carron, and D. Clewell.** 1979. Plasmid transfer in *Streptococcus faecalis*. Production of multiple sex pheromones by recipients. Plasmid **2:**454–465.

5. **Dunny, G., C. Funk, and J. Adsit.** 1981. Direct stimulation of the transfer of antibiotic resistance by sex pheromones in *Streptococcus faecalis*. Plasmid **6:**270–278.

6. **Dunny, G., C. Funk, and E. Ehrenfeld.** 1981. Genetic analysis of conjugation in *Streptococcus faecalis*, p. 597. *In* S. B. Levy, R. C. Clowes, and E. L. Koenig (ed.), Molecular biology, pathogenicity, and ecology of bacterial plasmids. Plenum Press, New York.

7. **Lacks, S. A.** 1977. Binding and entry of DNA in bacterial transformation, p. 177–232. *In* J. L. Reissig (ed.), Microbial interactions, series B. Receptors and recognition, vol. 3. Chapman and Hall, London.

Conjugative Transfer of Antibiotic Resistance Markers in Beta-Hemolytic Streptococci in the Presence and Absence of Plasmid DNA

THEA HORODNICEANU, CHANTAL LE BOUGUENEC, ANNIE BUU-HOÏ, AND GILDA BIETH

Reference Center of Streptococci (Unité de Bactériologie Médicale), Institut Pasteur, 75724 Paris Cedex 15, and Centre Hospitalo-Universitaire, Broussais-Hôtel Dieu, Paris, France

Beta-hemolytic Lancefield group A, B, C, and G streptococci are among the most common pathogens in humans and are involved in upper respiratory tract, skin, and neonatal infections. These strains are naturally susceptible to penicillins, macrolides and related drugs, tetracycline, and chloramphenicol, and are resistant to aminoglycoside antibiotics (low-level resistance). The appearance of antibiotic resistance in these strains has been reported for tetracycline, chloramphenicol, macrolides-lincosamides-streptogramin B (MLS resistance) (6–8, 20, 23, 25), and aminoglycosides (high levels of streptomycin and kanamycin) (18).

Evidence for the presence of MLS resistance plasmids (associated or not associated with chloramphenicol resistance) has been reported in beta-hemolytic streptococci of groups A (4, 22), B (9,14), C, and G (1), and of tetracycline-resistance plasmids in group B strains (2). More recently, conjugative genetic exchange of multiple antibiotic resistance in the apparent absence of plasmid DNA has been reported in strains of groups A, B, F, and G (15) as well as in other streptococcal species, such as *S. pneumoniae* (3, 26), *S. faecalis* (11), *S. bovis*, and viridans streptococci (18).

The purpose of this report is to provide information on the genetic and molecular basis of multiple antibiotic resistance of beta-hemolytic streptococci.

ANTIBIOTIC RESISTANCE PATTERNS OF WILD-TYPE STRAINS

Fifty clinical isolates of beta-hemolytic streptococci (14 group A, 23 group B, 2 group C, 11 group G) were resistant to one or several antibiotics: tetracycline (44 strains), macrolides and related drugs (39 strains), chloramphenicol (16 strains), and streptomycin and kanamycin (7 strains). Abbreviations of resistance markers are given in Tables 1 and 2. The minimal inhibitory concentrations (MICs) were determined for tetracycline (MIC, 32 to 64 µg/ml), erythromycin (MIC, 1 to 2,000 µg/ml), lincomycin (MIC, 1 to 500 µg/ml), chloramphenicol (MIC, 16 to 32 µg/ml), kanamycin (MIC, >8,000 µg/ml), and streptomycin (MIC, 1,000 to 8,000 µg/ml). The resistance patterns were found to be Tc, Cm, MLS, MLS Tc, Cm Tc, Cm MLS, Cm MLS Tc, Km Sm MLS Tc, Cm Km Sm Tc, Cm Km Sm MLS, and Cm Km Sm MLS Tc.

The phenotypic aspect of MLS resistance was investigated for 39 strains. Five different MLS phenotypes were found with respect to inhibition zones around susceptibility disks and to the existence of an antagonistic phenomenon between these drugs (16).

MATING AND CURING EXPERIMENTS AND PLASMID DNA ISOLATION

The 50 wild-type donor strains were initially crossed on membrane filters as described (3) with two streptococcal recipients: JH2-2 (*S. faecalis*) (19) and BM132 (group B *Streptococcus*) (17). Thirteen strains were further mated with 10 other streptococcal recipients (groups A, C, G, UV202 [27], *S. faecium*, *S. durans*, *S. bovis*, *S. sanguis*, two *S. pneumoniae* strains [3] [encapsulated and nonencapsulated]), and a *Staphylococcus aureus* restriction-deficient mutant strain (10). Selection was done separately for all resistance markers carried by the donor strains. The transconjugants obtained were analyzed for selected and unselected markers.

Curing procedures have been described (14).

Plasmid DNA was isolated from crude and cleared lysates of wild-type and transconjugant strains by dye-buoyant density centrifugation as described (15). For plasmid analysis by radioactive labeling, cells were incubated with [*methyl-³H*]thymidine as described (3).

PLASMID-BORNE ANTIBIOTIC RESISTANCE

Table 1 presents the results of conjugative transfer and of the isolation of plasmid DNA in nine wild-type strains and four of their cured

TABLE 1. R plasmids isolated from beta-hemolytic streptococci

Strain designation	Serogroup	Wild-type strain resistance markers[a]	Markers transferred[a]	Plasmid designation	Mol wt	Reference or origin
A449	A	Cm MLS Tc	No transfer	pIP955	22×10^6	MH613, S. Mitsuhashi, 15
BM6402	A	Tc	No transfer	No plasmid DNA		A449 cured for Cm MLS
B96	B	Cm MLS Tc	Cm MLS	pIP501	19.7×10^{6b}	14
BM6103	B	Tc	No transfer	No plasmid DNA		B96 cured for Cm MLS
B97	B	Cm MLS Tc	Cm MLS	pIP612	22.7×10^6	9, 17
BM6106	B	Tc	No transfer	No plasmid DNA		B97 cured for Cm MLS
B98	B	Cm MLS Tc	Cm MLS	pIP635	20×10^6	17
B110	B	MLS Tc	MLS	pIP639	17.5×10^6	17
B113	B	MLS Tc	MLS	pIP640	17.5×10^6	17
B115	B	MLS Tc	MLS	pIP642	17.5×10^6	17
C87	C	MLS Tc	MLS	pIP646	17.9×10^{6b}	1
BM6502	C	Tc	No transfer	No plasmid DNA		C87 cured for MLS
G49	G	Cm MLS Tc	Cm MLS	pIP920	20.4×10^{6b}	1

[a] Antibiotic resistance markers: Cm, chloramphenicol; MLS, macrolides (erythromycin, spiramycin)-lincos-amides (lincomycin, clindamycin)-streptogramin B; Tc, tetracycline.

[b] The molecular weight of these plasmids was calculated by addition of band sizes after cleavage with HindIII restriction endonuclease.

derivatives, as well as in their transconjugants. Strain A449 harbored a nonconjugative, 22×10^6-dalton, Cm MLS plasmid, which was not found in the cured derivative of this strain (BM6402). The six group B strains, as well as C87, transferred MLS or Cm MLS markers at a high frequency (10^{-1} to 10^{-3}) into both S. faecalis and group B Streptococcus recipients. Strain G49 transferred Cm MLS markers at a very low frequency (10^{-8}) and only into S. faecalis recipient. None of the MLS or Cm MLS transconjugants analyzed (>2,000 clones) carried tetracycline resistance. No transfer of a Tc marker either from wild-type or from cured-derivative donors could be detected when selection was done on tetracycline. MLS or Cm MLS markers were cured from both wild-type and transconjugant strains.

Plasmid DNA was found in both wild-type and transconjugant strains. These plasmids had molecular weights of 17.5×10^6, and 20×10^6 or 23×10^6, depending on the absence or presence of chloramphenicol marker, respectively. Plasmids pIP501, pIP646, and pIP920 were further analyzed by HindIII, EcoRI, and HpaI restriction endonuclease digestion. These plasmids were not cleaved by EcoRI and had very similar HindIII and HpaI restriction patterns. Cm MLS

TABLE 2. Host range of antibiotic resistance markers in plasmid-free beta-hemolytic streptococci

	Wild-type donors		Recipient strains[b]							
Designation	Serogroup	Resistance markers[a]	Group A	Group B	Group C	Group G	S. faecalis		S. sanguis	S. pneumoniae
							JH2-2	UV202[c]		
A454	A	MLS Tc	+[d]	+	+	+	+	+	+	+
A459	A	MLS Tc	+	+	+	+	+	−	+	−
A458	A	Cm Km Sm Tc	+	+	−	−	+	−	NT	NT
B109	B	Cm MLS Tc	+	+	+	+	+	−	+	−
B117	B	Cm Tc	−	+	+	+	−	−	−	−
B119	B	Tc	−	+	−	−	−	−	−	−
B121	B	MLS Tc	−	+	+	−	−	−	−	−
B122	B	MLS Km Sm Tc	−	+	−	−	+	−	NT	NT
G41	G	MLS Tc	+	+	+	+	+	−	+	−
G42	G	MLS Km Sm Tc	−	+	+	−	+	NT	NT	NT
G44	G	Cm MLS Tc	−	+	+	−	−	−	−	−

[a] For abbreviations see Table 1; Km, kanamycin; Sm, streptomycin.

[b] No transfer into S. faecium, S. durans, S. bovis, or Staphylococcus aureus.

[c] UV202 is a recombination-deficient mutant of JH2-2 (27).

[d] Symbols: +, antibiotic resistance transfer; −, no transfer; NT, not tested.

plasmids contained a fragment with a molecular weight of 4×10^6 not found in MLS plasmids (1, 13).

Plasmids pIP501 and pIP646 displayed a wide host range. They transferred into all recipients tested, except *S. bovis* and the encapsulated *S. pneumoniae*. The transfer frequency of pIP501 into the recombination-deficient strain UV202 was 10-fold lower (10^{-4}) than into JH2-2 (10^{-3}). pIP501 and pIP646 were stably maintained in the new streptococcal hosts, but a 97% spontaneous loss was observed after 20 generations in *Staphylococcus aureus*. The broad host range of other MLS plasmids, such as pAMβ1 (5) and pRI405 (10), harbored by *S. faecalis* strains was demonstrated by their conjugative transfer into several *Streptococcus* (10, 21), *Lactobacillus* (12), and *Staphylococcus* (10) recipients.

PLASMID-FREE ANTIBIOTIC RESISTANCE

Table 2 presents the results of conjugative transfer of resistance markers from 11 wild-type donors into 12 recipients. All strains transferred their resistance markers at a low frequency (10^{-5} to 10^{-8}). Similar frequencies of transfer were obtained when either erythromycin or tetracycline was the selective agent.

Analysis of transconjugants revealed that strains A454, A459, B109, B117, B121, G41, and G42 transferred their resistance markers en bloc (including Tc). However, in two of five mating experiments, strain G41 transferred only MLS markers into JH2-2 (*S. faecalis*) at a high frequency (10^{-3}). These markers were found to be carried by a plasmid designated pIP659. Strains A458 and G44 did not transfer their Tc marker, and strain B122 transferred Km Sm MLS as linked markers and Tc independently.

All strains transferred their resistance markers into group B *Streptococcus* but none of them transferred into *S. faecium*, *S. durans*, *S. bovis*, and *Staphylococcus aureus*. The frequency of transfer of resistance markers of strain A454 into the recombination-deficient strain UV202 was 10-fold lower (10^{-7}) than into JH2-2 (10^{-6}). Other donors transferred at a very low frequency into JH2-2 (10^{-8} to 10^{-9}), and no transfer could be detected into UV202.

All attempts to obtain antibiotic-susceptible derivatives by curing were unsuccessful.

Dye-buoyant centrifugation analysis demonstrated that, with two exceptions, none of the wild types nor their transconjugants contained detectable satellite DNA. Moreover, when [³H]thymidine-labeled lysates of these strains were fractionated on gradients, no radioactive plasmid DNA could be detected. The two exceptions were strains A458, which contained a small

(3×10^6 daltons), nonconjugative, cryptic plasmid, and JH2-2 (pIP659), which harbored a conjugative R plasmid (17.8×10^6 daltons) not found in the wild-type donor G41. The *Hin*dIII digestion pattern of pIP659 (15) was similar to that of other MLS plasmids (1, 13).

Plasmid pIP501 was transferred into one of the plasmid-free Tc^r MLS^r transconjugants obtained from the donor strain B109 (15). The entry of pIP501 was at least 1,000-fold lower (10^{-6}) than its normal transfer frequency (10^{-3}) into a plasmid-free, antibiotic-susceptible recipient. In addition to the entry exclusion, an apparent incompatibility phenomenon was also observed, since a 95% displacement of the incoming pIP501 was obtained (15).

In 30 strains (10 group A, 12 group B, 1 group C, 7 group G) after 18 h of mating, regardless of the drug used for selection, no detectable transfer could be obtained into either *S. faecalis* or group B *Streptococcus* recipients. Twelve of these 30 strains were examined for the presence of plasmid DNA. Dye-buoyant centrifugation analysis confirmed that none of them contained detectable satellite DNA.

CONCLUSIONS

Antibiotic resistance of beta-hemolytic streptococci can be one of four types: (i) nonconjugative and plasmid borne (2%), (ii) nonconjugative and plasmid free (60%), (iii) conjugative and plasmid borne (16%), and (iv) conjugative and plasmid free (22%).

The last two types have certain distinctive features. Type 3 displays a high frequency of transfer (10^{-1} to 10^{-3}), wide host range, curing, and physical evidence of plasmid DNA. No detectable transfer of tetracycline could be obtained. Type 4 displays a low frequency of transfer (10^{-5} to 10^{-8}) of resistance markers (including Tc), narrow host range, no curing, and no physical evidence of plasmid DNA.

The presence of pIP659 in one of the transconjugants obtained from strain G41 supports the hypothesis that conjugative elements could be inserted into the chromosome by a site-specific recombination mechanism (24). Since such elements lack autonomously replicating genes but possess transfer genes, they might be excised from the donor, transferred, and integrated into the chromosome of a new recipient. pIP659 is an example of such a naturally conjugative integrated element, which is also capable of autonomous replication (15).

ACKNOWLEDGMENTS

We are very grateful to Y. A. Chabbert for his support and helpful discussion. We thank Susan Michelson for criticism of the manuscript, Françoise Delbos for technical assistance, and Odette Rouelland for secretarial assistance.

The work which formed the basis of this report was supported by grant 78.4.137.1 from the Institut National de la Santé et de la Recherche Médicale to T.H.

LITERATURE CITED

1. **Bougueleret, L., G. Bieth, and T. Horodniceanu.** 1981. Conjugative R plasmids in group C and G streptococci. J. Bacteriol. **145**:1102–1105.

2. **Burdett, V.** 1980. Identification of tetracycline-resistant R-plasmids in *Streptococcus agalactiae* (group B). Antimicrob. Agents Chemother. **18**:753–760.

3. **Buu-Hoï, A., and T. Horodniceanu.** 1980. Conjugative transfer of multiple antibiotic resistance markers in *Streptococcus pneumoniae*. J. Bacteriol. **143**:313–320.

4. **Clewell, D. B., and A. E. Franke.** 1974. Characterization of a plasmid determining resistance to erythromycin, lincomycin, and vernamycin Bα in a strain of *Streptococcus pyogenes*. Antimicrob. Agents Chemother. **5**:534–537.

5. **Clewell, D. B., Y. Yagi, G. M. Dunny, and S. K. Schultz.** 1974. Characterization of three plasmid deoxyribonucleic acid molecules in a strain of *Streptococcus faecalis*: identification of a plasmid determining erythromycin resistance. J. Bacteriol. **117**:283–289.

6. **Dixon, J. M. S.** 1968. Group A *Streptococcus* resistant to erythromycin and lincomycin. Can. Med. Assoc. J. **99**:1093–1094.

7. **Dixon, J. M. S., and A. E. Lipinski.** 1974. Infections with beta-hemolytic *Streptococcus* resistant to lincomycin and erythromycin and observations on zonal-pattern resistance to lincomycin. J. Infect. Dis. **130**:351–356.

8. **Eickhoff, T. C., J. O. Klein, A. K. Daly, D. Ingall, and M. Finland.** 1964. Neonatal sepsis and other infections due to group B beta-hemolytic streptococci. N. Engl. J. Med. **271**:1221–1228.

9. **El-Solh, N., D. H. Bouanchaud, T. Horodniceanu, A. F. Roussel, and Y. A. Chabbert.** 1978. Molecular studies and possible relatedness between R plasmids from group B and D streptococci. Antimicrob. Agents Chemother. **14**:19–23.

10. **Engel, H. W. B., N. Soedirman, J. A. Rost, W. J. van Leeuwen, and J. D. A. van Embden.** 1980. Transferability of macrolide, lincomycin and streptogramin resistances between group A, B, and D streptococci, *Streptococcus pneumoniae*, and *Staphylococcus aureus*. J. Bacteriol. **142**:407–413.

11. **Franke, A. E. and D. B. Clewell.** 1981. Evidence for a chromosome-borne resistance transposon (Tn*916*) in *Streptococcus faecalis* that is capable of "conjugal" transfer in the absence of a conjugative plasmid. J. Bacteriol. **145**:494–502.

12. **Gibson, E. M., N. M. Chace, S. B. London, and J. London.** 1979. Transfer of plasmid-mediated antibiotic resistance from streptococci to lactobacilli. J. Bacteriol. **137**:614–619.

13. **Hershfield, V.** 1979. Plasmids mediating multiple drug resistance in group B *Streptococcus*: transferability and molecular properties. Plasmid **2**:137–149.

14. **Horodniceanu, T., D. H. Bouanchaud, G. Bieth, and Y. A. Chabbert.** 1976. R plasmids in *Streptococcus agalactiae* (group B). Antimicrob. Agents Chemother. **10**:795–801.

15. **Horodniceanu, T., L. Bougueleret, and G. Bieth.** 1981. Conjugative transfer of multiple-antibiotic resistance markers in beta-hemolytic group A, B, F and G streptococci in the absence of extrachromosomal deoxyribonucleic acid. Plasmid **5**:127–137.

16. **Horodniceanu, T., L. Bougueleret, and F. Delbos.** 1980. Phenotypic aspects of resistance to macrolides and related antibiotics in β-hemolytic group A, B, C and G streptococci, p. 122–131. *In* R. Facklam, G. Laurell, and I. Lind (ed.), Recent developments in laboratory identification techniques, Uppsala, 1979. Excerpta Medica, Amsterdam.

17. **Horodniceanu, T., L. Bougueleret, N. El Solh, D. H. Bouanchaud, and Y. A. Chabbert.** 1979. Conjugative R plasmids in *Streptococcus agalactiae* (group B). Plasmid **2**:197–206.

18. **Horodniceanu, T., A. Buu-Hoï, F. Delbos, and G. Bieth.** 1982. High-level amino-glycoside resistance in group A, B, G, D (*Streptococcus bovis*), and viridans streptococci. Antimicrob. Agents Chemother. **21**:176–179.

19. **Jacob, A. E., and S. J. Hobbs.** 1974. Conjugal transfer of plasmid-borne multiple antibiotic resistance in *Streptococcus faecalis* var. *zymogenes*. J. Bacteriol. **117**:360–372.

20. **Kahlmeter, G., and K. Kamme.** 1972. Tetracycline-resistant group A streptococci and pneumococci. Scand. J. Infect. Dis. **4**:193–196.

21. **Leblanc, D. J., R. J. Hawley, L. N. Lee, and E. J. St. Martin.** 1978. "Conjugal" transfer of plasmid DNA among oral streptococci. Proc. Natl. Acad. Sci. U.S.A. **75**:3484–3487.

22. **Malke, H., H. E. Jacob, and K. Storl.** 1976. Characterization of the antibiotic resistance plasmid ERL 1 from *Streptococcus pyogenes*. Mol. Gen. Genet. **144**:333–338.

23. **Mitsuhashi, S., M. Inoue, A. Fuse, Y. Kaneko, and T. Oba.** 1974. Drug resistance in *Streptococcus pyogenes*. Jpn. J. Microbiol. **18**:98–99.

24. **Philips, S., and R. P. Novick.** 1979. Tn554-a site-specific repressor-controlled transposon in *Staphylococcus aureus*. Nature (London) **278**:476–478.

25. **Sanders, E., M. T. Foster, and D. Scott.** 1968. Group A beta-hemolytic streptococci resistant to erythromycin and lincomycin. N. Engl. J. Med. **278**:538–540.

26. **Shoemaker, N. B., M. D. Smith, and W. R. Guild.** 1980. DNase-resistant transfer of chromosomal *cat* and *tet* insertions by filter mating in *Pneumococcus*. Plasmid **3**:80–87.

27. **Yagi, Y., and D. B. Clewell.** 1980. Recombination-deficient mutant of *Streptococcus faecalis*. J. Bacteriol. **143**:966–970.

Evidence for Transposition of the Conjugative R Determinants of *Streptococcus agalactiae* B109

MICHAEL D. SMITH AND WALTER R. GUILD

Biochemistry Department, Duke University, Durham, North Carolina 27710

Franke and Clewell found that a chromosomal *tet* in *Streptococcus faecalis* transferred by filter mating at a low frequency in the absence of plasmids and that transfer increased in the presence of the conjugative hemolysin plasmid pAD1 (3). Hemolysin defective (Hem⁻) and hyperhemolytic transconjugants carried mutant pAD1 plasmids containing a 10-megadalton insert which they designated Tn916. These pAD1::Tn916 plasmids transfer at a high frequency by conjugation (3). We report here similar results for the transposition to pAD1 of the conjugative $\Omega(cat\text{-}tet\text{-}erm)$ element found in the chromosome of *S. agalactiae* B109 (5).

Our approach was to (i) transfer the B109 element to *S. faecalis* JH2-2, (ii) introduce pAD1, (iii) use this strain as donor and select for transconjugants carrying B109 determinants, and (iv) examine these transconjugants further. Both Hem⁺ and Hem⁻ transconjugants were found, and the latter were of two types that yielded hemolysis between the colonies when they were close together. These proved to be similar to the HemA and HemL phenotypes described by Granato and Jackson in mutagenized *S. zymogenes* (4). When HemA and HemL cultures were cross-streaked on blood agar, spurs of hemolysis appeared at the junctions as described (4).

Table 1 summarizes the origin of pAD1 derivatives carrying part or all of the B109 *cat-tet-erm* element. B109 donated $\Omega(cat\text{-}tet\text{-}erm)$ to JH2-2, yielding Xg83, which then received pAD1 from DS16 to give Xg84. Mating of Xg84 with the Rec⁻ UV202 yielded a large number of Hem⁺ transconjugants (pAD1) and varying numbers of Hem⁺ and Hem⁻ transconjugants expressing either Em or Cm Tc Em resistances (Table 1, C). Most of the Hem⁺ Cm Tc Em transconjugants did not transfer the multiple resistance at high frequency and segregated Cmˢ Tcˢ Emʳ derivatives at a frequency that increased on growth on erythromycin (not shown). However, Xg87 eventually yielded a stable derivative, Xg89, as described below. Of the small number of Hem⁻ Cm Tc Em transconjugants, Xg92 transferred its phenotype to *S. faecalis* OG1 derivatives at moderately high frequency (Table 1, D), sug-

TABLE 1. Origin of pAD1 derivatives carrying B109 R determinants[a]

Donor	Relevant properties	Recipient[b]	Selection	Transconjugants/ml	Isolates
A. B109	Cm Tc Em	JH2-2	Rif Cm Tc Em	240	Xg83
B. DS16	pAD1	Xg83	Rif Hem⁺	9×10^6	Xg84
C. Xg84	Cm Tc Em pAD1	UV202 Strʳ	Str Hem⁺	8×10^6	—
			Str Hem⁺ Em	3,500	Xg90
			Str Hem⁻ Em	200	—
			Str Hem⁺ Cm Tc Em	1,200	Xg87
			Str Hem⁻ Cm Tc Em	30	Xg 85, Xg86, Xg92
D. Xg92	HemL Cm Tc Em	OG1 Spcʳ	Spc HemL Cm Tc Em	2.0×10^4	—
E. Xg91 (from Xg85)[c]	HemA Cm Tc Em	OG1 Spcʳ	Spc HemA Cm Tc Em	2.3×10^7	—
F. Xg88 (from Xg86)[c]	HemL Cm Tc Em	OG1 Strʳ	Str HemL Cm Tc Em	1.2×10^7	—
G. Xg89 (from Xg87)[c]	Hem⁺ Cm Tc Em	OG1 Spcʳ	Spc Hem⁺ Cm Tc Em	1.2×10^7	—
H. Xg90	Hem⁺ Em	OG1 Spcʳ	Spc Hem⁺ Em	2.1×10^5	—

[a] Filter matings (4 h) were done as described (6) and scored by the agar overlay method (8). Donors and recipients averaged 5×10^7 and 5×10^8/ml, respectively.

[b] DS16 (3), UV202 (9), and a Fusʳ Rifʳ OG1 (2) were obtained from D. Clewell. Spcʳ and Strʳ derivatives were selected for use as recipients.

[c] See text.

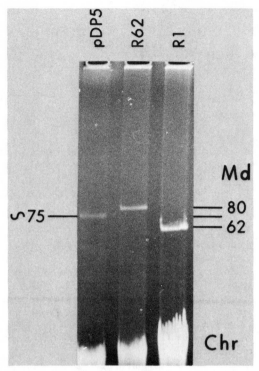

FIG. 1. Electrophoresis in agarose (0.5%) of plasmid-enriched lysates of Xg88 (pDP5) and *Escherichia coli* strains carrying R62 or R1drd19. Only the top portion of the gel is shown. Chr, chromosomal DNA; Md, megadaltons.

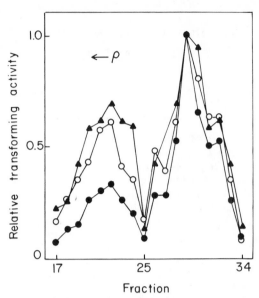

FIG. 2. Dye-buoyancy distribution of transforming activities of Xg88. Fractions were used as donor to DP1333 pneumococcal cells, which carry the *tet-3* variant of the *tet* region of BM6001 (7). The cells were scored for transformants to Cm^r (●), Tc^r (▲), and Em^r (○). A parallel gradient showed a peak of chromosomal genes centered at fraction 30.

gesting that it carried the R determinants inserted in pAD1. Stronger evidence came from derivatives of Xg85 (HemA) and Xg86 (HemL). These were mated with spectinomycin- or streptomycin-resistant OG1 strains by cross-streaking on agar, a procedure that is less efficient than filter mating and can select for high transfer efficiency (D. Clewell, personal communication). The intention was to select for a strain that did not lose its Cm and Tc, but we may have been selecting for transfer proficiency also. By several passes of this kind between spectinomycin- and streptomycin-resistant OG1, Xg91 was derived from Xg85, Xg88 from Xg86, and Xg89 from the Hem$^+$ Xg87. In filter mating, Xg88, Xg89, and Xg91 each transferred their Hem and resistance phenotypes to OG1 recipients at very high frequencies (Table 1, E, F, and G). These data strongly suggested that Ω(*cat-tet-erm*) had inserted into three different sites on pAD1. For Xg88, this conclusion was confirmed directly.

Plasmid pDP5 [pAD1::(*cat-tet-erm* B109)]

Examination of lysates of Xg88 enriched for plasmids by the Currier and Nester procedure

(1) showed that Xg88 contained a single plasmid of size near 75 megadaltons (Fig. 1), about 40 megadaltons larger than pAD1. In a dye-buoyancy gradient (Fig. 2), the peak of covalently closed circular DNA contained a substantial fraction of the *cat, tet,* and *erm* genes, as assayed by transformation of the *tet-3* pneumococcal strain DP1333 (7). Cotransformations were similar to those from B109 or pneumococcal derivatives carrying Ω*cat-tet-erm* in the chromosome (not shown). Therefore, the large plasmid in Xg88 carries the R determinants of B109, retains the transfer proficiency of pAD1, confers HemL phenotype, and is 40 megadaltons larger than the parent pAD1. We designate it pDP5.

Hem$^+$ Em^r and Hem$^-$ Em^r Strains

The initial cross of Xg84 and UV202 Str^r yielded about 3,500 Hem$^+$ Em^r and 200 Hem$^-$ Em^r transconjugants per ml (Table 1, C). A Hem$^+$ Em^r transconjugant (Xg90) transferred Hem$^+$ Em^r at a high frequency to OG1 Spc^r recipients, suggesting that Xg90 contained pAD1::*erm* (Table 1, D). A Hem$^+$ Em^r OG1 transconjugant contained plasmid DNA which was slightly larger than pAD1 by gel electrophoresis (not shown). These results suggest that *erm* may be capable of transposition independently of the rest of Ω(*cat-tet-erm*). However, the origin of Em^r strains like Xg90 is not clear; they may have resulted from transfer of pAD1::*erm* from Xg84 or from *cat-tet-erm* transconjugants which lost *cat* and *tet* at high frequency during selection for Em^r. This subject is under investigation.

SUMMARY AND CONCLUSIONS

We have isolated three *S. faecalis* strains, of differing hemolysin phenotype, in which *cat, tet,* and *erm* genes originating in the chromosomal Ω(*cat-tet-erm*) element of *S. agalactiae* B109 cotransfer at high frequency with hemolysin and transfer genes of pAD1. One of the strains has been shown to carry the genes on a 75-megadalton plasmid, pDP5, 40 megadaltons larger than pAD1. The results strongly suggest that the conjugative Ω(*cat-tet-erm*) element of B109 has transposed into three different sites of pAD1, and may therefore be called a "conjugative transposon." There is also a suggestion that *erm* may be able to transpose independently.

ACKNOWLEDGMENTS

We thank Judith Hageman for performing the transformation assays, Don Clewell and Thea Horodniceanu for strains, and Versie Lee for technical assistance.

This work was supported by grants from the National Institutes of Health and the Department of Energy.

LITERATURE CITED

1. **Currier, T. C., and E. W. Nester.** 1976. Isolation of covalently closed circular DNA of high molecular weight from bacteria. Anal. Biochem. **76:**431–441.
2. **Dunny, G. M., B. L. Brown, and D. B. Clewell.** 1978. Induced cell aggregation and mating in *Streptococcus faecalis:* evidence for a bacterial sex pheromone. Proc. Natl. Acad. Sci. U.S.A. **75:**3479–3483.
3. **Franke, A. E., and D. B. Clewell.** 1981. Evidence for a chromosome-borne resistance transposon (*Tn916*) in *Streptococcus faecalis* that is capable of "conjugal" transfer in the absence of a conjugative plasmid. J. Bacteriol. **145:**494–502.
4. **Granato, P. A., and R. W. Jackson.** 1969. Bicomponent nature of lysin from *Streptococcus zymogenes.* J. Bacteriol. **100:**865–868.
5. **Horodniceanu, T., L. Bougueleret, and G. Bieth.** 1981. Conjugative transfer of multiple-antibiotic resistance markers in beta-hemolytic group A, B, F, and G streptococci in the absence of extrachromosomal deoxyribonucleic acid. Plasmid **5:**127–137.
6. **Smith, M. D., and W. R. Guild.** 1980. Improved method for conjugative transfer by filter mating of *Streptococcus pneumoniae.* J. Bacteriol. **144:**457–459.
7. **Smith, M. D., S. Hazum, and W. R. Guild.** 1981. Homology among *tet* determinants in conjugative elements of streptococci. J. Bacteriol. **148:**232–240.
8. **Smith, M. D., N. B. Shoemaker, V. Burdett, and W. R. Guild.** 1980. Transfer of plasmids by conjugation in *Streptococcus pneumoniae.* Plasmid **3:**70–79.
9. **Yagi, Y., and D. B. Clewell.** 1980. Recombination-deficient mutant of *Streptococcus faecalis.* J. Bacteriol. **143:**966–970.

TRANSFORMATION, TRANSDUCTION, AND BACTERIOPHAGE

Phages, Transduction, and Phage-Associated Enzymes of Group A, C, and G Streptococci

LEWIS W. WANNAMAKER

Departments of Pediatrics and Microbiology, University of Minnesota, Minneapolis, Minnesota 55455

The bacteriophages and associated enzymes or lysins of hemolytic streptococci have attracted the attention of bacterial geneticists and also biomedical scientists interested in the antigenic structure of these bacteria (5, 11, 17), in markers for epidemiological studies (28, 32, 34), and in the pathogenesis of group A streptococcal infections and their sequelae (41, 42). Studies of lysogenic conversion and of transduction have demonstrated that phages have the capacity to transfer genetic determinants for a number of biologically important products and characteristics of group A, C, and G streptococci. This review will summarize some of the contributions by various investigators, with emphasis on those made since the reviews by Malke (21) and by Zabriskie et al. (42) in 1972.

INTRAGROUP TRANSDUCTION OF LABORATORY-INDUCED ANTIBIOTIC RESISTANCES

Transduction has been a particularly useful tool in studying genetic interchange in group A, C, and G streptococci. Early studies focused on intragroup transfers and utilized laboratory-induced antimicrobial resistance markers for which the determinants are probably chromosomal in location (Table 1). In addition to transfers between group A strains (7, 18, 19), transduction between group C strains was demonstrated (40). Streptomycin and erythromycin were the antibiotic resistance markers most often used.

Transductional analysis of chromosomal resistance to multiple antibiotics, by several laboratories (22, 35), culminated in the identification of three distinct linkage groups (Table 2). Resistance to some antibiotics has not been transducible, perhaps as a result of multiple mutations in chromosomal genes located some distance apart that determine resistance to the same antibiotic (35).

TRANSDUCING PHAGE A25

In these transduction studies a virulent phage, A25, has been especially useful. This phage contains double-stranded DNA. Morphologically, it has a long, noncontractile tail and a hexagonal head and is classified as a Bradley group B phage (21). In a study of strains from 30 different M types tested for transducibility to streptomycin and spectinomycin resistance by phage A25, all were found to absorb the phage and to take up phage DNA in an acid-precipitable form; yet only 50% of the strains were transducible. Irradiation of the phage lysates increased the frequency of transductions but did not convert nontransducible to transducible strains (26). A double temperature-sensitive mutant (ts1-2) of A25 has proved useful in preventing the killing of transduced cells by nondefective phage when transduction is performed at the restrictive temperature (19). In transduction experiments, lysogenization of the recipient strain has been shown to interfere with the replication of A25 phage DNA and at the same time to enhance transduction (23). Several different mechanisms appear to be involved in this prophage-mediated interference. Thus, lysogenization of group A streptococci, which is widespread in nature (42), may favor transduction and, in addition to classical phage DNA restriction, may be a means of contending with virulent bacteriophage infection (1).

The receptor site for A25 phage is peptidoglycan (Fig. 1) (5), the "backbone" of the streptococcal cell wall, responsible for its integrity. Peptidoglycan is less superficial than other cell wall components but may be more accessible for phage adsorption at some points on the surface, e.g., in the equatorial zone of active wall synthesis. This area of beginning septum formation appears to be relatively bald on electron microscopy as a result of the sparseness of hairlike fimbriae in this region (36). Adsorption of phage

TABLE 1. Intragroup transduction of laboratory-induced antimicrobial resistance[a]

Intragroup transduction	Marker	Phage	Reference
A → A	Streptomycin	A25 (virulent)	Leonard et al. (18)
A → A	Streptomycin	UV-irradiated A25	Colón et al. (7)
A → A	Erythromycin	A25 ts1-2	Malke (19)
C → C	Streptomycin	UV-irradiated A25	Wannamaker et al. (40)

[a] Presumably chromosomal.

TABLE 2. Chromosomal antibiotic resistance linkage groups in group A streptococci[a]

Group	Resistance
1	Spectinomycin-erythromycin-spiramycin
2	Streptomycin-fusidic acid-bacitracin-kasugamycin
3	Rifampin-streptolydigan

[a] From data of Stuart and Ferretti (35). Phage used in this transductional analysis was UV-irradiated A25 ts1-2.

A25 to group A streptococci occurs as a two-step reaction. The first step is a reversible attachment of the phage to the peptidoglycan component of the cell wall and is followed by a poorly understood second step in which the phage is irreversibly inactivated (5). The chemical structure of peptidoglycan is similar for group A, C, and G streptococci (30), which may account for the lack of strict group specificity of A25 and other streptococcal phages.

INTRAGROUP TRANSDUCTION OF NATURALLY OCCURRING ANTIBIOTIC RESISTANCE; ERL1 PLASMID AND PHAGE p13234 mo

Transduction studies of naturally occurring antimicrobial resistance (Table 3), which is usually extrachromosomally determined, may be of special pertinence. The multiply resistant strains common among clinical isolates from Japan, upon induction by mitomycin C, yield temperate phages which readily transduce sensitive recipient strains (39). Direct evidence for plasmid-determined antibiotic resistance in a clinical isolate of group A streptococcus was first provided by Clewell and Franke (6). A closely similar strain was the original host of the ERL1 plasmid determining inducible resistance to erythromycin, lincomycin, and staphylomycin S (27). This strain is naturally lysogenic for phage p13234 mo, which transduces at high frequencies and has an extraordinarily broad host range, thus providing a likely mechanism for spread of

the ERL1 plasmid in nature. Intragroup transduction of the ERL1 plasmid has been demonstrated for non-group A strains as well as for group A strains (31). The ERL1 plasmid has been recently characterized (13, 25).

INTERGROUP TRANSDUCTION OF ANTIBIOTIC RESISTANCE

Intergroup transduction of antibiotic resistance has been demonstrated in the closely related group A, C, and G streptococci (Table 4). Transduction has been accomplished in both directions (8, 24, 40), and in one study the circle has been completed, group A to group G and back to group A (31). This promiscuity may be facilitated by the chemical similarity of the peptidoglycan receptors of group A, C, and G streptococci (30) and may be responsible for the increasing prevalence of erythromycin resistance among streptococci of a variety of serological groups and types (9). Transduction of resistance to erythromycin (24, 31) and to bacitracin (40) may have clinical importance since erythromycin is commonly used for treatment of group A streptococcal infections in patients sensitive to penicillin, and bacitracin is often used for local treatment of streptococcal impetigo.

TRANSDUCTION OF OTHER BIOLOGICAL MARKERS

In addition to antibiotic resistance, transduction of the determinants for several other markers of biological importance has been reported in group A streptococci (Table 5). These include resistance to UV light (20), a possibly crucial factor in the ability of pyoderma strains to persist on the skin; bacteriocin production (37), which may play a role in the ecology of streptococci; and the production of streptolysin S (S. A. Skjold, W. R. Maxted, and L. W. Wannamaker, unpublished data), one of the two cytolytic toxins of group A streptococci and an almost indispensable marker for the identification of pathogenic streptococci in the clinical microbiology laboratory.

Of special interest is the role of bacteriophages in the production of M protein, the

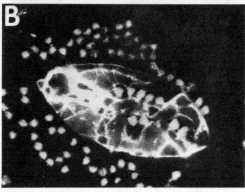

FIG. 1. (A) Cell wall peptidoglycan disks of group A streptococci. (B) Attachment of A25 phage to peptidoglycan disks. (Reproduced, with permission, from Cleary et al. [5].)

fimbrial protein of group A streptococci which confers virulence by its antiphagocytic properties. Transduction of M protein and the closely associated serum opacity factor has been reported (38) but has proved difficult to study and to reproduce, apparently as a result of the relatively low selectivity of the bactericidal systems used for identifying transformants. Other studies suggest that phage activates the synthesis of M protein by a mechanism not yet clarified (33).

PHAGE-ASSOCIATED HYALURONIDASES

The hyaluronidase activity associated with temperate bacteriophages provides a means of penetrating the capsule of the group A streptococcus (16). About 25% of the hyaluronidase activity is tightly bound to phage particles but can be released and solubilized by urea treatment (3). The enzyme activity of a temperate phage from a type 12 strain has been characterized as a hyaluronate lyase (EC 4.2.99.1) (29). In more recent studies, the hyaluronidase associated with a temperate phage obtained from a nephritogenic strain of type 49 streptococcus has been purified and characterized with respect to its physical, enzymatic, and immunological properties (2, 4). When examined immunologically, the phage-associated hyaluronidases have been found to be distinct from the bacterial hyaluronidase and indeed are remarkably heterogeneic among themselves, with immunological specificities that parallel but are not identical to those of the M proteins of the host streptococci (4, 16). The immunological diversity of the phage-associated hyaluronidases can be demonstrated by double-diffusion precipitin reactions in agar, by antibody neutralization of enzymatic activity, and by antibody inhibition of phage infection. Because of their immunological diversity, these phage-associated hyaluronidases provide useful antigenic markers for distinguishing temperate phages. Like the diversity of the M proteins, which may have evolved under the pressure of immunological selection in the human host, the multiple forms of the phage-associated hyaluronidases may have developed as a means of escaping the effects of antibody that would neutralize the phage-associated hyaluronidase and thereby inhibit phage infection.

TABLE 3. Intragroup transduction of naturally occurring antimicrobial resistance[a]

Intragroup transduction	Marker	Phage	Reference
A → A	Multiple antibiotics	Induced temperate	Ubukata et al. (39)
A → A	ERL1 plasmid (inducible erythromycin resistance)	p13234 mo (temperate)	Malke (24)
G → G	ERL1 plasmid (inducible erythromycin resistance)	A25 *ts*1-2	Skjold et al. (31)

[a] Probably or definitely extrachromosomal.

TABLE 4. Intergroup transduction of antibiotic markers in group A, C, and G streptococci

Intergroup transduction	Marker	Phage	Reference
A → G	Streptomycin	A25 (virulent), AT 298 (temperate)	Colón et al. (8)
C → A	Streptomycin, bacitracin	UV-irradiated A25	Wannamaker et al. (40)
A → C	ERL1 plasmid (inducible erythromycin resistance)	p13234 mo (temperate)	Malke et al. (27)
A → G			
A → G → A	ERL1 plasmid (inducible erythromycin resistance)	A25 ts1-2	Skjold et al. (31)

TABLE 5. Intragroup transduction of other biological markers

Intragroup transduction	Marker	Phage	Reference
A → A	UV resistance	A25 ts1-2	Malke (20)
A → A	Bacteriocin (A-FF22)	A25 ts1-2	Tagg et al. (37)
A → A	M protein, serum-opacity factor	CA1 (virulent), induced temperate	Totolian (38)
A → A	Streptolysin S	A25 ts1-2	Skjold et al.[a]

[a] S. A. Skjold, W. R. Maxted, and L. W. Wannamaker, unpublished data.

PHAGE-ASSOCIATED CELL WALL LYSINS

A potent cell wall lysin associated with a virulent group C streptococcal phage has been known for many years and has been invaluable in producing protoplasts and L-forms (12, 14) and in studying the antigenic composition of group A streptococci (17). This group C phage-associated lysin has been purified and characterized (10). Only recently has a similar but less potent cell wall lysin been identified in association with the A25 phage which is virulent for group A streptococci (15). In contrast to the lysin associated with the group C streptococcal phage, the A25-associated lysin is more active on chloroform-treated cells, is not bound to phage particles, and is active on a wider distribution of streptococcal groups. The function of this group A phage-associated cell wall lysin is unknown. It may play a role in the penetration of the streptococcal cell or in the release of mature phage. Although no autolytic system has been described for group A streptococci, some properties of this lysin suggest that it may have a mechanism similar to that of an autolysin or that the cell lysis observed may result from activation of a suppressed autolytic system (15).

CONCLUSION

Laboratory studies of phage-mediated interchange of genetic determinants among group A and other groups of streptococci and of the hyaluronidases and cell wall lysins associated with these streptococcal phages suggest that they may be important factors in the biology and in the ecology of these organisms. Eventually, however, the many fascinating tricks produced in the laboratory must be applied in epidemiological and clinical studies aimed at determining what really happens in nature.

ACKNOWLEDGMENTS

Studies from my laboratory were supported by Public Health Service grant AI 08724 from the National Institute of Allergy and Infectious Diseases. I am a Career Investigator of the American Heart Association.

I am indebted to Stephen A. Skjold for assistance in reviewing the literature.

LITERATURE CITED

1. Behnke, D., and H. Malke. 1978. Bacteriophage interference in Streptococcus pyogenes. I. Characterization of prophage-host systems interfering with the virulent phage A25. Virology 85:118–128.
2. Benchetrit, L., E. D. Gray, R. D. Edstrom, and L. W. Wannamaker. 1978. Purification and characterization of hyaluronidase associated with a temperate bacteriophage of group A, type 49 streptococci. J. Bacteriol. 134:221–228.
3. Benchetrit, L. C., E. D. Gray, and L. W. Wannamaker. 1977. Hyaluronidase activity of bacteriophages of group A streptococci. Infect. Immun. 15:527–532.
4. Benchetrit, L. C., L. W. Wannamaker, and E. D. Gray. 1979. Immunological properties of hyaluronidases associated with temperate bacteriophages of group A streptococci. J. Exp. Med. 149:73–83.
5. Cleary, P. P., L. W. Wannamaker, M. Fisher, and N. Laible. 1977. Studies of the receptor for phage A25 in group A streptococci: the role of peptidoglycan in reversible adsorption. J. Exp. Med. 145:578–593.
6. Clewell, D. B., and A. E. Franke. 1974. Characterization

of a plasmid determining resistance to erythromycin, lincomycin, and vernamycin B$_\alpha$ in a strain of *Streptococcus pyogenes*. Antimicrob. Agents Chemother. **5**:534–537.

7. **Colón, A. E., R. M. Cole, and C. G. Leonard.** 1970. Transduction in group A streptococci by ultraviolet-irradiated bacteriophages. Can. J. Microbiol. **16**:201–202.

8. **Colón, A. E., R. M. Cole, and C. G. Leonard.** 1972. Intergroup lysis and transduction by streptococcal bacteriophages. J. Virol. **9**:551–553.

9. **Dixon, J. M. S., and A. E. Lipinski.** 1974. Infections with β-hemolytic *Streptococcus* resistant to lincomycin and erythromycin and observations on zonal-pattern resistance to lincomycin. J. Infect. Dis. **130**:351–356.

10. **Fischetti, V. A., E. C. Gotschlich, and A. W. Bernheimer.** 1971. Purification and physical properties of group C streptococcal phage-associated lysin. J. Exp. Med. **133**:1105–1117.

11. **Fischetti, V. A., and J. B. Zabriskie.** 1968. Studies on streptococcal bacteriophages. II. Adsorption studies on group A and group C streptococcal bacteriophages. J. Exp. Med. **127**:489–505.

12. **Freimer, E. H., R. M. Krause, and M. McCarty.** 1959. Studies of L forms and protoplasts of group A streptococci. I. Isolation, growth, and bacteriologic characteristics. J. Exp. Med. **110**:853–874.

13. **Golubkov, V. I., T. V. Gupalova, I. M. Iontova, T. G. Kolesnichenko, and A. A. Totolyan.** 1977. Isolation and characterization of the plasmid determining multiple antibiotic resistance in strains of group A streptococci. Mol. Biol. (Moscow) **11**:909–916.

14. **Gooder, H., and W. R. Maxted.** 1958. Protoplasts of group A beta-haemolytic streptococci. Nature (London) **182**:808–809.

15. **Hill, J. E., and L. W. Wannamaker.** 1981. Identification of a lysin associated with a bacteriophage (A25) virulent for group A streptococci. J. Bacteriol. **145**:696–703.

16. **Kjems, E.** 1958. Studies on streptococcal bacteriophages. 3. Hyaluronidase produced by the streptococcal phage-host cell system. Acta Pathol. Microbiol. Scand. **44**:429–439.

17. **Krause, R. M.** 1958. Studies on the bacteriophages of hemolytic streptococci. II. Antigens released from the streptococcal cell wall by a phage-associated lysin. J. Exp. Med. **108**:803–821.

18. **Leonard, C. G., A. E. Colón, and R. M. Cole.** 1968. Transduction in group A streptococcus. Biochem. Biophys. Res. Commun. **30**:130–135.

19. **Malke, H.** 1970. Resistance pattern and genetics of erythromycin-resistant mutants of *Streptococcus pyogenes*. J. Gen. Microbiol. **64**:353–363.

20. **Malke, H.** 1970. Complementation between *uvr* mutants of *Streptococcus pyogenes*. Mol. Gen. Genet. **109**:278–284.

21. **Malke, H.** 1972. Transduction in group A streptococci, p. 119–133. *In* L. W. Wannamaker and J. M. Matsen (ed.), Streptococci and streptococcal diseases. Academic Press, Inc., New York.

22. **Malke, H.** 1972. Linkage relationships of mutations endowing *Streptococcus pyogenes* with resistance to antibiotics that affect the ribosome. Mol. Gen. Genet. **116**:299–308.

23. **Malke, H.** 1973. Phage A25-mediated transfer induction of a prophage in *Streptococcus pyogenes*. Mol. Gen. Genet. **125**:251–264.

24. **Malke, H.** 1975. Transfer of a plasmid mediating antibiotic resistance between strains of *Streptococcus pyogenes* in mixed cultures. Z. Allg. Mikrobiol. **15**:645–649.

25. **Malke, H., H. E. Jacob, and K. Störl.** 1976. Characterization of the antibiotic resistance plasmid ERL1 from *Streptococcus pyogenes*. Mol. Gen. Genet. **144**:333–338.

26. **Malke, H., and W. Köhler.** 1973. Transduction among group A streptococci: transducibility of strains representative of thirty different M types. Zentralbl. Bakteriol. Parasitenkd. Infektionskr. Hyg. Abt. 1 Orig. Reihe A **224**:194–201.

27. **Malke, H., R. Starke, W. Köhler, T. G. Kolesnichenko, and A. A. Totolian.** 1975. Bacteriophage P13234mo-mediated intra- and intergroup transduction of antibiotic resistance among streptococci. Zentralbl. Bakteriol. Parasitenkd. Infektionskr. Hyg. Abt. 1 Orig. Reihe A **233**:24–34.

28. **Mihalcu, F., and A. Vereanu.** 1978. Study on streptococcal bacteriophages—provisional lysotyping scheme. Arch. Roum. Pathol. Exp. Microbiol. **37**:217–222.

29. **Niemann, H., A. Birch-Andersen, E. Kjems, B. Mansa, and S. Stirm.** 1976. Streptococcal bacteriophage 12/12-borne hyaluronidase and its characterization as a lyase (EC 4.2.99.1) by means of streptococcal hyaluronic acid and purified bacteriophage suspensions. Acta Pathol. Microbiol. Scand. Sect. B **84**:145–153.

30. **Schleifer, K. H., and O. Kandler.** 1972. Peptidoglycan types of bacterial cell walls and their taxonomic implications. Bacteriol. Rev. **36**:407–477.

31. **Skjold, S. A., H. Malke, and L. W. Wannamaker.** 1979. Transduction of plasmid-mediated erythromycin resistance between group-A and -G streptococci, p. 274. *In* M. T. Parker (ed.), Pathogenic streptococci. Reedbooks Ltd., Chertsey, Surrey, U.K.

32. **Skjold, S. A., and L. W. Wannamaker.** 1976. Method of phage typing group A type 49 streptococci. J. Clin. Microbiol. **4**:232–238.

33. **Spanier, J. G., and P. P. Cleary.** 1980. Bacteriophage control of antiphagocytic determinants in group A streptococci. J. Exp. Med. **152**:1393–1406.

34. **Stringer, J.** 1980. The development of a phage-typing system for group-B streptococci. J. Med. Microbiol. **13**:133–143.

35. **Stuart, J. G., and J. J. Ferretti.** 1978. Genetic analysis of antibiotic resistance in *Streptococcus pyogenes*. J. Bacteriol. **133**:852–859.

36. **Swanson, J., K. Hsu, and E. Gotschlich.** 1969. Electron microscopic studies on streptococci. I. M antigen. J. Exp. Med. **130**:1063–1089.

37. **Tagg, J. R., S. Skjold, and L. W. Wannamaker.** 1976. Transduction of bacteriocin determinants in group A streptococci. J. Exp. Med. **143**:1540–1544.

38. **Totolian, A. A.** 1979. Transduction of M-protein and serum-opacity-factor production in group-A streptococci, p. 38–39. *In* M. T. Parker (ed.), Pathogenic streptococci. Reedbooks Ltd., Surrey, Chertsey, U.K.

39. **Ubukata, K., M. Konno, and R. Fujii.** 1975. Transduction of drug resistance to tetracycline, chloramphenicol, macrolides, lincomycin and clindamycin with phages induced from *Streptococcus pyogenes*. J. Antibiot. **28**:681–688.

40. **Wannamaker, L. W., S. Almquist, and S. Skjold.** 1973. Intergroup phage reactions and transduction between group C and group A streptococci. J. Exp. Med. **137**:1338–1353.

41. **Wannamaker, L. W., S. Skjold, and W. R. Maxted.** 1970. Characterization of bacteriophages from nephritogenic group A streptococci. J. Infect. Dis. **121**:407–418.

42. **Zabriskie, J. B., S. E. Read, and V. A. Fischetti.** 1972. Lysogeny in streptococci, p. 99–118. *In* L. W. Wannamaker and J. M. Matsen (ed.), Streptococci and streptococcal diseases. Academic Press, Inc., New York.

Phage Conversion and the Synthesis of Type A Streptococcal Exotoxin (Erythrogenic Toxin) in Group A Streptococci

JOSEPH J. FERRETTI, CLIFFORD W. HOUSTON,[1] LARRY K. McKANE,[2] AND S. KAY NIDA[3]

Department of Microbiology and Immunology, University of Oklahoma Health Sciences Center, Oklahoma City, Oklahoma 73190

The rash of scarlet fever is caused by the extracellular product of *Streptococcus pyogenes* variously known as Dick toxin, scarlatinal toxin (1), erythrogenic toxin (39), streptococcal pyrogenic exotoxin (40), or streptococcal exotoxin (29). Three antigenically distinct forms of streptococcal exotoxin exist, type A (23, 40), type B (23, 40), and type C (40). Only certain strains of *S. pyogenes* elaborate the type A exotoxin, and it was shown long ago that a filterable agent obtained from toxigenic cultures could convert nontoxigenic strains to the toxigenic state (4, 7, 15). In 1964, Zabriskie demonstrated that the nature of the filterable agent was a streptococcal bacteriophage capable of converting a group A nontoxigenic, nonlysogenic strain to a toxigenic, lysogenic strain (41) (Fig. 1). This phenomenon of toxigenic phage conversion has been well defined in *Corynebacterium diphtheriae* (13, 14), where evidence has been obtained detailing the role of a corynephage β determinant in the production of diphtheria toxin (17, 22).

The information reported here represents our progress toward understanding the mechanism of phage conversion and the synthesis of type A streptococcal exotoxin in group A streptococci.

TYPE A STREPTOCOCCAL EXOTOXIN

The biological activities reported to be associated with type A streptococcal exotoxin include the production of erythematous skin reactions in human and rabbit skin (11, 12, 23) thought to be enhanced by a secondary toxicity due to delayed hypersensitivity (36), pyrogenicity (5, 28, 40), mitogenic activity for human and rabbit lymphocytes (25, 26, 30, 32, 35), enhancement of lethal endotoxin shock and cardiotoxicity (28, 38, 40), and alterations in the immune system (3, 10, 18–21). Assay procedures for the detection of type A streptococcal exotoxin include the erythema-

tous skin reaction, pyrogenicity, mitogenic activity, *Limulus* amoebocyte lysate reaction (6), hemagglutination inhibition (37), and a number of immunological procedures such as immunodiffusion techniques and enzyme-linked immunosorbent assay. The enzyme-linked immunosorbent assay has been shown to be a sensitive and quantitative method for the detection of type A streptococcal exotoxin (24).

The type A streptococcal exotoxin is known to be associated with hyaluronic acid, and the protein component has been shown to have a minimum molecular weight of 8,500 and an isoelectric point of pH 5.2 (9, 24). Multimeric forms of type A exotoxin have been reported, as well as other estimates of its molecular weight (2, 16, 33). The type A streptococcal exotoxin is synthesized by toxigenic strains maximally during the mid-log phase of growth in a similar manner to other streptococcal extracellular products (24). Exposure of the type A exotoxin to various temperatures indicated that the component responsible for erythema was heat labile. Attempts to influence the levels of type A exotoxin production during growth of toxigenic strains included the following: varying nutrient additives, e.g., enriched medium plus combinations of 2% glucose, 0.5 mM cysteine, 60% yeast extract, 5% horse serum, 0.38% K_2HPO_4, and 1% $CaCl_2$; varying metal ion concentrations known to influence the production of toxins by other microorganisms (0.9 to 90 μM $CaCl_2$, $FeSO_4$, $MgCl_2$, $MnSO_4$); and varying incubation temperatures (24, 30, 37, 42°C). The incubation temperature of 42°C lowered both growth and the production of type A exotoxin, but none of

[1] Present address: Department of Microbiology, University of Texas Medical Branch, Galveston, TX 77550.
[2] Present address: Department of Biological Sciences, California State Polytechnic University, Pomona, CA 91768.
[3] Present address: Department of Microbiology, University of Minnesota, Minneapolis, MN 55455.

FIG. 1. Toxigenic phage conversion of *S. pyogenes* T25₃ by bacteriophage T12 to produce type A streptococcal exotoxin.

the factors significantly affected type A exotoxin synthesis. These results suggested that the regulation of synthesis of type A streptococcal exotoxin in group A streptococci occurred in a constitutive manner.

PHAGE SPECIFICITY, ROLE OF LYSOGENY

The mechanism by which phage T12 converts the $T25_3$ host bacterial strain to toxigenicity is unknown. It was of interest, therefore, to utilize a virulent (clear plaque-forming) mutant of phage T12, designated T12cp1, to determine whether type A exotoxin was still synthesized by a phage strain presumably unable to integrate into the host chromosome (31). The results of these experiments showed that type A exotoxin was still synthesized after infection by T12cp1. Another virulent phage, A25, unrelated to phage T12, however, was not able to effect conversion of the $T25_3$ host strain to production of type A exotoxin. Moreover, the temperate phage H4489A, which is unrelated to phage T12, was used to construct the lysogenic strain $T25_3$ (H4489A), and this lysogen was unable to produce type A exotoxin. These findings establish that conversion of group A streptococci to toxigenicity is phage specific and that integration of a phage chromosome into the host chromosome is not a requirement for toxigenic conversion.

SCOPE OF TOXIGENIC CONVERSION

Until the report of Nida et al. (34), there were only two bacteriophage strains (T12gl and 3GL16) and one bacterial recipient strain ($T25_3$) used to demonstrate toxigenic conversion in group A streptococci. The scope of toxigenic conversion has been expanded considerably by the construction of 18 new lysogens and one pseudolysogen by use of five bacterial recipient strains and 10 phages (33a). The phages were obtained by mitomycin C induction of *S. pyogenes* strains known to be associated with clinical cases of scarlet fever. Once obtained, the new lysogens were examined with type-specific antiserum for their ability to produce type A streptococcal exotoxin. All of the phages were able to convert the bacterial recipient strains to production of type A exotoxin once the lysogen was formed. Representative strains showing toxigenic conversion are listed in Table 1. Of interest is the conversion of strain T18P (exotoxin types $A^-B^-C^+$) to the synthesis of both exotoxin types A and B. This is the first report of conversion of a strain to synthesis of type B exotoxin. Colon-Whitt et al. (8) and Johnson et al. (27) have previously reported the conversion of strains to synthesis of type C exotoxin, thus

TABLE 1. Types of streptococcal exotoxin produced by recipient strains and newly constructed lysogens

Strain	Exotoxin type		
	A	B	C
$T25_3$	−	+	+
9440	−	+	+
K56	−	+	+
T18P	−	−	+
$T25_3$ (110)	+	+	+
$T25_3$ (119)	+	+	+
$T25_3$ (124)	+	+	+
K56 (T12)	+	+	+
K56 (107)	+	+	+
K56 (111)	+	+	+
9440 (113)	+	+	+
9440 (120)	+	+	+
9440 (124)	+	+	+
T18P (T19)	+	+	+
T18P (120)	+	+	+

indicating the phage conversion of all three exotoxin types. Also noteworthy is the conversion of strain T18P by phage T19, the latter phage originating from a host of exotoxin type $A^+B^+C^-$. The T18P (T19) lysogen synthesized all three exotoxins; the acquisition of phage T19 did not result in the absence of type C exotoxin production, as was characteristic of the phage donor bacterial strain. These results indicate that toxigenic phage conversion is not restricted to a few strains, but is a general phenomenon that may have significance in natural infection.

CHARACTERISTICS OF CONVERTING PHAGES

The converting phages were found to contain double-stranded DNA, and electron microscopy indicated that the phages possessed a polyhedral head with a long, unsheathed, non-contractile tail, characteristic of Bradley morphological group B1 (33a). The phages were extremely fragile and were disrupted by physical and chemical procedures tolerated by most other phages. Each phage had a unique host range, although two general classes of phages were identified by their ability to lyse some common strains. No correlation was made between phage host range and streptococcal M or T type. Antisera to phage T12 reacted with phage T12, but not with nine other converting phages, indicating the existence of at least two serological groups. Finally, the different electrophoretic mobilities of type A exotoxin and disrupted phage T12 components, and the lack of reactivity of phage components with antiserum to type A exotoxin, led to the conclusion that type A exotoxin was not a structural component of phage T12 (31).

SUMMARY

In summary, we have provided new information about the regulation and synthesis of type A streptococcal exotoxin, the scope of toxigenic conversion, the requirement of lysogeny for toxigenicity, phage specificity in conversion, and a characterization of phage properties. In spite of this progress, the mechanism of toxigenic phage conversion in group A streptococci remains unresolved. It is clear that the phage has a specific role in conversion of the bacterial host to production of type A streptococcal exotoxin. Whether the gene specifying type A exotoxin is located on the phage or bacterial chromosome remains to be determined, as does the actual mechanism of interaction and conversion. The recent application of recombinant DNA technology to the study of streptococci should provide an important tool for the future resolution of these important questions.

ACKNOWLEDGMENTS

This work was supported by grants from the American Heart Association, Oklahoma Affiliate, and the Roger McCormick Foundation, Chicago, Illinois.

LITERATURE CITED

1. Ando, K., K. Kurauchi, and H. Mishimura. 1930. Studies on the "toxins" of hemolytic streptococci. III. On the dual nature of the Dick toxin. J. Immunol. 18:223–255.
2. Barsumian, E. L., C. M. Cunningham, P. M. Schlievert, and D. W. Watson. 1978. Heterogeneity of group A streptococcal pyrogenic exotoxin type B. Infect. Immun. 20:512–518.
3. Barsumian, E. L., P. M. Schlievert, and D. W. Watson. 1978. Nonspecific and specific immunological mitogenicity by group A streptococcal pyrogenic exotoxins. Infect. Immun. 22:681–688.
4. Bingel, K. F. 1949. Heue untersuchungen zur scharlachatiologie. Dtsch. Med. Wochenschr. 74:703–706.
5. Brunson, K. W., and D. W. Watson. 1974. Pyrogenic specificity of streptococcal exotoxins, staphylococcal enterotoxin, and gram-negative endotoxin. Infect. Immun. 10:347–351.
6. Brunson, K. W., and D. W. Watson. 1976. Limulus amebocyte lysate reaction with streptococcal pyrogenic exotoxin. Infect. Immun. 14:1256–1258.
7. Cantacuzene, J., and O. Boncieu. 1926. Modifications subies par des streptocoques d'origine non-scarlatineuse qui contact des produits scarlatinuex filtres. C.R. Acad. Sci. 182:1185.
8. Colon-Whitt, A., R. S. Whitt, and R. M. Cole. 1979. Production of an erythrogenic toxin (streptococcal pyrogenic exotoxin) by a nonlysogenized group-A streptococcus, p. 64–65. In M. T. Parker (ed.), Pathogenic streptococci. Reedbooks Ltd., Chertsey, Surrey, U.K.
9. Cunningham, C. M., E. L. Barsumian, and D. W. Watson. 1976. Further purification of group A streptococcal pyrogenic exotoxin and characterization of the purified toxin. Infect. Immun. 14:767–775.
10. Cunningham, C. M. and D. W. Watson. 1978. Alteration of clearance function by group A streptococci and its relation to suppression of the antibody response. Infect. Immun. 19:51–57.
11. Dick, G. F., and G. H. Dick. 1924. A skin test for susceptibility to scarlet fever. J. Am. Med. Assoc. 82:265–266.
12. Dochez, A. R., and F. A. Stevens. 1927. Studies on the biology of Streptococcus. VI. Allergic reactions with strains from erysipelas. J. Exp. Med. 46:487–493.
13. Freeman, V. J. 1951. Studies on the virulence of bacteriophage-infected strains of Corynebacterium diphtheriae. J. Bacteriol. 61:675–688.
14. Freeman, V. J., and I. V. Morse. 1952. Further observations on the change to virulence of bacteriophage infected strains of Corynebacterium diphtheriae. J. Bacteriol. 63:407–414.
15. Frobisher, M., and J. H. Brown. 1927. Transmissible toxicogenicity of streptococci. Bull. Johns Hopkins Hosp. 41:167–173.
16. Gerlach, D., H. Knoll, and W. Köhler. 1980. Purification and characterization of erythrogenic toxins. 1. Investigation of erythrogenic toxin-A produced by Streptococcus pyogenes NY-5. Zentralbl. Bakteriol. Parasitenkd. Infektionskr. Hyg. Abt. 1. Orig. Reihe A 247:177–185.
17. Groman, N. B. 1955. Evidence for the active role of bacteriophage in the conversion of nontoxigenic Corynebacterium diphtheriae to toxin production. J. Bacteriol. 69:9–15.
18. Hanna, E. E., and M. Hale. 1975. Deregulation of mouse antibody-forming cells in vivo and in cell culture by streptococcal pyrogenic exotoxin. Infect. Immun. 11:265–272.
19. Hanna, E. E., and D. W. Watson. 1965. Host-parasite relationships among group A streptococci. III. Depression of reticuloendothelial function by streptococcal pyrogenic exotoxins. J. Bacteriol. 89:154–158.
20. Hanna, E. E., and D. W. Watson. 1968. Host-parasite relationships among group A streptococci. IV. Suppression of antibody response by streptococcal pyrogenic exotoxin. J. Bacteriol. 95:14–21.
21. Hanna, E. E., and D. W. Watson. 1973. Enhanced immune response after immunosuppression by streptococcal pyrogenic exotoxin. Infect. Immun. 7:1009–1011.
22. Holmes, R. K., and W. L. Barksdale. 1969. Genetic analysis of tox+ and tox− bacteriophages of Corynebacterium diphtheriae. J. Virol. 3:586–598.
23. Hooker, S. B., and E. M. Follensby. 1934. Studies on scarlet fever. II. Different toxins produced by hemolytic streptococci of scarlatinal origin. J. Immunol. 27:177–193.
24. Houston, C. W., and J. F. Ferretti. 1981. Enzyme-linked immunosorbent assay for detection of type A streptococcal exotoxin: kinetics and regulation during growth of Streptococcus pyogenes. Infect. Immun. 33:862–869.
25. Hribalova, V. 1974. Biological effects of scarlet fever toxin and the role of activation of lymphocytes. J. Hyg. Epidemiol. Microbiol. Immunol. 18:297–301.
26. Hribalova, V., and M. Pospisil. 1973. Lymphocyte-stimulating activity of scarlet fever toxin. Experientia 29:704–705.
27. Johnson, L. P., P. M. Schlievert, and D. W. Watson. 1980. Transfer of group A streptococcal pyrogenic exotoxin production to nontoxigenic strains by lysogenic conversion. Infect. Immun. 28:254–257.
28. Kim, Y. B., and D. W. Watson. 1970. A purified group A streptococcal pyrogenic exotoxin. Physicochemical and biological properties, including the enhancement of susceptibility to endotoxin lethal shock. J. Exp. Med. 131:611–628.
29. Kim, Y. B., and D. W. Watson. 1972. Streptococcal exotoxins: biological and pathological properties, p. 33–50. In

L. W. Wannamaker and J. M. Matsen (ed.), Streptococci and streptococcal diseases. Academic Press, Inc., New York.

30. **Knoll, H., F. Petermann, and W. Kohler.** 1978. Mitogenic activity of erythrogenic toxins. II. Determination of erythrogenic toxins in cultural supernatants of *Streptococcus pyogenes.* Zentralbl. Bakteriol. Parasitenkd. Infektinoskr. Hyg. Abt. 1 Orig. Reihe A **240**:466–473.

31. **McKane, L., and J. J. Ferretti.** 1981. Phage-host interactions and the production of type A streptococcal exotoxin in group A streptococci. Infect. Immun. **34**:915–919.

32. **Nauciel, C.** 1973. Mitogenic activity of purified streptococcal erythrogenic toxin on lymphocytes. Ann. Immunol. (Paris) **124**:383–390.

33. **Nauciel, C., J. Blass, R. Mangalo, and M. Raynaud.** 1969. Evidence for two molecular forms of streptococcal erythrogenic toxin. Eur. J. Biochem. **11**:160–164.

33a.**Nida, S. K., and J. J. Ferretti.** 1982. Phage influence on the synthesis of extracellular toxins in group A streptococci. Infect. Immun. **36**:745–750.

34. **Nida, S. K., C. W. Houston, and J. J. Ferretti.** 1978. Erythrogenic toxin production by group A streptococci, p. 66. *In* M. T. Parker (ed.), Pathogenic streptococci. Reedbooks Ltd., Chertsey, Surrey, U.K.

35. **Petermann, F., H. Knoll, and W. Kohler.** 1978. Mitogenic activity of erythrogenic toxins. I. Type-specific inhibition of the mitogenic activity of erythrogenic toxins by antitoxic antisera from the rabbit. Zentralbl. Bakteriol. Parasitenkd. Infektionskr. Abt. 1 Orig. Reihe A **240**:366–379.

36. **Schlievert, P. M., K. M. Bettin, and D. W. Watson.** 1979. Reinterpretation of the Dick test: role of group A streptococcal pyrogenic exotoxin. Infect. Immun. **26**:467–472.

37. **Schlievert, P. M., and D. W. Watson.** 1978. Group A streptococcal pyrogenic exotoxin: pyrogenicity, alteration of blood-brain barrier, and separation of sites for pyrogenicity and enhancement of lethal endotoxin shock. Infect. Immun. **21**:753–763.

38. **Schwab, J. H., D. W. Watson, and W. J. Cromartie.** 1955. Further studies of group A streptococcal factors with lethal and cardiotoxic properties. J. Infect. Dis. **96**:14–18.

39. **Stock, A. H.** 1939. Studies on the hemolytic streptococcus. I. Isolation and concentration of erythrogenic toxin of hemolytic streptococcus. J. Immunol. **36**:489–498.

40. **Watson, D. W.** 1960. Host-parasite factors in group A streptococcal infections. Pyrogenic and other effects of immunologic distinct exotoxins related to scarlet fever toxins. J. Exp. Med. **111**:255–284.

41. **Zabriskie, J.** 1964. The role of temperate bacteriophage in the production of erythrogenic toxin by group A streptococci. J. Exp. Med. **119**:761–779.

Plasmid Transformation in Pneumococcus: Behavior of the 20-Megadalton pIP501

CHARLES W. SAUNDERS[1] AND WALTER R. GUILD

Biochemistry Department, Duke University, Durham, North Carolina 27710

Our recent description of plasmid transformation in *Streptococcus pneumoniae* (2, 8–10) has provided a framework for interpretation of studies in a number of laboratories interested in cloning in gram-positive host-vector systems. Most of the work presented has been with the 3.5-megadalton *tet* plasmid pMV158. Examination of the 20-megadalton pIP501, conferring resistances to chloramphenicol and MLS antibiotics (macrolides-lincosamides-streptogramin B), showed quantitative differences in its behavior that can be significant in practical terms. We describe some of these below, after a brief review.

For pMV158, transforming activities in monomer and dimer forms were separated and analyzed by combinations of gel electrophoresis, sedimentation velocity, and dye-buoyancy, followed by examination of dose response and the dependence of transformation on time of exposure of cells to DNA. Monomer forms gave second-order responses and dimers gave first-order responses, with both time and concentration. Covalently closed (CC) forms were at least 35 times more active than open circular (OC) and linear forms. Unique linear forms produced by a restriction nuclease had no activity, but mixtures of linear forms produced by two different restriction enzymes were active, a result seen also by Barany and Tomasz with a different plasmid (1).

Coupled with evidence that plasmid DNA enters by the same pathway as does chromosomal DNA (1, 8), which involves entry of fragments of single strands cut from duplex donors on the cell surface (4–6, reviewed in 3), these results imply the pathway in Fig. 1, where repair synthesis before or after circularization leads to formation of a monomer replicon. It is worth emphasizing that there is no need for extended pairing between entering donor segments, but only enough to prime repair synthesis on strands long enough to eventually circularize. Further, the data suggest that circularization

usually involves only short lengths of complementary pairing (10). It could therefore even result from temporary mispairings sufficient to prime repair synthesis that would stabilize mutant structures, which have been seen by us and others. Also, the data do not exclude the possibility that, for dimers or higher multimers, no donor fragment may be needed for priming, inasmuch as it may be that DNA synthesis can initiate de novo at the normal origin (9).

Further work described elsewhere (11) gave two significant results. First, the unrelated pMV158 and pIP501 gave double transformants at frequencies equal to the product of the frequencies of the single transformations. This was the result expected if 100% of the cells were competent for transformation by plasmids, as they were for chromosomal markers. By excluding the possibility that only a minor fraction of the cells, perhaps with different properties, could be transformed by plasmids, this result strongly reinforced the evidence that the biologically active plasmid DNA follows the normal entry pathway. Second, in contrast to the above result, two related plasmids, pMV158 and a derivative constructed by in vitro cloning techniques (2), tended to transform the same cells 30 to 40 times more often than expected for independent events. When 0.1 to 0.2% of all cells had been transformed for one of the plasmids, 4 to 7% of these had also been transformed for the

[1]Present address: Genex Corp., Rockville, MD 20852.

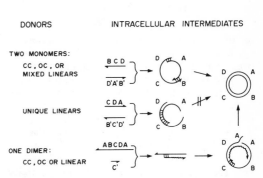

FIG. 1. Plasmid transformation in pneumococcus (from reference 10).

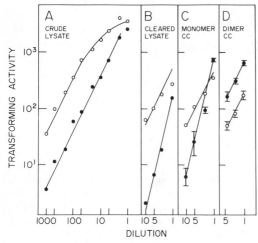

FIG. 2. Sedimentation of pIP501 transforming activity in neutral sucrose gradients (5 to 20%) run for 3 h at 24,000 rpm in an SW50.1 rotor. Input samples were 0.4 ml in A and B, and 0.2 ml in C. Ordinates are transformants counted in 0.2 ml (A, B) or 0.5 ml (C) of culture transformed by the indicated fractions. In A, 1, 2, and 3 indicate positions expected for 20-, 40-, and 60-megadalton CC DNAs. See text.

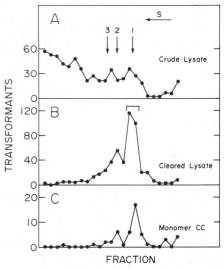

FIG. 3. Dose response for pIP501 (●) and chromosomal (○) transformants (see text). Unit dilution corresponds to plasmid DNA concentrations per milliliter of cells of approximately 50 ng (A), 100 ng (B), 20 ng (C), or undetectable (D). pIP501 transformants are expressed per 0.1 ml in A, per 0.01 ml in B, and per 1 ml in C and D. Where significant, error bars show one standard deviation of the colony counts.

other one, and both plasmids were present individually in the cotransformants (11). This is a result that should appear often when related plasmids are used. It could be due to cooperation in the low-efficiency formation of the primary intermediate, as in Fig. 1, or to one of the two plasmids first forming a replicon that is then transformed at high efficiency by a strand of the second plasmid. It was not due to congression in the sense of using an unlinked marker to select for the competent cells of the population, because the first result showed that essentially 100% of the cells were competent.

BEHAVIOR OF THE TRANSFORMING ACTIVITY OF pIP501

Because preparative fractionation of pIP501 on the continuous elution gel electrophoresis apparatus (9) was not successful (no activity ever eluted), we relied on sedimentation and dye-buoyancy gradients for identification of active forms. For pIP501, most of the transforming activity in a crude lysate sedimented more rapidly than monomer plasmid DNA (12; Fig. 2A). In a cleared lysate prepared by the sodium dodecyl sulfate-NaCl procedure, recovery of ^{3}H label in the CC region of a dye-buoyancy gradient was near 100%, but recovery of transforming activity was only 3 to 16% (8). Half of the remaining activity cosedimented with monomer CC forms (Fig. 2B). Whereas for pMV158 recovery of both ^{3}H and transforming activity was near 100% and much of the activity sedimented as multimeric DNA (8), for pIP501 the clearing procedure had removed much of the multimeric DNA that carried most of the transforming activity. The sodium dodecyl sulfate-NaCl procedure is well known to give poor recovery of large plasmids.

As with pMV158, an important question was whether the activity cosedimenting with monomer DNA was due to that form or to contaminating OC or linear multimers that may have cosedimented with it. The peak fractions indicated in Fig. 2B were pooled and banded in a dye-CsCl gradient; over 90% of the activity appeared in CC DNA (not shown). The fractions at the CC peak were resedimented in a sucrose gradient; again, most of the activity sedimented as expected for monomer CC (Fig. 2C). Thus, the activity was due to CC DNA that sedimented repeatedly with the velocity of monomer pIP501.

DOSE RESPONSE

For both pMV158 and pIP501, crude lysates showed first-order response curves, but pIP501 differed in that at higher DNA concentrations, where chromosomal transformation was starting to level off, its activity continued to rise (8; Fig.

TABLE 1. Transforming activities of monomer CC forms of pMV158 and pIP501[a]

| DNA concn | Transformants/ml | | Ratio, pMV158/ pIP501 |
	pMV158	pIP501	
6 ng/ml	8,800	75	120
4×10^8 molecules/ml	2,000	520	4

[a] Interpolated from points on second-order dose-response curves for peak fractions from the monomer CC region of sucrose gradients. See text.

3A). It was also much less affected by added competitor DNA than was pMV158 (8). A cleared lysate of pMV158 gave a mixed response curve, the sum of a linear component due to dimers and a second-order component due to monomers, which only became apparent at high concentrations (2, 8). For pIP501, the cleared lysate gave a second-order response curve without further separation of monomers from the multimers (Fig. 3B). This accounted for the variability in the assays of recovery in the cleared lysates and reinforced the fact that the relative peak heights in the gradients of Fig. 2 depended on the concentrations used for assay. An upper limit of 3% recovery of the activity due to multimers was estimated by assuming that all the transformants seen at the lowest concentration in Fig. 3B were due to a first-order response. The monomer and dimer peaks of the sucrose gradient gave second- and first-order responses as expected (Fig. 3C and D).

Besides differences in the proportions of forms in the initial lysates and in their recovery during subsequent procedures, the relative activities of two plasmids can be affected by differences in the effects of competing molecules that may be present and in the effects of cuts inflicted at the cell surface during binding and entry. The continued rise of transformation by pIP501 at high total DNA concentration (Fig. 3A) is reminiscent of transfection by the 33-megadalton ω3 phage DNA (7) and probably reflects fewer cuts per donor molecule as the surface binding sites become saturated. This would have more biological effect for large donors than for small, and pMV158 showed little or no such effect (8). Competitor DNA reduced transformation by monomer pMV158 by about the square of its effect on dimers, reflecting the difference in kinetics (10). Similar experiments on pIP501 showed (i) more effect on monomer than on dimer CC donors, but in each case less than on transformation for a chromosomal marker (which needs much shorter DNA for success); and (ii) a 1.2- to 1.7-fold *enhancement* of trans-

formation when, to a few nanograms of pIP501, 10 ng of competitor DNA was added per ml of cells (data not shown). At 10 ng of total DNA per ml, the response curve for chromosomal transformation is starting to deviate from linearity, and we estimate that the average cell is reacting with one to three donor DNA particles. The enhanced response for pIP501 may have been due to inhibition of second and third cuts having had more effect than reduction of available entry sites.

RELATIVE TRANSFORMATION BY PURIFIED MONOMER CC pMV158 AND pIP501

Cleared lysates of ^{3}H-labeled cultures carrying each plasmid were prepared and sedimented in sucrose gradients. Specific activities (counts per minute per nanogram of DNA) were measured on total DNAs prepared from each culture. Analytical gels showed little detectable DNA other than monomer CC, and the profiles of ^{3}H and transformants through the monomer peak suggested little contamination by chromosomal DNA in this region. Each monomer peak gave second-order dose-response curves, from which we could compare the transforming activities of the two plasmids under conditions where the above complications were absent (Table 1). For equal mass concentrations, the smaller plasmid gave 120 times more transformants; for equal numbers of donor molecules, the ratio was about 4. Two less thorough experiments also suggested comparable numbers of transformants for equal numbers of donor plasmids. The quantities of dimers have been too low to permit valid comparisons of this kind.

As with pMV158 (10), non-CC forms of pIP501 had significant transforming activity (10, 12), and there is no indication that the pathway for pIP501 is qualitatively different from that for pMV158, as in Fig. 1. Quantitatively, its behavior differs in ways that could be important for some kinds of studies.

ACKNOWLEDGMENTS

This work was supported by Public Health Service grant GM21887 from the National Institute of General Medical Sciences and contract DE-AS05-76EV03941 from the Department of Energy to W.R.G. C.W.S. was supported by a genetics training grant from the National Institutes of Health.

LITERATURE CITED

1. **Barany, F., and A. Tomasz.** 1980. Genetic transformation of *Streptococcus pneumoniae* by heterologous plasmid deoxyribonucleic acid. J. Bacteriol. **144**:698–709.
2. **Guild, W. R., and C. W. Saunders.** 1981. The pathway of plasmid transformation in pneumococcus, p. 227–235. *In* S. Levy, R. Clowes, and E. Koenig (ed.), Molecular

biology, pathogenicity, and ecology of bacterial plasmids. Plenum Publishing Corp., New York.

3. **Lacks, S.** 1977. Binding and entry of DNA in bacterial transformation, p. 179–232. *In* J. Reissig (ed.), Microbial interactions. Chapman and Hall, London.

4. **Morrison, D. A., and W. R. Guild.** 1972. Transformation and deoxyribonucleic acid size: extent of degradation on entry varies with size of donor. J. Bacteriol. **112**:1157–1168.

5. **Morrison, D. A., and W. R. Guild.** 1973. Breakage prior to entry of donor DNA in pneumococcus transformation. Biochim. Biophys. Acta **299**:545–556.

6. **Morrison, D. A., and W. R. Guild.** 1973. Structure of DNA on the cell surface during uptake by pneumococcus. J. Bacteriol. **115**:1055–1062.

7. **Porter, R. D., and W. R. Guild.** 1978. Transfection in pneumococcus: single strand intermediates in the formation of infective centers. J. Virol. **25**:60–72.

8. **Saunders, C. W., and W. R. Guild.** 1980. Properties and transforming activities of two plasmids in *Streptococcus pneumoniae*. Mol. Gen. Genet. **180**:573–578.

9. **Saunders, C. W., and W. R. Guild.** 1981. Monomer plasmid DNA transforms *Streptococcus pneumoniae*. Mol. Gen. Genet. **181**:57–62.

10. **Saunders, C. W., and W. R. Guild.** 1981. Pathway of plasmid transformation in pneumococcus: open circular and linear molecules are active. J. Bacteriol. **146**:517–526.

11. **Saunders, C. W., J. M. Hageman, and W. R. Guild.** 1982. Nonrandom cotransformation by related plasmids in *Streptococcus pneumoniae*, p. 43–50. *In* U. Streips, S. Goodgal, W. Guild, and G. Wilson (ed.), Genetic exchange. Marcel Dekker, Inc., New York.

12. **Shoemaker, N. B., M. D. Smith, and W. R. Guild.** 1979. Organization and transfer of heterologous chloramphenicol and tetracyline resistance genes in pneumococcus. J. Bacteriol. **139**:432–441.

Transformation of *Streptococcus pneumoniae* by Single-Stranded Plasmid-Phage Hybrid DNA

FRANCIS BARANY[1]

The Rockefeller University, New York, New York 10021

Heterologous plasmid DNA has recently been introduced into *Streptococcus pneumoniae* via transformation (2, 16) and conjugation (4, 20). Barany and Tomasz demonstrated that monomer plasmids, as well as mixtures of linear plasmids, exhibit transforming activity (2). This has been confirmed both in *S. pneumoniae* (17, 21) and in *S. sanguis* (3, 13). However, in *Bacillus subtilis* such DNA conformers are inactive (5, 8).

In this work single-stranded DNA (ssDNA) from phage-plasmid hybrids was used to study DNA uptake in *S. pneumoniae*.

MODEL SYSTEM FOR STUDYING DNA UPTAKE

Plasmid pFB3 is a high-copy-number derivative of pSA5700 (15; kindly provided by R. P. Novick) coding for inducible erythromycin (Em[r]) and chloramphenicol (Cm[r]) resistance (1a, 2). The Em[r] gene product methylates the 23S rRNA of the 50S ribosomal subunit, which can then no longer bind erythromycin (9, 10; B. Weisblum, this volume). This protein is induced by a low level of erythromycin; mutations in the control region of this gene causing constitutive synthesis confers resistance to two noninducing drugs, tylosin (Tyl[r]) and lincomycin (Linc[r]). Plasmid pFB9 (derived from pFB3) contains a 70-base pair (bp) insert in the Em[r] gene control region which confers constitutive resistance (Tyl[r] and Linc[r]) (1). Plasmids pFB3 and pFB9, two homologous plasmids differing only in a 70-bp insert which confers Tyl[r] and Linc[r], comprise the basic system for studying DNA uptake.

In classical pneumococcal transformation, where incoming DNA recombines with the homologous chromosome, transformation frequencies are low, about 1%, because only one piece out of every 100 contains the correct marker. With plasmid transformation, the DNA is pure, but the frequency is low (between 0.1 and 0.05% for purified monomer [2]) because the plasmid must establish itself. When the recipient contains a resident homologous plasmid (such as pFB3), the constitutive marker on pFB9 can be rescued, yielding transformation frequencies as high as 50 to 70% (1a, 2). Similar high frequencies have been obtained with cloned chromosomal DNA (7, 21). In the marker rescue experiments described below, transforming DNA contained the constitutive marker of pFB9, the recipient cells contained the inducible plasmid pFB3, and Tyl[r] (or Linc[r]) transformants were selected.

SINGLE-STRANDED DNA TRANSFORMS *S. PNEUMONIAE* WITH MARKER RESCUE

In 1962, Lacks proposed a model for DNA uptake in *S. pneumoniae* (11, 12). The model hypothesizes that a membrane-bound endonuclease binds and cuts double-stranded DNA (dsDNA), degrading one strand as the other strand is simultaneously internalized. The internalized strand can recombine with the chromosome, or (in the model system described here) with a resident homologous plasmid. According to the model, the energy for DNA uptake is provided by degradation of the opposite strand. The model thus has a stringent requirement for dsDNA, which was tested in early studies in which heat- or alkali-denatured DNA was used (14).

This model was tested using pure, cloned phage ssDNA, which has the following advantages over conventionally prepared ssDNA: (i) cloned DNA is homogeneous, (ii) either (+) or (−) strand may be tested, and (iii) filamentous phage package only ssDNA. During phage preparation, intact virions were treated with pancreatic DNase, thus totally eliminating contamination with dsDNA.

Plasmid pFB9 was cloned into the single-stranded phage f1 derivative CGF3 (N. D. Zinder and J. D. Boeke, submitted for publication) in both orientations (F. Barany, J. D. Boeke, and A. Tomasz, manuscript in preparation). Two phage-plasmid hybrids, called "phasmids" were isolated, fBB101 and fBB103, and their restriction maps are shown in Fig. 1. Phasmid fBB103 contains an 800-bp insertion directly

[1] Present address: Department of Molecular Biology and Genetics, The Johns Hopkins University School of Medicine, Baltimore, MD 21205.

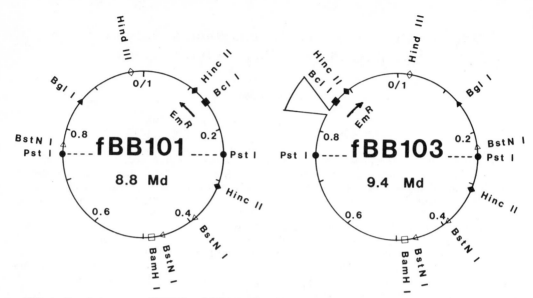

FIG. 1. Restriction maps of fBB101 and fBB103. Plasmid DNA containing pFB9 and pBB3 DNAs (1) (4.4 and 5.0 megadaltons) was cut with *Pst*I and ligated to f1 derivative CGF3 at its unique *Pst*I site to yield phasmids fBB101 and fBB103. The top half of each map represents pFB9 DNA; the bottom half represents f1 DNA. ssDNA isolated from virus particles grown in *E. coli* produced the strand coding for Em^r in fBB103 and the noncoding strand in fBB101. Phasmid fBB103 contains an 800-bp insert found in pBB3 (an unidentified insertion sequence) which fortuitously destroys constitutive (but not inducible) erythromycin resistance in *S. pneumoniae*.

in front of the Em^r gene which destroyed Tyl^r and Linc^r. This insert increases Em^r in *Escherichia coli* (1). Single-stranded fBB101 (ssfBB101, Tyl^r) was prepared from *E. coli* strain K414 (F$^+$, *recA*$^-$) (Zinder and Boeke, submitted for publication) and was tested for transforming activity into a recipient pneumococcus containing the resident inducible plasmid pFB3 and selecting for Tyl^r and Linc^r. At a DNA concentration of 1 µg/ml, ssDNA transformed 1% of the recipient pneumococcus to Tyl^r. This frequency is comparable to chromosomal transformation, but is 50-fold less than the frequency with double-stranded pFB9.

A competition experiment between ssDNA and dsDNA was performed to determine whether these two DNAs used the same or different entry sites on the pneumococcal surface. The results in Fig. 2 show that ssDNA barely competes with binding of dsDNA and that dsDNA competes with ssDNA threefold better than with dsDNA. Thus, ssDNA binds one-third as well as dsDNA, and it binds the pneumococcus at the same site as dsDNA.

TRANSFORMATION OF *S. PNEUMONIAE* WITH IMPERFECT HETERODUPLEXED DNA

ssfBB101 and ssfBB103 were heteroduplexed to pFB3 or pFB9 linearized by restriction endo-

nucleases, and the heteroduplexes were purified by gel electrophoresis. The heteroduplexes were tested for transforming activity of the Tyl^r marker into a recipient pneumococcus containing the homologous plasmid pFB3 (Fig. 3). When both strands contained the Tyl^r 70-bp insert marker (indicated by the black triangle)—as in pFB9 monomer (A), *Pst*I-linearized pFB9 (B), dsfBB101 (C), or *Pst*I-linearized pFB9 heteroduplexed with ssfBB101 (E)—transforming activity was high, from 31 to 83%. If the DNA heteroduplex was imperfect, i.e., containing either a 70-bp or 800-bp loop out, activity was just slightly higher than that of ssDNA: 3.3% for ssfBB103 heteroduplexed to ssfBB101 (H), 1.8% for *Hind*III-linearized CGF4 heteroduplexed with ssfBB101 (G), and 1.6% for *Pst*I-linearized pFB3 heteroduplexed with ssfBB101 (F), compared to 1.0% for ssfBB101 (D). With the heteroduplexed DNA, only one strand (ssfBB101) contains the Tyl^r marker, whereas with dsDNA both strands contain the marker, and one strand may be more active than the other. The possibility of such a strand bias in transformation was tested by heteroduplexing linearized pFB9 to an exc·ss of ssfBB101 (or fBB103) and purifying the displaced strand by electrophoresis in low-melting agarose. These strands were assayed for transforming activity of the Tyl^r marker into a recipient pneumococcus containing pFB3 (Fig. 4).

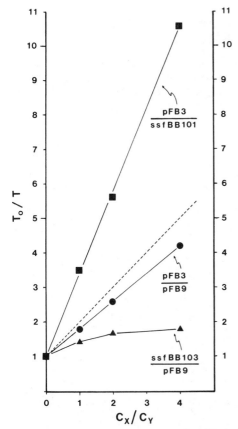

FIG. 2. Competition of ssDNA and dsDNA in pneumococcal transformation. Competent *S. pneumoniae* cells containing a resident inducible plasmid (pFB3) were transformed with DNA containing the constitutive marker (double-stranded pFB9 or ssfBB101) in the presence of competing DNA (inducible pFB3 or ssfBB103). Tyl^r and Linc^r transformants were selected (Barany, Boeke, and Tomasz, manuscript in preparation) and averaged. The number of transformants (average) obtained in the absence of competing DNA (T_o) divided by the number of transformants obtained in the presence of competing DNA (T) is plotted as a function of concentration of competing DNA (C_X) divided by the concentration of transforming DNA (C_Y). For double-stranded pFB9 (1 μg/ml) $T_o = 1.3 \times 10^7$ (71% transformation frequency); ssfBB101 (1 μg/ml) $T_o = 2.1 \times 10^5$ (1.0% transformation frequency), $C_Y = 1$ μg of DNA per ml, and C_X ranged from 1 to 4 μg of DNA per ml. Dashed line indicates ideal value for dsDNA competing with dsDNA. Symbols: ■, double-stranded pFB3 competing with ssfBB101; ●, double-stranded pFB3 competing with double-stranded pFB9; and ▲, ssfBB103 competing with double-stranded pFB9.

ssDNA of the "fBB103" orientation may be three- to fivefold more active than the "fBB101" strand. Rigorous confirmation of this will re-

quire isolation of "fBB102," same orientation as fBB103, without the 800-bp insert. Figure 4 also shows that a cut near to the marker (i.e., by *Hinc*II) diminishes activity. There is also no apparent difference in transforming activity if the marker is closer to the 3' or 5' end.

ssDNA TRANSFORMS *S. PNEUMONIAE* WITHOUT MARKER RESCUE

Without a resident homologous plasmid within a recipient pneumococcus, monomer plasmid pFB9 dsDNA gave a transformation frequency of 7.6×10^{-4}. Both ssfBB101 and ssfBB103 gave transformants, although at a 100-fold lower frequency. Furthermore, lysates of these transformants demonstrated phasmid DNA of the same molecular weight as starting dsfBB101 and dsfBB103 (Barany, Boeke, and Tomasz, manuscript in preparation). Hence, 12 kilobases of ssDNA can enter the pneumococcus intact and can also replicate to form dsDNA.

Imperfect heteroduplexed molecules containing Tyl^r marker on one strand and Tyl^s (800-bp insert) on the other strand were also tested for transforming activity into plasmid-free pneumococcus. Either strand of heteroduplexed DNA could enter, as seen in the ratio of Tyl^r/Tyl^s (Em^r) transformants obtained.

CONCLUSIONS

(i) ssDNA transforms *S. pneumoniae*. Without marker rescue, ssDNA gave 100-fold less activity than dsDNA; with marker rescue, it gave 50-fold less activity. (ii) dsDNA competitively reduced ssDNA transformation, indicating that ssDNA interacts with the pneumococcus at the same site as dsDNA. (iii) Under marker rescue conditions, heteroduplexed DNA containing a 70-bp or 800-bp loop showed 10 to 20-fold less activity than dsDNA. When these values are corrected for differing strand activities, the imperfect dsDNA demonstrated at least 3- to 5-fold less activity than perfect dsDNA. (iv) Either strand of heteroduplexed DNA can enter.

These findings are consistent with an uptake enzyme complex that has a higher affinity for processing perfect dsDNA, as is proposed in the Lacks model. However, these results indicate that simultaneous degradation of the alternate strand is neither required nor does it provide the energy for DNA uptake. Seto and Tomasz have demonstrated two essential requirements for uptake of prebound (with EDTA) DNA: (i) an energy source such as glucose and (ii) a specific requirement for calcium ions (18, 19). Glucose increased the number of transformants 4-fold (18), or up to 50-fold under low temperature (10°C) uptake conditions (Barany, unpublished

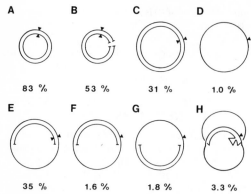

FIG. 3. Transformation of *S. pneumoniae* with heteroduplexed DNA. Competent *S. pneumoniae* cells containing pFB3 were transformed with various heteroduplexed DNA molecules containing the constitutive Tyl^r marker, indicated by the black triangle. Tyl^r transformation frequency is tabulated below schematic drawings of the molecules. (A) Double-stranded pFB9 monomer, (B) *Pst*I-linearized pFB9, (C) dsfBB101, (D) ssfBB101, (E) *Pst*I-linearized pFB9 heteroduplexed with ssfBB101, (F) ssfBB101 heteroduplexed to *Pst*I-linearized pFB3, (G) ssfBB101 heteroduplexed to *Hind*III-linearized CGF4, and (H) ssfBB101 heteroduplexed to ssfBB103.

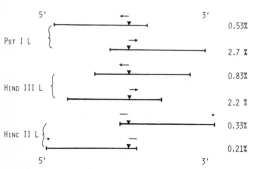

FIG. 4. Transforming activity of single-stranded pFB9 DNA. Plasmid pFB9, linearized by either *Pst*I, *Hind*III, or *Hinc*II, was heteroduplexed to an excess of either ssfBB101 or ssfBB103. The displaced strand was purified (by low-melting agarose gel electrophoresis) and assayed for transforming activity as described in Fig. 3. The top strand contains the sequence found in fBB101, and the bottom strand contains the sequence found in fBB103; transforming activity is indicated on the left. The black triangle indicates the Tyl^r marker, and the arrow indicates the direction of transcription of the Em^r gene. Circular ssfBB101 gave a transformation frequency of 1.0% under these conditions.

data). Furthermore, addition of the Ca^{2+}-Mg^{2+} ionophore A23187 inhibited uptake 100-fold, whereas valinomycin (K$^+$, H$^+$) only gave 2- to 3-fold inhibition (Barany, unpublished data).

The entry of a negatively charged macromolecule (DNA) into the pneumococcus might be ionically balanced by cation cotransport (Ca^{2+}). The membrane potential or calcium gradient, or both, required for such DNA uptake might be generated by the fermentation of glucose. Similar findings have been reported for *B. subtilis* transformation (6).

ACKNOWLEDGMENTS

I thank J. D. Boeke, T. Dougherty, S. Lacks, A. Tomasz, and B. Weisblum for helpful discussion, and R. Hamill for gifts of valinomycin, tylosin, and A23187.

This work was done in the laboratory of A. Tomasz and supported in part by Public Health Service grant AI-16170 from the National Institute of Allergy and Infectious Diseases and by grant PCM 79-10441 from the National Science Foundation. This work was carried out during the tenure of an Andrew W. Mellon Fellowship from The Rockefeller University.

LITERATURE CITED

1. **Barany, F., and J. D. Boeke.** 1982. Plasmid exchange between *Streptococcus pneumoniae* and *Escherichia coli*, p. 27–42. *In* U. N. Streips, S. Goodgal, W. Guild, and G. A. Wilson (ed.), Genetic exchange: a celebration and a new generation. Marcel Dekker Inc. New York.

1a. **Barany, F., J. D. Boeke, and A. Tomasz.** 1982. Staphylococcal plasmids that replicate and express erythromycin in both *Streptococcus pneumoniae* and *Escherichia coli*. Proc. Natl. Acad. Sci. U.S.A. **79**:2991–2995.

2. **Barany, F., and A. Tomasz.** 1980. Genetic transformation of *Streptococcus pneumoniae* by heterologous plasmid deoxyribonucleic acid. J. Bacteriol. **144**:698–709.

3. **Behnke, D.** 1981. Plasmid transformation of *Streptococcus sanguis* (Challis) occurs by circular and linear molecules. Mol. Gen. Genet. **183**:490–497.

4. **Buu-Hoi, A., and T. Horodniceanu.** 1980. Conjugative transfer of multiple antibiotic resistance markers in *Streptococcus pneumoniae*. J. Bacteriol. **143**:313–320.

5. **Canosi, U., G. Morelli, and T. A. Trautner.** 1978. The relationship between molecular structure and transformation efficiency of some *S. aureus* plasmids isolated from *B. subtilis*. Mol. Gen. Genet. **166**:259–267.

6. **Chaustova, L. P., L. L. Grinius, B. B. Griniuviene, A. A. Jasaitis, J. P. Kadziauskas, and R. J. Kiausinyte.** 1980. Studies on energy supply for genetic processes: involvement of membrane potential in genetic transformation of *Bacillus subtilis*. Eur. J. Biochem. **103**:349–357.

7. **Claverys, J. P., J. M. Louarn, and A. M. Sicard.** 1981. Cloning of *Streptococcus pneumoniae* DNA: its use in pneumococcal transformation and in studies of mismatch repair. Gene **13**:65–73.

8. **Contente, S., and D. Dubnau.** 1979. Characterization of plasmid transformation in *Bacillus subtilis*: kinetic properties and the effect of DNA conformation. Mol. Gen. Genet. **167**:251–258.

9. **Horinouchi, S., and B. Weisblum.** 1980. Posttranscriptional modification of mRNA conformation: mechanism that regulates erythromycin-induced resistance. Proc. Natl. Acad. Sci. U.S.A. **77**:7079–7083.

10. **Horinouchi, S., and B. Weisblum.** 1981. The control region for erythromycin resistance: free energy changes related to induction and mutation to constitutive expression. Mol. Gen. Genet. **182**:341–348.

11. **Lacks, S.** 1962. Molecular fate of DNA in genetic transformation of pneumococcus. J. Mol. Biol. **5**:119–131.

12. **Lacks, S.** 1977. Binding and entry of DNA in bacterial transformation, p. 177–232. *In* J. Reissig (ed.), Microbial interactions. Chapman and Hall, London.

13. **Macrina, F. L., K. R. Jones, and R. A. Welch.** 1981. Transformation of *Streptococcus sanguis* with monomeric pVA736 plasmid deoxyribonucleic acid. J. Bacteriol. **146:**826–830.

14. **Miao, R., and W. R. Guild.** 1970. Competent *Diplococcus pneumoniae* accept both single and double-stranded deoxyribonucleic acid. J. Bacteriol. **101:**361–364.

15. **Novick, R. P., E. Murphy, S. Iordanescu, I. Edelman, J. Korolewski, and M. Rush.** 1981. Hitchhiking transposons and other mobile genetic elements and site-specific recombination systems in *Staphylococcus aureus*. Cold Spring Harbor Symp. Quant. Biol. **45:**67–76.

16. **Saunders, C. W., and W. R. Guild.** 1981. Monomer plasmid DNA transforms *Streptococcus pneumoniae*. Mol. Gen. Genet. **181:**57–62.

17. **Saunders, C. W., and W. R. Guild.** 1981. Pathway of plasmid transformation in pneumococcus: open circular and linear molecules are active. J. Bacteriol. **146:**517–526.

18. **Seto, H., and A. Tomasz.** 1974. Early stages in DNA binding and uptake during genetic transformation of pneumococci. Proc. Natl. Acad. Sci. U.S.A. **71:**1493–1498.

19. **Seto, H., and A. Tomasz.** 1976. Calcium-requiring step in the uptake of deoxyribonucleic acid molecules through the surface of competent pneumococci. J. Bacteriol. **126:**1113–1118.

20. **Smith, M. D., N. D. Shoemaker, V. Burdett, and W. R. Guild.** 1980. Transfer of plasmids by conjugation in *Streptococcus pneumoniae*. Plasmid **3:**70–79.

21. **Stassi, D., P. Lopez, M. Espinosa, and S. Lacks.** 1981. Cloning of chromosomal genes in *Streptococcus pneumoniae*. Proc. Natl. Acad. Sci. U.S.A. **78:**7028–7032.

Effect of Chromosomal Homology on Plasmid Transfer and Transformation in *Streptococcus pneumoniae*

S. A. LACKS, D. L. STASSI,[1] P. LOPEZ,[2] M. ESPINOSA,[2] AND B. GREENBERG

Biology Department, Brookhaven National Laboratory, Upton, New York 11973

Molecular cloning depends on DNA-mediated transformation, and such transformation was first discovered in *Streptococcus pneumoniae*. Nevertheless, this species lagged far behind *Escherichia coli* as a host for cloned DNA. The reason was, in part, the absence of suitable plasmids, for only recently have selectable, multicopy plasmids been introduced into *S. pneumoniae* (1, 12). However, it was also thought that the processing undergone by DNA during uptake into pneumococcal cells would prevent establishment of a recombinant plasmid. This processing involves two types of degradation: single-strand breaks are made, initially, when DNA is bound to the cell, and then, during entry of a single-strand segment its complementary strand is hydrolyzed (8). Thus, the degradation associated with entry necessitates interaction between two separately entering strands to establish a plasmid. Such interaction gives a quadratic dependence of plasmid transfer on monomer plasmid DNA concentration, which was observed by Saunders and Guild (11). The obvious rarity of simultaneous uptake of two recombinant plasmids bearing the same chromosomal segment militated against the likelihood of cloning such segments by the conventional approach. However, it was possible to clone chromosomal genes in *S. pneumoniae*, and clones of two well-studied pneumococcal genes, *malM*, which codes for the amylomaltase essential for maltose utilization (6, 7, 16), and *sul-d*, which confers sulfonamide resistance (5), were obtained (13).

The availability of recombinant plasmids carrying DNA segments homologous to the chromosome allowed investigation of the effects of such homology on plasmid establishment. Plasmid transfer was increased 10-fold by the presence of chromosomal homology (8a). Such facilitation was frequently accompanied by introduction of the chromosomal allele into the plasmid during its establishment (8a). In addition to facilitation of plasmid establishment, evi-

dence was obtained for a subsequent process, in which alleles were equilibrated between the chromosome and the plasmid pool (8a).

CLONING OF CHROMOSOMAL GENES IN *S. PNEUMONIAE*

Vectors for cloning were either the 5.4-kilobase multicopy plasmid pMV158 (2, 10) or pLS1, a 4.3-kilobase derivative, both of which confer tetracycline resistance (Fig. 1A). Restriction fragments containing the *malM* and *sul-d* genes were partially purified by gel electrophoresis and ligated to the cut vectors. The *sul* plasmid pLS80 (Fig. 1B) was obtained by ligating the *Eco*RI *sul-d* chromosomal fragment to the linear form of pLS1, transforming a sulfonamide-sensitive recipient, and selecting for Tc[r] Sul[r] transformants. Details of the cloning procedures and results have been published (8a, 13, 14). To obtain the *mal* plasmid pLS70 (Fig. 1C), the *Pst*I *mal* chromosomal fragment was ligated to pMV158 partially cut with *Pst*I. The ligated DNA was used to transform recipient cells carrying the *581* deletion of the *mal* region (Fig. 1D), and Tc[r]Mal[+] clones were selected. Both pLS70 and pLS80 are multicopy plasmids, with a copy number estimated at ~30.

The pLS80 plasmid confers resistance to at least 10 times the level of sulfanilamide as does a single copy of the *sul-d* gene. Cells containing pLS70 synthesize approximately 10 times the normal level of amylomaltase, which in induced cells represents almost 10% of the cellular protein. In addition, they produce similar levels of a fragment of the X protein, which is a protein of unknown function, induced by maltose and coded by the gene adjacent to *malM* (Fig. 1D).

It should be pointed out that the *sul* recombinant plasmid was established in a cell with a chromosome that shared homology with the plasmid, whereas the *mal* plasmid was established in the absence of chromosomal homology. Cloning can be achieved in either circumstance. Given the unlikelihood of either the simultaneous uptake by a cell of two *mal* recombinant plasmids or the formation of a recombinant dimer, how was the recombinant DNA reconsti-

[1] Present address: Bristol-Myers, Syracuse, NY 13201.
[2] Present address: Instituto de Inmunologia y Biologia Microbiana, C.S.I.C., Velazquez, 144, Madrid-6, Spain.

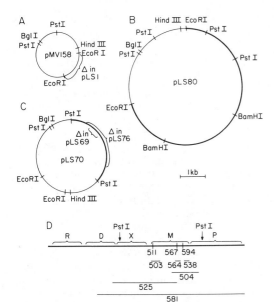

FIG. 1. Maps of (A) vector plasmids, (B) *sul* recombinant plasmid, (C) *mal* recombinant plasmids, and (D) chromosomal *mal* region. Light line, vector DNA; heavy line, DNA of chromosomal origin. Genes R, D, X, M, and P code, respectively, for repressor, maltotetraose permease, X protein, amylomaltase, and phosphorylase. Mutations are indicated below the chromosomal map, with line segments indicating the extent of deletions.

tuted from the strand fragments which entered the cell? The most plausible explanation is that a recombinant strand fragment, which contained the entire chromosomal segment and portions of the vector on each side, needed only to react with a vector strand fragment to reconstitute the entire recombinant plasmid (13). Inasmuch as the vector constituted a large fraction (10%) of the total DNA ligated, the frequency of vector segments in the cells would be sufficiently high for this rescue function.

The effect of various restriction cuts in the recombinant plasmid on its ability to transfer the cloned marker depended on the presence or absence of homologous DNA in the cell (13). In the absence of homology in either the chromosome or an endogenous plasmid in the recipient, for example, when the *mal-581* mutant was treated with pLS70, any restriction cut in the plasmid destroyed its ability to transform cells to either Tc^r or Mal^+. However, when that deletion mutant already contained the pMV158 plasmid, cuts in the vector portion of pLS70 by *Eco*RI, *Bgl*I, or both, did not prevent transformation to Mal^+. In the former case, the Mal^+ transformation depended on establishment of the plasmid

as an independent replicon. In the latter case the *mal* segment was presumably introduced into a preexisting plasmid by interaction of the homologous plasmid sequences adjacent to the *mal* insert. Removal of those sequences by *Pst*I destroyed the Mal^+ transforming activity in that case. We have proposed that the first type of transformation, which requires plasmid establishment, be called *plasmid transfer*, and that the second type, in which an endogenous plasmid is altered, be called *plasmid transformation* (13). When the chromosome carried *mal* homology, for example, with mutant *mal-594* as recipient, the *Pst*I-cut plasmid could still transform the chromosome and give Mal^+ transformants, but no Tc^r transformants could be obtained with any of the vector cut forms.

CHROMOSOMAL FACILITATION OF PLASMID TRANSFER

Comparison of Tc^r transformation by pLS70 by recipients with and without the homologous *mal* region in their chromosomes indicated significantly higher plasmid transfer frequencies in the presence of homology (8a, 13). This effect was particularly marked with isolated covalently closed monomers as the donor DNA (Table 1). With either wild-type or single-site mutant (*594*) alleles in the recipient, the facilitation of plasmid transfer, expressed as the ratio of transformation by pLS70 to pLS1 (which lacks chromosomal homology), was about 15-fold. A small *mal* deletion (*503*) in the chromosome did not prevent facilitation, but a larger deletion (*504*) that corresponded to approximately one-third of the *mal* insert in pLS70 greatly reduced facilitation. A still larger deletion (*525*) eliminated the effect entirely, and no facilitation was observed when the chromosomal deletion (*581*) removed all of the sequence homologous to the plasmid. Similar effects were found for deletions in the *mal* segment of the plasmid. The small deletion in pLS69 did not affect facilitation, but the large deletion in pLS76 abolished it (8a).

Analysis of the DNA concentration dependence of transformation by the recombinant plasmid pLS70 gave an interesting result. With monomeric plasmid DNA, a quadratic concentration dependence was observed for both Mal^+ and Tc^r transformation when the recipient cell (the *581* deletion mutant) contained no DNA homologous to the plasmid (8a). This behavior was found also for Tc^r transformation by pLS1 in any recipient, and it corresponds to the findings of Saunders and Guild (11). Transformation of a single-site mutant (*594*) to Mal^+ by pLS70 gave a linear concentration dependence, which

TABLE 1. Effect of chromosomal homology on plasmid transfer frequency

mal allele in recipient strain	Tc^r transformants per ml		Ratio, pLS70/pLS1
	pLS1	pLS70	
mal$^+$	4.2×10^3	6.0×10^4	14
594	8.0×10^2	1.3×10^4	16
503	3.2×10^3	4.3×10^4	13
504	3.7×10^3	8.0×10^3	2.2
525	2.6×10^3	1.3×10^3	0.7
581	6.0×10^2	5.0×10^2	0.8

was expected for this essentially chromosomal transformation. Surprisingly, however, Tc^r transformants in this cross were also linearly proportional to DNA concentration, although they were almost 100-fold less frequent than the Mal$^+$ transformants (8a). In every case the Tc^r transformant contained a plasmid the size of pLS70. The linear concentration dependence presumably reflects participation of the bacterial chromosome in reconstituting a plasmid from a single entering plasmid fragment. In the absence of chromosomal homology, two plasmid fragments are required for reconstitution.

A further effect of homology between chromosome and plasmid is its enabling of a restriction endonuclease-cut plasmid to become established in a cell. Normally, restriction endonuclease-cut plasmids cannot reconstitute an intact replicon because there are no strand fragments that would overlap the restriction site (1, 4). A particularly interesting study in this regard was carried out with the sul plasmid pLS80 (8a). Various restriction-cut fragments of pLS80 could transform cells to Sul^r because this transformation is predominantly chromosomal. When the plasmid was cleaved by BglI, which cuts it in the nonhomologous, vector portion, its ability to transfer Tc^r was destroyed, being reduced to <0.01% of the original. However, when pLS80 was cleaved by BamHI, which cuts only in the chromosomal insert (Fig. 1B), the cut plasmid retained Tc^r transforming activity, to the extent of 2% of the original activity. Such persistence of activity on restriction cutting of a plasmid sharing homology with the chromosome has been reported, also, in Bacillus subtilis (3). BamHI makes two cuts within the chromosomal insert of pLS80. When the large BamHI fragment, which lacks 3.3 kilobases of the original 10-kilobase insert but carries the entire vector sequence, was isolated and tested, it showed Tc^r transforming activity. All of these Tc^r transformants contained plasmids the size of pLS80. Thus, interaction with the chromosome not only enables a single linear plasmid fragment to establish itself

as a plasmid within the cell, but it can also compensate for a gap in the homologous portion.

INCORPORATION OF CHROMOSOMAL MARKERS INTO THE PLASMID

The ability of the chromosome to compensate for a gap in the introduced plasmid fragment shows that it can contribute information to the plasmid during its establishment. Such contribution was shown directly by the introduction of chromosomal markers into the plasmid (8a). When pLS70 was introduced into the single-site mutant 594, 16% of the Tc^r transformants carried the mal-594 mutation in their plasmid pool. In the reciprocal cross, where the mutant plasmid was introduced into wild-type cells, again 16% of the Tc^r transformants carried the wild-type pLS70. Small deletions, such as 564 and 503, were also readily incorporated. The frequency of incorporation of the chromosomal allele into the plasmid appeared to depend on its position in the PstI mal segment. Mutations in the center portion were transferred more frequently than those in the ends. That the transfer occurred during the establishment of the plasmid was evident from the generally homogeneous nature of the plasmid pool in each cell. The vast majority of the plasmids in a given cell contained either the mutant or wild-type form. Introduction of the chromosomal allele, therefore, must have preceded amplification of the established plasmid.

Once the plasmid was established, another process of gradual equilibration of the homologous alleles between chromosome and plasmid appeared to take place. This was demonstrated by the slow accumulation of mal$^+$ plasmids in the pool of cells originally containing a mal$^+$ chromosome and mal$^-$ plasmids (8a). The maximum proportion of mal$^+$ plasmids observed was 1:36, which presumably reflected the ratio of mal$^+$ genes to the total of mal genes in the chromosome and multicopy plasmid pool after mal$^-$ plasmid establishment and amplification. The mechanism of this postestablishment exchange is presumably insertion and subsequent excision of the plasmid in the chromosome by homologous duplex recombination events (8a).

Some speculations as to the mechanism of chromosomal facilitation in the original plasmid establishment have been offered (8a). Three possibilities were envisaged: (i) chromosomal copying, in which information but no material is transferred; (ii) chromosomal donation, in which a single-strand segment of the chromosome is transferred; (iii) integration into the chromosome followed by excision. Detailed molecular mechanisms have been proposed for each possibility (8a). The integration mechanism, in particular, was based on the proposal for integration of pBR322 recombinant plasmids in the *amiA* locus of *S. pneumoniae* (15). In all of the mechanisms envisaged, replacement by the chromosome of a portion of the plasmid missing in the entering strand fragment would introduce the chromosomal marker into the plasmid.

ACKNOWLEDGMENTS

This work was supported by the U.S. Department of Energy and by Public Health Service grants AI14885 and GM29721 from the National Institutes of Health. D.L.S. was a recipient of National Research Service Award GM06975, and P.L. was a recipient of a grant from the U.S.-Spanish Joint Committee for Scientific and Technological Cooperation.

LITERATURE CITED

1. **Barany, F., and A. Tomasz.** 1980. Genetic transformation of *Streptococcus pneumoniae* by heterologous plasmid deoxyribonucleic acid. J. Bacteriol. **144:**698–709.
2. **Burdett, V.** 1980. Identification of tetracycline resistant R-plasmids in *Streptococcus agalactiae* (group B). Antimicrob. Agents Chemother. **18:**753–760.
3. **Canosi, U., A. Iglesias, and T. A. Trautner.** 1981. Plasmid transformation in *Bacillus subtilis*: effects of insertion of *Bacillus subtilis* DNA into plasmid pC194. Mol. Gen. Genet. **181:**434–440.
4. **Contente, S., and D. Dubnau.** 1979. Marker rescue transformation by linear plasmid DNA in *Bacillus subtilis*. Plasmid **2:**555–571.
5. **Hotchkiss, R. D., and A. H. Evans.** 1958. Analysis of the complex sulfonamide resistance locus of pneumococcus. Cold Spring Harbor Symp. Quant. Biol. **23:**85–97.
6. **Lacks, S. A.** 1966. Integration efficiency and genetic recombination in pneumococcal transformation. Genetics **53:**207–235.
7. **Lacks, S. A.** 1968. Genetic regulation of maltosaccharide utilization in pneumococcus. Genetics **60:**685–706.
8. **Lacks, S. A.** 1977. Binding and entry of DNA in bacterial transformation, p. 179–232. *In* J. Reissig (ed.), Microbial interactions. Chapman and Hall, London.
8a. **Lopez, P., M. Espinosa, D. L. Stassi, and S. A. Lacks.** 1982. Facilitation of plasmid transfer in *Streptococcus pneumoniae* by chromosomal homology. J. Bacteriol. **150:**692–701.
9. **Lopez, P., D. L. Stassi, M. Espinosa, and S. A. Lacks.** 1982. Comparison of plasmid transformation and the cloning of recombinant DNA in *Streptococcus pneumoniae* and *Bacillus subtilis*, p. 247–259. *In* U. Streips, S. Goodgal, W. Guild, and G. Wilson (ed.), Genetic exchange. Marcel Dekker, New York.
10. **Saunders, C. W. and W. R. Guild.** 1980. Properties and transforming activities of two plasmids in *Streptococcus pneumoniae*. Mol. Gen. Genet. **180:**573–578.
11. **Saunders, C. W., and W. R. Guild.** 1981. Monomer plasmid DNA transforms *Streptococcus pneumoniae*. Mol. Gen. Genet. **181:**57–62.
12. **Smith, M. D., N. B. Shoemaker, V. Burdett, and W. R. Guild.** 1980. Transfer of plasmids by conjugation in *Streptococcus pneumoniae*. Plasmid **3:**70–79.
13. **Stassi, D. L., P. Lopez, M. Espinosa, and S. A. Lacks.** 1981. Cloning of chromosomal genes in *Streptococcus pneumoniae*. Proc. Natl. Acad. Sci. U.S.A. **78:**7028–7032.
14. **Stassi, D. L., P. Lopez, M. Espinosa, and S. A. Lacks.** 1982. Characterization of *mal* recombinant plasmids cloned in *S. pneumoniae*, p. 235–246. *In* U. Streips, S. Goodgal, W. Guild, and G. Wilson (ed.), Genetic exchange. Marcel Dekker, New York.
15. **Vasseghi, H., J. P. Claverys, and A. M. Sicard.** 1981. Mechanism of integrating foreign DNA during transformation in *Streptococcus pneumoniae*, p. 137–154. *In* M. Polsinelli (ed.), Transformation 1980. Cotswold Press, Oxford.
16. **Weinrauch, Y., and S. A. Lacks.** 1981. Nonsense mutations in the amylomaltase gene and other loci of *Streptococcus pneumoniae*. Mol. Gen. Genet. **183:**7–12.

Transformation, a Factor of Significance for the Genetic Flexibility of Oral *Streptococcus sanguis*

GUDRUN WESTERGREN

Department of Cariology, Faculty of Odontology, University of Göteborg, Göteborg, Sweden

Streptococcus sanguis is one of the predominant streptococci in human dental plaque. It is believed to have low cariogenic potential, whereas *Streptococcus mutans*, another member of the viridans group, is considered to play an important role in the development of caries (3, 4, 7).

A clinical study revealed that a considerable proportion of oral *S. sanguis* strains are transformable (11). The transformation marker in this study was chromosomally encoded streptomycin resistance, but recently some of these clinical isolates were also transformed to erythromycin resistance (unpublished data) by the erythromycin/lincomycin resistance streptococcal plasmid pSM7 (6). It would, however, be of interest to know whether other phenotypic traits associated with virulence can be acquired by competent strains of *S. sanguis* by transformation.

A previous study showed that DNA isolated from a rough variant of *S. sanguis* transformed smooth transformable strains of *S. sanguis* into variants with rough colonial morphology (Fig. 1A). The rough variant showed increased adherence ability, and this property was concomitantly transferred (11). As the initial bacterial adherence is of decisive importance for host-microbe interactions (2), this is of clinical significance. Another atypical colonial variant of the same *S. sanguis* strain formed flat, soft colonies on mitis-salivarius agar and was found to have impaired ability to synthesize extracellular polysaccharides from sucrose (Fig. 1b). This defective variant was transformed to the typical original colonial morphology (raised and firm colonies on mitis-salivarius agar) by DNA from various *S. sanguis* donors. The transformants had regained their ability to produce extracellular polysaccharides (unpublished data).

Further, Westergren and Emilson have demonstrated that resistance to chlorhexidine can be developed in vitro and subsequently transferred to originally sensitive strains of *S. sanguis* by transformation (Table 1; 11). Also, this observation is of clinical interest as this antibacterial agent has been widely used against plaque formation (5) and for elimination of *S. mutans* in caries prevention (I. Zickert, C.-G. Emilson, and B. Krasse, J. Dent. Res. Spec. Issue A **60**:363, abstr. 209, 1981).

Frequent exposure of the mouth to sorbitol (D-glucitol) induces increased acid production from this sugar alcohol in dental plaque (1). Various mechanisms have been suggested. Recently, it was shown that sorbitol-nonfermenting (Srl⁻) strains of *S. sanguis* could be transformed

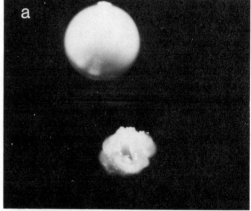
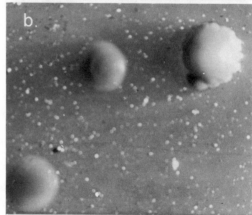

FIG. 1. Colonial variants of an oral *S. sanguis* strain on blood agar (a) and on mitis-salivarius agar (b).

TABLE 1. Transformation of the sensitive *S. sanguis* strains G26-S, BK1, and Challis to chlorhexidine resistance

Donor strain	No. of transformants on blood agar plates containing 64 μg of chlorhexidine/ml divided by total no. of viable cells		
	G26-S	BK1	Challis
G26-S (Chx^r)	0.05×10^{-5}	0.5×10^{-4}	0.78×10^{-6}
BK1 (Chx^r)	$<10^{-6}$	0.12×10^{-5}	$<10^{-6}$
ATCC 10558 (Chx^r)	$<10^{-6}$	0.02×10^{-5}	0.6×10^{-6}
Challis-1 (Chx^{r-32})[a]	$<10^{-6}$	0.11×10^{-3}	0.14×10^{-3}
Control	$<10^{-6}$	$<10^{-6}$	$<10^{-6}$

[a] Challis transformant isolated from blood agar containing 32 μg of chlorhexidine per ml of agar. Donor of DNA was G26-S (Chx^r).

TABLE 2. Transformation of *S. sanguis* to Srl$^+$ (number of positive tubes/number of tested tubes, pooled results)[a]

Donor species	Recipient strains of *S. sanguis*		
	Challis	BK1	G26-S
S. sanguis (4 strains)	33/35	10/30	29/30
S. mitior (1 strain)	5/5	0/10	3/5
S. salivarius (1 strain)	0/10	0/10	0/10
S. mutans (2 strains)	0/20	0/20	0/20
Lactobacillus (3 strains)	0/30	0/30	0/30
Control	1/50	0/50	0/50

[a] A series of tubes containing phenol red broth plus 1% sorbitol were inoculated with the transformation reaction mixture. A change in the color of the indicator from red to yellow was recorded as a positive result.

into ability to metabolize sorbitol by exposing them to DNA from sorbitol-fermenting (Srl$^+$) strains of *S. sanguis* and *S. mitior* (Table 2; 11). These findings indicate that genetic transformation could contribute to enhanced fermentability of sorbitol by the oral microflora.

The results from these various studies show that properties, other than resistance to antibiotics, can be transferred to transformable strains of *S. sanguis*, thus indicating that genetic exchange by transformation could be a factor of significance for the flexibility of oral *S. sanguis* and, consequently, also for the ecological balance in dental plaque.

LITERATURE CITED

1. **Birkhed, D., S. Edwardsson, B. Svensson, F. Moskowitz, and G. Frostell.** 1978. Acid production from sorbitol in human dental plaque. Arch. Oral Biol. 23:971–975.
2. **Gibbons, R. J.** 1977. Adherence of bacteria to host tissue, p. 395–406. *In* D. Schlessinger (ed.), Microbiology—1977. American Society for Microbiology, Washington, D.C.
3. **Hamada, S., and H. D. Slade.** 1980. Biology, immunology and cariogenicity of *Streptococcus mutans*. Microbiol. Rev. 44:331–384.
4. **Krasse, B.** 1976. Approaches to prevention, p. 867–878. *In* H. M. Stiles, W. J. Loesche, and T. C. O'Brien (ed.), Proceedings: Microbial Aspects of Dental Caries (a special supplement to Microbiology Abstracts), vol. 3. Information Retrieval Inc., Washington, D.C.
5. **Löe, H., and C. R. Schiött.** 1970. The effect of mouthrinses and topical application of chlorhexidine on the development of dental plaque and gingivitis in man. J. Periodontal Res. 5:79–83.
6. **Malke, H.** 1981. Deletion analysis of the streptococcal plasmid cloning vehicle pSM10. FEMS Microbiol. Lett. 11:27–30.
7. **van Houte, J.** 1980. Bacterial specificity in the etiology of dental caries. Int. Dent. J. 30:305–326.
8. **Westergren, G.** 1978. Transformation of *Streptococcus sanguis* to a rough colonial morphology with an increased ability to adhere. Arch. Oral Biol. 23:887–891.
9. **Westergren, G., and C.-G. Emilson.** 1977. Transformation of streptococci to streptomycin resistance by oral streptococcal DNA. Arch. Oral. Biol. 22:533–537.
10. **Westergren, G., and C.-G. Emilson.** 1979. *In vitro* development of chlorhexidine resistance in *Streptococcus sanguis* and its transmissibility by genetic transformation. Scand. J. Dent. Res. 88:236–243.
11. **Westergren, G., B. Krasse, D. Birkhed, and S. Edwardsson.** 1981. Genetic transfer of markers for sorbitol (D-glucitol) metabolism in oral streptococci. Arch. Oral Biol. 26:403–407

Competence for Transformation in *Streptococcus pneumoniae*: an Inducible High-Capacity System for Genetic Exchange

D. A. MORRISON, B. MANNARELLI, AND M. N. VIJAYAKUMAR

Department of Biological Sciences, University of Illinois, Chicago, Illinois 60680

One of the oldest and one of the most important tools available in streptococcal genetics is genetic transformation (1). Yet, the physiological status of the state of competence for transformation, as seen among naturally transformable species of bacteria, has remained obscure. Several factors have contributed to this obscurity. First, the conditions of culture governing competence are complex and poorly understood. Second, competence often occurs concomitantly with changes in culture nutritional conditions, so that effects or requirements specific to competence cannot readily be identified. Third, competence may be limited to a minority of the cells in a culture. Finally, it has not been clear whether competence reflects anything more than the appearance of an ability to absorb DNA, i.e., whether the processing of DNA after uptake reflects the fate of single-strand DNA fragments in cells at any stage or is specific to competence.

The genetic transformation system of the streptococci, as seen in *S. pneumoniae* and *S. sanguis*, presents perhaps fewer of these technical problems than those of other species. In cultures of these two species, competence occurs during exponential growth, often far from any known limiting nutritional conditions (24). Competence typically occurs in all cells of a competent culture at once (4, 16). Furthermore, the timing of competence is known to be controlled by an excreted protein, the "competence factor," which apparently acts as a population density monitor, inducing competence at a specific cell density during culture growth (15, 21, 24, 25) and permitting manipulation of competence with unusual facility.

The response of streptococcal cells to competence factor was shown by Tomasz to be dependent on protein synthesis (23). The nature of the response, however, remained vague until two groups undertook examination of the proteins synthesized by cells during the response to competence factor. Both investigations began with observations of unusual physical properties of DNA in the intermediate single-strand state ("eclipse" [2]) after uptake but before integra-

tion into the resident chromosome (6, 7, 17). These studies, proceeding along parallel lines for the *S. pneumoniae* (8–11, M. F. Baker, M.S. thesis, University of Illinois, Chicago, 1979) and the *S. sanguis* systems (18, 19), have developed a picture of competence as a temporary differentiation in which a few proteins are made in rather large quantities just at competence.

ECLIPSE COMPLEX

In a study of the processing of DNA by competent *S. pneumoniae* cells, we had found that the single strands of donor DNA generated during uptake formed part of a complex with unusual properties, including resistance to nuclease digestion, a lower buoyant density, and unique chromatographic behavior (6). We found that this eclipse complex contained a protein with a molecular weight of 19,000 (11) and examined its synthesis by pulse-labeling studies of cultures near competence (10; Baker, thesis). It was clear that the eclipse complex protein was made at competence, but not at other times in culture growth (8, 10).

The role of eclipse complex in recombination remains to be elucidated, although a high resistance to nuclease attack (12) suggests that such protection could be one in vivo role, and it is clear that DNA in eclipse complex does participate in recombination (M. N. Vijayakumar and D. A. Morrison, in preparation). However, the specific synthesis of the protein component of eclipse complex at competence may presumably be taken as an indication of an important role for this complex in transformation.

COMPETENCE-SPECIFIC PROTEINS

Our pulse-labeling experiments also revealed an unexpected phenomenon associated with competence: an abrupt and dramatic change in the pattern of proteins synthesized by a culture whenever it passed into the competent state (Baker, thesis). In what can best be described as a temporary differentiation event, the whole culture reduces synthesis of most protein products and makes a small array of proteins during competence (8–10; Baker, thesis), reversing the change as competence is lost. Controls show this not to be an isolation artifact arising from the fragility (5, 20) of competent cells, but a genuine global alteration in the pattern of protein synthesis (8). The proteins made at competence are not all synchronously induced.

Two-dimensional electrophoresis has shown that at least 16 of the polypeptides made at competence are new; i.e., they are not made during precompetent growth. Some others appear to be made by competent and noncompetent cells alike (8). Physical studies have already shown that the prominent competence proteins form parts of at least seven different native protein species.

Two of the prominent competence proteins have been implicated in the transformation process. The most prominent single band (molecular weight, 19,000) seen on sodium dodecyl sulfate-polyacrylamide gels has been shown to contain the eclipse complex protein (Baker, thesis). It has also been purified to radiochemical homogeneity (B. Mannarelli and D. A. Morrison, in preparation) and characterized as a DNA-binding protein of native molecular weight about 110,000 (Vijayakumar, unpublished data). A second, larger, polypeptide has, in addition, recently (9) been tentatively identified as possessing a role in transformation through mutant studies, as described below.

METABOLIC INTERRUPTION

In the light of these recent results, it is interesting to recall additional features of competent pneumococci that have been reported previously, some or all of which may be secondary effects of a major redirection of cell metabolism for transformation, arising as cells temporarily devote most of their ribosomal capacity to making an apparatus for transformation. These include: (i) a new surface antigen (13); (ii) an altered cell wall structure, as revealed by electron microscopy and by exposure of a new agglutinin (26); (iii) susceptibility of competent cells to autolysis when incubated in certain buffer systems (5, 20); (iv) a reduction of lysine incorporation at competence, apparently representing an interruption of cell wall synthesis (3); (v) release of DNA into the culture medium (14); and (vi) a special significance of choline in cell walls for competence development (22, 27).

COMPETENCE-DEFECTIVE MUTANTS

We have begun a screen of transformation-defective mutants to identify and examine those which exhibit a normal competence cycle and normal DNA uptake but fail to form recombinants. Among these we are searching for changes in structure of competence-specific proteins, to identify those essential for transformation. One mutation abolishing integration but not uptake of donor DNA has recently been identified with a shift of isoelectric point in one of the prominent proteins made at competence (molecular weight of about 50,000) (9). Further studies on competence-defective mutants will clearly be valuable.

DISCUSSION

In summary, observations obtained with *S. pneumoniae* and with *S. sanguis* each lead us to the hypothesis that the gross change in synthetic pattern at competence reflects the production of large quantities of proteins needed for extensive genetic recombination. Evidence linking these competence-specific proteins to transformation is mostly circumstantial. Two proteins in each species, however, are directly implicated: one by being bound to DNA in eclipse, the other by association with a Com⁻ mutation (9). The others are certainly prime candidates for roles in transformation, and their study is a promising avenue of approach to the mechanisms of this system of genetic exchange.

We suggest that competence for transformation in the streptococci represents an interruption in the normal metabolic life of the cell at least as significant as that occasioned by bacterial conjugation. It appears to be unique in that the entire metabolism is altered so as to provide the machinery for exchange of massive amounts of DNA, as up to 10% of the chromosome may be replaced, in scores of segments, all of this being accomplished in a small fraction of one generation time.

ACKNOWLEDGMENTS

Work of this laboratory reported here was supported in part by grants from the National Institutes of Health and the National Science Foundation.

LITERATURE CITED

1. **Avery, O., and M. McCarty.** 1944. Studies on the chemical nature of the substance inducing transformation of pneumococcal types. Induction of transformation by a DNA fraction isolated from pneumococcus type III. J. Exp. Med. **79**:147–168.
2. **Ephrussi-Taylor, H.** 1960. L'état du DNA transformant au cours des premières phases de la transformation bactérienne. C.R. Seances Soc. Biol. Paris **154**:1951–1955.
3. **Ephrussi-Taylor, H., and B. A. Freed.** 1964. Incorporation of thymidine and amino acids into deoxyribonucleic acid and acid-insoluble cell structures in pneumococcal cultures synchronized for competence to transform. J. Bacteriol. **87**:1211–1215.
4. **Javor, G., and A. Tomasz.** 1968. An autoradiographic study of genetic transformation. Proc. Natl. Acad. Sci. U.S.A. **60**:1216–1222.

5. **Lacks, S., and M. Neuberger.** 1975. Membrane location of a deoxyribonuclease implicated in the genetic transformation of *Diplococcus pneumoniae*. J. Bacteriol. **124:**1321–1329.

6. **Morrison, D. A.** 1977. Transformation in pneumococcus: existence and properties of a complex involving donor deoxyribonucleate single strands in eclipse. J Bacteriol. **132:**576–583.

7. **Morrison, D. A.** 1978. Transformation in pneumococcus: protein content of eclipse complex. J. Bacteriol. **136:**548–557.

8. **Morrison, D. A.** 1981. Competence-specific protein synthesis in *Streptococcus pneumoniae*, p. 39–53. *In* M. Polsinelli and G. Mazza (ed.), Transformation—1980, Proceedings of the 5th European Meeting on Bacterial Transformation and Transfection, Florence, Italy. Cotswold Press Ltd., Oxford.

9. **Morrison, D. A.** 1981. Competence-specific proteins in transformation-deficient mutants of *Streptococcus pneumoniae*, p. 171–177. *In* U. Streips (ed.), Genetic exchange: a celebration and a new generation. Marcel Dekker, New York.

10. **Morrison, D. A., and M. Baker.** 1979. Competence for genetic transformation in pneumococcus depends on synthesis of a small set of proteins. Nature (London) **282:**215–217.

11. **Morrison, D. A., M. Baker, and B. Mannarelli.** 1979. A protein component of the pneumococcal eclipse complex, p. 43–52. *In* S. W. Glover and L. O. Butler (ed.), Transformation—1978, Proceedings of the 4th European Meeting on Bacterial Transformation and Transfection, York, England. Cotswold Press Ltd., Oxford.

12. **Morrison, D. A., and B. Mannarelli.** 1979. Transformation in pneumococcus: nuclease resistance of deoxyribonucleic acid in the eclipse complex. J. Bacteriol. **140:**655–665.

13. **Nava, G., A. Galis, and S. M. Beiser.** 1963. Bacterial transformation: an antigen specific for "competent" pneumococci. Nature (London) **197:**903–904.

14. **Ottolenghi, E., and R. D. Hotchkiss.** 1962. Release of genetic transforming agent from pneumococcal cultures during growth and disintegration. J. Exp. Med. **116:**491–519.

15. **Pakula, R., and W. Walczak.** 1963. On the nature of competence of transformable streptococci. J. Gen. Microbiol. **31:**125–133.

16. **Porter, R. D., and W. R. Guild.** 1969. Number of transformable units per cell in *Diplococcus pneumoniae*. J. Bacteriol. **97:**1033–1035.

17. **Raina, J., and A. Ravin.** 1978. Fate of homospecific transforming DNA bound to *Streptococcus sanguis*. J. Bacteriol. **133:**1212–1223.

18. **Raina, J., and A. Ravin.** 1980. Presynaptic donor DNA-protein complexes in transformation of *Streptococcus sanguis*: identification of the protein component. Biochem. Biophys. Res. Commun. **93:**228–234.

19. **Raina, J., and A. Ravin.** 1980. Switches in macromolecular synthesis during induction of competence for transformation of *Streptococcus sanguis*. Proc. Natl. Acad. Sci. U.S.A. **77:**6062–6066.

20. **Seto, H., and A. Tomasz.** 1975. Protoplast formation and leakage of intramembrane cell components: induction by the competence activator substance of pneumococci. J. Bacteriol. **121:**344–353.

21. **Tomasz, A.** 1966. Model for the mechanism controlling the expression of the competent state in pneumococcus cultures. J. Bacteriol. **91:**1050–1061.

22. **Tomasz, A.** 1968. Biological consequences of the replacement of choline by ethanolamine in the cell wall of pneumococcus: chain formation, loss of transformability, and loss of autolysis. Proc. Natl. Acad. Sci. U.S.A. **59:**86–93.

23. **Tomasz, A.** 1970. Cellular metabolism in genetic transformation of pneumococci: requirement for protein synthesis during induction of competence. J. Bacteriol. **101:**860–871.

24. **Tomasz, A., and R. Hotchkiss.** 1964. Regulation of the transformability of pneumococcal cultures by macromolecular cell products. Proc. Natl. Acad. Sci. U.S.A. **51:**480–487.

25. **Tomasz, A., and J. Mosser.** 1966. On the nature of the pneumococcal activator substance. Proc. Natl. Acad. Sci. U.S.A. **55:**58–66.

26. **Tomasz, A., and E. Zanati.** 1971. Appearance of a protein "agglutinin" on the spheroplast membrane of pneumococci during induction of competence. J. Bacteriol. **105:**1213–1215.

27. **Tomasz, A., E. Zanati, and R. Ziegler.** 1971. DNA uptake during genetic transformation and the growing zone of the cell envelope. Proc. Natl. Acad. Sci. U.S.A. **68:**1848–1852.

Plasmid-Mediated Transformation of *Streptococcus mutans*

H. K. KURAMITSU AND C. M. LONG

Department of Microbiology-Immunology, Northwestern University Medical-Dental Schools, Chicago, Illinois 60611

Streptococcus mutans appears to play a significant role in the development of human dental caries (1). Despite the rapid accumulation of information regarding the potential cariogenic properties of this organism over the past few years (2), it has not been possible to extend these investigations by using genetic approaches. However, recent information from several laboratories suggests that it may now be possible to carry out genetic analysis of *S. mutans* cariogenicity. LeBlanc et al. (3) demonstrated the transfer of plasmid pAMβ$_1$ from a group F streptococcus species to *S. mutans* by a process resembling conjugation. More recently, Perry and Kuramitsu (7) reported the transformation of selected strains of *S. mutans* by homologous and heterologous DNA. The present report demonstrates that these same species of *S. mutans* are transformable with streptococcal plasmids capable of functioning as potential cloning vectors.

The bacterial strains as well as the transformation protocol utilized in the present investigation have been recently described (7). Plasmid pVA736, constructed by ligating an erythromycin resistance (Ery^r) coding fragment from plasmid pVA1 with naturally occurring *S. ferus* plasmid pVA380-1 (5), was isolated and purified from *S. sanguis* Challis V736 as previously described (5). Plasmid pVA1 was isolated by the same procedure from *S. sanguis* Challis V486. Both plasmid-bearing strains were obtained from F. L. Macrina (Virginia Commonwealth University, Richmond). Transformation frequencies were determined by scoring appropriate samples on brain heart infusion agar (Difco Laboratories) containing erythromycin (10 μg/ml) after anaerobic incubation for 48 h at 37°C.

When *S. mutans* GS-5 was exposed to plasmid pVA736 purified from strain Challis, a significant number of cells were transformed to Ery^r (Table 1). Since it may be possible that restriction-modification systems present in strain GS-5 could affect the expression of the Ery^r marker contained on the Challis plasmid, it was of interest to reisolate the plasmid from pVA736-transformed GS-5 cells for use in subsequent

TABLE 1. Plasmid pVA736-mediated transformation of *S. mutans* GS-5[a]

Plasmid	Source	No. of Ery^r transformants per 10^7 CFU[c]
pVA736	*S. sanguis* (Challis)	6
pVA736[b]	*S. mutans* GS-5	201

[a] *S. mutans* GS-5 was grown to optimal competence (5 h) and transformed as previously described (7) with plasmid DNA (approximately 0.7 μg).

[b] Plasmid extracted from *S. mutans* GS-5 cells previously transformed to erythromycin resistance by plasmid pVA736 (Challis).

[c] Control incubations in the absence of plasmid DNA yielded no spontaneous erythromycin-resistant colonies. Transformants represent the average of duplicate plates. CFU, Colony-forming units.

transformations. A comparison of the transformation rates obtained with Challis and GS-5–derived plasmid pVA736 demonstrated that the latter plasmid produced higher transformation frequencies in strain GS-5 (Table 1). Agarose gel electrophoresis of cleared lysates of transformed GS-5 cells revealed the presence of a plasmid DNA band which comigrated with purified pVA736 (data not shown). These results suggest that the plasmid is incorporated intact into GS-5 or that only small deletions occur. The plasmid is also stably maintained in strain GS-5 since Ery^r transformants remain resistant to the antibiotic when grown in the absence of erythromycin. Another streptococcal plasmid coding for erythromycin resistance, pVA1 (6), could also transform GS-5. In addition, pVA736 successfully transformed *S. mutans* strains MT557, HS-6, and V318 (4), but not strains LM-7 and 6715.

The ability to transform *S. mutans* with plasmid pVA736, originally constructed as a potential streptococcal cloning vector (5), suggests that it may be possible to develop an *S. mutans* cloning system. Such a system could prove useful in directly testing the biological properties of *S. mutans* gene fragments isolated in heterologous systems after incorporation of the genes into plasmid pVA736 or other suitable streptococcal cloning vectors.

ACKNOWLEDGMENT

This investigation was supported by Public Health Service grant DE-03258 from the National Institute of Dental Research.

LITERATURE CITED

1. **Gibbons, R. J., and J. van Houte.** 1975. Dental caries. Annu. Rev. Med. **26:**121–136.
2. **Hamada, S., and H. D. Slade.** 1980. Biology, immunology, and cariogenicity of *Streptococcus mutans.* Microbiol. Rev. **44:**331–384.
3. **LeBlanc, D. J., R. J. Hawley, L. N. Lee, and E. J. St. Martin.** 1978. "Conjugal" transfer of plasmid DNA among oral streptococcal. Proc. Natl. Acad. Sci. U.S.A. **75:**3484–3487.
4. **Macrina, F. L., J. L. Reider, S. S. Virgili, and D. J. Kopecko.** 1977. Survey of the extrachromosomal gene pool of *Streptococcus mutans.* Infect. Immun. **17:**215–226.
5. **Macrina, F. L., K. R. Jones, and P. H. Wood.** 1980. Chimeric streptococcal plasmids and their use as molecular cloning vehicles in *Streptococcus sanguis* (Challis). J. Bacteriol. **143:**1425–1435.
6. **Macrina, F. L., C. L. Keeler, K. R. Jones, and P. H. Wood.** 1980. Molecular characterization of unique deletion mutants of the streptococcal plasmid, pAMβ₁. Plasmid **4:**8–16.
7. **Perry, D., and H. K. Kuramitsu.** 1981. Genetic transformation of *Streptococcus mutans.* Infect. Immun. **32:**1295–1297.

Genetics and Biology of Pneumococcal Phages

R. LÓPEZ, P. GARCÍA, C. RONDA, AND E. GARCÍA

Instituto de Inmunologia y Biologia Microbiana (Consejo Superior de Investigaciones Cientificas), Velazquez, 144, Madrid, 6, Spain

The study of streptococcal bacteriophages has been hampered by several types of technical problems, such as the complex growth requirements of the bacterial hosts and the need of special media for good plaque formation, as well as the small burst size of the infected culture (3). Although some of these problems have been overcome, at present relatively little is known about the biophysical properties of streptococcal phage particles and their macromolecular components, with the exception of the temperate phage ϕ227 (10). *Streptococcus pneumoniae* would probably share with other streptococci many of the difficulties pointed out above for the isolation of bacteriophages. In fact, pneumococcal phages were not isolated until recently by two independent groups (9, 16). Since then, lytic and temperate phages have been isolated from a wide variety of geographical locales (2, 11, 12, 15), and indeed, pneumococcal phages seem to be of widespread occurrence. We have isolated and characterized several pneumococcal phages (Dp-1, Dp-4, and Cp-1), and these phages have proved to be an interesting tool for gaining information about the host bacterium, *S. pneumoniae*. This paper illustrates some of the ongoing studies with the pneumococcal bacteriophages.

CHARACTERISTICS OF SOME PNEUMOCOCCAL PHAGES AND THEIR MACROMOLECULAR COMPONENTS

Dp-1 has turned out to be the first lipid-containing phage with a gram-positive host (8). Thin-layer chromatography of lipid extracted shows the presence of neutral lipid, cardiolipin, and, in small proportion, phosphatidylethanolamine (7). Dp-1 and Dp-4 show similar morphology, with a polyhedral head and a long noncontractile tail without collar or appendages, a morphology that closely resembles that of most streptococcal phages. In contrast, the morphology of Cp-1 is entirely different: a short-tailed particle with a flattened base, neck appendages, and head projections, a structure that resembles *B. subtilis* phage ϕ29. Figure 1 shows the appearance of Dp-4 and Cp-1, and Table 1 compares various properties, as well as the characteristics of their macromolecular components (4, 5, 7, 12, 13, 15).

BACTERIOPHAGE RECEPTORS

The importance of the choline residues in the pneumococcal wall teichoic acid has been previously investigated. The biosynthetic replacement of choline by certain analogs (e.g., ethanolamine) results in important biochemical and physiological changes in a series of properties involving the cell surface (18). The role of the choline residues in Dp-1 adsorption has been previously pointed out (7, 9). The affinity of phage Dp-1 for choline residues has been used to demonstrate the incorporation and distribution of newly synthesized molecules of the teichoic acid-peptidoglycan complex into the cell wall of pneumococci (unpublished data). In short, ethanolamine-grown bacteria received a very small amount of choline; upon further incubation, the bacteria depleted the choline in the medium and returned to the utilization of ethanolamine in the growth medium (18). When phages were added to this culture at different times after the addition of the minipulse of choline, the phages were adsorbed exclusively at distinct zones, the position of which occupied the sites where the choline-containing cell wall teichoic acid residues are expected to be localized on the basis of the equatorial growth zone and conservative wall segregation model for pneumococci (1, 17, 18) (Fig. 2). Attempts to characterize the phage receptors in detail are in progress.

TRANSFECTION WITH Dp-4 DNA AND REPLICATION OF Dp-4 IN *S. PNEUMONIAE*

We have developed a transfection system in pneumococci, using mature phage DNA. In this system, both binding and uptake of phage DNA were stimulated by the presence of calcium ions (13). The use of *p*-hydroxyphenylazouracil has permitted us to carry out a detailed study of the infectious process (5, 6). We found a rapidly sedimenting complex in detergent lysates of bacteriophage Dp-4–infected cells by sedimenta-

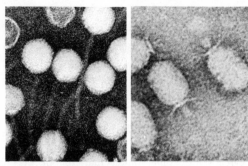

FIG. 1. Electron micrographs of mature phages Dp-4 (left) and Cp-1 (right).

tion in neutral sucrose gradients (5). This complex could be "chased" first into free DNA and subsequently into mature phage particles. This intermediate, which incorporated most of the radioactivity during a short pulse of [³H]thymidine, represents the replicating phage DNA attached to some other constituent of the infected cell.

LIBERATION OF THE PHAGE PROGENY

The involvement of the host autolytic system in the liberation of the progeny of Dp-1 phage to the medium has been suggested (7, 14). A variety of conditions that block the normal activity of the pneumococcal autolysin also blocked the liberation of the phage progeny (i.e., low pH, Forssman antigen, etc.). In contrast to the wild type, a lysis-defective mutant (defective in the murein hydrolase) would lyse only if infected at a multiplicity of infection (MOI) higher than 1. At low MOI, infection resulted in culture lysis provided that the bacteria were "coated" with wild-type autolysin (19) prior to phage infection (7). Nevertheless, the nature of the factor(s) involved in the liberation of phages at high MOI in the mutant (Cw-1) is under intensive investigation in our laboratory. Cw-1 labeled with [*methyl*-³H]choline and infected at high MOI was found to release most of the macromolecular choline-labeled material into the culture medium. This release was blocked in the presence of inhibitors of protein synthesis (e.g., streptomycin), suggesting de novo synthesis of a pro-

TABLE 1. Biophysical characteristics of Dp-4 and Cp-1

Characteristic	Measurement	
	Dp-4	Cp-1
Virion		
Particle density (g/cm³)	1.48	1.46
Diameter (nm)	60	60 by 45
Tail length (nm)	155	20
Appendages and fibers	No	Yes
Number of structural proteins	5	9
Presence of "envelope"	No	No
DNA		
Type	Linear duplex	Linear duplex
Contour length (μm)	17.5 ± 3	6.3 ± 0.3
Sedimentation coefficient ($S_{20,w}$)	ND[a]	19S
T_m (°C)	83.5	87
Guanine plus cytosine content (%)	33	41
Molecular weight (megadaltons)	37	12
Buoyant density (g/cm³)		
Neutral CsCl (native)	1.666	1.699
Neutral CsCl (heat denatured)	$\begin{cases}1.677\\1.692\end{cases}$	1.717
Cs₂SO₄	1.410	1.422
Transfection	Yes	Yes (?)
Restriction endonucleases		
Sensitive to (number of fragments)	*Alu*I (15)	*Alu*I (12)
	*Hae*II (ND)	*Hind*III (2)
		*Hae*III (2)
Resistant to	—[b]	—[c]

[a] ND, Not determined.
[b] *Dpn*I, *Dpn*II, *Hae*III, *Eco*RI, *Hind*III, *Pst*I, *Xba*I, *Mbo*I, *Bgl*II, *Sma*I, *Sal*I, *Bam*HI, *Hpa*II, *Hin*II.
[c] *Pst*I, *Xba*I, *Bgl*II, *Eco*RI, *Sal*I, *Mbo*I, *Sma*I, *Dpn*I, *Dpn*II, *Bam*HI, *Pst*I.

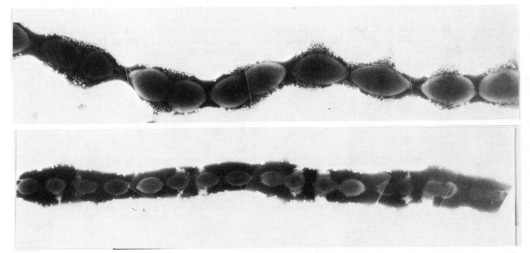

FIG. 2. Electron micrograph showing location of phage particles adsorbed to ethanolamine-grown cells minipulsed with choline. A culture of pneumococci growing at 37°C in ethanolamine-containing medium (40 μg/ml), received a "minipulse" (0.08 μg/ml) of choline at zero time, and incubation was continued for 5 min. At different times, samples were taken and incubated with purified bacteriophage Dp-1 (MOI, 100) at 4°C for 45 min. The samples were centrifuged and washed at 4°C (10,000 × g) and were prepared for electron microscopy. The figure shows the location of the phage particles when Dp-1 was added 5 min (top) or 45 min (bottom) (about one generation time) after the addition of choline.

tein(s). We have also detected this activity in vitro on choline-labeled cell walls, using lysates from such infected cultures of pneumococci. The activity was not inhibited by an antiserum prepared in our laboratory against the murein hydrolase present in the wild-type pneumococci (unpublished data). Experiments in progress show that this lytic activity is stimulated both in vivo and in vitro by the presence of reducing agents (2-mercaptoethanol, DDT, etc.) in a way similar to that with C phage-associated lysin of group C *Streptococcus* (2). In our case this lytic activity does not seem to be associated with the phage particles. The results suggest that more than one lytic activity (at least two) may be involved in the liberation of the phage progeny.

LITERATURE CITED

1. **Barak-Briles, E., and A. Tomasz.** 1970. Radioautographic evidence for equatorial wall growth in a Gram positive bacterium: segregation of H³-choline labeled teichoic acid. J. Cell Biol. **47:**786–790.
2. **Bernheimer, H. P.** 1979. Lysogenic pneumococci and their bacteriophages. J. Bacteriol. **138:**618–624.
3. **Fischetti, V. A., T. C. Gotschlich, and A. W. Bernheimer.** 1971. Purification and physical properties of group C streptococcal phage-associated lysin. J. Exp. Med. **133:**1105–1117.
4. **Garcia, E., C. Ronda, and R. Lopez.** 1979. Bacteriophages of *Streptococcus pneumoniae*: physiochemical properties of bacteriophage Dp-4 and its transfecting DNA. Eur. J. Biochem. **101:**59–64.
5. **Garcia, E., C. Ronda, and R. Lopez.** 1980. Replication of bacteriophage Dp-4 DNA in *Streptococcus pneumoniae*. Virology **105:**405–414.
6. **Lopez, R., E. Garcia, and C. Ronda.** 1980. Selective replication of diplophage Dp-4 deoxyribonucleic acid in 6-(p-hydroxyphenylazo)-uracil treated *Streptococcus pneumoniae*. FEBS Lett. **111:**66–68.
7. **Lopez, R., E. Garcia, and C. Ronda.** 1981. Bacteriophages of pneumococcus. Rev. Infect. Dis. **3:**212–223.
8. **Lopez, R., C. Ronda, A. Tomasz, and A. Portoles.** 1977. Properties of "Diplophage": a lipid-containing bacteriophage. J. Virol. **24:**201–210.
9. **McDonnell, M., C. Ronda, and A. Tomasz.** 1975. "Diplophage": a bacteriophage of *Diplococcus pneumoniae*. Virology **63:**577–582.
10. **Nuget, K. M., and R. M. Cole.** 1977. Characterization of group H streptococcal temperate bacteriophage φ227. J. Virol. **21:**1061–1073.
11. **Porter, D. D., and W. R. Guild.** 1976. Characterization of some pneumococcal phages. J. Virol. **19:**659–664.
12. **Ronda, C., R. López, and E. García.** 1981. Isolation and characterization of a new bacteriophage, Cp-1, infecting *Streptococcus pneumoniae*. J. Virol. **40:**551–559.
13. **Ronda, C., R. Lopez, A. Portoles, and E. Garcia.** 1979. DNA binding and entry during transfection in *Streptococcus pneumoniae*. FEMS Microbiol. Lett. **6:**309–312.
14. **Ronda, C., R. Lopez, A. Tapia, and A. Tomasz.** 1977. Role of the pneumococcal autolysin (Murein hydrolase) in the release of progeny bacteriophage and in the phage-induced lysis of the host cells. J. Virol. **21:**366–374.
15. **Ronda, C., R. Lopez, A. Tomasz, and A. Portoles.** 1978. Transfection of *Streptococcus pneumoniae* with bacteriophage DNA. J. Virol. **26:**221–225.
16. **Tiraby, J. G., E. Tiraby, and M. S. Fox.** 1975. Pneumococcal bacteriophages. Virology **68:**566–569.
17. **Tomasz, A., M. McDonnell, M. Westphal, and E. Zanati.** 1975. Coordinated incorporation of nascent peptidoglycan and teichoic acid into pneumococcal cell walls and con-

servation of peptidoglycan during growth. J. Biol. Chem. **250**:337–341.

18. **Tomasz, A., M. Westphal, E. B. Briles, and P. Fletcher.** 1975. On the physiological functions of teichoic acids. J. Supramol. Struct. **3**:1–16.

19. **Tomasz, A., and S. Waks.** 1975. Enzyme replacement in a bacterium: phenotypic correction by the experimental introduction of the wild type enzyme into a live enzyme defective mutant pneumococcus. Biochem. Biophys. Res. Commun. **65**:1311–1319.

Hyaluronidase Associated with a Temperate Bacteriophage of *Streptococcus equi*

J. F. TIMONEY, LISA PESANTE, AND CYNTHIA ERNST

Department of Microbiology, New York State College of Veterinary Medicine, Cornell University, Ithaca, New York 14853

Streptococcus equi is a heavily encapsulated group C streptococcus that causes strangles, a severe upper respiratory tract disease of horses. Many clinical isolates host one or the other of two serologically different but related groups of temperate bacteriophage that can change colonial morphology from mucoid to matt (Fig. 1), a change previously noted in group A streptococci when hyaluronidase was applied to fully developed mucoid colonies (6). *S. equi*, however, does not produce hyaluronidase (7) and therefore differs from other group C streptococci, which produce large amounts of the enzyme (4).

In the group A streptococci the demonstration (2) of phage-associated hyaluronidases serologically different from the enzyme produced by the host organism prompted us to investigate the possibility that the matt colony of lysogens of *S. equi* was due to phage-associated hyaluronidase. Our studies focused on the detection of hyaluronidase in purified phage suspensions, culture supernatants, and cell extracts of *S. equi* e23 and its lysogenic derivatives. Hyaluronidase was assayed by a modification of the sensitive Stainsol binding assay (1) and by the less sensitive turbidimetric method (3).

PHAGE-ASSOCIATED HYALURONIDASE

Two bacteriophage strains (P9 and P11) were concentrated from lysates of *S. equi* (e23) by

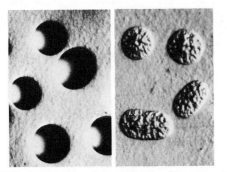

FIG. 1. Mucoid and matt colonies of *S. equi* and its lysogen.

polyethylene glycol to give a concentration of phage of approximately 3×10^9 PFU/ml. Hyaluronidase as assayed by the Stainsol method indicated that each of the phage suspensions contained enzyme activity equivalent to about 2.9 µg of bovine testicular hyaluronidase per 10^4 PFU (Fig. 2).

HYALURONIDASE ACTIVITY OF CULTURE SUPERNATANTS

Supernatants of 18-h cultures in Todd-Hewitt medium of three *S. equi* strains (e23, e80-1, and 35630) and of their lysogenic derivatives were tested for hyaluronidase by the turbidimetric assay. No enzyme activity was detected in any of the supernatants, a result opposite to that observed for a large number of strains of group C streptococci by MacLennan (4), who showed that hyaluronidase was easily detectable by the turbidimetric assay in culture supernatants. Since the sensitivity of the turbidimetric assay is ≥1.3 µg of hyaluronidase per ml, it is clear that the enzyme, if present, must be at very low concentration in culture supernatants of *S. equi*.

HYALURONIDASE ACTIVITY OF CELL EXTRACTS

Cell pellets from 16-h cultures of e23 and its lysogen (P9) were French pressed; the supernatant was saturated to 60% ammonium sulfate, and the precipitate was dissolved in buffer. The solution was then tested for enzyme activity by the Stainsol and turbidimetric assays. Enzyme activity was absent from both e23 and its lysogen. Small amounts (1.25 µg/ml) of bovine testicular hyaluronidase were, however, easily detectable after their addition to the extracts.

EFFECT OF HYALURONIDASE ON COLONY MORPHOLOGY

The addition of bovine testicular hyaluronidase (50 µg/ml) to blood agar resulted in development of glossy colonies by mucoid e23, a result previously noted by Wilson (6) in a similar

145

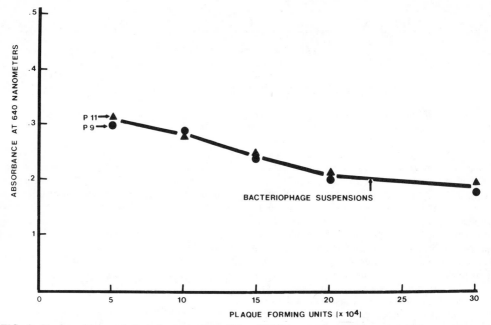

FIG. 2. Hyaluronidase activity in bacteriophage (P9 and P11) suspensions of *S. equi*. Activity was measured by the Stainsol method and was equivalent to that produced by 2.9 μg of bovine testicular hyaluronidase per 10^4 PFU.

experiment on mucoid group A streptococci. When the enzyme was applied to developed mucoid colonies of e23, these colonies collapsed and exhibited a matt texture. This is consistent with the hypothesis that matt colonies are a result of hyaluronidase action late in colony development.

In summary, our observations suggest that hyaluronidase associated with a temperate bacteriophage of *S. equi* is responsible for the matt colony form of the lysogen. The enzyme is not present in detectable amounts in either culture supernatants or extracts of cells of *S. equi*. The phage-associated enzyme of this group C streptococcus is therefore analogous to hyaluronidases similarly associated with group A streptococci (2).

It is probable that the function of the enzyme is to allow the phage to penetrate the capsule of new host cells. It is also probable that the gene(s) controlling synthesis of the enzyme is carried in the phage genome.

LITERATURE CITED

1. **Benchetrit, L. C., S. L. Pahuja, E. D. Gray, and R. D. Edstrom.** 1977. A sensitive method for the assay of hyaluronidase activity. Anal. Biochem. **79**:431–437.
2. **Benchetrit, L. C., L. W. Wannamaker, and E. D. Gray.** 1979. Immunological properties of hyaluronidases associated with temperate bacteriophages of group A streptococci. J. Exp. Med. **149**:73–83.
3. **Faber, V.** 1952. Streptococcal hyaluronidase—review and the turbidimetric method for its determination. Acta Pathol. Microbiol. Scand. **31**:345–350.
4. **McLennan, A. P.** 1956. The production of capsules, hyaluronic acid and hyaluronidase by 25 strains of group C streptococci. J. Gen. Microbiol. **15**:485–491.
5. **Spanier, J., and J. F. Timoney.** 1977. Bacteriophages of *Streptococcus equi*. J. Gen. Virol. **35**:369–375.
6. **Wilson, A.** 1959. The relative importance of the capsule and the M-antigen in determining colony form of group A streptococci. J. Exp. Med. **109**:257–270.
7. **Woolcock, J. B.** 1974. The capsule of *Streptococcus equi*. J. Gen. Microbiol. **85**:372–375.

DRUG RESISTANCE

Occurrence of Antibiotic Resistance in Hemolytic Streptococci

J. M. S. DIXON AND A. EUGENIA LIPINSKI

Provincial Laboratory of Public Health, University of Alberta, Edmonton, Alberta, Canada T6G 2J2

Penicillin is the antibiotic of choice for therapy of infections with group A hemolytic streptococci (*Streptococcus pyogenes*). Thus, it is fortunate that resistance to penicillin has not been reported in a clinical isolate or in strains of many other Lancefield groups of streptococci, a notable exception being enterococci of group D (26), which are not considered here. Resistance of hemolytic streptococci has been reported, however, to antibiotics often chosen as alternatives in patients unable to tolerate penicillin. Group A strains resistant to tetracycline were reported in England in 1954 (18) and in the United States in 1958 (27); to erythromycin in England in 1959 (19), in North America in 1968, the strains also being resistant to lincomycin (7, 31), and in Japan in 1971 (25); and to chloramphenicol in Japan in 1969 (25). Significant multiple resistance has developed: first in the United Kingdom to erythromycin, lincomycin, and tetracycline in 1968 (20), then in Japan to tetracycline and chloramphenicol in 1969, and finally to all four of these agents simultaneously in Japan beginning in 1971 (25).

GROUP A STREPTOCOCCI

Penicillin. We studied 101,590 strains of *S. pyogenes* isolated from clinical specimens in western Canada during 1968–1980. All were susceptible to benzylpenicillin by a 1.6-μg (2-U) disk diffusion test. During 1977–1980, strains were also tested with a 1-μg oxacillin disk, because of its value for detecting low-level penicillin resistance in pneumococci (10), and all strains were susceptible. This is in accord with all other published reports.

Erythromycin and lincosamides. The same 101,590 Canadian strains were tested with erythromycin, and 1,320 (1.3%) were resistant. Annual percentage resistance rates varied from 0.03% in 1968 to 2.9% in 1974. Erythromycin resistance was of two degrees: high, with minimal inhibitory concentrations (MICs) of ≥ 200 μg/ml, or low, with MICs of 0.78 to 3.1 μg/ml (8). Strains

of high erythromycin resistance were also highly lincomycin resistant; strains of low resistance, with very rare exceptions, either were highly lincomycin resistant or exhibited a zonal pattern of lincomycin resistance characterized by growth in subinhibitory concentrations of ≤ 0.05 μg/ml and in the range of 50 to 100 μg/ml but not in intermediate or higher concentrations (8, 9). More than 50% showed the zonal pattern. Zonally resistant strains may be missed in diffusion tests with lincomycin disks, but all are resistant in tests with a 2-μg erythromycin disk, use of which is recommended for their detection. Strains with regular-pattern lincomycin resistance were also clindamycin resistant, whereas many of the zonally resistant strains were susceptible to clindamycin (9).

Erythromycin resistance was detected in a variety of serotypes (Table 1). Types with T-antigen 12 were most common, but many other M and T types occurred, and type distribution differed in 1971–1972 and 1979–1981.

Reports from the United States noted erythromycin resistance rates of 0.5% in 1978 (32) and of 5% in 1980 (14), from France of 0.5 to 2% (13), and from Taiwan of 4.4% in 1975 (33). These are in contrast to experience in Japan, where rates of 15% in 1970–1973 (24) and rates exceeding 60% in 1974–1975 (21, 28) were reported. In Japan, erythromycin resistance was associated with resistance to tetracycline or chloramphenicol, or both, in more than 99% of strains in a 1972–1974 series (25); 97% of these strains were type T12. Zonal-pattern lincomycin resistance has been observed in both Australia (2) and France (13). The importance of incubating broth dilution tests with lincomycin for more than 24 h to ensure detection of zonal resistance was noted (9, 13). Clindamycin resistance has occurred in the United States (11) and has been associated with tetracycline resistance.

Tetracycline. Resistance of group A streptococci to tetracycline has fluctuated widely in time and place since its description in 1954 (18). In one English hospital, the incidence steadily

TABLE 1. Serotypes of group A strains resistant to erythromycin and lincomycin in western Canada

Type		No. of resistant strains	
T	M[a]	1971–1972	1979–1981[b]
2	2; —	3	13
4	4; 63; —	0	45
11	11; —	0	12
12	12	22⎫	17⎫
	22	9⎬ 44	9⎬ 41
	—	13⎭	15⎭
25	—	11	1
55	31	25	0
58	58	27	8
Imp. 19	2; —	9	28
3/13/B3264	33; 56; 80; or —	13	14
Others[c]		18	4

[a] M antigens associated with each T type; only one M antigen was detected in any single strain.
[b] To 30 June 1981.
[c] T antigens 3, 6, 9, 28, and 5/27/44.

increased from 0.4% in 1958 to 44% in 1965 (6) and then declined each year to 28% in 1970 (30). In western Canada we noted resistance in 3.3% of 13,889 strains isolated in 1979–1980, and they were of T-antigen types 6, 9, 11, 12, 14, and 3/13/B3264. The type 14 strains were also resistant to chloramphenicol.

· In 1960–1961, 20% of strains in a New York hospital were resistant, belonging to three T-antigen types (23). In a 1972 Swedish series, 6% were resistant (16). Resistance rates in Japanese reports have been very high: 73% in 1970–1973 (24) and 80% in 1974–1975 (28). In Taiwan over 90% of strains studied in 1975 were resistant (33). There was marked correlation between tetracycline resistance and serotype in Japan; in one study type T4 strains were commonly resistant to tetracycline alone, type T3 strains to tetracycline and chloramphenicol, and type T12 strains to macrolides, tetracycline, and chloramphenicol (25).

Chloramphenicol. Resistance to chloramphenicol has rarely been reported outside Japan, where published rates include 22% in 1970–1973 (24), and 57% (28) and 69% (21) in 1974–1975. Most strains were of type T12 and were also resistant to other antibiotics. In Canada our resistance rate has been less than 0.01%, and the strains have also been resistant to erythromycin.

Multiple resistance. Resistance to macrolides, lincosamides, tetracycline, and chloramphenicol (referred to hereafter as quadruple resistance) has rarely been reported except from Japan. From January 1979 to June 1981, we detected one strain (type M12 T12) with quadruple resist-

ance among 17,711 isolates. In two Japanese series, 51% (28) and 61% (21) showed quadruple resistance in 1974–1975, and almost all were of type T12.

GROUP B STREPTOCOCCI

Penicillin resistance of group B strains has not been reported, but the mean MIC of penicillin (1, 3) and the cephalosporins (5, 20) is higher than for group A strains.

Erythromycin and lincosamides. Erythromycin resistance was recorded in Boston in 4 (2.7%) of 149 group B isolates during 1962–1963 (12). Its prevalence has not changed greatly since then. During 1971–1980, 300 (1.7%) of 17,350 group B strains examined in this laboratory were erythromycin resistant. In a 1971–1973 California study, 1.6% were resistant (3). The Canadian strains were also lincomycin resistant, often with a zonal pattern (9), and the U.S. strains were clindamycin resistant (3). In Texas, 1.2% of 244 strains isolated in 1970–1975 were resistant to lincomycin and clindamycin (4).

Tetracycline. Resistance of group B strains to tetracycline is common. Resistance rates recorded include: in the United States 37% in 1962–1963 (12), 85% in 1971–1973 (3), and 87% in 1976 (4); and in Finland 80% in 1976 (15). Our Canadian experience is a resistance rate of 52.4% in 2,679 strains isolated in 1979–1980.

Chloramphenicol. Resistance to chloramphenicol is rare. In Canada in 1979–1980, we found resistance in 3 (0.1%) of 2,679 strains. In California 1.6% of 511 isolates studied in 1971–1973 were resistant (3), and none of 244 strains in Texas during 1970–1975 was resistant (4).

Multiple resistance. Quadruple resistance was observed in 1 of 1,293 strains isolated in our laboratory in 1980.

OTHER GROUPS

Penicillin tolerance, but not resistance, has been reported in group C strains (29). Group F strains with some resistance to penicillin (MIC ≥ 3.1 U/ml) have been observed (22). The highest MIC we have detected among strains of groups A, B, C, and G was 0.63 µg/ml in a group G strain isolated in 1978. Erythromycin resistance was found in our laboratory during 1971–1980 in 163 (1.7%) of 9,750 group C strains and in 311 (3.0%) of 10,546 group G strains; zonal-pattern lincomycin resistance was observed (9). In 1980, 1 of 807 group G strains had quadruple resistance. Resistance to lincomycin and clindamycin has been noted in occasional strains of groups F, H, M, O, P, and Q (17).

TABLE 2. Resistance of hemolytic streptococci in western Canada, 1979–80, to erythromycin (EM), clindamycin (CD), tetracycline (TC), and chloramphenicol (CM)

Group	Strains tested	Percentage resistant to			
		EM	CD	TC	CM
A	13,889	1.2	0.1	3.3	<0.01
B	2,679	2.5	0.4	52.4	0.1
C	1,431	1.3	0.1	12.8	0
G	1,829	3.8	1.0	32.6	0.1

DISCUSSION AND CONCLUSIONS

There are marked differences between North America and Japan in the occurrence and patterns of resistance of *S. pyogenes* to erythromycin, lincomycin, tetracycline, and chloramphenicol. Strains resistant to each antibiotic are far more common in Japan, but most striking is the enormously greater prevalence of strains resistant to combinations of these antibiotics, particularly to all four agents. Furthermore, the marked association in Japan between T-antigen serotype and certain resistance patterns has not been reported elsewhere.

The reason for these differences is not known but may be related to differences in antibiotic usage. Consumption is reported to be particularly high in Japan (21). Reduction of antibiotic usage might reduce the prevalence of resistant strains and may possibly have been responsible for some of the reported decline in tetracycline resistance. The present occurrence of resistance in group A strains in western Canada is shown in Table 2.

There is no indication for clinical laboratories to undertake routine testing of group A streptococci for susceptibility to penicillin. It is advisable, however, that in vitro testing be performed when other antibiotics are being considered for therapy of a serious infection with a hemolytic streptococcus of any group. This is especially important in regions where resistant strains commonly occur or where antibiotic usage is high. If lincomycin resistance is being sought, failure to detect zonally resistant strains is best avoided in disk diffusion tests by using a 2-μg erythromycin disk, and in broth dilution tests by using a sufficient range of concentrations of lincomycin and incubating tests for at least 48 h. The prevalence of resistance is such that tetracycline is not recommended for therapy of infections with hemolytic streptococci, especially those of groups B and G.

There is no evidence that *S. pyogenes* is developing resistance to penicillin, as has *S.*

pneumoniae, and penicillin remains the therapeutic agent of choice.

LITERATURE CITED

1. **Allen, J. L., and K. Sprunt.** 1978. Discrepancy between minimum inhibitory and minimum bactericidal concentrations of penicillin for group A and group B β-hemolytic streptococci. J. Pediatr. **93:**69–71.
2. **Annear, D. I.** 1978. Interaction between erythromycin and lincomycin in *Streptococcus pyogenes*. J. Med. Microbiol. **11:**193–196.
3. **Anthony, B. F., and N. F. Concepcion.** 1975. Group B *Streptococcus* in a general hospital. J. Infect. Dis. **132:**561–567.
4. **Baker, C. J., B. J. Webb, and F. F. Barrett.** 1976. Antimicrobial susceptibility of group B streptococci isolated from a variety of clinical sources. Antimicrob. Agents Chemother. **10:**128–131.
5. **Baker, C. N., C. Thornsberry, and R. R. Facklam.** 1981. Synergism, killing kinetics, and antimicrobial susceptibility of group A and B streptococci. Antimicrob. Agents Chemother. **19:**716–725.
6. **Dadswell, J. V.** 1967. Survey of the incidence of tetracycline-resistant haemolytic streptococci between 1958 and 1965. J. Clin. Pathol. **20:**641–642.
7. **Dixon, J. M. S.** 1968. Group A streptococcus resistant to erythromycin and lincomycin. Can. Med. Assoc. J. **99:**1093–1094.
8. **Dixon, J. M. S., and A. E. Lipinski.** 1972. Resistance of group A beta-hemolytic streptococci to lincomycin and erythromycin. Antimicrob. Agents Chemother. **1:**333–339.
9. **Dixon, J. M. S., and A. E. Lipinski.** 1974. Infections with β-hemolytic *Streptococcus* resistant to lincomycin and erythromycin and observations on zonal-pattern resistance to lincomycin. J. Infect. Dis. **130:**351–356.
10. **Dixon, J. M. S., A. E. Lipinski, and M. E. P. Graham.** 1977. Detection and prevalence of pneumococci with increased resistance to penicillin. Can. Med. Assoc. J. **117:**1159–1161.
11. **Drapkin, M. S., A. W. Karchmer, and R. C. Moellering, Jr.** 1976. Bacteremic infections due to clindamycin-resistant streptococci. J. Am. Med. Assoc. **236:**263–265.
12. **Eickhoff, T. C., J. O. Klein, A. K. Daly, D. Ingall, and M. Finland.** 1964. Neonatal sepsis and other infections due to group B beta-hemolytic streptococci. N. Engl. J. Med. **271:**1221–1228.
13. **Horodniceanu, T., L. Bougueletel, and F. Delbus.** 1979. Phenotypic aspects of resistance to macrolide and related antibiotics in β-haemolytic group A, B, C and G streptococci p. 122–131. *In* R. Facklam, G. Laurell, and I. Lind (ed.), Recent developments in laboratory identification techniques. Excerpta Medica, Amsterdam.
14. **Istre, G. R., D. F. Welch, M. I. Marks, and N. Moyer.** 1981. Susceptibility of group A beta-hemolytic *Streptococcus* isolates to penicillin and erythromycin. Antimicrob. Agents Chemother. **20:**244–246.
15. **Jokipii, A. M. M., and L. Jokipii.** 1976. Presumptive identification and antibiotic susceptibility of group B streptococci. J. Clin. Pathol. **29:**736–739.
16. **Kahlmeter, G., and C. Kamme.** 1972. Tetracycline-resistant group A streptococci and pneumococci. Scand. J. Infect. Dis. **4:**193–196.
17. **Karchmer, A. W., R. C. Moellering, Jr., and B. K. Watson.** 1975. Susceptibility of various serogroups of streptococci to clindamycin and lincomycin. Antimicrob. Agents Chemother. **7:**164–167.
18. **Lowbury, E. J. L., and J. S. Cason.** 1954. Aureomycin and erythromycin therapy for Str. pyogenes in burns. Br. Med. J. **2:**914–915.
19. **Lowbury, E. J. L., and L. Hurst.** 1959. The sensitivity of staphylococci and other wound bacteria to erythromycin,

oleandomycin, and spiramycin. J. Clin. Pathol. **12:**163–169.

20. **Lowbury, E. J. L., and A. Kidson.** 1968. Group A streptococci resistant to lincomycin. Br. Med. J. **2:**490–491.

21. **Maruyama, S., H. Yoshioka, K. Fujita, M. Takimoto, and Y. Satake.** 1979. Sensitivity of Group A streptococci to antibiotics. Am. J. Dis. Child. **133:**1143–1145.

22. **Matsen, J., and C. R. Coghlan.** 1972. Antibiotic testing and susceptibility patterns of streptococci, p. 189–204. *In* L. W. Wannamaker and J. M. Matsen (ed.), Streptococci and streptococcal diseases: recognition, understanding and management. Academic Press, Inc., New York.

23. **McCormack, R. C., D. Kaye, and E. W. Hook.** 1962. Resistance of group A streptococci to tetracycline. N. Engl. J. Med. **267:**323–326.

24. **Mitsuhashi, S., I. Matsuhisa, A. Fuse, Y. Kaneko, and T. Oba.** 1974. Drug resistance in *Streptococcus pyogenes.* Jpn. J. Microbiol. **18:**98–99.

25. **Miyamoto, Y., K. Takizawa, A. Matsushima, Y. Asai, and S. Nakatsuka.** 1978. Stepwise acquisition of multiple drug resistance by beta-hemolytic streptococci and difference in resistance pattern by type. Antimicrob. Agents Chemother. **13:**399–404.

26. **Moellering, R. C., Jr., and D. J. Krogstad.** 1979. Antibiotic resistance in enterococci, p. 293–298. *In* D. Schlessinger (ed.), Microbiology—1979. American Society for Microbiology, Washington, D.C.

27. **Mogabgab, W. J., and W. Pelon.** 1958. An outbreak of pharyngitis due to tetracycline-resistant group A, type 12 streptococci. Am. J. Dis. Child. **96:**696–698.

28. **Nakae, M., T. Murai, Y. Kaneko, and S. Mitsuhashi.** 1977. Drug resistance in *Streptococcus pyogenes* isolated in Japan (1974–1975). Antimicrob. Agents Chemother. **12:**427–428.

29. **Portnoy, D., J. Prentis, and G. K. Richards.** 1981. Penicillin tolerance of human isolates of group C streptococci. Antimicrob. Agents Chemother. **20:**235–238.

30. **Rees, T. A.** 1971. Decline in frequency of isolation of tetracycline-resistant beta-haemolytic streptococci from ear, nose and throat 1967–71. Lancet **1:**938–939.

31. **Sanders, E., M. T. Foster, and D. Scott.** 1968. Group A beta-hemolytic streptococci resistant to erythromycin and lincomycin. N. Engl. J. Med. **278:**538–540.

32. **Saroglou, G., and A. L. Bisno.** 1978. Susceptibility of skin and throat strains of group A streptococci to rosamicin and erythromycin. Antimicrob. Agents Chemother. **13:**701–702.

33. **Tadano, J., N. Kosakai, T. Oguri, and C. M. Wang.** 1978. A study on beta-hemolytic streptococci isolated from the throats of healthy schoolchildren in Taiwan: changing patterns of type distribution and drug susceptibility, p. 547–550. *In* W. Siegenthaler and R. Lüthy (ed.), Current chemotherapy. American Society for Microbiology, Washington, D.C.

Drug Resistance in *Streptococcus pyogenes* Strains Isolated in Japan

SUSUMU MITSUHASHI, MATSUHISA INOUE, KAZUKO SAITO, AND MASATAKA NAKAE

Department of Microbiology, Laboratory of Drug Resistance in Bacteria, School of Medicine, Gunma University, Maebashi, and Department of Microbiology, Nippon Dental University, Niigata, Japan

The emergence of bacterial strains resistant to antibacterial agents has become one of the more important problems in clinical medicine. Among these strains are staphylococci and gram-negative enteric rods which are known to possess multiple resistances to useful antibacterial agents (1, 2, 5). This paper deals with epidemiological studies of drug resistance in streptococci. In addition, plasmid DNA was isolated from streptococci and was transformed into *Bacillus subtilis*.

EXPERIMENTAL PROCEDURES

A total of 2,565 strains of *Streptococcus pyogenes* were isolated in Japan from clinical specimens, and 564 strains were isolated in Sweden, Belgium, and England. They were isolated and stored in this laboratory. The stock cultures were kept on slants of Trypticase soy agar supplemented with 5% sheep blood. Prior to use, cultures were transferred to P broth (brain heart infusion broth, 0.2% yeast extract, 10 μg of DL-tryptophan per ml, and 10^{-4} M $CaCl_2$). Heart infusion agar and peptone-water (10 g of polypeptone, 5 g of NaCl, and 1 liter of distilled water, pH 7.2) were used for the determination of drug resistance. Drug resistance of each strain was determined on agar containing serial two-fold dilutions of each drug. Susceptibility to chloramphenicol, tetracycline, erythromycin, streptomycin, penicillin G, and lincomycin was determined after incubation at 37°C for 18 h. Serotypes were determined by an agglutination test in which standard T antigens were used (9).

To eliminate drug resistance, an overnight brain heart infusion broth culture of each strain at 37°C was diluted 10-fold with fresh broth containing EDTA and was gently shaken at 37°C. The artificial elimination of resistance to tetracycline, chloramphenicol, or macrolide antibiotics was then examined by cultivation at 42°C or by addition of acriflavine or rifampin. After 18 h of incubation, the cultures were plated on brain heart infusion agar. Single colonies were picked, and the elimination of drug resistance in each colony was determined by plating on a brain heart infusion agar plate containing erythromycin (1.6 μg/ml), tetracycline (12.5 μg/ml), and chloramphenicol (12.5 μg/ml).

B. subtilis CRK3000 *ade* (derived from *B. subtilis* 168) carrying a plasmid was cultured in Penassay broth containing adenine (25 μg/ml) at 37°C. After overnight incubation, the culture was diluted with the same broth to 10^3 cells per ml. The diluted culture was supplemented with various concentrations of acridine orange or rifampin and was cultured at 37°C. After overnight incubation, the turbid culture containing the highest concentration of the drugs was spread on a heart infusion agar plate. The colonies formed after overnight incubation were replica plated on heart infusion agar and on plates containing tetracycline (12.5 μg/ml), chloramphenicol (12.5 μg/ml), or erythromycin (1.6 μg/ml). The frequency of elimination of drug resistance was determined after 18 h of incubation at 37°C. The diluted culture was incubated at 42°C, and after overnight incubation, the frequency of elimination of drug resistance was similarly examined by the replica-plating method.

Plasmid DNA was isolated (3) and was transformed into *B. subtilis* 168 mutant CRK3000 (8) in all cases.

The frequencies of drug resistance in isolates of group A beta-hemolytic streptococci are

TABLE 1. Frequency of drug resistance in group A beta-hemolytic streptococci isolated in Japan and Europe

Drug	% Resistant					
	Japan					Europe 1976–1977
	1972	1974	1975	1977	1978	
Tetracycline	47.4	84.3	78.0	95.2	68.2	23.6
Chloramphenicol	23.0	63.0	54.9	72.6	30.9	0
Erythromycin	11.9	61.3	60.0	83.1	35.4	0
Lincomycin	0.0	58.7	59.2	83.1	33.1	0
Susceptible	51.1	15.2	20.8	2.4	30.7	76.4

TABLE 2. Yearly changes of the serotype
distribution of group A beta-hemolytic streptococci
in Japan[a]

Serotype (T)	Percent			
	1972	1974	1976	1978
12	23.7	69.9	55.0	32.2
4	17.0	8.8	9.6	21.8
3	1.5	6.6	6.0	4.5
1	25.9	0.7	4.4	11.9
Others	28.2	9.6	19.0	20.7
Untypable	3.7	4.4	6.0	8.9

[a] Results based on surveys of 2,565 strains isolated
from 1972 to 1978 in various districts in Japan.

TABLE 3. Relationship between resistance patterns
and serotypes in group A streptococci

Resistance pattern	% of T type:					
	1	3	4	12	Others	Untypable
Tc Cm Mac	4.9	2.8	11.0	68.9	2.6	16.7
Mac Cm	0	0	0	0.1	2.6	0
Tc Cm	2.4	44.4	3.1	4.2	1.3	6.7
Mac Tc	4.9	0	4.7	11.5	1.3	3.3
Tc	0	22.2	76.6	9.1	10.5	6.7
Mac	0	0	0	0.9	1.3	0
Susceptible	87.8	30.6	4.6	5.0	81.4	66.6

shown in Table 1. Tetracycline resistance was
most often seen, followed by resistance to chloramphenicol, erythromycin, and lincomycin,
which occurred at almost equal frequencies.
However, the strains isolated in Europe differed
from the Japanese isolates in that most were
susceptible to chloramphenicol, erythromycin,
and lincomycin, but only 20% were tetracycline
resistant. It should be noted that almost all of the
strains were susceptible to penicillin G. The T-
type distributions of the strains isolated in Japan
are shown in Table 2.

Drug resistance patterns and their frequency
of occurrence in strains isolated in Japan are
shown in Fig. 1. Strains carrying triple resistance (Tc Cm Mac) were most frequently seen
among the isolates, followed by those with single (Tc) or double resistance (Mac Tc, Tc Cm,
Mac Cm). However, strains with single resistance (Mac or Cm) were rather few in number.

As shown in Table 3, Tc Cm Mac resistance
was most frequently seen in strains of T type 12.
However, the strains carrying Tc Cm and Tc

resistance were often isolated from those of T
types 3 and 4, respectively.

The frequency of elimination of drug resistance from streptococci was rather low because
of their formation of long chains. By contrast,
drug resistance of the B. subtilis transformants
was cured at a high frequency by treatment with
drugs or by cultivation at 42°C. Tetracycline
resistance was eliminated by Tc selection. By
contrast, resistance to both macrolides and
chloramphenicol was jointly cured by either
Mac or Cm selection, or by heat treatment.
These results indicated that two types of drug
resistance plasmid carrying either Tc or Mac Cm
resistance were found in streptococci (Table 4).

Transformation analysis of drug resistance in
streptococci indicated that Tc or Mac Cm resistance was separately transmitted and Mac Cm
resistance was jointly transformed into B. subtilis. These results confirmed the presence of two
types of drug resistance plasmid, i.e., Tc and
Mac Cm plasmids (Table 5).

Macrolide-resistant streptococci consistently

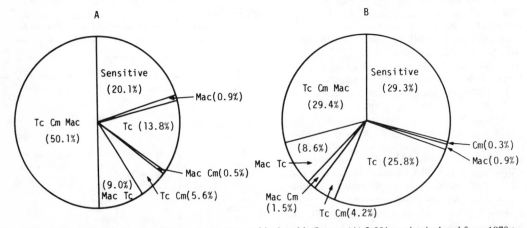

FIG. 1. Resistance patterns of group A streptococci isolated in Japan: (A) 2,001 strains isolated from 1970 to
1975; (B) 564 strains isolated from 1976 to 1978.

TABLE 4. Elimination of Tc and Mac Cm resistances in *B. subtilis* transformants by treatment at 42°C

Strain no.	Elimination of resistance in cells incubated at:	
	37°C	42°C
1	0/100[a]	3/250 (Tc)
2	0/100	4/125 (Tc)
3	0/100	0/95
4	0/84	1/251 (Mac Cm)
15	0/105	5/50 (Mac Cm)
24	0/100	1/120 (Mac Cm)
54	0/100	1/100 (Mac Cm)
75	0/150	1/250 (Mac Cm)

[a] Number of strains whose resistance was eliminated/total number of strains examined.

TABLE 5. Transformation of tetracycline, chloramphenicol, and macrolide resistance to *B. subtilis* CRK3000[a]

Strain no.	Selected on:		
	Tetracycline	Chloramphenicol	Macrolides
3	100 (Tc)	100 (Cm Mac)	100 (Mac Cm)
4	100 (Tc)	100 (Cm Mac)	100 (Mac Cm)
5	100 (Tc)	100 (Cm Mac)	100 (Mac Cm)
14	100 (Tc)	0	100 (Mac)
15	0	100 (Cm Mac)	100 (Mac Cm)
23	0	100 (Cm Mac)	100 (Mac Cm)
24	100 (Tc)	100 (Cm Mac)	100 (Mac Cm)
54	0	100 (Cm Mac)	100 (Mac Cm)
75	0	100 (Cm Mac)	100 (Mac Cm)

[a] Numbers indicate the transformants which were selected on tetracycline, chloramphenicol, or macrolide plates. Resistance patterns of the transformants selected are shown in parentheses.

carried lincomycin resistance. This trait was constitutive, indicating the difference from staphylococcal resistance to macrolides. It was characteristic that penicillin or streptomycin resistance was not found in streptococci.

The molecular weight of plasmid DNA was determined by agarose gel electrophoresis. That of the streptococcal Tc plasmid was 2.6×10^6 and was similar to that of the staphylococcal Tc plasmid. The molecular weight of the streptococcal Mac Cm plasmid (about 10×10^6) was larger than those of staphylococcal Mac (1.4×10^6) and Cm (2.6×10^6) plasmids. However, the molecular weight of the Mac Pc plasmid was 18×10^6.

DISCUSSION

We previously reported (6) on epidemiological studies of drug resistance in group A beta-hemolytic streptococci isolated from 1970 to 1973 in Japan. The results indicated that distinct group resistances to penicillin G and streptomycin could not be identified among the strains thus far examined. However, recent surveys from this and other laboratories have demonstrated strains resistant to chloramphenicol, tetracycline, and the macrolide antibiotics (1, 2, 4, 6). The frequency of isolation of strains resistant to macrolides is increasing in Japan as a result of the widespread use of these drugs.

Resistance patterns of streptococci were found to be quite different from those of staphylococci (7) in that no streptococcal strains resistant to penicillin or streptomycin were isolated. Strains carrying only tetracycline resistance were often seen, but those resistant only to chloramphenicol or macrolides were rather few in number. By contrast, the strains carrying double resistance (Mac Tc, Tc Cm, Mac Cm) were frequently isolated. These results indicated

that resistance patterns are increasing in occurrence in parallel with the widespread use of many drugs and that there is some tendency to multiple resistance, i.e., from single (Tc) to double resistance, and from double to triple (Tc Cm Mac) resistance. It was characteristic that penicillin or streptomycin resistance was not found in streptococci in spite of the high frequency of staphylococcal isolates resistant to penicillin or streptomycin (7). Macrolide resistance in streptococci was consistently accompanied by lincomycin resistance and was constitutive, whereas about half of macrolide resistance in staphylococci was inducible and was not accompanied by lincomycin resistance (7).

Our investigation of the relationship between resistance patterns and T type showed that strains with triple resistance (Tc Cm Mac) were often those of type T12. These results were quite similar to the multiple resistance found in staphylococcal strains with phage type 80/81 (7, 9).

The Mac Cm and Tc plasmids were often seen in streptococci. However, the Mac Cm plasmid was not isolated from staphylococci, whereas Mac and Mac Pc plasmids were often seen in staphylococci (7).

SUMMARY

Our survey of the drug resistance of 2,565 *S. pyogenes* strains isolated during 1972 and 1978 in various districts of Japan showed that tetracycline-, chloramphenicol-, and macrolide antibiotic-resistant strains were often isolated. Distinct group resistances to penicillin and aminoglycoside antibiotics could not be identified among the strains examined. It was characteristic that triple (Mac Tc Cm) and double (Mac Tc, Mac Cm) resistance were manifested among the strains resistant to macrolides, tetracycline, and chloramphenicol, and they were confined to the type T12. The emergence of multiply resistant streptococcal strains was due mostly to the rapid increase in the frequency of isolation of macrolide-resistant strains.

The Tc and Mac Cm plasmids were isolated at a high frequency from streptococci, and they were stably maintained in *B. subtilis* after transformation. The molecular weights of Tc and Mac Cm plasmids were 2.6×10^6 and 10.0×10^6, respectively.

LITERATURE CITED

1. **Dixon, J. M. S.** 1968. Group A streptococcus resistant to erythromycin and lincomycin. Can. J. Microbiol. **16**:201–202.
2. **Dixon, J. M. S., and A. E. Lipinski.** 1972. Resistance of group A beta-hemolytic streptococci resistant to lincomycin and erythromycin. Antimicrob. Agents Chemother. **4**:333–339.
3. **Kupersztoch Portnoy, Y. M., M. A. Lovett, and D. R. Helinski.** 1974. Strand and site specificity of the relaxation event for the relaxation complex of the antibiotic resistance plasmid R6K. Biochemistry **13**:5484–5490.
4. **Matsen, J. M., and C. R. Coghlan.** 1972. Antibiotic testing and susceptibility patterns of streptococci, p. 189–204. *In* L. W. Wannamaker and J. M. Matsen (ed.), Streptococci and streptococcal diseases: recognition, understanding and management. Academic Press, Inc., New York.
5. **Mitsuhashi, S.** 1977. Epidemiology of bacterial drug resistance, p. 3–24. *In* S. Mitsuhashi (ed.), R factor. Drug resistance plasmid. University of Tokyo Press, Tokyo.
6. **Mitsuhashi, S., M. Inoue, A. Fuse, Y. Kaneki, and T. Oba.** 1974. Drug resistance in *Streptococcus pyogenes*. Jpn. J. Microbiol. **18**:98–99.
7. **Mitsuhashi, S., M. Inoue, H. Kawabe, H. Oshima, and T. Okubo.** 1973. Genetic and biochemical studies of drug resistance in staphylococci, p. 144–165. *In* J. Jeljaszewicz (ed.), Staphylococci and staphylococcal infections. S. Karger, Basel.
8. **Stewart, C. R.** 1969. Physical heterogeneity among *Bacillus subtilis* deoxyribonucleic acid molecules carrying particular genetic markers. J. Bacteriol. **98**:1239–1247.
9. **Williams, R. E.** 1958. Laboratory diagnosis of streptococcal infections. Bull. W.H.O. **19**:153–176.

Multiple Tetracycline Resistance Determinants in
Streptococcus

VICKERS BURDETT, JULIA INAMINE, and SHRIN RAJAGOPALAN

Department of Microbiology and Immunology, Duke University Medical Center, Durham, North Carolina 27710

Bacterial resistance to tetracycline is widespread among both gram-positive and gram-negative bacteria and approaches 90% among streptococci in some surveys (5). Although tetracycline resistance in gram-negative bacteria is predominantly plasmid mediated, this appears not to be the case among clinical isolates of *Streptococcus* (1, 7). In a previous study in this laboratory (1), 30 tetracycline-resistant strains of *Streptococcus agalactiae* (group B) were examined in detail to elucidate the genetic basis of tetracycline resistance in this organism. Only three tetracycline resistance plasmids were found; pMV158 and pMV163 are small, nonconjugative multicopy plasmids (5.2 and 5.4 kilobases [kb], respectively) which are easily mobilized by streptococcal "sex-factors," whereas pMV120 is a 45-kb conjugative plasmid. The remaining strains contained no detectable plasmid DNA, and they were unable to transfer tetracycline resistance even when a known sex factor was introduced into the cell. Similar results were found among oral streptococci by LeBlanc (7). The failure to identify tetracycline resistance plasmids in most of the strains studied may reflect the presence of tetracycline resistance determinants which are part of the chromosome. Some of these insertions are conjugative and have been identified in *S. faecalis* (6), *S. agalactiae* (8), and *S. pneumoniae* (14); they are sometimes linked to chloramphenicol or erythromycin resistance determinants, or to both. One of these insertions, Tn916, has been shown to be a conjugative transposon (6). Further genetic analysis of plasmid- and nonplasmid (npTET)-associated tetracycline resistance is being carried out in this laboratory. To facilitate this analysis, we have cloned one plasmid and one nonplasmid tetracycline resistance determinant into *Escherichia coli* and have demonstrated the presence of at least three genetically unrelated tetracycline resistance determinants (*tetL, tetM, tetN*). We have also detected differences in phenotypic expression of tetracycline resistance of different origins with regard to tetracycline and minocycline, as reported elsewhere (2).

RESISTANCE TO TETRACYCLINE AND ANALOGS

A series of isogenic strains of *S. faecalis* JH2-2 were constructed to contain a single tetracycline resistance determinant. Measurements of resistance to tetracycline, minocycline, and chelocardin were then performed in liquid culture. Tetracycline resistance in all but one instance studied was found to be expressed constitutively (2; J. Inamine and V. Burdett, this volume). Thus, the resistance level of the strains tested was unaffected by pregrowth in subinhibitory concentrations of tetracycline. Growth of the strain containing the inducible tetracycline resistance determinant (*tetM*[1]) at high antibiotic concentrations was slowed unless it was pregrown in subinhibitory concentrations of tetracycline. Overall, one group of strains showed resistance to ≤6.25 μg of tetracycline per ml but wild-type susceptibility to minocycline and chelocardin (Table 1). This was the case for strains which carry pMV158, pMV163, pAMα1, and pJH1. Another group (pAM211, pIP614, pMV120, and npTET) showed resistance to minocycline (3.12 to 6.25 μg/ml) as well as high-level resistance to tetracycline (25 to 50 μg/ml). None of the tetracycline resistance determinants identified so far provides any resistance to chelocardin.

GENETIC COMPARISON OF TETRACYCLINE RESISTANCE

Our finding that tetracycline resistances from different sources express different sensitivities to tetracycline analogs suggested that there might be genetic diversity among these tetracycline resistances as well. We chose as prototypes of these classes pMV163 and a nonplasmid determinant (npTET) cloned from *S. agalactiae* B109. Direct analysis was carried out by using the DNA transfer method of Southern (16) to assess homology among determinants from diverse sources and also to assess the distribution of these determinants. Plasmid DNAs and whole cell DNAs isolated from tetracycline-resistant strains were digested with *Hinc*II, transferred to

155

TABLE 1. Streptococcal tetracycline resistance determinants

Determinant class	Plasmid or insertion	Tetracycline resistance (μg/ml)	Minocycline resistance (μg/ml)
tetL	pMV158, pMV163, pAMα1, pJH1	6.25	<0.1
tetM	pAM211, pIP614, npTET	25	3.125-6.25
tetN	pMV120	25–50	6.25

nitrocellulose filters (16), and hybridized with ^{32}P-labeled probe.

When pMV163 was utilized as a probe against a large number of DNAs representative of the two phenotypic classes, the only homology seen was against pMV158, pAMα1, and pJH1. No homology with pMV120, pAM211, or npTET was seen. When pMV158 or pAMα1 was used as the radioactive probe, similar results were obtained. To test whether the region of homology was due to the tetracycline resistance determinant or some other region of the plasmid, we carried out deletion analysis of pMV163. This analysis was facilitated by the construction of a hybrid plasmid in E. coli between pMV163 and pVH2124 (ColE1-amp). This hybrid plasmid pVB·B11 was able to express resistance to 25 μg of tetracycline per ml in E. coli (100-fold higher than background) and retained wild-type susceptibility to minocycline. From the hybridization data, it was known that HincII fragments B, D, and E hybridized with the heterologous probes. Deletions of pVB·B11 produced by partial cleavage with HincII confirmed that removing fragment B or D generated tetracycline-sensitive plasmids, whereas deletion of most of fragment E did not affect tetracycline resistance. Fragment A may be necessary for expression of tetracycline resistance. Although no hybridization to this fragment was observed, deletions of this fragment were never obtained. Maps of pMV158, pMV163, and pAMα1 (Fig. 1) show the tetracycline resistance region defined by hybridization and deletion analysis.

Analysis of non-plasmid-associated tetracycline resistance was carried out in a similar manner. S. agalactiae B109 is resistant to tetracycline, chloramphenicol, and MLS antibiotics (macrolides, lincosamides, and streptogramin B) (9). These resistances can be transferred en bloc by a mechanism which resembles conjugation (8; Inamine and Burdett, this volume), even in the absence of any demonstrable plasmid DNA. A tetracycline resistance determinant from B109 was cloned in E. coli. The plasmid DNA from one such transformant (pJI2) contained a 20-kb EcoRI fragment from B109. E. coli transformants containing pJI2 expressed resistance to 2.5 μg of tetracycline per ml and 1.6 μg of

minocycline per ml, consistent with npTET expression in Streptococcus. The region necessary and sufficient for tetracycline resistance in pJI2 was confined to a 5.0-kb HincII fragment which has been subcloned, generating pJI3, and this fragment was found to be sufficient for tetracycline resistance. Further mapping and deletion analysis is under way to locate the tetracycline resistance region precisely within the 5.0-kb HincII fragment.

Plasmid pJI2 was used as a probe in hybridization experiments with DNA from tetracycline-resistant and -susceptible strains as well as tetracycline-resistant transconjugants in MV762 (a S. agalactiae recipient strain) and JH2-2 (a S. faecalis recipient strain). All the tetracycline-resistant strains, including transconjugants, contain a number of fragments that share extensive homology with pJI2. Limited hybridization was also observed with MV762. This region is identical in endonuclease cleavage pattern with one end of the pJI2 probe. Thus, it is likely that the region of pJI2 in common with MV762 is normal cellular DNA contiguous with the tetracycline resistance region from B109, and the 20-kb EcoRI fragment cloned in pJI2 may include the junction region between a recipient genome and the inserted tetracycline resistance determinant. Further, these fragments were not observed in any S. faecalis transconjugants. When the 5.0-kb fragment containing the tetracycline resistance genes (as pJI3) was used as a probe in Southern hybridization experiments, only DNA from tetracycline-resistant strains showed homology with the probe. In many cases the homologous fragment was also 5.0 kb. No homology was seen with pMV158, pMV163, pAMα1, or pMV120.

Vigorous attempts have been made, without success, to clone the tetracycline resistance determinant from pMV120 in E. coli either as an intact linear molecule or as fragments generated by sequence-specific nucleases. Recently, this determinant has been cloned into S. sanguis Challis by using pVA736 (12) as the vector. Analysis of these hybrids is too preliminary to report here.

The three tetracycline resistance determinants identified in this study represent determinants

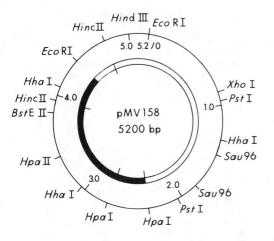

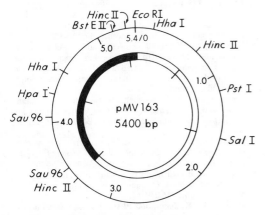

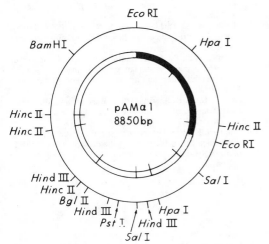

FIG. 1. Maps of pMV158, pMV163, and pAMα1 showing cleavage sites for the sequence-specific endonucleases studied. The filled portion on the inner circle indicates the *tet* region as defined by hybridization and deletion analysis. The inner circle has been subdivided by lines representing *Hinc*II sites. The plasmids

TABLE 2. Distribution of tetracycline resistance determinants

Source	Sample size	*tetL*	*tetM*
S. faecalis			
Human	14	14/14	14/14
Animal	17	17/17	16/17
Miscellaneous	4	1/4	3/4
S. agalactiae			
Human	13	2/13	12/13

which are unique to *Streptococcus*. Neither probe (pMV163 or pJI2) showed homology with any of the four tetracycline resistance determinants from *E. coli* (13), pT181 from *Staphylococcus aureus* (10), pBC3106 from *Bacillus sphaericus* (J. Polak, personal communication), or pMV120 from *S. agalactiae* (1). These naturally occurring tetracycline resistance determinants have been designated *tetL* (e.g., pMV163), *tetM* (e.g., npTET), and *tetN* (pMV120).

DISTRIBUTION OF TETRACYCLINE RESISTANCE DETERMINANTS

The available probes for tetracycline resistance determinants *tetL* and *tetM* were used in colony hybridization experiments to examine the relative frequency of these tetracycline determinants in nature. Our results so far show that *tetM*-like determinants are widespread among human and animal isolates (Table 2). Of the 31 isolates of *S. faecalis* assayed, 31 reacted with the *tetL* probe and 30 reacted with *tetM*. These isolates were all multiply drug resistant and contained from two to six plasmids (G. Dunny, unpublished data). Conversely, clinical isolates of *S. agalactiae* contained few plasmids and multiple resistance was infrequent; 13 tetracycline-resistant strains have been tested in all, of which 2 contained *tetL* and 12 reacted with *tetM*. Only one strain (B117) failed to react with either probe. The two strains which reacted with both *tetL* and *tetM* were the parental strains from which pMV158 and pMV163 were isolated. Many of the strains tested were also erythromycin resistant. Seventeen of 21 erythromycin-resistant *S. faecalis* strains and 3 of 3 erythromycin-resistant *S. agalactiae* isolates reacted

pMV158 and pMV163 contain no sequences cleaved by *Bam*HI, *Bal*II, *Hae*II, *Hae*III, *Kpn*I, *Pvu*I, *Sma*I, *Sst*I, *Sst*II, and *Xba*I; in addition, pMV158 contains no sites for *Sal*I and pMV163 contains no *Ava*I or *Hin*dIII sites.

with the erythromycin resistance determinant of pAMβ1 that is part of pVA736 (12).

SUMMARY REMARKS

We have defined three naturally occurring tetracycline resistance determinants (*tetL, tetM,* and *tetN*) in *Streptococcus* (2). The *tetL* and *tetM* determinants are widespread in nature, and both may be contained in a single isolate from nature. The ecology of *S. faecalis* and the presence of large numbers of plasmids and conjugative elements may provide a repository of diverse resistance determinants which are transmissible among the streptococci and other gram-positive bacteria.

The small nonconjugative *tetL*-containing plasmids pMV158 and pMV163 transform *S. sanguis* to tetracycline resistance (1), and pMV158 readily transforms *S. pneumoniae* (15). These plasmids are therefore potentially useful as molecular cloning vectors since the region necessary for tetracycline resistance has been identified and sequence-specific endonuclease cleavage maps are available. Based on the mapping/deletion data, miniplasmid derivatives of pMV158 and pMV163 could be constructed for use as cloning vectors.

Expression of heterologous tetracycline resistance has been demonstrated in several systems (3, 4, 11). The experiments reported here demonstrate that *tetL* and *tetM* confer tetracycline resistance when cloned in *E. coli*. The introduction of *tetL* increased the resistance of the streptococcal host to 6.25 μg of tetracycline per ml and of the *E. coli* host to 25 μg/ml. The npTET determinant (*tetM*) conferred resistance to 25 μg of tetracycline per ml and 6.25 μg of minocycline per ml in *Streptococcus* but only to 2.5 μg/ml and 1.6 μg/ml, respectively, in *E. coli*. Thus, the cross-resistance pattern is retained in the heterologous *E. coli* host. The reasons for differences in the expression of tetracycline resistance determinants, both in the streptococcal hosts and in *E. coli*, are not known but are currently under investigation.

LITERATURE CITED

1. **Burdett, V.** 1980. Identification of tetracycline-resistant R-plasmids in *Streptococcus agalactiae* (Group B). Antimicrob. Agents Chemother. **18**:753–760.
2. **Burdett, V., J. Inamine, and S. Rajagopalan.** 1982. Heterogeneity of tetracycline resistance determinants in *Streptococcus.* J. Bacteriol. **149**:995–1004.
3. **Eccles, S., A. Docherty, I. Chopra, S. Shales, and P. Ball.** 1981. Tetracycline resistance genes from *Bacillus* plasmid pAB124 confer decreased accumulation of the antibiotics in *Bacillus subtilus* but not in *Escherichia coli.* J. Bacteriol. **145**:1417–1420.
4. **Ehrlich, S. D.** 1977. Replication and expression of plasmids from *Staphylococcus aureus* in *Bacillus subtilus.* Proc. Natl. Acad. Sci. U.S.A. **74**:1680–1682.
5. **Finland, M.** 1979. Emergence of antibiotic resistance in hospitals, 1935–1975. Rev. Infect. Dis. **1**:4–21.
6. **Franke, A. E., and D. B. Clewell.** 1981. Evidence for a chromosome-borne resistance transposon (Tn*916*) in *Streptococcus faecalis* that is capable of "conjugal" transfer in the absence of a conjugative plasmid. J. Bacteriol. **145**:494–502.
7. **Hawley, R., L. Lee, and D. LeBlanc.** 1980. Effects of tetracycline on the streptococcal flora of peridontal pockets. Antimicrob. Agents Chemother. **17**:372–378.
8. **Horodniceanu, T., L. Bougueleret, and G. Bieth.** 1981. Conjugative transfer of multiple-antibiotic resistance markers in beta-hemolytic Group A, B, F, and G streptococci in the absence of extrachromosomal deoxyribonucleic acid. Plasmid **5**:127–137.
9. **Horodniceanu, T., L. Bouguelet, N. El-Solh, D. H. Bouanchaud, and Y. A. Chabbert.** 1979. Conjugative-R-plasmids in *Streptococcus agalactiae* (Group B). Plasmid **2**:197–206.
10. **Iordanescu, S.** 1976. Temperature sensitive mutant of a tetracycline resistance staphylococcal plasmid. Arch. Roum. Pathol. Exp. Microbiol. **35**:257–264.
11. **Kreft, J., K. Bernard, and W. Goebel.** 1978. Recombinant plasmids capable of replication in *B. subtilus* and *E. coli.* Mol. Gen. Genet. **162**:59–67.
12. **Macrina, F., K. Jones, and P. W. Wood.** 1980. Chimeric streptococcal plasmids and their use as molecular cloning vehicles in *Streptococcus sanguis* (Challis). J. Bacteriol. **143**:1425–1435.
13. **Mendez, B., C. Tachibana, and S. B. Levy.** 1980. Heterogeneity of tetracycline resistance determinants. Plasmid **3**:99–108.
14. **Shoemaker, N. B., M. D. Smith, and W. R. Guild.** 1980. DNase resistant transfer of chromosomal *cat* and *tet* insertions by filter mating in pneumococcus. Plasmid **3**:80–87.
15. **Smith, M., N. B. Shoemaker, V. Burdett, and W. Guild.** 1980. Transfer of plasmids by conjugation in *Streptococcus pneumoniae.* Plasmid **3**:70–79.
16. **Southern, E.** 1975. Detection of specific sequences among DNA fragments separated by gel electrophoresis. J. Mol. Biol. **98**:503–517.

Amino Acid Sequence Conservation in Two MLS Resistance Determinants

SUEHARU HORINOUCHI[1] AND BERNARD WEISBLUM

Department of Pharmacology, University of Wisconsin Medical School, Madison, Wisconsin 53706

Resistance to macrolide, lincosamide, and streptogramin type B (MLS) antibiotics is mediated by specific methylation of adenine in 23S rRNA, as a consequence of which bacterial cells become co-resistant to all members belonging to these three chemically dissimilar classes of 50S ribosome subunit inhibitors (6, 11, 12). Ribosomes which contain the specifically methylated adenine residues bind MLS antibiotics with reduced affinity (19).

The MLS phenotype is widely distributed in gram-positive bacteria, including streptococci (e.g., *Streptococcus pyogenes* [20], *S. faecalis* [2, 20], *S. pneumoniae* [4], *S. agalactiae* [7, 9], *S. sanguis* [21]), and the manifestations of this phenotype in the streptococci have been discussed by Clewell (1) in a review covering antibiotic resistance in this group of organisms. Not only is MLS resistance found in a wide range of naturally occurring strains of streptococci, but also the resistance determinant genes are easily transferred in the laboratory between various streptococcal strains (4, 5, 7, 13, 14) and have even been transferred to *Streptococcus pneumoniae* from *Staphylococcus aureus* (4).

Examination of relatedness of selected MLS determinants from staphylococci and streptococci at the nucleotide sequence level by use of the DNA blot hybridization method of Southern (17) under stringent hybridization conditions (i.e., in a medium containing 0.45 M NaCl and 0.045 M sodium citrate, pH 7.0) has revealed that some MLS determinants show sequence relatedness, whereas others do not (3, 15, 18; M. S. Gilmore, D. Behnke, and J. J. Ferretti, this volume; H. Ounissi and P. Courvalin, this volume). For example, the MLS determinant of staphylococcal plasmid pI258 showed homology with streptococcal plasmids pAM-β, pAC-1, and pAM77, as well as with (presumed) chromosomal DNA from MLS-resistant *S. pneumoniae*, whereas no homology was found with pE194, another plasmid from *S. aureus* which specifies MLS resistance (18). Docherty et al. (3) noted a lack of sequence homology in a comparison of the MLS determinants from plasmid pAM77, plasmid pE194, and *B. licheniformis* chromosomal DNA under similar stringent hybridization conditions. Likewise, the lack of relatedness between pE194 and other MLS determinants has been noted by Parisi et al. (15), Ounissi and Courvalin (this volume), and Gilmore et al. (this volume).

In this presentation we pose the question: Can any similarity be shown to exist for MLS resistance determinant structural genes which fail to show relatedness by nucleic acid hybridization methods? The answer to this question is "yes."

Underlying this question is the more general problem of whether the apparent differences in resistance determinants reflect qualitative diversity indicative of possible independent origin of these genes or whether the differences observed are only quantitative and therefore suggestive of a common origin. In one experimental system which we studied, our findings suggest the latter to be the case.

To compare two MLS determinants which fail to show sequence homology under stringent nucleic acid hybridization conditions, we therefore sequenced the MLS determinant of *S. sanguis* plasmid pAM77 (21) and compared the deduced amino acid sequence with that of pE194, which is already known (8, 16). For purposes of sequencing, pAM77 DNA fragments which carry the MLS determinant were prepared by digestion with restriction endonucleases and identified on the basis of their ability to hybridize with the MLS determinant of pAM-β from *S. faecalis*. Briefly, pAM77 DNA fragments obtained by digestion with restriction endonucleases were end labeled with [γ-^{32}P]ATP and T4 polynucleotide kinase, and were used as probes in DNA blot hybridization experiments against pAM-β DNA digested with *Hind*III used as target. We showed previously (18) that, under these conditions, homology between the MLS determinants and the *S. faecalis* *Hind*III target DNA could be localized in a single DNA fragment with electrophoretic mobility corresponding to approximately 2.1 megadaltons.

---

[1] Present address: Department of Agricultural Chemistry, The University of Tokyo, Tokyo 113, Japan.

The results of our analysis are shown in Fig. 1. The two MLS resistance determinant proteins differ in number by only one amino acid residue. Moreover, half of the amino acids are identical in sequence, and some are organized as uninterrupted clusters, one of which contains nine amino acids. The similarity between the two determinants is even greater if one counts residues at which chemical properties of the respective side chains are conserved. The striking similarity between the two amino acid sequences suggests that the two MLS determinants have a common origin.

Comparison of the nucleotide sequences of these structural genes reveals that approximately half of the nucleotides are correspondingly identical as well (data not shown), and in many instances the amino acid is conserved by coding degeneracy. Nucleotide mismatch in the two MLS determinants to an extent of 50% would produce hybrids which are too unstable to persist under the usual hybridization conditions.

Despite lack of demonstrable hybridization between the two MLS determinant sequences studied, our results suggest a common origin for the MLS determinants specified by pAM77 from *S. sanguis* and pE194 from *S. aureus*, respectively. These findings are germane to the accurate interpretation of data which suggest grouping MLS determinants according to criteria based on nucleic acid homology studies, particularly negative hybridization results. The findings we have reported suggest that negative hybridization data may indicate distinct classes of MLS determinants, but that the distinction made by such assays is one of degree rather than one based on fundamental qualitative differences. Our findings do not exclude the possibility that further sequence studies will uncover MLS determinants for which similarity to already characterized determinants cannot be demonstrated.

ACKNOWLEDGMENTS

This work was supported by research grant PCM-779730 from the National Science Foundation and by research grants from The Upjohn Co. and from Eli Lilly & Co.

LITERATURE CITED

1. **Clewell, D. B.** 1981. Plasmids, drug resistance, and gene transfer in the genus *Streptococcus*. Microbiol. Rev. **45:**409–436.
2. **Clewell, D. B., Y. Yagi, G. M. Dunny, and S. K. Schultz.** 1974. Characterization of three plasmid deoxyribonucleic acid molecules in a strain of *Streptococcus fecalis*: identification of a plasmid determining erythromycin resistance. J. Bacteriol. **117:**283–289.
3. **Docherty, A., G. Grandi, R. Grandi, T. J. Gryczan, A. G. Shivakumar, and D. Dubnau.** 1981. Naturally occurring macrolide-lincosamide-streptogramin B resistance in *Bacillus licheniformis*. J. Bacteriol. **145:**129–137.
4. **Engel, H. W., N. Soedirman, J. A. Rost, W. J. van**

```
                    1        10        20        30        40        50        60        70        80        90       100       110       120 125
pE194  MNEKNIKHSQNFITSKHNIDKIMTNIRLNEHDNIFEIGSGKGHFTLELVKRCNFVTAIEIDHKLCKTTENKLVDHDNFQVLNKDILQFKFPKNQSYKIVGNIPYNISTDIRRKIVFDSIANEIYL
       =  ==== ==== =  =  =    =     = = =  = ==== ==  =     =     ==    ==     ==  === =    ===  ==   ==  === ==  === ==       ==  === ==
pAM77  MK'KNIKYSQNFLTNEKVLNQIIKQLNLKETDTVYEIGTGKGHLTTKLAKISKQVTSIELDSHLFNLSSEKLKLNIRVTLIHQDILQFPNKQRYKIVGSIPYHLSTQIIKKVVFESHASDIYL
                    1        10        20        30        40        50        60        70        80        90       100       110       120 124

       126 130       140       150       160       170       180       190       200       210       220       230       240 244
pE194  IVEYGFAKRLLNTKRSLALLMAEVDISILSMVPREYFHPKVNSSLIRLSRKKSRISHKDKQKYNYFVMKWVMKEYKKIFTKNQFNNSLKHAGIDDLNNISFEQFLSLFNSYKLFNK
       === ==  = =  =   ==     ==   =   ==========  = ====  ==== =  ===  ====  =  ==== ====  ====  === ==
pAM77  IVEEGFYKRTLDIIHRSLGLLLHTQVSIQQLLKLPAECFHPKVNSVLIKLTRHTTDVPDKYWKLYTYFVSKWVNREYRQLFTKNQFHQAMKHAKVNNLSTVTYEQVLSIFNSYLLFNGRK
       125 130       140       150       160       170       180       190       200       210       220       230       240 245
```

FIG. 1. Comparison of amino acid sequences of the pE194 MLS determinant and the pAM77 determinants, both deduced from the respective DNA sequences. The pAM77 MLS determinant sequence contains 245 amino acid residues, whereas that of pE194 contains 244. If the two sequences are aligned as shown, 123 amino acid residues are identical. The symbols ' and = indicate, respectively, spaces added to bring the two amino acid sequences into alignment and the occurrence of identical amino acids in both sequences. Abbreviations: A, alanine; C, cysteine; D, aspartic acid; E, glutamic acid; F, phenylalanine; G, glycine; H, histidine; I, isoleucine; K, lysine; L, leucine; M, methionine; N, asparagine; P, proline; Q, glutamine; R, arginine; S, serine; T, threonine; V, valine; W, tryptophan; Y, tyrosine.

Leeuen, and J. D. A. van Embden. 1980. Transferability of macrolide, lincomycin, and streptogramin resistances between groups A, B, and D streptococci, *Streptococcus pneumoniae*, and *Staphylococcus aureus*. J. Bacteriol. 142:407–413.

5. Gibson, E. M., N. M. Chace, S. B. London, and J. London. 1979. Transfer of plasmid-mediated antibiotic resistance from streptococci to lactobacilli. J. Bacteriol. 137:614–619.

6. Graham, M. Y., and B. Weisblum. 1979. Altered methylation of adenine in 23S ribosomal RNA associated with erythromycin resistance in *Streptomyces erythreus* and *Streptococcus fecalis*. Contrib. Microbiol. Immunol. 6:159–164.

7. Hershfield, V. 1979. Plasmids mediating multiple drug resistance in group B streptococci: transferability and molecular properties. Plasmid 2:137–149.

8. Horinouchi, S., and B. Weisblum. 1980. Posttranscriptional modification of messenger RNA conformation: mechanism of erythromycin inducible resistance. Proc. Natl. Acad. Sci. U.S.A. 77:7079–7083.

9. Horodniceanu, T., L. Bougueleret, N. El-Solh, D. H. Bouanchaud, and Y. A. Chabbert. 1979. Conjugative R plasmids in *Streptococcus agalactiae* (group B). Plasmid 2:197–206.

10. Jacob, A. E., and S. J. Hobbs. 1974. Conjugal transfer of plasmid-borne multiple antibiotic resistance in *Streptococcus faecalis* var. *zymogenes*. J. Bacteriol. 117:360–372.

11. Lai, C.-J., J. E. Dahlberg, and B. Weisblum. 1973. Structure of an inducibly methylatable nucleotide sequence in 23S ribosomal ribonucleic acid from erythromycin-resistant *Staphylococcus aureus*. Biochemistry 12:457–463.

12. Lai, C.-J., and B. Weisblum. 1971. Altered methylation of ribosomal RNA in an erythromycin-resistant strain of *Staphylococcus aureus*. Proc. Natl. Acad. Sci. U.S.A. 68:856–860.

13. LeBlanc, D. J., and F. P. Hassell. 1976. Transformation of *Streptococcus sanguis* Challis by plasmid deoxyribonucleic acid from *Streptococcus faecalis*. J. Bacteriol. 128:347–355.

14. Malke, H. 1979. Conjugal transfer of plasmids determining resistance to macrolides, lincosamides, and streptogramin-B type antibiotics among group A, B, D, and H streptococci. FEMS Microbiol. Lett. 5:335–338.

15. Parisi, J. T., J. Robbins, B. C. Lampson, and D. W. Hecht. 1981. Characterization of a macrolide, lincosamide, and streptogramin resistance plasmid in *Staphylococcus epidermidis*. J. Bacteriol. 148:559–564.

16. Shivakumar, A. G., J. Hahn, G. Grandi, Y. Kozlov, and D. Dubnau. 1980. Posttranscriptional regulation of an erythromycin resistance protein specified by plasmid pE194. Nucleic Acids Res. 4:1569–1578.

17. Southern, E. M. 1975. Detection of specific sequences among DNA fragments separated by gel electrophoresis. J. Mol. Biol. 98:503–517.

18. Weisblum, B., S. B. Holder, and S. M. Halling. 1979. Deoxyribonucleic acid sequence common to staphylococcal and streptococcal plasmids which specify erythromycin resistance. J. Bacteriol. 138:990–998.

19. Weisblum, B., C. Siddhikol, C.-J. Lai, and V. Demohn. 1971. Erythromycin-induced resistance in *Staphylococcus aureus*: requirements for induction. J. Bacteriol. 106:835–847.

20. Yagi, Y., A. E. Franke, and D. B. Clewell. 1975. Plasmid-determined resistance to erythromycin: comparison of strains of *Streptococcus faecalis* and *Streptococcus pyogenes* with regard to plasmid homology and resistance inducibility. Antimicrob. Agents Chemother. 7:871–873.

21. Yagi, Y., T. S. McLellan, W. A. Frez, and D. B. Clewell. 1978. Characterization of a small plasmid determining resistance to erythromycin, lincomycin, and vernamycin B alpha in a strain of *Streptococcus sanguis* isolated from dental plaque. Antimicrob. Agents Chemother. 13:884–887.

Resistance of Streptococci to Aminoglycoside-Aminocyclitol Antibiotics

C. CARLIER AND P. COURVALIN

Laboratoire de Biochimie, L.A. CNRS 271, Unité de Bactériologie Médicale, Institut Pasteur, F-75724 Paris, France

The aminoglycoside-aminocyclitols (AGAC) constitute a large and clinically important family of antibiotics (for information on the structure and chemistry of these compounds, see 34). Group D enterococci (*Streptococcus faecalis, S. faecium,* and *S. durans*) are intrinsically resistant to low levels of AGACs (minimal inhibitory concentrations [MICs] ≤ 250 µg/ml) (43). Uptake of AGACs by the cells requires oxidatively generated energy (3). "Low-level" resistance of enterococci therefore probably reflects inefficient AGAC active transport due to a defect in oxidative membrane energization (2). The cell wall seems also to play some role in this "taxonomic" type of resistance (32).

Clinical isolates of group D streptococci resistant to high levels (MICs > 2 mg/ml) of virtually all the commercially available AGACs (this includes neomycin B, paromomycin, lividomycin A, ribostamycin, butirosin, kanamycin A, B, and C, tobramycin, dibekacin, gentamicin, sisomicin, netilmicin, and streptomycin) have been reported (21, 23, 41). This high-level resistance is mediated by AGAC-modifying enzymes (9, 13, 27, 28, 38), and many of the corresponding genes (R determinants) are located on self-transferable plasmids (R plasmids).

As in gram-negative bacteria (for a review, see 16), the enzymes can be divided into three classes depending upon the reaction catalyzed (phosphorylation or adenylylation of hydroxyl group, acetylation of an amino group) and are named according to the site they modify on the antibiotic molecule (Table 1). The enzymes vary in their substrate ranges, which are often very broad (Table 2). Some modify structurally related compounds only: for example, the APH(2″) enzyme inactivates exclusively the 4,6 disubstituted deoxystreptamines (9). Others can modify structurally unrelated drugs: the APH(3′)(5″) type III enzyme inactivates both the 4,5 and 4,6 disubstituted deoxystreptamines (13, 28, 38). The enzyme can recognize two different hydroxyl groups which are, presumably, in similar structural neighborhoods (44). The modifying activities detected in the streptococci constitute a subset of the staphylococcal enzymes: en-

zymes with identical site specificity were previously found in the latter bacterial genus (11, 17, 22, 26, 30). Some of the enzymes, e.g., APH(2″), appear to be specific for the gram-positive cocci: they have not been detected in gram-negative bacteria.

The comparison of expression, function, and structure of several enzymes, based on determination of MICs in vivo, substrate profiles in vitro, pH optimum for activity, apparent molecular weight, isoelectric point, crossed immuno-electrophoresis results, and Southern hybridization of the plasmid genes, showed that enzymes with identical site specificity from gram-positive cocci were very similar, but differed from the corresponding enzymes of gram-negative bacteria (9, 10; T. J. White, D. I. Smith, S. Rosenthal, and J. Davies, Program Abstr. Intersci. Conf. Antimicrob. Agents Chemother. 18th, Atlanta, Ga., abstr. no. 287, 1978). The common aspects of streptococcal and staphylococcal resistance to AGACs have also been observed in the chloramphenicol (20) and macrolide-lincosamide-streptogramin-B (MLS) (46; H. Ounissi and P. Courvalin, this volume) antibiotic resistance systems. These findings support the notion of easy exchange of R determinants between these two phylogenetically remote genera of pathogenic bacteria. Indeed, in vitro direct plasmid transfer between streptococci and staphylococci has recently been obtained (19).

Despite the differences between the modifying enzymes from gram-positive and gram-negative organisms, there are common features in bacterial resistance to AGACs. The enzymes are synthesized constitutively, and there is no gross inactivation of the antibiotics in the culture medium (9–11, 13, 24). This latter observation is consistent with the notion that resistance to AGAC antibiotics is due to a balance between the rate of uptake and the rate of detoxification of the antibiotic (3). The enzymes, which are both necessary and sufficient to confer resistance (25), allow the host to grow in the presence of higher concentrations of unmodified antibiotics (15).

Serious group D streptococcal infections in

TABLE 1. Classes of AGAC-modifying enzymes found in gram-positive and gram-negative bacteria[a]

Enzyme	Gram positive		Gram negative
	Strepto-coccus	Staphylo-coccus	
Phosphotransferases			
APH (6)	?	−	+
APH (3′)(5″)-I	−	−	+
(3′)-II	−	−	+
(3′)(5″)-III	+	+	−
APH (2″)	+	+	−
APH (3″)	?	+	+
APH (5″)	−	−	+
Nucleotidyltransferases			
AAD (6)	?	+	−
AAD (9)	−	+	−
AAD (4′)(4″)	−	+	−
AAD (2″)	?	?	+
AAD (3″)(9)	?	+	+
Acetyltransferases			
AAC (3)	−	?	+
AAC (2′)	−	−	+
AAC (6′)	+	+	+

[a] Symbols: +, presence of enzyme; −, absence of enzyme; ?, preliminary evidence that an enzyme of this type is present, but without complete characterization; APH, aminoglycoside phosphotransferase; AAD, aminoglycoside adenylyltransferase; AAC, aminoglycoside acetyltransferase.

humans (e.g., endocarditis) are treated with penicillin and AGAC antibiotics (24). Group D streptococci resistant to high levels of an AGAC are refractory to synergism of penicillin with this antibiotic (5, 8, 9, 28, 41). Considering the variety of AGAC-modifying enzymes detected in streptococci, their broad substrate ranges, and the existence of their genes on self-transferable plasmids, we anticipated the emergence of strains refractory to synergism of all possible combinations of β-lactam and AGAC antibiotics (9). Such a strain has recently been isolated (A. Buu-Hoï, M. D. Kitzis, F. W. Goldstein, and J. F. Acar, Abstr. Annu. Meet. Am. Soc. Microbiol. 1981, A8, p. 2), and its enzyme content is being investigated in this laboratory.

TRANSPOSABLE AMINOGLYCOSIDE (AG) AND MLS RESISTANCE IN S. PNEUMONIAE

S. pneumoniae strain BM4200 is resistant to kanamycin, MLS constitutively, chloramphenicol, penicillin, tetracycline (and its lipophilic analogs minocycline and chelocardine), sulfonamide, and trimethoprim, and belongs to serotype 23. Resistance to high levels of kanamycin and structurally related compounds is due to the constitutive synthesis of an APH(3′)(5″) type III enzyme (P. Courvalin, C. Carlier, and E. Collatz, Program Abstr. Lunteren Lectures, 11th, Lunteren, the Netherlands, abstr. no. 85, 1979); resistance to chloramphenicol is due to production of a chloramphenicol acetyltransferase. We did not detect any β-lactamase in this strain. We

TABLE 2. Substrate ranges of streptococcal AGAC-modifying enzymes[a]

Antibiotic	Phosphotransferase				Nucleotidyltransferase			Acetyl-trans-ferase
	(6)	(3′)(5″)-III	(2″)	(3″)	(6)	(2″)	(3″)(9)	(6′)
Neomycin B	−	+	−	−	−	−	−	(+)
Paromomycin	−	+	−	−	−	−	−	−
Lividomycin A	−	+	−	−	−	−	−	−
Ribostamycin	−	+	−	−	−	−	−	+
Butirosin	−	+	−	−	−	−	−	(+)
Kanamycin A	−	+	(+)	−	−	+	−	+
Kanamycin B	−	+	(+)	−	−	+	−	+
Kanamycin C	−	+	(+)	−	−	+	−	−
Tobramycin	−	−	(+)	−	−	+	−	+
Dibekacin	−	−	(+)	−	−	+	−	+
Amikacin	−	+	(+)	−	−	−	−	+
Gentamicin C$_{1a}$	−	−	+	−	−	+	−	+
Gentamicin C$_1$	−	−	+	−	−	+	−	−
Gentamicin C$_2$	−	−	+	−	−	+	−	−
Sisomicin	−	−	+	−	−	+	−	(+)
Netilmicin	−	−	+	−	−	−	−	(+)
Streptomycin	+	−	−	+	+	−	+	−
Spectinomycin	−	−	−	−	−	−	+	−

[a] Symbols: +, substrate; (+), weak substrate; −, nonsubstrate. The fact that an antibiotic is a substrate for an enzyme does not obligatorily mean that strains harboring this enzyme are resistant to this antibiotic (see text). For the approximate composition of commercially available AGAC complexes, see reference 8.

failed to detect the presence of extrachromosomal DNA in strain BM4200 by ultracentrifugation in cesium chloride-ethidium bromide (9, 29)
and by agarose gel electrophoresis of crude
bacterial lysates (18). Similar negative results
have been reported (4; W. R. Guild, S. Hazum,
and M. D. Smith, Plasmid **5**:226, 1981), and it
has been suggested, on the basis of cosedimenta-
tion data (37), that the chloramphenicol, tetracycline, MLS, and AG "conjugative" (4; Guild et
al., Plasmid **5**:226, 1981) R determinants were
located in the chromosome (Guild et al., Plasmid
5:226, 1981).

The AGAC-modifying enzyme from strain
BM4200 was compared with phosphotransfer-
ases of identical site specificity from *Staphylococcus aureus* strains BM4600 (10) and RN450/
pSH2 (11) and *Streptococcus faecalis* strain
JH2-2/pJH1 (13). There was no apparent difference in the substrate profile, pH optimum for
activity, molecular weight (22,000), and isoelectric point (5.3) of the phosphotransferase from
the gram-positive cocci (Courvalin et al., Program Abstr. Lunteren Lectures, 11th, abstr. no.
85, 1979).

The AG and MLS R determinants from
BM4200 were cloned on plasmid ColE1::Tn*3*
(RSF2124 [39]) into *Escherichia coli*. As for
Bacillus circulans (14), *S. aureus* (12), and *S.
faecalis* (Carlier and Courvalin, unpublished
data) genes, we obtained constitutive phenotypic expression of the phosphotransferase in the
new host. However, as opposed to previous
attempts (7, 12), we also obtained full constitutive expression of the MLS R determinant.
Because of the demonstrated relationship between N^6-dimethylation of adenine in 23S rRNA
and resistance to MLS antibiotics in staphylococci and streptococci (45), it has been suggested that the presence of N^6-monomethyl adenine
residues in 23S rRNA of gram-negative bacteria,
combined with cellular impermeability, was responsible for the clinical unresponsiveness of
gram-negative organisms to MLS antibiotics
(42). Our data indicate that *E. coli* 23S rRNA is a
substrate for the pneumococcal methylase and
that dimethylation, rather than monomethyla-
tion, of adenine is the chemical modification
responsible for, apparently useless, MLS resistance in gram-negative organisms.

Staphylococcal plasmid pSH2 confers resistance to AG by synthesis of an APH(3')(5'')-III
(11) which has been shown, by electron microscopic analysis of heteroduplexes and by DNA
annealing, to be representative of this type of
enzyme in staphylococci (12) and in streptococci
(10). Transposable element Tn*551* from *S. aureus* (33, 45) is representative of MLS R determi-

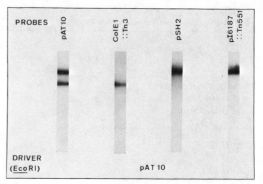

FIG. 1. Analysis of plasmid pAT10 DNA by hybridization. Total DNA from *S. pneumoniae* strain
BM 4200 and ColE1::Tn*3* (11 kilobases [14, 39]) DNA
digested with *Eco*RI and ligated was used to transform
E. coli as described (14). Clones were selected for their
ability to grow in the presence of ampicillin and
kanamycin. One transformant, which was also MLS
resistant, was studied further, and its hybrid plasmid
was called pAT10. Purified pAT10 (approximately 39
kilobases) DNA was digested with *Eco*RI. The resulting fragments were fractionated by electrophoresis
(36), transferred to a nitrocellulose sheet (40), and
hybridized (12) to in vitro ^{32}P-labeled (31) plasmid
DNA probes. Hybridization was revealed by autoradiography.

nants of class A (Ounissi and Courvalin, this
volume). The structural homology detected between the R determinants of pSH2, Tn*551*, and
BM4200 chromosome (Fig. 1) confirms the similarities observed at the enzyme level and constitutes further support for the notion of easy
exchange of genetic information within the
gram-positive cocci (10, 46).

The AG and MLS R determinants were transposed from pAT10 to the chromosome of a
recombination-deficient *E. coli* strain (data not
shown). The two R determinants were further
transposed from the host chromosome to various sites of a conjugative R plasmid (Fig. 2). The
structure and the properties of this new transposon, approximately 18.5 kilobases in length
and designated Tn*1545* (6), are being investigated in more detail.

Phenotypic expression of R determinants derived from gram-positive bacteria has been
shown to occur in gram-negative organisms (7,
12) and vice versa (35). We have demonstrated
full functional expression in *E. coli* of a transposable element originating in a gram-positive
bacterium. It seems, therefore, that the only
apparent barrier to the exchange and subsequent
spread of antibiotic resistance-mediating genes
between gram-positive and gram-negative bacte-

PROBE   PAT 10

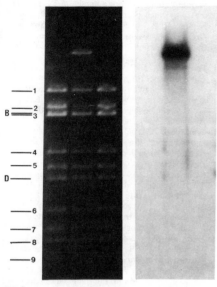

DRIVERS
(EcoR1)

pIP135-1
pIP135-1::Tn1545
pIP135-1

pIP135-1
pIP135-1::Tn1545
pIP135-1

FIG. 2. Transposition of pneumococcal Tn*1545* element in *E. coli*. The hybrid plasmid pAT10 was introduced into the recombination-deficient *E. coli* strain HB101 (1) by transformation. The AG and MLS R determinants were transposed into the host chromosome, and plasmid pAT10 was lost spontaneously (data not shown). Plasmid pIP135-1 (Tra$^+$, Inc M-7, Tc, Hg [A. Labigne-Roussel et al., submitted for publication]) was introduced into this latter strain by conjugation and was retransferred to *E. coli* strain BM694 (29) by conjugation with selection on nalidixic acid plus either kanamycin or erythromycin. Plasmid DNA from pIP135-1, from one of the transconjugants, and from a spontaneous AG-MLS–susceptible derivative of this transconjugant, was purified (29), digested with *Eco*RI, and analyzed by agarose gel electrophoresis (36) (left, from the left to the right). The DNA fragments were transferred to a nitrocellulose sheet (40) and hybridized (12) to an in vitro ^{32}P-labeled (31) pAT10 DNA probe (right). Comparative analysis of the *Eco*RI-generated fragment patterns (left) showed that Tn*1545* was integrated in pIP135-1 *Eco*RI fragment 2 and that the AG-MLS–susceptible derivative was generated by an apparently clean excision of Tn*1545*. The result of the hybridization experiment (right) is consistent with this interpretation.

ria lies in plasmid replication. To our knowledge, efficient replication of plasmids from gram-positive bacteria in gram-negative organisms or vice versa has not been reported.

ACKNOWLEDGMENTS

We thank F. W. Goldstein for the gift of *S. pneumoniae* strain BM4200, O. Rouelland for secretarial assistance, and Y. A. Chabbert for material support.

LITERATURE CITED

1. **Boyer, H. W., and D. Roulland-Dussoix.** 1969. A complementation analysis of the restriction and modification of DNA in *Escherichia coli*. J. Mol. Biol. **41**:459–472.
2. **Bryan, L. E., S. K. Kowand, and H. M. Van Den Elzen.** 1979. Mechanism of aminoglycoside antibiotic resistance in anaerobic bacteria: *Clostridium perfringens* and *Bacteroides fragilis*. Antimicrob. Agents Chemother. **15**:7–13.
3. **Bryan, L. E., and H. M. Van Den Elzen.** 1977. Effects of membrane-energy mutations and cations on streptomycin and gentamicin accumulation by bacteria: a model for entry of streptomycin and gentamicin in susceptible and resistant bacteria. Antimicrob. Agents Chemother. **12**:163-177.
4. **Buu-Hoï, A., and T. Horodniceanu.** 1980. Conjugative transfer of multiple antibiotic resistance markers in *Streptococcus pneumoniae*. J. Bacteriol. **143**:313–320.
5. **Calderwood, S. B., C. Wennerstein, and R. C. Moellering.** 1981. Resistance to antibiotic synergism in *Streptococcus faecalis*: further studies with amikacin and with a new amikacin derivate, 4′-deoxy, 6′-N-methylamikacin. Antimicrob. Agents Chemother. **19**:549–555.
6. **Campbell, A., D. E. Berg, D. Bostein, E. M. Lederberg, R. P. Novick, P. Starlinger, and W. Szybalski.** 1979. Nomenclature of transposable elements in prokaryotes. Gene **5**:197–206.
7. **Chang, A. C. Y., and S. N. Cohen.** 1974. Genome construction between bacterial species *in vitro*: replication and expression of *Staphylococcus* plasmid genes in *Escherichia coli*. Proc. Natl. Acad. Sci. U.S.A. **71**:1030–1034.
8. **Courvalin, P., and C. Carlier.** 1981. Resistance towards aminoglycoside-aminocyclitol antibiotics in bacteria. J. Antimicrob. Chemother. **8**(Suppl. A):57–69.
9. **Courvalin, P., C. Carlier, and E. Collatz.** 1980. Plasmid-mediated resistance to aminocyclitol antibiotics in group D streptococci. J. Bacteriol. **143**:541–551.
10. **Courvalin, P., C. Carlier, and E. Collatz.** 1980. Structural and functional relationships between aminoglycoside-modifying enzymes from streptococci and staphylococci, p. 309–320. *In* S. Mitsuhashi, L. Rosival, and V. Krcmery (ed.), Medical and biological aspects of resistant strains. Springer-Verlag, Berlin.
11. **Courvalin, P., and J. Davies.** 1977. Plasmid-mediated aminoglycoside phosphotransferase of broad substrate range that phosphorylates amikacin. Antimicrob. Agents Chemother. **11**:619–624.
12. **Courvalin, P., and M. Fiandt.** 1980. Aminoglycoside-modifying enzymes of *Staphylococcus aureus*: expression in *Escherichia coli*. Gene **9**:247–269.
13. **Courvalin, P. M., W. V. Shaw, and A. E. Jacob.** 1978. Plasmid-mediated mechanisms of resistance to aminoglycoside-aminocyclitol antibiotics and to chloramphenicol in group D streptococci. Antimicrob. Agents Chemother. **13**:716–725.
14. **Courvalin, P., B. Weisblum, and J. Davies.** 1977. Aminoglycoside-modifying enzyme of an antibiotic-producing bacterium acts as a determinant of antibiotic resistance in *Escherichia coli*. Proc. Natl. Acad. Sci. U.S.A. **74**:999–1003.
15. **Davies, J., and S. A. Kagan.** 1977. What is the mechanism of plasmid-determined resistance to aminoglycoside antibiotics, p. 207–215. *In* J. Drews and G. Hogenauer (ed.), R-factors: their properties and possible control. Springer-Verlag, New York.
16. **Davies, J., and D. I. Smith.** 1978. Plasmid-determined resistance to antimicrobial agents. Annu. Rev. Microbiol. **32**:469–518.

17. **Dowding, J. E.** 1977. Mechanisms of gentamicin resistance in *Staphylococcus aureus*. Antimicrob. Agents Chemother. **11**:47–50.

18. **Eckardt, T.** 1978. A rapid method for the identification of plasmid desoxyribonucleic acid in bacteria. Plasmid **1**:584–588.

19. **Engel, H. W. B., N. Soedirman, J. A. Rost, W. J. van Leeuwen, and J. D. A. van Embden.** 1980. Transferability of macrolide, lincomycin, and streptogramin resistances between group A, B, and D streptococci, *Streptococcus pneumoniae*, and *Staphylococcus aureus*. J. Bacteriol. **142**:407–413.

20. **Fitton, J. E., L. C. Packman, S. Harford, Y. Zaidenzaig, and W. V. Shaw.** 1978. Plasmids and the evolution of chloramphenicol resistance, p. 249–252. *In* D. Schlessinger (ed.), Microbiology—1978. American Society for Microbiology, Washington, D.C.

21. **Horodniceanu, T., L. Bougueleret, N. El Solh, G. Bieth, and F. Delbos.** 1979. High-level, plasmid-borne resistance to gentamicin in *Streptococcus faecalis* subsp. *zymogenes*. Antimicrob. Agents Chemother. **16**:686–689.

22. **Huang, T. S. R., and J. Davies.** 1979. Plasmid-determined aminoglycoside resistance in staphylococci, p. 225–234. *In* S. Mitsuhashi (ed.), Microbial drug resistance, vol. 2. Japan Scientific Societies Press, Tokyo.

23. **Jacob, A. E., and S. J. Hobbs.** 1974. Conjugal transfer of plasmid-borne multiple antibiotic resistance in *Streptococcus faecalis* var. *zymogenes*. J. Bacteriol. **117**:360–372.

24. **Jawetz, E., J. B. Gunnison, and V. R. Coleman.** 1950. The combined action of penicillin with streptomycin and chloromycetin on enterococci in vitro. Science **111**:254–256.

25. **Kagan, S. A., and J. E. Davies.** 1980. Enzymatic modification of aminocyclitol antibiotics: mutations affecting the expression of aminocyclitol acetyltransferase-3. Plasmid **3**:312–318.

26. **Kayser, F. H., M. Devaud, and J. Biber.** 1976. aminoglycoside 3′-phosphotransferase IV: a new type of aminoglycoside-phosphorylating enzyme found in staphylococci. Microbios Lett. **3**:63–68.

27. **Kono, M., H. Hamashima, and K. O'Hara.** 1981. Modification of aminoglycoside antibiotics by clinical isolates of *Streptococcus faecalis*. J. Antibiot. **34**:224–230.

28. **Krogstad, D. J., T. R. Korfhagen, R. C. Moellering, Jr., C. Wennersten, M. N. Swartz, S. Perzynsk, and J. Davies.** 1978. Aminoglycoside-inactivating enzymes in clinical isolates of *Streptococcus faecalis*. J. Clin. Invest. **62**:480–486.

29. **Labigne-Roussel, A., G. Gerbaud, and P. Courvalin.** 1981. Translocation of sequences encoding antibiotic resistance from the chromosome to a receptor plasmid in *Salmonella ordonez*. Mol. Gen. Genet. **182**:390–408.

30. **Le Goffic, F., A. Martel, N. Moreau, M. L. Capmau, C. J. Soussy, and J. Duval.** 1977. 2″-O-Phosphorylation of gentamicin components by a *Staphylococcus aureus* strain carrying a plasmid. Antimicrob. Agents Chemother. **12**:26–30.

31. **Maniatis, T., A. Jeffrey, and D. G. Kleid.** 1975. Nucleotide sequence of the rightward operator of phage λ. Proc. Natl. Acad. Sci. U.S.A. **72**:1184–1188.

32. **Moellering, R. C., Jr., and A. N. Weinberg.** 1971. Studies on antibiotic synergism against enterococci. II. Effect of various antibiotics on the uptake of ^{14}C-labelled streptomycin by enterococci. J. Clin. Invest. **50**:2580–2584.

33. **Novick, R. P., I. Edelman, M. D. Schwesinger, A. D. Gruss, E. C. Swanson, and P. A. Pattee.** 1979. Genetic translocation in *Staphylococcus aureus*. Proc. Natl. Acad. Sci. U.S.A. **76**:400–404.

34. **Price, K. E., J. C. Godfrey, and H. Kawaguchi.** 1977. Effect of structural modifications on the biological properties of aminoglycoside antibiotics containing 2-desoxystreptamine, p. 239–395. *In* D. Perlman (ed.), Structure-activity relationships among the semisynthetic antibiotics. Academic Press, Inc., New York.

35. **Schottel, J. L., M. J. Bibb, and S. N. Cohen.** 1981. Cloning and expression in *Streptomyces lividans* of antibiotic resistance genes derived from *Escherichia coli*. J. Bacteriol. **146**:360–368.

36. **Shinnick, T. M., E. Lund. O. Smithies, and F. R. Blattner.** 1975. Hydridization of labeled RNA to DNA in agarose gels. Nucleic Acids Res. **2**:1911–1929.

37. **Shoemaker, N. B., M. D. Smith, and W. Guild.** 1979. Organization and transfer of heterologous chloramphenicol and tetracycline resistance genes in *Pneumococcus*. J. Bacteriol. **139**:432–441.

38. **Slocombe, B.** 1978. Transmissible aminoglycoside resistance in *Streptococcus faecalis*, p. 801–893. *In* W. Siegenthaler and R. Lüthy (ed.), Current chemotherapy: proceedings of the 10th International Congress of Chemotherapy, vol. 2. American Society for Microbiology, Washington, D.C.

39. **So, M., R. Gill, and S. Falkow.** 1975. The generation of a ColE1-Apr cloning vehicle which allows detection of inserted DNA. Mol. Gen. Genet. **142**:239–249.

40. **Southern, E. M.** 1975. Detection of specific sequences among DNA fragments separated by gel electrophoresis. J. Mol. Biol. **98**:503–517.

41. **Standiford, H. D., H. B. de Maine, and W. M. M. Kirby.** 1970. Antibiotic synergism of enterococci. Arch. Intern. Med. **126**:255–259.

42. **Tanaka, T., and B. Weisblum.** 1975. Systematic difference in the methylation of ribosomal ribonucleic acid from gram-positive and gram-negative bacteria. J. Bacteriol. **123**:771–774.

43. **Toala, P., A. McDonald, C. Wilcox, and M. Finland.** 1969. Susceptibility of group D *Streptococcus* (*enterococcus*) to 21 antibiotics *in vitro*, with special reference to species difference. Am. J. Med. Sci. **258**:416–430.

44. **Umezawa, H.** 1979. Studies on aminoglycoside antibiotics: enzymic mechanism of resistance and genetics. J. Antibiot. **32**(Suppl.):1–14.

45. **Weisblum, B.** 1975. Altered methylation of ribosomal ribonucleic acid in erythromycin-resistant *Staphylococcus aureus*, p. 199–206. *In* D. Schlessinger (ed.), Microbiology—1974. American Society for Microbiology, Washington, D.C.

46. **Weisblum, B., S. B. Holder, and S. M. Halling.** 1979. Deoxyribonucleic acid sequence common to staphylococcal and streptococcal plasmids which specify erythromycin resistance. J. Bacteriol. **138**:990–998.

Heterogeneity of Macrolide-Lincosamide-Streptogramin B-Type Antibiotic Resistance Determinants

H. OUNISSI AND P. COURVALIN

Laboratoire de Biochimie, L.A. CNRS 271, Unité de Bactériologie Médicale, Institut Pasteur, F-75724 Paris, France

Resistance to macrolide-lincosamide-streptogramin B-type (MLS) antibiotics is widespread among clinical isolates (2, 3, 7, 9, 18; Table 2). This inducible or constitutive coresistance phenotype is generally associated with a specific N^6-dimethylation of adenine in 23S rRNA (23). Gram-positive cocci (streptococci-pneumococci and staphylococci) and anaerobes (gram-negative *Bacteroides fragilis* and gram-positive *Clostridium perfringens*) are both human pathogens which have common ecosystems (e.g., the human gut). Certain MLS R determinants from gram-positive cocci are located on transposons (Table 2), and there is no barrier to the expression of these resistance and transposition genes in *Escherichia coli* (C. Carlier and P. Courvalin, this volume). Transfer of genetic information between these phylogenetically remote bacterial genera may then occur in vivo and should influence the effectiveness of MLS therapy.

It has been suggested that antibiotic-producing organisms might represent the pool of origin of R determinants (22).

To test critically these two hypotheses, we compared, by the technique described by Southern (20), the MLS R determinants from clinical isolates of pathogenic bacteria and soil organisms; the results are summarized in Table 1.

We detected homology between some MLS R determinants from the gram-positive cocci but not between these and the genes from *Bacillus licheniformis* and *Bacteroides fragilis*. We did not find any homology between the streptococcal and staphylococcal plasmids tested. Based on these DNA-DNA hybridizations and on data obtained from the literature, we can define at least four distinct classes of MLS R determinants (Table 2).

The investigations, by DNA annealing, of the evolutionary origin and extent of transfer of genes which code for MLS resistance indicate the following. (i) There is substantial sequence diversity among the MLS R determinants, and our results do not support the hypothesis that these R determinants originated in soil organisms. (ii) As in the aminoglycoside-aminocyclitol (4, 5) and chloramphenicol (10) resistance systems, there is a recent common origin for the majority of MLS R determinants in streptococci-pneumococci and staphylococci. Our results

TABLE 1. Summary of the results of the hybridization experiments[a]

Driver (reference)	Probe				
	pI6187::Tn551	pC194	pC194Ω (pE194MLS)	pAD1::Tn917	pBD90
pI6187 (16)	+			−	
pI6187::Tn551 (15)	+	+	+	+	
pII147 (16)	+			−	
pII147::Tn554 (17)	+	+	+	−	
pC194 (12)		+	+		+
pC194Ω (pE194MLS) (13)		+	+		+
pBD90 (8)					+
pAD1 (21)				+	
pAD1::Tn917 (21)	−	−	−	+	
pDB201 (1)	−	−	−	+	
pIP411 (19)	−	−	−		−
pIP410 (19)	−	−	−		−

[a] Symbols: +, positive result; −, negative result. Driver plasmid DNAs were digested with restriction endonucleases *Eco*RI, *Taq*I, *Sau*3AI, or *Hin*dII. The resulting DNA fragments were fractionated by electrophoresis, transferred to nitrocellulose sheets (20), and hybridized to an in vitro ^{32}P-labeled plasmid cRNA (6) or a nick-translated DNA (14) probe, or to both. Hybridization was revealed by autoradiography.

TABLE 2. Classification of MLS R determinants[a]

Class	Inducibility or constitutivity	Genetic support	Original host	Reference
A	C	Tn551 (pI258)	S. aureus	24
	I	pAC-1	S. pyogenes (group A)	24
	C	pAMβ1	S. faecalis (group D)	24
	I	Tn917 (pAD2)	S. faecalis (group D)	This paper
	I	pAM77	S. sanguis (group H)	24
	I	pSM19035	S. sanguis (group H)	This paper
	C	Chromosome	S. pneumoniae B1,B363	24
	C	Tn1545 (chromosome)	S. pneumoniae BM4200	Carlier and Courvalin, this volume
B	I	pE194, pE5	S. aureus	8
C	I	Chromosome	B. licheniformis	8
D	C	pIP410	B. fragilis	This paper

[a] MLS R determinants of Tn554 (from S. aureus), Corynebacterium diphtheriae (7), Clostridium perfringens (9), and Streptomyces erythreus (11) were not classified.

support the notion of facile (direct or indirect) exchange of R determinants, but not of plasmids, within the gram-positive cocci. (iii) Gene transfer may not occur between gram-positive cocci and anaerobes (B. fragilis). (iv) The classes do not correlate with differences in regulation (inducibility or constitutivity). (v) Certain classes appear indigenous to particular bacterial species (e.g., B. licheniformis).

ACKNOWLEDGMENTS

We thank O. Rouelland for secretarial assistance and Y. A. Chabbert for material support.
H.O. was the recipient of a Bristol fellowship.

LITERATURE CITED

1. **Behnke, D., and J. J. Ferretti.** 1980. Molecular cloning of an erythromycin-resistance determinant in streptococci. J. Bacteriol. **144**:806–813.
2. **Chabbert, Y.** 1956. Antagonisme in vitro entre l'érythromycine et la spiramycine. Ann. Inst. Pasteur Paris. **90**:787–790.
3. **Courvalin, P. M., C. Carlier, and Y. A. Chabbert.** 1972. Plasmid-linked tetracycline and erythromycin resistance in group D "Streptococcus." Ann. Inst. Pasteur Paris **123**:755–759.
4. **Courvalin, P., C. Carlier, and E. Collatz.** 1980. Structural and functional relationships between aminoglycoside-modifying enzymes from streptococci and staphylococci, p. 309–320. In S. Mitsuhashi, L. Rosival, and V. Krcméry (ed.), Medical and biological aspects of resistant strains. Springer-Verlag, Berlin.
5. **Courvalin, P., C. Carlier, and E. Collatz.** 1980. Plasmid-mediated resistance to aminocyclitol antibiotics in group D streptococci. J. Bacteriol. **143**:541–551.
6. **Courvalin, P., and M. Fiandt.** 1980. Aminoglycoside-modifying enzymes of Staphylococcus aureus: expression in Escherichia coli. Gene **9**:247–269.
7. **Coyle, M. B., B. H. Minshew, J. A. Bland, and P. C. Hsu.** 1979. Erythromycin and clindamycin resistance in Corynebacterium diphteriae from skin lesions. Antimicrob. Agents Chemother. **16**:525–527.
8. **Docherty, A., G. Grandi, R. Grandi, T. J. Gryczan, A. G.** Shivakumar, and D. Dubnau. 1981. Naturally occurring macrolide-lincosamide-streptogramin B resistance in Bacillus licheniformis. J. Bacteriol. **145**:129–137.
9. **Dutta, G., and L. A. Devriese.** 1981. Macrolide-lincosamide-streptogramin resistance patterns in Clostridium perfringens from animals. Antimicrob. Agents Chemother. **19**:274–278.
10. **Fitton, J. E., L. C. Packman, S. Harford, Y. Zaidenzaig, and W. V. Shaw.** 1978. Plasmids and the evolution of chloramphenicol resistance, p. 249–252. In D. Schlessinger (ed.), Microbiology—1978. American Society for Microbiology, Washington, D.C.
11. **Graham, M. Y., and B. Weisblum.** 1979. 23S ribosomal ribonucleic acid of macrolide-producing Streptomyces contains methylated adenine. J. Bacteriol. **137**:1464–1467.
12. **Gryczan, T., A. G. Shivakumar, and D. Dubnau.** 1980. Characterization of chimeric plasmid cloning vehicles in Bacillus subtilis. J. Bacteriol. **141**:246–253.
13. **Horinouchi, S., and B. Weisblum.** 1980. Posttranscriptional modification of mRNA conformation: mechanism that regulates erythromycin-induced resistance. Proc. Natl. Acad. Sci. U.S.A. **77**:7079–7083.
14. **Maniatis, T., A. Jeffrey, and D. G. Kleid.** 1975. Nucleotide sequence of the rightward operator of phage λ. Proc. Natl. Acad. Sci. U.S.A. **72**:1184–1188.
15. **Novick, R. P., I. Edelman, M. D. Schwesinger, A. D. Gruss, E. C. Swanson, and P. A. Pattee.** 1979. Genetic translocation in Staphylococcus aureus Proc. Natl. Acad. Sci. U.S.A. **76**:400–404.
16. **Novick, R. P., and M. H. Richmond.** 1965. Nature and interaction of the genetic elements governing penicillinase synthesis in S. aureus. J. Bacteriol. **90**:467.
17. **Phillips, S., and R. P. Novick.** 1979. Tn554-a-site-specific repressor-controlled transposon in Staphylococcus aureus. Nature (London) **278**:476–478.
18. **Privitera, G., G. Botta, and M. Sebald.** 1981. Macrolide, lincosamide, streptogramin and tetracycline transferable resistance in the Bacteroides fragilis group. J. Antimicrob. Chemother. **8**(Suppl D):87–94.
19. **Privitera, G., A. Dublanchet, and M. Sebald.** 1979. Transfer of multiple antibiotic resistance between subspecies of Bacteroides fragilis. J. Infect. Dis. **139**:97–101.
20. **Southern, E. M.** 1975. Detection of specific sequences among DNA fragments separated by gel electrophoresis. J. Mol. Biol. **98**:503–517.
21. **Tomich, P. K., F. Y. An, and D. B. Clewell.** 1980. Proper-

ties of erythromycin-inducible transposon Tn9*17* in *Strep-tococcus faecalis*. J. Bacteriol. **141**:1366–1374.

22. **Walker, M. S., and J. B. Walker.** 1970. Streptomycin biosynthesis and metabolism. J. Biol. Chem. **245**:6683–6689.

23. **Weisblum, B.** 1975. Altered methylation of ribosomal ribonucleic acid in erythromycin-resistant *Staphylococ-*

cus aureus, p. 199–206. In D. Schlessinger (ed.), Microbiology—1974. American Society for Microbiology, Washington, D.C.

24. **Weisblum, B., S. B. Holder, and S. M. Halling.** 1979. Deoxyribonucleic acid sequence common to staphylococcal and streptococcal plasmids which specify erythromycin resistance. J. Bacteriol. **138**:990–998.

Genetic and Physical Characterization of Two Chromosomal Resistance Determinants of *Streptococcus agalactiae*

JULIA INAMINE AND VICKERS BURDETT

Department of Microbiology, Duke University Medical Center, Durham, North Carolina 27710

The presence of R plasmids has long been considered to be the sine qua non for infectious multiple antibiotic resistance among clinical isolates of bacteria. Indeed, these genetic elements are ubiquitous among gram-negative organisms. Recent studies indicate, however, that the conjugal transfer of resistance determinants among gram-positive isolates, especially the streptococci, may also occur in the absence of detectable extrachromosomal DNA (3). The report of a chromosome-borne tetracycline resistance transposon, Tn916, in *Streptococcus faecalis* (6) raises questions as to the relationship between the plasmid and nonplasmid resistance genes. We have detected three distinct, nonhomologous, tetracycline resistance determinants in *S. agalactiae* by DNA-DNA hybridization studies (2). One of these, designated *tetM*, is a chromosomal determinant which hybridizes to Tn916 and which shows genetic linkage to two other antibiotic resistance determinants. We present here the initial genetic and physical characterization of this chromosomal resistance region. In addition, we describe some of our preliminary results concerning the presence of these determinants in other resistant strains. The methods used for filter mating experiments, minimal inhibitory concentration (MIC) measurements, and the determination of the type of resistance expression are published procedures (see the footnotes to Tables 1, 2, and 3). Methods for cloning, restriction enzyme mapping, deletion analysis, and DNA transfer and hybridization are described in detail elsewhere (2; J. Inamine and V. Burdett, in preparation; see also V. Burdett, J. Inamine, and S. Rajagopalan, this volume).

The *tetM* determinant was isolated from *S. agalactiae* (group B) B109. This strain is also resistant to chloramphenicol and the MLS antibiotics (macrolides such as erythromycin, lincosamides, and the streptogramin B-type antibiotics). Horodniceanu et al. (8) showed that these resistance markers can be transferred en bloc by a conjugation-like process and that this transfer occurs in the absence of detectable plasmid DNA. We used this strain as the donor in filter mating experiments with group B, D, and H recipients (Table 1). The transfer frequencies, expressed as the number of transconjugants per donor colony-forming unit, ranged from 10^{-5} to 10^{-4} for transfer to group B recipients and from 10^{-8} to 10^{-7} for transfer to group D and H recipients. The tetracycline (Tc), chloramphenicol (Cm), and erythromycin (Em) resistance markers were cotransferred from B109 except in one mating with JH2-2$_D$. In this case, a transconjugant which had acquired only tetracycline resistance was also obtained. Four transconjugants were examined for their ability to retransfer the resistance determinants (Table 2). The Tc Cm Em resistance markers were co-transferred from the group B donors at frequencies similar to those seen with B109. Only one transconjugant among 100 colonies screened was chloramphenicol susceptible. The Tc and Tc Em resistance determinants were transferred from JH2-2 (B109T) and JH2-2 (B109 TCE), respectively, at frequencies similar to that seen from B109 to group D recipients. Both the transfer of Tc alone from B109 to JH2-2$_D$ and the transfer of Tc Em from JH2-2 (B109 TCE) to JH203 were detected only once in three independent but identical experiments; the data shown are from the experiments in which transfer was detected. All of the other transfer frequencies represent the average of at least two mating experiments (data not shown). These results suggest that the transfer of resistance determinants from *S. agalactiae* B109 is partially dependent on the recipient strain utilized. A conjugal Tc element was distinguished from a Tc Cm Em element by using the JH2-2$_D$ recipient; these two elements retransfer at their own characteristic frequencies from JH2-2$_D$ donors. The separation of these elements has not been detected in matings of B109 with group B or H recipients. JH2-2 (B109 TCE) and JH2-2 (B109 T) were chosen for further study because of this difference.

B109, JH2-2, JH2-2 (B109 TCE), and JH2-2 (B109 T) were characterized as to their levels of resistance to tetracycline, chloramphenicol, and erythromycin, and whether the expression of these resistances was inducible or constitutive.

TABLE 1. Transfer of resistance markers from B109[a]

Recipient[b]	Donor marker selected[c]	Frequency of transfer[d]	Phenotype of transconjugants	Designation of transconjugants
MV757$_B$	T	10^{-5}	TCE	MV757 (B109 TCE)
MV762$_B$	T	10^{-4}	TCE	MV762 (B109 TCE)
	C	10^{-5}	TCE	
	E	10^{-5}	TCE	
JH2-2$_D$	T	10^{-7}	TCE	JH2-2 (B109 TCE)
			T	JH2-2 (B109 T)
	C	10^{-7}	TCE	
	E	10^{-8}	TCE	
JH203$_D$	T	10^{-7}	TCE	JH203 (B109 TCE)
V481$_H$	T	10^{-7}	TCE	V481 (B109 TCE)
	E	10^{-7}	TCE	

[a] The filter mating procedure and strains MV157$_B$, MV762$_B$, JH2-2$_D$, and JH203$_D$ have been described (1). MV757$_B$ is a rifampin-resistant mutant derived from MV157$_B$. V481$_H$ is a rifampin-resistant *S. sanguis* Challis strain obtained from F. Macrina.

[b] Subscript indicates serotype B, D, or H.

[c] T, Tetracycline; C, chloramphenicol; E, erythromycin. Antibiotic concentrations were 10 µg/ml.

[d] Calculated as the number of transconjugants per donor colony-forming unit.

The results are summarized in Table 3. The growth in broth of the inducibly resistant strains was temporarily inhibited by a high concentration of antibiotic unless they were pregrown in a subinhibitory concentration of the same drug. The expression of tetracycline resistance could not be defined as either inducible or constitutive for B109, whereas JH2-2 (B109 TCE) is inducible and JH2-2 (B109 T) is constitutive. This observation was of special interest since a number of tetracycline-resistant group B streptococci (both plasmid- and non-plasmid-mediated), representing several genetically nonhomologous resistance determinants (2), were all found to express constitutive resistance to tetracycline (1).

To further study the genetic organization of the resistance region of B109, we cloned the tetracycline and chloramphenicol resistance genes in *E. coli* (2; Inamine and Burdett, in preparation). Those regions within the cloned fragments which are necessary and sufficient for resistance have been defined by deletion analysis. The tetracycline resistance gene resides within a 5-kilobase (kb) *Hinc*II fragment which has been subcloned into pACYC177; this plasmid has been designated pJI3. The chloramphenicol resistance gene has been cloned into

TABLE 2. Transfer of resistance markers from transconjugants[a]

Donor	Recipient[b]	Donor marker selected[c]	Frequency of transfer[d]	Phenotype of transconjugants
MV757 (B109 TCE)	MV762$_B$	T	10^{-6}	TCE
				TE
MV757 (B109 TCE)	MV759$_B$	T	10^{-5}	TCE
		C	10^{-6}	TCE
		E	10^{-6}	TCE
JH2-2 (B109 TCE)	JH203$_D$	T	10^{-8}	TE
JH2-2 (B109 T)	JH203$_D$	T	10^{-7}	T

[a] See footnote a of Table 1. MV759$_B$ is a streptomycin-resistant mutant of MV157$_B$.

[b] Subscript indicates serotype B, D, or H.

[c] T, Tetracycline; C, chloramphenicol; E, erythromycin. Antibiotic concentrations were 10 µg/ml.

[d] Calculated as the number of transconjugants per donor colony-forming unit.

TABLE 3. Resistance characteristics of selected strains[a]

Strain	Tetracycline		Chloramphenicol		Erythromycin	
	MIC	Expression	MIC	Expression	MIC	Expression
B109	40	I/C	40	I	640	I
JH2-2	0.63	—	5	—	0.31	—
JH2-2 (B109 TCE)	20	I	80	I	640	I
JH2-2 (B109 T)	40	C	5	—	0.31	—

[a] The broth dilution method used to determine the MIC has been described (2). The MIC represents the lowest concentration (μg/ml) of antibiotic at which complete inhibition occurs. The procedure for determining whether resistance is inducible or constitutive has also been described (7). Tetracycline, chloramphenicol, or erythromycin was used as the inducer and as challenge drug at 0.5 and 5 μg/ml, 0.5 and 10 μg/ml, or 0.05 and 5 μg/ml, respectively. I, Inducible; C, constitutive; —, not applicable.

pACYC177 on a 2.2-kb HindIII fragment, and this plasmid has been designated pJI5. These recombinant plasmids were used as probes in Southern transfer hybridization experiments with DNAs from tetracycline- and chloramphenicol-resistant strains, including the transconjugants JH2-2 (B109 TCE) and JH2-2 (B109 T). A summary of some of our results is shown in Table 4. Although the probes hybridize to specific fragments of chromosomal DNA from resistant strains, the organization of the resistance determinants appears to be different as judged by the size of these fragments. There was no detectable homology of either probe to DNAs

from tetracycline- and chloramphenicol-susceptible strains. Note that strain B109 contains two HincII fragments which hybridize to the Tc probe (pJI3): the fragments are 5.0 and 4.9 kb in size, and the Tc probe contains a cloned 5.0-kb HincII fragment. Examination of JH2-2 (B109 T) and JH2-2 (B109 TCE) revealed that the former contains only the 5.0-kb fragment whereas the latter contains a 4.9-kb fragment. Prolonged exposure of the autoradiogram allowed us to detect an additional 3.2-kb HincII fragment which hybridizes very poorly to the Tc probe (data not shown); this fragment was found in DNAs from B109 or JH2-2 (B109 TCE) but not

TABLE 4. Summary of selected Southern hybridization experiments[a]

Source of DNA electrophoresed on gel	Relevant cellular phenotype of strain[b]	Size of fragments hybridizing to probe (kb)	
		Tc probe[c]	Cm probe[d]
S. agalactiae[e]			
B109	Tc Cm MLS	5.0	2.2
		4.9	
MV107	Tc	12.0	NT
MV158	Tc Cm	5.0	3.0
MV762	—	NDH	NDH
S. faecalis[f]			
DS16C3	Tc	5.0	NT
JH2-2 (B109 TCE)	Tc Cm MLS	4.9	2.2
JH2-2 (B109 T)	Tc	5.0	NT
JH2-2	—	NDH	NDH
S. pneumoniae[g]			
BM6001	Tc Cm	20.6	2.2
N77	Tc Cm	5.0	2.2

[a] The methods for sequence-specific nuclease digestion, gel electrophoresis, and DNA transfer and hybridization have been described (2). Chromosomal DNAs were digested with HincII for hybridization to the Tc probe and HindIII for hybridization to the Cm probe. NT, Not tested; NDH, no detectable homology.

[b] Tc, Tetracycline resistance; Cm, chloramphenicol resistance; MLS, MLS resistance; —, susceptible to tetracycline, chloramphenicol, and the MLS antibiotics.

[c] The Tc probe was ³²P-labeled pJI3, which is a 5.0-kb HincII fragment of B109 DNA cloned into pACYC177.

[d] The Cm probe was ³²P-labeled pJI5, which is a 2.2-kb HindIII fragment of B109 DNA cloned into pACYC177.

[e] References: B109 (8), MV107 (5), MV158 (1), MV762 (1).

[f] References: DS16C3::Tn916 (6); JH2-2 (B109 TCE), this paper; JH2-2 (B109 T), this paper; JH2-2 (7).

[g] References: BM6001 (4), N77 (9).

from JH2-2 (B109 T). This, together with the differential transfer properties and expression of tetracycline resistance of these transconjugants, suggests that at least two Tc genes exist in the chromosome of B109. We have tested this hypothesis by cloning the tetracycline resistance determinant of JH2-2 (B109 TCE). Preliminary results show that this cloned insert contains both a 4.9- and a 3.2-kb *Hinc*II fragment and not a 5.0-kb fragment; the 4.9-kb fragment hybridizes to the Tc probe, but we have not established the identity of the 3.2-kb fragment. Although we have not yet defined the resistance region of this second Tc determinant by deletion analysis, the data suggest that the region(s) of homology corresponds to the region responsible for tetracycline resistance.

The study of the organization of the Tc Cm Em region of the B109 chromosome should provide some insights into the mechanism of transfer of chromosomal resistance determinants in *S. agalactiae*. To this end, we have also recently cloned the Em gene(s) from B109 and the Cm and Em genes from JH2-2 (B109 TCE). Studies on these clones are currently under way.

ACKNOWLEDGMENTS

This work was supported by Public Health Service grant AI 15619 from the National Institute of Allergy and Infectious Diseases. J.I. was supported by a Graduate Fellowship from the National Science Foundation.

We thank Dale Blazey for helpful suggestions and Dayle Wilkins for typing the manuscript.

LITERATURE CITED

1. **Burdett, V.** 1980. Identification of tetracycline-resistant R-plasmids in *Streptococcus agalactiae* (group B). Antimicrob. Agents Chemother. **18**:753–760.
2. **Burdett, V., J. Inamine, and S. Rajagopalan.** 1982. Heterogeneity of tetracycline resistance determinants in *Streptococcus*. J. Bacteriol. **149**:995–1004.
3. **Clewell, D. B.** 1981. Conjugation and resistance transfer in streptococci and other gram positive species: plasmids, sex pheromones and "conjugative transposons" (a review), p. 191–205. *In* S. B. Levy, R. C. Clowes, and E. L. Koenig (ed.), Molecular biology, pathogenicity, and ecology of bacterial plasmids. Plenum Press, New York.
4. **Dang-Van, A., G. Tiraby, J. F. Acar, W. V. Shaw, and D. H. Bouanchaud.** 1978. Chloramphenicol resistance in *Streptococcus pneumoniae*: enzymatic acetylation and possible plasmid linkage. Antimicrob. Agents Chemother. **13**:577–583.
5. **Dixon, J. M. S., and A. E. Lipinski.** 1974. Infections with β-hemolytic *Streptococcus* resistant to lincomycin and erythromycin and observations on zonal-pattern resistance to lincomycin. J. Infect. Dis. **130**:351–356.
6. **Franke, A. E., and D. B. Clewell.** 1981. Evidence for a chromosome-borne resistance transposon (Tn*916*) in *Streptococcus faecalis* that is capable of "conjugal" transfer in the absence of a conjugative plasmid. J. Bacteriol. **145**:494–502.
7. **Hershfield, V.** 1979. Plasmids mediating multiple drug resistance in Group B streptococcus: transferability and molecular properties. Plasmid **2**:137–149.
8. **Horodniceanu, T., L. Bougueleret, and G. Bieth.** 1981. Conjugative transfer of multiple-antibiotic resistance markers in beta-hemolytic Group A, B, F, and G streptococci in the absence of extrachromosomal deoxyribonucleic acid. Plasmid **5**:127–137.
9. **Miyamura, S., H. Ochiai, Y. Nitahara, Y. Nakagawa, and M. Terao.** 1977. Resistance mechanism of chloramphenicol in *Streptococcus haemolyticus, Streptococcus pneumoniae*, and *Streptococcus faecalis*. Microbiol. Immunol. **21**:69–76.

Evolutionary Relatedness of MLS Resistance and Replication Function Sequences on Streptococcal Antibiotic Resistance Plasmids

MICHAEL S. GILMORE, DETLEV BEHNKE, AND JOSEPH J. FERRETTI

Department of Microbiology and Immunology, and Department of Biochemistry and Molecular Biology, University of Oklahoma Health Sciences Center, Oklahoma City, Oklahoma 73190, and Academy of Sciences of the German Democratic Republic, Central Institute for Microbiology and Experimental Therapy, DDR-69 Jena, German Democratic Republic

Plasmid-mediated resistance to erythromycin and other antibiotics in the macrolide, lincosamide, and streptogramin B (MLS) group has been well documented in clinically significant streptococcal strains (J. M. S. Dixon and A. E. Lipinsky, this volume) and is being observed with increasing frequency (S. Mitsuhashi et al., this volume). Several patterns of MLS resistance in streptococci have been reported, including inducible and constitutive resistance as well as the recently described zonal resistance phenotype (8, 11). However, only a single mechanism for enzyme-mediated MLS resistance in streptococci has been described, specifically, the N^6 dimethylation of 23S RNA adenine residues (18).

The discovery that antibiotic-producing microorganisms contain enzymes that modify the antibiotics they produce and that resemble the plasmid-mediated enzymes of antibiotic-resistant clinical isolates has led to the suggestion that resistance determinants originated in the antibiotic-producing organisms and were spread to other organisms by various genetic exchange mechanisms (3, 16). Support for this theory, as it applies to streptococcal MLS resistance, is derived from the demonstration that a *Streptomyces erythreus* strain known to produce erythromycin exhibits MLS resistance by the same mechanism as was characterized in resistant strains of streptococci (6). Furthermore, Weisblum and co-workers (18) demonstrated that radiolabeled cRNA probe sequences derived from streptococcal plasmids pAM77 (group H) and PAMβ1 (group D), as well as staphylococcal plasmid pI258, cross-hybridized to immobilized restriction endonuclease digests of these three plasmids and also to digests of pAC1 (group A) and MLS-resistant *S. pneumoniae* chromosomal DNA. In these experiments, hybridization to immobilized pI258 endonuclease digests was localized to a fragment known to include the MLS resistance transposon Tn551 (18).

The present study was initiated to determine the evolutionary relatedness of a spectrum of MLS resistance determinants from the clinically relevant streptococcal groups A, B, D, and H, including both inducible and zonal resistance phenotypes. Also included were MLS resistance plasmids from *Bacteroides fragilis* (pIP410 or pBF4; 13, 19) and *Staphylococcus aureus* (pI258 and pE194) and chromosomal resistance determinants in *S. erythreus* NRRL 2338 and *Lactobacillus casei* ATCC 21053. We assessed the homology of these various MLS resistance determinants by using the hybridization technique described by Southern (14). A specific MLS resistance probe sequence was obtained from the well-characterized group A plasmid pSM19035 (1). By using this 1.7-kilobase (kb) MLS resistance determinant, it was intended to minimize false-positive signals derived from homology between non-MLS resistance coding regions and, additionally, to determine the location of the MLS resistance determinant on other MLS resistance plasmids.

It was also of interest to determine the relationship of the replicons carrying these determinants since the discovery of transposon-mediated resistance in both streptococci and staphylococci suggested that MLS resistance gene proliferation could occur independent of plasmid sequences. Since transposon-mediated resistance implies facultative association with plasmid replicons, restriction endonuclease digests of both MLS and non-MLS resistance plasmids were used in homology studies employing a 1.5-kb fragment known to contain the replication origin and copy control region of the group A plasmid pSM19035.

HOMOLOGY OF MLS RESISTANCE SEQUENCES

The phenotypic properties associated with plasmids used in this study, and their respective strains, are summarized in Table 1. Hybridiza-

174

TABLE 1. Bacterial strains, plasmids, and results of Southern hybridization with the MLS or replication copy control probes derived from *S. pyogenes* plasmid pSM19035 and immobilized restriction endonuclease digests of plasmids

Original host species	Host designation	Reference	Plasmid	Phenotype[a]	MLS	Rep
S. pyogenes	SM10	9	pSM10	MLS zonal	+[b]	+
S. pyogenes	SM10419	11	pSM10419	MLS zonal	+	+
S. pyogenes	SM13234L	10	ERL1	MLS, Tra	+	+
S. agalactiae	SM301	2	pGB301	MLS, Cm	+	+
S. agalactiae	B96	7	pIP501	MLS, Cm, Tra	+	+
S. faecalis	DS16	15	pAD2 (Tn917)	MLS, Km, Sm	+	−
S. faecalis	DS5	20	pAMα1	Tc	NT	−
S. faecalis	SF351	—[c]	pSF351C61	Tc	NT	−
S. faecalis	BM4100	5	pIP800/802	Cm, Gm, Km	NT	−
S. faecalis	SF9400	—[c]	pSF9400	MLS, Bcn	+	+
S. sanguis	A1	21	pAM77	MLS	+	−
S. aureus	RN453	12	pI258 (Tn551)	MLS, Pn, As, Hg, Pb, Cd	+	−
S. aureus	Rn2442	17	pE194	MLS	−	−
B. fragilis	92/77	13	pIP410	MLS, Tra	−	−
S. erythreus	NRRL 2338	6		MLS producer	−	−
L. casei	ATCC 21053	B. Chassy		MLS	−	−

[a] Resistance to: MLS, macrolide, lincosamide, streptogramin B; Zonal, zonal lincosamide resistance; Cm, chloramphenicol; Km, kanamycin; Sm, streptomycin; Gm, gentamicin; Tc, tetracycline; Pn, penicillin; Em, erythromycin; As, arsenate and arsenite; Hg, mercury; Pb, lead, Cd, cadmium. Also, Bcn, bacteriocin; and Tra, transmissible.

[b] Detectable hybridization to the MLS or replication origin/copy control (Rep) probe is indicated by +; lack of detectable hybridization, by −. NT, Not tested.

[c] B. A. Forbes, Ph.D. thesis, University of Oklahoma Health Sciences Center, Oklahoma City, 1979.

tion of the specific MLS resistance probe to immobilized restriction enzyme digests of the plasmid indicated that the streptococcal MLS resistance determinant, regardless of phenotypic permutation, was highly conserved. That is, detectable homology was observed between the MLS resistance probe and transposon-mediated MLS resistance sequence (Tn917), zonally expressed MLS resistance sequence, and MLS resistance sequences occurring on plasmids isolated from streptococcal groups A, B, D, and H (Table 1). DNA sequence homology between the radiolabeled streptococcal group A MLS resistance probe and staphylococcal plasmid pI258 was also observed, in agreement with earlier analogous experiments (18). However, no hybridization was observed between the MLS resistance probe and the determinants residing on *S. aureus* pE194 and *B. fragilis* pIP410 plasmids or chromosomal determinants derived from *S. erythreus* and *L. casei*.

HOMOLOGY OF REPLICATION ORIGIN/ COPY CONTROL SEQUENCES

Hybridization of the replication origin/copy control probe, derived from a 1.5-kb *Hind*III fragment of pSM19035, was observed with all MLS resistance plasmids giving a positive signal for MLS resistance homology in the previous paragraph, except for pAD2, pI258, and pAM77.

Lack of sequence homology between the replication origin/copy control probe and pAD2 and pI258, despite the intense hybridization observed with the MLS resistance determinants on these two plasmids, might have been expected since both pAD2 and pI258 possessed transposon-mediated genes. The lack of hybridization between the replication origin/copy control probe and pAM77 suggested the possibility that the MLS resistance determinant of pAM77 originated as a transposable element. In this regard, it is interesting to note that pAM77 (7 kb) is much smaller in size than most other naturally occurring MLS resistance plasmids (4). Additionally, no sequence homology between the replication origin/copy control probe and respective regions on non-MLS resistance probes was detected.

DISCUSSION

The results of this study indicate that the MLS resistance determinants in streptococci share a common ancestry and demonstrate little evolutionary divergence. Included among homologous MLS resistance determinants were those from Lancefield groups A, B, D, and H specifying inducible and zonal resistance and transposon-mediated MLS resistance. The MLS resistance determinant characteristic of this plasmid family (and probable incompatibility group) is homologous to both transposon Tn*917* (*S. faecalis*) and Tn*551* (*S. aureus*), and we conclude that these transposable elements share the same derivation. These results also suggest that the zonal MLS resistance phenotype is the consequence of a small and evolutionarily recent mutation. Lack of homology with the streptococcal MLS resistance determinant as assessed by hybridization was observed with plasmids pE194 (*S. aureus*) and pIP410 (*B. fragilis*) and chromosomal determinants from *L. casei* ATCC 21053 and *S. erythreus* NRRL 2338. The lack of observable hybridization to these MLS resistance determinants, most notably the MLS resistance sequence in the erythromycin-producing organism *S. erythreus*, may have been attributable to the stringent conditions under which hybridization was performed and the small size (1.7 kb) of the probe fragment, disallowing extensive mismatch. A direct comparison of these nucleotide sequences will therefore be necessary to demonstrate the relationship of nonhybridizing MLS resistance determinants. These MLS resistance genes may represent examples of evolutionary convergence or divergence; a discussion of the latter is presented in this volume (S. Horinouchi and B. Weisblum).

The concurrent existence of both MLS resistance and replication origin/copy control homology between the specific probes and respective regions on a broad sampling of MLS resistance plasmids from diverse streptococcal groups suggests a linkage between the replicon and the MLS resistance gene. This deduction is emphasized by the observance of strong hybridization of the probe to pIP501 (group B, Em^r, Cm^r) and not to pIP800/802 (group D, Cm^r, Gm^r, Km^r) or other non-MLS resistance plasmid sequences.

ACKNOWLEDGMENTS

This work was supported by a grant from the Chauncey and Marion Deering McCormick Foundation, Chicago, Ill., and the research exchange program between the National Academy of Sciences of the United States and the Academy of Sciences of the German Democratic Republic. M.S.G. is the recipient of a Colin Munroe MacLeod research fellowship.

LITERATURE CITED

1. **Behnke, D., and J. J. Ferretti.** 1980. Molecular cloning of an erythromycin resistance determinant in streptococci. J. Bacteriol. **144**:806–813.
2. **Behnke, D., M. S. Gilmore, and J. J. Ferretti.** 1981. Plasmid pGB301, a new multiple resistance streptococcal cloning vehicle and its use in cloning of a gentamicin/kanamycin resistance determinant. Mol. Gen. Genet. **182**:414–421.
3. **Benveniste, R., and J. Davies.** 1973. Aminoglycoside antibiotic inactivating enzymes in actinomycetes similar to those present in clinical isolates of antibiotic resistant bacteria. Proc. Natl. Acad. Sci. U.S.A. **70**:2276–2280.
4. **Clewell, D. B.** 1981. Plasmids, drug resistance, and gene transfer in the genus *Streptococcus*. Microbiol. Rev. **45**:409–436.
5. **Courvalin, P., C. Carlier, and E. Collatz.** 1980. Plasmid mediated resistance to aminocyclitol antibiotics in group D streptococci. J. Bacteriol. **143**:541–551.
6. **Graham, M. Y., and B. Weisblum.** 1979. 23S ribosomal ribonucleic acid of macrolide-producing streptomycetes contains methylated adenine. J. Bacteriol. **137**:1464–1467.
7. **Hershfield, V.** 1979. Plasmids mediating multiple drug resistance in group B *Streptococcus*: transferability and molecular properties. Plasmid **2**:137–149.
8. **Horodniceanu, T., L. Bougueleret, and F. Delbos.** 1980. Phenotypic aspects of resistance to macrolide and related antibiotics in 3-haemolitic group A, B, C, and G streptococci, p. 122–131. *In* Recent developments in laboratory identification techniques. Excerpta Medica, Amsterdam.
9. **Malke, H., L. G. Burman, and S. E. Holm.** 1981. Molecular cloning in streptococci: physical mapping of the vehicle plasmid pSM10 and demonstration of intergroup DNA transfer. Mol. Gen. Genet. **181**:259–267.
10. **Malke, H., H. E. Jacob, and K. Störl.** 1976. Characterization of the antibiotic resistance plasmid ERL1 from *Streptococcus pyogenes*. Mol. Gen. Genet. **144**:333–338.
11. **Malke, H., W. Reichardt, M. Hartmann, and F. Walter.** 1981. Genetic study of plasmid-associated zonal resistance to lincomycin in *Streptococcus pyogenes*. Antimicrob. Agents Chemother. **19**:91–100.
12. **Novik, R. P., E. Murphy, T. J. Gryczan, E. Baron, and I. Edelman.** 1979. Penicillinase plasmids of *Staphylococcus aureus*: restriction-deletion maps. Plasmid **2**:109–129.
13. **Privitera, G., A. Dublanchet, and M. Sebald.** 1979. Transfer of multiple antibiotic resistance between subspecies of *Bacteroides fragilis*. J. Infect. Dis. **139**:97–101.
14. **Southern, E. M.** 1975. Detection of specific sequences among DNA fragments separated by gel electrophoresis. J. Mol. Biol. **98**:503–517.
15. **Tomich, P., F. An, S. Damle, and D. B. Clewell.** 1979. Plasmid related transmissibility and multiple drug resistance in *Streptococcus fecalis* subsp. *zymogenes* strain D16. Antimicrob. Agents Chemother. **15**:828–830.
16. **Walker, M. S., and J. B. Walker.** 1970. Streptomycin biosynthesis and metabolism. J. Biol. Chem. **245**:6683–6689.
17. **Weisblum, B., M. Y. Graham, T. Cryczan, and D. Dubnau.** 1979. Plasmid copy number control: isolation and characterization of high-copy-number mutants of plasmid pE194. J. Bacteriol. **137**:635–643.
18. **Weisblum, B., S. B. Holder, and S. M. Halling.** 1979. Deoxyribonucleic acid sequence common to staphylococcal and streptococcal plasmids which specify erythromycin resistance. J. Bacteriol. **138**:990–998.
19. **Welch, R. A., K. R. Jones, and F. L. Macrina.** 1979. Transferable lincosamide-macrolide resistance in *Bacteroides*. Plasmid **2**:261–268.
20. **Yagi, Y., and D. Clewell.** 1976. Plasmid-determined tetracycline resistance in *Streptococcus fecalis*. Tandemly repeated resistance determinants in amplified forms of pAM1 DNA. J. Mol. Biol. **102**:583–600.
21. **Yagi, Y., T. McLellan, W. Frez, and D. Clewell.** 1978. Characterization of a small plasmid determining resistance to erythromycin, lincomycin, and vernamycin B in a strain of *Streptococcus sanguis* isolated from dental plaque. Antimicrob. Agents Chemother. **13**:884–887.

Multiple Antibiotic Resistance in *Streptococcus pneumoniae*

SONIA ZIGHELBOIM-DAUM AND ALEXANDER TOMASZ

The Rockefeller University, New York, New York 10021

Since the introduction of penicillin for the treatment of pneumococcal infections, pneumococci have been regarded as exquisitely sensitive to penicillin. However, scattered reports appeared in the literature between 1967 and 1977 indicating the existence of *Streptococcus pneumoniae* strains with increased levels of penicillin resistance. Finally, highly penicillin-resistant pneumococci appeared for the first time in South Africa in 1977, and since then strains with multiple antibiotic resistance have been described in South Africa, Australia, and the United States.

In this paper we summarize results of our studies on the biochemical basis of the mechanism that allows the highly penicillin-resistant South African pneumococci to grow in the presence of penicillin concentrations as high as 1,000 times the minimal inhibitory concentration (MIC) for susceptible strains.

After diffusing through the capsule and the cell wall, the β-lactam molecules seem to attach to penicillin-binding proteins (PBPs) which are located in the plasma membrane. Pneumococci contain five different PBPs (PBP 1a, PBP 1b, PBP 2a, PBP 2b, and PBP 3) of molecular weights ranging from 100,000 to 52,000. The attachment of penicillin to these PBPs, which are penicillin-sensitive enzymes involved in peptidoglycan biosynthesis (transpeptidases, carboxypeptidases, endopeptidases), causes the inhibition of these cell wall synthetic enzymes in a process that will eventually lead to inhibition of cell growth, cell death, and cell lysis. Bacteria can become resistant to penicillin by one or more of the following mechanisms:

(i) Destruction of the drug before it reaches its target, i.e., production of enzymes that destroy the β-lactam antibiotics. Data from several laboratories, including our own, indicate that the South African strains of pneumococci do not produce β-lactamases.

(ii) Decreased permeability to the antibiotic. Transformation experiments using encapsulated resistant organisms as DNA donors when the recipient was a susceptible rough strain allowed the elimination of the capsule as a factor determining resistance. At this point, the cell wall cannot be eliminated as a permeability barrier.

(iii) Intrinsic resistance to the drugs. The South African pneumococci represent cases of intrinsic resistance to the β-lactams, the mechanism of which has been studied with the aid of highly radioactive tritiated penicillin to label the PBPs.

Several strains of South African pneumococci (8249, D20, 140, CMR 40, A9229, A95210) show alterations in their PBP pattern when compared with the penicillin-susceptible rough laboratory strain R6. Two strains have been selected for a more detailed study: 8249 (MIC of benzylpenicillin, 6.2 μg/ml) and D20 (MIC of benzylpenicillin, 12.5 μg/ml) (Fig. 1).

This paper reviews data related to strain 8249, some of which have already been reported in several publications (9–12), and also new experimental observations on strain D20.

To determine whether the changes observed were accidental differences between unrelated strains or were directly related to penicillin resistance, the penicillin resistance marker was put in an isogenic background in a series of transformation experiments that were performed with the highly resistant strains as DNA donors (8249, D20) and the susceptible rough R6 laboratory strain as the recipient. Results from these experiments indicate the following:

(i) Penicillin resistance can be transformed in unique steps in several rounds of transformations where the recipients are either the R6 susceptible strain or transformants from lower levels of resistance. The process seems to be mediated by several genetic units which depend on each other for the manifestation of the different levels of resistance.

(ii) The frequency of transformation declines rapidly and progressively as selection for higher levels of resistance is attempted; thus, the very high level of resistance of the parental donor strain is never achieved. The cause for this phenomenon is unknown, since the level of competence does not decrease as penicillin resistance increases, as is demonstrated by the fact that high levels of streptomycin-resistant transformants are obtained in each round of transformation.

(iii) The stepwise acquisition of penicillin

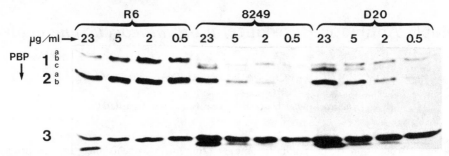

FIG. 1. PBPs of R6 and of South African strains 8249 and D20.

resistance is accompanied by unique changes in the PBPs characteristic of the particular resistance level. These PBP changes are sequential and cumulative.

(iv) The changes in PBPs associated with each resistance level are unique. Thus, in transformation experiments using either 8249 or D20 DNA as donor, individual transformant clones selected for the same level of resistance gave identical PBP changes, and clinical isolates from the Oklahoma Children's Hospital yielded PBP changes that were similar to the PBP alterations observed in the transformant class selected for

the same level of penicillin resistance and constructed with the South African DNA (5). This suggests that, at least in the strains studied, the PBP changes represent a unique biochemical strategy to achieve a particular level of penicillin resistance.

(v) Four of the five PBPs resolved by gel electrophoresis are changed during the gradual increase in penicillin resistance. It is concluded that these PBPs represent biologically important targets of penicillin action in pneumococci.

(vi) PBPs 1a, 1b, 2a, and 2b undergo a progressive decrease in their affinity for penicillin in

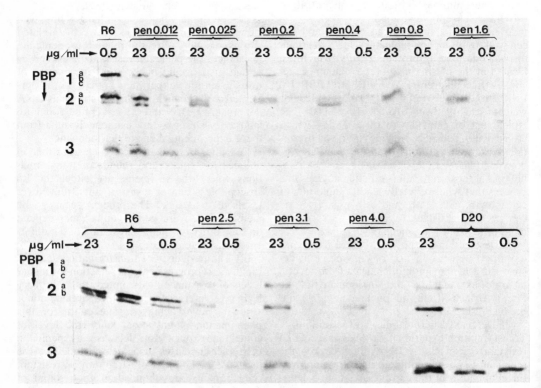

FIG. 2. PBPs of R6, D20, and a series of transformants resistant to different levels of penicillin. The transformants were obtained in successive rounds of transformations in which D20 DNA was used as donor.

parallel with gradually increasing resistance of the bacteria to the drug; PBPs 1a, 1b, and 2b, eventually disappear. In transformants with resistance levels higher than 0.4 μg of penicillin per ml, the bacteria contain an unchanged PBP 3, a PBP 2a with greatly lowered penicillin affinity, and a new binding protein (PBP 1c) of distinct electrophoretic mobility (Fig. 2).

The question to be asked is whether the PBP changes observed can explain the ability of the South African cells to grow in the presence of high concentrations of penicillin. Most of the changes are in the direction of lower affinity for the β-lactam, so more drug is needed to saturate the PBPs, which are penicillin-sensitive enzymes involved in peptidoglycan cross-linking whose inhibition is ultimately responsible for growth inhibition. In other words, it appears that in resistant organisms more penicillin is needed to inhibit the penicillin-sensitive enzymes. Biochemical alterations in the direction of lower β-lactam affinity have also been observed recently in intrinsically resistant *Staphylococcus aureus* (6), *Neisseria gonorrhoeae* (1–3), *Pseudomonas aeruginosa* (4, 7), and other intrinsically resistant pneumococci (8). Thus, lowering of PBP affinity for penicillin may be a general novel mechanism for achieving resistance to β-lactams.

Although most of the PBP changes are in the direction of decreased affinity, it is not possible to rule out completely the possibility of a decreased cellular concentration of the PBP or an increase in the turnover rate of the enzyme.

The fact that resistant organisms show altered PBPs, which are supposed to be enzymes involved in peptidoglycan metabolism, allows us to speculate that resistant strains may have a different cell wall and that the entire surface structure may have changed.

LITERATURE CITED

1. **Barbour, A. G.** 1981. Properties of penicillin binding proteins in *Neisseria gonorrhoeae*. Antimicrob. Agents Chemother. **19**:316–322.
2. **Dougherty, T. J., A. E. Koller, and A. Tomasz.** 1980. Penicillin binding proteins of penicillin susceptible and intrinsically resistant *Neisseria gonorrhoeae*. Antimicrob. Agents Chemother. **18**:730–737.
3. **Dougherty, T. J., A. E. Koller, and A. Tomasz.** 1981. Competition of beta lactam antibiotics for the penicillin binding proteins of *Neisseria gonorrhoeae*. Antimicrob. Agents Chemother. **20**:109–114.
4. **Godfrey, A. J., L. E. Bryan, and H. R. Rabin.** 1981. Beta lactam resistant *Pseudomonas aeruginosa* with modified penicillin binding proteins emerging during cystic fibrosis treatment. Antimicrob. Agents Chemother. **19**:705–711.
5. **Hackenbeck, R., M. Tarpay, and A. Tomasz.** 1980. Multiple changes of penicillin binding proteins in penicillin resistant clinical isolates of *Streptococcus pneumoniae*. Antimicrob. Agents Chemother. **17**:364–371.
6. **Hartman, B., and A. Tomasz.** 1981. Altered penicillin binding proteins in methicillin-resistant strains of *Staphylococcus aureus*. Antimicrob. Agents Chemother. **19**:726–735.
7. **Mirelman, D., Y. Nuchamowitz, and E. Rubinstein.** 1981. Insensitivity of peptidoglycan biosynthetic reactions to beta lactam antibiotics in clinical isolates of *Pseudomonas aeruginosa*. Antimicrob. Agents Chemother. **19**:687–695.
8. **Percheson, P. B., and L. E. Bryan.** 1980. Penicillin binding components of penicillin susceptible and resistant strains of *Streptococcus pneumoniae*. Antimicrob. Agents Chemother. **12**:390–396.
9. **Williamson, R., S. Zighelboim, and A. Tomasz.** 1981. Penicillin binding proteins of penicillin resistant and penicillin tolerant *Streptococcus pneumoniae*. *In* M. Salton and G. D. Shockman (ed.), Beta lactam antibiotics: mode of action, new developments and future prospects. Academic Press, Inc., New York.
10. **Zighelboim, S., and A. Tomasz.** 1979. Stepwise acquisition of resistance to oxacillin in *Streptococcus pneumoniae*, p. 290–292. *In* D. Schlessinger (ed.), Microbiology—1979. American Society for Microbiology, Washington, D.C.
11. **Zighelboim, S., and A. Tomasz.** 1980. Penicillin binding proteins of multiply resistant South African strains of *Streptococcus pneumoniae*. Antimicrob. Agents Chemother. **17**:434–442.
12. **Zighelboim, S., and A. Tomasz.** 1981. Multiple antibiotic resistance in South African strains of *Streptococcus pneumoniae*: mechanism of resistance to beta lactam antibiotics. Rev. Infect. Dis. **3**:267–276.

GENETICS AND PHYSIOLOGY

Plasmids in Genetic and Physiological Functions of Group A Streptococci

V. GOLUBKOV, T. GUPALOVA, T. KOLESNICHENKO, I. IONTOVA, A. SUVOROV, AND A. TOTOLIAN

Institute of Experimental Medicine, Leningrad, USSR

Our knowledge of the structural and biological peculiarities of the group A streptococcal plasmids determining resistance to MLS antibiotics (macrolides, lincosamides, streptogramin B) is more complete than that of the functions they determine in bacteria (1, 2, 8; V. Golubkov et al. and H. Malke et al., 8th International Symposium on Streptococci and Streptococcal Diseases, Lund, Sweden, p. 105 and 109, 1981). This stimulated our search for new plasmid functions. Below we present evidence that plasmids play a role in the expression of virulence and in the repair of a Rec⁻ mutant of *Streptococcus pyogenes*.

ROLE OF PLASMIDS IN EXPRESSION OF VIRULENCE

Genetic approaches to the study of *S. pyogenes* virulence have been suggested, with special emphasis on the role of plasmid or phage DNA in expression of the pathogenic phenotype (3, 6, 7). In this investigation a number of strains were surveyed for plasmids to confirm the existence of extrachromosomally encoded virulence traits and to study homology among well-known (pERL1, pSM22095) and newly isolated plasmids. Plasmid DNA was demonstrated in strains with different M^+ OF^+ serotypes (Table 1). The plasmids are unstable. Spontaneous elimination of them changed the virulence phenotype of the strains to an M^- OF^- avirulent one. Thus, new multicopy streptococcal miniplasmids were described. The plasmids pSL2, pSL28, and pSL63 were mapped with endonucleases (Fig. 1A). Plasmid pSL63 is cleaved with *Hin*dIII into two fragments of 2.0 and 0.3 megadaltons and has no site for *Eco*RI. Both pSL2 and pSL28 were found to be cleaved once with *Hin*dIII and *Eco*RI. The *Hin*dIII sites are in a functionally essential region of pSL63 and outside pSL2 and pSL28 replicons. Analysis of *Hin*dIII-digested plasmids revealed a fragment (2.0 megadaltons) common to cryptic plasmids as well as to pERL1

(C fragment) and pSM22095 (B fragment). DNA-DNA hybridization in solution (5) revealed a 100% homology between pSL63 and pERL1 as well as between pSL2 and pSL28; the latter were nonhomologous to the former. There was an 80% homology between pERL1 and pSM22095. pSL63 and pSM22095 were not found to be identical.

Taking into account these data, we concluded that: (i) pSL2 and pSL28 are identical although they originate from strains of different M^+ OF^+ types; (ii) they are completely different from pSL63; and (iii) the loss of the plasmids results in conversion of strains to the M^- OF^- phenotype. Transduction of pERL1, 100% homologous to pSL63, results in transductants that acquired M^+ OF^+ phenotypes (7). It is obvious that none of the plasmids contains the information on M-protein or opacity-factor synthesis because of the presence of identical plasmids in different types. It is more likely that plasmids can switch on chromosomally encoded M-protein and opacity-factor synthesis by suppressing chromosomal mutation or by coding substances responsible for assembly of cell wall filamentous protrusions. We showed that the plasmids contain, as a minimum, two different DNA sequences that take part in expression of the M^+ OF^+ phenotype (first in pSL2 and pSL28, second in pSL63 and pERL1). Thus, the system controlling the virulence phenotype in *S. pyogenes* seems to be polygenic. This is confirmed by data (6) showing that M-protein synthesis results from joint functions of chromosomal and prophage genes. Apparently, not only phage but also plasmid DNAs could be involved in the process.

For further study, the pSL2 and pSL28 were marked by cloning an MLS^r gene in *S. sanguis* and were banked in *Escherichia coli* via pBR322. New plasmids pGV202, pGT128, and pGSI28 containing pSL2 or pSL28 replicons were constructed. Both pGT128 and pGV202

TABLE 1. New class of cryptic plasmids in group A streptococci

Plasmid	Strain (source)	M⁺ OF⁺ serotype	Mol wt (mega-daltons)	Copy no.	Presence of the plasmid DNA in:	
					M⁺ OF⁺	M⁻ OF⁻ derivative
pSL2	1/69	2	2.03	43	+	−
pSL4	1115	4	ND[a]	ND	+	−
pSL28	48/58	28	2.03	43	+	−
pSL63	4/75	63	2.3	95	+	−

[a] ND, Not done.

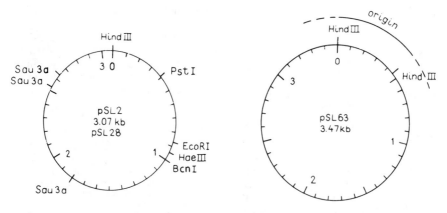

A.   RESTRICTION ENDONUCLEASE SITE MAPS OF
pSL2 (OR pSL28) AND pSL63

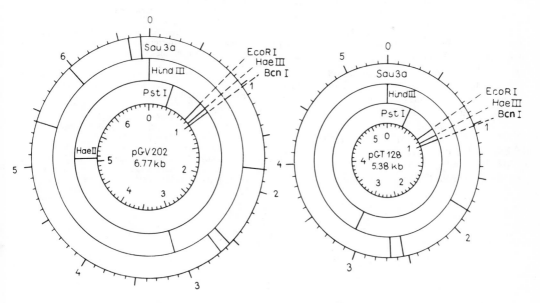

B.   RESTRICTION ENDONUCLEASE SITE MAPS OF
RECOMBINANT PLASMIDS pGV202 AND pGT128

FIG. 1. Restriction endonuclease site maps.

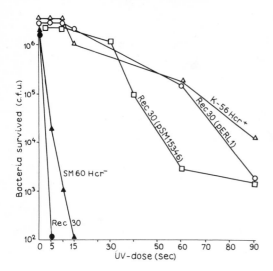

UV-SENSITIVITY OF Rec⁻ MUTANT AND THE
TRANSCONJUGANTS

FIG. 2. UV sensitivity of Rec⁻ mutant and the transconjugants.

were mapped and found to be cleaved once with four and five enzymes, respectively (Fig. 1B). Recombinant plasmids were stable in new hosts as a result of heterologous transformation and are used in molecular cloning.

ROLE OF PLASMIDS IN REPAIR OF A Rec⁻ MUTANT

Rec⁻ mutants of *S. pyogenes* have been obtained by Malke (4) from strain K-56. One of them, Rec⁻30, is characterized as follows: (i) it is not transduced by chromosomal markers; (ii) it is sensitive to UV rays (Uvr⁻); (iii) it cannot repair UV-irradiated phages (Hcr⁻); and (iv) its resident prophage cannot be induced by UV induction (Lys⁻). In our experiments strains SM60(pERL1), 56·188(pERL1) Sm^r, SM15346(pSM15346), and 56·188 Sm^r have been used as sources of pERL1, pSM15346, and chromosomal Sm^r marker, respectively. The strain Rec30 served as recipient in transduction by virulent A25 and temperate P15346 phages. Sixty-five Rec30(pERL1) and Rec30(pSM15346) transductants were studied. All of them became UV resistant (Fig. 2) and acquired the ability to repair the A25 phage damaged by UV irradiation. Twelve pERL1 and 27 pSM15346 transductants were found to be lysogenic by resident prophage. All transductants except two were transduced by chromosomal Sm^r marker with the frequency of 10^{-6} to 10^{-7}. Hence, when transduced with plasmids, a recombination-deficient mutant of *S. pyogenes* repaired the pleiotropic effect of *rec⁻* mutation. This is the first record of the phenomenon, and the mechanism is still under study.

In conclusion, we stress that the data presented focused our attention on plasmid-chromosomal interactions which play an important role not only in determination but also in expression of some essential functions of *S. pyogenes*.

LITERATURE CITED

1. **Behnke, D., H. Malke, M. Hartmann, and F. Walter.** 1979. Post-transformational rearrangement of an *in vitro* reconstructed group A streptococcal erythromycin resistance plasmid. Plasmid 2:605–616.
2. **Boitsov, A., V. Golubkov, I. Iontova, E. Zaitsev, H. Malke, and A. Totolian.** 1979. Inverted repeats on plasmids determining resistance to MLS antibiotics in group A streptococci. FEMS Microbiol. Lett. 6:11–14.
3. **Cleary, P., Z. Johnson, and L. Wannamaker.** 1975. Genetic instability of M protein and serum opacity factor of group A streptococci. Evidence suggesting extra-chromosomal control. Infect. Immun. 12:109–118.
4. **Malke, H.** 1975. Recombination-deficient mutants of *Streptococcus pyogenes* K56. Z. Allg. Mikrobiol. 15:31–37.
5. **Salzberg, S., Z. Levi, M. Aboud, and A. Goldberger.** 1977. Isolation and characterization of DNA-DNA and DNA-RNA hybrid molecules formed in solution. Biochemistry 16:25–29.
6. **Spanier, J., and P. Cleary.** 1980. Bacteriophage control of anti-phagocytic determinants in group A streptococci. J. Exp. Med. 152:1393–1406.
7. **Totolian, A.** 1979. Transduction of M-protein and serum-opacity-factor production in group-A streptococci, p. 38–39. *In* M. T. Parker (ed.), Pathogenic streptococci. Reedbooks, Chertsey, Surrey, England.
8. **Weisblum, B., S. Holder, and S. Halling.** 1979. Deoxyribonucleic acid sequence common to staphylococcal and streptococcal plasmids which specify erythromycin resistance. J. Bacteriol. 138:990–998.

Bacteriophage Requirement for Resistance to Phagocytosis in Group A Streptococci

P. PATRICK CLEARY AND JONATHAN SPANIER

Department of Microbiology, University of Minnesota, Minneapolis, Minnesota 55455

Unstable phenotypes have always caught the eye and interest of microbial geneticists. Over the years, numerous bacterial pathogens have been noted to be phenotypically unstable with respect to virulence, but only the variation of flagellar antigens among salmonellae is understood at the molecular level. In this case a promoter sequence controlling the synthesis of two flagellar proteins inverts alternatively between the two states (10).

To resist the immunological defenses of higher animals, most bacterial pathogens have evolved inhibitory somatic macromolecules, either proteins or polysaccharides. The M protein, a component of the fibrous matt which surrounds virulent group A streptococci, imparts antiphagocytic properties to this organism by blocking the opsonic activity of the alternate complement pathway (7). At various frequencies most M^+ cultures yield M^- variants which are susceptible to phagocytosis and fail to elicit extractable M antigen. This change has been noted to occur during growth in laboratory media and in the throats of convalescent and healthy carriers. M^+ and M^- colonies can be distinguished by their respective matt or glossy appearance, or by the presence or absence of opaque zones surrounding colonies on serum agar plates (3, 5). A molecular basis for this variability was the goal of the studies described here.

Curing experiments suggested the extrachromosomal DNA could in part be responsible for the variation in the M^+ phenotype (3). As predicted, a temperate bacteriophage, SP24, isolated from an $M12^+$ streptococcus, strain CS24, by mitomycin C induction has the potential, upon lysogenization, to convert the M^- strain, CS112, to the M^+ state (Fig. 1) (9). This recipient strain is a spontaneous M^- derivative of strain CS110 which produces on M76 antigen. Infection of the M^- recipient with either phage SP24 or a variant, phage SP272, results in both M^- and M^+ stable lysogens. The latter can be selected by exposing infected cultures to human leukocytes which phagocytically eradicate the M^- cells (2). Under the same conditions the uninfected recipient culture does not revert to the M^+ state at a detectable frequency. A few M^+ lysogens have been examined in detail; lysogens 157, 272, and 275 resist phagocytosis and readily grow in human blood lacking M76 antibody (Fig. 1). The recipient strain CS112 and isolates cured of the prophage, strains 272C and 157C, are highly sensitive to phagocytosis and are rapidly cleared from the blood. The M antigen extracted from these lysogens when examined by immunodiffusion has M76 rather than M12 determinants. Moreover, only M76 antibody is able to opsonize these lysogens (9).

The phage genome, therefore, does not encode the structural gene for the M antigen, but instead amplifies its biosynthesis or inhibits its destruction. Quantitative comparison of extractable M76 antigen by single radial immunodiffusion clearly demonstrates the impact of the prophage (Fig. 2). Lysogen 272 yields 35 times more M76 antigen than the uninfected recipient strain CS112. The latter does produce small quantities of a cross-reacting antigen; however, it has not yet been determined whether this antigen is qualitatively identical to the M76 protein.

REARRANGEMENT OF PROPHAGE DNA CORRESPONDS TO THE M^+ STATE

An unusual feature of this system is that some lysogens are M^- whereas others are M^+, even though infecting lysates had been plaque purified. It is unlikely that the "on-off" switch resides on the phage genome, because DNA from spontaneous M^- variants and M^+ parent cultures showed identical endonuclease maps when a variety of nucleases were used. Moreover, phage lysates from M^- cultures retain the potential to convert strain CS112 to the M^+ state. Therefore, we conclude that a specific interaction between the phage genome and the bacterial DNA is required for full expression of the M-protein structural gene. A specific integration or recombination event could explain our results.

To evaluate this possibility, we compared prophage DNA restriction fragments from M^+ and M^- lysogens of strain CS112. The cleavage

183

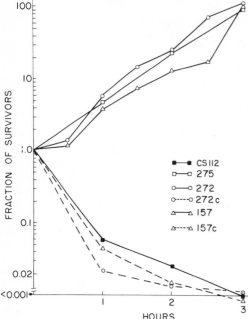

FIG. 1. Growth of lysogens in phagocytic human blood. Log-phase cells were inoculated into fresh heparinized human blood, and this mixture was rotated end over end at 37°C. Strain CS112 is the M⁻ recipient culture; strains 275 and 272 are independent phage SP24 lysogens of strain CS112; strain 157 is a CS112(SP44) lysogen, phage SP44 being a derivative of phage SP24; and strains 272C and 157C are phage-cured descendants of strains 272 and 157, respectively.

phenotype is the fact that the *Sal* C fragment, 5.8 kilobases, of the vegetative phage DNA (lanes A and E) is replaced by a larger fragment, 7.2 Kb (*Sal* C′) in DNA from M⁺ lysogens (lanes B, C, and H). Further examination of lanes B, C, and H reveals very low levels of the *Sal* C fragment. The next experiment led us to believe that this reflects the presence of a few M⁻ cells in the population from which the DNA was extracted. In this experiment phage-infected M⁻ cells were grown for 18 h before DNA was extracted and analyzed (Fig. 3, tract F). A second portion of this culture was then enriched for M⁺ cells by growth in phagocytic human blood for 3 h prior to DNA extraction (2). The DNA from predominantly M⁺ cultures contained an excess of the *Sal* C′ (7.2 kilobases) fragment (Fig. 3, tracts G and H), and as expected DNA from unenriched cultures, M⁺ and M⁻ cells contain both *Sal* C and *Sal* C′ fragments (Fig. 3, tract F). Hybridization of phage DNA to *Pvu*I digests of DNA from lysogens was consistent with the *Sal*I experiments; i.e., only one fragment increased in apparent weight (unpublished data).

A complete understanding of the molecular events required to establish a latent phage infection and subsequent conversion to the M⁺ state of strain CS112 awaits further experimentation. However, the prophage map could be explained if the phage *Sal* C fragment contains the phage *att* site, and in the integrated state splits into two junction fragments, only one of which was detected in the preceding experiment. More recent evidence supports this notion of a λ-like integra-

map of phage SP272 is a circle (Fig. 3); however, DNA isolated from mature virions is linear and has been shown to exist as a terminally redundant form of the unit-length phage genome (J. G. Spanier, Ph.D. thesis, University of Minnesota, Minneapolis, 1982). Terminally redundant DNA molecules are common to bacteriophage from both gram-positive and gram-negative organisms (4, 6).

The locations of the six phage *Sal*I sites in total DNA from lysogens were determined by the Southern blot procedure employing phage SP272 DNA labeled with ³²P by nick translation (8) as a probe. Phage SP272, a derivative of the wild-type phage SP24, carries a DNA substitution which originated from an endogenous prophage harbored by all descendants of the M76 streptococcal line (manuscript in preparation). Therefore, DNA fragments, 12.0 and 1.2 kilobases, from the M⁻ recipient strain hybridize to the phage probe (Fig. 3, lane D). The relevance of these fragments to the M⁺ lysogenic state is unclear at this time. More relevant to the M

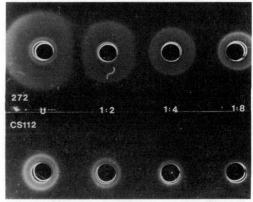

FIG. 2. Quantitation of M76 antigen by single radial immunodiffusion. Immunodiffusion agar contained RS4 antisera at a final dilution of 1:8. Wells contained the indicated dilutions of concentrated acid extracts of strains C112 and 272. U indicates undiluted extract. Slides were incubated at 25°C for 72 h.

tion state (1). The unintegrated form of the prophage is quasi-stable, but the lysogen retains its M$^-$ phenotype. In contrast, conversion to the M$^+$ state requires an integrated prophage. At this time, we are certain that concomitant with a phenotypic shift from the M$^-$ to M$^+$ state is an alteration of the *Sal* C prophage sequence; whether this change in phenotype is a direct consequence of the DNA rearrangement is unknown.

ACKNOWLEDGMENTS

This work was supported by a grant-in-aid from the American Heart Association with funds contributed in part by the Minnesota Heart Association and by Public Health Service grant AI16722 from the National Institute of Allergy and Infectious Diseases. J. G. S. was a predoctoral trainee supported by Public Health Service training grant 1T32HLI07114 from the National Heart, Lung and Blood Institute.

We sincerely thank Ann Partel for assistance in the preparation of this manuscript.

LITERATURE CITED

1. **Campbell, A., M. Bendek, and L. Heffernan.** 1979. Viruses and inserting elements in chromosomal evolution, p. 51–59. *In* A. S. Dion (ed.), Concepts of the structure and function of DNA, chromatin and chromosomes. Year Book Medical Publishers, Chicago.
2. **Cleary, P. P., and Z. Johnson.** 1977. Possible dual function of M protein: resistance to bacteriophage A25 and resistance to phagocytosis by human leukocytes. Infect. Immun. **16:**280–292.
3. **Cleary, P. P., Z. Johnson, and L. W. Wannamaker.** 1975. Genetic instability of M protein and serum opacity factor of group A streptococci: evidence suggesting extrachromosomal control. Infect. Immun. **12:**109–118.
4. **Ikeda, H., and J. Tomizawa.** 1968. Prophage P1, an extrachromosomal replication unit. Cold Spring Harbor Symp. Quant. Biol. **33:**791–798.
5. **Lancefield, R. C., and E. W. Todd.** 1928. Antigenic differences between matt hemolytic streptococci and their glossy variants. J. Exp. Med. **48:**769–790.
6. **Moynet, D. J., and C. F. Garom.** 1981. Streptococcal bacteriophage φ42 has a terminal repetition and a circular permutation. Virology **109:**211–214.
7. **Peterson, P., D. Schmeling, P. Cleary, B. Wilkinson, Y. Kim, and P. Quie.** 1979. Inhibition of alternate complement pathway opsonization by group A streptococcal M proteins. J. Infect. Dis. **189:**575–585.
8. **Southern, E. M.** 1975. Detection of specific sequences among DNA fragments separated by gel electrophoresis. J. Mol. Biol. **98:**503–517.
9. **Spanier, J. G., and P. Cleary.** 1980. Bacteriophage control of antiphagocytic determinants in group A streptococci. J. Exp. Med. **152:**1393–1406.
10. **Zeig, J., M. Hilman, and M. Simon.** 1978. Regulation of gene expression by site-specific inversion. Cell **15:**237–244.

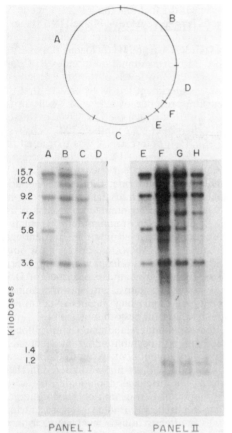

FIG. 3. Hybridization of *Sal*I-digested phage and prophage DNAs to phage SP272 DNA. Phage DNA and total DNA isolated from bacterial cultures were digested to completion with *Sal*I and electrophoresed for 15 h at 50 V on 0.7% agarose gels. DNA was blotted onto nitrocellulose and hybridized to phage SP272 DNA labeled with ^{32}P by nick translation (8). Tracts A and E contain DNA from phage SP272 particles; tracts B and C contain DNA from two independent, highly M$^+$ lysogens; tract D contains DNA from the recipient, M$^-$ culture, strain CS112; tract F contains DNA from phage SP272-infected survivors of strain CS112 prior to their subjection to phagocytosis; tract G contains DNA from the same infected cultures as tract F after 3 h of phagocytic enrichment; and tract H is the same as tract B. Autoradiographs shown in panels I and II represent separate experiments.

Use of Mutants to Study the Glucan-Associated Pathophysiology of *Streptococcus mutans*

M. L. FREEDMAN AND J. M. TANZER

Department of Oral Diagnosis, School of Dental Medicine, University of Connecticut Health Center, Farmington, Connecticut 06032

In the past decade, research into the pathophysiology of the mutans streptococci has burgeoned (reviewed in 10) as approaches and techniques from molecular biology have been applied to these important bacteria. There is broad agreement that the genetically and biochemically heterogeneous microbes grouped beneath the banner *Streptococcus mutans*, though not the sole, are certainly prime multisurface cariogens in diverse mammalian hosts. (The mutans-type streptococci include *S. mutans, S. rattus, S. cricetus,* and *S. sobrinus* [2], as well as a mutans-like inhabitant of wild rats, *S. ferus.*) The taxonomy of these bacteria has been studied at length (2), and it is thought that the mutans streptococci have persisted as residents of the oral cavity (of man) prior to the recent and common dietary use of sucrose. Thus, residing for eons in dental backwaters and naturally retentive locales have been potentially cariogenic representatives of the mutans streptococci, constitutively producing enzymes with sucrose or sucrose-derived polymers as their obligate substrates.

Approximately 100 reports in the literature have used these bacteria, producing, isolating, and characterizing mutants with defects in caries-associated traits (reviewed in 6). A smaller number have combined such biochemically based studies with assays of virulence in characterized hosts feeding on caries-conducive diets (6). This report covers the progress we have made in the study of three mutant types which are related through their involvement with dental plaque formation and bacterial accretion. Adherent plaque formation on teeth and the acidogenic metabolism of bacteria contained therein are requisites for caries formation. The characteristics of the three mutant types are summarized in Table 1.

PLAQUE FORMATION-DEFECTIVE MUTANTS

Mutants defective in plaque formation have been studied by many (4, 6, 11, 13), and the enzymology of both under- and overproducers of plaque polysaccharides has been described. One means of isolating such variants makes use of the distinctive morphology of the mutans streptococci on sucrose-containing nutrient agar (5, 8). Under such conditions, extracellular polysaccharides synthesized from sucrose by a constitutive glucosyl transferase enzyme(s) (GTF) give the colonies a dense, granular appearance, whereas colonies growing on glucose-containing nutrient agar have a smooth morphology. Mutagenized cells which yielded glucose-morphology colonies on sucrose-containing nutrient agar were selected as putative, glucan synthesis-defective variants and were characterized further. Of special interest was the effect of such a phenotypic alteration of colony appearance on other traits potentially related in plaque formation, e.g., on the abilities of bacteria (i) to form an adhesive deposit on a solid substratum when cultured in the presence of sucrose, (ii) to cleave $\alpha(1\rightarrow6)$ dextran. (Several caries-associated traits in mutans are customarily verified—intracellular glycogen-like polysaccharide synthesis, storage, and degradation during times of exogenous nutrient privation; acidogenic metabolism favoring lactate production; aciduric growth at pH values lower than 5; ability to hydrolyze levan; etc.)

As shown in Table 1, the notable defect in glucan synthesis-defective mutants such as 4, 27, and 33 was the loss of ability to form, in vitro, the water-insoluble, $\alpha(1\rightarrow3)$ linkage-rich polymers of the dental plaque matrix (4). Thus, altered colony morphology and the inability to form an adherent deposit on a surface could be traced to the absence of water-insoluble glucans rich in $\alpha(1\rightarrow3)$ linkages and, hence, to some defect in the cells' GTF complement. Dextranase activity was reported to be compromised when assayed in colonies growing on nutrient agar containing blue dextran (3), but has been shown to be unaltered in some isolates by the affinity chromatographic isolation of extracellular enzymes and their subsequent electrophoret-

TABLE 1. Effects of mutation on glucan-related characteristics and virulence of S. sobrinus (2) 6715-13 wild type (WT) and S. mutans UCHC-EHL WT

Trait[a]	S. sobrinus defective in extracellular glucan synthesis				Defective in extracellular, endohydrolytic glucan hydrolase (dextranase)					S. sobrinus defective in exogenous, dextran-mediated agglutination			
					S. sobrinus		S. mutans						
	WT	4	27	33	201	206	WT	108	111	2	3	7	18
In vitro plaque formation	Yes	No	No	No	Yes	Yes	Yes	Yes	Yes	Yes	Yes	Yes	Yes
Extracellular glucan synthesis													
Water-soluble, α(1→6) linkage-rich polymer	Low	High	High	High	Low	Low	Low	Low	Low	Low	Low	Low	Low
Water-insoluble, α(1→3) linkage-rich polymer	High	Absent	Absent	Absent	High	High	High	High	High	High	High	High	High
Extracellular dextranase activity	Yes	Yes[c]	Yes[c]	Yes	No	No	Yes	No	No	Yes	Yes	Yes	Yes
Agglutination of glucose-cultured cells by α(1→6)-linked dextran	Yes	Yes	Yes	Yes	Yes	Yes	Yes	Yes	Yes	R	R	R	Absent
Virulence[b] SPF, smooth tooth surfaces	GR	GR	GR	GR	GR	GR	Yes	GR	GR	Yes	Yes	Yes	Yes
SPF, pits and fissures	SR	SR	SR	SR	SR	SR	Yes	SR	SR	SR	SR	Yes	Yes
GF, smooth tooth surfaces	Yes	Absent	Absent	Absent	SR	SR	NT	NT	NT	Yes	Yes	Yes	Yes
GF, pits and fissures	Yes	R	R	R	Yes	Yes	NT	NT	NT	Yes	Yes	Yes	Yes

[a] Checked, in addition to the traits listed here, were acidogenic and aciduric carbohydrate metabolism, growth rate, intracellular polysaccharide synthesis, levanase activity, streptomycin resistance, etc. R, reduced; GR, greatly reduced; SR, slightly reduced; NT, not tested.

[b] Assayed in conventionalized, specific pathogen-free (SPF) Sprague-Dawley and/or Osborne-Mendel rats and in germfree (GF) gnotobiotic Sprague-Dawley rats consuming a caries-conducive, sucrose-rich diet, ad libitum. Uninfected controls were used.

[c] May be dextranase activity variable (3).

ic separation in blue dextran-containing polyacrylamide gels (unpublished data; M. M. McCabe and M. L. Freedman, submitted for publication).

These in vitro plaque formation-defective mutants, streptomycin resistant to assure their reisolation, have been used to infect specific pathogen-free rats and to monoassociate germfree gnotobiotic rats which consumed, ad libitum, a sucrose-rich, caries-conducive diet (14). Quantitation of carious lesions showed a drop in or elimination of smooth surface, adhesive plaque-dependent dental disease (Table 1), reflecting the obligate dependence of microbial proliferation at these tooth sites on the production, from sucrose, of water-insoluble $\alpha(1\rightarrow3)$-rich glucans. Notably, decay at naturally retentive tooth loci, e.g., pits and fissures, was also diminished. This indicates a role for the same plaque polymers in blocking the diffusion of demineralizing acids of microbial metabolism out of and of buffering and diluting saliva into the plaque matrix. Thus, the cause of the specific phenotypic change in colony morphology affects both in vitro adhesion and the type and amount of glucan formed, as well as the distribution and severity of disease in vivo.

EXTRACELLULAR DEXTRANASE ACTIVITY

S. mutans produces, constitutively, an endohydrolytic glucan hydrolase (dextranase) which is inactive on the $\alpha(1-3)$ linkages of S. mutans' glucans (9, 12). Some functions of this enzyme in the bacterium's pathophysiology have been speculated to be (i) the postsynthetic modification of native glucan through the removal of linear $\alpha(1\rightarrow6)$ sequences, thereby rendering the residue more $\alpha(1\rightarrow3)$ rich and hence more insoluble, and (ii) the provision of stimulatory $\alpha(1\rightarrow6)$ sequences (from i, above, or other source) to the GTF, thereby increasing the rate of glucan polymer initiation by these (nonprimer dependent) glucosyl transferase enzymes (9).

Selection of dextranase-defective mutants (Table 1) for further characterization consisted of spreading mutagenized cells on nutrient agar supplemented with blue dextran and selecting colonies not surrounded by zones of decolorization. Further characterization consisted of the quantitative and qualitative analysis, by gas-liquid chromatography, of methylated derivatives of the glucans produced both by putative mutants and by wild-type controls, as well as the standard verification of the constancy of other disease-related traits.

Subsequent detailed characterization of these mutants by the molecular exclusion chromatography of blue dextran substrate after prolonged exposure to concentrated culture medium or cell-free extracts, and by polyacrylamide gel electrophoresis in blue dextran-containing gels, showed that dextranase activity was undetectable. However, the cells agglutinated when exposed to exogenous, pure $\alpha(1-6)$ dextran (molecular weight, 2×10^6; concentration less than one dextran molecule per bacterium), as had the glucan synthesis-defective mutants previously described, and, notably, synthesized quantitatively and qualitatively normal extracellular glucans. Thus, S. mutans' dextranase did not appear to be directly related to glucan binding to the cells or to be a requirement for supplying primer/acceptor dextrans for endogenous glucose polymer synthesis by the cells' GTFs.

Two experimental animal caries models were infected with selected dextranase-defective mutants and suitable controls (Table 1). The first harbored a specific pathogen-free indigenous microbial flora; the second was germfree. The mutants were essentially avirulent in the specific pathogen-free model, like uninfected but unlike wild-type–infected controls, and caused little multisurface decay. However, in the germfree caries model, where no competing flora was present, levels of decay resembling those in the wild-type–infected rats were obtained. Thus, a new function for S. mutans dextranase activity in this organism's pathogenic potential can be advanced: the bacterium's endohydrolytic glucan hydrolase may play a role in fostering the invasion, by mutans streptococci, of preexisting oral ecosystems. Clinical studies commonly show S. sanguis preceding S. mutans in the development of an oral flora (1), and S. sanguis produces $\alpha(1\rightarrow6)$-rich polymers (12), as opposed to the $\alpha(1\rightarrow3)$ dextranase-resistant polymers of S. mutans (4). Our recent studies used the specific pathogen-free rats' mixed oral flora to produce, in vitro, an isotopically labeled, poorly adherent, non-plaque-like "deposit" on solid surfaces. As shown by the liberation of radioactivity into the surrounding medium, virulent wild-type cells more effectively dislodged the preceding oral flora's residue than did the dextranase-defective mutants. It is unlikely that oral bacteria could have remote hydrolytic effects on the oral ecosystem, given their size, numbers, and salivary dilution effect. However, in the microenvironment of an S. mutans cell, bound via its cell surface receptors for $\alpha(1\rightarrow6)$ linkages to an endogenous, microbially derived deposit, it is conceivable that constitutive dextranases could facilitate the entry of a cariogen into a preexisting microbial deposit.

DEXTRAN RECEPTOR REACTIONS

S. mutans cultures were enriched for dextran binding-defective variants by exposure to $\alpha(1\rightarrow6)$-linked glucan during post-mutagen-treatment growth. Unaltered cells bound the dextran, agglutinated, and settled (7), whereas receptor-defective cells remained in suspension and were harvested and used as inocula for further enrichment cycles. In this way several agglutination-defective mutants were isolated and characterized. They showed a range of dextran-mediated agglutination refractilities from complete insensitivity to 10^2–10^4-fold less sensitive. Studies on a completely defective isolate (Table 1), cultured in defined medium supplemented with dialyzed sucrose, showed normal glucan synthesis, indicating that cell-associated GTF is not the receptor involved in agglutination. Also, these mutants were unaltered in dextranase activity, as in other customarily screened traits. Thus, growth of dental plaque seems to result more from the entrapment of growing and dividing bacteria in an expanding glucan matrix, perhaps secondary to a degree of cell binding to dextrans in the plaque. In support of this are several peripheral lines of evidence. First, an adherent plaque cannot be formed from the components of plaque; i.e., it cannot be reconstituted from dextran and receptor-competent bacteria. De novo, in situ glucan synthesis coupled with bacterial growth and division is required, obligately. Second, the glucans of *S. mutans*, which are predominantly insoluble, branched, and $\alpha(1\rightarrow3)$ rich, are inefficient stimuli of agglutination; most efficient are linear $\alpha(1\rightarrow6)$ homopolymers not predominant in plaque. The short $\alpha(1\rightarrow6)$-linked runs of glucose residues occurring in the glucans of *S. mutans*, if available to cells for agglutination via dextranase action, should be of little effect, inasmuch as agglutination efficiency declines with decreasing molecular weight.

The final evidence of the dispensability of dextran-mediated agglutination in disease is the seemingly unaffected plaque formation and virulence of these variants in rat caries models (Table 1). Such mutants penetrate, persist, and proliferate in the oral ecology, are acidogenic and aciduric, and cause rampant multisurface decay. If there is a role for such agglutination phenomena, mediated by dextran, saliva, or salivary antibodies, it may be one that protects the host by abetting the clearance of *S. mutans* from the oral cavity. Perhaps agglutination could foster intraoral dissemination of competent bacteria. Other workers have recently reported that the sucrose-induced agglutination phenomenon was labile (8) and was not detected in bacteria recovered from animal experiments.

SUMMARY AND CONCLUSION

The three traits described are among many in *S. mutans'* pathophysiological armamentarium. They are unique in that they all involve the cell surface-associated or extracellular processes of glucose polymer synthesis, degradation, or binding. Furthermore, all three activities are constitutive, are recoverable from the culture medium, and may be isolated from an $\alpha(1\rightarrow6)$-linked, glucan affinity matrix, which suggests that there is a common molecular (recognition) structure in these three diverse traits or proteins. One property, $\alpha(1\rightarrow3)$ linkage-rich glucan (plaque) formation, is of vital importance to the carious process at diverse tooth sites, albeit by different mechanisms. Another, dextranase activity, has perhaps variable importance, playing a role in the presence of a competing flora but otherwise being dispensable. The third, agglutination resulting from exogenous dextran binding by the cells, also appears dispensable to the bacteria, but is perhaps of importance to the host's self-protective capabilities.

Efforts directed toward the isolation and characterization of a common structure or sequence are under way and may provide a specific immunogen for protection against caries.

ACKNOWLEDGMENT

This research was supported by Public Health Service grant DE 03758 from the National Institute of Dental Research.

LITERATURE CITED

1. **Carlsson, J., H. Grahnen, G. Jonsson, and S. Wikner.** 1970. Establishment of *Streptococcus sanguis* in the mouths of infants. Arch. Oral Biol. **15:**1143–1148.
2. **Coykendall, A.** 1977. Proposal to elevate the subspecies of *Streptococcus mutans* to species status, based on their molecular compositions. Int. J. Syst. Bacteriol. **27:**26–30.
3. **Donkersloot, J., and R. Harr.** 1979. A more sensitive test agar for detection of dextranase-producing oral streptococci and identification of two glucan synthesis-defective mutants of *Streptococcus mutans*. J. Clin. Microbiol. **10:**919–922.
4. **Freedman, M., D. Birkhed, and K. Granath.** 1978. Analyses of glucans from cariogenic and mutant *Streptococcus mutans*. Infect. Immun. **21:**17–27.
5. **Freedman, M. L., and J. M. Tanzer.** 1974. Dissociation of plaque formation from glucan-induced agglutination in mutants of *Streptococcus mutans*. Infect. Immun. **10:**189–196.
6. **Freedman, M. L., J. M. Tanzer, and A. L. Coykendall.** 1981. The use of genetic variants in the study of dental caries, p. 247–269. *In* J. M. Tanzer (ed.), Proceedings of the Symposium and Workshop on Animal Models in Cariology. Information Retrieval, Inc., Washington, D.C.
7. **Gibbons, R. J., and R. J. Fitzgerald.** 1969. Dextran-induced agglutination of *Streptococcus mutans* and its potential role in the formation of microbial dental plaques. J. Bacteriol. **98:**341–346.

8. **Gibbons, R., and J. Qureshi.** 1980. Virulence-related physiological changes and antigenic variation in populations of *Streptococcus mutans* colonizing gnotobiotic rats. Infect. Immun. **29:**1082–1091.

9. **Guggenheim, B., and J. T. Burckhardt.** 1974. Isolation and properties of a dextranase from *Streptococcus mutans* OMZ 176. Helv. Odontol. Acta **18:**101–113.

10. **Hamada, S., and H. Slade.** 1980. Biology, immunology and cariogenicity of *Streptococcus mutans*. Microbiol. Rev. **44:**331–384.

11. **Michalek, S. M., J. Shiota, T. Ikeda, J. M. Navia, and J. R. McGhee.** 1975. Virulence of *Streptococcus mutans*:

biochemical and pathogenic characteristics of mutant isolates. Proc. Soc. Exp. Biol. Med. **150:**498–502.

12. **Pulkownik, A., and G. Walker.** 1977. Purification and substrate specificity of an endodextranase of *Streptococcus mutans* U1-R. Carbohydr. Res. **54:**237–251.

13. **Schachtele, C. F., G. R. Germaine, and S. K. Harlander.** 1975. Production of elevated levels of dextransucrase by a mutant of *Streptococcus mutans*. Infect. Immun. **12:**934–937.

14. **Tanzer, J. M., M. L. Freedman, R. J. Fitzgerald, and R. H. Larson.** 1974. Diminished virulence of glucan synthesis-defective mutants of *Streptococcus mutans*. Infect. Immun. **10:**197–203.

Analysis of Lactate Dehydrogenase Mutants of *Streptococcus mutans* and Their Potential Use in Replacement Therapy for Caries Prevention

JEFFREY D. HILLMAN

Department of Microbiology, Forsyth Dental Center, Boston, Massachusetts 02115

The human oral cavity harbors a large variety of bacteria, including an estimated nine species of streptococci. Of these, *Streptococcus mutans* seems to be the principal cause of dental caries (2, 11, 13). Several of the features which predispose this organism to cause decay include its ability to stick to tooth surfaces (3, 5) and its ability to produce large amounts of acid from the metabolism of dietary sugars (8, 17). This acid appears to be directly involved in the decay process: by reducing the pH in the microenvironment of the tooth surface below a threshold level, dissolution of the mineral phase of enamel and dentin is promoted. Eventually, cavitation of the weakened surface occurs, yielding clinically observable caries.

Metabolism of carbohydrates by *S. mutans* characteristically yields lactate as the chief end product (17, 18). Under certain conditions of growth, such as glucose limitation (18) or with mannitol or sorbitol as the sole energy source (1), *S. mutans* produces significant amounts of ethanol, formate, and acetate. These findings suggest the existence of alternate pathways for the dissimilation of pyruvate. Mutants of *S. mutans* strain BHT-2 lacking one of these pathways, that leading to lactate, were isolated on glucose tetrazolium medium (12) as bright-red colonies amid a background of white wild-type colonies. Cell-free extracts of the isolated red colonies lacked the enzyme activity L(+)-lactate dehydrogenase (LDH).

ACID-PRODUCING PROPERTIES

LDH-deficient mutants were significantly less effective than their parent in reducing the pH of glucose-containing broth (4). As shown in Table 1, the differences observed did not reflect differences in the amount of glucose consumed or in the cell yields. Gas-liquid chromatography of culture liquors of the mutant demonstrated high levels of ethanol, formate, and acetate, and no detectable lactate. A more accurate appraisal of the mutants' acid-producing capabilities was obtained by pH-controlled glucose fermentation studies of washed, resting cells. At pH 5, 6, and 7, LDH-deficient mutants produced, respectively, 60, 70, and 80% of the total titratable acid produced by their parent.

GENETIC STUDIES

A total of 18 independent LDH-deficient derivatives of strain BHT-2 have been isolated as red colonies on glucose tetrazolium medium. One strain, JH145, was obtained without the use of a mutagenic agent and, therefore, was the strain used in most of the following studies.

After mutagenesis, temperature-sensitive revertants of several LDH-deficient strains were obtained which produced white colonies when grown on glucose tetrazolium medium at 30°C and red colonies when grown at 42°C. Cell-free extracts of these revertants grown at the permissive temperature contained a thermolabile LDH activity. This finding suggests the likelihood that a structural gene mutation is responsible for the observed phenotype. Mutagenesis of BHT-2 with nitrosoguanidine, followed by selection of mutants resistant to the antibiotic bacitracin, yields a relatively high frequency (ca. 0.4%) of isolates also deficient in LDH. Thus, the locus for LDH appears to be linked to the locus responsible for conferring resistance to bacitracin.

TABLE 1. Growth properties of BHT-2 and LDH-deficient mutants[a]

Strain	Terminal pH	Cell yield (OD_{580})	Glucose consumed (µmol/ml)	Lactic acid produced (µmol/ml)
BHT-2	4.38	2.4	47.2	33.9
LDH	4.80	2.4	45.6	<1.0

[a] Strains were subcultured 1:100 into Todd-Hewitt broth containing 1% glucose. After 48 h of incubation in candle jars at 37°C, the absorbance at 580 nm (OD_{580}) and pH of the cultures were determined. Lactic acid production and glucose consumption were determined by gas-liquid chromatography and glucose oxidase assays, respectively, of the culture liquors.

Of interest is the fact that attempts to isolate LDH-deficient derivatives from other laboratory strains of *S. mutans* have to date been unsuccessful. This is of concern since serogroup c strains tend to predominate in human populations whereas serotype b strains, such as BHT-2, are most frequently isolated from rodents. Recently, I have noted that aerobically grown glucose-broth cultures of BHT-2 contain two- to threefold more formate and acetate than do culture liquors from most serogroup c strains. BHT-2 also distinguishes itself from most serogroup c strains on Lederberg's glucose tetrazolium medium in which 2,3,5-triphenyl tetrazolium is replaced by neotetrazolium. Under these conditions BHT-2 produces deep-blue colonies compared with pink or light blue colonies of serogroup c strains. Mutants of serogroup c strain OMZ 176 have been obtained that produce relatively dark blue colonies on neotetrazolium medium. Compared with their parent, culture liquors of these mutants appear to contain increased amounts of formate and acetate. Thus, I currently speculate that BHT-2 has a fortuitous mutation rendering the biosynthesis or activity, or both, of its pyruvate-formate lyase system insensitive to the inhibitory effects of oxygen (19). BHT-2 would, thus, have an alternate pyruvate-dissimilating pathway available to it under the aerobic conditions employed to screen for LDH-deficient mutants.

CARIOGENIC PROPERTIES

The mutants' altered ability to produce acid suggested the possibility that they would demonstrate an altered cariogenic potential. A number of studies were performed to test this possibility (4, 6). For example, it was found that, when human teeth were immersed in a sucrose-containing broth culture of BHT-2 and fresh medium was added daily, incipient carious lesions called *white spots* were visible after 10 days of incubation. In contrast, teeth exposed to cultures of an LDH-deficient strain were free from visible pathology even after 21 days of incubation.

More direct evidence for the mutants' decreased cariogenic potential was obtained in studies of germfree and conventional Sprague-Dawley rats (6). In these experiments, separate groups of animals were infected with BHT-2 or an LDH-deficient mutant, or were sham infected. After 14 weeks, during which time the animals were fed a high-sugar diet to promote decay, the teeth of the animals were examined. As shown in Fig. 1, conventional rats infected with the mutant had an incidence and severity of carious lesions comparable to the sham-infected control group. Both of these groups developed significantly fewer and less extensive lesions than did BHT-2–infected animals. Since the mutant populated the oral cavity of the rats to the same extent as BHT-2, the observed difference in cariogenic potential could be attributed directly to the difference in their acid-producing capabilities.

CONCLUSIONS

For over 100 years, microbiologists have speculated that certain bacterial infections might be prevented by purposefully colonizing susceptible host tissues with nonpathogenic microorganisms (14–16). The basis for this approach, which has recently been termed *replacement therapy*, depends on the ability of the harmless, so-called *effector strain* to occupy the niche in susceptible host tissues normally occupied by the pathogen. Once established there, the effector strain could follow one of several courses to prevent infection by a particular pathogen (15).

The decreased cariogenicity of LDH-deficient mutants has suggested their possible application as effector strains in the replacement therapy of dental caries. In this approach, the LDH-deficient mutants would be introduced into the mouths of subjects after elimination of their indigenous *S. mutans* or, preferably, into the mouths of children prior to their acquisition of naturally occurring strains. Once established, the effector strain could conceivably provide lifelong protection against caries by preventing colonization of the oral cavity by naturally occurring *S. mutans*. In this regard, we have found that colonization of conventional rats by an LDH-deficient mutant causes a 10- to 10,000-fold increase in the minimal infectious dose for colonization by wild-type strains of *S. mutans* (14). This finding is in accord with previous studies which demonstrated the difficulty of supplanting an established strain of *S. mutans* with another strain (9, 10).

The replacement therapy approach to the prevention of dental caries has the likely added advantage of providing so-called *herd protection* by the natural transmission of the effector strain within the population. Finally, it should be noted that almost any bacterial or viral infection should be amenable to control by this approach. The application of these methods requires a basic understanding of the identity, ecology, and pathogenic mechanisms of the infectious agent. Once these are established, as in the case of *S. mutans*, the application of current genetic techniques may provide a useful effector strain for use in the control of the disease.

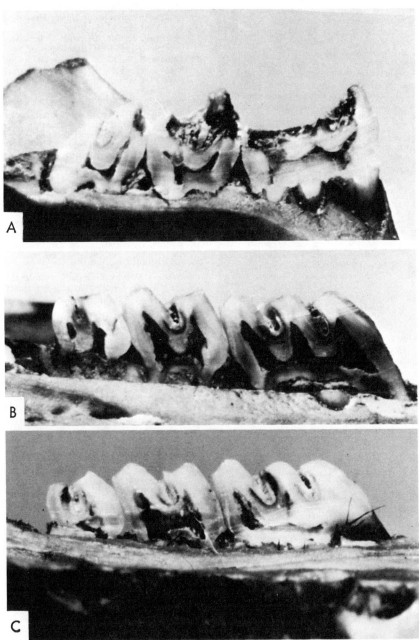

FIG. 1. Cariogenicity of parent and LDH-deficient strains in conventional rats. After 14 weeks of infection, the molar teeth of conventional Sprague-Dawley rats infected with (A) BHT-2 or (B) JH145 (*ldh*) or (C) sham-infected were sagitally sectioned and stained for areas of demineralization.

LITERATURE CITED

1. **Brown, A. T., and C. E. Patterson.** 1973. Ethanol production and alcohol dehydrogenase activity in *Streptococcus mutans*. Arch. Oral Biol. **18**:127–131.
2. **deStoppelaar, J. D., J. van Houte, and O. Backer Dirks.** 1969. The relationship between extracellular polysaccharide producing streptococci and smooth surface caries in 13-year old children. Caries Res. **3**:190–199.
3. **Gibbons, R. J., and R. J. Fitzgerald.** 1969. Dextran induced agglutination of *Streptococcus mutans*, and its potential role in the formation of microbial dental plaques. J. Bacteriol. **98**:341–346.
4. **Hillman, J. D.** 1978. Lactate dehydrogenase mutants of *Streptococcus mutans*: isolation and preliminary characterization. Infect. Immun. **21**:206–212.
5. **Hillman, J. D., J. van Houte, and R. J. Gibbons.** 1970. Sorption of bacteria to human enamel powder. Arch. Oral Biol. **15**:899–903.
6. **Johnson, C. P., S. M. Gross, and J. D. Hillman.** 1980. Cariogenic potential *in vitro* in man and *in vivo* in the rat of lactate dehydrogenase mutants of *Streptococcus mutans*. Arch. Oral Biol. **25**:707–713.
7. **Johnson, C. P., and J. D. Hillman.** 1982. Competitive properties of lactate dehydrogenase mutants of *Streptococcus mutans*. Arch. Oral Biol. (in press).
8. **Jordan H. V.** 1965. Bacteriological aspects of experimental dental caries. Ann. N.Y. Acad. Sci. **131**:905–912.
9. **Jordan, H. V., H. R. Englander, W. O. Engler, and S. Kulczyk.** 1972. Observations on the implantation and transmission of *Streptococcus mutans* in humans. J. Dent. Res. **51**:515–518.
10. **Krasse, B., S. Edwardsson, I. Svensson, and L. Trell.** 1967. Implantation of caries-inducing streptococci in the human oral cavity. Arch. Oral Biol. **12**:231–236.
11. **Krasse, B. H., H. V. Jordan, S. Edwardsson, I. Svensson, and L. Trell.** 1968. The occurrence of certain "caries inducing" streptococci in human dental plaque material. Arch. Oral Biol. **13**:911–918.
12. **Lederberg, J.** 1948. Detection of fermentative variants with tetrazolium. J. Bacteriol. **56**:695.
13. **Littleton, N. W., S. Kakehashi, and R. J. Fitzgerald.** 1970. Recovery of specific "caries-inducing" streptococci from carious lesions in the teeth of children. Arch. Oral Biol. **15**:461–463.
14. **Pasteur, L., and J. F. Joubert.** 1877. Charbon et septicemie. C.R. Acad. Sci. **85**:101–115.
15. **Sanders, E.** 1969. Bacterial interference. I. Its occurrence among the respiratory tract flora and characterization of inhibition of group A streptococci by viridans streptococci. J. Infect. Dis. **120**:698–707.
16. **Shinefield, H. R., J. C. Ribble, and M. Boris.** 1971. Bacterial interference between strains of *Staphylococcus aureus*, 1960 to 1970. Am. J. Dis. Child. **121**:148–152.
17. **Tanzer, J. M., M. I. Krichevsky, and P. H. Keyes.** 1969. The metabolic fate of glucose catabolized by a washed stationary phase caries conducive streptococcus. Caries Res. **3**:167–177.
18. **Yamada, T., and J. Carlsson.** 1975. Regulation of lactate dehydrogenase and change of fermentation products in streptococci. J. Bacteriol. **124**:55–61.
19. **Wood, N. P.** 1966. Formate-pyruvate exchange system: *Streptococcus faecalis*. Methods Enzymol. **9**:718–722.

Genetic and Physiological Determinants of the Enterococcal Response to Antimicrobial Synergism

DONALD J. KROGSTAD AND ROBERT C. MOELLERING, JR.

Divisions of Laboratory Medicine and Infectious Diseases, Departments of Medicine and Pathology, Washington University School of Medicine, St. Louis, Missouri 63110, and Departments of Medicine, New England Deaconess Hospital and Harvard Medical School, Boston, Massachusetts 02215

In 1947, it first became apparent that enterococci, unlike other streptococci, were resistant to killing with penicillin alone (3). Although the basis of enterococcal resistance to penicillin inhibition and killing remains incompletely defined (see below), a number of investigators have demonstrated that the addition of an aminoglycoside to penicillin produces antibiotic synergism in vitro (5) and a satisfactory clinical outcome in vivo (3, 16).

MECHANISM OF ANTIMICROBIAL SYNERGY

Penicillin, vancomycin, cycloserine, and other agents that act on the cell wall (including EDTA) all produce antibiotic synergism against enterococci (a ≥100-fold reduction in colony-forming units per milliliter after overnight incubation at 37°C) when combined with an aminoglycoside (Fig. 1A) (12). By use of ^{14}C-labeled streptomycin, it has also been shown that these agents facilitate aminoglycoside uptake (10). Thus, the mechanism of penicillin plus aminoglycoside synergism against enterococci presumably depends on the ability of penicillin to facilitate the aminoglycoside uptake necessary for its bactericidal effect(s).

HIGH-LEVEL AMINOGLYCOSIDE RESISTANCE

Aminoglycosides alone are relatively inactive against enterococci. In the absence of penicillin, strains susceptible to penicillin plus aminoglycoside synergism require aminoglycoside concentrations 10 to 50 times greater than those achievable clinically for inhibition and killing in vitro (100 to 1,000 µg/ml). These isolates, for which minimal inhibitory concentrations of aminoglycosides are much greater than the achievable serum concentrations, are nevertheless susceptible to antimicrobial synergism with those aminoglycosides.

Initially, it seemed that all enterococcal isolates would be susceptible to antibiotic synergism with penicillin plus streptomycin. However, it subsequently became apparent that organisms with high-level resistance (minimal inhibitory concentrations of >2,000 µg/ml) to a given aminoglycoside were resistant to synergism with penicillin plus that aminoglycoside (Fig. 1B) (11, 14). The high-level aminoglycoside resistance of clinical isolates is almost invariably mediated by the production of aminoglycoside-inactivating enzymes (1, 6, 13, 17) (Fig. 2), although one clinical isolate has recently been shown to have defective gentamicin uptake (9) and a laboratory mutant studied in 1971 was found to have ribosomal resistance to streptomycin (18).

With one exception (17), these enzymes are plasmid determined. The evidence for their extrachromosomal location includes their transfer by conjugation, which also produces high-level aminoglycoside resistance in the transconjugant and renders it resistant to antimicrobial synergism (1, 6, 7). In our initial experiments, a 45-megadalton plasmid was documented in both donor and transconjugant strains (by cesium chloride-ethidium bromide ultracentrifugation, agarose gel electrophoresis, and electron microscopy) (7). It produced a phosphotransferase (APH 3') that mediated resistance to kanamycin and amikacin and a streptomycin adenylyltransferase (6), and was similar to the strains described by both Jacob and Hobbs (4) and Slocombe (13). Recently, Courvalin et al. reported plasmid-mediated production of a phosphotransferase (APH 2″) and an acetyltransferase (AAC 6') that mediate high-level resistance to gentamicin (1), and Murray et al. showed that strains with these enzymes are resistant to synergism with penicillin plus gentamicin (B. E. Murray, J. Tsao, and P. Jayanetra, ASM Int. Conf. Streptococcal Genetics, abstr. P-15, 1981).

In contrast, the AAC 6' enzyme produced by *S. faecium* (which produces high-level tobramycin resistance) appears to be chromosomally determined (17). Thus, clinical isolates of enterococci may be resistant to synergism with any

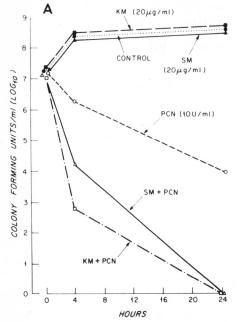
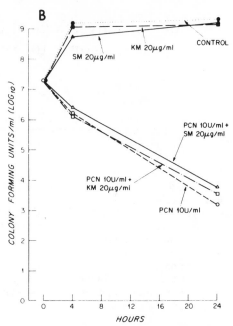

FIG. 1. (A) Killing of enterococcal strains without high-level aminoglycoside resistance by penicillin (PCN) plus aminoglycoside (SM, streptomycin; Km, kanamycin) combinations. (B) Lack of synergism against strains with high-level resistance to aminoglycosides. (Reproduced with permission from the *Journal of Clinical Investigation*, reference 7.)

or all of the aminoglycosides in common clinical use.

PENICILLIN RESISTANCE

Unlike most other streptococci, enterococci are resistant to penicillin. The concentrations of penicillin necessary to inhibit and kill enterococci in vitro (2 to 4 and 250 to 500 μg/ml) are much greater than those necessary to inhibit and kill the penicillin-susceptible streptococci (0.01 to 0.03 μg/ml) (8). In contrast to high-level aminoglycoside resistance (1, 6, 13), enterococcal resistance to penicillin is not transferable by conjugation and is presumably chromosomal.

The biochemical bases of this resistance may include both the penicillin-binding proteins (PBPs) and the autolytic enzyme system of the enterococcus. The PBPs of enterococci bind penicillin less well than those of penicillin-susceptible streptococci and *Staphylococcus aureus* (2; R. Williamson et al., Program Abstr. Intersci. Conf. Antimicrob. Agents Chemother. 20th, New Orleans, La., abstr. no. 714, 1980). In addition, those of *S. faecium* (which is more penicillin resistant than *S. faecalis*) bind penicillin less well than those of *S. faecalis* (Williamson et al., 20th ICAAC, abstr. no. 714, 1980). Thus, there is a generally inverse relationship between

the minimal inhibitory concentrations for these strains and the affinity of their PBPs for penicillin. However, the recent report of Eliopoulos et al. indicates that striking increases in the penicillin susceptibility of *S. faecium* may occur without detectable alterations in their PBPs (G. M. Eliopoulos, C. B. G. Wennersten, and R. C. Moellering, Jr., 21st ICAAC, Chicago, Ill., abstr. no. 502, 1981). Thus, PBPs alone do not appear to satisfactorily explain the resistance of enterococci to penicillin.

In particular, the autolytic enzyme system may be an important factor in enterococcal resistance to penicillin killing. Recent studies indicate that activation of the autolytic enzyme system is necessary for penicillin to lyse and kill enterococci and that human serum inhibits penicillin-induced lysis and killing in vitro (15). Thus, the inhibitory effect of human serum on penicillin killing may help to explain the failure of penicillin alone to cure serious enterococcal diseases, such as enterococcal endocarditis.

CONCLUSIONS

In conclusion, the enterococcus is an important human pathogen that requires treatment with penicillin plus an aminoglycoside to produce antimicrobial synergism in vitro and a

Penicillin Plus: Penicillin Plus:

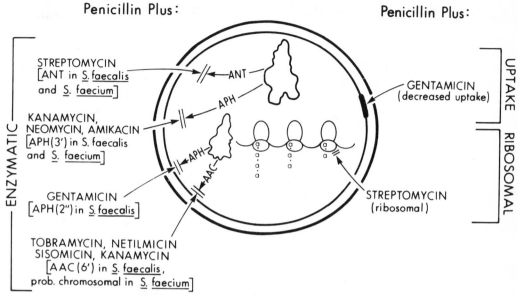

FIG. 2. Enterococcal resistance to penicillin-aminoglycoside synergism. High-level aminoglycoside resistance in clinical isolates of enterococci usually results from the plasmid synthesis of aminoglycoside-inactivating enzymes. ANT, Adenylyltransferase; APH, phosphotransferase; AAC, acetyltransferase.

successful clinical outcome in vivo. Plasmid-mediated synthesis of aminoglycoside-inactivating enzymes and chromosomally determined penicillin resistance are the major genetic factors responsible for resistance to synergism and to penicillin killing. However, the ability of penicillin alone to lyse and kill enterococci in vivo may be critically dependent on the environment in which the drug exposure occurs. Thus, as yet unknown factors in human serum may also be important physiological determinants of the enterococcal response to antimicrobial agents in vivo.

ACKNOWLEDGMENTS

We gratefully acknowledge the contributions of Steven B. Calderwood, George M. Eliopoulos, Thomas R. Korfhagen, Barbara E. Murray, and Gregory A. Storch, and the assistance of Arlene R. Parquette and Christine B. G. Wennersten.

LITERATURE CITED

1. **Courvalin, P. M., C. Carlier, and E. Collatz.** 1980. Plasmid-mediated resistance to aminocyclitol antibiotics in group D streptococci. J.Bacteriol. **143**:541–551.
2. **Georgopapadakou, N. H., and F. Y. Liu.** 1980. Binding of β-lactam antibiotics to penicillin-binding proteins of *Staphylococcus aureus* and *Streptococcus faecalis*: relation to antibacterial activity. Antimicrob. Agents Chemother. **18**:834–836.
3. **Hunter, T. H.** 1947. Use of streptomycin in the treatment of bacterial endocarditis. Am. J. Med. **2**:436–442.
4. **Jacob, A. E., and S. J. Hobbs.** 1974. Conjugal transfer of plasmid-borne multiple antibiotic resistance in *Strepto-*

coccus faecalis var. *zymogenes*. J. Bacteriol. **117**:360–372.
5. **Jawetz, E., J. B. Gunnison, and V. R. Coleman.** 1950. The combined action of penicillin with streptomycin or chloromycetin on enterococci *in vitro*. Science **111**:254–256.
6. **Krogstad, D. J., T. R. Korfhagen, R. C. Moellering, Jr., C. B. G. Wennersten, S. Perzynski, J. E. Davies, and M. N. Swartz.** 1978. Aminoglycoside inactivating enzymes: an explanation for resistance to antibiotic synergism in *Streptococcus faecalis*. J. Clin. Invest. **62**:480–486.
7. **Krogstad, D. J., T. R. Korfhagen, R. C. Moellering, Jr., C. B. G. Wennerstein, and M. N. Swartz.** 1978. Plasmid-mediated resistance to antibiotic synergism in enterococci. J. Clin. Invest. **61**:1645–1653.
8. **Krogstad, D. J., and A. R. Parquette.** 1980. Defective killing of enterococci: a common property of antimicrobials that act on the cell wall. Antimicrob. Agents Chemother. **17**:965–968.
9. **Moellering, R. C., Jr., B. E. Murray, S. C. Schoenbaum, J. Adler, and C. B. G. Wennersten.** 1980. A novel mechanism of resistance to penicillin gentamicin synergism in *Streptococcus faecalis*. J. Infect. Dis. **141**:81–86.
10. **Moellering, R. C., Jr., and A. N. Weinberg.** 1971. Studies on antibiotic synergism against enterococci. II. Effects of various antibiotics on the uptake of ^{14}C-labelled streptomycin by enterococci. J. Clin. Invest. **50**:2580–2584.
11. **Moellering, R. C., Jr., C. B. G. Wennersten, T. Medrek, and A. N. Weinberg.** 1971. Prevalence of high-level resistance to aminoglycosides in clinical isolates of enterococci, p. 335–340. Antimicrob. Agents Chemother. 1970.
12. **Moellering, R. C., Jr., C. B. G. Wennersten, and A. N. Weinberg.** 1971. Studies on antibiotic synergism against enterococci. I. Bacteriologic studies. J. Lab. Clin. Med. **77**:821–828.
13. **Slocombe, B.** 1978. Transmissible aminoglycoside resistance in *Streptococcus faecalis*, p. 891–893. *In* W. Siegenthaler and R. Lüthy (ed.), Current chemotherapy, vol.

II. American Society for Microbiology, Washington, D.C.

14. **Standiford, H. D., H. B. de Maine, and W. M. M. Kirby.** 1970. Antibiotic synergism of enterococci. Arch. Intern. Med. **125:**225–229.

15. **Storch, G. A., and D. J. Krogstad.** 1981. Antibiotic-induced lysis of enterococci. J. Clin. Invest. **68:**639–645.

16. **Weinstein, A. J., and R. C. Moellering, Jr.** 1973. Penicillin and gentamicin therapy for enterococcal infections. J. Am. Med. Assoc. **223:**1030–1032.

17. **Wennersten, C. B., and R. C. Moellering, Jr.** 1980. Mechanism of resistance to penicillin-aminoglycoside synergism in *Streptococcus faecium*, p. 710–712. *In* J. D. Nelson and C. Grassi (ed.), Current chemotherapy and infectious diseases, vol. I. American Society for Microbiology, Washington, D.C.

18. **Zimmerman, R. A., R. C. Moellering, Jr., and A. N. Weinberg.** 1971. Mechanism of resistance to antibiotic synergism in enterococci. J. Bacteriol. **105:**873–879.

Penicillin Tolerance and Resistance in *Streptococcus faecium*

L. DANEO-MOORE AND MICHAEL PUCCI

Department of Microbiology and Immunology, Temple University School of Medicine, Philadelphia, Pennsylvania 19140

Studies of several streptococci indicate that penicillin can cause a whole spectrum of different responses. For example, *Streptococcus pneumoniae* is both killed and lysed by penicillin, *S. pyogenes* is killed but not lysed, and *S. sanguis* is neither killed nor lysed (12). Figure 1 summarizes all of these responses to penicillin. The minimal inhibitory concentration of penicillin G for our laboratory strain of this organism, ATCC 9790S, is 0.6 µg/ml in complex media. This relatively high minimal inhibitory concentration is characteristic of enterococci (15). At 5 µg of penicillin G per ml, both killing and lysis occur (Fig. 1A). Over a wide range of conditions, the killing rate is about four times the lysis rate (E. T. Hinks, Ph.D. thesis, Temple University, Philadelphia, 1977). Figure 1B shows the response to penicillin G of an autolytic enzyme-defective strain (Aut 1), isolated after nitrosoguanidine mutagenesis (18). On addition of penicillin, the organism is killed rapidly after a brief lag, whereas the rate of lysis is slow. Figure 1C shows the "tolerant" response exhibited by the parent type culture collection strain, *S. faecium* ATCC 9790. A penicillin-tolerant response is typical of blood isolates of enterococci (14), but was observed by us in only 3 of 25 enterococcal isolates from various clinical sources (unpublished data).

There is some controversy as to whether a true qualitative difference exists between the responses shown in Fig. 1B and 1C. Shockman and collaborators have argued that the extent of killing and of lysis varies in so-called penicillin-tolerant organisms (17). For example, the viability after the equivalent of two generations of exposure to 10 times the inhibitory concentration of penicillin G ranged from 3 to 61% among various strains of tolerant oral streptococci. In a test for tolerance based on viability after 24 to 48 h of incubation (16), survivors ranged from 0.5 to 2%. Since "tolerant" and "nonlytic" streptococci usually grow in chains of various lengths, viability determinations by colony counts can be misleading unless corrected for chain length (17).

The organisms exhibiting the responses shown in Fig. 1B and 1C are all deficient in cellular autolytic functions. Penicillin-induced cell lysis and cell death are reduced also in three strains deficient in autolytic functions that were isolated by Cornett et al. (2, 18). Three temperature-conditional strains isolated in our laboratory for growth on Triton X-100 plates at 25°C have interesting characteristics in that they are lysed and die slowly in the presence of penicillin G at 25°C but not at 37°C (Fig. 2). However, the strains are lysed at the wild-type rate at both 25 and 37°C by several other inhibitors of cell wall biosynthesis, including bacitracin, cycloserine, vancomycin, and ampicillin. The strains exhibit the wild-type phenotype when pregrown in the presence of an unsaturated fatty acid. Thus, these conditional lysis strains appear to be tolerant to penicillin lysis as a result of a change in the amount of saturated fatty acids in their membranes. Increases in the saturated fatty acids in the membranes of bacteria resistant to detergent have been reported (13).

S. faecium ATCC 9790, which is tolerant to penicillin lysis and killing, exhibits deficient cellular autolytic activity. There is some evidence that the glycolipid content of the susceptible and tolerant strains are different. The tolerant strain contains primarily glycerol phosphate kojibiose diglyceride (5, 6), whereas the susceptible strain contains phosphatidyl diglucosyldiglyceride which is also the anchor lipid for the lipoteichoic acid of the susceptible strain (9). A role for lipoteichoic acid in the regulation of autolytic activity in exponentially growing cells has been questioned (1).

Figure 3 shows that the tolerant strain is identical to the ATCC 9790S strain in its penicillin-binding protein (PBP) profile. Since the tolerant strain was moderately resistant to cephalothin, methicillin, and oxacillin in a Kirby-Bauer disk assay, we examined the binding of penicillin to membranes after prebinding with cephalothin. In both strains the results were identical (Fig. 3). Williamson et al. (19) also found no difference in the PBPs of *S. pneumoniae* grown under lytic and tolerant conditions.

The PBPs of *S. faecium* shown in Fig. 4 are labeled 1 through 6. PBP 6 binds the bulk of the penicillin in a 10- to 15-min binding assay. The

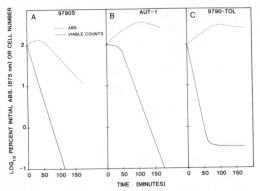

FIG. 1. Schematic pattern of effects of penicillin G (5 µg/ml) addition on viable cell counts and absorbance at 675 nm. (A) *S. faecium* ATCC 9790S. (B) *S. faecium* Aut-1. (C) *S. faecium* ATCC 9790-Tol. Solid lines show viable cell counts and dashed lines show absorbance at 675 nm.

protein was isolated by Coyette et al. (3) and found to have DD-carboxypeptidase activity. The half-life of this protein is much longer than that of its complex with penicillin, and this protein is thought to cleave penicillin slowly to phenylacetylglycine and *N*-formyl-D-penicillamine (4). PBP 1, the slowest-moving protein component, also has a longer half life than its penicillin complex. The product of the complex breakdown is thought to be penicilloic acid, indicating that the protein may have a weak β-lactamase activity (4).

The other PBPs are of most interest in the present context, since resistance to penicillin is accompanied by alterations in some of these proteins. All of these proteins have half-lives comparable to those of their complex with penicillin (Fig. 4). The enzymatic function of these PBPs is currently unknown. On the basis of binding properties at the minimal inhibitory concentration at 45 and 32°C, Fontana et al. (7) suggested that PBP 3 may be the lethal target for penicillin in *S. faecium*. On entirely different considerations, based on morphological appearance at subinhibitory concentrations of certain antibiotics, in particular of thienamycin, we believe that PBP 3 may be involved in functions concerned with surface enlargement. This conclusion is tentative, since PBP 3 can be subdivided into two proteins, PBP 3a and 3b (4). Moreover, a penicillin-resistant clinical isolate of *S. faecium* has no PBP 3 band(s), but is morphologically normal (see below). However, loss of penicillin-binding activity need not be accompanied by loss of a putative enzymatic function in peptidoglycan assembly. PBP 3 is cleaved proteolytically on prolonged incubation

at 37°C to a product of 75,000 to 80,000 daltons (4).

Also on the basis of morphological appearance of cells exposed to subinhibitory concentrations of certain antibiotics, in particular of cefoxitin, we suggest that PBP 2 may have a function in septum formation and cell division. Again, these conclusions are tentative. PBP 2 appears to double (to PBP 2a and 2b) in some penicillin-resistant clinical isolates that are morphologically normal (see below).

PBP 4 is the most unstable band in *S. faecium* and has been shown to break down at 37°C to a 73,000-dalton product. Two high-level penicillin-resistant clinical isolates appear to lack PBP 4 (see below).

From the standpoint of penicillin resistance, PBP 5 is of great interest. It was recently reported that this protein bound penicillin very slowly, reaching saturation only after 60 to 90 min of incubation (8). Consequently, PBP 5 appeared to be a minor component after 10 to 15 min of incubation, but increased in importance when membranes were incubated for longer times. We have confirmed these observations in our laboratory. Of even greater interest, however, was the observation by Fontana and Cerini (8) that

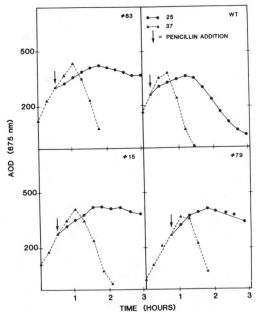

FIG. 2. Lysis of *S. faecium* ATCC 9790 wild type (WT) and cold-sensitive mutants 15, 79, and 83 at 25°C and 37°C after the addition of penicillin G (20 µg/ml). Cells were grown in chemically defined medium, and antibiotic addition occurred in early exponential phase. Symbols: ▲, 37°C; ●, 25°C.

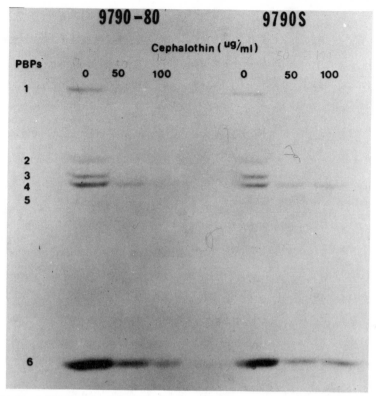

FIG. 3. PBP pattern of *S. faecium* ATCC 9790S and *S. faecium* 9790-80. Cell membranes were pre-incubated at 37°C for 15 min with cephalothin at 0, 50, and 100 μg/ml before a 10-min binding with 3.2 μg of ^{14}C-benzylpenicillin per ml at 37°C.

PBP 5 was increased in all penicillin-resistant isolates, including clinical and laboratory isolates. They reported that the increasing binding of PBP 5 in these strains was roughly proportional to the level of resistance. Again, our preliminary observations of clinical isolates and of several laboratory strains confirm these findings. Figure 5 shows the scanning of an autoradiograph of *S. faecium* ATCC 9790S, and of a clinical isolate (CH-2) resistant to 16 μg of penicillin G per ml. The scan also shows two other changes alluded to above, i.e., a broadening (possibly doubling) of PBP 2 and the absence of PBP 3.

Still other changes have been observed. For example, in CH-1, a penicillin-resistant clinical isolate, PBP 2 is clearly doubled, PBP 4 is missing, and PBP 5 is slightly increased. We are also currently analyzing spontaneous penicillin-resistant isolates obtained from *S. faecium* ATCC 9790S. An unexpected feature of these strains, as well as of the clinical isolates, is an alteration in the overall mobility of membrane proteins, which is also found in laboratory derivatives of *S. faecium* 9790S resistant to various levels of penicillin (12, 15, and 25 μg/ml).

In summary, the genetic basis for penicillin tolerance and for nonlytic death in *S. faecium* appears to reside at various levels of autolytic enzyme function and regulation. Detailed study of the derivatives obtained from *S. faecium* ATCC 9790 should provide important information in the regulation of autolytic enzyme expression during normal growth, during the cell division cycle (11, 17), and after antibiotic treatments.

Low- and high-level penicillin resistance in *S. faecium* appears to be accompanied by an increase in the binding of penicillin to a 75,000-dalton component(s). In the susceptible organism, this component exhibits relatively slow saturation kinetics. Some uncertainty exists about the identity of PBP 5 and some of the proteolytic cleavage products reported by Coyette et al. (4). Currently, two hypotheses can be proposed as a useful basis for further study. PBP 5 may be increased in levels or in binding affinity in all low-level penicillin-resistant *S.*

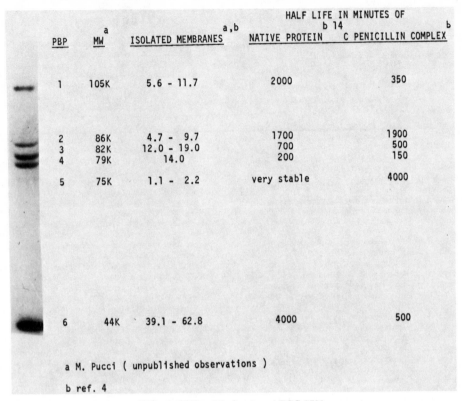

PBP	MW[a]	ISOLATED MEMBRANES[a,b]	HALF LIFE IN MINUTES OF	
			NATIVE PROTEIN[b]	[14]C PENICILLIN COMPLEX[b]
1	105K	5.6 - 11.7	2000	350
2	86K	4.7 - 9.7	1700	1900
3	82K	12.0 - 19.0	700	500
4	79K	14.0	200	150
5	75K	1.1 - 2.2	very stable	4000
6	44K	39.1 - 62.8	4000	500

a M. Pucci (unpublished observations)

b ref. 4

FIG. 4. PBPs of *S. faecium* ATCC 9790.

faecium strains, possibly compensating for the loss of another PBP. Alternatively, an endogenous proteolytic activity capable of cleaving PBP 2, 3, and possibly 4 may be elevated in low-level penicillin-resistant *S. faecium* strains. This proteolytic activity would in turn generate a band(s) with the mobility of PBP 5. In view of the altered membrane protein mobility of all penicillin-resistant strains examined recently, we think that the second hypothesis should be given consideration. It is also interesting to note that apparently new penicillin-binding bands were observed in penicillin-resistant *S. pneumoniae* (10, 20).

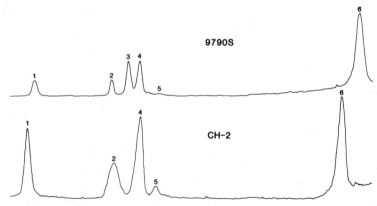

FIG. 5. Soft laser scanning densitometry of the PBP patterns of *S. faecium* 9790S and *S. faecium* CH-2. Cell membranes were bound with 32 μg of ^{14}C-benzylpenicillin per ml at 37°C for 10 min.

ACKNOWLEDGMENTS

We thank J. Campos and G. Dunny for providing the clinical isolates and G. D. Shockman for discussions and encouragement.

This work was supported by Public Health Service grant AI 05044 from the National Institute of Allergy and Infectious Disease.

LITERATURE CITED

1. **Carson, D. D., R. A. Pieringer, and L. Daneo-Moore.** 1981. Effect of cerulenin on cellular autolytic activity and lipid metabolism during inhibition of protein synthesis in *Streptococcus faecalis*. J. Bacteriol. **146**:590–604.

2. **Cornett, J. B., B. E. Redman, and G. D. Shockman.** 1978. Autolytic defective mutant of *Streptococcus faecalis*. J. Bacteriol. **133**:631–640.

3. **Coyette, J., J. M. Ghuysen, and R. Fontana.** 1978. Solubilization and isolation of membrane-bound DD-carboxypeptidase of *Streptococcus faecalis*. ATCC 9790. Eur. J. Biochem. **88**:297–305.

4. **Coyette, J., J. M. Ghuysen, and R. Fontana.** 1980. The penicillin-binding proteins in *Streptococcus faecalis* ATCC 9790. Eur. J. Biochem. **110**:445–456.

5. **Fischer, W., I. Ishizuka, H. R. Landgraf, and J. Herrmann.** 1973. Glycerophosphoryl diglucosyl diglyceride, a new phosphoglycolipid from streptococci. Biochim. Biophys. Acta **296**:527–545.

6. **Fischer, W., H. R. Landgraf, and J. Herrman.** 1973. Phosphatidyldiglucosyl diglyceride from streptococci and its relationship to other polar lipids. Biochim. Biophys. Acta **306**:353–367.

7. **Fontana, R., P. Canepari, G. Satta, and J. Coyette.** 1980. Identification of the lethal target of benzylpenicillin in *Streptococcus faecalis* by *in vivo* penicillin binding studies. Nature (London) **287**:70–72.

8. **Fontana, R., and R. Cerini.** 1982. The mechanism of penicillin resistance in *Streptococcus faecalis*, p. 225–226. *In* P. Periti and G. G. Grassi (ed.), Current chemotherapy and infectious disease. American Society for Microbiology, Washington, D.C.

9. **Ganfield, M., and R. A. Pieringer.** 1975. Phosphatidylkojibiosyl diglyceride: the covalently linked lipid constituent of the membrane lipoteichoic acid from *Streptococcus faecalis (faecium)* ATCC 9790. J. Biol. Chem. **250**:702–709.

10. **Hakenbeck, R., M. Tarpay, and A. Tomasz.** 1980. Multiple changes of penicillin-binding proteins in penicillin-resistant clinical isolates of *Streptococcus pneumoniae*. Antimicrob. Agents Chemother. **17**:364–471.

11. **Hinks, R. P., L. Daneo-Moore, and G. D. Shockman.** 1978. Cellular autolytic activity in synchronized populations of *Streptococcus faecium*. J. Bacteriol. **133**:822–829.

12. **Horne, D., and A. Tomasz.** 1977. Tolerant response of *Streptococcus sanguis* to β-lactams and other cell wall inhibitors. Antimicrob. Agents Chemother. **11**:888–896.

13. **Inoue, K., and T. Kitagawa.** 1976. Effect of lipid composition on sensitivity of lipid membranes to Triton X-100. Biochim. Biophys. Acta **426**:1–16.

14. **Krogstadt, D. J., and A. R. Parquette.** 1980. Defective killing of enterococci: a common property of antimicrobial agents acting on the cell wall. Antimicrob. Agents Chemother. **17**:965–968.

15. **Moellering, R. C., Jr., and D. J. Krogstad.** 1979. Antibiotic resistance in enterococci, p. 293–298. *In* D. Schlessinger (ed.), Microbiology—1979. American Society for Microbiology, Washington, D.C.

16. **Sabath, L. D., N. Wheeler, M. Laverdiere, D. Blazevic, and B. J. Wilkinson.** 1977. A new type of penicillin resistance of *Staphylococcus aureus*. Lancet **2**:443–447.

17. **Shockman, G. D., L. Daneo-Moore, T. D. McDowell, and W. Wong.** 1981. Function and structure of the cell wall—its importance in the life and death of bacteria, p. 31–65. *In* M. Salton and G. D. Shockman (ed.), β-Lactam antibiotics. New York.

18. **Shungu, D. L., J. B. Cornett, and G. D. Shockman.** 1979. Morphological and physiological studies of autolytic-defective *Streptococcus faecium* strains. J. Bacteriol. **138**:598–608.

19. **Williamson, R., R. Hakenbeck, and A. Tomasz.** 1980. The penicillin-binding proteins of *Streptococcus pneumoniae* grown under lysis-permissive and lysis-protective (tolerant) conditions. FEMS Microbiol. Lett. **7**:127–131.

20. **Zighelboim, S., and A. Tomasz.** 1980. Penicillin-binding proteins of multiple antibiotic resistant South African strains of *Streptococcus pneumoniae*. Antimicrob. Agents Chemother. **17**:434–442.

Lack of UV-Induced Mutation in Several Streptococci

NICOLE SICARD

Centre de Recherche de Biochimie et de Génétique Cellulaires du C.N.R.S., 31062 Toulouse, France

Various agents that damage DNA induce an array of functions in bacteria (4–10) and mammalian cells (2). One step is the "SOS response" (7). Many genes are induced in a coordinated fashion regulated by the *recA* and *lexA* genes in *Escherichia coli* (5). Although it is likely that such a repair process may occur in other organisms (11), my colleagues and I recently reported a lack of Weigle reactivation and a lack of induction of mutations by UV irradiation, thymidine starvation, or isogenic transformation in several strains of *Streptococcus pneumoniae*,

suggesting a lack of SOS repair functions in these bacteria (1). However, it has been reported that UV irradiation induced streptomycin-resistant mutants in five different streptococcal strains of group A (8) under experimental conditions with which no such mutants could be detected in pneumococci. The different behavior of these serologically distinct groups may be due to a quite divergent background. In this communication I show that a variety of *S. sanguis* related to pneumococci belonging to group H and *S. mutans* do not respond to UV induction

TABLE 1. Frequency of mutants after UV treatment of *S. sanguis* strains[a]

Strain	Survival (%)	Ami^r ($\times 10^{-5}$)	Rif^r ($\times 10^{-6}$)	Str^r ($\times 10^{-6}$)
Challis	100	2	0.2	0.3
	40	2.8	0.5	0.2
	13	3.1	0.1	0.2
	4	2.9	0.2	0.4
	0.2	3	0.1	0.9
Wicky	100	3.5	1.1	1.1
	83	2.4	0.5	0.8
	32	2.6	0.8	1.3
	7	3.8	2.1	0.4
	2	2	0.4	1.2
Blackburn (7122)	100	Resistant	4.9	Resistant
	41		4.6	
	8		3.7	
Channon (7126)	100	7.8	2.9	Resistant
	15	9.8	5.8	
	2	8.1	3.0	
ATCC 10558 (7233)	100	Resistant	6.9	0.2
	11		9.3	0.3
	1		12.0	0.2
NCTC 7863 (7234)	100	11.1	7.1	Resistant
	35	10.1	13.2	
	6	14.1	11.1	

[a] UV irradiation was performed on exponential-phase cultures in synthetic medium with a germicidal lamp giving an incident dose rate of 5 J/m^2 per s. Survival was determined by plating on complete medium. Control and treated cultures were diluted 100-fold into complete medium and incubated to full growth. The total number of viable cells and the number of bacteria resistant to antibiotics were determined by plating on complete medium or medium containing 10^{-5} M aminopterin (Ami^r), 2 µg of rifampin per ml (Rif^r), or 50 µg of streptomycin per ml (Str^r). The frequency of mutants is the ratio of resistant bacteria to viable cells.

of mutations as first observed for pneumococci.

Six different cultures of *S. sanguis*, strains Challis, Wicky, Blackburn (7122), Channon (7126), ATCC 10558 (7233), and NCTC 7863 (7234) were exposed to UV light, and survival was determined. After phenotypic expression, bacteria resistant to aminopterin, rifampin, and streptomycin were scored. The results are summarized in Table 1.

Irradiation with doses sufficient to reduce survival to a few percent caused no detectable increase in the frequency of aminopterin-, rifampin-, or streptomycin-resistant mutants. However, spontaneous mutants were easily detected without overloading the plates with bacteria. When a strain was naturally resistant to the chosen level of antibiotic, no mutant could be scored. None of the phenotypes was induced to mutate by UV irradiation although the spontaneous level of rifampin- and streptomycin-resistant mutants was considerably lower than the level of aminopterin-resistant mutants.

Similar experiments were performed with two strains of *S. mutans* and similar results were observed for both strains.

The lack of UV-induced mutability in such a variety of bacteria suggests that one of the repair pathways involved in SOS functions may be deficient, in contrast to wild-type *E. coli* (10) and *Bacillus subtilis* (11). In that respect, pneumococcus is similar to *Haemophilus influenzae* (6), *Micrococcus radiodurans* (9), and *Proteus mirabilis* (3). It is quite possible that the repair system has evolved differently in some bacteria. This raises the question of whether other, unknown repair processes substitute for the missing steps.

ACKNOWLEDGMENTS

I am grateful to Dr. Tiraby and Dr. Cole for the supply of bacterial strains.

LITERATURE CITED

1. **Gasc, A. M., N. Sicard, J. P. Claverys, and A. M. Sicard.** 1980. Lack of SOS repair in *Streptococcus pneumoniae*. Mutat. Res. **70**:157–165.
2. **Hanawalt, P. C., P. K. Cooper, A. K. Ganesan, and C. A. Smith.** 1979. DNA repair in bacteria and mammalian cells. Annu. Rev. Biochem. **48**:783–836.
3. **Hofemeister, J., and H. Böhme.** 1975. DNA repair in *Proteus mirabilis*. Mol. Gen. Genet. **141**:147–161.
4. **Howard-Flanders, P.** 1973. DNA repair and recombination. Br. Med. Bull. **29**:226–235.
5. **Kenyon, C. J., and G. C. Walker.** 1980. DNA-damaging agents stimulate gene expression at specific loci in *Escherichia coli*. Proc. Natl. Acad. Sci. U.S.A. **77**:2819–2823.
6. **Kimball, R. F., M. E. Boling, and S. W. Perdue.** 1977. Evidence that UV inducible error-prone repair is absent in *Haemophilus influenzae* Rd. Mutat. Res. **44**:183–196.
7. **Radman, M.** 1975. SOS repair hypothesis: phenomenology of an inducible DNA repair which is accompanied by mutagenesis, p. 355–368. *In* P. C. Hanawalt and B. Setlow (ed.), Molecular mechanisms for repair of DNA. Plenum Press, New York.
8. **Ravin, A. W., and A. K. Mishra.** 1965. Relative frequencies of different kinds of spontaneous and induced mutants of pneumococci and streptococci capable of growth in the presence of streptomycin. J. Bacteriol. **90**:1161–1170.
9. **Sweet, D. M., and B. E. B. Moseley.** 1974. Accurate repair of UV induced damage in *Micrococcus radiodurans*. Mutat. Res. **23**:311–318.
10. **Witkin, E. M.** 1976. Ultraviolet mutagenesis and inducible DNA repair in *Escherichia coli*. Bacteriol. Rev. **40**:869–907.
11. **Yasbin, R. E.** 1977. DNA repair in *Bacillus subtilis*. Mol. Gen. Genet. **153**:219–225.

Isolation and Characterization of a *Streptococcus sanguis* FW213 Mutant Nonadherent to Saliva-Coated Hydroxyapatite Beads

PAULA FIVES-TAYLOR

Department of Medical Microbiology, University of Vermont, Burlington, Vermont 05401

Dental caries and periodontal disease are two of the most common infectious diseases in the United States today. The causal relationship between these diseases and dental plaque was demonstrated many years ago (3, 6, 11, 15, 16). Early plaque development involves aerobic, predominantly coccal flora which are succeeded by a complex, filamentous, largely anaerobic population (17). It seems probable that the first organism to adhere initiates plaque development by altering the environment to favor the attachment of the later flora. Investigations of the succession of oral flora from birth onwards revealed that the recovery of *Streptococcus sanguis* from the mouth is closely correlated with the eruption of the first teeth (1, 5). When recolonization of cleaned teeth occurs, *S. sanguis* is the first organism to appear on the tooth surface and becomes 70% of the cultivable microflora in 2 days (18). Of the microorganisms found in dental plaque, *S. sanguis* has one of the highest affinities for the teeth and for saliva-coated spheroidal hydroxyapatite beads (SC-SHA) as measured by an in vitro assay mimicking the salivary pellicle of the tooth surface (4, 7, 10, 13). For these reasons, studies of the surface structures of *S. sanguis* were undertaken in the hope of identifying those structures which are

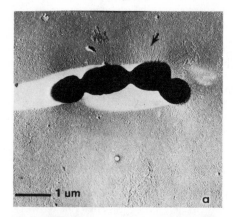

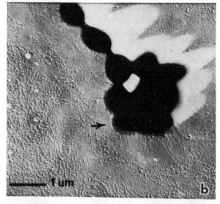

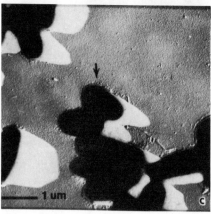

FIG. 1. Platinum-shadowed electron micrographs of *S. sanguis*. The cells were grown aerobically at 36°C in Todd-Hewitt broth and were harvested at the late logarithmic phase of growth. Portions of 1.5 ml were washed three times in 0.85% saline at 0°C. The final pellet was suspended in 3.7% formaldehyde. A drop of this suspension was allowed to settle on a Formvar-coated grid for approximately 30 min. The excess liquid was removed by gentle suction, and the grids were fixed by drying at 60°C for 10 min. The grids were shadowed at a 14° angle with platinum and observed in a Phillips 300 electron microscope. (a) *S. sanguis* FW213 showing fimbriae (→) surrounding the entire cell. (b) *S. sanguis* JD262, the nontwitching mutant that has lost the polar fimbriae (→) associated with the parent strain FW213. (c) *S. sanguis* JL7, the nonadherent mutant that possesses only very short, stubby fimbriae (→).

involved in the adhesion of this organism to the salivary pellicle of the tooth.

S. sanguis FW213 possesses an abundance of fimbriae (pili), hairlike surface fibers surrounding the entire cell (Fig. 1a) (S. Fachon and P. Fives-Taylor, Abstr. Annu. Meet. Am. Soc. Microbiol. 1978, J2, p. 77). This paper is a report of work on the isolation of an isogenic, nonfimbriated mutant of the parent strain. The final mutant, JL7, was obtained in a two-step process. In 1975, Henriksen and Henrichsen reported a positive correlation between the possession of polar fimbriae and the ability of an organism to express twitching motility, a nonflagellar translocation on the surface of an agar plate (8, 9). Twitching motility can be recognized when colonies have a narrow, thin spreading zone, with more or less irregular dentate edges (Fig. 2a). It seemed probable that this twitching phenomenon could be used as a way of screening a large number of mutagenized cells and selecting the ones most likely to be nonfimbriated. Consequently, logarithmic, aerobically grown cells of FW213 were mutagenized with 50 μg of nitrosoguanidine per ml, a concentration calculated to yield only one mutation per cell (14). Survivors, diluted to give no more than 100 colonies per plate, were plated on tryptose blood agar plates. These plates were then taped and incubated at 37°C in a CO_2 incubator set for high humidity for 5 to 7 days. Cells not possessing a narrow, thin, irregular spreading zone were selected as possible nontwitchers (Fig. 2b). These nontwitchers were replated and examined again to ensure that phase variation or growth conditions were not responsible for the loss of twitching motility. A screening of 23,690 isolates produced only 2 stable nontwitchers. Electron microscopy revealed that these mutants had lost the polar fimbriae associated with the parent strain but still possessed many fimbriae surrounding the cell surface (Fig. 1b). The ability of these organisms to adhere to saliva-coated hydroxyapatite was tested by the adherence assay of Gibbons et al. (4). The Langmuir adsorption isotherms derived from these data showed that the mutants had the same type of specific binding to SC-SHA as FW213 (Fig. 3b) and the same number of binding sites (3.41×10^8). However, their affinity for SC-SHA was 7.96×10^{-10}, which is 25% reduced from that of the parent strain (Table 1).

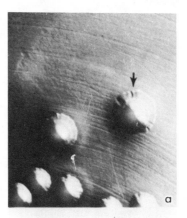

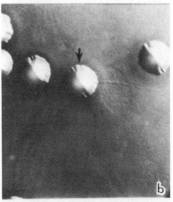

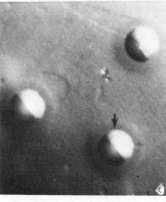

FIG. 2. Light micrographs of colonies of *S. sanguis* plated for twitching motility. *S. sanguis* cells, mutagenized with nitrosoguanidine, were diluted and plated on blood agar so as to give no more than 100 colonies per plate. These plates were taped and incubated with high humidity for 7 days in 5% CO_2 at 36°C. The colonies were examined for twitching motility with a stereomicroscope illuminated with oblique lighting. (a) Colonies of *S. sanguis* FW213 showing the transparent zone with undulating edges characteristic of twitching motility (→). (b) Colonies of JD262 that have lost the transparent zone characteristic of twitching motility but still have some dentate edges on the colony itself (→). (c) Colonies of the nonadherent mutant JL7 showing no twitching zone and having smooth edges to the colony (→). The zone seen around the colony is alpha-hemolysis, which was deemphasized in Fig. 2a by the twitching motility zone.

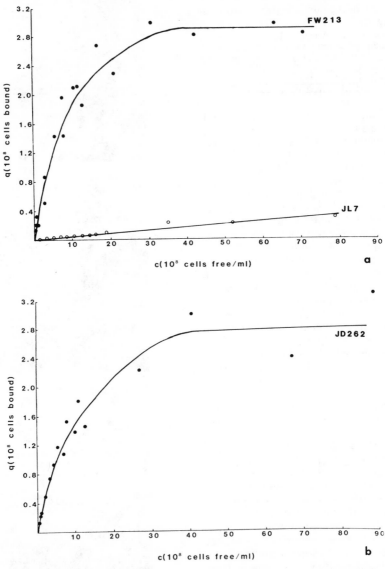

FIG. 3. Langmuir adsorption isotherms of *S. sanguis*. Cells were grown as described in Fig. 1 except that 2 μC of [³H]thymidine per ml was added to the media. Washed, labeled cells in phosphate buffer were added to 40 mg of SC-SHA. The beads were incubated on a sample mixer at 37°C for 1 h. The beads and adsorbed cells were allowed to settle, and the supernatant was removed. The amount of radioactivity associated with the beads and the supernatant was determined in a Beckman LS7500 liquid scintillation counter, and the counts were converted to number of cells bound to 40 mg of SC-SHA (q) and number of free cells (c). (a) Langmuir adsorption isotherms of *S. sanguis* FW213 and JL7. *S. sanguis* FW213 displays the curvilinear relationship characteristic of specific binding. Saturation of the binding sites is reached when the free cell concentration approaches 3×10^9 cells per ml. The straight line of positive slope shown by *S. sanguis* JL7 suggests that these cells have lost all specific binding to SC-SHA. (b) Adsorption isotherm of *S. sanguis* JD262 showing the same specific binding to SC-SHA shown by FW213.

TABLE 1. Number of binding sites (N) and affinity constant (K_a) for *S. sanguis* FW213 and JD262[a]

Strain	N	K_a
FW213	3.4×10^8	1.0×10^{-9}
JD262	3.4×10^8	7.9×10^{-10}

[a] The Langmuir adsorption isotherms of Fig. 3 were plotted as c versus c/q, which results in a straight line of positive slope. N was determined from the reciprocal of the slope of this line, and K_a was calculated from the negative reciprocal of the x intercept.

These data imply that the polar fimbriae associated with twitching motility may strengthen the adsorption bond but are not the receptors involved in the bond itself.

One of the nontwitching mutants, JD262, and its parent strain, FW213, were selected and mutagenized in the manner described above, and an attempt was made to isolate nonadherers by an enrichment procedure. These mutagenized cells, as well as unmutagenized FW213 and JD262, were mixed with SC-SHA until an adsorption equilibrium was reached. Previous experiments showed that this occurred in less than 1 h (12). After 1 h, the beads and the adsorbed cells were allowed to settle out, and the supernatant was again mixed with fresh SC-SHA. After each transfer, the cells were plated on Trypticase soy agar and screened with a stereomicroscope for any differences in colonial morphology. After 16 transfers, a total of six different morphologies were observed. Representative samples of each of these were selected and tested for adherence to SC-SHA. A large, opaque, smooth colony, JL7, derived from mutagenized JD262, was the only isolate showing significantly decreased adherence to SC-SHA. Upon further study, it was determined that the 10% adherence characteristic of JL7 was nonspecific (Fig. 3a). When examined by electron microscopy, JL7 possessed only very short, stubby fimbriae (Fig. 1c) characteristic of cells such as *S. salivarius* (S. Fachon and P. Fives-Taylor, Abstr. Annu. Meet. Am. Soc. Microbiol. 1978, J2, p. 77) that do not adhere to teeth (7). When plated on blood agar and incubated to produce twitching zones, JL7 was negative for twitching motility as expected. However, it also had lost the undulating edge of the colony associated with its parent, JD262 (Fig. 2c).

In summary, these data imply that *Streptococcus sanguis* FW213 possesses at least three distinct classes of fimbriae: (i) polar fimbriae necessary for twitching motility, (ii) peritrichous fimbriae associated with adherence to SC-SHA, and (iii) short fimbriae whose function to date is unknown. These data also suggest that the fimbriae necessary for twitching motility may be involved in stabilizing the adherence bond.

ACKNOWLEDGMENTS

This investigation was supported by Public Health Service grant RO1 05606-02 from the National Institute of Dental Research and by National Institutes of Health General Research Support grant 5429-19-6.

LITERATURE CITED

1. **Carlson, J., H. Grahnen, G. Jonsson, and S. Wikner.** 1970. Establishment of *Streptococcus sanguis* in the mouths of infants. Arch. Oral Biol. **15:**1143–1148.
2. **Clark, W. B., L. L. Bammann, and R. J. Gibbons.** 1978. Comparative estimates of bacterial affinities and adsorption sites on hydroxyapatite surfaces. Infect. Immun. **19:**846–853.
3. **Fitzgerald, R. J., and P. H. Keyes.** 1960. Demonstration of the etiologic role of streptococci in experimental caries in the hamster. J. Am. Dent. Assoc. **61:**9–19.
4. **Gibbons, R. J., E. C. Moreno, and D. M. Spinell.** 1976. Model delineating the effects of a salivary pellicle on the adsorption of Streptococcus miteor onto hydroxyapatite. Infect. Immun. **14:**1109–1112.
5. **Gibbons, R. J., S. S. Socransky, S. deAranjo, and J. Van Houte.** 1964. Studies of predominant cultivated microbiota of dental plaques. Arch. Oral Biol. **9:**365–370.
6. **Gibbons, R. J., and J. Van Houte.** 1973. On the formation of dental plaques. J. Periodontol. **44:**347–360.
7. **Gibbons, R. J., and J. Van Houte.** 1975. Bacterial adherence in oral microbial ecology. Annu. Rev. Microbiol. **29:**19–44.
8. **Henrichsen, J., and J. Blom.** 1975. Correlation between twitching motility and possession of polar fimbriae in *Acinetobacter calcoaceticus*. Acta Pathol. Microbiol. Scand. Sect. B **83:**103–115.
9. **Henriksen, S. D., and J. Henrichsen.** 1975. Twitching motility and possession of polar fimbriae in spreading *Streptococcus sanguis* isolates from the human throat. Acta Pathol. Microbiol. Scand. Sect. B **83:**133–140.
10. **Hillman, J. D., J. Van Houte, and R. J. Gibbons.** 1970. Sorption of bacteria to human enamel powder. Arch. Oral Biol. **15:**899.
11. **Jenkins, G. N.** 1968. The mode of formation of dental plaque. Caries Res. **2:**130.
12. **Liljemark, W. F., and S. V. Schauer.** 1975. Studies on the bacterial components which bind *Streptococcus sanguis* and *Streptococcus mutans* to hydroxyapatite. Arch. Oral Biol. **20:**609–615.
13. **Liljemark, W. F., and S. V. Schauer.** 1977. Competitive binding among oral streptococci to hydroxyapatite. J. Dent. Res. **56(2):**157–165.
14. **Miller, J. H.** 1972. Experiments in molecular genetics, p. 125–129. Cold Spring Harbor Laboratory, Cold Spring Harbor, N.Y.
15. **Orland, F., J. Blaney, R. Harrison, J. Reymers, P. Trexier, M. Wagner, M. Gordon, and T. Luckey.** 1954. Use of the germ free animal technic in the study of experimental dental caries. I. Basic observations on rats reared free of all microorganisms. J. Dent. Res. **33:**147–174.
16. **Socransky, S. S.** 1970. Relationship of bacteria to the etiology of periodontal disease. J. Dent. Res. **49:**203.
17. **Socransky, S. S., and A. D. Manganiello.** 1971. The oral microbiota of man from birth to senility. J. Periodontol. **42:**485.
18. **Socransky, S. S., A. D. Manganiello, D. Propas, V. Oram, and J. Van Houte.** 1977. Bacteriological studies of developing supragingival dental plaque. J. Periodontal Res. **12:**90–106.
19. **Van Houte, J., R. J. Gibbons, and S. B. Banghart.** 1970. Adherence as a determinant of the presence of *Streptococcus salivarius* and *Streptococcus sanguis* on the tooth surface. Arch. Oral Biol. **15:**1025.

METABOLIC AND BACTERIOCIN-RELATED PLASMIDS

Characterization and Transferability of Plasmids Among Group N Streptococci

LARRY L. McKAY and KATHLEEN A. BALDWIN

Department of Food Science and Nutrition, University of Minnesota, St. Paul, Minnesota 55108

Our laboratory has been examining group N streptococci (*Streptococcus lactis, S. cremoris,* and *S. lactis* subsp. *diacetylactis*) for presence of plasmid DNA in an attempt to correlate the spontaneous loss of metabolic properties observed in these organisms to plasmid DNA, as well as an attempt to find or develop DNA transfer systems to allow genetic studies in this industrially important group of microorganisms. Three metabolic properties of these organisms vital for successful dairy fermentations include the ability to ferment lactose, the ability to release amino acids and peptides from casein (proteolytic activity), and the ability of *S. diacetylactis* to utilize citrate. It is now known that variants of parental strains can be isolated (spontaneously, by curing with acridine dyes, or by incubation at elevated temperatures) which have lost one or more of the following: ability to ferment lactose (Lac⁻), ability to produce proteinase (Prt⁻), or ability to utilize citrate (Cit⁻). These phenotypic data suggested that these metabolic traits were plasmid mediated (12).

To obtain physical evidence for this linkage, we compared plasmid profiles of the parent and variant strains. Table 1 shows the diversity of plasmid sizes found in group N streptococci. It has become apparent that these organisms characteristically harbor many plasmid species (4, 6–10, 16). The number observed ranges from 2 to 11, but most strains contain from 4 to 7 plasmid species. Most of the plasmids observed in these organisms are cryptic, but some appear to carry identifiable traits. For example, Lac⁺ Prt⁻ variants of *S. cremoris* HP lose an 8-megadalton (Mdal) plasmid (9), and Lac⁺ Prt⁻ derivatives of *S. lactis* C2 lose both a 12- and an 18-Mdal plasmid (7, 12). Lac⁻ Prt⁺ variants of *S. cremoris* B₁ are missing a 36-Mdal plasmid (1), and Lac⁻ Prt⁻ variants of *S. lactis* strains C2, ML3, C10, and M18 each lose a single plasmid of 30-, 33-, 40-, and 45-Mdal, respectively (7, 8). Why a strain can become Lac⁻ Prt⁻ or Lac⁺ Prt⁻ and lose different plasmids has not been resolved.

Cit⁻ variants of *S. diacetylactis* lose a single plasmid of about 5.5 Mdal, and on the basis of restriction endonuclease digestion patterns, the same plasmid appears to be present in different strains of *S. diacetylactis* (4). Plasmids have also been implicated by LeBlanc and associates in the fermentation of sucrose, glucose, mannose, and xylose, and in the production of nisin (10). Galactose utilization via the phosphoenolpyruvate-dependent phosphotransferase system also appears to be plasmid mediated (11, 15).

Genetic evidence that lactose metabolism is plasmid mediated was obtained by transduction and conjugation. Lac⁺ Prt⁺ *S. lactis* C2 possesses a 30-Mdal plasmid which is lost when the strain becomes Lac⁻ Prt⁻. Upon transduction (using a temperate phage induced from C2) to a Lac⁺ phenotype, the acquisition of a 20- to 21-Mdal plasmid by the Lac⁻ recipient was observed. This was lost when the transductant became Lac⁻. The plasmid was smaller in the

TABLE 1. Apparent distribution of plasmid sizes found in some group N streptococci

Organism	Plasmid sizes (Mdal)
S. lactis	
C2	1, 2, 5, 12, 18, 30
ML3	1, 2, 5, 33
M18	1, 4.5, 25, 29, 45
C10	1, 4.5, 25, 40
C₂O	1.5, 2.2, 23, 29
S. diacetylactis	
18-16	3, 3.4, 5.5, 6.4, 28, 41
DRC-3	1.8, 3.2, 3.8, 5.5, 26.5, 34, 40, 52
11007	4.8, 5.5, 18, 27, 32
WM4	3.6, 4.3, 5.5, 28, 30
S. cremoris	
B₁	9, 36
C3	2, 2.8, 12, 16, 21, 27, 34
AM2	9.5, 16, 27, 42
EB₇	1.2, 1.5, 4, 5, 9, 20, 27, 30, 40, 42
Z₈	1.5, 2.6, 7, 11, 17, 27
R₁	1.5, 1.8, 2, 6.5, 11, 15, 17, 23, 27, 30, 34

transductants because the small head size of the phage allowed only a portion of the 30-Mdal plasmid to be packaged (12). Kinetics of UV irradiation inactivation of lactose-transducing ability confirmed the plasmid location of this trait (3). Transduction was also used to construct a variant in which the Lac plasmid, or a portion of it, integrated into the chromosome of *S. lactis*, thus stabilizing lactose-fermenting ability (13).

The conjugal transfer of plasmid DNA among group N streptococci has recently been demonstrated (4, 14, 17, 18), and the conjugal transfer of plasmids responsible for lactose-fermenting ability has provided additional proof that this trait is plasmid mediated in many strains. Phenotypic and physical evidence indicated that lactose metabolism in *S. diacetylactis* 18-16 was linked to a 41-Mdal plasmid. Conjugal transfer of the 41-Mdal plasmid from 18-16 to a Lac⁻ plasmid-cured derivative of *S. lactis* C2 (LM2301) converted the strain to the Lac⁺ phenotype (5). Lac⁺ transconjugants resulting from matings between *S. lactis* ML3 and LM2301 possessed a single plasmid of approximately 60 Mdal, which is nearly twice the size of the lactose plasmid of the donor (18). The majority of these Lac⁺ transconjugants aggregated in broth and were able to transfer lactose-fermenting ability at a frequency higher than 10^{-1} per donor. The appearance of the cell aggregates was similar to that described by Dunny et al. (2) for *S. faecalis* mating mixtures and by Gasson and Davies for *S. lactis* 712 (4). There were differences between the ML3 system and the *S. faecalis* system. In the ML3 system Lac⁺ transconjugants alone but not the original parental mating mixtures formed aggregates when grown in broth. Cell-free filtrates of clumping strains did not induce nonclumping strains to aggregate or to mate at higher frequency. The results suggested that the genes responsible for cell aggregation and high-frequency conjugation are on the segment of DNA which recombined with the 33-Mdal lactose plasmid in ML3.

We have found it difficult, at least in comparison with *S. lactis* and *S. diacetylactis*, to obtain phenotypic and physical evidence that lactose metabolism is mediated by plasmid DNA in *S. cremoris* strains. The apparent stability of lactose metabolism in some strains of *S. cremoris* might be due to a stable Lac plasmid in these strains because the transfer of a Lac plasmid was observed when several Lac⁺ *S. cremoris* strains were used as donors in conjugal matings (17).

S. diacetylactis WM4 exhibits the conjugal transfer of the ability to produce a bacteriocin-like substance (Bac⁺; unpublished data). Two types of Lac⁺ transconjugants were obtained when WM4 was mated with LM2301: Lac⁺ Bac⁺ and Lac⁺ Bac⁻. The ability to produce Bac, however, has not yet been linked to plasmid DNA. The Lac⁺ Bac⁺ transconjugants, upon losing the transferred Lac plasmid, retain the ability to produce Bac (Lac⁻ Bac⁺). The Lac⁺ Bac⁻ transconjugants possessed a large recombinant plasmid. Lac⁺ transconjugants of *S. diacetylactis* DRC-3 exhibited normal turbidity in broth, some possessed a recombinant plasmid of approximately 100 Mdal, and many formed colonies demonstrating cohesive properties (unpublished data).

The development of a transformation system has been a prerequisite for the application of recombinant DNA technology to the group N streptococci. In our laboratory, Jeffery Kondo recently used protoplasts and Lac plasmid DNA to transform Lac⁻ *S. lactis* ML3 to lactose-fermenting ability (submitted for publication).

It is now known that group N streptococci harbor plasmids of diverse sizes and that some of these plasmids code for properties vital for successful dairy fermentations. The presence of more than one plasmid in some transconjugants (14), as well as the presence of plasmids larger than those found in the donor, suggests that mobilization of plasmids and some recombination events are occurring. The conjugal transfer of chromosomal markers in the absence of extrachromosomal DNA has also been demonstrated (14). Further investigations should determine whether different plasmids undergo recombination within the host and whether recombination between plasmid and chromosomal DNA occurs.

ACKNOWLEDGMENTS

The research reported from our laboratory was supported in part by the Minnesota Agricultural Experiment Station, by the Biotechnology Group, Miles Laboratories, Inc., Elkhart, Ind., and by Dairy Research Inc., Chicago, Ill.

LITERATURE CITED

1. **Anderson, D. G., and L. L. McKay.** 1977. Plasmids, loss of lactose metabolism and appearance of partial and full lactose-fermenting revertants in *Streptococcus cremoris* B₁. J. Bacteriol. 129:367–377.
2. **Dunny, G. M., B. L. Brown, and D. B. Clewell.** 1978. Induced cell aggregation and mating in *Streptococcus faecalis*: evidence for a bacterial sex pheromone. Proc. Natl. Acad. Sci. U.S.A. 75:3479–3483.
3. **Efstathiou, J. D., and L. L. McKay.** 1977. Inorganic salts resistance associated with a lactose-fermenting plasmid in *Streptococcus lactis*. J. Bacteriol. 130:257–265.
4. **Gasson, M. J., and F. L. Davies.** 1980. High-frequency conjugation associated with *Streptococcus lactis* donor cell aggregation. J. Bacteriol. 143:1260–1264.
5. **Kempler, G. M., and L. L. McKay.** 1979. Genetic evidence for plasmid-linked lactose metabolism in *Strepto-*

coccus lactis subsp. *diacetylactis*. Appl. Environ. Microbiol. **37**:1041–1043.

6. **Kempler, G. M., and L. L. McKay.** 1981. Biochemistry and genetics of citrate utilization in *Streptococcus lactis* subsp. *diacetylactis*. J. Dairy Sci. **64**:1527–1539.

7. **Klaenhammer, T. R., L. L. McKay, and K. A. Baldwin.** 1978. Improved lysis of group N streptococci for isolation and rapid characterization of plasmid DNA. Appl. Environ. Microbiol. **35**:592–600.

8. **Kuhl, S. A., and L. L. McKay.** 1979. Plasmid profiles of lactose-negative and proteinase-deficient mutants of *Streptococcus lactis* C10, ML3, and M18. Appl. Environ. Microbiol. **37**:1193–1195.

9. **Larsen, L. D., and L. L. McKay.** 1978. Isolation and characterization of plasmid DNA in *Streptococcus cremoris*. Appl. Environ. Microbiol. **36**:944–952.

10. **Le Blanc, D. J., V. L. Crow, and L. N. Lee.** 1980. Plasmid mediated carbohydrate catabolic enzymes among strains of *Streptococcus lactis*, p. 31–41. *In* C. Stuttard and K. R. Rozee (ed.), Plasmids and transposons: environmental effects and maintenance mechanisms. Academic Press, Inc., New York.

11. **Le Blanc, D. J., V. L. Crow, L. N. Lee, and C. F. Garon.** 1979. Influence of the lactose plasmid on the metabolism of galactose by *Streptococcus lactis*. J. Bacteriol. **137**:878–884.

12. **McKay, L. L.** 1978. Microorganisms and their instability in milk and milk products. Food Technol. **32**:181–185.

13. **McKay, L. L., and K. A. Baldwin.** 1979. Stabilization of lactose metabolism in *Streptococcus lactis* C2. Appl. Environ. Microbiol. **36**:360–367.

14. **McKay, L. L., K. A. Baldwin, and P. M. Walsh.** 1980. Conjugal transfer of genetic information in group N streptococci. Appl. Environ. Microbiol. **40**:84–91.

15. **Park, Y. H., and L. L. McKay.** 1982. Distinct galactose phosphoenolpyruvate-dependent phosphotransferase system in *Streptococcus lactis*. J. Bacteriol. **149**:420–425.

16. **Pechmann, H., and M. Teuber.** 1981. Plasmids in lactic streptococci. Kiel. Milchwirtsch. Forschungsber. **32**:143–175.

17. **Snook, R. J., and L. L. McKay.** 1981. Conjugal transfer of lactose-fermenting ability among *Streptococcus cremoris* and *Streptococcus lactis* strains. Appl. Environ. Microbiol. **42**:904–911.

18. **Walsh, P. M., and L. L. McKay.** 1981. Recombinant plasmid associated with cell aggregation and high-frequency conjugation of *Streptococcus lactis* ML3. J. Bacteriol. **146**:937–944.

Bacteriophage DNA Restriction and the Lactic Streptococci

CHARLES DALY and GERALD F. FITZGERALD

Dairy and Food Microbiology Department, University College, Cork, Ireland

The group N lactic streptococci are major components of starter cultures essential for the production of a variety of fermented dairy products. In contrast to most microbial fermentations, those of the dairy industry are very vulnerable to bacteriophage attack. This is explained, at least in part, by the fact that a nonsterile medium (pasteurized or raw milk) is used in the process. Although considerable effort is required to counteract the phage problem (15, 24), the performance of cultures in cheese making has long suggested that some strains possess marked phage insensitivity (7, 10), and this has been confirmed in recent reports (5, 11, 12, 17, 27). However, there has been little detailed study of the molecular basis of phage-host relationships in the lactic streptococci which would explain the mechanism(s) of insensitivity observed and possibly suggest approaches to modifying sensitive strains which have otherwise desirable characteristics.

The phenomenon of restriction-modification of phage DNA has been well characterized in several genera and is considered to play a role in phage insensitivity (1, 3, 21). Although circumstantial evidence for its presence in lactic streptococci was presented (6, 13) before the phenomenon was explained in *Escherichia coli* on the basis of the enzymatic restriction of phage DNA (8), there has been no detailed study of the genetics or biochemistry of restriction-modification in the lactic streptococci. Recent reports have focused on the biological evidence for the presence of restriction-modification, the properties of modified phage, the heat sensitivity of the restriction system, the possible involvement of plasmid DNA, and the significance to commercial cheese making (2, 16, 18, 19, 20, 22, 23).

In our studies of phage-host interactions, including restriction-modification systems, in the lactic streptococci, we have used restriction enzyme analysis to characterize phage DNAs. Alterations in restriction digest patterns of phage DNA modified by growth in different hosts have been observed. In addition, we have demonstrated the presence of a type II restriction endonuclease in *Streptococcus cremoris* F and have established its activity in vitro. These findings are reviewed in this paper and will be published in detail elsewhere.

RESTRICTION ENZYME ANALYSIS OF PHAGE DNA CARRYING DIFFERENT MODIFICATIONS

A preliminary survey revealed the presence of several restriction-modification systems among strains of lactic streptococci (see examples in Table 1). *S. cremoris* KH showed restricting ability against 8 of 24 phages examined, with an efficiency of plaquing as low as 10^{-9} in some cases. The phage adsorbed to their restricting hosts with 40 to 90% efficiency. The data in Table 1 indicate that *S. cremoris* strains C3, AMI, F, and KH all possess modifying and restricting activity and that the modification they possess determines the ability of phages c3 and f to grow on a particular host.

The DNA of phage c3 grown in restricting (AMI) and nonrestricting (C3) hosts was examined by restriction enzyme analysis. The *Eco*RI digest pattern of c3 DNA (four fragments, track D, Fig. 1) was distinctly different from that of c3.AM1 DNA (seven fragments, track E, Fig. 1). Similar results, but with enzyme-specific cleavage patterns, were observed for *Hin*dIII, *Sal*I, *Taq*I, *Hpa*II, *Sau*3A, and *Mbo*I (unpublished data). *Bam*HI and *Dpn*I did not cut either DNA. Phage c3.AMI.C3 gave the same response as c3 for all the enzymes used (*Eco*RI digest, track F, Fig. 1).

These results indicate that the particular modifications carried by the phage DNA dictated the number and location of specific cleavage sites. It is noteworthy that this was true for a variety of enzymes. Alternative possibilities were that phage c3 infection of AMI triggered release of a prophage or that a recombination event had occurred. In an effort to determine the molecular basis of our observations, we established that the restriction-modification efficiency data and the enzyme digest patterns were reproducible for phage recycled between the restricting and nonrestricting hosts. In addition, the molecular weights of c3, c3.AMI, and c3.AMI.C3 DNAs, as quantified from the *Eco*RI digests (Fig. 1),

TABLE 1. Plaque-forming ability of bacteriophage on modifying and restricting *S. cremoris* hosts

Phage	Previous host	Plaqued on host	PFU/ml
c3	C3	C3	1.3×10^9
		AMI	1.0×10^2
c3.AMI	AMI	C3	9.7×10^2
		AMI	3.5×10^9
c3.AMI.C3	C3	C3	3.0×10^8
		AMI	1.0×10^1
f	F	F	4.5×10^8
		KH	3.0×10^5
f.KH	KH	F	1.4×10^5
		KH	2.0×10^9
f.KH.F	F	F	7.0×10^8
		KH	1.5×10^4

18.7, 18.6, and 18.7 megadaltons, respectively, were the same within the margins of experimental error. Further evidence that the c3 and c3.AMI phage were homologous was provided by the Southern (26) hybridization technique (unpublished data). Homology was detected be-tween the *Eco*RI/*Hin*dIII double digests of c3 (seven bands) and c3.AMI (eight bands) with α-^{32}P-labeled c3 DNA in vitro. Control, λ, f (host *S. cremoris* F), and c10 (host *S. lactis* C10) DNA showed no homology. The *Eco*RI restriction pattern of the mitomycin C-induced phage from AMI (nine fragments, track G, Fig. 1), its molecular weight (27.1 Mdal), and the fact that it did not proliferate on strain C3 show that it is distinct from phage c3.

In summary, the most likely interpretation of the present data is that the same phage is giving a different restriction pattern after propagation on two alternative hosts. Each pattern is reproducible on recycling. Strikingly, the alteration is detectable with a variety of enzymes with different specificities.

ISOLATION OF A RESTRICTION ENDONUCLEASE FROM *S. CREMORIS* F

What is the nature of the DNA restricting ability evident among lactic streptococci (Table 1)? To answer this question, cultures showing the ability to restrict unmodified DNA were screened for the presence of type II restriction endonucleases. The ability to digest λ DNA was

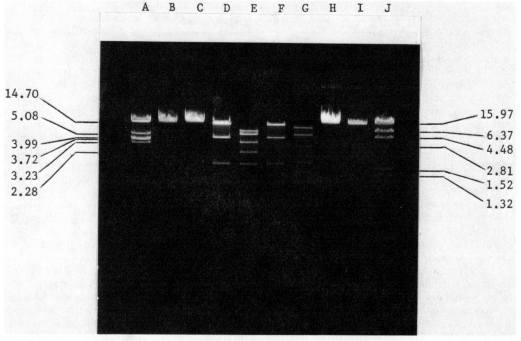

FIG. 1. Agarose (1%) gel electrophoresis pattern of *Eco*RI digests of phage c3 carrying the *S. cremoris* C3 and *S. cremoris* AMI modifications. A, λ DNA, *Eco*RI digest; B, c3 DNA; C, c3.AMI DNA; D, c3.DNA, *Eco*RI digest; E, c3.AM1 DNA, *Eco*RI digest; F, c3.AMI.C3 DNA, *Eco*RI digest; G, DNA from induced phage of *S. cremoris* AMI, *Eco*RI digest; H, c3.AM1.C3 DNA; I, DNA induced phage of AMI, and J, λ DNA, *Hin*dIII digest. Molecular weights of standards are shown in megadaltons.

detected in the case of *S. cremoris* F. Successive purifications on DEAE-cellulose (Whatman DE-52), phosphocellulose (Whatman P11), and hydroxylapatite (Bio-Gel HTP) columns were used to remove contaminating exonuclease activity. The purified enzyme gave site-specific cleavage of λ, φX174, simian virus 40, and pBR322 DNAs, producing >30, 2, >8, and >7 fragments, respectively, as detected by agarose (1 and 2%) gel electrophoresis. Using a reduced concentration of enzyme which gave partial digests of substrate DNA, we examined the effects of selected parameters on enzyme activity. There was an absolute requirement for Mg^{2+} (optimal concentration 6 to 8 mM) but not ATP or *S*-adenosylmethionine. Neither NaCl nor KCl was essential; greater than 80 mM of the former had an inhibitory effect. The optimal pH was 7.0, with a range of 6.0 to 9.0. The enzyme was active over the temperature range 21 to 48°C, with an optimum at approximately 40°C (more active at 43 than at 37°C). In addition, heating the enzyme in a 20 mM phosphate buffer (pH 7.0) containing 7.0 mM $MgCl_2$ at 40°C for up to 40 min had no effect on activity. The response to temperature is interesting in view of the reported heat sensitivity in vivo of restriction systems present in *S. cremoris* strains 799 and KH (18,

22) and is significant from a practical viewpoint since 40°C is the cooking temperature used in Cheddar cheese manufacture. The observed properties are those of a type II restriction endonuclease, and following the nomenclature of Smith and Nathans (25), we call the enzyme endonuclease R·*Scr*FI. Further analysis, including double digests with characterized enzymes, and, possibly, sequence studies, will be necessary to determine the specific cleavage site of *Scr*FI and establish whether it is a new enzyme or an isoschisomer of a previously characterized one.

EFFECT OF endo R·*Scr*FI ON PHAGE f DNAs

Although a large number of site-specific endonucleases have been isolated from a variety of bacteria, only a few have been shown to be involved in the restriction of foreign DNA (14, 21). The availability of a restriction-modification system active on phage f in *S. cremoris* strains F and KH (Table 1) enabled us to examine the activity of *Scr*FI on f DNA carrying either the F or KH modification. *Scr*FI cleaved f.KH into four fragments (track D, Fig. 2) but did not cleave f DNA, i.e., modified for F (track C, Fig. 2). Although these results suggest a potential

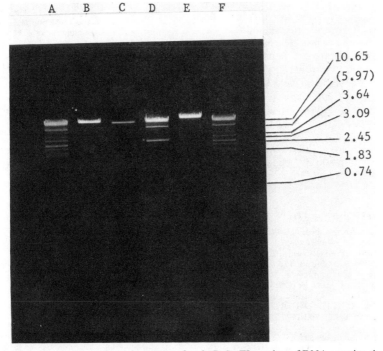

FIG. 2. Agarose (1%) gel electrophoresis pattern of endo R·*Scr*FI on phage f DNA carrying the *S. cremoris* F and *S. cremoris* KH modifications. A and F, λ DNA *Eco*RI/*Bam*HI double digests; B, f DNA; C, f DNA, *Scr*FI digest; D, f.KH DNA, *Scr*FI digest; E, f.KH DNA. Molecular weights of standards are shown in megadaltons.

biological role for *Scr*FI, we have not determined whether this enzyme is responsible for the in vivo restriction ability of *S. cremoris* F. Although the nature of the modification activity present in lactic streptococci has not been examined, it is apparent from the results described that *S. cremoris* F has modifying ability on the specific cleavage site of *Scr*FI.

ACTIVITY OF endo R·*Scr*FI ON SELECTED STREPTOCOCCAL PHAGE DNAs

Phage-host interactions are of major practical importance among the lactic streptococci (9, 15, 24), and individual strains often find themselves exposed to a variety of phages in the factory environment. Since, in other genera, restriction enzymes are considered to have a role in the phage insensitivity of the producing strains (4, 21), it was of interest to determine whether *Scr*FI had activity on the DNA of phage active on various lactic streptococci, other than *S. cremoris* F. The DNAs of phages homologous for *S. lactis* ML8, SK3, and C10, *S. lactis* subsp. *diacetylactis* 18-16, and *S. cremoris* C3 and P2 were all digested, producing from 2 to >16 fragments. The site-specific cleavage patterns of phage DNA obtained with *Scr*FI and commercially available restriction enzymes (unpublished data) may help to establish the molecular weight of phage DNA, to map the phage genomes, and to determine the relatedness between phages, provided that the possible effects of different modifications are considered. The observed wide spectrum of activity of *Scr*FI on lactic phage DNAs would suggest that the cloning of genes for this and other restriction enzymes into selected strains of lactic streptococci may greatly increase their phage insensitivity and make them very attractive for dairy fermentations. In this regard, studies on the genetic location of restriction activity being undertaken by Klaenhammer's group (23) and in our laboratory will be useful.

LITERATURE CITED

1. **Arber, W.** 1974. DNA modification and restriction. Prog. Nucleic Acid Res. Mol. Biol. **14**:1–37.
2. **Boussemaer, J. P., P. P. Schrauwen, J. L. Sourrouille, and P. Guy.** 1980. Multiple modification/restriction systems in lactic streptococci and their significance in defining a phage-typing system. J. Dairy Res. **47**:401–409.
3. **Boyer, H.** 1971. DNA restriction and modification mechanisms in bacteria. Annu. Rev. Microbiol. **25**:153–176.
4. **Chater, K. F., and L. C. Wilde.** 1976. Restriction of a bacteriophage of *Streptomyces albus* G involving endonuclease Sal I. J Bacteriol. **128**:644–650.
5. **Chopin, M. C., A. Chopin, and C. Roux.** 1976. Definition of bacteriophage groups according to their lytic action on mesophilic lactic streptococci. Appl. Environ. Microbiol. **32**:741–746.
6. **Collins, E. B.** 1956. Host-controlled variations in bacteriophages active against lactic streptococci. Virology **2**:261–271.
7. **Crawford, R. J. M., and J. H. Galloway.** 1962. Bacteriophage contamination of mixed-strain cultures in cheesemaking, p. 785–791. *In* Proceedings of the 16th International Dairy Congress, vol. B.
8. **Dussoix, D., and W. Arber.** 1962. Host specificity of DNA produced by *Escherichia coli*. II. Control over acceptance of DNA from infecting phage λ. J. Mol. Biol. **5**:37–49.
9. **Erickson, R. J.** 1980. Bacteriophage problems in the dairy industry. Their cause, characterization and cure. Dairy Ind. Int. **45**:40–43.
10. **Galesloot, T. H. E., F. Hassing and J. Stadhouders.** 1966. Differences in phage sensitivity of starters propagated in practice and in a dairy research laboratory, p. 491–498. *In* Proceedings of the 17th International Dairy Congress, vol. D2.
11. **Heap, H. A., and R. C. Lawrence.** 1976. The selection of starter strains for cheesemaking. N.Z. J. Dairy Technol. **11**:16–20.
12. **Hull, R. R.** 1977. Control of bacteriophage in cheese factories. Aust. J. Dairy Technol. **32**:65–66.
13. **Hunter, G. J. E.** 1939. Examples of variation within pure cultures of *Streptococcus cremoris*. J. Dairy Res. **10**:464–470.
14. **Ikawa, S., T. Shibata, K. Matsumoto, T. Iijima, H. Saito, and T. Ando.** 1981. Chromosomal loci of genes controlling site-specific restriction endonucleases of *Bacillus subtilis*. Mol. Gen. Genet. **183**:1–6.
15. **Lawrence, R. C., H. A.Heap, G. Limsowtin, and A. W. Jarvis.** 1978. Cheddar cheese starters: current knowledge and practices of phage characteristics and strain selection. J. Dairy Sci. **61**:1181–1191.
16. **Limsowtin, G. K. Y., H. A. Heap, and R. C. Lawrence.** 1978. Heterogeneity among strains of lactic streptococci. N.Z. J. Dairy Technol. **13**:1–8.
17. **Limsowtin, G. K. Y., and B. E. Terzaghi.** 1976. Phage resistant mutants: their selection and use in cheese factories. N.Z. J. Dairy Sci. Technol. **11**:251–256.
18. **Pearce, L. E.** 1978. The effect of host-controlled modification on the replication rate of lactic streptococcal bacteriophage. N.Z. J. Dairy Sci. Technol. **13**:166–171.
19. **Pearce, L. E., and R. J. Lowrie.,** 1974. Host-controlled modification and restriction on bacteriophage host range by strains of *Streptococcus cremoris* and *Streptococcus lactis* used as starters in cheese making, p. 410. *In* Proceedings of the 19th International Dairy Congress, vol. 1E.
20. **Potter, N. N.** 1970. Host-induced changes in lactic streptococcal bacteriophages. J. Dairy Sci. **53**:1358–1362.
21. **Roberts, R. J.** 1976. Restriction endonucleases. Crit. Rev. Biochem. **4**:123–164.
22. **Sanders, M. E., and T. R. Klaenhammer.** 1980. Restriction and modification in group N streptococci: effect of heat on development of modified lytic bacteriophage. Appl. Environ. Microbiol. **40**:500–506.
23. **Sanders, M. E., and T. R. Klaenhammer.** 1981. Evidence for plasmid linkage of restriction and modification in *Streptococcus cremoris* KH. Appl. Environ. Microbiol. **42**:944–950.
24. **Sandine, W. E.** 1979. Lactic starter culture technology. Pfizer Inc., New York.
25. **Smith, H. O., and D. Nathans.** 1973. A suggested nomenclature for bacterial host modification and restriction systems and their enzymes. J. Mol. Biol. **81**:419–423.
26. **Southern, E. M.** 1975. Detection of specific sequences among DNA fragments separated by gel electrophoresis. J. Mol. Biol. **98**:503–517.
27. **Thunell, R. K., and W. E. Sandine.** 1980. Standardizing Cheddar cheesemaking using phage-insensitive starters. J. Dairy Sci. **63** (Suppl I):37.

Identification of the Lactose Plasmid in *Streptococcus lactis* 712

M. J. GASSON

National Institute for Research in Dairying, Shinfield, Reading RG2 9AT, Berkshire, United Kingdom

Streptococcus lactis strain NCDO 712 carries a temperate bacteriophage, φT712, which has classical properties; the prophage was curable, producing strains which indicated plaque formation and which could be readily relysogenized (8). By using prophage-cured derivatives as recipients, the erythromycin resistance plasmid pAMβ was introduced from *S. faecalis* DS-5 to provide a wide-host-range conjugation system in lactic streptococci (6). High-frequency transfer of lactose genes by conjugation was demonstrated for variant *S. lactis* 712 donor strains which

exhibited constitutive cell aggregation (7). In addition, the temperate phage φT712 has been shown to transduce both pAMβ and lactose genes (4). In the latter case, but not the former, an elevated frequency of transfer was found in subsequent rounds of transduction (high-frequency transfer phenomenon) (4). Transfer of the 17-megadalton (Mdal) plasmid pAMβ by conjugation and transduction was readily followed by agarose gel electrophoresis of covalently closed circular DNA (6, 9). Although lactose plasmids have been identified in the

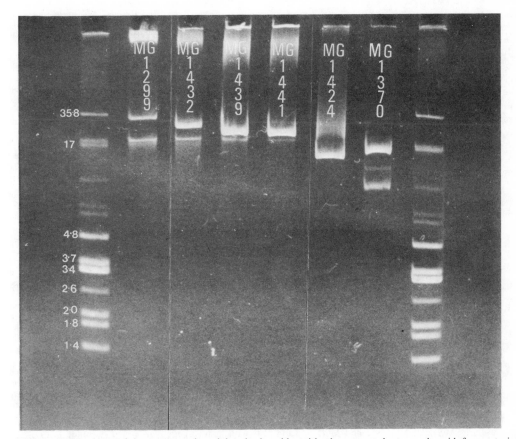

FIG. 1. Comparison of lactose-negative deleted plasmids with the parent lactose plasmid from strain MG1299.

plasmid complements of various lactic strepto-cocci (1, 11–15), the physical demonstration of a lactose plasmid in *S. lactis* 712 has proved complex. The lactose utilization phenotype was often irreversibly lost, but conventional curing experiments did not reveal a consistent correlation between this event and loss of any of the strain's five plasmid molecules (1.8, 2.5, 5.2, 9.7, and 33 Mdal) (2, 7). Early gene transfer experiments involved nonrevertable lactose-defective recipient strains which had lost only the 9.7-Mdal plasmid (4, 7, 9). Lactose gene transfer by conjugation did not lead to a change in the recipient strain's plasmid profile (7). After lactose gene transfer by transduction, novel plasmids of 22 to 25 Mdal, and in two cases of 42 and 54 Mdal, were found. In curing experiments these novel molecules and the lactose utilization phenotype did show concomitant loss (9). Hence, a lactose plasmid has been identified after transduction but not in the parent strain *S. lactis* 712 (2, 7, 9).

The development of a protocol for the efficient production and regeneration of protoplasts from lactic streptococci (5) has facilitated a new approach to plasmid curing in these species. For *S. lactis* 712 plasmid curing during protoplast regeneration occurred at a very high frequency and has been used to investigate lactose plasmid identification in this strain. Random protoplast regenerants were screened in a microscale cleared lysate procedure to identify strains in which a plasmid(s) had been cured. Only subsequently were changes in the lactose phenotype sought. The results of these experiments were that strains which had lost the 33-Mdal plasmid always became lactose defective, whereas strains which retained this plasmid were either lactose defective or lactose positive. Strains cured of any other plasmid were also either lactose defective or lactose positive. This suggested that the 33-Mdal plasmid may be involved in lactose metabolism in *S. lactis* 712. In a different plasmid curing experiment, lactose-

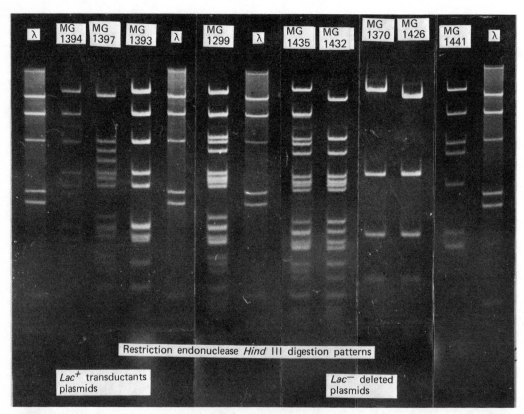

FIG. 2. Comparison of the 33-Mdal lactose plasmid from MG1299 with 22-Mdal transduced lactose plasmids from strains MG1393, MG1397, and MG1394, and also with lactose-negative deleted plasmids from strains MG1435, MG1432, MG1370, MG1426, and MG1441. Plasmid DNA was digested with restriction endonuclease *Hind*III and subjected to electrophoresis on 0.7% agarose gels.

TABLE 1. Comparison of the restriction endonuclease *Hin*dIII fragmentation pattern produced from the lactose plasmid in MG1299 with those from lactose-negative deleted plasmids and lactose-positive transductants[a]

Size (kilobases)	Parent strain MG1299	Lactose-negative deletions					Lactose-positive transductants	
		MG1532	MG1434	MG1441	MG1370	MG1426	MG1393	MG1397
10.80	+	8.50	+	+	8.95	8.05	+	9.69
6.45	+		+	+			+	
4.55	+		+	(4.25)				(3.41)
4.30	+						+	+
3.85	+	+	+	+				+
2.85	+	+					+	+
2.62	+	+						+
2.52	+	+	+	+	+	+		
2.43	+	+					+	+
1.60	+	+	+					+
1.40	+	+		+			+	+
1.30	+	+					+	+
1.13	+	+	+	+	+	+	+	
0.95	+	+						+
0.88	+						+	+
0.81	+	+						+
0.63	+	+	+	+	+	+	+	+
0.54	+	+						
0.49	+	+					+	
0.43	+	+					+	
Total kilobases	50.53	36.65	31.53	31.03	13.23	12.33	33.09	33.23
Mdal	33.35	24.19	20.81	20.48	8.73	8.14	22.12	22.29

[a] Plus signs indicate the presence of a fragment, and numbers in parentheses indicate a novel fragment. These numbers and those in the left-hand column are sizes in kilobases determined by comparison with λ *Hin*dIII fragments.

positive protoplast regenerants were selected and screened for random plasmid loss. Isolates cured of a cryptic plasmid were then used in sequential rounds of protoplast regeneration and plasmid screening until a lactose-positive strain carrying only the 33-Mdal plasmid (MG1299) was isolated. Lactose-defective variants of strain MG1299 were then isolated by using both protoplast regeneration and conventional curing methods. Of 33 lactose-defective derivatives from protoplast curing, 7 had lost the 33-Mdal molecule, whereas 2 appeared to retain this plasmid. In the remaining 23 strains a plasmid smaller than 33-Mdal was present (Fig. 1), the smallest molecule found being one of 8 Mdal. In acriflavine and heat curing experiments 86% of the lactose-defective strains isolated had lost the 33-Mdal plasmid whereas 14% carried a smaller plasmid. The conclusion from these observations is that the 33-Mdal plasmid of *S. lactis* 712 encodes lactose genes but is subject to an unusually high rate of deletion formation. In wild-type *S. lactis* 712 lactose gene deletions of this plasmid occurred frequently but were of small size. In a strain carrying only the lactose plasmid,

much larger deletions were frequently isolated.

The relationship between the various shortened plasmids found in deleted strains and the 33-Mdal plasmid was investigated by using restriction enzyme digestion. Plasmid DNA was prepared by cesium chloride-ethidium bromide centrifugation of cleared lysates and was purified by isoamyl alcohol extraction and dialysis against TE buffer (10 mM Tris, 1mM EDTA, pH 8.0). Plasmid DNA was digested with restriction endonucleases *Eco*RI, *Hin*dIII, and *Hae*II and was examined by agarose gel electrophoresis. For all enzymes clear evidence was produced to show that the smaller plasmids were indeed deleted derivatives of the 33-Mdal plasmid (e.g., Fig. 2, Table 1).

Confirmation that the 33-Mdal plasmid was a lactose plasmid was sought by comparing it with lactose plasmids formed after transduction. The temperate phage φT712 was used to transduce lactose genes from MG1299 into a plasmid-free strain, creating lactose plasmids of approximately 22 Mdal. These plasmids were always cured together with the lactose utilization phenotype. Such plasmids were transduced at an elevated frequency in subsequent transduction experiments, raising the possibility that recombination with phage ϕT712 DNA may have occurred (10). Accordingly, representative transduced lactose plasmids were compared both with the 33-Mdal plasmid DNA from strain MG1299 and with DNA extracted from bacteriophage ϕT712, again by using restriction endonucleases EcoRI, HindIII, and HaeII. Those transduced plasmids examined were clearly similar to the 33-Mdal plasmid (Fig. 2, Table 1) and appeared to be lactose-positive deletions of this plasmid. No evidence for the inclusion of phage DNA in the transduced lactose plasmids was found by comparison of the restriction fragment patterns. These observations confirm that the 33-Mdal plasmid of S. lactis 712 encodes lactose genes. The deletion phenomenon characteristic of this plasmid may account for the formation of shortened lactose-positive plasmids capable of accommodation in the ϕT712 phage head. In this event transducing phage induced from S. lactis 712 would merely select spontaneously deleted lactose plasmids. The high-frequency transfer phenomenon characteristic of lactose gene transduction would then be accounted for without the need to postulate recombination between phage and plasmid DNA. Further investigation of this possibility will involve the use of Southern hybridization to probe the source of DNA in the transduced plasmids.

The original gene transfer experiments using S. lactis 712 involved lactose-defective recipient strains which retained a plasmid of approximately 33-Mdal (7, 9). This plasmid probably carried a deletion which inactivated or removed the lactose genes without causing a change in molecular weight detectable on agarose gels. As a result, transfer of a 33-Mdal lactose plasmid by conjugation would not be detected. Using plasmid-free recipient strains, transfer of the 33-Mdal lactose plasmid by conjugation has been observed. However, in some instances novel plasmids of 60 Mdal have been found in progeny strains, as have plasmid-free lactose-utilizing progeny (2). The occasional isolation of lactose-positive transductants with larger-molecular-weight plasmids (42 and 54 Mdal) (9) may be explained by recombination between an incoming transduced lactose plasmid and the deleted 33-Mdal plasmid present in the recipient.

In conclusion, the lactose plasmid of S. lactis 712 has been identified as a 33-Mdal molecule, which is subject to an unusually high rate of deletion formation. This situation is consistent with the reports of 33- and 29-Mdal lactose plasmids in S. lactis strains ML3 and C2 (11, 12,

15), which are known to be related to S. lactis 712 (3). The occurrence of deletions on plasmids may be a more widespread phenomenon in lactic and other streptococci. It may account for problems in identifying lactose and proteinase plasmids in other S. lactis and S. cremoris strains (F. L. Davies and M. J. Gasson, unpublished data).

ACKNOWLEDGMENTS

I am indebted to my colleagues Lyndon Davies and Phil Warner for advice and support, to Phil Warner for preparing ϕT712 DNA, and to Jan Elkins for invaluable expert technical assistance.

LITERATURE CITED

1. **Anderson, D. G., and L. L. McKay.** 1977. Plasmids, loss of lactose metabolism, and appearance of partial and full lactose-fermenting revertants in *Streptococcus cremoris* B_1. J. Bacteriol. **129**:367–377.
2. **Davies, F. L., and M. J. Gasson.** 1981. Reviews of the progress of dairy science: genetics of lactic acid bacteria. J. Dairy Res. **48**:363–376.
3. **Davies, F. L., H. M. Underwood, and M. J. Gasson.** 1981. The value of plasmid profiles for strain identification in lactic streptococci and the relationship between *Streptococcus lactis* 712, ML3 and C2. J. Appl. Bacteriol. **51**:325–337.
4. **Davies, F. L., H. M. Underwood, and M. J. Gasson.** 1982. Transduction in *S. lactis* 712. J. Gen. Microbiol., in press.
5. **Gasson, M. J.** 1980. Production, regeneration and fusion of protoplasts in the lactic streptococci. FEMS Microbiol. Lett. **9**:99–102.
6. **Gasson, M. J., and F. L. Davies.** 1980. Conjugal transfer of the drug resistance plasmid pAMβ in the lactic streptococci. FEMS Microbiol. Lett. **7**:51–53.
7. **Gasson, M. J., and F. L. Davies.** 1980. High frequency conjugation associated with donor cell aggregation in *Streptococcus lactis*. J. Bacteriol. **143**:1260–1264.
8. **Gasson, M. J., and F. L. Davies.** 1980. Prophage cured derivatives of *Streptococcus lactis* and *Streptococcus cremoris*. Appl. Environ. Microbiol. **40**:964–966.
9. **Gasson, M. J., and F. L. Davies.** 1982. Plasmid analysis and conjugation in lactose transductants of *S. lactis* 712. J. Gen. Microbiol., in press.
10. **Klaenhammer, T. R., and L. L. McKay.** 1976. Isolation and examination of transducing bacteriophage particles from *Streptococcus lactis* C2. J. Dairy Sci. **59**:396–404.
11. **Klaenhammer, T. R., L. L. McKay, and K. A. Baldwin.** 1978. Improved lysis of group N streptococci for isolation and rapid characterization of plasmid DNA. Appl. Environ. Microbiol. **35**:592–600.
12. **Kuhl, S. A., L. D. Larsen, and L. L. McKay.** 1979. Plasmid profiles of lactose-negative and proteinase-deficient mutants of *Streptococcus lactis* C10, ML3, and M18. Appl. Environ. Microbiol. **37**:1193–1195.
13. **LeBlanc, D. J., U. L. Crow, L. N. Lee, and C. F. Garon.** 1979. Influence of the lactose plasmid on the metabolism of galactose by *Streptococcus lactis*. J. Bacteriol. **137**:878–884.
14. **McKay, L. L., and K. A. Baldwin.** 1974. Simultaneous loss of proteinase- and lactose-utilizing enzyme activities in *Streptococcus lactis* and reversal of loss by transduction. Appl. Microbiol. **28**:342–346.
15. **McKay, L. L., K. A. Baldwin, and J. D. Efstathiou.** 1976. Transductional evidence for plasmid linkage of lactose metabolism in *Streptococcus lactis* C2'. Appl. Environ. Microbiol. **32**:45–52.

Production of Diplococcin by *Streptococcus cremoris* and Its Transfer to Nonproducing Group N Streptococci

GRAHAM P. DAVEY AND LINDSAY E. PEARCE

New Zealand Dairy Research Institute, Palmerston North, New Zealand

Antibiotic-producing streptococci were first described by Whitehead and Riddet (20), who isolated strains from raw milk that were capable of inhibiting growth and acid production of starter cultures during cheese making. Further studies (19) identified one such producer as *Streptococcus cremoris* and showed that the inhibitory agent was protein in nature. Mattick and Hirsch isolated inhibitor-producing strains of *S. lactis* from milk and starters. The inhibitor from these strains, which was termed nisin (15), had a wide spectrum of activity, including activity against bacilli, clostridia, and lactobacilli, and was recognized as a potential food preservative. Extensive studies established nisin in this role and provided basic data on its synthesis, chemical structure, and mode of action (10). In contrast, the earlier-described inhibitor from *S. cremoris* was inactive against *Bacillus subtilis* (19) or other sporeformers. Oxford (16) partially purified an antibiotic-like substance from *S. cremoris* which he termed "diplococcin." He identified diplococcin as a protein deficient in sulfur or phosphorus with a limited activity spectrum, *S. cremoris* strains being most sensitive.

S. cremoris is now the species of group N streptococci most commonly used in starter cultures for the manufacture of Cheddar-type cheeses (12, 13, 18). Our research program has thus placed emphasis on the study of characters that differentiate the various group N streptococci in an effort to improve strain selection methods. Initially, this involved examining the chemical and physical properties of diplococcin, and more recently its genetic behavior.

PURIFICATION AND PROPERTIES OF DIPLOCOCCIN

Diplococcin production in either milk or broth media parallels bacterial growth, reaching maximum titer as the cells enter stationary phase. *S. cremoris* 346 diplococcin was purified by ammonium sulfate precipitation followed by chromatography on carboxymethyl cellulose CM 32 and sodium dodecyl sulfate-polyacrylamide gels (4). Specific activity was increased 1,000-fold with 45% recovery. Purified diplococcin is stable at −75°C but unstable at 4°C or at higher temperatures. No satisfactory stabilizer of defined composition has been found, and addition of a complex broth was necessary to achieve stability.

Diplococcin can be clearly distinguished from nisin by a number of properties (Table 1). In particular, the absence of any of the four unusual amino acids found in nisin, the sensitivity to proteolytic enzymes, and the more limited activity spectrum are characteristic.

MODE OF ACTION OF DIPLOCOCCIN

Diplococcin is rapidly and nonspecifically bound to sensitive, resistant (nonproducing), and immune (producing) cells of *S. cremoris* or *S. lactis* as well as to *Staphylococcus aureus* (2). This binding is equally efficient with either viable or heat-killed cells, as is the case with other bacteriocins (17). The lethal effect is dependent on active cellular metabolism. Uptake of [^{3}H]thymidine and [^{3}H]uracil into the trichloroacetic acid-insoluble material of logarithmic-phase cells of *S. cremoris* 448 showed that both DNA and RNA syntheses were halted within 2 min. Protein synthesis was also rapidly affected but not completely stopped (2).

STABILITY OF DIPLOCOCCIN PRODUCTION

The group N streptococci have a higher plasmid content than the other serological groups, most strains carrying at least four plasmids. Characters known or suspected of being plasmid associated include lactose metabolism, proteinase synthesis, citrate utilization, and nisin production (5). We examined whether diplococcin-negative (Dip⁻) strains could be isolated from producers (Dip⁺) by growth at higher than optimal temperatures (3). Dip⁻ isolates were obtained from *S. cremoris* 346, 378, and 486 after growth at 35.5°C at a frequency of 0.1 to 0.2%, which was higher than expected from a chromosomal mutation but not indicative of a readily cured plasmid. Phage sensitivity and acid production were similar to those of the parent strains. No revertants to Dip⁺ were detected after 40 subcultures of independent Dip⁻ iso-

TABLE 1. Comparison of group N streptococcal bacteriocins

Property	Diplococcin[a]	Nisin[b]
Producer organism	S. cremoris	S. lactis
Activity spectrum	S. cremoris/S. lactis only	S. cremoris/S. lactis, many gram positive but not gram negative
Molecular weight	5,300	3,300 (7,000)
Heat resistance, 100°C/ 1 h, pH 5.0	+	+
Enzyme sensitivity		
Trypsin	+	−
Pronase	+	−
α-Chymotrypsin	+	+
Amino acid composition	No sulfur-containing amino acids	Unusual sulfur-containing amino acids: lanthionine and β-methyl lanthionine. Also unusual amino acids: dehydrobutyrine and dehydroalanine

[a] Taken from reference 4.
[b] Taken from references 8 and 10.

lates from the different strains. It was of considerable interest to find that Dip⁻ isolates of *S. cremoris* 346 retained the desirable cheese-making characteristics of the parent. One such isolate, *S. cremoris* 582, has been successfully used as a paired starter for commercial cheese manufacture (4).

CONJUGAL TRANSFER OF DIPLOCOCCIN PRODUCTION

Transfer of the conjugative drug resistance plasmid pAMβ₁ from *S. faecalis* to other streptococci, as well as to members of other genera, is now well established (7). By using filter matings, pAMβ₁ (Emʳ) was transferred from *S. faecalis* DS₅ to Smʳ mutants of *S. lactis* ML₃ and *S. cremoris* P₂ 4030 and 4008, respectively. As DS₅ carries a low-level SMʳ (50 μg/ml), it was necessary to use recipients resistant to 5,000 μg of streptomycin per ml to obtain efficient selection. Transconjugants receiving pAMβ₁ were identified by unselected markers and plasmid profiles. The transferred plasmid was incorporated into the transconjugant without affecting the stability of the resident plasmids. Transfer frequencies were 10⁻⁶ and 10⁻⁴ per donor, respectively.

The group N streptococci are sensitive to the bacteriocin(s) produced by DS₅, and after overnight filter matings on nonselective media the recipient count can be as low as 1% of the initial level. In an attempt to improve conjugation frequencies, a hemolysin (Hly)- and bacteriocin (Bcn)-negative strain, 4085, was isolated for use as a donor. Conjugation frequencies were increased 40- to 100-fold by using strain 4085. From the initial transconjugants, pAMβ₁ was readily transferred to other *S. lactis* or *S. cremoris* recipients.

We investigated whether Dip⁺ donors carrying pAMβ₁ would also transfer Dip unselected to *S. cremoris* C₁₃. At the same time, control crosses were set up with wild-type Dip⁺ donors. Both sets of crosses successfully gave rise to Dip⁺ transconjugants of strain C₁₃. There was no significant difference in frequency with or without the presence of pAMβ₁ in the donor. Results from preliminary experiments with four wild-type donors showed Dip⁺ transfer at a frequency of approximately 10⁻⁵ per donor (Table 2). The Dip⁺ transconjugants retained the phage sensitivity and physiological characteristics of the recipient. Transconjugants produced diplococcin at the same level as the donor, and the bacteriocin was unaltered in activity spectrum or proteolytic enzyme sensitivity. Transconjugants were able to retransfer Dip⁺ to *S. lactis* ML₃, and from ML₃ to *S. lactis* C₁₀. The genetic transfer depended on cell to cell contact, was insensitive to DNase, and did not take place with donor filtrates.

Plasmid profiles of all strains used in curing and conjugation experiments were prepared to examine whether the presence or acquisition of Dip⁺ could be associated with any particular plasmid species. We were unable to correlate any plasmid with the ability to produce diplococcin. In an attempt to provide a clear background in which to observe any plasmid transfer, we isolated a plasmid-free strain of *S. lactis* H₁ (Nis⁺) by growth at higher than optimal temperature. It was anticipated that Nis would be removed by the curing treatment, as this character has been reported to be plasmid linked (11). Interestingly, the plasmid-free strain H₁ 4125 was still Nis⁺. A Nis⁻ mutant H₁ 4198 was isolated but reverted to Nis⁺ too frequently to be useful for selecting Dip⁺. Plasmid-free strains

TABLE 2. Conjugal transfer of diplococcin production in group N streptococci[a]

Donor	Recipient	Transconjugant	Frequency[b]
S. cremoris	*S. cremoris*	*S. cremoris*	
346 Dip$^+$ WT	C$_{13}$ Dip$^-$ (4092)	C$_{13}$ Dip$^+$ (4276)	ca. 10^{-5}
378 Dip$^+$ WT	C$_{13}$ Dip$^-$ (4092)	C$_{13}$ Dip$^+$ (4277)	
918 Dip$^+$ WT	C$_{13}$ Dip$^-$ (4092)	C$_{13}$ Dip$^+$ (4278)	
486 Dip$^+$ WT	C$_{13}$ Dip$^-$ (4092)	C$_{13}$ Dip$^+$ (4279)	
S. cremoris	*S. lactis*	*S. lactis*	
C$_{13}$ Dip$^+$ (4277)	ML$_3$ Dip$^-$ Nis$^-$ (4090)	ML$_3$ Dip$^+$ Nis$^-$ (4280)	ca. 10^{-4}
C$_{13}$ Dip$^+$ (4276)	ML$_3$ Dip$^-$ Nis$^-$ (4090)	ML$_3$ Dip$^+$ Nis$^-$ (4281)	
S. lactis	*S. lactis*	*S. lactis*	
ML$_3$ Dip$^+$ Nis$^-$ (4280)	C$_{10}$ Dip$^-$ Nis$^-$ (4150)	C$_{10}$ Dip$^+$ Nis$^-$ (4282)	10^{-5}

[a] Membrane filter matings (6) were for 16 h at 30°C on nonselective agar plates. Recipient strains were mutants resistant to either streptomycin (250 µg/ml) or fusidic acid (50 µg/ml). Filter populations were plated on media containing the appropriate antibiotic. Dip$^+$ transconjugants were detected by soft-agar overlay of the colonies with *S. cremoris* 480 B$_1$ and further incubation for 16 to 18 h at 22°C. WT, Wild type.

[b] Frequency is calculated as transconjugants per donor at the end of mating.

derived from non-bacteriocin-producing *S. cremoris* and *S. lactis* are currently being sought.

DISCUSSION

Diplococcin and nisin differ both structurally and physiologically. They represent that most marked single-character difference established between these two types of streptococci. Nisin bears a close structural affinity with the *Bacillus subtilis* antibiotic subtilin, both being pentacyclic peptides of 34 and 32 residues, respectively, and containing four unusual amino acids (8). By contrast, diplococcin, with a minimum of 51 amino acid residues, is clearly of a quite different evolutionary origin. Nevertheless, we have shown that the Dip genes can be readily transferred to, and fully expressed in, *S. lactis*.

Despite the relative ease of Dip transfer among the lactic streptococci, Dip$^+$ isolates of *S. lactis* have not been reported among natural strains of this organism. The majority of isolates from raw milk are *S. lactis*, of which a proportion are Nis$^+$ (9). As nisin is more active against *S. cremoris* than diplococcin is against *S. lactis*, *S. cremoris* producers may not prove overly effective in nature, a possible contributing factor to the apparent scarcity of *S. cremoris* isolates from natural sources.

There is no evidence at present to determine whether the Dip genes are plasmid borne. In favor are the relatively high frequency of isolation of Dip$^-$ strains and the failure to detect reversion of such isolates. On the other hand, the absence of plasmid changes in Dip$^-$ isolates or in Dip$^+$ transconjugants suggests a chromosomal location for Dip. A definitive answer to the question, however, awaits the isolation and characterization of plasmid-free recipients able to accept Dip by conjugal transfer.

Immunity to their own bacteriocin is a characteristic feature of producing cells. Loss of ability to produce by Nis$^+$ cultures, however, was not associated with loss of immunity (11). It was interesting, therefore, to observe in the present work that loss of Dip in four different strains was also unaccompanied by loss of immunity. This observation at present remains unexplained. *S. cremoris* C$_{13}$ was unique among over 100 different nonproducing wild-type *S. cremoris* strains examined in that it was Dip resistant, a point previously observed by Collins (1). This may be due either to lack of receptors or to C$_{13}$ being derived from a Dip$^+$ parent and still carrying immunity.

Just as drug resistance genes can be carried on either plasmid or chromosome, so it appears that the Nis genes of *S. lactis* may be in either state. Our observation that the plasmid-free *S. lactis* strain H$_1$ 4125 retains its Nis$^+$ character is in contrast to the finding of Le Blanc et al. that in *S. lactis* DR1251 there is a strong association of Nis and Suc with the 28-megadalton plasmid (14). It is not unlikely that other characters of lactic streptococci which are plasmid associated in some strains might prove to be chromosomal in others.

LITERATURE CITED

1. **Collins, E. B.** 1961. Domination among strains of lactic streptococci with attention to antibiotic production. Appl. Microbiol. 9:200–205.
2. **Davey, G. P.** 1981. Mode of action of diplococcin, a bacteriocin from *Streptococcus cremoris* 346. N.Z. J. Dairy Sci. Technol. 16:187–190.
3. **Davey, G. P., and L. E. Pearce.** 1980. The use of *Streptococcus cremoris* strains cured of diplococcin production as cheese starters. N.Z. J. Dairy Sci. Technol. 15:51–57.
4. **Davey, G. P., and B. C. Richardson.** 1981. Purification and some properties of diplococcin from *Streptococcus cremoris* 346. Appl. Environ. Microbiol. 41:84–89.

5. **Davies, F. L., and M. J. Gasson.** 1980. Reviews of the progress of dairy science: genetics of lactic acid bacteria. J. Dairy Res. **48:**363–376.
6. **Franke, A. E., G. M. Dunny, B. L. Brown, F. An, D. R. Oliver, S. P. Damle, and D. B. Clewell.** 1978. Gene transfer in *Streptococcus faecalis*: evidence for the mobilization of chromosomal determinants by transmissible plasmids, p. 45–47. *In* D. Schlessinger (ed.), Microbiology— 1978. American Society for Microbiology, Washington, D.C.
7. **Gibson, E. M., N. M. Chace, S. B. London, and J. London.** 1979. Transfer of plasmid-mediated antibiotic resistance from streptococci to lactobacilli. J. Bacteriol. **137:**614–619.
8. **Gross, E.** 1977. Chemistry and biology of amino acids in food proteins. Lysinoalanine, p. 37–51. *In* R. E. Feeney and J. R. Whitaker (ed.), Food proteins. Improvement through chemical and enzymatic modification. American Chemical Society, Washington, D.C.
9. **Heap, H. A., G. K. Y. Limsowtin, and R. C. Lawrence.** 1978. Contribution of *Streptococcus lactis* strains in raw milk to phage infection in commercial cheese factories. N.Z. J. Dairy Sci. Technol. **13:**16–22.
10. **Hurst, A.** 1978. Nisin, p. 297–314. *In* F. A. Skinner and L. B. Quesnel (ed.), Streptococci. Academic Press, London.
11. **Kozak, W., M. Rajchert-Trzpil, and W. T. Dobrzanski.** 1974. The effect of proflavin, ethidium bromide and an elevated temperature on the appearance of nisin-negative clones in nisin-producing strains of *Streptococcus lactis*. J. Gen. Microbiol. **83:**295–302.
12. **Lawrence, R. C., and L. E. Pearce.** 1972. Cheese starters under control. Dairy Ind. **37:**73–78.
13. **Lawrence, R. C., and T. D. Thomas.** 1979. The fermentation of milk by lactic acid bacteria. Symp. Soc. Gen. Microbiol. **29:**187–219.
14. **Le Blanc, D. J., V. L. Crow, and L. N. Lee.** 1980. Plasmid-mediated carbohydrate catabolic enzymes among strains of *Streptococcus lactis*, p. 31–41. *In* C. Stuttard and K. R. Rozee (ed.), Plasmids and transposons, environmental effects of maintenance. Academic Press, Inc., New York.
15. **Mattick, A. T. R., and A. Hirsch.** 1947. Further observations on an inhibitory substance (nisin) from lactic streptococci. Lancet **ii:**5–12.
16. **Oxford, A. E.** 1944. Diplococcin, an antibacterial protein elaborated by certain milk streptococci. Biochem. J. **38:**178–182.
17. **Tagg, J. R., A. S. Dajani, L. W. Wannamaker, and E. D. Gray.** 1973. Group A streptococcal bacteriocin. Production, purification, and mode of action. J. Exp. Med. **138:**1168–1183.
18. **Thomas, T. D., and R. J. Lowrie.** 1975. Starters and bacteriophages in lactic acid casein manufacture. J. Milk Food Technol. **38:**269–274.
19. **Whitehead, H. R.** 1933. A substance inhibiting bacterial growth, produced by certain strains of lactic streptococci. Biochem. J. **27:**1793–1800.
20. **Whitehead, H. R., and W. Riddet.** 1933. Slow development of acidity in cheese manufacture. Investigation of a typical case of "non-acid" milk. N.Z. J. Agric. **46:**225–229.

Lactostrepcins: Bacteriocins of Lactic Streptococci

WŁADYSŁAW T. DOBRZAŃSKI, JACEK BARDOWSKI, WITOLD KOZAK, AND JOLANTA ZAJDEL

Department of Pharmaceutical Microbiology, Medical Academy, Oczki 3, 02-007 Warsaw, Poland

When starting our studies on lactic streptococci, we were interested in the genetic mechanisms of a phenomenon known for a long time, namely, the antagonism among the strains of lactic streptococci and between the lactic streptococci and other bacteria.

At the beginning of our studies, a possible plasmid localization was shown for the gene coding for nisin, a polypeptide antibiotic produced by some *Streptococcus lactis* strains (8), as well as for the occurrence of lysogeny in lactic streptococci (11). These studies have led us to demonstrate that antibiotic substances hitherto not described are produced by many strains of lactic streptococci (3, 10, 14). These substances have been classified as bacteriocins, the term "lactostrepcins" being proposed for them.

OCCURRENCE AND PROPERTIES OF LACTOSTREPCINS

Table 1 shows the occurrence of lactostrepcins among lactic streptococci. Lactostrepcins were found to be produced by all non-nisin-producing *S. lactis* strains tested, by almost all strains of *S. lactis* subsp. *diacetylactis*, and by only 1 of the 17 strains of *S. cremoris* tested. *S. lactis* strains producing nisin did not produce lactostrepcins. As reported recently by Davey and Richardson, bacteriocins, which they called "diplococcins," were produced by 11 of 150 *S. cremoris* strains (7).

In our collection of lactic streptococci some strains produced bacteriocins active against only one of the indicator strains (*S. lactis* 60), and others produced bacteriocins active against all three indicator strains used.

Several strains produced at least two lactostrepcins. The production of two bacteriocins by *S. lactis* strain 300 is illustrated in Fig. 1.

All lactostrepcins are susceptible to proteolytic enzymes, and the majority of them are also inactivated by phospholipases A and C and lipases. They show bactericidal effects without causing cell lysis, and most of them show maximum activity at a pH of about 5.0. Lactostrepcins fail completely or almost completely to dialyze through Visking dialysis tubing (Union Carbide Corp.), thus suggesting their molecular weight to be 10,000 or more; they are heat stable and do not sediment upon ultracentrifugation (3, 10, 14). Therefore, they can be classified into group I bacteriocins in the system of Bradley (4).

At least five different lactostrepcins are produced by lactic streptococci. Some differences in their properties are shown in Table 2. At neutral pH, lactostrepcins are either active, partly active, or reversibly inactivated. The inactivation does not seem to depend on modified susceptibility of indicator strains to lactostrepcins.

Lactostrepcins are the only bacteriocins which either act at acid pH only or show maximum activity at such pH.

The yield of lactostrepcin production depends on quality of the medium. Highest concentrations of these bacteriocins can be obtained in rich complex media, in which lactostrepcin activity is more or less stabilized (10, 14). Lactostrepcin production could not be demonstrated in a rich, fully synthetic medium in which nisin was produced (3). Lactostrepcins are produced in milk (J. Bardowski and W. Kozak, unpublished data). A semisynthetic medium for *S. lactis* strain 71 has also been prepared in which only lactostrepcin inactive at pH 7.0 was synthesized, whereas lactostrepcin active at this pH was not produced at all (J. Bardowski, unpublished data). About 1 to 10% of lactostrepcin activity may occur intracellularly (3, 14).

Besides the activity against a number of strains of lactic streptococci, and depending on type, lactostrepcins may kill the cells of group A, C, and G streptococci, *Bacillus cereus*, and only some strains of *Leuconostoc citrovorum*, *Leuconostoc paracitrovorum*, and *Lactobacillus helveticus*. Other gram-positive and gram-negative bacteria used in the study were not susceptible to these bacteriocins (10, 14).

Lactostrepcin 5 produced by *S. cremoris* 202 (this strain seems to produce only one lactostrepcin which contains no lipid component) was purified by salting out, heating, dialysis, and electrophoresis. Its molecular weight, determined as described by Laemli and Favre (12), seems to be about 20,000, and it has an isoelectric point at 4.8 (J. Zajdel and M. Kawczyński, unpublished data). Recently, a method of purification for another *S. cremoris* bacteriocin has been described by Davey and Richardson (6).

TABLE 1. Occurrence of lactostrepcins in lactic streptococci

Species	Total no. of strains tested	No. of lactostrepcin-producing strains active against indicator strains		% of strains
		S. lactis 60	S. lactis 60, S. lactis 51, S. cremoris 1P5	
S. lactis				
Non-nisin-producing	47	38	9	100
Nisin-producing	6	0	0	0
S. lactis subsp. diacetylactis	13	6	6	92
S. cremoris	17	0	1	6

According to the authors, this bacteriocin, with a molecular weight of ca. 6,000, contains no rare amino acids. It is worth emphasizing that nisin contains certain unusual amino acids.

Sensitive lactic streptococci are killed very quickly by lactostrepcins. For instance, over 99% of S. cremoris 1P$_5$ cells are killed by lactostrepcin 5 in moderate concentration within 3 min of incubation. Although to a lower degree than whole cells, protoplasts of S. lactis 60 strain are also susceptible to this bacteriocin (J. Zajdel and I. Glińska, unpublished data).

Some lactostrepcins (e.g., those produced by S. lactis 71 and S. cremoris 202) are adsorbed by both susceptible and nonsusceptible strains of lactic streptococci. On the other hand, we could not show the adsorption of lactostrepcin 1 by the indicator cells.

Some lactostrepcin-resistant mutants of lactic streptococci were isolated.

PRELIMINARY TRIALS OF BACTERIOCIN TYPING OF LACTIC STREPTOCOCCI

An attempt was also made to check whether lactostrepcins could be applied for typing the lactic streptococci (2). In these observations active supernatants containing one or two lactostrepcins were used of necessity, not the purified lactostrepcin.

The results obtained to date permit the following conclusions: (i) lactostrepcin typing of lactic streptococci seems to be possible, since the majority of strains are sensitive to one or more lactostrepcins; (ii) in the system applied, seven lactostrepcin types of lactic streptococci could be distinguished; and (iii) lactostrepcin sensitiv-

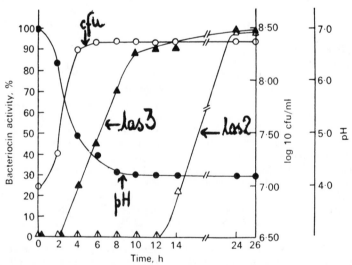

FIG. 1. Production of two bacteriocins by S. lactis strain 300. Bacteriocin activity was determined as follows. To 1 ml of the supernatant of the S. lactis 300 culture was added 0.1 ml (10^4 colony-forming units) of a dilution of a 3-h culture of a streptomycin-resistant indicator strain. After incubation for 60 min at 30°C, the number of surviving cells was determined. It was arbitrarily assumed that the supernatant contained a bacteriocin if it killed at least 90% of the indicator cells; other details have been described (10). Symbols: △, lactostrepcin 2; ▲, lactostrepcin 3; ○, colony-forming units; ●, pH.

TABLE 2. Type-differentiating properties of
lactostrepcins[a]

Lactostrepcin type	A	B	C	D	E	F
1	−	+	+	−	−	No
2	−	+	+	?	+	No
3	−	+	−	+	ND[b]	Partial (30%)
4	+	+	+	+	ND	No
5	15% (residual)	−	+	+	+	Partial (10%)

[a] Key to column heads: A, activity at pH 7.0; B, inactivation by phospholipases and lipases; C, activity against *S. lactis* 60 indicator strain; D, activity against *S. cremoris* 1P5 indicator strain; E, activity against *S. lactis* 60 indicator mutant resistant to lactostrepcin 1; F, dialysis.

[b] Not done.

ity does not correspond with classification of lactic streptococci.

Of interest is whether a correlation exists between bacteriocin type and industrial potential of lactic streptococci.

PRELIMINARY OBSERVATIONS ON THE LOCALIZATION OF A DETERMINANT(S) FOR LACTOSTREPCIN PRODUCTION

Using gel electrophoresis, we surveyed for plasmid content in cleared lysates of 40 strains of lactostrepcin-producing and -nonproducing lactic streptococci. All strains contained plasmids. No differences could be found between the producing and nonproducing strains.

We then demonstrated that ability to produce lactostrepcins is common among clones originating from single cells of *S. cremoris* 202 (this strain contains four or five plasmids) and *S. lactis* 71 (this strain contains three plasmids and produces two bacteriocins, lactostrepcins 3 and 4). Some 400 clones from both strains were tested.

After treatment of both strains with ethidium bromide, acridine, or elevated temperature (39°C), very few (yield ca. 0.5%) permanently lactostrepcin-negative (Las) clones were isolated. Such clones were not found when rifampin or novobiocin was used as a plasmid curing factor. Pechmann and Teuber [13] reported a possibility of elimination, but only of some plasmids of lactic streptococci, by treatment of cell populations with nalidixic acid and elevated temperature. Of interest would be the possibility of successively removing the plasmids of lactic streptococci by repeated protoplasting of the cells (M. J. Gasson and F. L. Davies, Abstr. ASM Int. Conf. Streptococcal Genetics, 1981, abstr. S-25).

In *S. cremoris* 202, five Las⁻ variants were isolated [14]. However, after numerous passages and some months of storage, two of these variants spontaneously started to produce lactostrepcin, though in much lower amounts than the parental strain. From the three remaining variants, permanently Las⁻, plasmid DNA was isolated and purified, and electrophoretic patterns of these DNAs were compared with that of the parental strain. These observations revealed that: (i) when the experiments were repeated with the same or different clones of the parental Las⁺ strain, the number of plasmid DNA bands in gels ranged from 9 to 13, thus making the analysis very difficult; and (ii) plasmid DNA patterns of *S. cremoris* 202, as compared with patterns of Las⁻ variants of this strain, may be almost identical or different.

To check these differences or similarities, the DNAs under study were digested with restriction enzymes *Xba* or *Hind*III and subjected to gel electrophoresis. The results essentially confirmed the observed similarities or differences [14].

If it is assumed that the Las⁻ variants used did not emerge by plasmid mutation, these observations may suggest a chromosomal localization of the determinant of lactostrepcin production, at least in some variants, and do not exclude plasmid localization in other variants.

Attempts were also made to transform the determinant(s) of lactostrepcin production. Taking into account that transformation has not been described in lactic streptococci as yet, we decided to use as DNA recipient the plasmid-free *Bacillus subtilis* MT 120 *recE, leu*, Km^s (minimal inhibitory concentration of kanamycin, 0.4 μg/ml) and to perform the protoplast transformation by the method of Chang and Cohen [5]. Markers for bacteriocin production are only semiselective. Therefore, an accessory selective marker of kanamycin resistance (Km^r) was applied. This could be done since some strains in our collection of lactic streptococci were characterized by Km^r. Purified plasmid DNA from *S. lactis* 71 *las⁺*, Km^r (minimal inhibitory concentration of kanamycin, 50 μg/ml) was used as donor DNA.

Upon repeated transformations, only very few *B. subtilis* transformants (minimal inhibitory concentration 25 μg/ml) were obtained (Fig. 2). Plasmid DNA patterns of the transformants differ from that of the *S. lactis* 71 donor. The transformants do not produce lactostrepcin.

From one of the transformants, plasmid DNA was isolated and purified, and again transformed into *B. subtilis* MT 120. A very high yield of transformation of the Km^r gene was obtained.

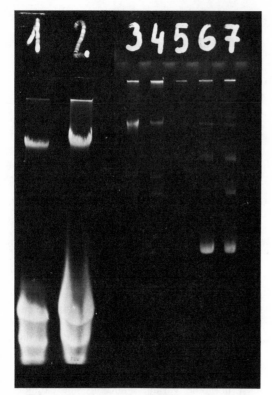

FIG. 2. Plasmid patterns of strains used in transformation of Km[r] marker from *S. lactis* 71 to *B. subtilis* MT 120. Isolation and purification of plasmid DNA from the donor *S. lactis* 71 were performed as described by Klaenhammer et al. (9) with some modifications. Isolation and purification of plasmid DNA from the recipient *B. subtilis* MT 120 and its transformants were performed as described by Clewell and Helinski (6). Transformation of *B. subtilis* MT 120 protoplasts was done by the method of Chang and Cohen (5), with a selective kanamycin concentration of 100 μg/ml. Lanes 1 and 2: Cleared lysates of *B. subtilis* MT 120. Lanes 3–7: Purified plasmid DNA (3 and 4) *S. lactis* 71; (5) *B. subtilis* MT 120 transformant no. 1; (6 and 7) *B. subtilis* MT 120 transformants obtained after transformation of the recipient with plasmid DNA isolated from the transformant no. 1 (lane 5).

Some 50% of colonies that developed after regeneration of the protoplasts were Km[r]. Plasmid DNA was isolated from 16 such transformants and subjected to gel electrophoresis. For 15 of these transformants, plasmid DNA patterns were identical; for 1, they were different (Fig. 2, lanes 6 and 7). Under conditions of selective pressure, plasmid material in *B. subtilis* MT 120 is stable, as is also the case with kanamycin resistance of the transformants. It is worth mentioning that in 1980, at the 5th European Meeting

on Bacterial Transformation and Transfection in Florence, Bal, Cegłowski, and Maciag from our laboratory reported that *S. sanguis* DNA fragments could be cloned in *B. subtilis* (1).

The data presented on *B. subtilis* MT 120 transformation suggest strongly that the Km[r] gene in certain strains of lactic streptococci is plasmid located. (Evidence on genes carried by numerous and divergent plasmids of these bacteria is very scarce to date.) The data also indicate the possibility of exploiting *B. subtilis* as recipient in experiments on transfer of genetic material of lactic streptococci and on cloning of their genes in *Bacillus*.

Experiments now in progress in our laboratory are aimed at determinating in which of the *S. lactis* 71 plasmids the Km[r] gene is located and at elaborating a method for protoplast transformation in lactic streptococci.

Little is known on the role of bacteriocins in nature. Lactostrepcins, however, may be of essential importance in the dairy industry, in technological processes for which lactic streptococci are applied.

Data now available on lactostrepcins already permit more detailed genetic research on their production and on their use as genetic markers. The data also make it possible to study the role they may play in the dairy industry.

LITERATURE CITED

1. Bal, J., P. Cegłowski, and I. Maciag. 1982. New bifunctional plasmid vector for transformation of *Escherichia coli* and *Bacillus subtilis*. Acta Microbiol. Polon., in press.
2. Bardowski, J., and W. Kozak. 1981. Preliminary attempts at bacteriocin typing of lactic streptococci. Acta Microbiol. Polon. **30:**227–230.
3. Bardowski, J., W. Kozak, and W. T. Dobrzański. 1979. Further characterization of lactostrepcins—acid bacteriocins of lactic streptococci. Acta Microbiol. Polon. **28:**93–99.
4. Bradley, D. E. 1967. Ultrastructure of bacteriophages and bacteriocins. Bacteriol. Rev. **31:**230–314.
5. Chang, S., and S. N. Cohen. 1979. High frequency transformation of *Bacillus subtilis* protoplasts by plasmid DNA. Mol. Gen. Genet. **168:**111–115.
6. Clewell, D. B., and D. R. Helinski. 1972. Effect of growth conditions on the formation of the relaxation complex of supercoiled ColE1 deoxyribonucleic acid and protein in *Escherichia coli*. J. Bacteriol. **110:**1135–1146.
7. Davey, G. P., and B. C. Richardson. 1981. Purification and some properties of diplococcin in *Streptococcus cremoris* 346. Appl. Environ. Microbiol. **41:**84–89.
8. Fuchs, P. G., J. Zajdel, and W. T. Dobrzański. 1975. Possible plasmid nature of the determinant for production of the antibiotic nisin in some strains of *Streptococcus lactis*. J. Gen. Microbiol. **88:**189–192.
9. Klaenhammer, T. R., L. L. McKay, and K. A. Baldwin. 1978. Improved lysis of group N streptococci for isolation and rapid characterization of plasmid DNA. Appl. Environ. Microbiol. **35:**592–600.
10. Kozak, W., J. Bardowski, and W. T. Dobrzański. 1978. Lactostrepcins—acid bacteriocins produced by lactic streptococci. J. Dairy Res. **45:**247–257.

11. **Kozak, W., M. Rajchert-Trzpil, J. Zajdel, and W. T. Dobrzański.** 1973. Lysogeny in lactic streptococci producing and not producing nisin. Appl. Microbiol. **25**:305–308.

12. **Laemli, U. K., and M. Favre.** 1973. Maturation of the head of bacteriophage T4. I. DNA packing events. J. Mol. Biol. **80**:575–599.

13. **Pechmann, H., and M. Teuber.** 1981. Plasmide bei Milchsäurestreptokokken. Kiel. Milchwirtsch. Forschungsber. **33**:143–175.

14. **Zajdel, J., and W. T. Dobrzański.** 1982. Isolation and preliminary characterization of *Streptococcus cremoris* (strain 202) bacteriocin. Acta Microbiol. Polon., in press.

Virulent and Temperate Bacteriophages of the Mesophilic Lactic Streptococci

MICHAEL TEUBER AND JÜRGEN LEMBKE

Institute of Microbiology, Federal Dairy Research Center, D-2300 Kiel, Germany

The mesophilic lactic streptococci play an important role in the fermentation processes for cheese, sour milk, yogurt, and butter. The worldwide production totals about 2×10^{10} kg per year (7). Since most of these fermentations are conducted under nonsterile conditions, bacteriophages constitute a major problem for the industry. The sources of these phages seem to be the raw milk, cheese, and whey used, and possibly temperate phages are released from the starter cultures employed (4, 5). In addition to these practical aspects, these virulent and temperate phages could be important genetic vehicles for the transfer of genes within the lactic streptococci by transduction (3) and transfection procedures (A. Geis, in preparation). As a basis for general and applied research, we have initiated an elaborate and careful investigation of the ultrastructure of the virulent and inducible phages of the mesophilic lactic streptococci (*Streptococcus lactis, S. lactis* subsp. *diacetylactis*, and *S. cremoris*).

ULTRASTRUCTURE OF LYTIC (VIRULENT) PHAGES (5)

Using an indicator set of 55 strains of *S. lactis, S. lactis* subsp. *diacetylactis*, and *S. cremoris*, we have isolated and checked about 300 lytic phages from raw milk, whey, and starter cultures in German cheese factories where all the internationally operating starter culture producers were represented. More than 14 morphologically distinct phage types were identified. However, more than 80% of the phages investigated belonged to only four morphotypes (P001, P008, P047, and P109). The most virulent types are depicted in Fig. 1 (P001 and P008). P109 is distinct from P001 only by the presence of a collar. The DNA of phage P001 has a guanine plus cytosine content of 41%. Recently, the guanine plus cytosine content of phage P008 was shown to be 37.5% (M. Loof, Master's thesis, University of Kiel, 1982). The genome sizes determined by electron microscopy are about 13 and 20 megadaltons, respectively. Very potent restriction systems have been detected for phage types P001, P008, and P109 (H. Protz, Master's

thesis, University of Kiel, 1979). Within the morphologically uniform phage type P001, a further differentiation into five subgroups has been achieved by immunoelectron microscopy (6). A comparison of our morphological differentiation system with the lytic system established by Chopin et al. (1) is under way and promises to yield a common basis for the identification of lactic streptococcal phages.

INDUCTION AND ULTRASTRUCTURE OF TEMPERATE PHAGES

To test a large number (about 300) of streptococcal strains, J. Lembke has devised a simple and rapid method for the induction of prophages by UV light or mitomycin C. The test is conducted on solid M 17 medium in petri dishes inoculat-

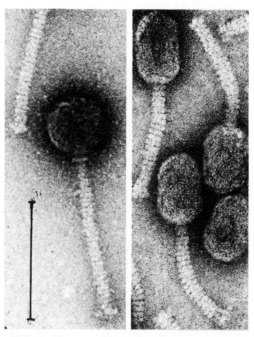

FIG. 1. Electron micrographs of the two most common bacteriophage types of lactic streptococci (P001 at right, P008 at left). Bar, 100 nm.

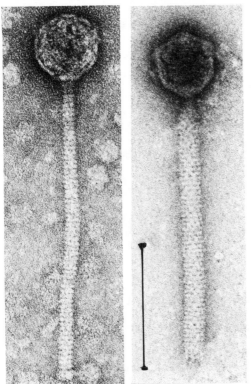

FIG. 2. Electron micrographs of two bacteriophages released from two streptococcal strains by UV induction. Bar, 100 nm.

ed with up to 96 different strains per plate by use of the Dynatech Inoculator MIC-2000 apparatus. For the induction by UV light, parallel plates are inoculated, incubated for 3 h at 30°C to get the bacteria into the logarithmic growth phase, and irradiated with a suitable UV source at a suitable distance for 0, 5, 15, 30, and 60 s. No colonies will develop from strains containing inducible prophages after further incubation of the irradiated plates at 30°C. Inducible strains detected by this method can then be examined by the usual procedure in liquid medium. Induction with mitomycin C was detected on parallel plates containing 0, 1, 2, 5 and 10 µg of antibiotic per ml of medium by the same simple method. Of the 300 strains tested, 80% proved to be inducible by UV or mitomycin C. Eighty of these strains have been induced in liquid medium with UV: 28 strains did not reveal phages in the lysate, 4 strains produced three phages, 17 strains produced two, and 22 strains produced one phage type in the lysate. Nine strains showed incomplete phage particles such as heads, empty

heads, or tails only. Only phages having isometric heads were detected (21 morphologically distinct types). Examples are shown in Fig. 2. Within 51 lysates tested from the mentioned indicator set, only 5 lysates contained lytic phages for streptococcal strains Wg2, 3079, and 3107 (M. Erttmann, Master's thesis, University of Kiel, 1979). From this obvious lack of sensitive indicator strains for the induced prophages, we conclude that temperate phages are not of major importance for the induction of phage problems in the cheese industry. A few of the induced phages were morphologically identical with previously isolated lytic phages (P047, P107, P204, P142) (5). A detailed biochemical and immunological study of these relationships is in active progress.

CONCLUSION

The mesophilic lactic streptococci and their lytic and temperate bacteriophages constitute an interesting and integrated part of the microbial ecosystem of the dairy industry. The recent and exciting discovery of plasmids and their vital role in the fermentation properties of lactic streptococci (for review, see 2, 3) cannot be fully evaluated without examination of the implication of the prophage systems present in almost every strain. In view of the economic impact, the large body of experience, and the nonexisting toxicological risks of these bacteria for human consumption, all efforts should be made to develop the genetics of these microorganisms to a point that will ensure safe production of conventional and future "genetically engineered" products.

LITERATURE CITED

1. Chopin, M.-C., A. Chopin, and C. Roux. 1976. Definition of bacteriophage groups according to their lytic action on mesophilic lactic streptococci. Appl. Environ. Microbiol. 32:741–746.
2. Clewell, D. B. 1981. Plasmids, drug resistance, and gene transfer in the genus Streptococcus. Microbiol. Rev. 45:409–436.
3. Davies, F. L., and M. J. Gasson. 1981. Reviews of the progress of dairy science: genetics of lactic acid bacteria. J. Dairy Res. 48:363–376.
4. Lawrence, R. C. 1978. Action of bacteriophage on lactic acid bacteria: consequences and protection. N.Z. J. Dairy Sci. Technol. 13:129–136.
5. Lembke, J., U. Krusch, A. Lompe, and M. Teuber. 1980. Isolation and ultrastructure of bacteriophages of group N (lactic) streptococci. Zentralbl. Bakteriol. Parasitenkd. Infektionskr. Hyg. Abt. 1 Orig. Reihe C 1:79–91.
6. Lembke, J., and M. Teuber. 1981. Serotyping of morphologically identical bacteriophages of lactic streptococci by immunoelectron microscopy. Milchwissenschaft 36:10–12.
7. Teuber, M., and A. Geis. 1981. The family Streptococcaceae (nonmedical aspects), p. 1614–1630. In M. P. Starr, H. Stolp, H. G. Trüper, A. Balows, and H. G. Schlegel (ed.), The prokaryotes. Springer-Verlag, Berlin.

Genetic Analysis of Carbohydrate Metabolism in Streptococci

EDWARD J. ST. MARTIN, LINDA N. LEE, AND DONALD J. LeBLANC

Laboratory of Microbiology and Immunology, National Institute of Dental Research, Bethesda, Maryland 20205, and Laboratory of Molecular Microbiology, National Institute of Allergy and Infectious Diseases, Frederick, Maryland 21701

Lactose fermentation by *Streptococcus lactis* and sucrose metabolism by *S. mutans* are of economic and public health interest. Regretfully, most of the strains for which these traits are important are not competent for genetic transformation, and detailed analysis and manipulation of their catabolic genes have not been possible. To overcome this problem, we have taken advantage of the ability of *S. sanguis* strain Challis to be transformed by heterologous DNA (2, 3) and attempted to transfer different lactose and sucrose genes into Challis where they can be analyzed and compared. Because Challis also has the ability to use lactose and sucrose, specific negative mutants were isolated to serve as recipients for heterologous genes. A double mutant of *S. sanguis* (*lac-83*) that lacked lactose phosphotransferase transport activity and phospho-β-galactosidase activity was used as the first recipient (Table 1). Homologous *S. sanguis* chromosomal DNA that was isolated from a streptomycin-resistant mutant was capable of transforming the *lac-83* recipient to streptomycin resistance and lactose utilization at equal frequencies. Therefore, both lactose mutations in *lac-83* must be closely linked on the chromosome. Lactose utilization by *S. lactis* ATCC 11454, unlike that by *S. sanguis*, is an unstable phenotype that is associated with the presence of a 32-megadalton plasmid (1). To determine which, if any, of the lactose catabolic enzymes in *S. lactis* are coded for by this plasmid, we used purified *S. lactis* plasmid DNA to transform the *lac-83* mutant (Table 1). Analysis of these plasmid transformants indicated that they had acquired a lactose phosphotransferase activity with the same substrate specificity (galactose/lactose phosphotransferase activity ratio) as the *S. lactis* donor strain (Table 2). In addition, molecular sizing of the phospho-β-galactosidase activity in the transformants by use of polyacrylamide gradient gels revealed that it was the same size as the donor strain enzyme. Therefore, the lactose plasmid present in *S. lactis* must code for the synthesis of both lactose phosphotransferase and phospho-β-galactosidase activities. The stability of the lactose trait and lack of detectable plasmid DNA in the transformants suggest that the *S. lactis* plasmid genes were integrated into the Challis chromosome.

S. sanguis has two pathways for sucrose metabolism. Sucrose can either be cleaved outside the cell by the action of an extracellular glucosyltransferase or be transported into the cell by a sucrose phosphotransferase followed by cleavage of intracellular sucrose 6-phosphate by a hydrolase (4, 5). A double mutant of *S. sanguis* (*sac-324*) that lacked extracellular glucosyltransferase and intracellular sucrose 6-phosphate hydrolase activity was used as the second recipient (Table 1). Chromosomal DNA from streptomycin-resistant mutants of *S. sanguis* and *S. mutans* DR0001 was capable of

TABLE 1. Transformation of *S. sanguis* mutants

Donor	Recipient	Transformation frequency[a]		
		Str[r]	Lac[+]	Sac[+]
S. sanguis chromosome	*lac-83*	2×10^{-3}	2×10^{-3}	—
S. lactis plasmid	*lac-83*	—	1×10^{-6}	—
S. sanguis chromosome	*sac-324*	5×10^{-3}	—	4×10^{-3}
S. mutans chromosome	*sac-324*	4×10^{-5}	—	1×10^{-5}

[a] Str[r], Resistance to streptomycin; Lac[+] and Sac[+], growth on lactose and sucrose, respectively.

TABLE 2. Characterization of transformants

Organism	Gal/Lac PTS[a]	Mol wt of P-β-GAL[b]
S. lactis (donor)	0.30	40,000
S. sanguis (recipient)	0.05	52,000
S. sanguis (transformants)	0.29	40,000

[a] Galactose/lactose phosphotransferase activity ratio.
[b] Molecular weight of phospho-β-galactosidase.

232

transforming *sac-324* to streptomycin resistance and sucrose utilization at similar frequencies. However, transformation by heterologous *S. mutans* DNA was reduced by approximately two orders of magnitude. Enzymatic analysis of these transformants indicated that hydrolase but not transferase activity was restored. Therefore, the two sucrose mutations in *sac-324* are not linked on the chromosome. In addition, molecular sizing of the hydrolase activity in the transformants revealed that the smaller (47,000) *S. mutans* sucrose 6-phosphate hydrolase did not replace the larger (64,000) enzyme in the recipient strain. Because sucrose-positive revertants of *sac-324* always become constitutive for sucrose 6-phosphate hydrolase activity, we suspect that the mutation in *sac-324* is not in the structural gene for this enzyme but rather in its regulation. Chromosomal DNA from *S. mutans* can apparently repair this regulatory defect.

The ability of *S. sanguis* Challis to be transformed by heterologous chromosomal and plasmid DNA makes it an ideal recipient for analysis of diverse streptococcal genes. We have shown that heterologous genes that code for lactose transport, phospho-β-galactosidase, and regulation of sucrose 6-phosphate hydrolase synthesis can be transformed into and expressed by *S.*

sanguis. The use of specific double-negative mutants permitted positive selections for these rare heterologous DNA transformants (Table 1). Other reports in this volume (D. Behnke, M. S. Gilmore, and J. J. Ferretti; F. L. Macrina et al.; H. Malke and S. E. Holm) describe the development of plasmid cloning vectors that can carry heterologous DNA and be introduced into *S. sanguis* Challis. With this new capability it will be possible to isolate, analyze, and manipulate many streptococcal metabolic genes.

LITERATURE CITED

1. **LeBlanc, D. J., V. L. Crow, L. N. Lee, and C. F. Garon.** 1978. Influence of the lactose plasmid on the metabolism of galactose by *Streptococcus lactis*. J. Bacteriol. **137:**878–884.

2. **LeBlanc, D. J., and F. P. Hassell.** 1976. Transformation of *Streptococcus sanguis* Challis by plasmid deoxyribonucleic acid from *Streptococcus faecalis*. J. Bacteriol. **128:**347–355.

3. **Perry, D., and H. D. Slade.** 1964. Intraspecific and interspecific transformation in streptococci. J. Bacteriol. **88:**595–601.

4. **St. Martin, E. J., and C. L. Wittenberger.** 1979. Characterization of a phosphoenolpyruvate-dependent sucrose phosphotransferase system in *Streptococcus mutans*. Infect. Immun. **24:**865–868.

5. **St. Martin, E. J., and C. L. Wittenberger.** 1979. Regulation and function of sucrose 6-phosphate hydrolase in *Streptococcus mutans*. Infect. Immun. **26:**487–491.

DEVELOPMENT AND USE OF RECOMBINANT DNA TECHNOLOGY

Molecular Cloning Strategies for the *Streptococcus sanguis* Host-Vector System

FRANCIS L. MACRINA, JANET ASH TOBIAN, R. PAUL EVANS, AND KEVIN R. JONES

Department of Microbiology, Virginia Commonwealth University, Richmond, Virginia 23298

The first reports describing the development and use of a streptococcal host-vector molecular cloning system appeared in 1980 (2, 8). A number of suitable plasmid vectors for this system have since been described (3, 9, 11), and one such vector recently reported bears a chloramphenicol resistance determinant that may be insertionally inactivated (3). This newly developed recombinant DNA system promises to facilitate the analysis of streptococcal plasmids in their natural hosts. Such recombinant DNA methodologies also will afford novel means for dissecting the genetic basis of virulence in a number of streptococcal pathogens.

The cloning of plasmid gene sequences by using streptococcal vectors proved to be straightforward (2, 8). However, early attempts to achieve "shotgun cloning" of chromosomal gene sequences by using the *S. sanguis* host-vector system met with the unexpected finding that many of the recovered chimeric plasmids had suffered deletions after their entry into the streptococcal cell (1, 8, 9). Reports from two laboratories (1, 9) have now shed light on this observation and, in addition, have led to the development of alternative strategies to circumvent this problem. In this communication we highlight the development of the *S. sanguis* host-vector system and review the strategies currently available for molecular cloning in this species.

VECTOR CONSTRUCTION

S. sanguis is able to develop genetic competence naturally and can be transformed with chromosomal or plasmid DNA at relatively high efficiency (see 15 for review). This made it suitable as a host in a recombinant DNA system; however, naturally occurring plasmids in this species were rare (10). Our initial efforts, then, were centered around the construction of cloning vectors by using plasmids from other strep-

tococcal species that could be transferred by natural means to *S. sanguis*. The primary family of vectors constructed in our laboratory were derived from the in vitro ligation of two separate replicons. pVA380-1 was a 4.2-kilobase multicopy plasmid initially isolated from a strain of *S. ferus*. It carried no detectable phenotypic markers. pVA1 was an 11-kilobase multicopy plasmid bearing a determinant conferring resistance to erythromycin (Em^r; growth on >25 μg/ml). A number of different strategies of restriction endonuclease digestion and ligation were used to insert the Em^r marker of pVA1 into pVA380-1. The resultant plasmids, recovered after transformation into *S. sanguis*, were mapped by using restriction endonucleases and deletion analysis (8). The unique restriction endonuclease sites present on such plasmids into which passenger DNA could be inserted without perturbing plasmid function were determined. This information was deduced from vector construction strategies, deletion analysis, and direct testing of sites by insertion of passenger DNA (8, 9). One such cloning vehicle is shown in Fig. 1. This plasmid, pVA736, has been used successfully to clone heterologous plasmid sequences in *S. sanguis* (8). Although it has only one selectable marker (Em^r), the relatively large number of restriction enzymes that can be used alone or in combination to insert passenger DNA into it make it useful as a vector plasmid.

Finally, it should be noted that the pVA380-1 plasmid used to construct pVA736 is a cloning vehicle in its own right despite the fact that it is phenotypically cryptic. Any marker that allows direct selection (e.g., antibiotic resistance) can be inserted into pVA380-1 at one of a number of unique restriction sites (e.g., *Hin*dIII, *Eco*RI, *Ava*I, *Hin*cII). Within this context, we have found pVA380-1 to be a useful plasmid vector as well (8; J. A. Tobian and F. L. Macrina, submitted for publication).

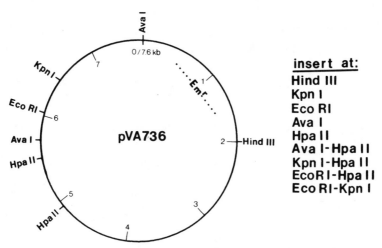

FIG. 1. Restriction site map of pVA736. The numbers on the inside of the circle represent plasmid size in terms of kilobase pairs. The location of the Em^r determinant is noted at kilobase coordinates 0.5 to 1.5. The sites (single or combination) at which passenger DNA can be inserted are noted to the right of the map.

PLASMID TRANSFORMATION OF S. SANGUIS

The transformation of *S. sanguis* and *S. pneumoniae* is marked by conversion of the incoming DNA molecule to a single-stranded form. This has been clearly established for chromosomal DNA (12, 13) and is assumed to be the case in plasmid transformation as well (7). A model consistent with the events of plasmid transformation in *S. pneumoniae* (and extrapolated to *S. sanguis* [9]) has been put forward by Saunders and Guild (14). Their model proposes that two monomeric single-stranded plasmid molecules enter the competent cell and that these donor molecules have sequence overlap to facilitate recircularization. This accounts for the two-hit kinetics observed when monomeric plasmid DNA is used to transform *S. sanguis* (1, 9). Oligomeric plasmid molecules transform with one-hit kinetics, presumably because such molecules can recircularize via a replication-repair event after they have entered the competent cell as single-stranded DNA. These considerations raised serious questions about the efficiency of molecular cloning in the *S. sanguis* host. Clearly, however, the feasibility of plasmid-plasmid cloning experiments was established by the construction of our pVA380-1 vector family. Our feeling is that plasmid-plasmid cloning experiments work because ligation of vector and passenger (both plasmid sequences) fragments result in the formation of significant numbers of the same monomeric chimera needed to effect two-hit kinetics. In addition, such conditions would favor the formation of desired oligomeric molecules consisting of vector and passenger fragments. Either of these situations would result in the recovery of transformants bearing the desired recombinant plasmid. These two nonexclusive pathways are illustrated in Fig. 2.

RECOMBINATIONAL RESCUE OF PLASMID CHIMERAS

As previously mentioned, the molecular requirements for the successful transformation of *S. sanguis* with plasmid DNA had serious implications for the shotgun cloning of chromosomal gene sequences in this host. The formation of multimers carry a given chromosomal insert seemed remote as a result of the large size of the bacterial genome. Similarly, the formation of large numbers of monomers of a given chimera seemed very likely. To solve this problem, we adapted to our system the *Bacillus subtilis* "helper plasmid" cloning method of Gryczan et al. (6). This system allows for the recombinational rescue of chimeras entering the cell by a plasmid that shares homology with the cloning vector. Our system was ideally suited for such a method. All of our vectors were constructed with the pVA380-1 replicon. This plasmid, although phenotypically cryptic, had been introduced into *S. sanguis* by indirect selection (10). Because this plasmid is multicopy (~30 copies per chromosome) and carried no selectable markers, it provides an ideal "target" for the recovery of inserts and selective markers carried by, for example, pVA736 (see Fig. 1). We have demonstrated (9; submitted for publication) that the rescue of linearized pVA736 molecules by

Cloning system:
Plasmid-Plasmid(phage)

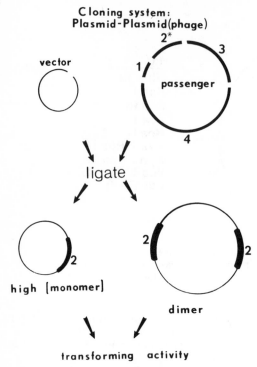

FIG. 2. Cloning plasmid sequences in *S. sanguis*. This illustration depicts how cloning plasmid-derived sequences in *S. sanguis* is envisioned to work. Both the vector plasmid and the passenger plasmid DNA have been cleaved with the same enzyme, yielding one and four fragments, respectively. In this case, fragment 2 of the passenger plasmid is the one being sought. Ligation can result in relatively high concentrations of the desired chimera (left-side pathway) which would transform with the needed two-hit kinetics. In addition, the desired multimer (vector-fragment 2) could be formed (right-side pathway). Such a multimer could transform with one-hit kinetics, giving rise to a clone bearing the desired chimera.

the pVA380-1–bearing *S. sanguis* host is a highly efficient process. This indicated that such "helper plasmid" cloning would work in *S. sanguis*. Using the "helper plasmid" method, we have recently cloned a determinant for tetracycline resistance from the chromosome of a clinical isolate of *S. mutans* (Tobian and Macrina, submitted for publication). This clearly demonstrates the ability to recover directly selectable genes from the chromosome of a heterologous host in *S. sanguis*. However, attempts thus far to clone fragments bearing nonselectable genes (e.g., dextranase gene of *S. mutans*) by the "helper plasmid" method have been unsuccessful. More work is needed to assess this system in

terms of cloning determinants that may not be directly selected. The events that are postulated to occur during the molecular cloning by the "helper plasmid" method are depicted in Fig. 3.

TRANS-GENERIC PLASMID SHUTTLE VECTOR

An obvious alternative to the "helper plasmid" method for shotgun cloning of chromosomal gene sequences in *S. sanguis* was the use of an *Escherichia-Streptococcus* shuttle vector plasmid. Such a plasmid would be defined as one that would be able to replicate in *E. coli* as well as *S. sanguis* and would carry at least one antibiotic resistance determinant that would be expressed in each genus. Shotgun cloning of

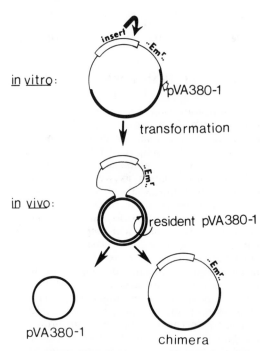

FIG. 3. "Helper plasmid" cloning method. This method was adapted from the system of Gryczan et al. (6) used in *B. subtilis*. A hypothetical chimera formed in vitro can be seen at the top of the figure. It contains pVA380-1 sequences (thick line). This chimeric plasmid enters an *S. sanguis* host which carries the pVA380-1 cryptic plasmid. Pairing between the chimera and the resident pVA380-1 is thought to occur. The chimeric sequences are likely single stranded upon entering the *S. sanguis* cell (13, 15). Extensive (i.e., complete) pairing between the pVA380-1 sequences of the chimera and the resident plasmid is probably not needed. The fragment bearing the directly selectable Em[r] gene and the desired insert recombine into the multicopy resident pVA380-1, giving rise to the recombination products seen at the bottom of the figure.

chromosomal gene sequences would be accomplished by first establishing a "gene bank" of chromosomal fragments in *E. coli* by using the shuttle vector. Standard recombinant DNA methodology would be employed here, and the number of clones needed to ensure the total representation of the host genome in the bank could be computed by the relationship described by Clark and Carbon (5). Once such a gene library was established in *E. coli*, chimeric plasmids, either singly or in small groups, could be introduced into *S. sanguis* by direct transformation. Because such plasmid preparations would be homogeneous in molecular composition, they would be expected to transform *S. sanguis* readily. In this regard, minimal problems associated with deletion formation of newly formed chimeras would be expected.

We have constructed an *Escherichia-Streptococcus* shuttle vector for use in making streptococcal gene banks. Two separate plasmids were used in the construction of our shuttle vector. pACYC184 is a 4-kilobase *E. coli* cloning vehicle originally described by Chang and Cohen (4). It carries chloramphenicol (Cm^r) and tetracycline (Tc^r) resistance determinants and is present to the extent of about 15 copies per chromosomal equivalent in *E. coli*. pACYC184 contains a number of unique restriction endonuclease sites into which passenger DNA can be inserted. pVA749, a streptococcal chimeric plasmid, is 5.2 kilobases in size and carries an erythromycin resistance determinant (9). It has unique *Hpa*II, *Ava*I, and *Hind*III sites into which passenger DNA may be inserted. pVA749 and pACYC184 were joined together in vitro by using their single *Hind*III sites, and the resultant chimera was recovered after transformation into *E. coli* V850 (an erythromycin-sensitive mutant of *E. coli* kindly supplied to us by Julian Davies). This plasmid was found to express Cm^r (25 μg/ml) in *E. coli* V850. The Tc^r gene of the chimera was inactivated by the insertion of pVA749 into pACYC184. Attempts to restore tetracycline resistance by reversing the orientation of the pVA749 replicon in pACYC184 were unsuccessful. The Em^r determinant of pVA749 was constitutively expressed in *E. coli* V850, with the strain showing a 100% plating efficiency on media containing 10 μg of erythromycin per ml. Without the pACYC184-pVA749 chimera, V850 fails to form colonies on solid media containing 10 μg of erythromycin per ml (5 × 10^7 cells plated).

The pACYC184-pVA749 chimera was designated pVA838, and its restriction endonuclease cleavage site map is shown in Fig. 4. Passenger DNA may be inserted into the unique *Bam*HI,

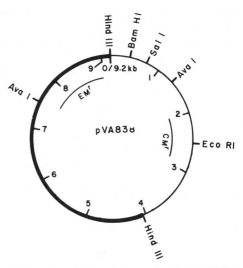

FIG. 4. Restriction site map of pVA838. Kilobase coordinates are given on the inside of the circle, and the positions of the Cm^r and Em^r genes are noted. The thick line corresponds to the pVA749 component of this plasmid, and the thin line corresponds to the pACYC184 sequences.

*Sal*I, and *Eco*RI sites. Because the *Eco*RI site resides within the Cm^r determinant, this gene may be inactivated by the insertion of passenger DNA. pVA838 was 9.2 kilobases (6 × 10^6 daltons) in size and was present to the extent of about eight copies per chromosomal equivalent. pVA838 DNA could be readily transformed into *E. coli* by using either the Cm^r or Em^r markers for selection (~5 × 10^{-5} transformants per survivor). It also could be transformed into *S. sanguis* (Challis) by using the Em^r marker for selection at comparable frequencies. The Cm^r marker of pVA838 was not expressed in *S. sanguis*. pVA838 DNA isolated from *S. sanguis* was able to transform *S. sanguis* to Em^r at frequencies that were about 10-fold higher than those obtained when pVA838 of *E. coli* origin was used. The origin of the pVA838 DNA did not influence the transformation frequencies obtained with *E. coli* V850 as a recipient (V850 is known to be a restrictionless mutant [J. Davies, personal communication]). The copy number of pVA838 in *S. sanguis* was about 15 copies per chromosomal equivalent.

We have recently used pVA838 to clone in *E. coli* V850 both plasmid-derived and chromosomally derived *Eco*RI restriction fragments from *S. mutans* and *S. sanguis*. Chimeric plasmids were readily obtained, and such plasmid DNA present in mini-cleared lysates could be used to transform *S. sanguis* at frequencies of about 10^{-5} per recipient (in preparation). Thus, the pVA838 shuttle vector has been shown to be functional within the context that it was designed. We are currently using pVA838 to construct an *S. mutans* gene library in *E. coli*. Plasmids bearing desired chromosomal fragments from this collection will be introduced by transformation into *S. sanguis* so that we can better study streptococcal gene expression.

ACKNOWLEDGMENTS

Our research was supported by Public Health Service grant DE04224 from the National Institute for Dental Research. F.L.M. is the recipient of Research Career Development Award DE00081 from the National Institute for Dental Research.

We gratefully acknowledge the helpful suggestions and comments of D. B. Clewell and D. Behnke.

LITERATURE CITED

1. **Behnke, D.** 1981. Plasmid transformation of *Streptococcus sanguis* (Challis) occurs by circular and linear molecules. Mol. Gen. Genet. **183**:490–497.
2. **Behnke, D., and J. J. Ferretti.** 1980. Molecular cloning of an erythromycin resistance determinant in streptococci. J. Bacteriol. **144**:806–813.
3. **Behnke, D., and M. S. Gilmore.** 1981. Location of antibiotic resistance determinants, copy control, and replication functions on the double selective streptococcal cloning vector pGB301. Mol. Gen. Genet. **184**:115–120.
4. **Chang, A. C. Y., and S. Cohen.** 1978. Construction and characterization of amplifiable multicopy DNA cloning vehicles derived from the P15A cryptic miniplasmid. J. Bacteriol. **134**:1141–1156.
5. **Clark, L., and J. Carbon.** 1979. Selection of specific clones from colony banks by suppression or complementation tests. Methods Enzymol. **68**:396–408.
6. **Gryczan, T., S. Contente, and D. Dubnau.** 1980. Molecular cloning of heterologous chromosomal DNA by recombination between a plasmid vector and a homologous resident plasmid in *Bacillus subtilis*. Mol. Gen. Genet. **177**:459–467.
7. **Lacks, S.** 1979. Uptake of circular deoxyribonucleic acid and mechanism of deoxyribonucleic acid transport in genetic transformation of *Streptococcus pneumoniae*. J. Bacteriol. **138**:404–409.
8. **Macrina, F. L., K. R. Jones, and P. H. Wood.** 1980. Chimeric streptococcal plasmids and their use as molecular cloning vehicles in *Streptococcus sanguis* (Challis). J. Bacteriol. **143**:1425–1435.
9. **Macrina, F. L., J. A. Tobian, R. P. Evans, and K. R. Jones.** 1981. Molecular cloning in the streptococci, p. 195–210. *In* A. Hollaender (ed.), Genetic engineering of microorganisms for chemicals. Plenum Press, New York.
10. **Macrina, F. L., P. H. Wood, and K. R. Jones.** 1980. Genetic transformation of *Streptococcus sanguis* (Challis) with cryptic plasmids from *Streptococcus ferus*. Infect. Immun. **28**:692–699.
11. **Malke, H., L. G. Burman, and S. E. Holm.** 1981. Molecular cloning in streptococci: physical mapping of the vehicle plasmid pSM10 and demonstration of intergroup transfer. Mol. Gen. Genet. **181**:254–267.
12. **Morrison, D. A., and W. R. Guild.** 1972. Transformation and deoxyribonucleic acid size: extent of degradation on entry varies with size of donor. J. Bacteriol. **112**:1157–1168.
13. **Raina, J. L., and A. W. Ravin.** 1978. Fate of homospecific transforming DNA bound to *Streptococcus sanguis*. J. Bacteriol. **133**:1212–1223.
14. **Saunders C. W., and W. R. Guild.** 1981. Monomer plasmid DNA transforms *Streptococcus pneumoniae*. Mol. Gen. Genet. **181**:57–62.
15. **Smith, H. O., D. B. Danner, and R. A. Deich.** 1981. Genetic transformation. Annu. Rev. Biochem. **50**:41–68.

pGB3,01 Vector Plasmid Family and Its Use for Molecular Cloning in Streptococci

DETLEV BEHNKE, MICHAEL S. GILMORE, AND JOSEPH J. FERRETTI

Academy of Sciences of the German Democratic Republic, Central Institute for Microbiology and Experimental Therapy, DDR-69 Jena, German Democratic Republic, and Department of Microbiology and Immunology, University of Oklahoma Health Sciences Center, Oklahoma City, Oklahoma 73109

The introduction of recombinant DNA technology into streptococcal genetics is expected to obviate many of the problems that have made progress in this field of research difficult in the past. Toward this goal several streptococcal cloning vectors have recently been developed (3, 9, 11), and on the basis of studies of the plasmid transformation mechanism (2, 10), the efficiency of molecular cloning experiments has been improved (10). A new line of streptococcal vector plasmids and their use in cloning experiments are the subject of this communication.

CHARACTERISTICS OF pGB301 AND DERIVED PLASMIDS

Plasmid pGB301 was isolated as a spontaneous deletion mutant after transformation of *Streptococcus sanguis* (Challis) by the naturally occurring 29.7-kilobase (kb) group B streptococcal plasmid pIP501 (5, 8). Although pGB301 retained the chloramphenicol and MLS (macrolides-lincosamides-streptogramin B) resistance genes of its ancestor, it was no longer conjugative. From restriction enzyme analysis it was obvious that pGB301 originated from a single deletion event (5). The plasmid had a molecular size of 9.8 kb and was present at an estimated 10 copies per cell.

Cleavage of pGB301 with a number of restriction enzymes allowed the construction of a physical map, part of which is shown in Fig. 1 (4, 5). The plasmid featured unique cleavage sites for eight restriction endonucleases generating either sticky (*Ava*I, *Bcl*I, *Bst*EII, *Hpa*II, *Kpn*I) or blunt (*Bsp*RI, *Hpa*I, *Pvu*II) ends. Seven of these unique cleavage sites were located outside of essential plasmid regions, and one site (*Bst*EII) may be used for insertional inactivation of the chloramphenicol resistance gene (Fig. 1). The enzymes *Hin*dIII, *Hin*dII, *Hae*II, and *Ava*II cleaved the plasmid into four, three, four, and two fragments, respectively.

A number of deletion derivatives of pGB301 have been isolated either after transformation with mixtures of in vitro-generated recombinant plasmids (see also next paragraph) or by in vitro removal of *Bsp*RI-*Hin*dII flanked fragments (4). Twelve derivatives of pGB301 which were examined had DNA segments deleted ranging in size from 0.3 to 4.1 kb. The positions of these deletions have been mapped and are shown in Fig. 2. Those deletions located to the left of the single *Bsp*RI site inactivated the chloramphenicol resistance, whereas all deletions to the right of the *Bsp*RI site impaired the MLS resistance. The deletion Δ354 also affected the copy control of pGB301. The corresponding plasmid, pGB354, was present at the elevated copy number of 49 plasmid molecules per cell. Together, the two largest deletions, Δ307 and Δ354, spanned a continuous region of 7.7 kb without impairing functions pertaining to plasmid replication or maintenance. These functions were,

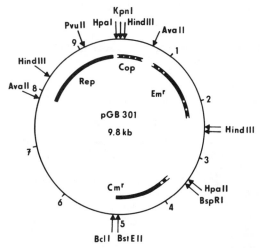

FIG. 1. Location of biological functions in relation to the restriction enzyme cleavage site map of plasmid pGB301. Map coordinates are given in kilobases. The single *Kpn*I site was arbitrarily chosen to map at zero position. Em^r, Inducible resistance to erythromycin and lincomycin; Cm^r, resistance to chloramphenicol; Cop, copy control region; Rep, replication region/function(s).

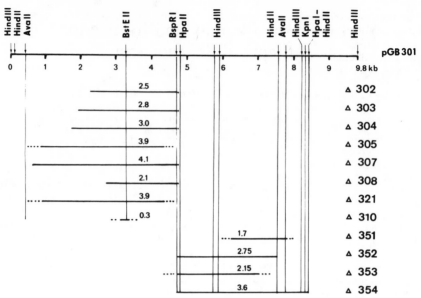

FIG. 2. Map positions of deletions inactivating either the chloramphenicol or erythromycin resistance and/or the copy control mechanism of plasmid pGB301. The linearized restriction map is calibrated in kilobases. Vertical lines indicate the positions of restriction endonuclease cleavage sites.

therefore, assigned to the remaining 2.1-kb DNA segment. The locations of biological functions of pGB301 in relation to its physical map are presented in Fig. 1.

Introduction of pGB301 and its deletion derivatives pGB305, pGB351, and pGB354 into the minicell-producing *Bacillus subtilis* strain CU403 revealed that three proteins were specified by this plasmid, one associated with erythromycin resistance, a second associated with chloramphenicol resistance, and a third which was likely to be associated with plasmid replication or maintenance, or both.

MOLECULAR CLONING

Passenger DNA of both plasmid and chromosomal origin has been successfully inserted into several of the unique restriction enzyme cleavage sites of pGB301. In experiments in which *Hpa*II fragments of the 69-kb group D streptococcal plasmid pSF351C61 (B. A. Forbes, Ph.D. thesis, University of Oklahoma, Oklahoma City, 1979) were cloned into pGB301, about 37% of the transformant clones screened for their plasmid content harbored recombinant plasmids (5). None of these plasmids, however, expressed the tetracycline resistance carried by pSF351C61. The failure to clone this resistance gene is believed to reflect an expression problem in Challis. A similar yield of transformants harboring recombinant plasmids was observed when frag-

ments of chromosomal *Staphylococcus aureus* DNA were spliced into the *Hpa*II site of pGB301. No phenotypic activity could be attributed to these cloned segments of staphylococcal DNA.

Both *Hind*II- and *Bsp*RI-generated fragments of the multiple resistance group B streptococcal plasmid pIP800 (71 kb; 6) have been inserted into the single *Bsp*RI site of pGB301. The recombinant plasmids pGB3011, pGB3012, and pGB3013, isolated from three gentamicin-resistant transformant clones, had molecular sizes of 9.5, 12.7, and 15.8 kb, respectively. They shared a 1.7-kb passenger DNA sequence which was found in either insertion orientation and is likely to carry the gentamicin resistance gene or part of it. Two of the recombinant plasmids (pGB3011, pGB3013) suffered deletions affecting both the passenger DNA and the vector. Nevertheless, a minimum size of 6.8 kb was estimated for the passenger DNA of pGB3013. The deletion in pGB3011 rendered the recombinant plasmid smaller than the vector itself, thereby causing loss of the sequences coding for the chloramphenicol resistance of pGB301 (5).

Chloramphenicol-susceptible transformants were also observed with high frequency in experiments designed to clone blunt-ended chromosomal *S. aureus* DNA fragments into the single *Bsp*RI site of pGB301. Many of these plasmids had lost the passenger DNA completely as well as vector plasmid sequences bracketing the site used for cloning. (See also Fig. 2, Δ302 through Δ309.)

Deletions that affected both the vector and passenger DNA (chromosomal *S. aureus* fragments) or completely removed the insert plus flanking vector sequences (e.g., Δ310, Fig. 2) were also found with considerable frequency in cloning experiments which involved the single *Bst*EII site of pGB301. Recombinant plasmids that carried inserts recoverable by *Bst*EII cleavage failed to express chloramphenicol resistance. Therefore, insertional inactivation of this gene occurred as a consequence of cloning into the *Bst*EII site.

The high frequency of deletions observed after transformation of plasmids into strain Challis, an observation also reported by others (10), made a shotgun approach to gene cloning in streptococci inefficient. The generation of deletions was not a specific characteristic of pGB301 (as opposed to an earlier interpretation [5]), but rather was the result of the plasmid transformation mechanism of Challis (2, 10).

PLASMID TRANSFORMATION MECHANISM IN CHALLIS

Plasmid transformation of *S. sanguis* strain Challis apparently follows a mechanism similar or identical to that recently described for *S. pneumoniae* (1, 14). According to this model, plasmid molecules are randomly linearized at the surface of competent cells, and only single-stranded DNA enters the cell. Restoration of a circular plasmid molecule inside the cell then occurs by annealing of complementary strands originating from two different donor molecules which were linearized at points distant enough to provide a sufficiently long overlapping sequence.

The following experimental results support this model of plasmid transformation of Challis. Plasmid and chromosomal DNA (which is known to enter the cell in single-stranded form [13]) competed for transformation. A second-order dependence of the transformation frequency on the DNA concentration was observed for monomeric plasmid DNA (2). Open circular plasmid DNA transformed Challis at a reduced frequency (Table 1). Plasmid molecules linearized at a single restriction site failed to transform Challis (Table 1). However, mixing of two plasmid DNA preparations linearized at different sites restored the transforming activity with high efficiency (Table 1). Finally, a mixture of linearized pGB301 and one of its deletion derivatives (each linearized at a different site) gave rise to transformants containing only the smaller plasmid, thus supporting reannealing between complementary strands from two different donor molecules as the mechanism of plasmid restoration (2).

According to this plasmid transformation mechanism, the probability for an annealing of two complementary strands originating from two recombinant plasmid molecules (of a ligation mixture) with identical inserts in the same orientation decreases as the number of passenger DNA fragments increases. Annealing of only partly homologous molecules most likely leads to mispairings which eventually result in the deletion of DNA segments. Consequently, for DNA cloning in streptococci, approaches different from those developed for *Escherichia coli* had to be deployed.

CLONING BY RECOMBINATION

Dubnau and co-workers recently introduced a cloning approach for *B. subtilis* which takes advantages of homologous recombination in the course of which passenger DNA from an incoming recombinant plasmid is rescued by a resident homologous plasmid (7). This approach, which has also been applied to streptococcal cloning systems (10), allows circumvention of the problems posed by the transformation mechanism of Challis. In model experiments both the erythromycin and the chloramphenicol resistance determinants could be rescued from linear pGB301 molecules by resident deletion derivatives of pGB301 (e.g., pGB302 or pGB351) at frequencies up to 5%. The frequency depended on the size of the fragment to be rescued and decreased with increasing length of the nonhomologous

TABLE 1. Effect of DNA conformation on transformation

Plasmid/enzyme[a]	Conformation	Transformants/0.1 ml
pGB301/none	Covalently closed circular	3.7×10^5
pGB301/none	Open circular	6×10^2
pGB301 × *Bsp*RI	Linear	52^b
pGB301 × *Hpa*II	Linear	0
pGB301 × *Kpn*I	Linear	69^b
pGB301 × *Bsp*RI + pGB301 × *Kpn*I	Linear	3.8×10^4
pGB301 × *Hpa*II + pGB301 × *Kpn*I	Linear	6.4×10^4

[a] Restriction enzymes used to cleave pGB301 had only single sites on the plasmid molecule. See also Fig. 1.

[b] The residual transforming activity is due to traces of uncleaved plasmid DNA.

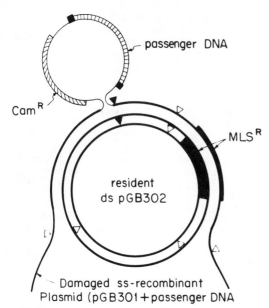

FIG. 3. Hypothetical intermediate occurring during molecular cloning by recombinational rescue of passenger DNA by a partly homologous resident plasmid. The presence of the chloramphenicol resistance gene within the region of nonhomology allows direct selection for transformants carrying recombinant plasmids. Heavy and medium lines indicate regions of homology and nonhomology, respectively; $\triangledown$, HindIII sites; $\blacktriangledown$, HpaII sites; $\blacksquare$, BspRI sites.

DNA. Rescue of nonhomologous DNA was also demonstrated between the resident plasmids pGB302 or pGB351 and the recombinant plasmid pGB3012. In these arrangements rescue of DNA segments with a minimum length of 5 kb occurred at frequencies between 10^{-5} and 10^{-6}. No rescue was observed when a linearizing cut was present within the region of nonhomology.

Cloning of markers that can be directly selected for may, therefore, easily be accomplished by the described approach. However, when no selective pressure can be applied, incompatibility reactions inside of the transformed cell will severely reduce the efficiency of this cloning approach. The pGB301 vector family allows circumvention of this problem by directly selecting for recombinant plasmids via co-rescue of either one of its antibiotic resistance markers. Passenger DNA inserted into the HpaII or BspRI site of pGB301 is co-rescued along with the antibiotic resistance marker of pGB301 which is missing on the resident deletion derivative (Fig. 3). In experiments in which pGB302 was used as a resident plasmid and the linearized recombinant plasmid pGB3012 served as donor DNA, chloramphenicol-resistant transformants

were always resistant to gentamicin, thus demonstrating 100% co-rescue of passenger DNA.

CONCLUSIONS

The pGB301 vector family has been shown to be a useful tool for molecular cloning experiments in streptococci. Besides featuring all of the essential, and most of the desirable, characteristics for cloning vehicles, the pGB301 plasmid family offers new possibilities for alternative cloning strategies, such as cloning by recombination. This cloning approach, together with the deployment of shuttle vector systems (12; F. L. Macrina et al., this volume) which allow initial cloning in E. coli, will make molecular cloning a powerful tool for streptococcal genetics too.

LITERATURE CITED

1. **Barany, F., and A. Tomasz.** 1980. Genetic transformation of *Streptococcus pneumoniae* by heterologous plasmid DNA. J. Bacteriol. **144:**698–709.
2. **Behnke, D.** 1981. Plasmid transformation of *Streptococcus sanguis* (Challis) occurs by circular and linear molecules. Mol. Gen. Genet. **183:**490–497.
3. **Behnke, D., and J. J. Ferretti.** 1980. Physical mapping of pDB101: a potential vector plasmid for molecular cloning in streptococci. Plasmid **4:**130–138.
4. **Behnke, D., and M. S. Gilmore.** 1981. Location of antibiotic resistance determinants, copy control, and replication functions on the double-selective streptococcal cloning vector pGB301. Mol. Gen. Genet. **184:**115–120.
5. **Behnke, D., M. S. Gilmore, and J. J. Ferretti.** 1981. Plasmid pGB301, a new multiple resistance streptococcal cloning vehicle and its use in molecular cloning of a gentamicin/kanamycin resistance determinant. Mol. Gen. Genet. **183:**414–421.
6. **Courvalin, P., C. Carlier, and E. Collatz.** 1980. Plasmid-mediated resistance to aminocyclitol antibiotics in group D streptococci. J. Bacteriol. **143:**541–551.
7. **Gryczan, T., S. Contente, and D. Dubnau.** 1980. Molecular cloning of heterologous chromosomal DNA by recombination between a plasmid vector and a homologous resident plasmid in *Bacillus subtilis*. Mol. Gen. Genet. **177:**459–467.
8. **Horodniceanu, T., P. H. Bouanchaud, G. Bieth, and Y. A. Chabbert.** 1976. R-plasmids in *Streptococcus agalactiae* (group B). Antimicrob. Agents Chemother. **10:**795–801.
9. **Macrina, F. L., K. R. Jones, and P. H. Wood.** 1980. Chimeric streptococcal plasmids and their use as molecular cloning vehicles in *Streptococcus sanguis* (Challis). J. Bacteriol. **143:**1425–1435.
10. **Macrina, F. L., J. A. Tobian, K. R. Jones, and R. P. Evans.** 1981. Molecular cloning in the streptococci, p. 195–210. *In* A. Hollaender (ed.), Genetic engineering of microorganisms for chemicals. Plenum Press, New York.
11. **Malke, H., L. G. Burman, and S. E. Holm.** 1981. Molecular cloning in streptococci. Physical mapping of the vehicle plasmid pSM10 and demonstration of intergroup DNA transfer. Mol. Gen. Genet. **181:**259–267.
12. **Malke, H., and S. E. Holm.** 1981. Expression of streptococcal plasmid determined resistance to erythromycin and lincomycin in *Escherichia coli*. Mol. Gen. Genet. **184:**283–285.
13. **Raina, J. L., and H. E. Ravin.** 1978. Fate of homospecific transforming DNA bound to *Streptococcus sanguis*. J. Bacteriol. **133:**1212–1223.
14. **Saunders, C. W., and W. R. Guild.** 1981. The pathway of plasmid transformation in *Pneumococcus*. Open circular and linear molecules are active. J. Bacteriol. **146:**517–526.

Helper Plasmid System for DNA Cloning with pSM10-Related Vehicles

HORST MALKE AND STIG E. HOLM

Academy of Sciences of the German Democratic Republic, Central Institute of Microbiology and Experimental Therapy, Jena, German Democratic Republic, and Department of Clinical Bacteriology, University of Umeå, Umeå, Sweden

Streptococcus pneumoniae and *S. sanguis* can be transformed by a variety of plasmid DNA forms including open and covalently closed circular monomers, oligomers, and linear monomeric and oligomeric molecules (1, 5, 8, 11). Monomer linear forms must represent a mixture of molecules linearized by cutting at different places if they are to be active in transformation. Analysis of the kinetics and efficiencies of transformation by the different DNA species led Saunders and Guild (11) to arrive at a model for pneumococcal plasmid transformation according to which two monomeric plasmid molecules or a single oligomeric molecule are needed to yield a viable transformant. In the transformation process plasmid replicons are reassembled by pairing of independent single-strand fragments derived from duplex donors cut on the cell surface. The essential features of this model, which is analogous to that proposed to explain transfection (10), have been adopted for the Challis transformation system as well (1, 5). In molecular cloning, the low overall efficiency of establishing new replicons in the recipient cell calls for a system able to rescue damaged vector DNA. As documented for a *Bacillus subtilis* host vector system (3), the frequency of plasmid marker transformation can be increased by allowing incoming plasmid DNA to be repaired by recombination with resident homologous plasmid DNA. We have developed and tested such a helper plasmid system for molecular cloning with pSM10-related vector plasmids in the Challis strain of *S. sanguis*.

CONSTRUCTION OF THE HELPER PLASMID, pSM102210

As reported previously (9), a plasmid chimera, pSM10221 (12.8 kilobases [kb]), constructed by fusion of the streptococcal erythromycin resistance (Em^r) plasmid pSM10 (8.3 kb) and the staphylococcal chloramphenicol resistance (Cm^r) plasmid pC221 (4.5 kb) at their single *Eco*RI sites, expresses resistance to both antibiotics in *S. sanguis*. pSM10 and its deletion derivatives pSM9 (7.3 kb), pSM8 (6.7 kb), and pSM7 (6.4 kb) constitute a group of physically mapped plasmids which have been shown to be suitable as streptococcal cloning vehicles (6–9). To provide them with sequence homology in the recipient cell, Challis (pSM10221) was mutagenized with 100 μg of nitrosoguanidine per ml for 30 min at 37°C and was screened for Em^s Cm^r survivors. To eliminate a possible host mutation background, plasmid DNA from one such mutant was isolated and used to retransform the wild-type Challis strain to Cm^r. All transformants examined contained a plasmid, indistinguishable in size from pSM10221, which failed to confer Em^r and lincomycin resistance (Lm^r) on its host (minimal inhibitory concentrations of ≤0.05 and 0.5 μg/ml, respectively). A strain carrying the mutant plasmid, designated as pSM102210, was capable of reversion to Em^r at a frequency of $4.9 \pm 0.8 \times 10^{-7}$, with all revertants tested exhibiting levels of resistance to erythromycin, lincomycin, and chloramphenicol identical to those determined by the wild-type plasmid pSM10221 (minimal inhibitory concentrations of 1,000, 250, and 25 μg/ml, respectively). This analysis shows that pSM102210 carried a point mutation which completely inactivated expression of Em^r.

KINETICS OF TRANSFORMATION OF CHALLIS (pSM102210) BY MONOMER COVALENTLY CLOSED CIRCULAR DNA

Using the standard transformation protocol of LeBlanc and Hassell (4), we compared Challis wild type with Challis(pSM102210) with respect to their transformability by the Em^r marker of pSM10221. Monomer covalently closed circular DNA was purified by agarose gel electrophoresis and was used at concentrations ranging from 0.15 to 5 ng/ml of competent cultures containing 7×10^7 to 9×10^7 colony-forming units. As shown in Fig. 1, double log plots of transformation frequency versus DNA concentration revealed two-hit kinetics for wild-type transformation (slope of the dose-response curve = 2.02 by

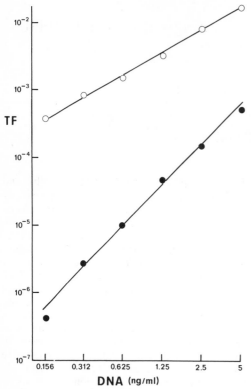

FIG. 1. Dose response for transformation of Challis ($\bullet$; two-hit kinetics) and Challis(pSM102210) ($\bigcirc$; one-hit kinetics) by monomeric pSM10221 DNA. The transformation frequency (TF) is expressed as number of Em^r transformants per total colony-forming units at the time of plating.

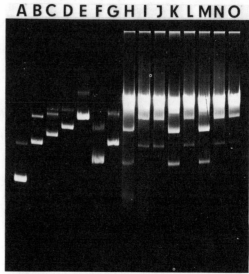

FIG. 2. Plasmid screening (2) of Em^r Cm^s transformants (lanes H-O) that arose by transformation of Challis(pSM102210) with pSM72 DNA linearized by *Kpn*I digestion (see Table 1). The gel (0.8%) shows that five transformants carried a plasmid indistinguishable in size from pSM72 (lane G) and three transformants carried plasmids of the size of pSM7 (lane F). Lanes A–E contained additional plasmid size markers: A, pBR322 (4.4 kb); B, pSM102 (8.6 kb) (7); C, pSM7322 (10.8 kb) (8); D, pSM10221 (12.8 kb); E, pSM102211 (16.6 kb).

linear regression analysis), whereas transformation of Challis carrying the homologous plasmid followed first-order kinetics (slope = 1.08 by linear regression analysis). Over the entire DNA concentration range, transformation of Challis(pSM102210) was much more efficient than that of the wild-type; the differences in the yield of transformants for the two strains varied with the DNA concentrations between one and three orders of magnitude. On the basis of the Saunders and Guild model, we interpret these results to mean that one monomeric pSM10221 molecule was sufficient to give a successful transformation event with Challis(pSM102210), whereas two molecules were needed when wild-type Challis was used. From the dose-response curves it can be estimated that 10^8 monomeric pSM10221 molecules, corresponding to 1.4 ng of DNA, gave approximately 4×10^4 transformants per ml with the Challis recipient and 3×10^6 transformants with Challis(pSM102210). The

former value is 10^2- to 10^3-fold lower than that predicted by the Poisson distribution for the fraction of cells infected by two molecules. This shows that successful transformation of wild-type Challis was a rare event even when the recipient cells had been infected by the necessary minimum of donor molecules.

FATE OF RECOMBINANT PLASMIDS AFTER TRANSFORMATION OF CHALLIS(pSM102210)

To test the potential of the Challis(pSM102210) recipient for rescuing nonhomologous DNA, pSM10-related vector plasmids with group C streptococcal chromosomal DNA inserts at defined sites were used to select Em^r transformants which then were scored with respect to Cm^r. The plasmids of a limited number of both Cm^r and Cm^s colonies were identified by virtue of their characteristic sizes on agarose gels (Fig. 2). To ensure that all transformants arose by recombination between incoming and resident plasmid DNA, the donor DNAs were uniquely cut with appropriate restriction enzymes before being used for transformation.

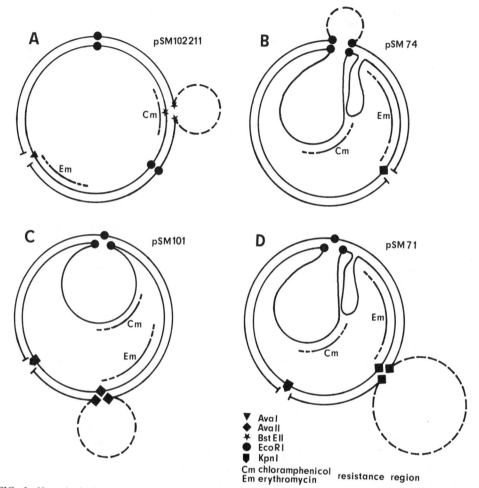

FIG. 3. Hypothetical paired intermediates between the resident plasmid pSM102210 (inner circles) and different recombinant donor plasmids (outer circles) whose inserts are depicted as broken loops. Relevant restriction sites, the location of the resistance determinants, and the position of the linearizing cuts in the donor plasmids are indicated. Loops belonging to the resident plasmid represent sequences lacking homology to vector DNA. The sizes of the different domains of the donor plasmids may be taken from Table 1 and information given in the text.

Unless stated otherwise, these linearizing cuts were placed outside the inserts. The principal transformation reactions performed and the structures of the hypothetical paired intermediates are depicted in Fig. 3. The results, together with additional information on important experimental parameters such as insert sizes, distances between insertion and cleavage sites, etc., are given in Table 1. The following findings are worth noting.

(i) Regardless of the donor plasmid used, transformant clones doubly resistant to erythromycin and chloramphenicol invariably contained a plasmid indistinguishable in size from pSM10221. Obviously, this transformant type was the result of recombinational substitution of the mutant Em^s site by the wild-type marker. The failure to find pSM10221 (or pSM102210) together with the donor plasmids in the same cell showed that these plasmids expressed the desired property of being strongly incompatible.

(ii) Cm^s transformants invariably contained the donor plasmids provided that their inserts were in the BstEII or EcoRI sites. Since DNA insertion into the BstEII site inactivates Cm^r (8), this finding was to be expected. It implies that a single-strand insertion loop can be rescued along with homologous DNA formally capable of

TABLE 1. Co-rescue of H46A (group C) chromosomal DNA inserts in pSM10-related vector plasmids after transformation of *S. sanguis* Challis(pSM102210) to Em^r

Recombinant donor plasmid	Derived from	Site of H46A DNA insertion	Insert size (kb)	Distance between linearizing cut and insertion site (kb)	Ratio of Cm^s/total transformants scored (%)	No. of Cm^s transformants:			Paired intermediate depicted in Fig. 1
						Screened for plasmid type	Containing donor plasmid	With insert deleted	
pSM102211	pSM10221	*Bst*EII	3.8	5.5	25/590 (4)	8	8	0	A
pSM74	pSM7	*Eco*RI	1.0	2.1	77/995 (8)	24	24	0	B
pSM101	pSM10	*Ava*II	3.0	1.4	18/160 (11)	17	8	9	C
pSM71	pSM7	*Ava*II	4.3	1.4	39/351 (11)	8	4	4	D
pSM72	pSM7	*Ava*II	2.1	1.4	81/650 (12)	8	5	3	D

forming a complete circle of paired DNA with the resident plasmid (Fig. 3A). The potential of the system to rescue donor plasmids with *Eco*RI inserts is even more remarkable since hybridization between incoming and resident plasmid DNA can give rise to only an incomplete circle of paired DNA consisting of pSM10 sequences. The circle is completed by a substitution loop, one arm of which is the pC221 component of the resident plasmid and the other arm of which is the foreign DNA inserted into the *Eco*RI site (Fig. 3B). The special design of the system thus ensures that Cm^s transformants are committed to containing the intact *Bst*EII and *Eco*RI inserts. The segregational loss of Cm^r may thus be exploited in the same way as insertional inactivation for the rapid identification of clones bearing recombinant plasmids.

(iii) When the inserts were in the *Ava*II site of the recombinant donor plasmids (Fig. 3C and D), they were recovered in about 50% of the Cm^s transformants. The remainder contained the insert-free original vehicle, suggesting that an insertion loop at this site had a 50% chance of being precisely excised at the two vector-fragment junctions.

(iv) Donor plasmids linearized by cutting in the insert (*Eco*RI insert tested) never gave rise to Cm^s transformants. This proves that DNA damage in the nonhomologous moiety leads to an irreversible loss of foreign DNA inserts.

(v) The proportion of Cm^s transformants was a function of the distance between the selective marker (Em^r) and the insertion site. This distance was greatest in the case of pSM102211 (carrying a *Bst*EII insert) and smallest in the case of pSM71, pSM72, and pSM101 (carrying *Ava*II inserts). Accordingly, the ratio of Cm^s/total transformants was highest when the latter plasmids served as donors, intermediate in the case of pSM74 (carrying an *Eco*RI insert), and smallest in the case of pSM102211 as donor DNA. Since, however, the transforming activity

of a marker carried on the nonhomologous donor moiety would also seem to depend on the distance between the insertion site and a unique cleavage site within the homologous moiety (see Table 1), the apparent frequency of Cm^s transformants may additionally be influenced by this factor.

CONCLUSIONS

Although the state of donor DNA in the model experiments described is not representative of that in an actual cloning experiment, we thought it important to study the potential of the system under well-defined conditions. The experiments provided quantitative data showing that nonhomologous DNA inserted into at least three different sites is rescued along with the homologous selective vector marker, although, as expected, at lower frequencies. Cm^s clones have a very high chance of containing recombinant plasmids. The system, which takes advantage of segregational loss of Cm^r, thus appears to have a potential approaching that of systems exploiting insertional inactivation for identifying clones carrying recombinant plasmids. For molecular cloning, small vehicles with sites for insertion close to the selective marker may be most effective. Furthermore, quasi-complete homology (disturbed by probably only a single base pair mismatch) between the selective donor marker and the corresponding locus on the resident plasmid, as demonstrated in the present system, seems to be advantageous. The rule that a linearizing cut must not occur within the nonhomologous sequence (nor at the junction between the homologous and nonhomologous segments) in order for the foreign DNA to be perpetuated constitutes an inherent weakness of the streptococcal cloning systems. The actual co-rescue frequencies of foreign DNA inserts may be drastically influenced by DNA-damaging processes that occur during or after entry of the donor DNA into the competent cell. Mutational alteration of this host property would be desirable to make the streptococcal cell a better host for molecular cloning.

ACKNOWLEDGMENTS

Most of this work was done during H.M.'s tenure of a Visiting Scientist Award of the Medical Faculty of the University of Umeå and was supported by the Royal Swedish Academy of Sciences.

We express our thanks and gratitude to Don Clewell and the American Society for Microbiology for their liberal financial support, without which this work could not have been presented at the meeting.

LITERATURE CITED

1. **Behnke, D.** 1981. Plasmid transformation of *Streptococcus sanguis* (Challis) occurs by circular and linear molecules. Mol. Gen. Genet. **182:**490–497.

2. **Burdett, V.** 1980. Identification of tetracycline-resistant R plasmids in *Streptococcus agalactiae* (group B). Antimicrob. Agents Chemother. **18:**753–760.

3. **Gryczan, T., S. Contente, and D. Dubnau.** 1980. Molecular cloning of heterologous chromosomal DNA by recombination between a plasmid vector and a homologous resident plasmid in *Bacillus subtilis.* Mol. Gen. Genet. **177:**459–467.

4. **LeBlanc, D. J., and F. P. Hassell.** 1976. Transformation of *Streptococcus sanguis* Challis by plasmid deoxyribonucleic acid from *Streptococcus faecalis.* J. Bacteriol. **128:**347–355.

5. **Macrina, F. L., K. R. Jones, and R. A. Welch.** 1981. Transformation of *Streptococcus sanguis* with monomeric pVA736 plasmid deoxyribonucleic acid. J. Bacteriol. **146:**826–830.

6. **Malke, H.** 1981. Deletion analysis of the streptococcal plasmid cloning vehicle pSM10. FEMS Microbiol. Lett. **11:**27–30.

7. **Malke, H., L. G. Burman, and S. E. Holm.** 1981. Molecular cloning in streptococci: physical mapping of the vehicle plasmid pSM10 and demonstration of intergroup DNA transfer. Mol. Gen. Genet. **181:**259–267.

8. **Malke, H., and S. E. Holm.** 1982. Streptococcal DNA cloning vehicles derived from a plasmid associated with zonal lincomycin resistance. *In* S. E. Holm and P. Christensen (ed.), Basic concepts of streptococci and streptococcal diseases. Redbooks Ltd., Chertsey, England, in press.

9. **Malke, H., W. Reichardt, M. Hartmann, and F. Walter.** 1981. Genetic study of plasmid-associated zonal resistance to lincomycin in *Streptococcus pyogenes.* Antimicrob. Agents Chemother. **19:**91–100.

10. **Porter, R. D., and W. R. Guild.** 1978. Transfection in pneumococcus: single-stranded intermediates in the formation of infective centers. J. Virol. **25:**60–72.

11. **Saunders, C. W., and W. R. Guild.** 1981. Pathway of plasmid transformation in pneumococcus: open circular and linear molecules are active. J. Bacteriol. **146:**517–526.

Relationship Between Base Mismatches and Integration Efficiency in Transformation of *Streptococcus pneumoniae*

J. P. CLAVERYS, V. MÉJEAN, A. M. GASC, AND A. M. SICARD

Centre de Recherche de Biochimie et de Génétique Cellulaires du Centre National de La Recherche Scientifique, 31062 Toulouse, France

In genetic crosses the recombination frequency strongly depends upon the nature of the markers (3, 5, 9, 12, 13, 16; for a review, see 17). This "marker effect" was extensively studied in *Streptococcus pneumoniae*, for which discrete classes of transformation efficiency were described: very high (VHE), high (HE), intermediate (IE), and low (LE) efficiency in the relative ratio of 2.0:1.0:0.4:0.15 (5, 9, 22). In transformation a strand of donor DNA is paired with the opposite recipient strand. It has been proposed that excision and correction of donor DNA induced by some mismatched base pairs of donor-recipient heteroduplexes account for the low efficiency of some markers (4). This hypothesis was substantiated by the identification of mutant strains, denoted *hex*, which are transformed with very high efficiency for all single-site markers (10, 23). We have initiated a program of sequence analysis of a variety of mutants to determine their nucleotide changes from wild type and correlate these changes to their recombinational proficiency. Mutations at the aminopterin resistance locus (*amiA*) were used for this study since many mutations differing in integration efficiency have been mapped both genetically and by restriction enzyme analysis. In this communication we report our results on the relationship between base mispairing and integration efficiencies in transformation of *S. pneumoniae*.

CHOICE OF MARKERS

A partial genetic map of the *amiA* locus which shows the position of some restriction sites pertinent to this study is shown in Fig. 1.

The *amiA22*, *amiA29*, *amiA9*, *amiA10*, and *amiA141* sites were taken for DNA sequence analysis. These sites were chosen because they are located close to a *Bam*HI or an *Eco*RI restriction site, a favored situation for sequence analysis, and because they covered a large spectrum of integration efficiencies. It has been reported that the efficiency of a marker depends on the strand which is used for transformation:

both strands (referred to as light [L] and heavy [H]; 2, 18) are equally corrected for LE markers (2) and neither is corrected for VHE markers (2, 18), whereas the complementary strands are not equally effective in producing transformants for HE markers (2, 18). This last property was called strand preference (18). It is interpreted as correction of one of the two reciprocal mismatched base pairs; the more efficient (preferred) strand can be either the H or the L strand, depending on the marker (18). Markers in the same gene may exhibit opposite strand preference (2).

With a wild-type recipient strain, *amiA9* and *amiA10* behave as LE markers, and *amiA22*, *amiA29*, and *amiA141* are HE markers (2, 5) with a strand preference toward the H strand. Spontaneous reversions of some of these mutations can be isolated in a synthetic medium (19). The revertants exhibit a wild-type phenotype but are not true revertants since the integration efficiency of each marker is changed when the strain carrying their respective reversions is used as recipient (21). Thus, *amiA29* behaved as a VHE marker when the 29*rev* strain was used as recipient, and *amiA9* behaved as an HE marker in the 9*rev* recipient strain. The efficien-

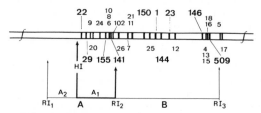

FIG. 1. Physical and genetic map of the *amiA* locus. Markers are ordered according to their map position established from genetic crosses (20). RI and HI designate, respectively, *Eco*RI and *Bam*HI restriction sites. *Eco*RI-generated fragments A and B are, respectively, 1,800 and 2,500 base pairs long. Fragments A₁ and A₂ are by-products of the *Bam*HI hydrolysis of the A fragment. Large numbers correspond to HE and VHE markers; small numbers, to LE markers.

cy of *amiA10* was intermediate (0.4) when tested on the 6*rev*3 strain, which is a reversion at the site of 10 or 6, since *amiA6* and *amiA10* are homoallelic (Fig. 1).

In addition, it is possible to determine the integration efficiency of the mismatches between wild-type and revertant sequences (1). This was done by testing the effect of these mismatches on the integration of neighboring markers normally integrated as HE markers. On the basis of whether the integration of these markers is affected (exclusion effect) or unaffected by the presence of a given mismatch, the efficiency of this mismatch can be deduced.

For example, the mismatched base pair between 29*rev* and wild type does not affect the integration of *amiA22* or *amiA144*, two linked HE markers with opposite strand preference. This mismatch is therefore concluded to be of the VHE type. The mismatch between 9*rev* and wild type, affecting the integration of both *amiA22* and *amiA144* markers, is deduced to be of the LE type (1). In similar experiments the mismatch between wild type on the donor DNA and 6*rev*3 on the recipient behaved as HE with a strand preference for the L strand. Thus, at least one example of each described efficiency class (LE, IE, HE, VHE) can be found in this investigation in which wild-type, mutant, and reverted sequences have been characterized.

MUTATIONAL CHANGES

The starting material for DNA sequence analysis was recombinant plasmids described elsewhere (15). Each carried either a 1,050-base pair *Bam*HI-*Eco*RI fragment (A_1 fragment), on which were located the five genetic sites, or a longer fragment of the *amiA* locus. The strategy used for sequence determination of sites *amiA22*, *amiA29*, and *amiA9* was to linearize the plasmid with *Bam*HI and label either the 5′ or the 3′ end. For *amiA10* and *amiA141*, the 5′ end was labeled after *Eco*RI digestion. These fragments were sequenced by the Maxam and Gilbert method (14). Six hundred twenty bases of the A_1 fragment have been sequenced. Of a possible 6 reading frames, 1 is open and the others contain from 5 to more than 20 stop codons. This enabled us to define the transcribed strand (1).

The mutational changes are shown in Fig. 2. The four strains bearing *amiA22*, *amiA9*, *amiA10*, and *amiA141* carry point mutations. All four mutations introduce nonsense codons in the open reading frame defined above. This is also in agreement with genetic analysis showing that the *amiA9* mutation is suppressible by an informational suppressor of nonsense codons (8).

The *amiA29* mutation is a complex change: the sequence ATGGAT is mutated to ATTTGCT, which results in a frame shift of +1 base. This frame shift mutation leads to a stop codon a few bases downstream. It is not surprising that these five mutants are well blocked by stop codons since most *amiA* mutants were selected for their resistance to the highest concentration of drug expressed by this gene. In Fig. 2 are also shown the sequences for the sites when revertant DNAs were studied. At site 10, three different base pairs were found. The corresponding amino acids would be tryptophan for the wild type and cysteine for the revertant. The reversion 9*rev* is a transversion A→C in the third base of the codon, whereas mutation 9 results from a substitution at the first base. The reversion 29*rev* restores a normal reading frame by deletion of 34 bases covering the mutation *amiA29*.

RELATION BETWEEN THE TYPE OF MISMATCH AND TRANSFORMING EFFICIENCY

When donor and recipient DNAs differ by one-base changes, four pairs of mismatches are expected. Each of these pairs has been found in this study and related to transforming efficiency (Table 1). When there is a transitional change, it results in an LE marker. The two mismatches A/C and G/T are equally strongly corrected since there is no strand preference and the total efficiency of markers carried by these strands is low (0.15). The HE markers result from two transversions, AT↔CG and CG↔GC, leading to two pairs of mismatches: A/G and C/T, C/C and G/G. One member of each pair is corrected and the other is not. The last transversion, AT↔TA, leads to A/A and T/T mismatches and results in an IE marker. Both strands must be corrected, but the relative extent of correction has not yet been determined. This agrees with the proposal that some IE markers are point mutations (9). There is no pair of single-site mismatches to account for VHE markers. The sequence analysis of *amiA29* reveals that a deletion of 34 base pairs behaves as a VHE marker, and as previous genetic work has shown that larger deletions are not recognized by the *hex* system (2, 10, 11) and exhibit a high efficiency of transformation, it is likely that deletions and additions, even of one base, account for VHE markers. As the size of these mutations affects their efficiency of transformation, only short deletions or additions will transform with an efficiency of 1.8 to 2. Therefore, VHE markers are best defined as markers without strand preference that yield transformants with such high efficiency.

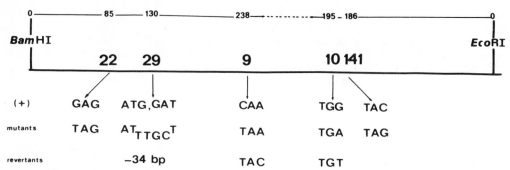

FIG. 2. Base changes at five genetic sites of the *amiA* locus. The A₁ fragment (1,050 base pairs long) limited by *Bam*HI and *Eco*RI restriction sites has been partially sequenced from both ends. The A₁ fragment was obtained from plasmids carrying the wild type, a mutant, or a revertant sequence (15). On the first line are indicated the locations of the genetic sites, taking the *Bam*HI or *Eco*RI site as position O. The second line represents the genetic map. For each site, bases are arrayed by triplets. The partial nucleotide sequence is displayed for the mRNA strand (L strand). The transcribed strand has been defined through phenotypic expression studies (2). The transcription is from left to right (1). The reversion of mutation 29 is a deletion of 34 bases which restores a correct reading frame.

Mismatches of the same type are found at different sites, and they have the same transformation efficiency whatever their location. This suggests that the neighboring sequences do not affect their efficiency. However, since some mismatches have been found only once, more examples are required to test this proposal. Of the eight mismatches, two (A/G and C/C) were not corrected. However, one cannot exclude a very limited correction. The main conclusion of these studies is that the *hex* system is specific for single-site substitution and is able to discriminate between A/G, C/C, and the other six mismatches. A simple explanation of the correction specificity built upon the complementary base-pairing model proposed by Topal and Fresco (24) cannot account for our observations. It seems to be the structure between the mispaired bases which is recognized, rather than a given base per se involved in a mismatch, as we suggested previously (1).

Another open question concerns frame shift mutations. It has been shown that acridine-induced mutations were mainly of the LE type, and evidence has been presented that these mutations were frame shift mutations (7). Our results suggest that the mispairing between wild type and one frame shift mutation (*amiA29*) is

TABLE 1. Efficiency of correction of mismatched bases

Cross			No. of cases	Mismatched base pairs		Relative efficiency[a]
A $\overrightarrow{}\overleftarrow{}$ T	×	G $\overrightarrow{}\overleftarrow{}$ C	2	A/C corrected	G/T corrected	LE (0.15)
A $\overrightarrow{}\overleftarrow{}$ T	×	C $\overrightarrow{}\overleftarrow{}$ G	4	A/G not corrected	C/T corrected	HE (1.1)
C $\overrightarrow{}\overleftarrow{}$ G	×	G $\overrightarrow{}\overleftarrow{}$ C	1	C/C not corrected	G/G corrected	HE (1.1)
A $\overrightarrow{}\overleftarrow{}$ T	×	T $\overrightarrow{}\overleftarrow{}$ A	1	A/A corrected[b]	T/T corrected[b]	IE (0.4)

[a] The relative efficiency is the ratio of aminopterin-resistant or -susceptible transformants to streptomycin-resistant (*str-41*) transformants. For LE markers both strands are equally corrected. For HE markers the corrected strands are fivefold less efficient than the uncorrected strands.

[b] For the IE marker the relative extent of correction has not been determined.

not recognized by the *hex* system. It is possible that the acridine-induced mutations that were studied were a complex of base substitution and frame shift mutations. This could explain the low efficiency of transformation of these mutations without need for recognition of frame shift per se by the *hex* system.

CONCLUSION

The marker effect in pneumococci results from the nature of the mutation. If the mutation is a short deletion (or addition), the relative transformation efficiency is maximal (1.8 to 2). The longer the deletion, the smaller will be the efficiency (9). If the mutation is a single-site substitution, different mismatches are possible. When the mismatched bases are A/G-C/T or C/C-G/G, one strand is well transformed without correction; the other, being strongly corrected, is transformed poorly. The total efficiency of such markers is high (1 to 1.2). When the mismatched bases are A/A-T/T, transformation efficiency is 0.4. When the transition type of mismatch occurs, i.e., A/C and G/T, both strands are poorly transformed, and the resulting efficiency is 0.10 to 0.15 (LE). This explains why the mutagens we have used—nitrous acid, hydroxylamine, ethyl ethane sulfonate (6, 20), which are known to induce transitions preferentially—yield only LE mutants. Interestingly, three of the four mismatch couples were correctly assigned by Lacks to their efficiency class on the basis of deductions from mutagen specificity (nitrous acid, ethyl methane sulfonate, and H_2O_2; 9). However, it was assumed that H_2O_2, by attacking G, induced the transversion GC→CG, although there was no chemical evidence for such specificity. Moreover, this assignment was deduced from studies of mutation and reversion induction at only one genetic site, with the assumption that sequence changes occurred at the same base, which may not necessarily be true (see, for examples, *amiA9*, *9rev*; *amiA29*, *29rev*).

It was the selection and the study of spontaneous mutants and revertants that led us to all kinds of mismatches. It is possible that marker effects have been observed only rarely in other bacteria, such as *Enterobacteriaceae* (3), because most markers tested were induced by these mutagens. In any case it will be interesting to learn whether the specificity of recognition that we have described is general and applies to other genetic systems.

LITERATURE CITED

1. **Claverys, J. P., V. Mejean, A. M. Gasc, F. Galibert, and A. M Sicard.** 1981. Base specificity of mismatch repair in *Streptococcus pneumoniae*. Nucleic Acids Res. **9**:2267–2280.
2. **Claverys, J. P., M. Roger, and A. M. Sicard.** 1980. Excision and repair of mismatched base pairs in transformation of *Streptococcus pneumoniae*. Mol. Gen. Genet. **178**:191–201.
3. **Drapeau, G. R., W. J. Brammar, and C. Yanofsky.** 1957. Aminoacid replacements of the glutamic acid residue at position 48 in the tryptophan synthetase A protein of *Escherichia coli*. J. Mol. Biol. **35**:357–367.
4. **Ephrussi-Taylor, H., and T. C. Gray.** 1966. Genetic studies of recombining DNA in pneumococcal transformation. J. Gen. Physiol. **49**:211–231.
5. **Ephrussi-Taylor, H., A. M. Sicard, and R. Kamen.** 1965. Genetic recombination in DNA-induced transformation of pneumococcus. I. The problem of relative efficiency of transforming factors. Genetics **51**:455–475.
6. **Gasc, A. M., and A. M. Sicard.** 1972. Mutagénèse induite par l'hydroxylamine sur l'ADN du pneumocoque. C. R. Acad. Sci. **275**:285–287.
7. **Gasc, A. M., and A. M. Sicard.** 1978. Genetic studies of acridine-induced mutants in *Streptococcus pneumoniae*. Genetics **90**:1–18.
8. **Gasc, A. M., J. Vacher, R. Buckingham, and A. M. Sicard.** 1979. Characterization of an amber suppressor in pneumococcus. Mol. Gen. Genet. **172**:295–301.
9. **Lacks, S.** 1966. Integration efficiency and genetic recombination in pneumococcal transformation. Genetics **53**:207–235.
10. **Lacks, S.** 1970. Mutants of *Diplococcus pneumoniae* that lack deoxyribonucleases and other activities possibly pertinent to genetic transformation. J. Bacteriol. **101**:373–383.
11. **Lataste, H., J. P. Claverys, and A. M. Sicard.** 1980. Physical and genetic characterization of deletions in *Streptococcus pneumoniae*. J. Bacteriol. **144**:422–424.
12. **Leblon, G.** 1972. Mechanism of gene conversion in *Ascobolus immersus*. I. Existence of a correlation between the origin of mutants induced by different mutagens and their conversion spectrum. Mol. Gen. Genet. **115**:36–48.
13. **Lieb, M.** 1976. Mapping missense and nonsense mutations in gene CI of bacteriophage lambda: marker effects. Mol. Gen. Genet. **146**:285–290.
14. **Maxam, A. M., and W. Gilbert.** 1980. Sequencing end-labeled DNA with base-specific chemical cleavages. Methods Enzymol. **65**:499–560.
15. **Mejean, V., J. P. Claverys, H. Vasseghi, and A. M. Sicard.** 1981. Rapid cloning of specific DNA fragments of *Streptococcus pneumoniae* by vector integration into the chromosome followed by endonucleolytic excision. Gene **15**:289–293.
16. **Norkin, L. C.** 1970. Marker-specific effects in genetic recombination. J. Mol. Biol. **51**:633–655.
17. **Radding, C. M.** 1978. Genetic recombination: strand transfer and mismatch repair. Annu. Rev. Biochem. **47**:847–880.
18. **Roger, M.** 1977. Mismatch excision and possible polarity effects result in preferred deoxyribonucleic acid strand of integration in pneumococcal transformation. J. Bacteriol. **129**:298–304.
19. **Sicard, A. M.** 1964. A new synthetic medium for *Diplococcus pneumoniae* and its use for the study of reciprocal transformation at the *amiA* locus. Genetics **50**:31–44.
20. **Sicard, A. M., and H. Ephrussi-Taylor.** 1965. Genetic recombination in DNA-induced transformation of pneumococcus. II. Mapping the *amiA* region. Genetics **52**:1207–1227.
21. **Sicard, A. M., and H. Ephrussi-Taylor.** 1966. Recombination génétique dans la transformation chez le pneumocoque. Etude des reversions au locus *amiA*. C.R. Acad. Sci. **262**:2305–2308.
22. **Tiraby, G., and A. M. Sicard.** 1973. Integration efficien-

cies of spontaneous mutant alleles of *amiA* locus in pneumococcal transformation. J. Bacteriol. **116**:1130–1135.

23. **Tiraby, G., and A. M. Sicard.** 1973. Integration efficiency in DNA-induced transformation of pneumococcus. II. Genetic studies of mutant integrating all the markers with a high efficiency. Genetics **75**:35–48.

24. **Topal, M. D., and J. R. Fresco.** 1976. Complementary base pairing and the origin of substitution mutations. Nature (London) **263**:285–289.

Synthesis and Function of *Streptococcus mutans* Cell Surface Proteins in *Escherichia coli*

R. CURTISS III, J. P. ROBESON,[1] R. BARLETTA, Y. ABIKO,[2] AND M. SMORAWINSKA[3]

Institute of Dental Research and Department of Microbiology, University of Alabama in Birmingham, Birmingham, Alabama 35294

Streptococcus mutans is a principal etiological agent of dental caries (5). On the basis of the isolation and characterization of enzymes and proteins and the identification of mutants defective in cariogenicity, it has been proposed that *S. mutans* virulence is due to (i) a sucrose-independent adherence to the pellicle-coated tooth surface, (ii) a sucrose-dependent adherence and aggregation of *S. mutans* cells to the tooth surface to result in the formation of dental plaque, and (iii) the production of lactic acid from the degradation of extracellular and intracellular complex polysaccharides and the metabolism of mono-, di-, and trisaccharides. The last event results in demineralization of the tooth surface and the commencement of tooth decay (3).

A complete genetic and biochemical definition of the proteins and processes necessary for pathogenicity would require the ability to manipulate *S. mutans* genetically. Unfortunately, means for the genetic analysis of *S. mutans* are, at this stage, primitive at best. Thus, we chose to use recombinant DNA techniques to analyze *S. mutans* gene products thought to be involved in pathogenicity by cloning the genes encoding these proteins into suitable strains of *Escherichia coli* K-12. Ultimately, one could use the cloned gene products or genes to introduce specific gene mutations into *S. mutans* to evaluate their impact on cariogenicity.

EXPRESSION OF *S. MUTANS* GENES IN *E. COLI*

We have demonstrated that both plasmid and chromosomal genetic information is expressed in *E. coli* (2). Proteins specified by streptococcal plasmids are synthesized in *E. coli* although such streptococcal plasmids are unable to replicate in *E. coli* without the aid of either DNA

polymerase I or an *E. coli* replicon (4). About 35% of the mutations that confer upon *E. coli* the inability to synthesize amino acids, purines, and pyrimidines and the inability to metabolize carbohydrates can be complemented by *S. mutans* genetic information (2). Indeed, the *S. mutans* gene for aspartic acid semialdehyde dehydrogenase (*asd*) functions in *E. coli* better than do most *E. coli* genes, and the promoter for this *S. mutans* gene has a higher affinity for *E. coli* RNA polymerase than do the vast majority of *E. coli* promoters (2). The presence of the *S. mutans asd* gene on the multicopy plasmid pBR322 results in an *E. coli* cell which synthesizes 7% of its total protein as the *asd* gene product (E. K. Jagusztyn-Krynicka, M. Smorawinska, and R. Curtiss III, J. Gen. Microbiol., in press).

SELECTION OF *S. MUTANS* GENES THAT SPECIFY CELL SURFACE-ASSOCIATED PROTEINS

We have been able to identify *E. coli* recombinant clones containing *S. mutans* genetic information specifying *S. mutans* cell surface-associated proteins and enzymes. Two different methods have been employed. In the first, shotgun cloning was done with cosmid cloning vectors (1), with screening of recombinant vectors contained in *E. coli* cells with the thermosensitive λcI857 prophage on agarose medium containing high-titer antibodies raised to *S. mutans* extracellular proteins (Fig. 1). After overnight incubation of clones at 30°C to form colonies, lysis of cells within colonies was effected by shifting the temperature to 42°C. Release of *S. mutans* protein antigens and diffusion in the agarose resulted in precipitin bands around those colonies expressing a gene for an *S. mutans* cell surface protein. In this way, many recombinant clones have been identified, one of which specifies the *spaA* protein, a 210,000-molecular-weight protein on the cell surface of *S. mutans* (R. G. Holt, S. Saito, Y. Abiko, M. Smorawinska, and R. Curtiss III, unpublished data). We believe that this protein may be involved in sucrose-independent adherence to the

---

[1] Present address: Laboratorio de Microbiologia, Universidad Catolica de Valparaiso, Casilla 4059, Valparaiso, Chile.
[2] Present address: Department of Biochemistry, Nihon University, Tokyo, Japan.
[3] Present address: Institute of Microbiology, University of Warsaw, Warsaw, Poland.

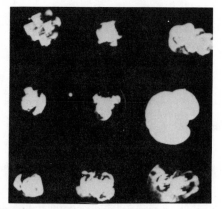

FIG. 1. In situ immunoassay for *S. mutans* extracellular proteins. An immunoprecipitin ring surrounds the bacterial colony that produces an antigen reacting with antisera against *S. mutans* cell surface proteins. All colonies contain λcI857 and are ampicillin resistant. Precipitin formation was dependent on prior induction of cell lysis by growth at 42°C.

pellicle-coated tooth surface. The second method for obtaining such clones has been to directly select clones able to metabolize raffinose or sucrose. The latter selection on sucrose has worked since many *S. mutans* cell surface proteins synthesized by *E. coli* are transported across the cytoplasmic membrane into the *E. coli* periplasm where they can hydrolyze sucrose. One clone specifying a glucosyltransferase has been studied most thoroughly (J. P. Robeson, Ph.D. thesis, University of Alabama, Birmingham, 1981; J. P. Robeson, R. G. Barletta, and R. Curtiss III, in preparation).

CHARACTERIZATION OF THE PRODUCT OF THE *S. MUTANS gtfA* GENE CLONED INTO *E. COLI*

Approximately 20 recombinant clones that grow on raffinose plus isopropyl β-thiogalactopyranoside, but grow more slowly on sucrose, were obtained by shotgun cloning of DNA from derivatives of the serotype *c S. mutans* strains PS14 and GS-5 (Robeson, Ph.D. thesis; Robeson et al., in preparation). Toluene treatment of the

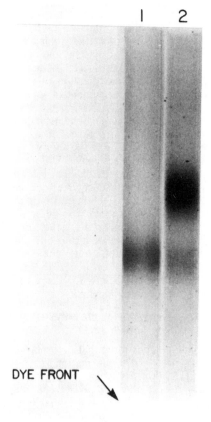

FIG. 3. Analysis in nondenaturing polyacrylamide gels of sucrose-cleaving enzymes present in crude cell extracts. Lane 1: χ1274(pYA601). Lane 2: *S. mutans* UAB90. Gels were incubated in 0.1 M sucrose in 0.5 M sodium phosphate buffer, pH 7, for 2 h at 37°C and then placed for 30 min in 0.1% triphenyl tetrazolium chloride in 1 N NaOH.

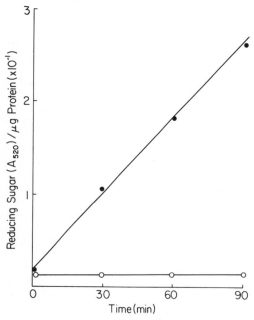

FIG. 2. Presence of a sucrose-cleaving enzyme in χ1274(pYA601) toluene-treated cells. Symbols: ●, χ1274(pYA601) cells; ○, χ1274(pBR322) cells.

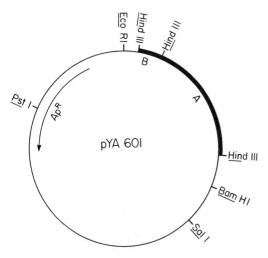

FIG. 4. Physical map of pYA601. The narrow line represents pBR322 DNA, 4,362 base pairs in length, and the thick line represents *S. mutans* UAB90 DNA that contains the coding sequence for the *gtf*A enzyme. The *S. mutans* DNA insert consists of two *Hind*III restriction fragments, A and B, of 1,360 and 370 base pairs in length, respectively. The arrow that runs counterclockwise with respect to the *Eco*RI restriction site of pBR322 spans the pBR322 coding sequence specifying ampicillin resistance (Ap^r). The total molecular mass of pYA601 is about 3.9 megadaltons.

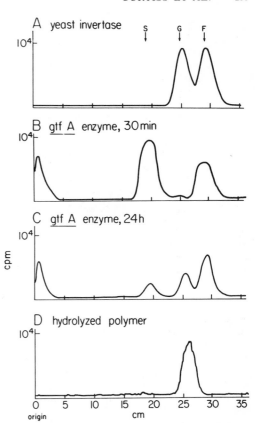

FIG. 5. Scan of descending paper radiochromatograms of enzyme reaction products from [^{14}C]sucrose. (A) Products of reaction with yeast invertase. (B) Products after 30 min of reaction with purified *gtfA* enzyme from χ1274(pYA601) cells. (C) Products after 24 h of reaction with purified *gtfA* enzyme from χ1274(pYA601) cells. (D) Product of acid hydrolysis of radioactive material near the origin in B. Arrows indicate the places at which nonradioactive sucrose (S), glucose (G), and fructose (F) migrated in the chromatogram.

cells containing one such recombinant clone, pYA601, resulted in the linear generation of reducing sugar from sucrose (Fig. 2). Analysis of proteins specified by this *E. coli* recombinant on nondenaturing polyacrylamide gels indicated that the rapidly migrating activity was also present in *S. mutans* strains and distinct from a slower-migrating sucrose-hydrolyzing activity (Fig. 3). Restriction enzyme analysis of pYA601 plasmid DNA resulted in a restriction enzyme map (Fig. 4) which indicates the presence of a 1,730-base-pair insert containing two *Hind*III fragments inserted in the *Hind*III site of pBR322. Both *Hind*III fragments A and B are necessary for ability to grow on sucrose or raffinose plus isopropyl β-thiogalactopyranoside and ability to generate reducing sugar from sucrose. The sucrose-hydrolyzing enzyme has a molecular weight of 55,000, based on studies using minicells purified from a minicell-producing strain containing the pYA601 plasmid. On the basis of this molecular weight characterization, it was possible to purify the gene product to homogeneity by using a combination of DEAE-cellulose chromatography, gel-filtration chromatography, and ammonium sulfate precipitation (Robeson, Ph.D. thesis). Using the purified en-

zyme and uniformly ^{14}C-labeled sucrose as a substrate, we found that this enzyme is a glucosyltransferase yielding stoichiometric amounts of fructose and glucan (Fig. 5). Elution of the slowly migrating radioactive compound from the paper chromatograms (Fig. 5B and C) and hydrolysis with trifluoroacetic acid resulted in conversion of the product to glucose (Fig. 5D). The addition of dextran T10 did not enhance the rate of glucan synthesis. The use of sucrose labeled in the fructose moiety did not result in the generation of any radioactive glucan. Thus, this particular glucosyltransferase does not require a dextran primer, and probably uses water as the initial acceptor. Of some interest was the finding

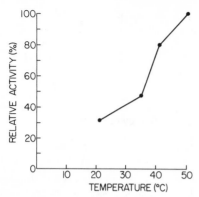

FIG. 6. Effect of temperature on the rate of reaction of *gtfA* enzyme from χ1274(pYA601). Purified enzyme was incubated at the indicated temperatures in 50 mM sodium phosphate buffer, pH 7. Enzyme activity was measured and expressed as a percentage of the maximum rate obtained.

FIG. 7. Effect of incubation at 52°C on the sucrose-cleaving enzyme activity in *S. mutans* UAB90 crude cell extract. Lane 1: *S. mutans* crude cell extract treated at 52°C for 5 min. Lane 2: Unheated control. The enzyme activities were analyzed in nondenaturing polyacrylamide gels (see Fig. 3 legend).

(Fig. 5C) that longer times of incubation of the enzyme with the substrate sucrose yielded not only a diminished amount of sucrose but the appearance of glucose. This particular glucosyltransferase enzyme thus has a glucanase activity which can degrade the glucan, with liberation of glucose. Such glucanase activity seems to be stimulated, however, by the presence of free fructose.

The *gtfA* gene product has a pH optimum of about 6.5 and a K_m for sucrose of 1.25 mM, whether the rate of reducing sugar generation or the rate of glucan synthesis is measured. Using the purified enzyme obtained from *E. coli* recombinant clones, we were able to raise antibodies against the glucosyltransferase and to show that 10 to 20% of this *S. mutans* cell surface protein is transported across the *E. coli* cytoplasmic membrane into the periplasmic space. This explains why *E. coli* strains containing the pYA601 recombinant plasmid can grow on sucrose as the sole carbon source. The *gtfA* gene product in the *E. coli* periplasm also permits *E. coli* to synthesize glucan. *E. coli perA* mutants defective in transport of *E. coli* periplasmic proteins (6) do not affect translocation of the *S. mutans gtfA* gene product into the *E. coli* periplasm (Robeson, Ph.D. thesis; Robeson et al., in preparation). Characterization of the periplasmic and cytoplasmic forms of the *gtfA* protein in *E. coli* failed to reveal any molecular differences, a result that suggests a new means for protein translocation.

Using antibodies against the *gtfA* protein, we were able to immunoprecipitate the activity in *E. coli* as well as the rapidly migrating activity on nondenaturing gels specified by *S. mutans* strains (see Fig. 3). Also of interest is the fact that this particular enzyme activity is reasonably thermostable and has increased activity even at 50°C (Fig. 6). As a consequence, treatment of *S. mutans* cell extracts at 50°C for 5 min resulted in the total inactivation of the slowly migrating sucrose-hydrolyzing activity with only a minor diminution of the activity of the rapidly migrating material on nondenaturing polyacrylamide gels (Fig. 7).

It is evident that recombinant DNA techniques for cloning *S. mutans* genetic information in *E. coli* have resulted in much useful information. Streptococcal genes are readily expressed in *E. coli*, and we have been able to characterize gene products not heretofore isolatable from *S. mutans* in the absence of competing or contaminating *S. mutans* gene products, or both. As a consequence, we have identified a glucosyl-transferase enzyme activity not previously described which may serve in an important capacity for the virulence of *S. mutans*. Using the cloned *gtfA* gene in *E. coli* and antibodies directed against this protein, we are now selecting *S. mutans* mutants devoid of this enzyme activity as a means of characterizing the influence of this enzyme on the cariogenicity of *S. mutans*.

It should be evident from our initial results that these techniques can be used effectively for the genetic analysis of other streptococcal species of medical and agricultural importance.

ACKNOWLEDGMENTS

We thank Pat Pierce for help in the preparation of this manuscript.

Research was supported by Public Health Service grant DE-02670 from the National Institute of Dental Research.

LITERATURE CITED

1. **Collins, J., and B. Hohn.** 1978. Cosmids: a type of plasmid gene-cloning vector that is packageable *in vitro* in bacteriophage λ heads. Proc. Natl. Acad. Sci. U.S.A. **75**:4242–4246.
2. **Curtiss, R., III, E. K. Jagusztyn-Krynicka, J. B. Hansen, M. Smorawinska, Y. Abiko, and G. Cardineau.** 1981. Expression of *Streptococcus mutans* plasmid and chromosomal genes in *Escherichia coli* K-12. Third Symposium of Drug Resistance in Bacteria. In press.
3. **Gibbons, R. J., and J. Van Houte.** 1975. Dental caries. Annu. Rev. Med. **26**:121–136.
4. **Hansen, J. B., Y. Abiko, and R. Curtiss III.** 1981. Characterization of the *Streptococcus mutans* plasmid pVA318 cloned into *Escherichia coli*. Infect. Immun. **31**:1034–1043.
5. **Littleton, N. W., S. Kakehashi, and R. J. Fitzgerald.** 1970. Recovery of specific "caries-inducing" streptococci from carious lesions in the teeth of children. Arch. Oral Biol. **15**:461–463.
6. **Wanner, B. L., A. Sarthy, and J. Beckwith.** 1979. *Escherichia coli* pleiotropic mutant that reduces amounts of several periplasmic and outer membrane proteins. J. Bacteriol. **140**:229–239.

III. BACTERIAL ADHESION IN PATHOGENESIS

(from the ASM Conference on Bacterial Adhesion in Pathogenesis, held 2–4 December 1981 in Atlanta, Georgia)

Bacterial Adhesion in Pathogenesis: an Introductory Statement

S. C. HOLT

Department of Microbiology, University of Massachusetts, Amherst, Massachusetts 01003

Morphological observation of diverse environments has revealed the existence of specific associations between bacteria and various substrates of their environment. The bacteria involved in these associations have, as integral parts of their cell surface, one or more surface-associated structures or components which most probably take part in adherence phenomena. These components include pili, fimbriae, surface antigens, surface-associated mucopolysaccharides, and lipoteichoic acids (see, for example, 3, 9–11, 23, 29, 40, 67). Some of the earliest studies of these associations were done by marine and soil scientists (73, 74), and revealed quite clearly that at least two phases of attachment occurred: an initial attachment phase, which was reversible and under van der Waals forces, and an irreversible phase, which was mediated by the synthesis of extracellular polymeric material (1, 32, 38, 44, 49, 73, 74).

The last several years have witnessed a considerable explosion of information about the resident microflora of selected ecological niches in humans, primates, rodents, and ruminants, all of which contain complex microbiotas (6, 55, 56). The microbiota of the mouth is especially complex, since numerous bacterial attachment mechanisms are possible—attachment to hard enamel surfaces and to epithelial and mucosal surfaces, as well as bacterium-bacterium interactions (18, 19, 65). Studies of the microbial ecology of the human mouth led to early convincing evidence of a relationship between bacterial adherence and natural colonization. Thus, the variety of surfaces in the oral cavity provide a focal point for exacting microbial specificities. Interestingly, many analyses of these bacterium-surface associations follow Langmuir isotherm kinetics. Since these kinetics are limited to monolayer adsorption, they may not adequately describe cell-cell interactions. The kinetics observed are also dependent upon a variety of culture-related variables, including reaction temperature, culture age, bacterial cell concentration, and hydrogen ion concentration. In a majority of these kinetic studies, laboratory-maintained bacterial strains adhered much more weakly to a substrate than did fresh bacterial isolates.

The specificity of bacterial adherence and the role that this selective adherence plays in tropisms and colonization by both invading and autochthonous bacteria is well documented (8, 12, 43). For example, members of the genus *Lactobacillus* colonize the surface of nonsecreting, keratinized epithelial cells in the rat and mouse stomach, but not the surface of secreting stomach epithelia. *Streptococcus pyogenes* shows a specificity of attachment to the tongue, whereas *Escherichia coli* for the most part attaches to bladder mucosa and similar tissues (18). Similarly, fresh clinical isolates of bacteria associated with genital tract infections attach in higher numbers to genital tract cells than do noninfecting microorganisms. In addition, several investigators (16, 26, 62) have observed that *E. coli* isolated from acute pyelonephritis patients adhered with greater tenacity to uroepithelial cells from normal women than did strains isolated from patients with asymptomatic bacteriuria. Group A streptococci isolated from rheumatic fever patients attached in greater numbers to buccal epithelial cells of rheumatic fever patients than to those of normal individuals (58). The greater adherence of *Pseudomonas aeruginosa* to damaged heart valves when compared with normal heart valves suggests rather strongly that the adherence process is a very specific one (Ramirez-Ronda, Clin. Res. 26:404A, 1978). These studies point strongly to a high degree of bacterial cell-tissue specificity.

The surface characteristics of the host's epithelial tissue itself must also play a role in the adherence phenomenon. Epithelial tissues most probably have limited receptor sites which can absorb a given number of bacteria. Further, the binding of bacteria to specific epithelial cell receptors may be through specific carbohydrate molecules, notably, through mannose-containing carbohydrates (46). However, the role of mannose-containing carbohydrates in adherence is open to interpretation. Further, several observations point to the possibility that there may be multiple surface components involved in bacterial colonization of host tissue. For example, *S. mutans* specifically interacts with several high-molecular-weight mucinous glycoproteins in whole saliva and parotid secretions (42, 66). In addition, *S. mutans* also synthesizes extracellular glucans which result in cellular accumulation on hard surfaces (31, 41, 42, 57). Glycosyl transferases elaborated by these organisms also bind to glucan molecules, possibly serving as an additional glucan-binding receptor (30, 33).

The ability of bacterial cells to interact with host tissue in a specific manner is thought to be a primary event in which most indigenous and pathogenic microorganisms initiate the colonization of a host. The autochthonous bacteria with a pathogenic potential are referred to as opportunistic pathogens (6). Thus, bacteria from one tissue or organ can take advantage of the loss of a normal host defense barrier, colonize, and possibly infect a normally "sterile" organ. According to Cheng and his associates (6), bacteria entering a favorable natural environment produce mixtures of attached bacteria as well as motile cells. The attached bacteria can grow and colonize large areas of an organ or tissue, and the motile cells extend the colonization to new surfaces, producing new microcolonies. The movement of these "swarmer cells" to new locations where they establish microcolonies has been demonstrated with gliding strains of *Capnocytophaga* (51). The microcolonies which are able to survive in the new and possibly "adverse environment" do so by being protected by a ruthenium red-attached glycocalyx. This persistence can lead to a pathogenic situation or potential in these new locations.

Surface fibrils and pili (the term pilus should be reserved for conjugative fibrils) have long been implicated in attachment of bacteria to tissue surfaces, with a strong positive correlation between adhesion and virulence, especially as related to mucous surfaces (see 64 for pertinent references). Early observations showed that, for the most part, adherent bacteria, especially gram-negative ones, were usually covered with thin, straight surface hairs or fibrils (23, 61, 63, 64). Nonadherent strains were free from these hairs. For the most part, these early observations dealing with pili (that is, fimbriae) were concentrated on *Neisseria gonorrhoeae* and *E. coli*. Substantial evidence indicates that fimbriated gonococci adhere to tissue surfaces in human gonococcal infections (22, 53, 63).

In an interesting study, McGee et al. (34–36), Melley et al. (37), and Johnson et al. (24) employed human fallopian tube organ culture to ascertain the course of infection of the gonococcus. Two phases of infection were noticed: an attachment phase and an invasive phase. Fimbriated gonococci attached to the cultured fallopian tubes with a much higher frequency and caused concomitantly greater damage than non-

fimbriated organisms. The damage to the ciliated cells was probably mediated by one or more toxic factors, possibly lipopolysaccharide. Of interest was their observation that, although greater numbers of fimbriated gonococci attached to fallopian tube mucosa, nonfimbriated cells also attached and damaged the mucosa, albeit more slowly than the fimbriated gonococci. Thus, factors other than fimbriae may mediate gonococcal attachment in the fallopian tube organ culture system (35, 36).

In addition to fimbriae, other surface structures, sometimes referred to as fibrils and capsules, have been investigated as possible mediators of bacterial attachment (see 2, 61, 66 for pertinent references). A variety of gram-negative bacteria and several gram-positive ones have been observed to possess such surface components (7, 21, 27, 28, 47, 48, 52, 72). In *Actinomyces viscosus*, for example, a prerequisite for virulence is the ability to attach to and colonize both the tooth surface and gingival crevice areas (57, 66). Avirulent strains of *A. viscosus* lack surface fibrils, do not attach to surfaces, do not colonize a host, and presumably do not cause disease (4).

Other surface components which have received attention as mediators of adhesion are the K88 and K99 antigens (5, 35, 39). These surface antigens, which cover the surface of *E. coli* and other gram-negative procaryotes, are thinner and more undulate than type 1 fimbriae. Recent investigations reveal that these antigens are coded for by plasmids, or more precisely, "the plasmids which code for them may contribute to host-parasite specificity" (59, 60, 69–71). Similar to the K88 and K99 antigens, and also plasmid coded, is Evan's colonization or virulence factor antigen, CFA/1 (13–15). Loss of the CFA/1 plasmid in certain *E. coli* strains which retain their ability to secrete enterotoxin results in the loss of strain pathogenicity. Interestingly, these *E. coli* strains still retain their ability to synthesize type 1 fimbriae—thus, these fimbriae may not alone be sufficient for virulence in these *E. coli* strains.

Not to be overlooked as a possible virulence-associated factor is the flagellum of certain gram-negative organisms. *Vibrio cholerae* cells, for example, possess multiple recognition systems which are separately associated with attachment to erythrocytes, brush borders, and intestinal mucosa (17, 18, 20, 25, 54). Nonmotile *V. cholerae* cells are both less virulent and less adhesive to intestinal brush border membranes, as well as possessing little hemagglutination activity. Jones and Freter (25) suggested that the flagellum of *V. cholerae* may carry, or have associated with it, some adhesive recognition component.

I have already mentioned that the surface of most bacteria is covered with amorphous material, in morphology similar to procaryotic capsules, microcapsules, or fuzzy coat layers, that is, the glycocalyx described by Costerton et al. (8). This surface layer consists of densely distributed surface fibrils of glycosaminoglycan composition. The anionic character of these compounds may permit them to function to trap nutrients and cations, as well as to protect against attack by viruses and phagocytes. The glycocalyx may also function as a protective barrier against the humoral defense system. This ruthenium red-positive material clearly permits bacteria to adhere to host cell surfaces. Kasper et al. (29) and Onderdonk et al. (48) have performed experiments to show that the ruthenium red capsule of *Bacteroides fragilis* may play a role in abscess formation. Their work with purified *B. fragilis* capsules shows quite clearly that it may have a major function in virulence.

The capsular K-1 antigen of *E. coli* may function similarly to that found in *Bacteroides*, being responsible for invasiveness of the bacteria (50, 54). Similar observations point to the fuzzy coat, or M protein, of *S. pyogenes* as a major determinant of host cell adherence as well as cell virulence (11).

Finally, Beachey and Ofek (3) and Ofek et al. (45) have shown that streptococcal lipoteichoic acid will bind to epithelial cell surfaces in addition to blocking the absorption of intact cells. The binding of lipoteichoic acid is of interest because of its potential role in the initiation of certain inflammatory diseases. Wicken and Knox (68) suggested that lipoteichoic acid may serve to carry various streptococcal antigens and to bind them to specific organ tissues where they could provoke immunocytotoxic effects.

It is clear that the adherence of bacteria to mammalian cells is determined by highly specific interactions, in many instances interactions which are mediated by specific macromolecules. The nature of these interactions most probably involves the formation of specific protein-carbohydrate complexes, similar to that observed in plant lectin interactions with their specific sugar substrates.

In several instances the bacterial component thought responsible for adherence has been isolated, purified, and chemically characterized, so that the degree of specificity which exists between these purified adhesions and mammalian receptors is now starting to be investigated and understood (see, for example, 2).

The results of numerous experiments already reported, as well as new observations reported in this volume, will surely reinforce the notion that adherence is an extremely complex process and that both bacterial and mammalian cell properties play a paramount role in determining the selective adherences involved.

LITERATURE CITED

1. **Beachey, E. H. (ed.).** 1980. Bacterial adherence (Receptors and recognition, series B, vol. 6). Chapman and Hall, London.
2. **Beachey, E. H.** 1981. Bacterial adherence: adhesion-receptor interactions mediating the attachment of bacteria to mucosal surfaces. J. Infect. Dis. **143:**325–345.
3. **Beachey, E. H., and I. Ofek.** 1976. Epithelial cell binding of Group A streptococci by lipoteichoic acid on fimbriae denuded of M protein. J. Exp. Med. **143:**759–771.
4. **Brecher, S. M., J. van Houte, and B. F. Hammond.** 1978. Role of colonization in the virulence of *Actinomyces viscosus* strains T14-Vi and T14-Av. Infect. Immun. **22:**603–614.
5. **Burrows, M. R., R. Sellwood, and R. A. Gibbons.** 1976. Haemagglutinating and adhesive properties associated with the K99 antigen of bovine strains of *Escherichia coli.* J. Gen. Microbiol. **96:**269–275.
6. **Cheng, K.-J., R. T. Irvin, and J. W. Costerton.** 1981. Autochthonous and pathogenic colonization of animal tissues by bacteria. Can. J. Microbiol. **27:**461–490.
7. **Clark, W. B., L. L. Bammann, and R. J. Gibbons.** 1978. Comparative estimates of bacterial affinities and adsorption sites on hydroxyapatite surfaces. Infect. Immun. **19:**846–853.
8. **Costerton, J. W., G. G. Geesey, and K.-J. Cheng.** 1978. How bacteria stick. Sci. Am. **238:**86–95.
9. **Duguid, J. P., and R. R. Gillies.** 1957. Fimbriae and adhesive properties in dysentery bacilli. J. Pathol. Bacteriol. **74:**397–411.
10. **Duguid, J. P., I. W. Smith, G. Dempster, and P. N. Edmunds.** 1955. Nonflagellar filamentous appendages ("fibriae") and haemagglutinating activity in *Bacterium coli.* J. Pathol. Bacteriol. **70:**335–348.
11. **Ellen, R. P., and R. J. Gibbons.** 1972. M protein associated adherence of *Streptococcus pyogenes* to epithelial surfaces: prerequisite for virulence. Infect. Immun. **5:**826–830.
12. **Ellen, R. P., and R. J. Gibbons.** 1974. Parameters affecting the adherence and tissue tropisms of *Streptococcus pyogenes.* Infect. Immun. **9:**85–91.
13. **Evans, D. G., and D. J. Evans, Jr.** 1978. New surface-associated heat-labile colonization factor antigen (CFA/II) produced by enterotoxigenic *Escherichia coli* of serogroups O6 and O8. Infect. Immun. **21:**638–647.
14. **Evans, D. G., D. J. Evans, Jr., W. S. Tjoa, and H. L. Dupont.** 1978. Detection and characterization of colonization factor of enterotoxigenic *Escherichia coli* isolated from adults with diarrhea. Infect. Immun. **19:**727–736.
15. **Evans, D. G., R. P. Silver, D. J. Evans, Jr., D. G. Chase, and S. L. Gorbach.** 1975. Plasmid-controlled colonization factor associated with virulence in *Escherichia coli* enterotoxigenic for humans. Infect. Immun. **12:**656–667.
16. **Fowler, J. E., Jr., and T. A. Stamey.** 1977. Studies of introital colonization in women with recurrent urinary infections. VII. The role of bacterial adherence. J. Urol. **117:**472–476.
17. **Freter, R.** 1969. Studies on the mechanism of action of intestinal antibody in experimental cholera. Tex. Rep. Biol. Med. **27:**299–316.
18. **Gibbons, R. J., and J. Van Houte.** 1971. Selective bacterial adherence to oral epithelial surfaces and its role as an ecological determinant. Infect. Immun. **3:**567–573.

19. **Gibbons, R. J., and J. Van Houte.** 1975. Bacterial adherence in oral microbial ecology. Annu. Rev. Microbiol. **29**:19–44.

20. **Guentzel, M. N., and L. J. Berry.** 1975. Motility as a virulence factor for *Vibrio cholerae*. Infect. Immun. **11**:890–897.

21. **Holt, S. C., A. C. R. Tanner, and S. S. Socransky.** 1980. Morphology and ultrastructure of oral strains of *Actinobacillus actinomycetemcomitans* and *Haemophilus aphrophilus*. Infect. Immun. **30**:588–600.

22. **James, A. N., J. M. Knox, and R. P. Williams.** 1976. Attachment of gonococci to sperm. Influence of physical and chemical factors. Br. J. Vener. Dis. **52**:129–135.

23. **Jephcott, A. E., A. Reyn, and A. Birch-Anderson.** 1971. *Neisseria gonorrhoeae*. III. Demonstration of presumed appendages to cells from different colony types. Acta Pathol. Microbiol. Scand. Sect. B **79**:437–439.

24. **Johnson, A. P., D. T. Taylor-Robinson, and Z. A. McGee.** 1977. Species specificity of attachment and damage to oviduct mucosa by *Neisseria gonorrhoeae*. Infect. Immun. **18**:833–839.

25. **Jones, G. W., and R. Freter.** 1976. Adhesive properties of *Vibrio cholerae*: nature of the interaction with isolated rabbit brush border membranes and human erythrocytes. Infect. Immun. **14**:240–245.

26. **Kallenius, G., and J. Winberg.** 1978. Bacterial adherence to periurethral epithelial cells in girls prone to urinary-tract infections. Lancet **ii**:540–543.

27. **Kasper, D. L.** 1976. The polysaccharide capsule of *Bacteroides fragilis* subspecies *fragilis*: immunochemical and morphologic definition. J. Infect. Dis. **133**:79–87.

28. **Kasper, D. L., M. E. Hayes, B. G. Reinap, F. O. Craft, A. B. Onderdonk, and B. F. Polk.** 1977. Isolation and identification of encapsulated strains of *Bacteroides fragilis*. J. Infect. Dis. **136**:75–81.

29. **Kasper, D. L., A. B. Onderdonk, and J. G. Bartlett.** 1977. Quantitative determination of the antibody response to the capsular polysaccharide of *Bacteroides fragilis* in an animal model of intraabdominal abscess formation. J. Infect. Dis. **136**:789–795.

30. **Koga, T., and M. Inoue.** 1978. Cellular adherence, glucosyltransferase adsorption, and glucan synthesis of *Streptococcus mutans* AHT mutants. Infect. Immun. **19**:402–410.

31. **Kuramitsu, H. K.** 1974. Adherence of *Streptococcus mutans* to dextran synthesized in the presence of extracellular dextransucrase. Infect. Immun. **9**:764–765.

32. **Labrec, E. H., H. Schneider, T. J. Magnani, and S. B. Formal.** 1964. Epithelial cell penetration as an essential step in the pathogenesis of bacillary dysentery. J. Bacteriol. **88**:1503–1518.

33. **McCabe, R. M., and J. A. Donkersloot.** 1977. Adherence of *Veillonella* species mediated by extracellular glucosyltransferase from *Streptococcus salivarius*. Infect. Immun. **18**:726–734.

34. **McGee, Z. A., A. P. Johnson, and D. Taylor-Robinson.** 1976. Human fallopian tubes in organ culture: preparation, maintenance, and quantitation of damage by pathogenic microorganisms. Infect. Immun. **13**:608–618.

35. **McGee, Z. A., A. P. Johnson, and D. Taylor-Robinson.** 1981. Pathogenic mechanisms of *Neisseria gonorrhoeae*: observations on damage to human Fallopian tubes in organ culture by gonococci of colony type 1 or type 4. J. Infect. Dis. **143**:413–422.

36. **McGee, Z. A., M. A. Melly, C. R. Gregg, R. G. Horn, D. Taylor-Robinson, A. P. Johnson, and J. A. McCutchan.** 1978. Virulence factors of gonococci: studies using human fallopian tube organ cultures, p. 258–262. *In* G. F. Brooks, E. C. Gotschlich, K. K. Holmes, W. D. Sawyer, and F. E. Young (ed), Immunobiology of *Neisseria gonorrhoeae*. American Society for Microbiology, Washington, D.C.

37. **Melley, M. A., C. R. Gregg, and Z. A. McGee.** 1981.

38. **Miller, M. A., J. C. Rapean, and N. F. Whedon.** 1948. The role of slime film in the attachment of fouling organisms. Biol. Bull. **94**:143–157.

39. **Morris, J. A., A. E. Stevens, and W. J. Sojka.** 1977. Preliminary characteristics of cell-free K99 antigen isolated from *Escherichia coli* B41. J. Gen. Microbiol. **99**:353–357.

40. **Morris, J. A., C. J. Thorns, and W. J. Sojka.** 1980. Evidence for two adhesive antigens on the K99 reference strain of *Escherichia coli* B41. J. Gen. Microbiol. **118**:107–113.

41. **Mukasa, H., and H. D. Slade.** 1973. Mechanism of adherence of *Streptococcus mutans* to smooth surfaces. I. Roles of insoluble dextran-levan synthetase enzymes and cell wall polysaccharide antigen in plaque formation. Infect. Immun. **8**:555–562.

42. **Mukasa, H., and H. D. Slade.** 1974. Mechanism of adherence of *Streptococcus mutans* to smooth surfaces. II. Nature of the binding site and the adsorption of dextran-levan synthetase enzymes on the cell-wall surface of the streptococcus. Infect. Immun. **9**:419–429.

43. **Nagy, B., H. W. Moon, and R. E. Isaacson.** 1977. Colonization of porcine intestine by enterotoxigenic *Escherichia coli*: selection of piliated forms in vivo, adhesion of piliated forms to epithelial cells in vitro, and incidence of pilus antigen among porcine enteropathogenic *E. coli*. Infect. Immun. **16**:344–352.

44. **Neihof, R., and G. Loeb.** 1972. Molecular fouling of surfaces in seawater, p. 710–718. *In* Proceedings of the Third International Congress on Marine Corrosion and Fouling. National Bureau of Standards, Gaithersburg, Md.

45. **Ofek, I., E. H. Beachey, W. Jefferson, and G. L. Campbell.** 1975. Cell membrane-binding properties of Group A streptococcal lipoteichoic acid. J. Exp. Med. **141**:990–1003.

46. **Ofek, I., D. Mirelman, and N. Sharon.** 1977. Adherence of *Escherichia coli* to human mucosal cells mediated by mannose receptors. Nature (London) **265**:623–625.

47. **Okuda, K., J. Slots, and R. J. Genco.** 1981. *Bacteroides gingivalis, Bacteroides asaccharolyticus*, and *Bacteroides melaninogenicus* subspecies: cell surface morphology and adherence to erythrocytes and human buccal epithelial cells. Curr. Microbiol. **6**:7–12.

48. **Onderdonk, A. B., D. L. Kasper, R. L. Cisneros, and J. G. Bartlett.** 1977. The capsular polysaccharide of *Bacteroides fragilis* as a virulence factor: comparison of the pathogenic potential of encapsulated and unencapsulated strains. J. Infect. Dis. **136**:82–89.

49. **O'Neill, T. B., and G. L. Wilcox.** 1971. The formation of a "primary film" on materials submerged in the sea at Port Hueneme, California. Pac. Sci. **25**:1–12.

50. **Ørskov, F.** 1978. Virulence factors of the bacterial cell surface. J. Infect. Dis. **137**:630–633.

51. **Poirier, T. P., S. J. Tonelli, and S. C. Holt.** 1979. Ultrastructure of gliding bacteria: scanning electron microscopy of *Capnocytophaga sputigena, Capnocytophaga gingivalis*, and *Capnocytophaga ochracea*. Infect. Immun. **26**:1146–1158.

52. **Progulske, A., and S. C. Holt.** 1980. Transmission-scanning electron microscopic observations of selected *Eikenella corrodens* strains. J. Bacteriol. **143**:1003–1018.

53. **Punsalang, A. P., Jr., and W. D. Sawyer.** 1973. Role of pili in the virulence of *Neisseria gonorrhoeae*. Infect. Immun. **8**:255–263.

54. **Richards, K. L., and S. D. Douglas.** 1978. Pathophysiological effects of *Vibrio cholerae* and enterotoxigenic *Escherichia coli* and their exotoxins on eucaryotic cells. Microbiol. Rev. **42**:592–613.

55. **Savage, D. C.** 1977. Microbial ecology of the gastrointestinal tract. Annu. Rev. Microbiol. **31**:107–133.

Studies of toxicity of *Neisseria gonorrhoeae* for human fallopian tube mucosa. J. Infect. Dis. **143**:423–431.

56. **Savage, D. C., R. Dubos, and R. W. Schaedler.** 1968. The gastrointestinal epithelium and its autochthonous bacterial flora. J. Exp. Med. **127:**67–75.

57. **Schachtele, C. F., R. H. Staat, and S. K. Harlander.** 1975. Dextranases from oral bacteria: inhibition of water-insoluble glucan production and adherence to smooth surfaces by *Streptococcus mutans*. Infect. Immun. **12:**309–317.

58. **Selinger, D. S., N. Julie, W. P. Reed, and R. C. Williams, Jr.** 1978. Adherence of Group A streptococci to pharyngeal cells: a role in the pathogenesis of rheumatic fever. Science **201:**455–457.

59. **Smith, H. W., and M. A. Linggood.** 1971. Observations on the pathogenic properties of the K88, Hly and Ent plasmids of *Escherichia coli* with particular reference to porcine diarrhoea. J. Med. Microbiol. **4:**467–485.

60. **Stirm, S., F. Ørskov, I. Ørskov, and B. Mansu.** 1967. Episome carried surface antigen K88 of *Escherichia coli*. II. Isolation and chemical analysis. J. Bacteriol. **93:**731–739.

61. **Svanborg-Eden, C., and H. A. Hansson.** 1978. *Escherichia coli* pili as possible mediators of attachment to human urinary tract epithelial cells. Infect. Immun. **21:**229–237.

62. **Svanborg Edén, C., L. A. Hanson, U. Jodal, U. Lindberg, and A. Sohl Akerlund.** 1976. Variable adherence to normal human urinary tract epithelial cells of *Escherichia coli* strains associated with various forms of urinary tract infection. Lancet **ii:**490–492.

63. **Swanson, J.** 1973. Studies on gonococcus infection. IV. Pili: their role in attachment of gonococci to tissue culture cells. J. Exp. Med. **137:**571–589.

64. **Swanson, J., S. J. Kraus, and E. C. Gotschlich.** 1971. Studies on gonococcus infection. I. Pili and zones of adhesion: their relation to gonococcal growth patterns. J. Exp. Med. **134:**886–906.

65. **Van Houte, J., and V. N. Upeslacis.** 1976. Studies of the mechanism of sucrose-associated colonization of *Streptococcus mutans* on teeth of conventional rats. J. Dent. Res. **55:**216–222.

66. **Wheeler, T. T., and W. B. Clark.** 1980. Fibril-mediated adherence of *Actinomyces viscosus* to saliva-treated hydroxyapatite. Infect. Immun. **28:**577–584.

67. **Wheeler, T. T., W. B. Clark, and D. C. Birdsell.** 1979. Adherence of *Actinomyces viscosus* T14V and T14AV to hydroxyapatite surfaces in vitro and human teeth in vivo. Infect. Immun. **25:**1066–1074.

68. **Wicken, A. J., and K. W. Knox.** 1977. Biological properties of lipoteichoic acids, p. 360–365. *In* D. Schlessinger (ed.), Microbiology—1977. American Society for Microbiology, Washington, D.C.

69. **Williams, P. H., N. Evans, P. Turner, R. H. George, and A. S. McNeish.** 1977. Plasmid mediating mucosal adherence in human enteropathogenic *Escherichia coli*. Lancet **i:**1151.

70. **Williams, P. H., M. I. Sedgwick, N. Evans, P. J. Turner, R. N. George, and A. S. McNeish.** 1978. Adherence of an enteropathogenic strain of *Escherichia coli* to human intestinal mucosa is mediated by a colicinogenic conjugative plasmid. Infect. Immun. **22:**393–402.

71. **Williams, P. H., M. I. Sedgwick, and A. S. McNeish.** 1978. Characterization of a plasmid of *Escherichia coli* controlling adherence to human intestinal mucosa. Heredity **40:**329.

72. **Woo, D. D. L., S. C. Holt, and E. R. Leadbetter.** 1979. Ultrastructure of *Bacteroides* species: *Bacteroides asaccharolyticus, Bacteroides fragilis, Bacteroides melaninogenicus* subspecies *melaninogenicus*, and *Bacteroides melaninogenicus* subspecies *intermedius*. J. Infect. Dis. **139:**534–546.

73. **Woods Hole Oceanographic Institution.** 1952. Marine fouling and its prevention, p. 236–261. Woods Hole Oceanographic Institution, Woods Hole, Mass.

74. **Zobell, C. E.** 1943. The effect of solid surfaces upon bacterial activity. J. Bacteriol. **46:**39–56.

AUTOCHTHONOUS POPULATIONS

Colonization of Tissue Surfaces by Autochthonous Bacteria

J. W. COSTERTON AND K.-J. CHENG

Biology, University of Calgary, Calgary, Alberta, Canada T2N-1N4, and Animal Science, Agriculture Canada Research Station, Lethbridge, Alberta, Canada, T1J-4B1

The fields of medical microbiology and of microbial ecology have evolved as separate entities with widely divergent basic premises. The host, or the habitat, has been the basis for research affiliations so that divisions of aquatic microbiology and urinary tract microbiology have rarely made useful contact even though both study *Pseudomonas aeruginosa* in an aqueous milieu. The unifying factor of the common bacteria found in various systems has been ignored even though it seems illogical that a particular species could employ significantly different physiological mechanisms or survival strategies in different ecosystems without divergent evolution. In this brief review we propose to present evidence that the protected and adherent microcolony mode of bacterial growth that has been found to predominate in natural environments is also adopted by these bacteria as they grow as autochthonous populations on plant and animal tissues, and as they invade compromised humans to grow as opportunistic pathogens.

MODE OF GROWTH OF BACTERIA IN NATURE

The direct examination of soil and water ecosystems has shown that bacteria grow in glycocalyx-enclosed microcolonies adherent to surfaces within the environment (10). The glycocalyx, which is defined in references 12 and 13, is an extensive fibrous anionic exopolysaccharide structure that surrounds the bacterial cell and mediates both microcolony formation and adhesion to surfaces (8, 12, 13). Perhaps because the enveloping glycocalyx provides protection from the bacteriophages and phagocytic amoebae that abound in natural environments, quantitative examinations of natural ecosystems have determined that the bacteria growing in glycocalyx-enclosed adherent microcolonies on surfaces outnumber mobile (planktonic) bacteria to a very significant extent (15). Recent examinations of industrial aquatic systems (11) have shown that bacterial cells within adherent micro-

colonies are significantly more resistant to chemical biocides than are the corresponding planktonic organisms. The protective effect of the bacterial glycocalyx can only be fully appreciated when we combine chemical evidence of its anionic nature (33), physical evidence of its high degree of organization (27), and morphological evidence of its considerable thickness (2). Whereas the glycocalyx is often diminished or lost during in vitro culture, because of overgrowth by fast-growing glycocalyx-negative mutants, it is universally found to surround bacteria in more challenging environments, where its phenomenal thickness can be illustrated by stabilizing it against collapse during dehydration by using specific antibodies and staining it with ruthenium red (Fig. 1).

MODE OF GROWTH OF AUTOCHTHONOUS BACTERIA ON TISSUES

When we note that the outermost component of the animal cell surface is a relatively inert predominantly polysaccharide glycocalyx (29) and that bathing fluids contain antibacterial factors such as surfactants, enzymes, serum factors, specific antibodies, and phagocytic cells (12), it is not surprising that direct examination of animal tissues colonized by autochthonous (30) bacteria shows that these organisms grow in glycocalyx-enclosed adherent microcolonies (Fig. 2). Some exposed tissues (e.g., the lung) possess such an effective battery of defense mechanisms that their surfaces are kept relatively free from bacterial colonization, whereas other tissues "encourage" colonization by selected beneficial autochthonous organisms (8). However, host defense factors are rarely suspended altogether, and these tissue-associated bacteria must grow in a protective mode (viz., the glycocalyx-enclosed microcolony) to persist.

BACTERIAL GROWTH ON NONSECRETORY SQUAMOUS TISSUES

Squamous tissues provide a unique bacterial habitat because their distal cells, being dead and

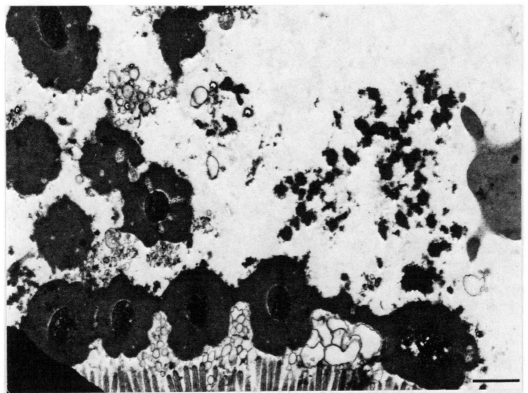

FIG. 1. Transmission electron microscopy of a section of the ileum of a newborn calf infected with a K99[+] K30[+] strain of enterotoxigenic *E. coli*. The glycocalyces of the infecting bacteria have been stabilized with specific anti-K30 antibodies, prior to staining with ruthenium red, to show the very extensive extracellular matrix that surrounds these pathogenic cells and mediates their formation of adherent microcolonies on the intestinal surface. Bar indicates 1.0 μm.

extensively keratinized, provide a nutritive substrate for proteolytic bacteria, and direct examination shows that they are often extensively digested by a single bacterial morphotype before their detachment (6). Very extensive glycocalyx-enclosed bacterial microcolonies form thick accretions on the squamous tissues of the bovine rumen (Fig. 2) and on human skin, and the extent of colonization seems to be limited only by physical factors such as abrasion (24). On the other hand, only approximately one-third of the sloughed squamous and transitional epithelial cells recovered from the urethral urine of healthy female volunteers were colonized (Fig. 3) by distinct microcolonies of bacteria (22), indicating that bacterial colonization of the proximal two-thirds of this organ is limited by host defense factors. Because of the continuous sloughing of distal cells from stratified squamous epithelia, the bacteria must proliferate and colonize newly exposed cells to maintain their colonization. Some tissues (e.g., the bladder) used

accelerated cell sloughing as a defense mechanism against pathogenic colonization (26).

BACTERIAL GROWTH ON MUCUS-COVERED TISSUES

The mucus produced by goblet cells in the respiratory and intestinal systems forms a continuous "blanket" that is moved over the tissue surface by ciliary action or by peristalsis. This mucus blanket is the preferred habitat of many bacteria that display a strong chemotactic attraction to its constituents (R. Freter, this volume), but these organisms are rarely seen in topographic examinations of colonized tissue by scanning electron microscopy because the mucus blanket is usually lost during preparation (K. R. Rozee et al., submitted for publication). We have developed procedures for the stabilization of the mucus of the mouse intestine, by reaction with antibodies against its protein component, and these methods aid in the retention of the mucus blanket overlying this tissue which is

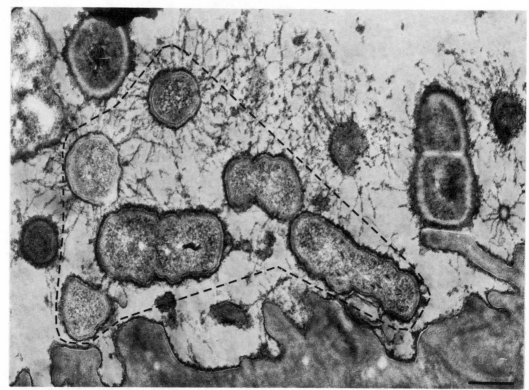

FIG. 2. Transmission electron microscopy of a section of the bovine rumen epithelium showing extensive colonization by autochthonous bacteria. This unstabilized preparation has been treated with ruthenium red which stains the condensed glycocalyx matrix that encloses this adherent bacterial population, including the microcolony of morphologically identical cells outlined by the dotted line. Bar indicates 1.0 μm.

seen to contain very large numbers of both bacteria and protozoa (Fig. 4). The mucus blanket of the intestine may attain a thickness of 400 μm, as measured in hydrated systems by light microscopy (20), and this structure constitutes a physiologically important "unstirred" layer at the tissue surface (35). When the mucus blanket is lost from normal broncheoles, we see the uncolonized surfaces of ciliated and secretory cells, but intestinal tissues are often colonized by bacteria and protozoa with specialized adhesion mechanisms that allow their persistence at the tissue surface in spite of the shear forces exerted by the moving viscous mass of mucus (30). These organisms exist at the tissue-mucus interface, and they depend on specialized holdfast mechanisms rather than on microcolony formation for their persistence and adhesion.

ROLE OF AUTOCHTHONOUS BACTERIA IN ORGAN SYSTEMS

Many animal tissues are regularly colonized by bacterial species selected from the thousands of species in their immediate environment by specific adhesion mechanisms, and these autochthonous organisms have been characterized in both the bovine rumen (7) and the human urethra (23). In the former the adherent autochthonous species, which are taxonomically distinct from lumenal autochthonous species, are acquired early in life and are maintained in spite of dietary changes (9). In the latter the autochthonous species are related to the autochthonous organisms found on neighboring tissues, and they are seen to vary with age and hormonal status (23). The consistent presence of certain autochthonous species on particular tissues raises the interesting question of the bacterial role in these ecologically stable relationships.

PHYSIOLOGICAL COOPERATIVITY OF BACTERIA WITH THE COLONIZED TISSUES

Although bacteria are commonly conceded to play an important role in such general processes as cellulose digestion by ruminants (17), their

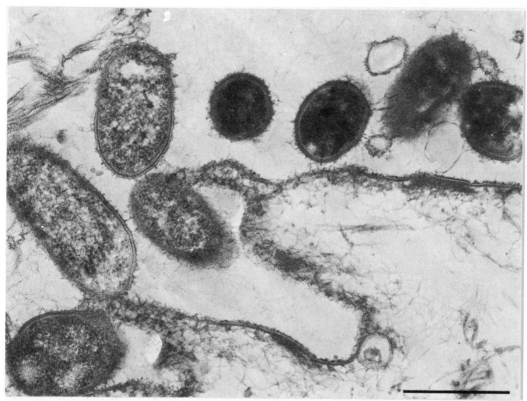

FIG. 3. Transmission electron microscopy of a section of a sloughed epithelial cell from the urethra of a healthy human female volunteer showing colonization by autochthonous bacteria. This unstabilized preparation has been treated with ruthenium red, which stains the condensed glycocalyx fibers that enclose the cells of two microcolonies composed of gram-positive cells (right) and one composed of gram-negative cells (left). Bar indicates 1.0 μm.

actual enzymatic integration into tissue physiology is often suggested but rarely documented. We have recently shown that the urease of the bovin rumen, which is necessary for the important conversion to ammonia of the urea that diffuses through the wall of this organ from the bloodstream, is not produced by the epithelial tissue but by several species of autochthonous bacteria that adhere to the rumen wall and effect this vital enzymatic transformation (7). This single instance of the enzymatic integration of autochthonous bacteria into the overall physiological activity of a tissue leads us to suggest that the consistent colonization of animal tissues by a particular species of bacteria may reflect a possible instance of physiological cooperativity.

PROTECTION OF COLONIZED TISSUES FROM PATHOGENIC COLONIZATION

The intestinal surface of newborn calves and lambs is exquisitely susceptible to colonization (Fig. 1) by K99 pilus-bearing enterotoxigenic strains of *Escherichia coli* which cause a potentially fatal form of diarrhea in these animals (25). Similar K88 pilus-bearing strains are potentially pathogenic to newborn piglets. This susceptibility decreases sharply with age, and 4 to 6 days after birth, the intestinal tissues of these animals are sufficiently colonized with autochthonous bacteria that their susceptibility to enterotoxigenic *E. coli* is sharply decreased. Similarly, the loss of autochthonous urethral bacterial flora as a result of treatment with broad-spectrum antibiotics often results in the development of an ascending cystitis caused by the same serotype of *E. coli* that is autochthonous in that person's intestine (32). These studies suggest that a vigorous autochthonous bacterial population may provide a barrier to pathogenic colonization by spatial occlusion of potential adhesion sites or by physiological competition with the pathogenic organisms (12). Direct examination of colonized digestive tract tissues (Fig. 2 and 4) and of

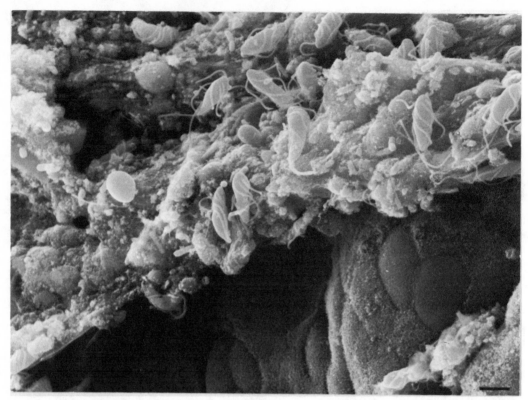

FIG. 4. Scanning electron microscopy of a preparation from the ileum of a mouse in which the mucus "blanket" overlying the tissue surface had been retained, and partially stabilized, by reaction with antibodies to protein components of the mucus. Bacteria and protozoa are seen within the mucus layer, which is 50 to 70 μm thick in these preparations, and very few bacteria are actually associated with the tissue surface. Bar indicates 5 μm.

colonized cells from the distal human female urethra (Fig. 3) shows a mode of bacterial growth in which the adherent bacterial cells and their enveloping glycocalyces appear almost completely to occlude the tissue surfaces.

MANIPULATION OF AUTOCHTHONOUS BACTERIAL POPULATIONS

When autochthonous bacteria are well established as a vigorous and integrated population on a tissue surface, these populations are ecologically stable and they resist manipulation by the introduction of extraneous bacteria (7). However, profound changes occur in these autochthonous populations when the tissue that they colonize changes its surface chemistry and no longer presents the specific ligands necessary for the adhesion of these autochthonous organisms. A case in point is the removal of the cell surface protein fibronectin from oropharyngeal epithelial cells by increased protease activity in the saliva of patients stressed by surgery or by

underlying disease (36) and the consequent replacement of this autochthonous population by a confluent growth of *P. aeruginosa* (18). Tissues may also change their adherent autochthonous populations in response to hormonal changes, as when the predominant flora of the distal human urethra changes from *Lactobacillus* to *Bacteroides* at menopause (23). Thus, there are "windows" in time in which the autochthonous bacterial population of a tissue is in transition, as a result of a change in tissue surface chemistry, and these populations may be susceptible to manipulation within these temporal "windows." Further, treatment with antibiotics also kills autochthonous bacteria, and broad-spectrum agents produce profound changes in the bacterial flora of major organ systems (5). The pristine microbial state of the tissues of newborn animals presents an excellent opportunity for the manipulation of autochthonous bacterial populations in that their naturally slow and random acquisition of beneficial flora can be accelerated by the introduction of suitable organisms in the first few hours of life.

We (K.-J. Cheng and J. W. Costerton, unpublished data) have selected 39 bacterial isolates from the beneficial adherent and nonadherent autochthonous bacterial populations of the major organs of the ruminant digestive tract (7) and have introduced them into newborn lambs in a study using identical twins as controls. The treated animals showed a very rapid acquisition of autochthonous bacterial flora, based on electron microscopy and on the urease activity of epithelial tissues, and they showed a statistically significant increase in early weight gain. Previous experiments had clearly shown that an autochthonous species of *Staphylococcus* could be introduced into the rumen of a gnotobiotic lamb (34) to form a vigorous, adherent, urease-producing population. Trials are presently being planned to assess the degree of protection from enterotoxigenic *E. coli* conferred by the early establishment of an autochthonous bacterial population in lambs, and Sprunt et al. (31) have implanted alpha-hemolytic streptococci in human neonates as a means of protection from pharyngeal pathogens. Perhaps the most extensive tests of the protective effects of autochthonous bacterial flora are those of Barnum et al. (1), who have used uncharacterized mixtures of bacteria from the cecal contents of healthy 4-week-old turkey poults to inoculate thousands of 0- to 3-day-old poults and have produced a very significant decrease in the incidence of salmonellosis in the treated animals by a process that they call "competitive exclusion." B. W. Brooks and D. A. Barnum (personal communication) are assessing the efficacy of an autochthonous species from the bovine udder, *Corynebacterium bovis*, in the prevention of mastitis, and we are examining the reestablishment of the autochthonous flora of the rat urethra after treatment with broad-spectrum antibiotics.

MODE OF GROWTH OF OPPORTUNISTIC PATHOGENS

The glycocalyx-enclosed adherent microcolony mode of growth that protects the bacteria in natural ecosystems from bacteriophages and phagocytic amoebae also protects the autochthonous bacteria on tissue surfaces from surfactants, specific antibodies, and activated phagocytes. When one of these environmental or autochthonous organisms is allowed, by a lapse in the defense mechanisms of a compromised host, to enter an organ system in which it is a potential pathogen, it uses the same protective microcolonial mode of growth to persist in spite of activated host defense mechanisms (13). A case in point is the colonization of the oropharynx of cystic fibrosis patients with *P. aeruginosa* (18), which serves as a reservoir population for the production of glycocalyx-enclosed aggregates of these organisms which, like the polysaccharide-enclosed cells in the agar beads used by Cash et al. (4) to initiate chronic pulmonary infections in normal rats, can then be aspirated into the lung to serve as protected foci from which the bacteria may emerge to form glycocalyx-protected microcolonies and cause a persistent "cyptic" infection of the lung (19). Once established, these protected microcolonies can withstand the vigorous immune response of the infected host (16) and can only be controlled when antibiotics are used in high and sustained doses (28) that build up pulmonary concentrations sufficient to penetrate the protective structures and to reach the infecting cells. The success of high single doses of antibiotics in controlling persistent urinary tract infections (14) may be added to direct morphological evidence (21) that the infecting cells grow in glycocalyx-enclosed microcolonies to suggest that these persistent infections are also "cryptic." Autochthonous bacteria from one organ system are particularly well suited to become opportunistic pathogens in another organ system of the same host because they have already persisted on a tissue surface in spite of the host's production of specific antibodies and in spite of the host's activated phagocytes.

Of course, an environmental or autochthonous bacterium is not forced to adopt its glycocalyx-enclosed protected microcolonial mode of growth if the compromised host's defense mechanisms have been destroyed, as in burned tissue, or if they have been overwhelmed by huge numbers of the pathogen, as in certain model pulmonary infections (3), and it will then cause an acute, often bacteremic infection by using its mobile "swarmer" cells. These acute infections must be expected to respond very well to immune or antibiotic therapy because the bacterial cells are in their unprotected mode of growth.

EPILOGUE

Studies of infectious disease have recently come to emphasize pathogenic adhesion, and the most common "experimental" approach has been to identify a particular bacterial surface structure (e.g., the pili of *Neisseria gonorrhoeae*) and to establish that this structure is a sine qua non of adhesion to the target tissue and of the ability to cause the disease. In certain relatively simple diseases (e.g., enterotoxigenic *E. coli* infections of newborn ruminants) a single surface structure (the K99 pilus) was the predominant ligand in adhesion, and a useful antipilus vaccine (Vicogen) was produced. Gradually, we have come to realize that pathogenesis is much more complex than we had imagined and that bacteria grow in many different modes, target tissues change their ligands, bacteria may use more than one surface structure as a ligand in adhesion, and most bacteria must not only adhere but also persist and multiply on their target tissue to cause disease. Thus, we find many seemingly "cut-and-dried" theories of the etiology of particular bacterial diseases lapsing into confusion and fascinating complexity. At this time, our knowledge of the molecular architecture of the cell surface of bacterial pathogens in their pathogenic mode of growth is as rudimentary as our knowledge of cell wall structure was in the early 1960s. Goal-oriented research by descriptive scientists will simply produce more attempts to correlate the presence of single structures with the complex process of the etiology of each bacterial disease. What is needed is the development of a broad parallel program in which analytical scientists use sophisticated probes (e.g., monoclonal antibodies and crossed immunoelectrophoresis) to develop a molecular "portrait" of the surface of the bacterial cell, and in which ecologists examine the roles of these bacterial cell surface components in the pathogen's adhesion to the target tissue, in its relation to autochthonous bacteria already on the tissues, in its persistence in the face of body defense mechanisms, in its proliferation on the tissue surface, and in the molecular mechanisms of its pathogenicity.

LITERATURE CITED

1. **Barnum, D. A., W. Anderson, C. Reid, E. Davis, and W. R. Mitchell.** 1981. The application of competitive exclusion in the prevention of salmonella colonization in turkeys, p. 88–93. *In* Proceedings of the 8th International Symposium of the World Association of Veterinary Food Hygienists.
2. **Bayer, M. E., and H. Thurow.** 1977. Polysaccharide capsule of *Escherichia coli*: microscopic study of its size, structure, and sites of synthesis. J. Bacteriol. **130**:911–936.
3. **Blackwood, L. L., and J. E. Pennington.** 1981. Influence of mucoidy on clearance of *Pseudomonas aeruginosa* from lungs. Infect. Immun. **32**:443–448.
4. **Cash, H. A., D. E. Woods, B. McCullough, W. G. Johanson, Jr., and J. A. Bass.** 1979. A rat model of chronic respiratory infection with *Pseudomonas aeruginosa*. Am. Rev. Resp. Dis. **119**:453–459.
5. **Chang, T. W., J. G. Bartlett, S. L. Gorbach, and A. B. Onderdonk.** 1978. Clindamycin-induced enterocolitis in hamsters as a model of pseudomembrane colitis in patients. Infect. Immun. **20**:526–529.
6. **Cheng, K.-J., D. E. Akin, and J. W. Costerton.** 1977. Rumen bacteria: interaction with dietary components and response to dietary variation. Fed. Proc. Fed. Am. Soc. Exp. Biol. **36**:193–197.
7. **Cheng, K.-J., and J. W. Costerton.** 1980. Adherent rumen bacteria: their role in the digestion of plant material, urea

and epithelial cells, p. 227–250. *In* Y. Ruckebush and P. Thivend (ed.), Digestive physiology and metabolism in ruminants. MTP Press, Lancaster, U.K.
8. **Cheng, K.-J., and J. W. Costerton.** 1981. Autochthonous and pathogenic colonization of animal tissues by bacteria. Can. J. Microbiol. **27**:461–490.
9. **Cheng, K.-J., R. P. McCowan, and J. W. Costerton.** 1979. Bacterial colonization of feed particles and tissue surfaces in the bovine rumen. Am. J. Clin. Nutr. **32**:139–148.
10. **Costerton, J. W., G. G. Geesey, and K.-J. Cheng.** 1978. How bacteria stick. Sci. Am. **238**:86–95.
11. **Costerton, J. W., and G. G. Geesey.** 1979. Microbial contamination of surfaces, p. 211–221. *In* K. L. Mittal (ed.), Surface contamination. Plenum Press, New York.
12. **Costerton, J. W., R. I. Irvin, and K.-J. Cheng.** 1981. The bacterial glycocalyx in nature and disease. Annu. Rev. Microbiol. **35**:299–324.
13. **Costerton, J. W., R. I. Irvin, and K.-J. Cheng.** 1981. The role of bacterial surface structures in pathogenesis. Crit. Rev. Microbiol. **8**:303–338.
14. **Fang, L. S. T., N. E. Tolkoff-Rubin, and R. H. Rubin.** 1978. Efficacy of single-dose and conventional amoxicillin therapy in urinary-tract infection localized by the antibody coated bacteria technique. N. Engl. J. Med. **298**:413–416.
15. **Geesey, G. G., R. Mutch, J. W. Costerton, and R. B. Green.** 1978. Sessile bacteria: an important component of the microbiol population in small mountain streams. Limnol. Oceanogr. **23**:1214–1223.
16. **Høiby, N., and N. H. Axelsen.** 1973. Identification and quantitation of precipitins against *Pseudomonas aeruginosa* in patients with cystic fibrosis by means of crossed immunoelectrophoresis with intermediate gel. Acta Pathol. Microbiol. Scand. Sect. B **81**:298–310.
17. **Hungate, R. E.** 1966. The rumen and its microbes. Academic Press, Inc., New York.
18. **Johanson, W. G., Jr., J. H. Higuchi, T. R. Chandhuri, and D. E. Woods.** 1980. Bacterial adherence to epithelial cells in bacillary colonization of the respiratory tract. Am. Rev. Resp. Dis. **121**:55–63.
19. **Lam, J., R. Chan, K. Lam, and J. W. Costerton.** 1980. Production of mucoid microcolonies by *Pseudomonas aeruginosa* within infected lungs in cystic fibrosis. Infect. Immun. **28**:546–556.
20. **Levin, R. J.** 1979. Fundamental concepts of structure and function of the intestinal epithelium, p. 307. *In* H. L. Duthie (ed.), Scientific basis of gastroenterology. Churchill Livingstone, New York.
21. **Marrie, T. J., G. K. M. Harding, A. R. Ronald, J. Dikema, J. Lam, S. Hoban, and J. W. Costerton.** 1979. Influence of antibody coating of *Pseudomonas aeruginosa*. J. Infect. Dis. **19**:357–361.
22. **Marrie, T. J., J. Lam, and J. W. Costerton.** 1980. Bacterial adhesion to uroepithelial cells: a morphological study. J. Infect. Dis. **142**:239–246.
23. **Marrie, T. J., C. A. Swante, and M. Hartlen.** 1980. Aerobic and anaerobic urethral flora of healthy females in various age groups and in females with urinary tract infections. J. Clin. Microbiol. **11**:654–659.
24. **McCowan, R. P., K.-J. Cheng, C. B. M. Bailey, and J. W. Costerton.** 1978. Adhesion of bacteria to epithelial cell surfaces within the reticulorumen of cattle. Appl. Environ. Microbiol. **35**:149–155.
25. **Moon, H. W.** 1974. Pathogenesis of enteric diseases caused by *Escherichia coli*. Adv. Vet. Sci. Comp. Med. **18**:179–211.
26. **Mooney, J. K., J. S. Mooney, and F. Hinman.** 1976. The antibacterial effect of the bladder surface; an electron microscopic study. J. Urol. **115**:381–386.
27. **Moorehouse, R., W. T. Winter, S. Arnoot, and M. E. Bayer.** 1977. Conformation and molecular organization in

fibers of capsular polysaccharide from *Escherichia coli* M41 mutant. J. Mol. Biol. **109**:373–391.

28. **Rabin, H. R., F. L. Harley, L. E. Bryan, and G. L. Elfring.** 1980. Evaluation of a high dose tobramycin and ticarcillin treatment protocol in cystic fibrosis based on improved susceptibility criteria and antibiotic pharmacokinetics, p. 370–375. *In* J. M. Sturgess (ed.), Perspectives in cystic fibrosis. Canadian Cystic Fibrosis Foundation, Toronto.

29. **Roseman, S.** 1974. Complex carbohydrates and intercellular adhesion, p. 317–337. *In* E. Y. C. Lee and E. E. Smith (ed.), Biology and chemistry of eukaryotic cell surfaces. Academic Press, London.

30. **Savage, D. C.** 1977. Microbiol ecology of the gastrointestinal tract. Annu. Rev. Microbiol. **31**:107–133.

31. **Sprunt, K., G. Leidy, and W. Redman.** 1980. Abnormal colonization of neonates in an I.C.U.: conversion of normal colonization by pharyngeal implantation of alpha hemolytic Streptococcus strain 215. Pediatr. Res. **14**:308–313.

32. **Stamey, T. A.** 1975. A clinical classification of urinary tract infections based upon origin. South. Med. J. **68**:934–939.

33. **Sutherland, I. W.** 1977. Bacterial polysaccharides: their nature and production, p. 27–96. *In* I. W. Sutherland (ed.), Surface carbohydrates of the prokaryotic cell. Academic Press, Inc., New York.

34. **Wallace, R. J., K.-J. Cheng, D. Dinsdale, and E. R. Ørskov.** 1979. An independent microbial flora of the epithelium and its role in the ecomicrobiology of the rumen. Nature (London) **279**:424–426.

35. **Winne, D.** 1976. Unstirred layer thickness in perfused rat jejunum. Experientia **32**:1278–1279.

36. **Woods, D. E., D. C. Straus, W. G. Johanson, Jr., V. K. Berry, and J. A. Bass.** 1980. Role of pili in adherence of *Pseudomonas aeruginosa* to mammalian buccal epithelial cells. Infect. Immun. **29**:1146–1151.

Colonization of the Intestine by Autochthonous Bacteria

L. R. INMAN AND AKIO TAKEUCHI

Department of Pathology, Medical University of South Carolina, Charleston, South Carolina 29425, and Department of Experimental Pathology, Walter Reed Army Institute of Research, Walter Reed Army Medical Center, Washington, D.C. 20012

The concept of autochthonous intestinal bacterial populations has been recognized and studied for some time (3, 19). In recent years, the term autochthonous has been well defined and reviewed (1, 9, 14, 16–18). This evaluation and evolution of the term autochthony have resulted in a term which implies the fulfillment of several criteria when applied to intestinal organisms.

The organism must (i) be capable of growth in an anaerobic environment, (ii) always be found in normal adults, (iii) colonize a particular area, and (iv) colonize that area during succession in infant animals and achieve stable climax populations in normal adults (17). Presently, autochthonous and indigenous are used synonymously (16).

The fulfillment of all of these criteria may not, however, be critical to the application of the term autochthonous to a given bacterial type in the intestine of an animal species, but should be seen within a population of that species (3).

At times, presumptive application of the term autochthonous is acceptable when applied to a monospecific population or when bacterial morphological specialization occurs (1). This presumptive identification has been necessitated by the inability, in many instances, to isolate and culture the organisms under study (1, 9, 18).

Topographically, bacteria and other parasites, autochthonous and pathogenic, may be classified according to their horizontal and vertical localization within the gut (13, 20).

Vertical characterization can be made by observing whether the organism is localized within the crypts of Lieberkuhn or prefers more luminal locations. Further vertical characterization may be made by noting those organisms which distribute freely in the lumen, localize at the mucus or glycocalyx, or localize at the microvilli. Certain pathogenic organisms, of course, may further proceed to localize within the epithelial cells or penetrate into the lamina propria.

Horizontally, an organism may be classified according to the particular area of the intestine in which it characteristically resides (9, 17).

Typically, organisms presumed to be autochthonous localize consistently in the same vertical and horizontal environment within the intestine, elicit little or no inflammatory response, and are not associated with any clinical syndrome. These observations have been considered a concession of the host to the bacteria (1).

Among the most specialized autochthonous bacteria are those which associate intimately with the intestinal epithelial cell membrane. Representative of these are the segmented filamentous microbes of the rodent small intestine (4, 15; J. E. Snellen and D. C. Savage, Am. J. Clin. Nutr. 32:266, 1979), and the spirochetes (12, 22, 23) and flagellated organisms (12, 22, 23) of the rhesus monkey colon.

SEGMENTED FILAMENTOUS MICROBES

The most direct physical associations between an indigenous microbe and its host is that observed in the association of the segmented filamentous microbe found in the small intestine of asymptomatic rats (4) and mice (15). This organism is commonly seen associated with the apical third of villi, and it reaches greater density in the distal ileum.

A structurally distinct holdfast segment of the microbe displaces the epithelial cell microvilli, invaginates the host cell membrane, and forms a morphologically unique attachment site adjacent to the area of the epithelial cell terminal web (4).

The life cycle of this organism also appears to be an adaptation to its environment. As the mucosal epithelial cell to which the organism is attached migrates toward the apex of the villus and toward ultimate desquamation, segments on the free end of mature microbes form and release new holdfast segments which then may attach to less mature cells, maintaining colonization.

At the area of holdfast attachment, the epithelial cell membrane appears intact (4, 15); however, in freeze-fracture preparations the membrane has a reduced number of intramembranous particles (Snellen and Savage, Am. J. Clin. Nutr. 32:266, 1979). Within the cytosol of the epithelial cell is an electron-dense plaque immediately underlying the cell membrane in areas of close association with the cell wall of the microbe. A condensed filamentous layer lies within that. These intracellular features have been interpreted as stabilizing the attachment site (4), possibly by a sol-gel transformation (Snellen and Savage, Am. J. Clin. Nutr. **32**:266, 1979).

SPIROCHETES AND FLAGELLATES

The close association of spirochetes and flagellated microbes to the colonic brush border of the rhesus monkey (22, 23) shows characteristics similar to those of the filamentous microbe in the mouse. The association of these microbes with the epithelial cells causes displacement of the microvilli and invagination of the lumenal mucosal epithelial cell membrane; the association is not consistently accompanied by clinical symptoms and produces no inflammatory response. These organisms are rarely found penetrating into the crypts, in contrast to the spiral-shaped microbes found in the rodent large bowel (2, 15), and may localize anywhere between the cecum and the rectum. When they are found in the crypts they are not attached.

Although not as ubiquitous as the filamentous microbe in the rodent small gut, spirochetes and flagellates have been present in as many as 28% of a rhesus monkey population (21) in numbers as high as 1,700 organisms per mm^2 (23).

The attached spirochete obliterates the host cell glycocalyx, orients perpendicularly to and

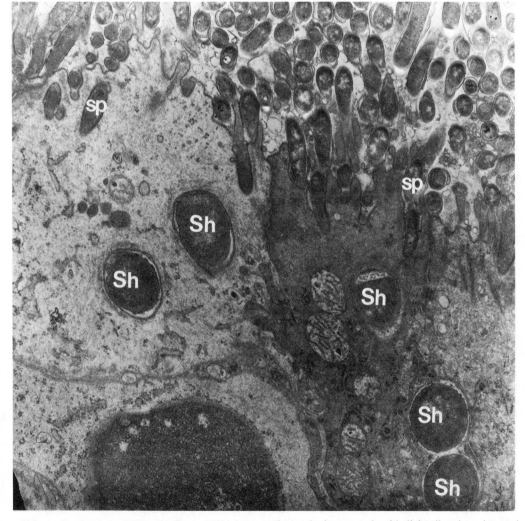

FIG. 1. Penetration of *Shigella flexneri* (Sh) into monkey colonic mucosal epithelial cells whose lumenal surface is diffusely coated with spirochetes (Sp).

indents the plasma membrane, and obscures the terminal web, but seldom penetrates farther (20). The approximation of the bacterial outer membrane with that of the mucosal epithelial cell maintains a consistent 6- to 8-nm distance (12).

The flagellated organism behaves similarly to the spirochete. It attaches perpendicularly to the host cell membrane with its blunt, flagellated pole, displacing the microvilli. The flagellate, however, indents the host cell plasma membrane shallowly, and the membrane-membrane distance varies along the microbe (12).

Recently, freeze-fracture studies of spirochete-flagellate-associated monkey colonic tissue have demonstrated membrane specialization in the outer membrane of both microbes only in the area of attachment (12).

SPECIALIZATION AND SPECIFICITY

The three microbes reviewed above demonstrate morphological specialization for attachment, and therefore they warrant presumptive designation as autochthonous. These organisms also demonstrate both vertical and horizontal localization.

Such close attachment may involve specific surface components of the mucosal epithelium which act as receptors for the microbes (13). It is known that there are both vertical and horizontal differences in cell membrane-associated substances in the intestinal tract. Qualitative differences exist in mucosal epithelial cell surface carbohydrates as the cells move up the villi in the small intestine (5). Differences also occur between cells as a function of the cell's distance from the pyloris (5). Quantitative differences in the number of intramembrane proteins occur as cells mature from crypt to villus (11).

It seems logical to conclude from this that, if bacterial specialization for attachment involves a close association with specific proteins, glycoproteins, or carbohydrates, this specialization would also serve to restrict the bacterium to areas where these membrane components are expressed. Specialization for attachment and localization could thus be a result of the same evolutionary event.

CONCEPT OF BARRIER POPULATION

Although the concept of a barrier population of autochthonous bacteria preventing disease caused by pathogenic organisms has been proposed (1, 19), such an effect has not yet been proven. The opposite possibility has also been suggested, i.e., that colonization by autochthonous bacteria may create or expose areas for attachment of other organisms (6). There is some evidence that autochthonous bacteria may physiologically inhibit colonization by pathogenic microbes (8). If autochthonous organisms were to present a barrier to infection by pathogens, they would need to form a continuous blanket over the mucosa to prevent establishment of the pathogen. This blanket colonization often occurs in colonization of the rhesus large bowel by spirochetes and flagellates (20, 23).

Takeuchi et al. (21) have used the rhesus monkey as a model for acute bacterial colitis due to *Shigella flexneri*. Data have indicated that *Shigella* must penetrate the mucosal epithelial cell to produce disease (7). During the course of these studies, animals later found to have colonic involvement with intestinal spirochetes were excluded. However, there was no difference in attack rate of the *Shigella* bacterium in monkeys when spirochetes were diffusely present (A. Takeuchi, unpublished data). Neither was there any apparent obstacle to epithelial cell penetration by the pathogen when spirochetes were present in large numbers over the cell surface (Fig. 1).

SUMMARY

We have described the characteristics of autochthonous bacteria on the intestinal mucosa and have reviewed what is known about three of these organisms adapted for firm attachment to mucosal epithelia cells of the gut. We have suggested that this adaptation may result in the type of tissue localization commonly seen with these organisms. We have also reported new observations on what appears to be the lack of protection afforded by a continuous blanket of autochthonous colonic bacteria to a colonic pathogen.

Clearly, much more work is needed to adequately understand the association of autochthonous organism with tissue surfaces. Such work will be facilitated when these organisms can be cultured and characterized (9). Already there has been some success with efforts to culture spiral-shaped bacteria in the rodent colon (10). Perhaps efforts to isolate and culture similar microbes in other hosts will be successful.

LITERATURE CITED

1. Cheng, K. J., R. T. Irvin, and J. W. Costerton. 1981. Autochthonous and pathogenic colonization of animal tissues by bacteria. Can. J. Microbiol. 27:461–490.
2. Davis, C. P., D. Mulcahy, A. Takeuchi, and D. C. Savage. 1972. Location and description of spiral-shaped microorganisms in the normal rat cecum. Infect. Immun. 6:184–192.
3. Dubos, R., R. W. Schaedler, R. Costell, and P. Hoet. 1965. Indigenous, normal, and autochthonous flora of the gastrointestinal tract. J. Exp. Med. 122:67–75.
4. Erlandsen, S. L., and D. G. Chase. 1974. Morphological alterations in the microvillus border of villous epithelial

cells produced by intestinal microorganisms. Am. J. Clin. Nutr. **27**:1277–1286.

5. **Etzler, M. E.** 1979. Lectins as probes in studies of intestinal glycoproteins and glycolipids. Am. J. Clin. Nutr. **32**:133–138.

6. **Freter, R.** 1980. Prospects for preventing the association of harmful bacteria with host mucosal surfaces, p. 440–458. *In* E. H. Beachey (ed.), Bacterial adherence (Receptors and recognition, series B, vol. 6). Chapman and Hall, London.

7. **Gemski, P., A. Takeuchi, O. Washington, and S. B. Formal.** 1972. Shigellosis due to *Shigella dysenteriae*. 1. Relative importance of mucosal invasion versus toxin production in pathogenesis. J. Infect. Dis. **126**:523–530.

8. **Hentges, D. J.** 1975. Resistance of the indigenous intestinal flora to the establishment of invading microbial populations, p. 116–119. *In* D. Schlessinger (ed.), Microbiology—1975. American Society for Microbiology, Washington, D.C.

9. **Lee, A.** 1980. Normal flora of animal intestinal surfaces, p. 145–173. *In* B. Bitton and K. C. Marshall (ed.), Adsorption of microorganisms to surfaces. John Wiley & Sons, Inc., New York.

10. **Lee, A., and M. Phillips.** 1978. Isolation and identification of spirochetes and other spiral-shaped bacteria associated with the cecal mucosa of rats and mice. Appl. Environ. Microbiol. **35**:610–613.

11. **Madara, J. L., J. S. Trier, and M. R. Neutra.** 1980. Structural changes in the plasma membrane accompanying differentiation of epithelial cells in human and monkey small intestine. Gastroenterology **78**:963–975.

12. **Neutra, M. R.** 1980. Prokaryotic-eukaryotic cell junctions. Attachment of spirochetes and flagellated bacteria to primate large intestinal cells. J. Ultrastruct. Res. **70**:186–203.

13. **Savage, D. C.** 1972. Survival on mucosal epithelia, epithelial penetration and growth in tissues of pathogenic bacteria. Symp. Soc. Gen. Microbiol. **22**:25–57.

14. **Savage, D.C.** 1975. Indigenous microorganisms associating with mucosal epithelial in the gastrointestinal exosystem, p. 120–123. *In* D. Schlessinger (ed.), Microbiology—1975. American Society for Microbiology, Washington, D.C.

15. **Savage, D. C.** 1977. Electron microscopy of bacteria adherent to epithelia in the murine intestinal canal, p. 422–426. *In* D. Schlessinger (ed.), Microbiology—1977. American Society for Microbiology, Washington, D.C.

16. **Savage, D. C.** 1977. Interactions between the host and its microbes, p. 277–310. *In* R. T. J. Clarke and T. Bauchop (ed.), Microbial ecology of the gut. Academic Press, London.

17. **Savage, D. C.** 1977. Microbial ecology of the gastrointestinal tract. Annu. Rev. Microbiol. **31**:107–133.

18. **Savage, D. C.** 1979. Introduction to mechanisms of association of indigenous microbes. Am. J. Clin. Nutr. **32**:113–118.

19. **Schaedler, R. W., R. Dubos, and R. Costello.** 1965. Association of germfree mice with bacteria isolated from normal mice. J. Exp. Med. **122**:77–82.

20. **Takeuchi, A.** 1973. Penetration of the intestinal epithelium by various microorganisms. Curr. Top. Pathol. **54**:1–27.

21. **Takeuchi, A., S. B. Formal, and H. Sprinz.** 1968. Experimental acute colitis in the rhesus monkey following peroral infection with *Shigella flexnari*. Am. J. Pathol. **52**:503–529.

22. **Takeuchi, A., H. R. Jervis, H. Nakazawa, and D. M. Robinson.** 1974. Spiral shaped organisms on the surface colonic epithelium of monkey and man. Am. J. Clin. Nutr. **27**:1287–1296.

23. **Takeuchi, A., and J. A. Zeller.** 1972. Scanning electron microscopic observations on the surface of the normal and spirochete-infected colonic mucosa of the rhesus monkey. J. Ultrastruct. Res. **40**:313–324.

Bacterial Association with the Mucus Gel System of the Gut

ROLF FRETER

Department of Microbiology, The University of Michigan, Ann Arbor, Michigan 48109

The "mucus" materials of mucosal surfaces are of two types. The first includes glycoproteins and glycolipids synthesized by the epithelial cell, which form an integrated glycocalyx. The second type, which is the subject of this paper, consists of glycoproteins that differ in various characteristics from those of the glycocalyx. This material, hereafter referred to as the "mucus gel," is secreted by specialized cells of the mucosa and often forms a layer covering the epithelium. The basic organization of mucus gels from different species and organs appears to be similar: large glycoprotein molecules that are cross-linked to various degrees by disulfide bridges between peptide chains (2, 7, 23, 25). Mucus is thus a true gel rather than a viscous fluid, and its peculiar rheological properties are due to this fact (23).

Mucous membranes which, by definition, are covered with mucus gel are found on the surfaces of many organs that have widely different functions in the mammalian body. It is therefore not surprising that many different functions have been ascribed also to the mucus gel itself, as will be discussed below.

POTENTIAL FUNCTIONS OF THE MUCUS GEL

Lubrication and chemical protection. The stomach is thought to owe its remarkable resistance to acid and to peptic digestion at least in part to the covering blanket of mucus which acts as an unstirred layer allowing acid that diffuses from the lumen to be neutralized by bicarbonate secreted by the epithelial cells (1, 26). The lubricating properties of mucus are thought to protect the mucosal surfaces of the gastrointestinal tract from abrasive damage by passing ingesta (1, 7). Chemical protection by mucus gel against the activity of proteolytic enzymes has also been envisaged for the small intestine. The relative resistance of native mucus gel to proteolytic degradation has been ascribed to the presence of the carbohydrate side chains which are thought to protrude from the protein backbone like the bristles of a bottle brush. In this view, significant proteolytic degradation of mucus gel occurs in vivo only after the carbohydrate side chains have been degraded by glycosidases of the intestinal microflora (24).

Protection against invading microorganisms. Best studied in this regard is the bronchial mucus gel that is expelled, together with entrapped microorganisms and other particles, by the activity of the ciliary epithelium. Effective propulsion of mucus gel by cilia appears to require a critical match between the rheological properties of the mucus gel and the characteristics of the cilia (23). Florey (6) observed in 1933 that the mucus gel of exteriorized cat or rabbit small intestine could envelop carbon particles and thereby cause their removal when the mucus was subsequently expelled by the pumping action of the intestinal villi. Walker and co-workers (21) have shown that soluble antigen-antibody complexes (or antigen alone in immunized animals) can stimulate the release of mucus gel from intestinal goblet cells. If such a reaction were to be triggered by microorganisms in the immune host, it would constitute a potentially powerful deterrent to mucosal colonization by pathogens.

As late as 1978, Edwards (4) considered the mucus gel to be a "particle and macromolecule proof coating for cell surfaces" through which bacteria must "bore a channel" by means of special virulence mechanisms. This view is no longer tenable, however, because there is considerable published evidence indicating that macromolecules can cross mucosal epithelia with some regularity (reviewed in 29). Evidence of bacterial penetration of mucus gel will be presented next.

Mucus gel as a habitat for bacteria. Dubos and co-workers first drew attention to the large bacterial populations covering the walls of the large intestine (3). They considered these to be embedded in the "mucous layer," but it is not clear whether the material surrounding these populations is of host or bacterial origin. Schrank and Verwey (27) showed that cholera vibrios were present in small intestinal mucus gel of rabbits within 2 h after experimental infection. In contrast, they found carbon particles to be excluded by the mucus gel in their studies. They considered bacterial motility to be the mechanism by which cholera vibrios penetrate the mucus layer. Consistent with this view are the studies by Berry and co-workers (31) showing a definite correlation between vibrio motility and virulence in experimental cholera, again implicating mucus penetration by means of bacterial motility. This straightforward interpretation became more problematical, however, when Jones and Freter (19) reported that motility correlated with the ability of vibrios to adhere to brush border membranes of intestinal epithelial cells, thereby furnishing an alternative explanation for the relationship between motility and virulence in these bacteria. More recent evidence from this laboratory will be discussed later in relation to the effects of bacterial chemotaxis.

Mucus gel as a directional pathway. Gibbons and Sellwood (15) reported that sperm moves in cervical mucus along planes of stress created by stretching of the gel. Jones and Freter (19) showed that cholera vibrios likewise moved along lines of strain created by stretching mucus gel from rabbit small intestine. In contrast, when the same mucus gel was simply deposited on a microscope slide, vibrios penetrated poorly, presumably because there were no parallel lines of stress. It is tempting to speculate that similar tracks may also be formed by the natural stress that is created when mucus gel is extruded by goblet cells. In the intestine, such lines of stress may be expected to parallel the villi and thus to create channels leading from the lumen deep into the intervillous spaces and onto the epithelial surface.

Mucus gel as a nutritional substrate. It has been known for some time that large concentrations of glycoproteins of host origin accumulate in the cecum of axenic rodents (17, 22), thus implicating the indigenous microflora in the normal degradation of these substances. The studies of Hoskins and co-workers (24), as well as those of others, have demonstrated this bacterial activity more directly. Most likely, mucus serves in vivo as a nutritional substrate for at least some of the indigenous gut bacteria. This idea is supported by data suggesting that bacteria capable of degrading the host's blood group-specific glycoproteins may have an ecological advantage in the human gut (16).

Mucus as an inhibitor of bacterial adhesion. In addition to presenting a physical barrier which restricts the access of bacteria to epithelial cell surfaces, components of the mucus gel may also act as competitive inhibitors of bacterial adhesion to epithelial cells. Although mucus gel differs chemically from the cell-associated glycocalyx (with which adherent bacteria interact [18]), there are likely to be sufficient similarities

in the structure of the component oligosaccharides to allow them to react with bacterial adhesins. Indeed, mucosal extracts can inhibit bacterial adhesion to brush border membranes of gut epithelial cells (11), and salivary mucin competes for streptococcal adhesins with receptors on buccal epithelium (30).

Adherent mucus gel as a receptor for bacterial adhesion. Mucus gel may adhere to epithelial cell surfaces with some tenacity (5, 8). M. N. Guentzel et al. (Abstr. Annu. Meet. Am. Soc. Microbiol. 1980, B24, p. 21) reported on electron micrographs showing that adherence of cholera vibrios to gut epithelial cell surfaces can be mediated by a reaction between the bacteria and mucus gel adhering to the mammalian cell. Thus, adherent mucus may provide mucosal epithelia with additional receptors for bacterial adhesion.

Chemotaxis and bacterial penetration of mucus gel. Recent data from this laboratory have implicated the chemotactic attraction of motile bacteria into the mucus gel as a major force aiding such microorganisms in the penetration of the intestinal mucus layer (10, 12–14). Penetration was rapid, requiring less than 15 min when intestinal slices were incubated in bacterial suspensions in vitro or when the bacteria were injected into intestinal loops of mice or rabbits. Inert polystyrene particles in the size range of bacteria or yeast cells also penetrated mucus gel, but at a much slower rate. One must conclude, therefore, that the mucus layer did indeed present a barrier to mucosal penetration, but that this barrier was imperfect and could be negotiated with ease by suitably equipped bacteria.

Taxins (e.g., mucosal extracts), when present on the lumenal side of the mucosa, could prevent the active penetration of the mucus layer by motile bacteria, presumably by blocking the taxin receptors on the bacterial surface and hence preventing chemotaxis. Superior ability to penetrate mucus gel was correlated with superior ecological fitness: nonchemotactic mutants were rapidly outgrown by their chemotactic parents in rabbit intestinal loops and in gnotobiotic mice. Interestingly, nonmotile mutants rapidly outgrew motile, but nonchemotactic, vibrios in gnotobiotic mice. Thus, motility appeared to confer an ecological disadvantage on bacteria in this animal, unless the motility was also guided by chemotactic stimuli.

Motile, chemotactic strains of *Pseudomonas aeruginosa* had a superior ability to infect the bladders of guinea pigs, as compared with normally motile, but nonchemotactic, mutants. As can be seen in Table 1, the ratio of chemotactic

TABLE 1. Recovery of chemotactic and
nonchemotactic *P. aeruginosa* strains from the
bladders of guinea pigs

Determination	Days after infection		
	3	5	6
Ratios:	154[a]	12	18
chemotactic/	390	11	26
nonchemotactic	2.4	6.4	56
Pseudomonas	17		
cultured	22		
from bladder	4.4		
	8.0		
Fraction of	1.5×10^{-7}	3×10^{-8}	2×10^{-9}
inoculum			
recovered[b]			

[a] Each figure represents one animal.
[b] Inoculum was approximately 10^{11} bacteria in-
stilled into the bladder in a 0.5-ml volume. Equal
numbers of a chemotactic plus a nonchemotactic
strain were given to each animal.

to nonchemotactic pseudomonads shifted from a
ratio of 1:1 in the original inoculum to a much
higher preponderance of the chemotactic parent
within 3 to 6 days after instillation of the bacteria
into the bladder (unpublished data).

ROLE OF MUCUS GEL IN BACTERIAL COLONIZATION

A discussion of the role of mucus gel is
pertinent in a symposium on bacterial adhesion
for several reasons. It seems self-evident that
active or passive penetration of mucus gel by
bacteria can have an ecological function similar
to that of binding to the epithelial cell surfaces;
i.e., in either case the bacteria are protected
from physical removal by virtue of their association with the mucosa. Of necessity, penetration
of the mucus gel must be the first stage of
mucosal association. In some instances, trapping and multiplication in the mucus gel may
even represent the only manner in which pathogenic bacteria colonize the mucosa. Even when
adhesion to epithelial cells constitutes the final
mechanism of colonization, the first stage of
bacterial association with the mucus gel may be
quite prolonged and therefore may be of considerable importance in pathogenesis.

For these reasons, the effects of the mucus gel
may at least in part explain the current difficulties encountered by various investigators of bacterial adhesion. After the first exciting successes
(e.g., with K88, K99, and CF antigens), it has
become increasingly difficult to definitively correlate specific adhesive properties of human
pathogens with their pathogenicity, as is docu-

mented in several papers of the present symposium. The various in vivo functions of mucus gel
almost certainly contribute to these difficulties
by modifying—or entirely substituting for—bacterial adhesion to epithelial cell surfaces. Unfortunately, the latter phenomenon is often the only
one considered by contemporary investigators
studying "adhesion" of pathogens to the host's
body surfaces. As discussed above, mucus gel
has the potential for many, often contradictory,
in vivo functions that may modify or even super-
sede bacterial adhesion to epithelial cells: mucus
gel may protect against microbial penetration,
but it may also form a habitat for suitably
equipped bacteria. It may prevent bacterial adhesion to epithelial cells by competitive inhibition, but it may also provide channels leading to
the epithelial cells and it may attract chemotactic bacteria into the mucosa. The mucus gel may
wash away entrapped bacteria but it may also
represent an important nutritional substrate for
other bacteria.

It is a major purpose of the present paper to
suggest that significant progress in our understanding of the interactions of microbial pathogens with mucosal surfaces will require a better
understanding of the various interactions between bacterial virulence mechanisms and the
peculiarities of a given microenvironment that
cause a given potential function of the mucus gel
to become the actually predominant one. For
example, a nonmotile *Escherichia coli* strain
which carries the K99 adhesin may not be significantly affected by the mucus layer because the
few bacteria which traverse it passively (in the
same manner as inert particles) may adhere so
strongly to the epithelial cells that they cannot
be washed away and therefore will be able to
multiply and form large populations. For other
bacteria which adhere only weakly to epithelial
cells, the mucus gel may represent a prohibitive
barrier, except when such bacteria are highly
motile and are attracted deeply into the mucus,
in which case the mucus blanket may become
their habitat and perhaps their food as well.

Another factor that must be considered in
evaluating the role of bacterial adhesion is
whether bacterial "sticking" is indeed a prerequisite for the colonization of a given in vivo
microhabitat. For example, K88 antigen is an
indispensable virulence factor for *E. coli* in
conventional piglets, but is not necessary for
pathogenicity when these animals are germfree
(20). As another example, one may cite the work
of Shedlofsky and Freter, who showed that the
(presumably antiadhesive) effect of local immunity for cholera vibrios significantly reduced the
vibrio populations in mice harboring a compet-

ing microflora, but not in mice monoassociated with the vibrios (28), where adhesion was probably of lesser importance for bacterial colonization. Moreover, it should be intuitively obvious that close association with the mucosa must be outright detrimental to a bacterial pathogen when there is a bactericidal mechanism operating on the mucosal surface. Such antibacterial mechanisms have actually been demonstrated (9), and an instance in which an increased capacity for mucosal association by *Vibrio cholerae* correlated with a reduced ability to colonize infant mice has been described (13).

In summary, then, a better understanding of the relationships between the numerous host and bacterial mechanisms that either promote or inhibit bacterial colonization appears to be necessary before the role of bacterial adhesion in colonization and pathogenicity can be properly evaluated. Prominent among these relationships are the interactions between bacterial pathogens and the mucus gel.

LITERATURE CITED

1. **Allen, A., and A. Garner.** 1980. Mucus and bicarbonate secretion in the stomach and their possible role in mucosal protection. Gut **21**:249–262.
2. **Clamp, J. R., A. Allen, R. A. Gibbons, and G. P. Roberts.** 1978. Chemical aspects of mucus. Br. Med. Bull. **34**:25–41.
3. **Dubos, R., R. W. Schaedler, R. Costello, and P. Hoet.** 1965. Indigenous, normal, and autochthonous flora of the gastrointestinal tract. J. Exp. Med. **122**:67–76.
4. **Edwards, P. A. W.** 1978. Is mucus a selective barrier to macromolecules? Br. Med. Bull. **34**:55–56.
5. **Etzler, M.** 1979. Lectins as probes in studies of intestinal glycoproteins and glycolipids. Am. J. Clin. Nutr. **32**:133–138.
6. **Florey, H. W.** 1933. Observations on the functions of mucus and the early stages of bacterial invasion of the intestinal mucosa. J. Pathol. Bacteriol. **37**:283–289.
7. **Forstner, J. F.** 1978. Intestinal mucins in health and disease. Digestion **17**:234–263.
8. **Forstner, J. F., N. Taichman, V. Kalnins, and G. Forstner.** 1973. Intestinal goblet cell mucus: isolation and identification by immunofluorescence of a goblet cell glycoprotein. J. Cell Sci. **12**:585–602.
9. **Freter, R.** 1970. Mechanism of action of intestinal antibody in experimental cholera. II. Antibody mediated antibacterial reaction at the mucosal surface. Infect. Immun. **2**:556–562.
10. **Freter, R., B. Allweiss, P. C. M. O'Brien, S. A. Halstead, and M. S. Macsai.** 1981. Role of chemotaxis in the association of motile bacteria with intestinal mucosa: in vitro studies. Infect. Immun. **34**:241–249.
11. **Freter, R., and G. W. Jones.** 1976. Adhesive properties of *Vibrio cholerae*: nature of the interaction with intact mucosal surfaces. Infect. Immun. **14**:246–256.
12. **Freter, R., and P. C. M. O'Brien.** 1981. Role of chemotaxis in the association of motile bacteria with intestinal mucosa: chemotactic responses of *Vibrio cholerae* and

description of motile nonchemotactic mutants. Infect. Immun. **34**:215–221.
13. **Freter, R., and P. C. M. O'Brien.** 1981. Role of chemotaxis in the association of motile bacteria with intestinal mucosa: fitness and virulence of nonchemotactic *Vibrio cholerae* mutants in mice. Infect. Immun. **34**:222–233.
14. **Freter, R., P. C. M. O'Brien, and M. S. Macsai.** 1981. Role of chemotaxis in the association of motile bacteria with intestinal mucosa: in vivo studies. Infect. Immun. **34**:234–240.
15. **Gibbons, R. A., and R. Sellwood.** 1973. The macromolecular biochemistry of cervical secretions, p. 251–265. *In* R. J. Blandau and K. Moghissi (ed.), The biology of the cervix. University of Chicago Press, Chicago.
16. **Hoskins, L. C., and E. T. Boulding.** 1976. Degradation of blood group antigens in human colon ecosystems. II. A gene interaction in man that affects the fecal population density of certain enteric bacteria. J. Clin. Invest. **57**:74–82.
17. **Hoskins, L. C., and N. Zamcheck.** 1968. Bacterial degradation of gastrointestinal mucins. I. Comparison of mucus constituents in the stools of germ-free and conventional rats. Gastroenterology **54**:210–217.
18. **Jones, G. W.** 1977. The attachment of bacteria to surfaces of animal cells, p. 141–176. *In* J. L. Reissig (ed.), Microbial interactions. Chapman and Hall, London.
19. **Jones, G. W., and R. Freter.** 1976. Adhesive properties of *Vibrio cholerae*. Infect. Immun. **14**:232–245.
20. **Jones, G. W., and J. M. Rutter.** 1972. Role of K88 antigen in the pathogenesis of neonatal diarrhea caused by *Escherichia coli* in piglets. Infect. Immun. **6**:918–927.
21. **Lake, A. M., K. J. Bloch, M. R. Neutra, and W. A. Walker.** 1979. Intestinal goblet cell mucus release. II. In vivo stimulation by antigen in the immunized rat. J. Immunol. **122**:834–837.
22. **Loesche, W. J.** 1968. Accumulation of endogenous protein in the cecum of the germfree rat. Proc. Soc. Exp. Biol. Med. **129**:380–384.
23. **Meyer, R. A., and A. Silverberg.** 1980. The rheology and molecular organization of epithelial mucus. Biorheology **17**:163–168.
24. **Miller, R. S., and L. C. Hoskins.** 1981. Mucin degradation in human colon ecosystems. Fecal population densities of mucin-degrading bacteria estimated by a "most probable number" method. Gastroenterology **81**:759–765.
25. **Pain, R. H.** 1980. The viscoelasticity of mucus: a molecular model. Symp. Soc. Exp. Biol. **34**:359–376.
26. **Ross, I. N., H. M. M. Bahari, and L. A. Turnberg.** 1981. The pH gradient across mucus adherent to rat fundic mucosa in vivo and the effect of potential damaging agents. Gastroenterology **81**:713–718.
27. **Schrank, G. D., and W. F. Verwey.** 1976. Distribution of cholera organisms in experimental *Vibrio cholerae* infections: proposed mechanisms of pathogenesis and antibacterial immunity. Infect. Immun. **13**:195–203.
28. **Shedlofsky, S., and R. Freter.** 1974. Synergism between ecologic and immunologic control mechanisms of intestinal flora. J. Infect. Dis. **129**:296–303.
29. **Warshaw, A. L., C. A. Bellini, and W. A. Walker.** 1977. The intestinal mucosal barrier to intact antigenic protein: difference between colon and small intestine. Am. J. Surg. **133**:55–58.
30. **Williams, R. C., and R. J. Gibbons.** 1975. Inhibition of streptococcal attachment to receptors on human buccal epithelial cells by antigenically similar salivary glycoproteins. Infect. Immun. **11**:711–718.
31. **Yancey, R. J., D. L. Willis, and L. J. Berry.** 1978. Role of motility in experimental cholera in adult rabbits. Infect. Immunol. **22**:387–392.

Influence of Salivary Components on Bacterial Adhesion

R. J. GIBBONS

Forsyth Dental Center, Boston, Massachusetts 02115

In addition to their lubrication and moistening properties, mucosal secretions are thought to protect the underlying epithelium from infectious agents and noxious substances. However, how secretions provide this protection has not been well studied. Interest in this area is increasing, because it is now realized that bacteria introduced into a mucosal environment must become attached to a surface before they can colonize; otherwise, they are removed by the flow of secretions. The attachment of bacteria to several host tissues has been found to be surprisingly specific, and the selectivity of this process can account for differences in the innate resistance or susceptibility of various hosts and tissues to infection. It is now clear that components of mucosal secretions can affect the attachment of bacteria to surfaces in a relatively specific manner, and this can influence their colonization. Therefore, the influence of secretions should be taken into account in any study of the role of bacterial adherence in the colonization process. The following discussion summarizes some information concerning the influence of secretions on the adherence and colonization of bacteria in the mouth; more extensive reviews are available (4, 8). Several of the principles which have evolved should prove applicable to other mucosal environments.

FEATURES OF THE MOUTH

Surfaces of the mouth available for bacterial colonization include those of the teeth, tongue, palate, gingiva, and buccal mucosa (4, 8). Oral secretions are derived from the parotid, submaxillary, sublingual, and minor salivary glands (10). Parotid secretion is a serous fluid which contains mostly cationic, nonviscous glycoproteins. Secretions from the other salivary glands are more viscous as a result of the presence of anionic, high-molecular-weight mucins and other glycoproteins. Humans secrete approximately 1 to 1.5 liters of saliva each day. Though secretions from the minor salivary glands account for only a small percentage of the total fluid, their glycoprotein content is high, and they contribute roughly half of the blood group-reactive mucins and secretory immunoglobulin A found in mixed oral fluid.

BACTERIAL ATTACHMENT TO SURFACES OF THE MOUTH

Interest in the attachment of bacteria to surfaces of the mouth stemmed from the recognition that dental caries and periodontal diseases are caused by bacterial accumulations, called dental plaques, which develop on the surfaces of teeth. Teeth are covered by a thin membranous film, termed the "acquired pellicle," which is formed by the selective adsorption of salivary components to hydroxyapatite mineral of enamel (4, 8). Components regularly detected in pellicles include blood group-reactive mucins, proteins which are rich in tyrosine, proline, and histidine, immunoglobulin A, and lysozyme. Amylase and immunoglobulin G are sometimes present, but muramic and diaminopimelic acids are usually not detectable; this suggests that pellicles do not contain appreciable quantities of bacterial cells. Pellicles are thought to protect the teeth from demineralization after exposure to acidic foods or beverages. However, to colonize a tooth, bacteria suspended in oral fluids must attach to the pellicle; this implies that surface components of the organism interact with adsorbed salivary macromolecules comprising this film.

In vitro models for studying bacterial attachment to teeth have used natural or synthetic hydroxyapatite adsorbents which were treated with human saliva to form an experimental pellicle (4, 8). Bacterial attachment to such saliva-treated hydroxyapatite surfaces can be quantitated by use of radiolabeled organisms or by turbidometric, cultural, or visual techniques. In vitro studies of bacterial attachment to epithelial surfaces have mainly used buccal cells obtained by scraping the cheek surfaces of volunteers. Such cells are incubated with washed bacteria, and the number which attach is determined by microscopy or other means. Use of such in vitro models has demonstrated that different bacterial species attach to quite different extents to saliva-treated hydroxyapatite surfaces and to buccal cells.

The specificity of bacterial adhesion has also been demonstrated directly in the mouth (7). This has been accomplished by introducing mixtures of streptomycin-resistant strains of benign indigenous bacteria into the mouths of volunteers. The proportions of one species relative to another which attach to a given surface are determined by culturing swab samples collected shortly afterwards on streptomycin-containing media. It has also been possible to study the attachment to thoroughly cleaned teeth of organisms which are naturally present in easily measurable concentrations in saliva.

Use of such in vitro and in vivo models has demonstrated that indigenous streptococci and other bacteria attach to oral surfaces in a highly selective manner, and their relative adherence, as determined experimentally, correlates with the extent to which they naturally colonize a site (7). These studies revealed the surprising recognition capabilities of the bacterial cell surface, and they also made it clear that bacterial colonization in the mouth, or in other environments which contain surfaces exposed to a fluid flow, requires that organisms attach to a surface to avoid being washed away. Attachment, therefore, is a major determinant of colonization of several host tissues.

MECHANISMS OF BACTERIAL ATTACHMENT

The high degree of specificity involved in the attachment of bacteria to oral tissues suggests the participation of a well-developed recognition system. Though bacteria can become loosely associated with surfaces by ionic and other physical forces of low specificity, a variety of data suggest that the affinity necessary for colonization requires the interaction of lectin-like ligands of the organism, called "adhesins," which can effectively link it to components in the pellicle or on epithelial cell surfaces (4, 8). These ligands may be fimbriae, various sugar-binding proteins, or surface-bound enzymes with specific binding properties; they may also represent surface components with hydrophobic properties. They are thought to interact with glycoprotein or glycolipid receptors on mucosal cell surfaces.

CLEANSING FORCES OPERATIVE IN THE MOUTH

Several bacteria and yeasts have been shown to be cleared rapidly after their introduction into the mouth, and therefore it is clear that potent cleansing forces are present. The existence of effective oral cleansing forces is suggested by several other observations. For example, sparse bacterial populations are present on the buccal mucosa and palate which are bathed by parotid and minor gland secretions, respectively, despite their frequent exposure to mixed oral fluids which contain more than 10^8 organisms per ml (7). In contrast, the dorsal surface of the tongue, which lacks major and minor glands, harbors over 100 bacteria per epithelial cell. The importance of saliva in protecting oral tissues also becomes painfully evident when a malfunction of the salivary glands occurs as a result of head and neck irradiation which results in xerostomia or "dry mouth" (10). Under such conditions, the mucosa bleeds easily and is highly prone to infection. Also, heavy accumulations of bacteria develop on the teeth, and dental caries and periodontal diseases are extensive.

Humans vary in the rate at which bacteria accumulate on their teeth and also in the rate at which bacteria are cleared from their mouths. These differences are often unrelated to the volume of salivary flow, and this suggests that the composition of oral fluids is at least as significant as their volume in the cleansing processes (4, 8). This is also suggested by studies which have shown that macromolecular components of saliva are highly effective in inhibiting the attachment of bacteria to experimental pellicles (2, 12) and to oral epithelial cells (14, 16). Such components include blood group-reactive mucins and other high-molecular-weight glycoproteins, antibodies, and lysozyme (3, 6, 9, 13, 15, 16); these have also been shown to bind to various bacteria, and this often causes aggregation.

The interaction of salivary macromolecules with bacteria can affect their attachment in several ways. First, some salivary components are similar, if not identical, to constituents of the enamel pellicle, and hence, they can compete for bacterial adhesins involved in attachment. Also, blood group-reactive mucins, and probably other components, are structurally related to glycoproteins and glycolipids on epithelial cell surfaces which act as bacterial receptors; therefore, they may also act as competitive inhibitors of attachment. Second, components which bind to bacteria may sterically mask adhesins. Third, salivary components which aggregate bacteria can affect attachment by this physical clumping per se. In fact, Liljemark and co-workers (9) recently showed that increased numbers of streptococci attach to experimental pellicles when the organisms are present as small aggregates of two or three cocci, but much lower numbers attach when they are in the form of large aggregates. Fourth, salivary components which mimic receptors and can compete for bacterial adhesins may also promote desorption of previously attached organisms.

The interactions of some salivary components with bacteria are highly specific (4, 8). For example, adsorption isotherms indicate that the number of binding sites on saliva-treated hydroxyapatite varies widely for different species; this suggests that different organisms interact with different pellicle receptors. This is also indicated by experiments which have shown that different oral *Streptococcus* species do not compete with one another for binding sites on experimental pellicles. In addition, saliva treated with various quantities of hydroxyapatite loses the ability to aggregate some bacterial species but not others. Furthermore, repeated adsorption of saliva or blood group-reactive mucin preparations with cells of one species renders them unreactive for additional cells of that species, but not for other organisms. Finally, it has been shown that treatment of a purified salivary glycoprotein with neuraminidase rendered it unreactive with cells of *S. sanguis*, but it still reacted with *S. mutans*.

INFLUENCE OF ORAL CLEARANCE ON BACTERIAL COLONIZATION

Several observations suggest that oral cleansing mechanisms do affect bacterial colonization. Thus, organisms such as *S. mutans* and lactobacilli, which have a relatively weak affinity for pellicles, preferentially colonize occlusal fissures and contact points between teeth which are relatively protected from cleansing activities (7). Conversely, bacteria which adhere avidly to experimental pellicles, such as *Actinomyces viscosus*, *S. mitis*, and *S. sanguis*, usually are found in significant proportions in plaques on most tooth surfaces. Specific components of salivary secretions have also been shown to affect colonization in some instances. Thus, secretory immunoglobulin A antibodies induced to *S. mutans* affect the extent to which it accumulates on teeth, and this may be associated with a reduction in dental caries (11). Also, populations of oral streptococci undergo antigenic fluctuations while colonizing experimental animals and humans, and this is thought to be modulated by the host's immune response.

Salivary mucins also may affect bacterial colonization. For example, strains of *Bacteroides gingivalis* contain several types of fimbriae, and buffer-suspended cells of this organism attach in high numbers to erythrocytes and to epithelial cells derived from buccal mucosa or from the gingival crevice area (14). *B. gingivalis* cells also attach, though less well, to experimental pellicles. However, when the organism is suspended in saliva, adherence to all of these surfaces is either greatly reduced or totally eliminated. The adherence-inhibiting activity is mainly associated with the blood group-reactive mucin fraction, though other salivary components also possess some activity. *B. gingivalis* cells coaggregate with *Actinomyces* and various other gram-positive bacteria, but saliva does not affect these interactions. The significance of these various adherent interactions has been assessed in the mouths of humans by introducing streptomycin-resistant mutants of *B. gingivalis*. After 150 min, *B. gingivalis* cells could be recovered only from preexisting dental plaques which harbor *Actinomyces* and other gram-positive organisms. This observation strongly suggests that the most significant receptors available to *B. gingivalis* cells entering the mouth are those present on the surfaces of gram-positive bacteria. Evidently, the potent adherence-inhibiting effects of salivary mucins negate the organisms' potential for attaching to other surfaces. It seems clear from this example that it may be difficult or even impossible to evaluate the in vivo significance of the adherence properties of an organism as determined in vitro unless the effects of secretions are considered.

Strains of *A. viscosus* and *A. naeslundii* possess a galactose-binding lectin, and this enables them to coaggregate with oral streptococci which contain galactosyl moieties on their surface (1). These coaggregation reactions are inhibited by lactose and also by saliva, and therefore, they differ significantly from those between *B. gingivalis* and *Actinomyces* (K. Komiyama and R. J. Gibbons, J. Dent. Res. Spec. Issue A, in press). Their susceptibility to saliva inhibition would seem to decrease the likelihood that they occur to a significant extent in the mouth.

It is interesting to note that many foods contain lectin-like components which can interact with components of saliva and various oral bacteria. Treatment of experimental pellicles, or of epithelial cells, with various lectins has been shown to either inhibit or enhance bacterial attachment. Also, the interaction of lectins with mammalian cells has been associated with a multitude of effects which range from mitogenic stimulation through cell death. However, when many lectins are dissolved in saliva, their binding to experimental pellicles or to buccal cells is reduced by 70 to 90% (J. Dankers and R. J. Gibbons, J. Dent. Res. Spec. Issue A **59**:542, abstr. 1091, 1980). Therefore, the ability of components of secretions to decrease the interaction of food lectins, as well as bacterial adhesins, with mucosal surfaces would appear to be one of the major functions of saliva and other secretions of the alimentary canal.

OTHER CONSEQUENCES OF SALIVA-BACTERIUM INTERACTIONS

On the one hand, components of saliva may help to protect oral surfaces from infectious agents and noxious substances; however, on the other hand, they may promote bacterial colonization of the teeth. Salivary components comprising the pellicle provide the receptors to which bacteria attach. However, since teeth do not desquamate, bacteria may accumulate in masses several hundreds of micrometers thick, especially in the more protected sites. Substances which bind to bacteria proliferating on the teeth and cause their aggregation are thought to promote such accumulations, and in fact, the matrices of plaques have been shown to contain macromolecules with bacterial aggregating activity, including high-molecular-weight mucinous glycoproteins (7, 8).

Mucins may affect colonization in other ways. Organisms suspended in mucin often survive for long periods of time, and this may promote their transmission in droplets and on contaminated objects. Also, because blood group-reactive mucin molecules bind avidly to bacteria and cannot be readily removed by washing, the organisms acquire part of the antigenic makeup of their host (6). This may help the organisms escape recognition by the host. It may also influence their transmission between individuals. For example, organisms proliferating in an individual of blood type A acquire A reactivity, and they would be expected to be affected by anti-A antibodies present in the secretions of individuals of other blood types.

MODIFICATION OF BACTERIAL RECEPTORS BY SALIVARY ENZYMES

We have recently observed that mixed oral fluid contains heat-labile substances, presumably enzymes, which can modify or destroy the receptors for strains of *S. mutans* and *S. sanguis* on experimental pellicles (5). Commercially obtained preparations of certain glycoside hydrolases produce similar effects. Enzymes found in mixed oral fluids may be derived from bacteria, which have been shown to synthesize an array of glycosidases, from the lysosomes of leukocytes, or from secretory cells in the salivary glands. Their presence may enable secretions to modify or destroy bacterial receptors throughout the alimentary canal.

LITERATURE CITED

1. Cisar, J. O., P. E. Kolenbrander, and F. C. McIntire. 1970. Specificity of coaggregation reactions between human oral streptococci and strains of *Actinomyces viscosus* and *Actinomyces naeslundii*. Infect. Immun. **24:**742–752.
2. Clark, W. B., and R. J. Gibbons. 1977. Influence of salivary components and extracellular polysaccharide synthesis from sucrose on the attachment of *Streptococcus mutans* 6715 to hydroxyapatite surfaces. Infect. Immun. **18:**514–523.
3. Ericson, T., and J. Magnusson. 1976. Affinity for hydroxyapatite of salivary substances inducing aggregation of oral streptococci. Caries Res. **10:**8–18.
4. Gibbons, R. J. 1980. Adhesion of bacteria to surfaces of the mouth, p. 351–388. *In* R. C. W. Berkeley, J. M. Lynch, J. Melling, P. R. Rutter, and B. Vincent (ed.), Microbial adhesion to surfaces. Society for Chemistry and Industry, Ellis-Horwood, Ltd., Chichester, England.
5. Gibbons, R. J., and I. Etherden. 1982. Enzymatic modification of bacterial receptors on saliva-treated hydroxyapatite surfaces. Infect. Immun. **36:**52–58.
6. Gibbons, R. J., and J. V. Qureshi. 1979. Selective binding of blood group reactive salivary mucins by *Streptococcus mutans* and other oral organisms. Infect. Immun. **22:**665–671.
7. Gibbons, R. J., and J. van Houte. 1975. Bacterial adherence in oral microbial ecology. Annu. Rev. Microbiol. **29:**19–44.
8. Gibbons, R. J., and J. van Houte. 1980. Bacterial adherence and the formation of dental plaques, p. 424–435. *In* E. H. Beachey (ed.), Bacterial adherence (Receptors and recognition, series B, vol. 6). Chapman and Hall, London.
9. Liljemark, W. F., C. S. Bloomquist, and G. R. Germaine. 1981. Effect of bacterial aggregation on the adherence of oral streptococci to hydroxyapatite. Infect. Immun. **31:**935–941.
10. Mandel, I. D., and S. Wotman. 1976. The salivary secretions in health and disease. Oral Sci. Rev. **8:**25–47.
11. McGhee, J. R., and S. M. Michalek. 1981. Immunobiology of dental caries; microbial aspects and local immunity. Annu. Rev. Microbiol. **35:**595–638.
12. Orstavik, D., F. W. Kraus, and L. C. Henshaw. 1974. In vitro attachment of streptococci to the tooth surface. Infect. Immun. **9:**794–800.
13. Pollock, J. J., V. J. Iacono, H. G. Bicker, B. J. MacKay, L. Katona, and L. B. Taichman. 1976. The binding, aggregation and lytic properties of lysozyme, p. 325–352. *In* H. M. Stiles, W. J. Loesche, and T. C. O'Brien (ed.), Microbial aspects of dental caries. Information Retrieval Inc., Washington, D.C.
14. Slots, J., and R. J. Gibbons. 1978. Attachment of *Bacteroides melaninogenicus* subsp. *asaccharolyticus* to oral surfaces and its possible role in colonization of the mouth and of periodontal pockets. Infect. Immun. **19:**254–264.
15. Williams, R. C., and R. J. Gibbons. 1971. Inhibition of bacterial adherence by secretory immunoglobulin A: a mechanism of antigen disposal. Science **177:**697–699.
16. Williams, R. C., and R. J. Gibbons. 1975. Inhibition of streptococcal attachment to receptors on human buccal epithelial cells by antigenically similar salivary glycoproteins. Infect. Immun. **11:**711–718.

ROLE OF SURFACE PROTEINS INVOLVED IN SURFACE ADHESION

Adherence to Uroepithelia In Vitro and In Vivo

C. SVANBORG EDÉN, R. FRETER, L. HAGBERG, R. HULL, S. HULL, H. LEFFLER, H. LOMBERG, AND G. SCHOOLNIK

Departments of Clinical Immunology, Pediatrics, and Medical Biochemistry, University of Göteborg, Göteborg, Sweden; Department of Microbiology, University of Michigan, Ann Arbor, Michigan 48109; Department of Microbiology and Immunology, Baylor School of Medicine, Houston, Texas 77025; and Division of Infectious Diseases, Stanford School of Medicine, Palo Alto, California 94305

The interactions of bacteria with host mucosal surfaces, as they occur during the pathogenesis of urinary tract infection (UTI), have proved useful in the study of bacterial adhesion. In a suitable host, *Escherichia coli* from the intestine proceeds to colonize the outer genital area and ascends to the urinary tract (16, 17). Depending on the susceptibility of the host and the virulence of the *E. coli* strain, the ensuing infection may be severe, involving the kidney as in acute pyelonephritis, limited to the bladder as in acute cystitis, or unnoticed as asymptomatic bacteriuria. A role of bacterial adhesion both in the selection of uropathogenic *E. coli* from the intestine (20) and in determining the level and severity of urinary tract infection (UTI) (19) was suggested by our earlier work (recently reviewed in 16 and 17). Subsequent identification of epithelial cell receptors and bacterial ligands involved in the adhesion process has allowed a more detailed analysis of the role of bacterial adhesion both in vitro and in vivo, as will be illustrated in this paper.

MECHANISMS OF ADHESION

Adherence, as determined by microscopy or other means, is the end result of multiple interactions of bacterial adhesins with host cell receptors. Uropathogenic *E. coli* can participate in several binding reactions, each involving a distinct set of receptors and ligands. The specificity of binding of one strain will depend on its complement of adhesins, and it will bind to a cell that possesses receptors for these adhesins (12). Work with wild-type strains with "single" specificities, and more recently with genetically manipulated strains has allowed a separate analysis of adhesins that are expressed simultaneously on the same wild-type strain.

Globoseries glycolipid receptors. The known species and tissue specificity of glycolipids (12),

as well as their function as blood group antigens (22) and as receptors for bacterial toxins (4), prompted our investigation of the role of glycolipids as receptors for specific bacterial adhesins. Globoseries glycolipids (11) with the minimal saccharide sequence αGal 1→4 βGal (7) fulfilled the criteria of receptors for the mannose-resistant adhesins of uropathogenic *E. coli* in the following way: (i) these *E. coli* strains adhered only to cells in which these substances were present naturally and not to cells free from globoseries glycolipids; (ii) attachment to human uroepithelial cells could be inhibited by neutral glycolipids isolated from reactive cells (11) as well as by purified globoseries glycolipids; and (iii) binding to unreactive cells could be induced when those cells were coated with globoside (11). The inhibition of adhesion in vitro by receptor analogs is illustrated in Table 1. As can be seen, relatively low concentrations of globotetraose (9 to 30 µg/ml) were required for 50% inhibition of adhesion. Mannosides had no effect. The capacity of receptor analogs to inhibit in vivo infections is mentioned below.

Bacterial ligands. Piliform bacterial appendages have been indirectly identified as ligands in many binding reactions (for review, see 1 and 2). Pili isolated by the improved technique of Korhonen et al. (9) retain the binding properties of whole bacteria (8) and react with globoside receptors (10). Interaction of pili with mannose residues has previously been shown (15). The interaction with globoseries glycolipid receptors results in attachment to uroepithelial cells; binding to mannose residues may be important for the association with urinary slime (14).

In spite of the marked difference in function and binding specificity, the pili binding to globoseries glycolipids and those with binding inhibited by mannosides are extremely similar in origin and primary protein structure (18). The genes of

TABLE 1. Inhibition of adhesion to human urinary sediment epithelial cells by receptor sugar

E. coli strain[a]	Adhesins	Control mean adherence[b]	Concn (µg/ml) of globotetraose[c] required for 50% inhibition of adhesion
3669	MR	41	11.5 ± 0.02
3048	MR MS	40	29.1 ± 0.04
824	MR	38	8.9 ± 3.8
849	MR	40	17.4 ± 7.6
742	MS	0	—

[a] E. coli 3669 and 3048 are wild-type pyelonephritis strains, previously used as model strains (8, 12); E. coli 824 and 742 are nitrosoguanidine-derived mutants from a pyelonephritic isolate, retaining only the mannose-resistant (MR) or mannose-sensitive (MS) adhesins. E. coli 849 is E. coli K-12 with the genes coding for MR pilus formation and expression cloned with pACY184 as a vector. (For more details see Svanborg Edén et al., in manuscript; Hull et al., in manuscript.)

[b] The bacterial concentration was ~10^9 bacteria per ml. Mean number of bacteria attached to 40 epithelial cells.

[c] Globotetraose was obtained by ozonolysis from globotetraosylceramide, as detailed in footnote d of Table 4.

both are chromosomally located (5) in contrast to other "mannose-resistant adhesins," most of which are coded for by plasmids (for review, see 3). The amino acid compositions of E. coli 3669, 3048, and Bam pilus proteins are very similar, as are their N-terminal amino acid sequences (18; C. Svanborg Edén et al., in manuscript). Certain variations in primary structure of different globoside-binding as well as mannose-binding pili have been observed. In spite of the similarities in primary protein structure, these pilus proteins are antigenically distinct. The lack of cross-reactivity between the globoside-binding pili on the urinary tract strains is an obstacle in the search for a pilus vaccine against recurrent UTI. Search for a common pilus antigen, probably the common receptor binding site shared by most of these pili, is in progress (see G. K. Schoolnik, J. Y. Tai, and E. C. Gotschlich, this volume).

ROLE OF ADHESION FOR ASCENDING UTI IN MICE

Globoseries glycolipids are the major nonacid glycolipids of human and mouse kidney. E. coli strains causing UTI in humans adhere to the same degree to epithelial cells from the sediment of human urine and the mouse bladder (Table 2). Both adhesion reactions can be inhibited in vitro by preincubation of the bacteria with globoseries glycolipids or their isolated sugars. Mice were, therefore, chosen as experimental animals to

TABLE 2. Properties of the E. coli strains used to infect mice

E. coli strain[a]	Adhesion to uroepithelial cells (bacteria/cell)		Hemagglutination pattern[b]	
	Human	Mouse	Human	Guinea pig
734	98	65	MR	MS
742	0	10	—	MS
824	90	51	MR	—

[a] E. coli 734, 742, and 824 were nitrosoguanidine-derived mutants from a wild-type pyelonephritic strain, differing only in adhesive properties.

[b] MR, Mannose resistant; MS, mannose sensitive.

investigate the role of adherence and the protective effect of receptor analogs in ascending UTI by strains relevant to human disease.

The mice were infected by catheterization of the urethra and injection of 0.05 ml of a bacterial suspension. At different times after infection the animals were sacrificed, kidneys and bladders were homogenized, and viable counts were performed (L. Hagberg et al., in manuscript).

The roles of adhesion per se and of the different types of adhesins were investigated by using genetically defined E. coli strains (Table 2). E. coli 734, 824, and 742 were derived by nitroso-guanidine mutagenesis from a wild-type E. coli strain isolated from a patient with acute pyelonephritis. This parent strain attached to human uroepithelial cells in vitro and carried surface ligands binding to globoseries glycolipids as well as to mannose-containing compounds. By hemagglutination and adhesion testing, mutants were selected to have only one of those binding properties. E. coli 734, 824, and 742 thus had identical chromosomal electromorph type, plasmid pattern, serotype, and sugar fermentation pattern (API 20E), were resistant to the bactericidal effect of normal human serum, and produced hemolysin, but E. coli 824 bound only to globoseries glycolipids and E. coli 742 bound only to mannose residues. E. coli 734 retained both binding properties (for details, see R. Hull et al., in manuscript).

To circumvent the problems of variation inherent in most animal models, a mixed infection protocol was chosen (Table 3). Each mouse was infected with a mixture of the two E. coli strains labeled with resistance to streptomycin or nalidixic acid. The exact proportions of each strain in the inoculum and in the homogenates of kidneys and bladders of the infected mice were determined by viable counts on agar containing streptomycin and nalidixic acid. The recovery of each strain was determined as the fraction of bacteria inoculated.

TABLE 3. Outcome of ascending experimental UTI in mice[a]

Inoculum	Tissue	Recovery of bacteria after 16 h		
		No. of animals with		Significance, P (sign-rank test)
		734<742	734>742	
734 Str[r] + 742 Nal[r]	Kidney	0	22	<0.001
	Bladder	0	22	<0.001
		734<824	734>824	
734 Str[r] + 824 Nal[r]	Kidney	6	8	NS[b]
	Bladder	1	14	0.01

[a] Each animal was infected with a mixture of the *E. coli* strains mentioned under inoculum, distinguishable by resistance to 1 mg of streptomycin per ml (Str[r]) or 50 μg of nalidixic acid per ml (Nal[r]). The exact proportions of each strain in the inoculum and in the homogenates of kidneys and bladders of the infected mice were determined as a fraction of the bacteria inoculated. The table shows the number of animals in which one or the other strain in the inoculum was recovered in higher numbers.
[b] Not significant.

E. coli 734, which had globoside- and mannose-binding properties, was more virulent in both the kidney and the bladder, when compared with *E. coli* 742, which expressed only the mannose-binding pili. Equal efficiency in colonizing the kidney was obtained when *E. coli* 734 and 824, both binding to globoside receptors, were compared. In the bladder, however, *E. coli* 734 was a more efficient colonizer (Table 3). These results are consistent with the theory that mannose-binding adhesins are sufficient for bladder colonization in the mouse model, whereas globoside recognition is more important for kidney infection.

The inhibition of experimental infection by receptor analogs was tested as detailed in the footnotes of Table 4. A mixed inoculum of *E. coli* 824 and 742, one strain binding to globotetraose and the other to mannose, was used. After preincubation of the mixed inocula with globotetraose, α-methyl-mannoside, or phosphate-buffered saline, mice were infected as described above. The ratio of recovery of 824/742 from each animal was calculated. This ratio would be lower if the recovery of strain 824 from the animals was decreased relative to the recovery of strain 742. If, for example, treatment of the inoculum with globotetraose were to reduce the colonization of the animal by strain 824, one would expect a lower number of this strain recovered relative to strain 742, which is not affected by this inhibitor. Pretreatment with globotetraose produced a significant decrease in the ratio, indicating protection against *E. coli* 824. No significant change in the ratio was seen after preincubation with α-mannoside (Svanborg Edén et al., in manuscript).

CLINICAL CONSIDERATIONS

The new knowledge about mechanisms of adhesion of uropathogenic *E. coli* might tentatively be used for diagnostic, prognostic, or therapeutic purposes. About 80% of *E. coli* isolates from infants with first-time acute pyelonephritis attach to human uroepithelial cells, and about 90% of those recognize globoseries glycolipids as epithelial cell receptors (6, 12, 16, 17, 21). Globoside binding is a simple test and has been suggested as a diagnostic tool for detecting "dangerous" bacteria. In how many patients with clinical signs of acute pyelonephritis would the diagnosis or treatment be changed by the outcome of this test? Probably very few. As shown in Table 5, the correlation between attaching bacteria and pyelonephritis holds true only for patients without reflux or other underlying problems. Regardless of the properties of the infecting strain, patients with clinical signs of acute pyelonephritis must be treated, since risk factors like reflux cannot be excluded.

The globoseries glycolipids are antigens in the P blood group system, and the P blood group phenotype seems to play a role in susceptibility to recurrent pyelonephritis. Persons of blood group P_1 phenotype have three antigens (p^k, P_1, and P) in their cell membranes, whereas those of blood group P_2 have two (p^k and P). We have suggested (13) that people of blood group P_1 may have a higher density of receptors for bacterial adhesins than those of blood group P_2. Indeed, the P_1 blood group phenotype is overrepresented in patients with recurrent pyelonephritis without reflux (Table 5), who have only about 3% P_2 compared with its frequency of 25% in the overall population (13). The majority of infecting strains in those patients recognize the globoseries glycolipid receptor (12) (Table 5). Could P blood group determination be used prognostically, to identify patients at risk for recurrent pyelonephritis or renal damage? Not as the only test. The incidence of P_1 blood group in the normal population is 75%. The probability is therefore high that a UTI patient will belong to this group, regardless of the severity of infection.

TABLE 4. Inhibitor of experimental infection by receptor analogs[a]

Animal group	Time (h)	No. of animals	Ratio of recovery, 824 Str^r/742 Nal^r[b]			
			Common median[c]	No. of animals <median>		Avg rank	Significance, P (x^2 for the median)
Globo inhibition[d]							
PBS, all cultures	2	8	0.986	1	7	11.375	<0.01
Globo, all cultures	2	7		6	0	4.143	
PBS, all cultures	16	32	0.470	12	20	30.063	<0.03
Globo, all cultures	16	19		13	5	19.158	
PBS, all cultures	All	49	0.352	19	30	48.204	<0.019
Globo, all cultures	times	36		23	12	35.917	
α-Mm inhibition[e]							
PBS, all cultures	16	22	1.379	9	12	30.273	0.24
α-Mm, all cultures	16	31		17	14	24.677	
PBS, kidneys	All	6	2.660	3	2	9.500	0.53
α-Mm, kidneys	times	13		6	7	10.231	
PBS, bladders	All	16	1.092	7	9	20.750	0.37
α-Mm, bladders	times	18		10	8	14.61	

[a] E. coli 824 and 742 were nitrosoguanidine-derived mutants from the wild-type E. coli strain GR12 isolated from a patient with acute pyelonephritis. E. coli 824 bound to globotetraosylceramide receptors; E. coli 742 bound to mannose residues.

[b] To allow separate detection of the two strains from a mixture, mutants of E. coli 824 resistant to 1 mg of streptomycin per ml (824 Str^r) and of E. coli 742 resistant to 50 μg of nalidixic acid per ml (742 Nal^r) were selected by serial passage on gradient plates. The resistant mutants were considered stable when they grew equally well on media with or without antibiotic after one passage on an antibiotic-free medium. E. coli 824 Str^r and 742 Nal^r also had the same adhesion and hemagglutination specificities as their parent strains. Furthermore, no difference was found in the recovery of E. coli 824 parent and 824 Str^r or E. coli 742 parent and 742 Nal^r from mice infected with mixtures of each parent and resistant mutant (not shown). Bacteria were preincubated with phosphate-buffered saline (PBS) alone or PBS with globotetraose (for experiment 1, 50 μg/ml = three times the concentration required for 50% inhibition of the adhesion of 10^9 E. coli 824 cells in vitro; for experiment 2, 30 μg/ml = two times the inhibitory concentration). The inocula per mouse were as follows: for experiment 1 in PBS 3.9×10^8 824 Str^r and 8.3×10^7 742 Nal^r cells; for experiment 2 in PBS 3.0×10^8 824 Str^r and 3.9×10^7 742 Nal^r cells and in globotetraose 2.9×10^8 824 Str^r and 3.3×10^7 Nal^r cells. After sacrifice, homogenization of tissue, and parallel culture on Trypticase soy agar without antibiotic and with 1 mg of streptomycin or 50 μg of nalidixic acid per ml, the ratios of recovery of 824 Str^r/742 Nal^r as a percentage of their respective inocula were determined for each animal and each tissue. The ratios were ranked within the groups compared. The average rank in each group as well as the median in each group is shown. Differences were evaluated by the Mann-Whitney U test or a x^2 test for the median. The P values show the outcome of the latter.

[c] The median ratios of the recoveries from animals in the PBS and the sugar groups are shown. The number of animals yielding a recovery lower than (<) or higher than (>) this common median are represented. The statistical test is a x^2 test for the median. For comparison, the average ranks in each subgroup, obtained by ranking of individual ratios of 824 Str^r/742 Nal^r within each group are shown.

[d] Globotetraose (Globo) was obtained by ozonolysis from globotetraosylceramide (10) and was purified by partitioning and repeated lyophilization. The product showed one band on thin-layer chromatography. The nuclear magnetic resonance spectrum in D_2O (21; Falk et al. to be published) showed signals from three anomeric protons with chemical shifts as expected from globotetraose: β-hexose, β-hexoseamine, α-hexose. The fourth anomeric signal from the reducing glucose residue was split into two, corresponding to the α and β forms in the proportions 1:2.

[e] Bacteria were preincubated with PBS or α-methyl-mannoside (α-Mm), 5 mg/ml.

TABLE 5. Binding properties of the infecting *E. coli* strain in relation to the P blood group phenotype of the patient

E. coli strains isolated from UTI episodes		P blood group phenotype	Bacterial hemagglutination pattern (%)[a]		
Diagnosis	No.		MR ± MS	MS	—
No reflux					
Pyelonephritis	51	P$_1$	84	16	0
	6	P$_2$	(50)	(50)	0
Asymptomatic bacteriuria	138	P$_1$	22	49	29
	29	P$_2$	34	31	35
With reflux					
Pyelonephritis	48	P$_1$	33	29	38
	13	P$_2$	62	23	15
Asymptomatic bacteriuria	32	P$_1$	10	31	59
	9	P$_2$	(56)	(33)	(11)

[a] MR, Agglutination of human erythrocytes not affected by α-methyl-mannoside; MS, agglutination of guinea pig or human erythrocytes, or both inhibited by α-methyl-mannoside. Parentheses indicate too few to validate percentages.

In contrast, both P blood group determination and characterization of the infecting strain might be useful in asymptomatic bacteriuria patients, to decide which cases may or may not require treatment. Patients of blood group P$_1$ infected with bacteria binding to globoseries glycolipid receptors may run a higher risk of developing acute pyelonephritis, and should probably be treated (H. Lomberg et al., in manuscript).

The inhibition of experimental infection by receptor analogs illustrates a possible approach to prophylaxis and treatment of infections occurring via mucous membranes. Compounds mimicking the host receptors may competitively bind to bacterial surface ligands. This might sufficiently decrease the number of bacteria attaching to the mucosa and thus alter the delicate balance of host-parasite interaction in favor of the host.

ACKNOWLEDGMENTS

This study was supported by grants from The Swedish Medical Research Council (Projects 215 and 3967, 6034), The University of Göteborg, The Ellen, Walter and Lennart Hesselman Foundation for Scientific Research, The Swedish board for Technical Development, and the Volkswagen Foundation. C.S.E. was supported by a Fogarthy Fellowship (no. 018497).

LITERATURE CITED

1. **Brinton, C. C.** 1978. The piliation phase syndrome and the use of purified pili in disease control, p. 33–70. XIII U.S.-Japan Conference on Cholera, Atlanta, Ga. Department of Health, Education, and Welfare Publication No. 78-1590.
2. **Duguid, J. P., and D. C. Old.** 1980. Adhesive properties of enterobacteriacae, p. 187–217. *In* E. H. Beachey (ed.), Bacterial adherence (Reception and recognition, series B, vol. 6). Chapman and Hall, London.
3. **Elwell, L. P., and P. L. Shipley.** 1980. Plasmid-mediated factors associated with virulence of bacteria to animals. Annu. Rev. Microbiol. **34**:465–496.
4. **Holmgren, J.** 1981. Actions of cholera toxin and the prevention and treatment of cholera. Nature (London) **292**:413–417.
5. **Hull, R. A., R. E. Gill, P. Hsu, B. H. Minshew, and S. Falkow.** 1981. Construction and expression of recombinant plasmids encoding type 1 or D-mannose-resistant pili from a urinary tract infection *Escherichia coli* isolate. Infect. Immun. **33**:933–938.
6. **Källenius, G., R. Möllby, S. B. Svensson, I. Helin, H. Hultberg, B. Cedergren, and J. Winberg.** 1982. Incidence of p-fimbriated *Escherichia coli* in urinary tract infections. Lancet, in press.
7. **Källenius, G., R. Möllby, S. B. Svensson, J. Winberg, A. Lundblad, S. Svensson, and B. Cedergren.** 1980. The p^k antigen as receptor for the hemagglutinin of pyelonephritic *Escherichia coli*. FEMS Microbiol. Lett. **7**:297–302.
8. **Korhonen, T. K., H. Leffler, and C. Svanborg Edén.** 1981. Binding specificity of piliated strains of *Escherichia coli* and *Salmonella typhimurium* to epithelial cells, *Saccharomyces cerevisiae* cells, and erythrocytes. Infect. Immun. **32**:796–804.
9. **Korhonen, T. K., E. L. Nurmiaho, H. Ranta, and C. Svanborg Edén.** 1980. A new method for the purification of *Escherichia coli* pili. Infect. Immun. **27**:569–575.
10. **Leffler, H., H. Lomberg, E. Gotschlich, L. Hagberg, U. Jodal, T. K. Korhonen, B. E. Samuelsson, G. Schoolnik, and C. Svanborg Edén.** 1981. Chemical and clinical studies on the interaction of *E. coli* with host glycolipid receptors in urinary tract infection. Scand. J. Infect. Dis. Suppl. in press.
11. **Leffler, H., and C. Svanborg Edén.** 1980. Chemical identification of a glycosphingolipid receptor for *Escherichia coli* attaching to human urinary tract epithelial cells and agglutinating human erythrocytes. FEMS Microbiol. Lett. **8**:127–134.
12. **Leffler, H., and C. Svanborg Edén.** 1981. Glycolipid receptors for uropathogenic *Escherichia coli* on human erythrocytes and uroepithelial cells. Infect. Immun. **34**:920–929.
13. **Lomberg, H., U. Jodal, C. Svanborg Edén, H. Leffler, and B. Samuelsson.** 1981. A genetic basis for susceptibility to infection: role of the P blood group in urinary tract infection. Lancet i:551–552.

14. Ørskov, I., F. Ørskov, and A. Birch-Andersen. 1980. A fimbria *Escherichia coli* antigen, F7, determining uroepithelial adherence. Comparison with type 1 fimbriae which attach to urinary slime. Infect. Immun. **27**:657–666.

15. Salit, I. E., and E. C. Gotschlich. 1977. Hemagglutination by purified type 1 *Escherichia coli* pili. J. Exp. Med. **146**:1169–1181.

16. Svanborg Edén, C., A. Fasth, L. Hagberg, L. Å. Hanson, T. Korhonen, and H. Leffler. 1982. Host interaction with *Escherichia coli* in the urinary tract, p. 113–131. *In* J. B. Robbins, J. C. Hill, and G. Sadoff (ed.), Bacterial vaccines, vol. 4. Thieme Stratton, New York.

17. Svanborg Edén, C., L. Hagberg, L. Å. Hanson, T. Korhonen, H. Leffler, and S. Olling. 1981. Adhesion of *Escherichia coli* in urinary tract infection, p. 161–187. *In* Adherence and microorganism pathogenicity. Ciba Symposium 80. Pittman Medical, Tunbridge Wells.

18. Svanborg Edén, C., L. Hagberg, R. Hull, S. Hull, and G. Schoolnik. 1981. Structure of *E. coli* pili in relation to receptor specificity and antigenicity. *In* E. C. Boedeher (ed.), Attachment of microorganisms to the gastrointestinal mucosal surface. CRC Press.

19. Svanborg Edén, C., L. Å. Hanson, U. Jodal, and A. Sohl Åkerlund. 1976. Variable adherence to normal human urinary tract epithelial cells of *Escherichia coli* strains associated with various forms of urinary tract infection. Lancet **ii**:490–492.

20. Svanborg Edén, C., G. Lidin-Janson, and U. Lindberg. 1979. Adhesion to human uroepithelial cells of faecal and urinary *E. coli* isolates from patients with symptomatic urinary tract infections or asymptomatic bacteriuria of varying duration. J. Urol. **122**:185–188.

21. Väisänen, V., J. Elo, L. Tallgren, A. Siitonen, P. H. Mäkelä, C. Svanborg Edén, G. Källenius, S. B. Svensson, H. Hultberg, and T. Korhonen. 1982. Mannose-resistant hemagglutination and P antigen recognition characteristic of *E. coli* causing primary pyelonephritis. Lancet, in press.

22. Yamakawa, T., and Y. Nagai. 1978. Glycolipids at the cell surface and their biological functions. Trends Biochem. Sci. **3**:128–131.

Role of Attachment in the Pathogenesis of Disease Caused by *Neisseria gonorrhoeae* and *Neisseria meningitidis*

ZELL A. McGEE, DAVID S. STEPHENS, M. ANN MELLY, CLARK R. GREGG, WALTER F. SCHLECH III, AND LOREN H. HOFFMAN

George Hunter Laboratory, Division of Infectious Diseases, Department of Medicine, and Department of Anatomy, Vanderbilt University School of Medicine, Nashville, Tennessee 37232

The ability of many bacterial pathogens to cause disease is associated with their ability to attach to epithelial surfaces (3, 6, 14, 18, 20, 22, 23). This attachment appears to involve the interaction between bacterial surface structures (ligands or adhesins) and host cell surface components (receptors) (1, 11, 21). The molecular mechanisms of attachment of some bacteria have been determined (1, 12). Although attachment may serve to secure the microorganism in the host, attachment per se does not result in tissue damage. To help determine the role of attachment in the disease process, we have used experimental models of gonococcal infection of human fallopian tube mucosa in organ culture and meningococcal infection of human nasopharyngeal mucosa in organ culture.

GONOCOCCAL INFECTIONS

As has been demonstrated with the interaction of gonococci with other human cells (9, 19, 23), piliated gonococci attach to human fallopian tube mucosa in greater numbers than nonpiliated gonococci (14). However, nonpiliated gonococci attach to human fallopian tube mucosa in far greater numbers than commensal neisseriae. This observation suggests that there are factors other than pili which mediate attachment of gonococci to host cells. A high degree of specificity or selectivity of attachment resides in the microorganisms. For instance, we found that piliated gonococci attached in relatively large numbers to fallopian tube mucosal cells, whereas a piliated commensal *Neisseria* species, *N. subflava*, did not attach. A high degree of specificity or selectivity also resides in the host tissues. For instance, piliated gonococci attached only to the nonciliated cells of fallopian tube mucosa (Fig. 1). Further, gonococci attached only to fallopian tube mucosa from humans, not to fallopian tube (oviduct) mucosa from rabbits, pigs, or cows (10).

The course of gonococcal infection of human fallopian tubes in organ culture included two major phases: (i) the attachment phase, during which organisms were attached to the surface of the epithelium and a majority of the damage occurred, and (ii) the invasion phase, during which the organisms entered the epithelial cells and were transported across the epithelial barrier by these cells. Damage to the mucosa, which was manifested primarily by sloughing of ciliated cells (Fig. 1), was produced more readily by piliated than by nonpiliated gonococci. A number of studies performed by Melly et al. (16) demonstrated that damage to the mucosa was mediated by one or more toxins elaborated by gonococci. Further studies by Melly et al. (Abstr. Annu. Meet. Am. Soc. Microbiol. 1980, B90, p. 32) and Gregg et al. (8) have indicated that peptidoglycan monomers and lipopolysaccharide, both of which are elaborated into their milieu by gonococci, are capable of damaging fallopian tube mucosa. It was of particular note that piliated gonococci attached to and damaged the fallopian tube mucosa more readily than nonpiliated gonococci (14); yet, we found that the amount of toxic activity and the concentrations of lipopolysaccharide in supernatant fluid from organ cultures infected with piliated or with nonpiliated gonococci were virtually identical (16). These findings suggest that the greater attachment of piliated gonococci enables them to deliver lipopolysaccharide and perhaps other toxic moieties more effectively to target cells in the mucosa.

Attachment may also play a vital role in the invasion of host cells by gonococci. Initial attachment of gonococci to microvilli on the surface of nonciliated cells was followed by active interaction of gonococci with these microvilli, which entrapped them and pulled them against the surface of nonciliated cells. Host cell membranes with the attached gonococci then invaginated, enclosing gonococci in phagocytic vacuoles in a manner analogous to phagocytosis by macrophages or polymorphonuclear leukocytes (13). The phagocytic vacuoles were rapidly transported to the base of the cells and remained there for 24 to 48 h, during which time the number of microorganisms increased by multi-

FIG. 1. Human fallopian tube mucosa infected with a piliated clone of *N. gonorrhoeae* strain 2686, transparent colony type. Note sloughing ciliated cell in foreground and gonococci attaching almost exclusively to microvilli of nonciliated cells. Scanning electron micrograph. ×4,000.

plication, coalescence of multiple phagocytic vacuoles, or both. Only occasionally was a lysosome-like structure seen in a mucosal cell, and there was no evidence of lysosomal fusion with the phagocytic vacuoles. Beginning about 48 h after infection, the phagocytic vacuoles were emptied through the base of the epithelial cells into the subepithelial tissues. The organisms in the subepithelial tissues had the morphological appearance of viable gonococci. Studies by W. F. Schlech III and Z. A. McGee (Clin. Res. **27**:788A, 1979), using various antimicrobials with different degrees of cell penetration, suggest that the gonococci remain alive inside the epithelial cells during the invasion phase. If this process of transport of gonococci across the mucosa takes place in vivo, as is suggested by pathological studies (7, 17), the organisms in the subepithelial tissues might cause localized inflammation (e.g., salpingitis) or might enter blood vessels to cause disseminated gonococcal infection.

The findings described above suggest that attachment may be important in the pathogenesis of gonococcal salpingitis in at least three ways: (i) in initial colonization—establishing the organism in the host; (ii) in positioning the organism to more effectively deliver toxic factors to target cells in the epithelium; and (iii) in facilitating phagocytosis and transport of the organisms across the mucosal barrier by epithelial cells.

MENINGOCOCCAL INFECTIONS

Virtually all meningococci are piliated on primary isolation (4, 22). In early studies meningococci lost piliation after one or two passages in vitro (5). Techniques developed in this laboratory have made it possible to maintain piliation of meningococci during serial passage in vitro (15). Greater attachment to human buccal epithelial cells by piliated than by nonpiliated meningococci has been demonstrated by Craven and Frasch, who used piliated and nonpiliated me-

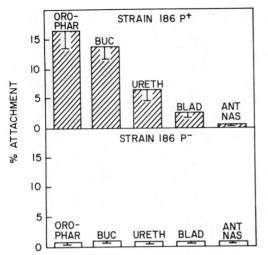

FIG. 2. Effect of type of receptor cell on attachment of isogenic piliated and nonpiliated clones of *N. meningitidis* strain 186, transparent colony type. OROPHAR, Nasopharyngeal epithelial cells; BUC, buccal epithelial cells; URETH, urethral epithelial cells; BLAD, transitional bladder cells; ANT NAS, anterior nasal epithelial cells. Nonpiliated meningococci (bottom) attached in low but equal numbers to all cell types, whereas piliated meningococci (top) attached to cells from some mucosal sites in high numbers and to cells from other mucosal sites in low numbers. (Figure from reference 22.)

ningococci from different sources (2), and by Stephens and McGee, who used isogenic piliated and nonpiliated clones of meningococci (22). In the latter studies, the attachment of meningococci to human cells depended both on the surface factors present on the meningococci and on the type of human cells employed (Fig. 2). Whereas nonpiliated meningococci attached to cells from different mucosal surfaces in low but equal numbers, piliated meningococci attached to nasopharyngeal and buccal cells in high numbers, to urethral and bladder cells in intermediate to low numbers, and to anterior nasal cells in very low numbers. The preferential attachment in vitro of meningococci to cells from the nasopharynx and oropharynx parallels the selective isolation of meningococci from these sites in vivo. These data suggest that the number and distribution of receptor sites for meningococcal pili or pili-associated factors differ among human cells and determine sites of meningococcal colonization.

To assess possible parallels between meningococcal and gonococcal infections, meningococci were used to infect human fallopian tube organ cultures. The events observed—selective attachment to microvilli of nonciliated cells, endo-cytosis by these cells, and probable exocytosis into subepithelial tissues—indicated that the pathogenic processes were similar if not identical.

To study the interaction of meningococci with a mucosal surface that is their natural habitat and the most likely site for their invasion, meningococci were used to infect human nasopharyngeal mucosa in organ culture (D. S. Stephens and Z. A. McGee, Program Abstr. Intersci. Conf. Antimicrob. Agents Chemother. 21st, Chicago, Ill., abstr. no. 370, 1981). The nasopharyngeal mucosa, like fallopian tube mucosa, has an epithelium consisting of ciliated and nonciliated columnar cells; however, there is a greater variety of nonciliated cells, and in most areas, the epithelium is pseudostratified columnar rather than simple columnar. In preliminary studies meningococci attached almost exclusively to nonciliated cells of the human nasopharyngeal mucosa. There was interaction with microvilli on the nonciliated cells, and the meningococci were phagocytosed by these cells. Although studies of the mechanism whereby meningococci traverse the epithelium are not yet complete, meningococci were seen inside cells and free beneath the epithelium by 24 to 36 h after infection. It is clear that the initial stages of interaction of meningococci with human nasopharyngeal mucosa are morphologically indistinguishable from those that result in phagocytosis and transport of gonococci and meningococci across the fallopian tube mucosa.

Attachment by pili, and probably other surface factors, appears important in the pathogenesis of infections with pathogenic neisseriae. Attachment not only establishes the organism in the host, but also may aid in more effective delivery of toxin to target cells in the mucosa and may facilitate phagocytosis and transport of *N. gonorrhoeae* and possibly *N. meningitidis* across mucosal barriers by nonciliated epithelial cells. This latter process may result in local inflammatory disease or bloodstream infection. Success as an invasive pathogen may require that the organisms, in addition to having factors which promote attachment and possibly phagocytosis, also have factors antagonistic to host defenses.

ACKNOWLEDGMENTS

We are grateful to Terry Wright, Patricia Argabrite, Sylvie Cousar, Jane Griffin, and Patricia McGraw for excellent technical assistance and to Jeanne Woodall for help in preparation of the manuscript. We thank R. T. Birmingham, D. D. Cannale, G. B. Crafton, V. Hutton, H. T. Lavely, Jr., R. R. Oldham, R. W. Parker, and N. E. Witthauer for providing fallopian tubes and J. P. Crook, W. L. Downey, and D. R. Hightower for providing nasopharyngeal tissue.

The various studies reported here were supported by Public Health Service research grants AI-13488, AI-17612, and AI-18329 from the National Institute of Allergy and Infectious Diseases and by a grant from the John A. Hartford Foundation.

LITERATURE CITED

1. **Beachey, E. H.** 1981. Bacterial adherence: adhesin-receptor interactions mediating the attachment of bacteria to mucosal surfaces. J. Infect. Dis. **143:**325–345.
2. **Craven, D. E., and C. E. Frasch.** 1978. Pili-mediated and nonmediated adherence of *Neisseria meningitidis* and its relationship to invasive disease, p. 250–252. *In* G. F. Brooks, E. C. Gotschlich, K. K. Holmes, W. D. Sawyer, and F. E. Young (ed.), Immunobiology of *Neisseria gonorrhoeae*. American Society for Microbiology, Washington, D.C.
3. **Deneke, C. F., G. M. Thorne, and S. L. Gorbach.** 1980. Adhesive pili from enterotoxigenic *Escherichia coli* (ETEC) pathogenic for humans, p. 777–781. *In* J. D. Nelson and C. Grassi (ed.), Current chemotherapy and infectious disease. American Society for Microbiology, Washington, D.C.
4. **DeVoe, I. W., and J. E. Gilchrist.** 1975. Pili on meningococci from primary cultures of nasopharyngeal carriers and cerebrospinal fluid of patients with acute disease. J. Exp. Med. **141:**297–305.
5. **DeVoe, I. W., and J. E. Gilchrist.** 1978. Piliation and colonial morphology among laboratory strains of meningococci. J. Clin. Microbiol. **7:**379–384.
6. **Duguid, J. P., and R. R. Gillies.** 1957. Fimbriae and adhesive properties in dysentery bacilli. J. Pathol. Bacteriol. **74:**397–411.
7. **Findley, P.** 1908. Gonorrhea in women, p. 27. C. V. Mosby Medical Book and Publishing Co., St. Louis, Mo.
8. **Gregg, C. R., M. A. Melly, C. G. Hellerqvist, J. G. Coniglio, and Z. A. McGee.** 1981. Toxic activity of purified lipopolysaccharide of *Neisseria gonorrhoeae* for human fallopian tube mucosa. J. Infect. Dis. **143:**432–439.
9. **James-Holmquest, A. N., J. Swanson, T. M. Buchanan, R. D. Wende, and R. P. Williams.** 1974. Differential attachment by piliated and nonpiliated *Neisseria gonorrhoeae* to human sperm. Infect. Immun. **9:**897–902.
10. **Johnson, A. P., D. Taylor-Robinson, and Z. A. McGee.** 1977. Species specificity of attachment and damage to oviduct mucosa by *Neisseria gonorrhoeae*. Infect. Immun. **18:**833–839.
11. **Keusch, G. T.** 1979. Specific membrane receptors: pathogenetic and therapeutic implications in infectious diseases. Rev. Infect. Dis. **1:**517–529.
12. **Leffler, H., and C. Svanborg-Eden.** 1980. Chemical identification of a glycosphingolipid receptor for *Escherichia coli* attaching to human urinary tract epithelial cells and agglutinating human erythrocytes. FEMS Microbiol. Lett. **8:**127–134.
13. **McGee, Z. A., and R. G. Horn.** 1979. Phagocytosis of gonococci by nonprofessional phagocytic cells, p. 158–161. *In* D. Schlessinger (ed.), Microbiology—1979. American Society for Microbiology, Washington, D.C.
14. **McGee, Z. A., A. P. Johnson, and D. Taylor-Robinson.** 1981. Pathogenic mechanisms of *Neisseria gonorrhoeae*: observations on damage to human fallopian tubes in organ culture by gonococci of colony type 1 or type 4. J. Infect. Dis. **143:**413–422.
15. **McGee, Z. A., C. H. Street, C. L. Chappell, E. S. Cousar, F. Morris, and R. G. Horn.** 1979. Pili of *Neisseria meningitidis*: effect of media on maintenance of piliation, characteristics of pili, and colonial morphology. Infect. Immun. **24:**194–201.
16. **Melly, M. A., C. R. Gregg, and Z. A. McGee.** 1981. Studies of toxicity of *Neisseria gonorrhoeae* for human fallopian tube mucosa. J. Infect. Dis. **143:**423–431.
17. **Norris, C. C.** 1913. Gonorrhea in women, p. 259. W. B. Saunders Co., Philadelphia.
18. **Pedersen, K. B., L. O. Froholm, and K. Bovre.** 1972. Fimbriation and colony type of *Moraxella bovis* in relation to conjunctival colonization and development of keratoconjunctivitis in cattle. Acta Pathol. Microbiol. Scand. Sect. B **80:**911–918.
19. **Punsalang, A. P., and W. D. Sawyer.** 1973. Role of pili in the virulence of *Neisseria gonorrhoeae*. Infect. Immun. **8:**255–263.
20. **Silverblatt, F. J., and L. S. Cohen.** 1979. Antipili antibody affords protection against experimental ascending pyelonephritis. J. Clin. Invest. **64:**333–336.
21. **Smith, H.** 1977. Microbial surfaces in relation to pathogenicity. Bacteriol. Rev. **41:**475–500.
22. **Stephens, D. S., and Z. A. McGee.** 1981. Attachment of *Neisseria meningitidis* to human mucosal surfaces: influence of pili and type of receptor cell. J. Infect. Dis. **143:**525–532.
23. **Swanson, J.** 1973. Studies on gonococcus infection. IV. Pili: their role in attachment of gonococci to tissue culture cells. J. Exp. Med. **137:**571–589.

Bacterial Surface Structures Involved in Adhesion to Phagocytic and Epithelial Cells

ITZHAK OFEK AND FREDRIC J. SILVERBLATT

Department of Human Microbiology, Sackler School of Medicine, Tel Aviv University, Tel Aviv, Israel, and Department of Medicine, Sepulveda Veterans Administration Medical Center, Sepulveda, California 91343

Bacterial surface structures (adhesins), which combine stereospecifically with macromolecules on host cell membranes (receptors), may be either advantageous or disadvantageous to the pathogen during the infectious process. On the one hand, adhesins bind the organisms to epithelial cells and allow bacterial colonization of mucosal surfaces. After bacterial invasion into deep tissues, on the other hand, the same adhesins can also attach the organisms to phagocytic cells and thus enhance the elimination of the invading pathogen by phagocytosis.

Adhesin receptors may be accessible on both epithelial and phagocytic cells or on only one of the two types of host cells. For example, the mannose-specific (also called mannose-sensitive) type 1 fimbriae (MSF) of *Escherichia coli* (2, 13, 20), the fimbrial adhesin of *Proteus mirabilis* (21), and lipoteichoic acid of *Streptococcus pyogenes* (3, 6) are adhesins which bind the organisms to receptors that are accessible on both epithelial and phagocytic cells. The gonococcal fimbriae (24) and the mannose-resistant fimbriae (MRF) of *E. coli* (4) combine with receptors which are accessible only on epithelial cells, whereas the leukocyte association factor of gonococci attaches the organisms only to phagocytes (24).

The potentially adverse effects of adhesin-phagocyte interactions may have promoted the development of mechanisms that allow bacterial pathogens to avoid attachment to phagocytic cells via their surface adhesins. One such mechanism is the synthesis of surface polymers which interfere with the adhesin-receptor interaction. These polymers may inhibit adhesin-mediated binding of bacteria to host cells by altering the net surface charge, the surface hydrophobicity, or the presenting orientation of the adhesins on the bacterial surfaces (25). The polysaccharide capsules of meningococci (7) and pneumococci (18), as well as the hyaluronic capsule of *S. pyogenes* (27), have been found to interfere with the binding of these organisms to both epithelial and phagocytic cells.

Bacteria that produce adhesins which are indispensable for their survival are most likely to express interfering polymers. An example of an indispensable adhesin is the lipoteichoic acid of *S. pyogenes* (26). In contrast, many gram-negative species produce fimbrial adhesins which are dispensable bacterial products (15). Although these organisms may also produce interfering polymers to avoid phagocytic attachment, they may avoid phagocytic attachment by a second mechanism as well—simply by not expressing their dispensable adhesins at a critical stage of the infectious process. Most fimbriated organisms, in fact, display nonfimbriated and fimbriated phenotypes in vitro, depending on the conditions of growth (5, 8, 9).

It is not widely appreciated that variable phenotypic expression of adhesins may be an important adaptive mechanism for some bacterial pathogens. We first became aware of this possibility during an electron microscopy study of ascending *Proteus* pyelonephritis in rats. We observed that bacteria colonizing the renal pelvic epithelium were heavily fimbriated, whereas those proliferating within the renal parenchyma appeared to be in a nonfimbriated phase (21). Subsequent experiments have suggested how variable expression of adhesins may contribute to bacterial virulence in this model. When introduced directly into the renal parenchyma, nonfimbriated organisms were found to be cleared much less rapidly than heavily fimbriated forms (22). The nonfimbriated organisms may have had a selective advantage in the kidney because in vitro studies showed that they were ingested and killed much less efficiently by granulocytes than were fimbriated bacteria (21). In contrast, with ascending infection, in which bacteria reach the kidney by colonizing and penetrating the renal pelvic mucosa, the fimbriated form was more virulent (19). In this setting the enhanced ability of fimbriated bacteria to bind to uroepithelial cells may have accounted for their advantage (21). Thus, the ability to express or not express the fimbrial adhesins may help *Proteus* adapt to the requirements of each of these two microenvironments.

We would like to support the hypothesis that variation in expression of adhesins is an impor-

TABLE 1. Mannose-binding activity (yeast aggregation) of *E. coli* obtained from patients with urinary tract infections[a]

No. of patients	Yeast aggregation of bacteria	
	Shed in urine	Subculture for 48 h
11	0	++++
2	+	0
11	0	0

[a] Data from reference 14.

tant adaptive mechanism in bacterial infections by reviewing recent observations that we have made on the MSF adhesins of isolates of another uropathogen, *E. coli*, focusing on two main issues: (i) the expression of MSF adhesin in vivo during natural urinary tract infections in humans and (ii) the interaction of the fimbriated and nonfimbriated phenotypes with human granulocytes in the presence and absence of antibodies.

EXPRESSION OF MSF IN HUMAN URINARY TRACT INFECTIONS

The development of antibodies against MSF in pyelonephritic patients (17) and experimental animals infected with MSF-producing *E. coli* (23) suggests that the MSF adhesins are produced in vivo by the bacteria in sufficient quanti-

ties to trigger an immune response. It was of interest, therefore, to see whether the organisms manifest an MSF⁻ phenotype during one or more stages of the infectious process in humans as does *P. mirabilis* in the rat. For this purpose, urine samples from 24 patients with *E. coli* urinary tract infection were collected (14). Production of MSF adhesins by the bacteria excreted in the urine and by the same isolates after growth in broth was assayed by the yeast cell aggregation test (14). The results revealed that only 2 of 24 isolates of *E. coli* excreted in the urine exhibited MSF activity, whereas about half of the same specimens did so after cultivation in broth (Table 1). Examination of representative specimens of *E. coli* excreted in urine showed that coating antibodies, mannose-containing glycoproteins, and encapsulation were not responsible for the lack of MSF activity. These and other results (14) suggest that *E. coli* strains that are genetically capable of exhibiting MSF adhesin may, when growing in the human bladder, exist in a phase which lacks the MSF adhesin.

INTERACTION OF MSF⁺ AND MSF⁻ PHENOTYPES WITH HUMAN GRANULOCYTES

The ability of cells of the MSF⁺ and MSF⁻ phenotypes to attach to and stimulate antimicro-

TABLE 2. Stimulation of human granulocytes by mannose-specific fimbrial adhesins of *E. coli*

Assay	Activity		Reference
	Fimbriated phenotype (+ AMM[a])	Nonfimbriated phenotype (+ antibody)	
Metabolic stimulation			
Chemiluminescence, peak cpm	35 × 10³ (15 × 10³)	ND[b]	Mangan and Synder (12)
	1,100 (53)	0 (1,000)	Silverblatt (unpublished data)
Protein iodination (nmol of I₂/10⁷ polymorphonuclear leukocytes per h)	8.4 (0.07)	0.11 (7.2)	Perry, Ofek and Silverblatt (unpublished data)
	2.6 ND	0.09 (1.1)[c]	Pryor, Willen, and Silverblatt (16)
Attachment			
Bacteria per 100 macrophages	563 (37)	53 (697)	Bar-Shavit et al. (2)
Granulocytes with attached bacteria, %	16.1 (0)	0 (27.3)	Perry, Ofek, and Silverblatt (unpublished data)
Killing			
Percent survival after 60 min	10 (70)	85 (1)[c]	Silverblatt, Dreyer, and Schauer (21)

[a] α-Methyl-D-mannoside.
[b] ND, Not done.
[c] Normal human serum used as opsonin.

TABLE 3. Granulocyte stimulation (myeloperoxidose-mediated protein iodination) by *E. coli* pretreated with various concentrations of antibody

Antibody specificity	Protein iodination (nmol of $I_2/19^7$ polymorphonuclear leukocytes per h) induced by MSF$^+$ *E. coli* pretreated with the following antibody concentrations:						
	1:4	1:8	1:16	1:32	1:64	1:128	1:256
Antibody to whole *E. coli*							
Unabsorbed	53.8	85.1	68.1	*86.9*[a]	42.2	26.8	18.6
Absorbed with MSF$^-$ phenotype	46.3	64.3	66.7	*83.8*	98.2	40.7	16.6
Antibody to MSF							
Immunoglobulin G anti-MSF	45.0	61.0	70.4	*70.3*	66.6	36.6	28.4
Immunoglobulin G + α-methyl mannoside	14.2	5.8	2.1	0.4	0	0	0
Immunoglobulin G + protein A	—	31.3	37.3	*78.1*	68.5	58.6	42.6
(Fab)$_2$ anti-MSF	11.0	11.4	*58.5*	39.9	45.2	35.2	26.6
(Fab)$_2$ + α-methyl mannoside	1.9	0.03	0.06	0.08	0.07	0.2	0.2
(Fab)$_2$ + protein A	16.3	27.6	*51.5*	56.5	56.7	54.2	31.3

[a] Italics indicate that maximum inhibition of MSF activity occurred at a similar antibody concentration.

bial systems in human granulocytes is summarized in Table 2. As compared with the MSF$^+$ phenotype, the MSF$^-$ phenotype was much less active. When cells of the MSF$^-$ phenotype were coated with antibodies, they were approximately equivalent to cells of the MSF$^+$ phenotype in the absence of antibodies (Table 2), suggesting that MSF on intact organisms is as efficient as the Fc portion of antibodies coating the bacteria in stimulating granulocytes.

As mentioned previously, MSF antibodies are acquired during the course of human and experimental *E. coli* pyelonephritis (17, 23). The interaction of these two ligands on granulocyte activity was recently examined by us (A. Perry, I. Ofek, and F. J. Silverblatt, in preparation). MSF$^+$ bacteria were coated with antibodies in amounts sufficient to either block or not block MSF activity, and their ability to stimulate human granulocytes was assayed, with myeloperoxide-mediated protein iodination used as an indicator of granulocyte microbicidal activity. Results of a representative experiment are depicted in Table 3. Up to a 10-fold increase in stimulation was observed when the granulocytes were incubated with cells of the MSF$^+$ phenotype pretreated with anti-MSF immunoglobulin G. Studies of the absorption of the antibody to whole *E. coli* cells with MSF$^-$ phenotype or with purified MSF revealed that the enhanced stimulation was largely due to antibody to MSF alone. Although MSF activity was partially blocked at concentrations of antibody which caused optimal granulocyte stimulation, the effect on the granulocyte appeared to be mediated by MSF ligands rather than the Fc portion of the antibody, as iodination could be inhibited by α-methyl-D-mannoside but not by staphylococcal protein A. Moreover, anti-MSF (Fab)$_2$ fragments, which lack the Fc portion, were as active as intact immunoglobulin G. We postulate that anti-MSF antibodies enhanced iodination by cross-linking the MSF on the surface of the bacteria. In fact, we have seen such clumping of the MSF by anti-MSF antibodies (data not shown). We postulate that, although cross-linking reduced the density of functional MSF over the surface of antibody-treated bacteria, and consequently reduced the ability of these organisms to agglutinate yeast cells, the resulting bundles of MSF fimbriae were far more effective at stimulating granulocytes because, bound together, they were better able to aggregate the MSF receptors on the granulocyte surface. Aggregation of surface receptors is important for many membrane-initiated events, and ligands with multiple valence are more effective than univalent or bivalent ligands in this regard. For example, native tetrameric concanavalin A causes a manyfold greater stimulation of phagocytic cell activity than does the succinylated bivalent form of the lectin (10).

The evidence presented thus far suggests that the MSF$^+$ phenotype does not predominate in the bladder or kidney and indeed may even be deleterious to the pathogen when humoral antibody and phagocytic cells are present. If MSF does play any role at all in the pathogenesis or urinary tract infection, it may help *E. coli* to persist in the intestinal reservoir and enable the bacteria to colonize the vaginal introitus or bladder at the onset of the infection, as has been shown with experimental models (1). It is not known, however, what is the predominant phenotype of *E. coli* in the fecal flora. If MSF is not expressed by bacteria in the intestines, then the invading uropathogen must produce another adhesin to enable it to attach to epithelial cells and to withstand the cleansing mechanism of the urinary flush. In this regard, Hagberg and his colleagues have shown that uropathogenic *E. coli*, especially pyelonephritic isolates, produce MRF in addition to the MSF adhesin (11). Since receptors for MRF are not accessible on phagocytic cells (4), it may well be that the predominant phenotype of *E. coli* in the kidney is MSF$^-$/MRF$^+$. As mentioned previously, however, antibody to MSF has been detected during the course of pyelonephritis in humans and experimental animals, indicating that some MSF$^+$ phenotypes are present in the kidney. Because of their greater susceptibility to phagocytosis, such MSF-bearing bacteria are likely to be readily cleared. Results of this study suggest that, although the enhanced stimulation of granulocyte by MSF–anti-MSF complexes observed may lead to a better clearance of the organisms, it may at the same time escalate the inflammation as a result of chemical mediators released from stimulated phagocytic cells.

In summary, previous studies on experimental *Proteus* pyelonephritis (19, 21, 22) and those described above emphasize the role of phenotypic variations in the production and expression of dispensable adhesins which bind bacteria to phagocytic and epithelial cells. Such variations may be mechanisms by which bacteria evade the host defense mechanisms at different stages of the infectious process. A better understanding of the molecular basis of these phenotypic variations should permit development of new and efficient tools for preventing pyogenic infections such as pyelonephritis.

ACKNOWLEDGMENTS

This work was supported by the Binational U.S.-Israel grant 2138/80 and by the medical research service of the Veterans Administration.

LITERATURE CITED

1. Aronson, M., O. Medalia, L. Schori, D. Mirelman, N. Sharon, and I. Ofek. 1979. Prevention of colonization of the urinary tract of mice with *Escherichia coli* by blocking of bacterial adherence with methyl α-D-mannopyranoside. J. Infect. Dis. **139**:329–332.

2. Bar-Shavit, Z., I. Ofek, R. Goldman, D. Mirelman, and N. Sharon. 1977. Mannose residues on phagocytes as receptors for the attachment of *Escherichia coli* and *Salmonella typhi*. Biochem. Biophys. Res. Commun. **78**:455–461.

3. Beachey, E. H., and I. Ofek. 1976. Epithelial cell binding of group A streptococci by lipoteichoic acid on fimbriae denuded of M protein. J. Exp. Med. **143**:759–771.

4. Blumenstock, E., and K. Jann. 1981. Adhesion of piliated *Escherichia coli* strains to phagocytes: differences between bacteria with mannose-sensitive pili and those with mannose-resistant pili. Infect. Immun. **35**:264–269.

5. Brinton, C. C., Jr. 1977. The piliation phase syndrome and the uses of purified pili in disease control, p. 33–70. Proceedings of the 13th Joint U.S.-Japan Conference on Cholera, Atlanta, Ga. Department of Health, Education, and Welfare Publication No. 78-1590.

6. Courtney, H., I. Ofek, A. Limfsore, and E. H. Beachey. 1981. Characterization of lipoteichoic acid binding to polymorphonuclear leucocytes of human blood. Infect. Immun. **32**:625–631.

7. Craven, D. E., and C. E. Frasch. 1978. Pili-mediated and non-mediated adherence of *Neisseria meningitidis* and its relationship to invasive disease, p. 250–257. *In* G. Brooks, E. L. Gotschlich, K. K. Holmes, W. D. Sawyer, and F. E. Young. (ed.), Immunobiology of *Neisseria gonorrhoeae*. American Society for Microbiology, Washington, D.C.

8. Duguid, J. P., and D. C. Old. 1980. Adhesive properties of enterobacteriacea, p. 186–217. *In* E. H. Beachey (ed.), Bacterial adherence (Receptors and recognition, series B, vol. 6). Chapman and Hall, London.

9. Fader, R. C., and D. W. Tempest. 1972. Effects of environment on bacterial wall content and composition. Adv. Microbial Physiol. **7**:83–115.

10. Goldman, R., N. Sharon, and R. Lotan. 1976. A differential response elicited in macrophages on interaction with lectins. Exp. Cell Res. **99**:408–422.

11. Hagberg, L., U. Jodal, T. K. Korhonen, G. Lidin-Janson, U. Lindberg, and C. Svanborg-Eden. 1981. Adhesion, hemagglutination, and virulence of *Escherichia coli* causing urinary tract infections. Infect. Immun. **31**:564–570.

12. Mangan, D. F., and I. S. Snyder. 1979. Mannose-sensitive stimulation of human leukocyte chemiluminescence by *Escherichia coli*. Infect. Immun. **26**:1014–1019.

13. Ofek, I., D. Mirelman, and N. Sharon. 1977. Adherence of *Escherichia coli* to human mucosal cells mediated by mannose receptors. Nature (London) **265**:623–625.

14. Ofek, I., A. Mosek, and N. Sharon. 1981. Mannose-specific adherence of *Escherichia coli* freshly excreted in the urine of patients with urinary tract infections, and of isolates subcultured from the infected urine. Infect. Immun. **34**:708–711.

15. Ottow, J. C. G. 1975. Ecology, physiology and genetics of fimbriae and pili. Annu. Rev. Microbiol. **29**:79–107.

16. Pryor, E. P., J. Willen, and F. J. Silverblatt. 1980. Piliated *Escherichia coli* activate polymorphonuclear leukocyte killing mechanisms, p. 817–818. *In* J. D. Nelson and C. Grassi (ed.), Current chemotherapy and infectious diseases. Proceedings of the 11th ICC and 19th ICAAC. American Society for Microbiology, Washington, D.C.

17. Rene, P., and F. J. Silverblatt. 1980. Serological response to *Escherichia coli* pili in pyelonephritis, p. 782–783. *In* J. D. Nelson and C. Grassi (ed.), Current chemotherapy and infectious diseases. Proceedings of the 11th ICC and 19th ICAAC. American Society for Microbiology, Washington, D.C.

18. Selinger, D., and W. P. Reed. 1979. Pneumococcal adherence to human epithelial cells. Infect. Immun. **23**:545–548.

19. Silverblatt, F. J. 1974. Host-parasite interactions in the rat renal pelvis: a possible role for pili in the pathogenesis of pyelonephritis. J. Exp. Med. **140**:1696–1711.

20. Silverblatt, F. J., J. S. Dreyer, and S. Schauer. 1979. Effect of pili on susceptibility of *Escherichia coli* to phagocytosis. Infect. Immun. **24**:218–223.

21. Silverblatt, F. J., and I. Ofek. 1978. Effects of pili on susceptibility of *Proteus mirabilis* to phagocytosis and on adherence to bladder cells, p. 49–59. *In* E. Kass and W. Brumfitt (ed.), Infections of the urinary tract. Proceedings of the 3rd International Symposium Pyelonephritis. University of Chicago Press, Chicago.

22. Silverblatt, F. J., and I. Ofek. 1978. The influence of pili on the virulence of *Proteus mirabilis* in experimental hematogenous pyelonephritis. J. Infect. Dis. **138**:664–667.

23. Smith, J. W., S. Wagner, and R. M. Swenson. 1981. Local immune response to *Escherichia coli* pili in experimental pyelonephritis. Infect. Immun. **31**:17–20.

24. Swanson, J., E. Sparks, D. Young, and G. King. 1975. Studies on gonococcus infection. X. Pili and leukocyte

association factor as mediators of interactions between gonococci and eukaryotic cells in vitro. Infect. Immun. **11:**1352–1361.

25. **Van Oss, C. J.** 1978. Phagocytosis as a surface phenomenon. Annu. Rev. Microbiol. **32:**19–39.

26. **Ward, J. B.** 1981. Teichoic and teichuronic acids: biosynthesis, assembly and location. Microbiol. Rev. **45:**211–243.

27. **Whitnack, E., A. L. Bisno, and E. H. Beachey.** 1981. Hyaluronate capsule prevents attachment of group A streptococci to mouse peritoneal microphages. Infect. Immun. **31:**985–991.

Role of Surface Proteins in the Adhesion of *Neisseria gonorrhoeae*

J. E. HECKELS

Microbiology, Southampton University Medical School, Southampton General Hospital, Southampton, England

The adhesion of gonococci to mucosal cells of the genital tract is a crucial early event in the pathogenesis of gonorrhea, enabling the bacteria to become established despite the fluid flows of mucus and other secretions. Electron microscopic studies with human fallopian tubes in vitro (19) have suggested the sequence of events leading to symptomatic infection, which is characterized by the destruction of the urethral mucosa, with accumulation of gonococci and polymorphs in the subepithelial connective tissues. Shortly after challenge of fallopian tube organ cultures, gonococci can be seen adherent to the microvilli of columnar epithelial cells which then surround the bacterium. Some organisms become totally enclosed by the host cell membrane and lie inside a phagocytic vacuole within the cell. Intracellular multiplication then occurs, and cells filled with gonococci rupture into the submucosa or onto the mucosal surface. Initial penetration is blocked by cytochalasin B, which disrupts microfilament activity, confirming that invasion occurs by means of epithelial cell phagocytosis (20). It is the ability to invade the nonciliated columnar epithelial cells which distinguishes gonococci from commensal neisseriae and other normal flora organisms which preferentially attach to squamous epithelium without penetrating. It has been suggested that gonococci possess adhesins which allow attachment to susceptible cells with high avidity and that an inevitable consequence of this close adhesion is some uptake by mucosal cells (20). The efficiency of the adhesion is shown by the observations that the infectious dose in human volunteers may be as low as 10^3 organisms and that micturition immediately after intercourse does not prevent naturally acquired gonorrhea (20). This paper outlines the evidence which suggests that adhesion is a two-component process involving both pili and proteins of the gonococcal outer membrane and that structural variations in these components which affect the adhesive properties of the organism may occur in vivo.

ROLE OF PILI IN ADHESION

Following the observation that virulent colonial forms of gonococci differed from avirulent forms in their possession of pili (16), considerable evidence has accumulated to show that pili facilitate adhesion to a range of host cells (2). The possible role of pili in attachment has been indicated in experiments in which gonococci were chemically modified to alter their surface charge (5). Like other bacteria and human cells, gonococci possess an overall net negative charge, but blocking free carboxyl and amino groups abolished this. The modified gonococci showed increased attachment to WISH cells, growing as a monolayer, but piliated organisms no longer showed any advantage in attachment. The implication of these experiments is that one role of pili in gonococcal adhesion is to overcome the repulsive electrostatic barrier which exists between any two negatively charged surfaces. The mechanism by which gonococci overcome this barrier is unclear, one possibility being that because of their small surface area pili are less sensitive to the electrostatic forces. Initial attachment by pili would then increase the probability of a closer approach, thus favoring attachment, since attractive forces act over a much shorter range than the electrostatic repulsive force. This second stage of attachment involves direct interaction between the surfaces of the bacterium and the host cell and may occur even when the bacterial cell is nonpiliated. This close approach is confirmed by electron micrographs of urethral cells from patients with early gonorrhea, where the gonococcal outer membrane is seen in intimate contact with the host cell surface (20).

The specificity of the pilus-host cell interaction has been investigated by comparing the adhesion of ^{3}H-labeled piliated and nonpiliated variants of strain P9 to human buccal epithelial cells (17). A variety of sugars were tested in the system and showed no inhibition of attachment.

However, modification of the host cell surface by treatment with a mixture of glycosidases reduced attachment of the piliated variant to that of the nonpiliated variant. Similarly, attachment of purified ^{125}I-labeled pili was inhibited by pretreatment of buccal cells with mixed glycosidases (2, 12). Thus, it was concluded that an oligosaccharide unit, perhaps a ganglioside, on the surface of the epithelial cell might act as pilus receptor. However, recent studies with different pilus types obtained from colonial variants suggest that the situation may be more complex than this and that structural modifications may alter the receptor specificity of the pilus.

STRUCTURAL VARIATIONS IN SURFACE COMPONENTS ASSOCIATED WITH ATTACHMENT

Outer membrane protein II. The outer membranes of gonococci contain a restricted number of proteins which may vary considerably between variants even of a single strain. A single major outer membrane protein (protein I) is present in variants which grow as transparent colonies, whereas more opaque colonies also have one or more additional proteins (proteins II) which show characteristic heat-modifiable properties on sodium dodecyl sulfate-polyacrylamide gels (9, 15). Structural studies suggest that the proteins II comprise a family of related molecules which share a common region embedded in the membrane and also have a variable region exposed on the surface (4). Such variations might be expected to have a considerable influence on the surface properties, including adhesive interactions. This is confirmed by the studies on the attachment of variants of strain P9 to buccal epithelial cells. A series of opaque variants of strain P9, each with a different protein II profile, showed considerably enhanced attachment to buccal cells over the transparent variant containing only protein I (10).

To investigate the contribution of protein II to adhesion, the attachment to buccal cells of isolated ^{125}I-labeled outer membranes has been studied (6). Membranes containing protein II showed considerably enhanced attachment over those containing only protein I. The data were subjected to Langmuir isotherm analysis (7), which showed that, although there were approximately equivalent numbers of binding sites for each membrane type, membranes containing both proteins I and II had a fivefold greater affinity for buccal cells than those containing protein I alone. When membranes were first treated with trypsin (1), little difference was seen with membranes from transparent gonococci, but the attachment of protein II-containing membranes was reduced to a similarly low level. Sodium dodecyl sulfate-polyacrylamide gel electrophoresis revealed that on trypsin treatment protein I (molecular weight of 36,000 [36K]) was cleaved, with the concomitant appearance of a 27.5K fragment, but that protein II was cleaved to fragments which were not retained in the membrane. A variety of sugars were tested in the system and showed no inhibition of attachment, but modification of the host cell surface with glycosidases reduced the attachment of protein II-containing membranes to those from transparent organisms. These observations confirm the importance of protein II in adhesion to buccal cells and suggest that protein I does not play a significant role in this system. As with pili, the evidence suggests the involvement of surface carbohydrates of the host cell in the adhesion process.

Although these data demonstrate the importance of protein II species in the attachment of opaque colonial forms, by using the buccal cell adhesion model, other workers have demonstrated that with different cell types transparent variants may attach more readily than opaque forms (7) and have suggested that isolation of transparent colonial forms from cases of salpingitis is due to the increased adhesion of these types to human fallopian tubes (3). Specificity in attachment is shown not only between transparent and opaque colonial forms but also between opaque variants of the same strain which have different protein II types (10). Comparison of two variants of strain P9 with proteins II of 28.5K or 28.0K reveals that, although both variants attach more avidly to epithelial cells than does the transparent variant, the 28.5K protein II is more effective in attachment to buccal cells and the 28.0K protein is more effective with the Chang conjunctival cell line (Table 1). An even more dramatic difference can be seen in the attachment to leukocytes, with variants that contain the 28.5K protein II showing sevenfold greater association. This differential adhesion to different cell types suggests that variations in outer membrane protein structure may play an important role in the ability of the gonococcus to colonize different sites in natural infection and to evade host defenses.

Pili. Pili isolated from different colonial variants of the same strain have also been shown to vary in subunit molecular weight (12), and additional types have been isolated from gonococci after applying a selection pressure by growth in plastic chambers subcutaneously implanted into guinea pigs (11, 14). Thus, pili with molecular weights of 21K, 20.5K, 19.5K, and 18.5K have

TABLE 1. Influence of outer membrane protein II on the attachment of *N. gonorrhoeae* P9 variants to different cell types

Variant	Protein II	Attachment[a] to:			
		Buccal epithelium[b]	Chang conjunctiva[c]	Leukocyte[b]	Erythrocyte[b]
P9-1	—	1.0	1.0	1.0	1.0
P9-13	28.5K	2.2	1.2	3.2	0.6
P9-16	28.0K	1.3	2.0	0.4	0.4

[a] Attachment to each cell type was measured by use of ^{3}H-labeled gonococci. Results for each cell type are expressed relative to the attachment obtained with P9-1, the variant lacking protein II.
[b] Reference 10.
[c] Reference 18.

been isolated from variants of strain P9. Peptide mapping has revealed that, like the proteins II, the variant pili show considerable structural homology but only limited antigenic cross-reactivity (P. Lambden, submitted for publication). Preliminary experiments carried out with the four pilus types show differential cell specificity in adhesion (Table 2), again suggesting the importance of structural variations for gonococcal colonization.

ROLE OF SURFACE PROTEIN VARIATIONS IN NATURAL INFECTION

Although evidence has accumulated to show that the gonococcal surface is capable of considerable structural variations during growth in vitro which directly affect the adhesive and other pathogenic properties of the organism, there is limited information on the extent of these variations during the course of natural infection. One study of isolates taken at different times of the menstrual cycle found a cyclic variation in the proportions of opaque and transparent colony types isolated (8). It was concluded that the gonococcal population changed in response to host factors, perhaps variations in the levels of proteolytic enzymes present during the menstrual cycle. Use of the guinea pig subcutaneous chamber model of gonococcal infection as an in vivo selection pressure has also revealed considerable potential for antigenic variations during growth in vivo. Differences occur not only in the protein II (13) but also in the pilus type (11, 14) of gonococci isolated during the course of chamber infections.

In an attempt to study the frequency of such variations in natural infection, different isolates of the same strain of gonococcus grown from partners and from different sites in the same patient were examined (M. Duckworth, D. Jackson, and J. E. Heckels, unpublished data). Preliminary results indicate that considerable variations in surface proteins occur during the course of natural infection which affect the pathogenic properties of the organism. Gonococci were cultured from the urethra of males and the cervix and urethra of female partners directly onto a nonselective gonococcal typing medium, and representative colonies were selected for further culture. In most groups of contacts, all the isolates had the same auxotype and protein I type, but sodium dodecyl sulfate-polyacrylamide gel electrophoresis of whole cell lysates showed differences in protein profile. Purification of the individual components revealed that isolates from the cervix and urethra of the same female frequently had differences in both pilus and protein II type and that further variation occurred in the male partner. The data from one such set of isolates reveal that such variations profoundly affect the adhesive properties of the organisms to both leukocytes and buccal epithelial cells (Table 3).

CONCLUSIONS

The ability of the gonococcus to adhere to mucosal surfaces at different anatomical sites and to invade and damage the epithelial cells is a critical determinant of gonococcal virulence. Both pili and outer membrane protein II play an

TABLE 2. Relative adhesion of pili from *N. gonorrhoeae* P9 to different cell types

Pilus mol wt	Adhesion[a] to:			
	Buccal epithelium	Chang conjunctiva	HEp-2 cells	Sheep erythrocytes
21K	1.0	0.3	0.8	0.3
20.5K	0.2	1.0	0.7	0.3
19.5K	0.9	0.5	1.0	0.3
18.5K	0.2	1.0	0.7	1.0

[a] Attachment was determined by use of ^{125}I-labeled pili and cells separated from nonattached pili by centrifugation on a cushion of 6% Dextran 110 (12). Results are expressed relative to the pilus type which showed greatest attachment for each cell type.

TABLE 3. Variation in surface protein and adhesive properties in variants of a gonococcal strain isolated at different anatomical sites[a]

Anatomical site	Protein		Pilus[b]	Leukocyte association (%)[c]	Buccal cell adhesion (%)[c]
	I[b]	II[b]			
Male urethra	35.5K	29 + 28K	17.5K	44	7
Female cervix	35.5K	28.5K	18K	18	35
Female urethra	35.5K	28.5K	17.7K	24	30

[a] All variants were of the arginine-requiring auxotroph.
[b] Subunit molecular weight as determined by sodium dodecyl sulfate-polyacrylamide gel electrophoresis (4).
[c] Determined as described previously (10).

important role in gonococcal adhesion to host cells, and during growth in vivo these components are capable of structural variations which modify their affinity for different cell types. It would appear that antigenic variations play an important role in the pathogenesis of gonorrhea, allowing the gonococcus to adapt to different cell surfaces found in the natural history of the disease. Indeed, it is likely that the ability to undergo such variations in response to environmental selection pressures makes a significant contribution to the success of this highly effective pathogen.

LITERATURE CITED

1. **Blake, M. S., E. C. Gotschlich, and J. Swanson.** 1981. Effects of proteolytic enzymes on the outer membrane proteins of *Neisseria gonorrhoeae*. Infect. Immun. 33:212–222.

2. **Buchanan, T. M., W. A. Pearce, and K. C. S. Chen.** 1980. Attachment of *Neisseria gonorrhoeae* to human cells, and investigations of the chemical nature of the receptor for gonococcal pili, p. 242–249. *In* G. F. Brooks, E. C. Gotschlich, K. K. Holmes, W. D. Sawyer, and F. E. Young (ed.), American Society for Microbiology, Washington, D.C.

3. **Draper, D. L., E. A. Donegan, J. F. James, R. L. Sweet, and G. F. Brooks.** 1980. *In vitro* modelling of acute salpingitis caused by *Neisseria gonorrhoeae*. Am. J. Obstet. Gynecol. 138:996–1002.

4. **Heckels, J. E.** 1981. Structural comparison of *Neisseria gonorrhoeae* outer membrane proteins. J. Bacteriol. 145:736–742.

5. **Heckels, J. E., B. Blackett, J. S. Everson, and M. E. Ward.** 1976. The influence of surface charge on the attachment of *Neisseria gonorrhoeae* to human cells. J. Gen. Microbiol. 96:359–364.

6. **Heckels, J. E., and L. T. James.** 1981. The structural organisation of the gonococcal cell envelope and its influence on pathogenesis, p. 25–28. *In* D. Danielsson and S. Normark (ed.), Genetics and immunobiology of pathogenic Neisseria. University of Umea, Umea, Sweden.

7. **James, J. F., C. J. Lammel, D. L. Draper, and G. F. Brooks.** 1980. Attachment of *N. gonorrhoeae* colony phenotype variants to eukaryotic cells, p. 213–216. *In* D. Danielsson and S. Normark (ed.), Genetics and immuno-

biology of pathogenic Neisseria. University of Umea, Umea, Sweden.

8. **James, J. F., and J. Swanson.** 1978. Studies on gonococcus infection. XIII. Occurrence of color-opacity colonial variants in clinical cultures. Infect. Immun. 19:332–340.

9. **Lambden, P. R., and J. E. Heckels.** 1979. The influence of outer membrane protein composition on the colonial morphology of *Neisseria gonorrhoeae* strain P9. FEMS Microbiol. Lett. 5:262–265.

10. **Lambden, P. R., J. E. Heckels, L. T. James, and P. J. Watt.** 1979. Variations in surface protein composition associated with virulence properties in opacity types of *Neisseria gonorrhoeae*. J. Gen. Microbiol. 114:305–312.

11. **Lambden, P. R., J. E. Heckels, H. McBride, and P. J. Watt.** 1981. The identification of novel pilus types produced by variants of *N. gonorrhoeae* P9 following selection *in vivo*. FEMS Microbiol. Lett. 10:339–341.

12. **Lambden, P. R., J. N. Robertson, and P. J. Watt.** 1980. Biological properties of two distinct pilus types produced by isogenic variants of *Neisseria gonorrhoeae* P9. J. Bacteriol. 141:393–396.

13. **McBride, H. M., P. R. Lambden, J. E. Heckels, and P. J. Watt.** 1981. The role of outer membrane proteins in the survival of *Neisseria gonorrhoeae* P9 within guinea pig subcutaneous chambers. J. Gen. Microbiol. 126:63–67.

14. **Penn, C. W., N. J. Parsons, D. R. Veale, and H. Smith.** 1980. Antigenic heterogeneity associated with pilus aggregation and autoagglutination in *Neisseria gonorrhoeae*. J. Gen. Microbiol. 121:195–202.

15. **Swanson, J.** 1978. Studies on gonococcus infection. XIV. Cell wall protein differences among color/opacity colony variants of *Neisseria gonorrhoeae*. Infect. Immun. 21:292–302.

16. **Swanson, J., S. J. Kraus, and E. C. Gotschlich.** 1971. Studies on gonococcus infection. I. Pili and zones of adhesion: their relation to gonococcal growth patterns. J. Exp. Med. 134:886–906.

17. **Trust, T. J., P. R. Lambden, and P. J. Watt.** 1980. The cohesive properties of variants of *Neisseria gonorrhoeae* strain P9: specific pilus-mediated and non-specific interactions. J. Gen. Microbiol. 119:179–187.

18. **Virji, M., and J. S. Everson.** 1981. Comparative virulence of opacity variants of *Neisseria gonorrhoeae* strain P9. Infect. Immun. 31:965–970.

19. **Ward, M. E., P. J. Watt, and J. N. Robertson.** 1974. The human fallopian tube: a laboratory model for gonococcal infection. J. Infect. Dis. 129:650–659.

20. **Watt, P. J., and M. E. Ward.** 1980. Adherence of *Neisseria gonorrhoeae* and other Neisseria species to mammalian cells, p. 253–288. *In* E. H. Beachey (ed.), Bacterial adherence (Receptors and recognition, series B, vol. 6). Chapman and Hall, London.

Analysis of Pilus-Mediated Pathogenic Mechanisms with Monoclonal Antibodies

T. SÖDERSTRÖM, C. C. BRINTON, JR., P. FUSCO, A. KARPAS, S. AHLSTEDT, K. STEIN, A. SUTTON, S. HOSEA, R. SCHNEERSON, AND L. Å. HANSON

Department of Clinical Immunology, Institute of Medical Microbiology, University of Göteborg, Göteborg, Sweden; Department of Life Sciences, University of Pittsburgh, Pennsylvania 15213; Bureau of Biologics, Food and Drug Administration, Bethesda, Maryland 20205; and National Institutes of Health, Bethesda, Maryland 20205

Most *Escherichia coli* strains causing disease in humans express or can be cloned to express type 1 pili, which are defined as a family of serologically related somatic pili (2). They are often characterized by their ability to mediate α-methyl mannoside (α-Mm)-inhibitable agglutination of guinea pig erythrocytes (9). The genes encoding their production are chromosomal (14). The role of type 1 pili in the pathogenesis of infectious disease is poorly understood. A strong link was shown between D-mannose inhibition of adherence of *E. coli* to certain human epithelial cells and the presence of type 1 pili on the bacteria (7, 8). Type 1 pilus binding has also been demonstrated to Vero cell monolayers (12) and to bovine mammary gland epithelial cells (4). It is known that many of the enterotoxigenic *E. coli* strains that colonize the intestine and cause diarrheal disease lack colonization factor antigens I and II (3, 5, 6, 10), but possess type 1 pili (1, 6). The component responsible for epithelial adhesion of such strains has not been identified.

In this study we have looked at the antigenic complexity of type 1 pili and the protective capacity of antibodies to such pili, using monoclonal antibodies against two different *E. coli* type 1 pilus preparations. In addition, we have analyzed the capacity of type 1 piliated *E. coli* to cause mannose-inhibitable adherence to and agglutination of human spermatozoa.

CHARACTERIZATION OF TYPE 1 PILI WITH MONOCLONAL ANTISERA

Monoclonal antisera were produced by fusion of spleen cells from mice immunized against purified type 1 pili from *E. coli* H10407 or *E. coli* E2528C1 with the SP2 0 nonsecreting mouse plasmacytoma cell line. Antibody-producing cells were detected by enzyme-linked immunosorbent assay and were then cloned. The monoclonal antibodies were characterized by isoelectric focusing and were analyzed for isotype by solid-phase radioimmunoassay using ^{3}H-labeled subclass-specific antisera. The monoclonal antibodies belonged to the immunoglobulin M (IgM), IgG1, and IgG2a subclasses. Antigenic specificity was characterized by immunodiffusion, capillary precipitation, agglutination, and enzyme-linked immunosorbent assay. The specificity of two of the antisera against *E. coli* H10407 was tested in an enzyme-linked immunosorbent assay (Table 1). Binding of the antisera to nine different *E. coli* type 1 pili and two unrelated pilus preparations (987-5/987 and H10407/NMS) was calculated as a percentage of the homologous reaction. The antibody 7F2 seems specific for a variable antigenic determinant of H10407 type 1 pili, whereas 1B69 shows broad cross-reactivity. The antibody 7F2, but not 1B69, still binds when the pilus preparation is brought to pH 9.5, and both antisera again precipitate the antigen when the pH is brought back to neutral. Interestingly, the antibody-pilus precipitation in immunodiffusion is blocked by α-Mm for 1B69, but not for 7F2. This suggests that the variable antigenic determinant is not related to a mannose-binding site, whereas the common determinant is.

TABLE 1. Reactivities of mouse hybridoma monoclonal antibodies to purified *E. coli* type 1 pili

E. coli pilus type	Relative reactivities (%)	
	Monoclonal antibody 1B6	Monoclonal antibody 7F2
H10407/type 1	100.0	100.0
51301/type 1	35.2	<0.1
BamP⁺/type 1	27.7	0.112
B7A/type 1	13.3	<0.01
TD225C4/type 1	11.1	<0.01
B9/AHA⁺/REV/type 1	9.7	<0.01
RDEC-1/Nal 1-2/type 1	7.2	<0.01
E2831/70/type 1	3.0	<0.01
E2528C1/type 1	1.4	<0.01
987-5/987	0	0
H10407/NMS	0	0

305

TABLE 2. Hemagglutination patterns of *E. coli* and agglutination of human spermatozoa[a]

E. coli strain	Guinea pig erythrocytes		Human erythrocytes		Spermatozoa donor			
	−M	+M	−M	+M	1	2	3	4
A	−	−	+	+	−	−	−	−
B	−	−	−	−	−	−	−	−
C	+ +	−	+ + +	+ + +	+ + +	+ + +	+ + +	+ + +
D	+	−	−	−	+ +	+ +	+ +	+ +
E	+ +	−	−	−	+ + +	+ + +	+ + +	+ + +
F	−	−	−	−	−	−	−	−
G	+ + +	−	+	−	+ + +	+ + +	+ + +	+ + +
H	+ + +	−	+	−	+ +	+ +	+ +	+ +
I	−	−	−	−	−	−	−	−
J	−	−	+ +	+ + +	−	−	−	−
K	+ + +	−	+ + +	−	+ + +	+ + +	+ + +	+ + +
L	−	−	−	−	−	−	−	−

[a] −, No hemagglutination; +, + +, and + + +, increasing strength of hemagglutination. M, D-Mannose.

Many of the other monoclonal antibodies show broad cross-reactivity when tested against different preparations of type 1 pili in immunodiffusion. Most, but not all, of these reactions to heterologous pili can be blocked with α-Mm. This means that shared antigenic sites not related to mannose binding exist on different type 1 pili.

Immunoglobulins are glycoproteins in that they contain conjugated carbohydrates, often present in complex chains. D-Mannose is a dominant carbohydrate constituting between 1% (IgG) and 3.6% (IgM) of the human immunoglobulin molecules (15). Interaction with these oligosaccharides could explain a nonspecific lectin-like mannose-inhibitable adhesion of monoclonal antibodies to heterologous pili. To check the binding of type 1 pili to different mouse immunoglobulin subclasses, *E. coli* H10407 type 1 pili were tested against mouse myeloma proteins of different subclasses and a series of monoclonal antibodies to unrelated antigens. In no case was any precipitation of type 1 pili seen. This does not support a nonspecific binding of such pili to the carbohydrate moiety of immunoglobulin molecules outside the antigen-combining site.

ANTIBODIES TO TYPE 1 PILI IN HOST DEFENSE

Among the host defense mechanisms that could be affected by induction of specific antisera against type 1 pili are (i) attachment and invasion, (ii) opsonization-phagocytosis, and (iii) complement-mediated bactericidal reactions. Depending on the site and type of infection, these mechanisms could be of different relative importance.

Many of the monoclonal antisera to type 1 pili were capable of in vitro agglutination of homologous and heterologous type 1 piliated bacteria. This reaction showed specificity, as the different antisera did not agglutinate the same bacteria. Agglutination in combination with the attachment of type 1 pili to urinary slime and probably mucosal slime at other sites (11) could facilitate removal of large masses of bacteria.

We found that all *E. coli* strains investigated, mediating α-Mm–inhibitable hemagglutination, adhered to and caused agglutination of human spermatozoa (Table 2). This agglutination was mannose sensitive, and our results agreed with earlier findings of a specificity in the lectin-like adherence of pili to mannose-containing structures on cell surfaces. A crystalliform type 1 pilus preparation showed the same capacity. Monoclonal antisera to type 1 pili inhibited both hemagglutination and sperm agglutination.

In a bactericidal assay (Table 3) with the addition of polymorphonuclear leukocytes

TABLE 3. Opsonization of *E. coli* O6:K13:H1 with monoclonal antibodies to the K13 capsular polysaccharide and to *E. coli* O78:K80:H1 type 1 pili[a]

Antiserum	% killing at 60 min	
	+ PMNs	− PMNs
None	25	—
Anti-K13 (IgM)	95	36
Anti-K13 (IgG1)	95	38
Anti-pili (IgG1)	28	3
Anti-pili (IgG2a)	28	—
Anti-pili (IgM)	31	—

[a] *E. coli* O6:K13:H1 (10^6 cells) mixed with 1% normal serum (complement) and PNMs was tested in a bactericidal assay with monoclonal antisera at 10% down to 0.001%; only the results for 0.1% are shown, but the tendency was uniform.

TABLE 4. Intraperitoneal infection of CBA mice with *E. coli* O6:K13 carrying type 1 pili

Antiserum	LD_{50}[a]
NaCl	3.3×10^6
Rabbit anti-*E. coli* O6	2.5×10^7
Mouse monoclonal anti-*E. coli* K13	4×10^7
Mouse monoclonal anti-*E. coli* type 1 pili	9.2×10^6

[a] LD_{50}, 50% lethal dose.

(PMNs) and normal serum as complement source, we found significant bacterial killing in the presence of from 1 to 0.001% of monoclonal antisera to the capsular polysaccharide. The monoclonal antibodies to heterologous type 1 pili did not enhance killing. Addition of similar amounts of antibody and normal human serum without PMNs resulted in background levels of killing only. Earlier investigations demonstrated that presence of type 1 pili on *E. coli* facilitated phagocytosis and that the viability of piliated organisms was reduced when they were incubated with PMNs (13). Low doses of monoclonal antibodies against type 1 pili, given subcutaneously 1 day before challenge, did not protect against bacteremia in neonatal rats challenged intragastrically with a heterologous *E. coli* K1 strain carrying type 1 pili.

In a single experiment with intraperitoneal challenge of adult CBA mice with *E. coli* type O6:K13:H1 grown for piliation, subcutaneously administered monoclonal antibodies to the K13 capsular polysaccharide increased survival as efficiently as a high-titer polyclonal rabbit anti-O6 antiserum. Monoclonal antibodies to heterologous *E. coli* type 1 pili showed little protective capacity (Table 4).

CONCLUSIONS

Type 1 pili are ubiquitous among *E. coli* strains causing disease, but are common also among carrier isolates. No definite role has been shown for type 1 pili as a virulence factor in human infections. The existence of shared antigenic sites, some mannose-related and some not, was shown between different type 1 pili. The remarkable finding that antibodies to type 1 pili did not induce in vitro phagocytosis or bacterial killing might mean that these antibodies do not cause an inflammatory response but could be protective at the mucosal level. Once invasion has occurred, no significant advantage of antibodies to type 1 pili was shown in the animal models.

The clinical relevance of the pilus-mediated agglutination of human spermatozoa is not known. It is striking, however, that prostatitis so often is caused by *E. coli* known to often carry type 1 pili.

LITERATURE CITED

1. **Brinton, C. C., Jr.** 1977. The piliation phase syndrome and the uses of purified pili in disease control, p. 33–70. Proceedings of the 13th Joint U.S.-Japan Conference on Cholera, Atlanta, Ga. Department of Health, Education and Welfare Publication 78-1590.
2. **Brinton, C., P. Fusco, S. Wood, S. Polen, A. To, S. To, M. Levine, T. Söderström, L. Hanson, R. Schneerson, and J. Robbins.** 1980. The development of *Escherichia coli* pilus vaccines for human and animal diseases. Proceedings International Symposium on Bacterial Vaccines, Washington, D.C.
3. **Gross, R. J., A. Cravioto, S. M. Scotland, T. Cheasty, and B. Rowe.** 1978. The occurrence of colonization factor (CF) in enterotoxigenic *Escherichia coli*. FEMS Microbiol. Lett. 3:231.
4. **Harper, M., A. Turvey, and A. J. Bramley.** 1978. Adhesion of fimbriate *Escherichia coli* to bovine mammary gland epithelial cells in vitro. J. Med. Microbiol. 11:117–123.
5. **Levine, M. M.,** 1981. Adhesion of enterotoxigenic *Escherichia coli* in humans and animals, p. 142–154. *In* Adhesion and pathogenicity Ciba Foundation Symposium. Pitman Medical, Tunbridge Wells, England.
6. **Levine, M. M., M. B. Rennels, V. Daya, and T. P. Hughes.** 1980. Hemagglutination and colonization factors in enterotoxigenic and enteropathogenic *Escherichia coli* that cause diarrhea. J. Infect. Dis. 141:738.
7. **Ofek, I., and E. H. Beachey.** 1978. Mannose binding and epithelial cell adherence of *Escherichia coli*. Infect. Immun. 22:247–254.
8. **Ofek, I., D. Mirelman, and N. Sharon.** 1977. Adherence of *Escherichia coli* to human mucosal cells mediated by mannose receptors. Nature (London) 265:623–625.
9. **Old, D. C.** 1972. Inhibition of the interaction between fimbrial haemagglutinations and erythrocytes by D-mannose and other carbohydrates. J. Gen. Microbiol. 71:149.
10. **Ørskov, I., and F. Ørskov.** 1977. Special O:K:H serotypes among enterotoxigenic *E. coli* strains from diarrhea in adults and children. Occurrence of the CF (colonization factor) antigen and hemagglutinating abilities. Med. Microbiol. Immunol. 163:99.
11. **Ørskov, I., F. Ørskov, and A. Birch-Andersen.** 1980. A fimbria *Escherichia coli* antigen, F7, determining uroepithelial adherence. Comparison with type 1 fimbriae which attach to urinary slime. Infect. Immun. 27:657–666.
12. **Salit, I. E., and E. C. Gotschlich.** 1977. Type 1 *Escherichia coli* pili: characterization of binding to monkey kidney cells. J. Exp. Med. 146:1182–1194.
13. **Silverblatt, F. J., J. S. Dreyer, and S. Schauer.** 1979. Effect of pili on susceptibility of *Escherichia coli* to phagocytosis. Infect. Immun. 24:218–223.
14. **Swaney, L. M., Y.-P. Liu, K. Ippen-Ihler, and C. C. Brinton, Jr.** 1977. Genetic complementation analysis of *Escherichia coli* type 1 somatic pilus mutants. J. Bacteriol. 130:506.
15. **Wasserman, R. L., and J. D. Capra.** 1977. Blood glycoproteins, p. 323–348. *In* M. I. Horowitz and W. Pigman (ed.), The glycoconjugates, vol 1. Academic Press, Inc., New York.

Genetic Control of Type 1 Fimbriae in *Escherichia coli*

BARRY I. EISENSTEIN

Departments of Medicine and Microbiology and Immunology, University of Tennessee Center for the Health Sciences, Memphis, Tennessee 38163

The recent appreciation of the importance of bacterial adherence in the interaction of host and parasite has resulted in an explosion of interest in the field. In many gram-negative bacteria, such as *Escherichia coli*, adherence is mediated by protein organelles, called fimbriae or pili, which are arranged on the bacterial surface and which bind to specific receptors on the host cell (12). Type 1 fimbriae, which are found on the majority of clinical isolates of *E. coli* (5), bind to mannose-containing receptors and mediate bacterial binding to a variety of eucaryotic cells (13), including monkey kidney cells (15), human epithelial cells (4, 9), intestinal cells (4), and leukocytes (1).

KNOWN GENETICS OF FIMBRIATION IN *E. COLI*

Most of the genetic studies of fimbriae have been reported from the laboratories of Brinton and Duguid (4, 5, 10, 11, 21, 22). Working with a K-12 strain of *E. coli*, Brinton and co-workers mapped the genes for fimbriation and showed them to be chromosomal, consisting of four complementation classes defining three alleles, *pilA, pilB,* and *pilC,* all of which mapped at 98 min on the K-12 chromosome (21, 22). Although all *pilA* and *pilB* mutants complemented *pilC* mutants, many *pilA* and *pilB* strains did not complement one another and were designated class AB (21); thus, either AB was one gene, with some cases of intracistronic complementation, or A and B were separate but contiguous genes under coordinate control. Since all *pil* mutations were recessive to the wild type, it was suspected that C and A-B were separate operons, with C perhaps being the positive control gene for A-B (or AB) (21).

The gene products of these three cistrons are unknown (21, 22), although one presumably codes for the multimeric fimbrial subunit. These studies demonstrate the feasibility of mutagenizing a strain of *E. coli* and selecting for Pil⁻ derivatives by cloning mutants with altered colonial morphology (22). Candidate nonfimbriate colonies are easily identified by their lack of pellicle formation when grown in broth, their lack of agglutination by anti-fimbrial antiserum, or their lack of fimbriae when observed by electron microscopy (8, 10, 22).

PHASE VARIATION AND ENVIRONMENTAL REGULATION OF FIMBRIATION

Despite these careful genetic studies, only a few observations have been made about the genetic regulation of fimbrial synthesis and expression. Brinton and co-workers have demonstrated that in *pil⁺* strains at least two different mechanisms operate in this regulation: (i) phase variation, which consists of the all-or-none alteration between fimbriate and nonfimbriate cells during growth; and (ii) growth cycle variation, which consists of quantitative changes in number of fimbriae per cell under different growth and environmental conditions (22). Phase variation is marked by a relatively high rate of change of phase type (1 per 1,000 bacteria per generation). Duguid, Old, and co-workers found that growth in static broth enhanced the population of fimbriate bacteria, whereas growth on agar plates selectively enriched the population of nonfimbriate bacteria (10). Growth cycle variation has been shown to depend greatly on the metabolic state of the culture. When bacteria are grown in static broth, cells grown with glucose are less fimbriate than those grown without glucose. Since exogenous glucose suppresses intracellular concentrations of cyclic AMP, it has been postulated that the glucose effect might be cyclic AMP-mediated via the permissive action of cyclic AMP on the transcription of "catabolite-sensitive" operons (14). Nevertheless, the work of my colleagues and I indicates that the glucose effect on fimbriae may be cyclic AMP independent (7; see below).

A major stumbling block in the evaluation of fimbrial synthesis and regulation has been the difficulty in quantitating synthesis of subunits and expression of organelles. The former has never been accomplished and the latter is either cumbersome, since it requires counting individual fimbriae observed by electron microscopy, or only semiquantitative (as with agglutination

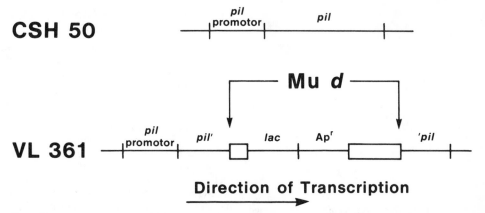

Direction of Transcription

FIG. 1. Construction of the *pil-lac* operon fusion. Lac⁻ strain CSH50 was transduced to Apʳ with bacteriophage Mu *d* (Apʳ *lac*), and single colonies were scored for Lac⁺ and Pil⁻. The stability of Pil⁻ was determined by growing potential Pil⁻ isolates in static broth and observing for the lack of pellicle formation and Pil⁺ outgrowth. One such Pil⁻ clone, VL361, was demonstrated to contain a single Mu *d* insertion by the fact that its transduction to Pil⁺ by P1 bacteriophage propagated on strain CSH50 always resulted in simultaneous loss of Lac⁺ and Apʳ. (Reproduced with permission from reference 6.)

tests). Recently though, a simple one-step method of fusing the structural gene for β-galactosidase to any operon of interest has been perfected by Casadaban (2, 3). The resulting operon fusion, with β-galactosidase production now coupled to the gene promoter of interest, allows the investigator to determine the transcriptional control of that gene by following β-galactosidase activity rather than the original gene product.

OPERON FUSION AS A PROBE OF PHASE VARIATION

Using the operon fusion method, I have developed a means of investigating the genetic control of type 1 fimbriae. To accomplish the fusion, I began with the Lac⁻ K-12 strain of *E. coli*, CSH50, and lysogenized it with bacteriophage Mu *d* (Apʳ, *lac*) (3). By selecting for Apʳ and screening the lysogens for acquisition of Lac⁺ and loss of type 1 fimbriae, I was able to position *lac* within a *pil* operon (Fig. 1 and 2). To demonstrate that one and only one Mu insertion occurred, I showed that transduction of the fusion strain, VL361, back to Pil⁺ (11) resulted in loss of both Apʳ and Lac⁺ (6). Since type 1 fimbriae in *E. coli* undergo phase variation, it was not surprising that when the fusion strain was grown on lactose-MacConkey agar both Lac⁺ (phase-positive) and Lac⁻ (phase-negative) colonies were found (Fig. 3). Moreover, Lac⁺ colonies gave rise to both Lac⁺ and Lac⁻ colonies (the former predominant), and Lac⁻ colonies gave rise to both Lac⁺ and Lac⁻ colonies (the latter predominant).

EFFECTS OF GLUCOSE AND CYCLIC AMP ON FIMBRIATION

Having thereby demonstrated that the enzyme was expressing the transcription of a *pil* operon, it was possible to determine whether it was a catabolite-sensitive operon. When the fusion strain was grown in broth in the absence and in the presence of glucose, there was only a 50% reduction in enzyme production in the glucose-

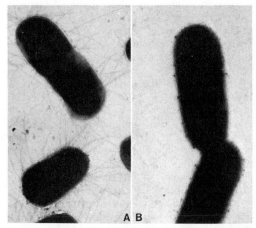

FIG. 2. Electron micrographs of Pil⁺ strain CSH50 and Pil⁻ strain VL361. Bacteria were grown in broth and stained with phosphotungstic acid. (8). (A) Strain CSH50, showing fimbriae on each bacterium. (B) *pil lac* fusion strain VL361, showing loss of fimbriae. ×18,000.

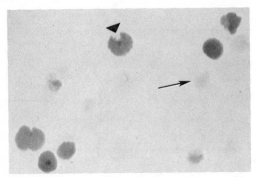

FIG. 3. Phase-variant colonies of strain VL361 stained for the presence or absence of β-galactosidase. Bacteria were grown in a layer of soft agar and stained as previously reported (6). Note that some colonies are dark, demonstrating the presence of enzyme (positive phase), and that some colonies are light, demonstrating the absence of enzyme (negative phase). When phase transition rates were determined by methods recently described (6), it was found that the phase transition rate from Lac$^+$ to Lac$^-$ was 1.05×10^{-3} per cell per generation and that from Lac$^-$ to Lac$^+$ was 3.12×10^{-3} per cell per generation. Arrow, difficult-to-see negative colony; arrowhead, negative sector arising out of a positive colony. (Reproduced with permission from reference 6.)

grown sample, compatible with the polarity effects that have been observed with the operon fusion technique (16). When both the parent strain, CSH50, and the fusion derivative, strain VL361, were transduced to Δcya (thereby preventing endogenous synthesis of cyclic AMP), there were minimal effects on either the degree of fimbriation or the synthesis of β-galactosidase in the respective derivatives. Therefore, the *pil* operon under investigation, as judged by a variety of methods, was found not to be catabolite sensitive.

I conclude that the genetic control of type 1 fimbriae in *E. coli* is, at least in part, directed by phase variation at the transcriptional level. In this regard, type 1 fimbriae may be similar genetically to flagella in *Salmonella*, where phase variation has been shown to be regulated by an invertible DNA switch that positions the flagellar promoter in either the "on" or the "off" configuration (19, 20, 23). Moreover, the effects of glucose on the degree of fimbriation do not appear to be due to events at the genetic level. It is more likely that the presence of glucose in static media merely prevents the outgrowth of fimbriate bacteria. In glucose-free broth, fimbriate bacteria possess a marked growth advantage because of their ability to form a pellicle at the air-liquid interface (10).

PATHOGENIC SIGNIFICANCE OF PHASE VARIATION

The presence of fimbriae may be advantageous or detrimental to the organism, depending on the environmental circumstances. Thus, at the mucosal surface, fimbriae promote bacterial adherence and colonization, whereas in deeper tissues, which contain leukocytes, fimbriae allow leukocyte recognition and phagocytosis (1), even in the absence of immunoglobulin. For example, in *Proteus mirabilis*, which undergoes phase variation, only fimbriate bacteria adhere well to uroepithelial cells and readily produce ascending urinary tract infection in an animal model (17). But when the route of inoculation is via the bloodstream, the fimbriate bacteria are ingested by phagocytes and are therefore unable to produce infection (18). In this latter model, only nonfimbriate organisms are able to produce hematogenous pyelonephritis. The on-off switch is, therefore, a virulence factor in that it causes random oscillation of fimbriation and nonfimbriation. This rapid switching permits a proportion of the infecting population, being in the proper pathogenic mode, to withstand selective environmental pressure. Thus, understanding the mechanisms of the genetic control of bacterial fimbriae may permit new insights into bacterial pathogenesis and may allow novel approaches to the control of infection.

ACKNOWLEDGMENTS

I thank V. Long, L. Hatmaker, and P. Swann for technical assistance.

This study was supported in part by Clinical Investigator Award AM-00686 from the National Institute of Arthritis and Metabolic Disease.

LITERATURE CITED

1. **Bar-Shavit, Z., I. Ofek, R. Goldman, D. Mirelman, and N. Sharon.** 1977. Mannose residues on phagocytes as receptors for the attachment of *Escherichia coli* and *Salmonella typhi*. Biochem. Biophys. Res. Commun. **78:**455–460.
2. **Casadaban, M. J.** 1976. Transposition and fusion of the *lac* genes to selected promoters in *Escherichia coli* using bacteriophage lambda and Mu. J. Mol. Biol. **104:**541–556.
3. **Casadaban, M. J., and S. N. Cohen.** 1979. Lactose genes fused to exogenous promoters in one step using a Mu-*lac* bacteriophage: *in vivo* probe for transcriptional control sequences. Proc. Natl. Acad. Sci. U.S.A. **76:**4530–4533.
4. **Duguid, J. P., and R. R. Gillies.** 1957. Fimbriae and adhesive properties in dysentery bacilli. J. Pathol. Bacteriol. **74:**397–411.
5. **Duguid, J. P., and D. C. Old.** 1980. Adhesive properties of Enterobacteriaceae, p. 185–217. *In* E. H., Beachey (ed.), Bacterial adherence (Receptors and recognition, series B, vol. 6). Chapman and Hall, London.
6. **Eisenstein, B. I.** 1981. Phase variation of type 1 fimbriae in *Escherichia coli* is under transcriptional control. Science **214:**337–339.
7. **Eisenstein, B. I., E. H. Beachey, and S. S. Solomon.** 1981. Divergent effects of cyclic adenosine 3′,5′-monophosphate on formation of type 1 fimbriae in different K-12 strains of *Escherichia coli*. J. Bacteriol. **145:**620–623.

8. **Eisenstein, B. I., I. Ofek, and E. H. Beachey.** 1979. Interference with the mannose binding and epithelial cell adherence of *Escherichia coli* by sublethal concentrations of streptomycin. J. Clin. Invest. **63:**1219–1228.

9. **Ofek, I., and E. H. Beachey.** 1978. Mannose binding and epithelial cell adherence of *Escherichia coli*. Infect. Immun. **22:**247–254.

10. **Old, D. C., and J. P. Duguid.** 1970. Selective outgrowth of fimbriate bacteria in static liquid medium. J. Bacteriol. **103:**447–456.

11. **Old, D. C., and J. P. Duguid.** 1971. Selection of fimbriate transductants of *Salmonella typhimurium* dependent on motility. J. Bacteriol. **107:**655–658.

12. **Ottow, J. C. G.** 1975. Ecology, physiology and genetics of fimbriae and pili. Annu. Rev. Microbiol. **29:**79–108.

13. **Pearce, W. A., and T. M. Buchanan.** 1980. Structure and cell membrane-binding properties of bacterial fimbriae, p. 289–344. *In* E. H. Beachey (ed.), Bacterial adherence (Receptors and recognition, Ser. B, vol. 6). Chapman and Hall, London.

14. **Saier, M. H., Jr., M. R. Schmidt, and M. Liebowitz.** 1978. Cyclic AMP-dependent synthesis for fimbriae in *Salmonella typhimurium*: effects of *cya* and *pts* mutations. J. Bacteriol. **122:**338–340.

15. **Salit, I., and E. C. Gotschlich.** 1977. Type 1 *Escherichia coli* pili: characterization of binding sites on monkey kidney cells. J. Exp. Med. **146:**1182–1194.

16. **Schwartz, M., and A. Ullmann.** 1980. The use of gene fusions to study polar effects in the *gal* operon of *Escherichia coli*. FEMS Microbiol. Lett. **8:**147–150.

17. **Silverblatt, F. J.** 1974. Host-parasite interaction in the rat renal pelvis: a possible role of pili in the pathogenesis of pyelonephritis. J. Exp. Med. **140:**1696–1711.

18. **Silverblatt, F. J., and I. Ofek.** 1978. Effects of pili on susceptibility of *Proteus mirabilis* to phagocytosis and on adherence to bladder cells, p. 49–59. *In* E. H. Kass (ed.), Infections of the urinary tract. University of Chicago Press, Chicago.

19. **Silverman, M., and M. Simon.** 1980. Phase variation: genetic analysis of switching mutants. Cell **19:**845–854.

20. **Silverman, J., J. Zieg, G. Mandel, and M. Simon.** 1981. Analysis of the functional components of the phase variation system. Cold Spring Harbor Symp. Quant. Biol. **45:**17–26.

21. **Swaney, L. M., Y.-P. Liu, K. Ippen-Ihler, and C. C. Brinton, Jr.** 1977. Genetic complementation analysis of *Escherichia coli* type 1 somatic pilus mutants. J. Bacteriol. **130:**506–511.

22. **Swaney, L. M., Y.-P. Liu, C.-M. To, C.-C. To, K. Ippen-Ihler, and C. C. Brinton, Jr.** 1977. Isolation and characterization of *Escherichia coli* phase variants and mutants deficient in type 1 pilus production. J. Bacteriol. **130:**495–505.

23. **Zieg, J., M. Silverman, M. Hilmen, and M. Simon.** 1977. Recombinational switch for gene expression. Science **196:**170–172.

Receptor Binding and Antigenic Domains of Gonococcal Pili

G. K. SCHOOLNIK, J. Y. TAI, AND E. C. GOTSCHLICH

The Rockefeller University, New York, New York 10021

Pili are proteinaceous, nonflagellar surface appendages which mediate the adherence of gonococci to human mucosa. Each pilus filament is an assembly of thousands of identical protein subunits which polymerize to form a linear structure approximately 6 nm in diameter and 1,000 to 4,000 nm in length (1, 16). Pili purified from different gonococcal strains possess subunit molecular weights which vary between 17,500 and 21,000 (2, 5, 12). The subunit molecular weights of pili from isogenic opaque (Op) and transparent (Tr) opacity variants may also differ (10, 13). Moreover, interstrain and intrastrain differences occur in the isoelectric point and buoyant density of pili (13). Thus, the molecular organization of gonococcal pili from different strains and isogenic opacity variants is similar, but not identical.

Pili attach to human cell surfaces: piliated gonococci adhere to spermatozoa (9), tissue culture cell lines derived from epithelial cells (15), the fallopian tube in organ culture (18), and erythrocytes (4). A quantitative hemagglutination assay, employed to measure the adherence function of pili, detected differences in the hemagglutinating capacity of pili from different strains and isogenic opacity variants. Pili from the opaque and transparent clones of four gonococcal strains agglutinated erythrocytes in protein concentrations of 0.2 to 82.5 µg/ml. In two of four strains, the hemagglutinating concentrations of pili from the opaque clone were 55 to 65 times lower than those from its transparent mate (14). Quantitative differences in the adherence function of pili therefore exist between and within strains (10, 14).

Gonococcal pili also adhere to animal cell surfaces. Erythrocytes from seven species of animals were agglutinated by pilus concentrations 2 to 100 times greater than human cells (12, 14). The capacity of pili to discriminate between the cell surfaces of animal and human erythrocytes is evidence for the specificity of the binding event.

Gonococcal pili are immunogenic (2, 3, 5, 17). Humoral and secretory antibody which forms in response to natural infection or systemic immunization detects both type-specific (homologous) and cross-reactive (common) antigenic determinants (2, 5). The antigenic diversity of gonococcal pili has been characterized with human and rabbit anti-pili antisera prepared by systemic immunization. Human antisera detect less than 50% and rabbit antisera less than 10% shared antigenicity between pili from heterologous strains (2, 5).

The physical, functional, and serological diversity of gonococcal pili is presumed to reside in their covalent structure. The amino acid compositions and minimal molecular weights of the protein of pili from several gonococcal strains have been determined and are similar but not identical (8, 14). The N-terminal amino acid sequence was found to be identical through the 49th residue for pili from the opaque and transparent variants of two strains (14) and through the 29th residue for pili from four strains sequenced by Hermodson et al. (8). However, tryptic peptide maps of pili from two strains resolved 22 peptides of which only 14 were identical (Fig. 1). Thus, differences in the primary structure of pili from different gonococcal strains exist and may be responsible for the functional and serological diversity of these organelles.

STRUCTURE-FUNCTION ANALYSIS OF GONOCOCCAL PILI

The properties attributed to gonococcal pili by these studies are determined by structurally independent regions of the pilus subunit which separately effect receptor binding function and antigenicity. The *receptor binding domain* mediates the adherence of pilus protein to specific cell surface receptor molecules. The *type-specific antigenic domain* is immunodominant and confers antigenic diversity.

Peptides encompassing these domains were sought by cyanogen bromide cleavage of pilus protein at methionine residues (7). The resulting fragments were purified by reverse-phase high-pressure liquid chromatography and were tested for receptor binding function and antigenicity. The cyanogen bromide fragments of the subunit of gonococcal pili, aligned as indicated in Fig. 2, are (14): CNBr-1 (N-terminal, 7 residues), CNBr-2 (residues 8 to ca. 84), and CNBr-3

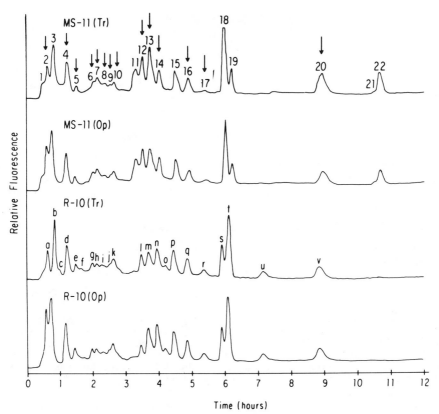

FIG. 1. Tryptic peptide maps (6) of reduced and alkylated gonococcal pili from the isogenic transparent (Tr) and opaque (Op) clones of strains MS11 and R10. Of the 22 peptides from MS11 (Tr) pili resolved by this technique, 14 (indicated by arrows, ↓) were identical to peptides of R10 pili. No significant differences were noted between the tryptic peptides of pili from the isogenic Tr and Op clones of the same strain.

(residues ca. 85 to 160, the carboxy-terminal portion of the molecule).

THE RECEPTOR BINDING DOMAIN

Fragments CNBr-2 and CNBr-3 were tested for their capacity to inhibit the agglutination of human erythrocytes by filaments of homologous and heterologous gonococcal pili. In this system, hemagglutination inhibition is a measure of the efficiency with which the peptides of pili compete with uncleaved pili for a finite number of erythrocyte surface receptor sites. CNBr-2, but not CNBr-3, inhibited hemagglutination by homologous and heterologous native gonococcal pili from both opacity variants. These results suggest the following:

(i) CNBr-2 fragment encompasses the amino acid sequence which binds the erythrocyte receptor site for gonococcal pili.

(ii) Gonococcal pili from the opaque and transparent variants of different gonococcal strains bind the same receptor.

(iii) Each pilus subunit possesses a receptor binding domain which, if expressed in the assembled state, results in a linear array of binding regions along the longitudinal axis of the pilus filament.

(iv) The receptor binding domain of CNBr-2 is highly conserved for pili from different gonococcal strains. This is implied by the observation that CNBr-2 fragments prepared from pili which are physically and serologically diverse inhibit hemagglutination by homologous and heterologous pili equally well. Accordingly, the amino acid compositions of CNBr-2 fragments from different gonococcal strains are similar, 87% of the CNBr-2 tryptic peptides are identical, and the N-terminal amino acid sequences of CNBr-2 fragments from heterologous pili are identical through the 42nd residue (14).

In contrast, tryptic peptide maps of CNBr-3 fragments from heterologous gonococcal pili indicate significant differences in the primary structure of the carboxy-terminal region of the

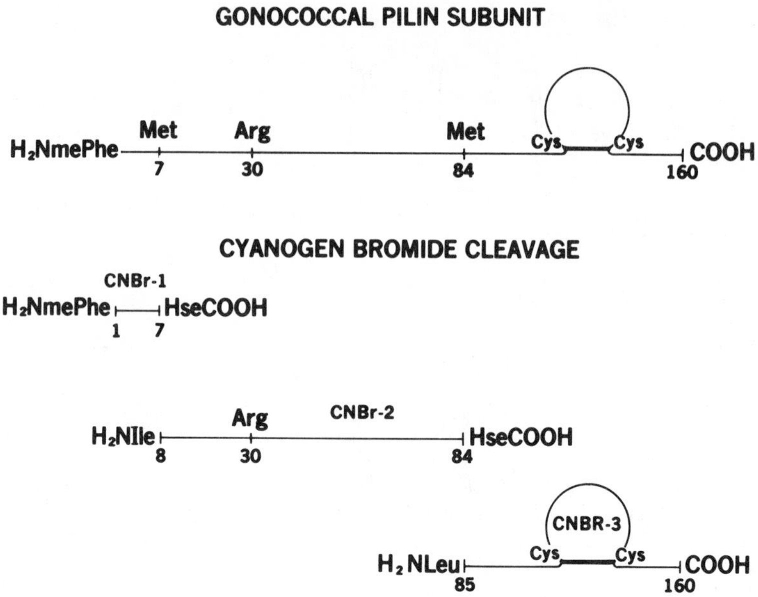

GONOCOCCAL PILIN SUBUNIT

CYANOGEN BROMIDE CLEAVAGE

FIG. 2. Cyanogen bromide cleavage (7) of pilus protein from the isogenic transparent clone of gonococcal strain MS11. Cleavage at methionine residues in positions 7 and ca. 84 of the sequence resulted in three fragments, CNBr-1, CNBr-2, and CNBr-3, which were purified by high-pressure liquid chromatography and tested for their ability to inhibit the agglutination of human erythrocytes by native pili. CNBr-3 contains a pair of half-cystine residues. Because no sulfhydryl group is detected by alkylation with iodoacetamide in 6 M guanidine HCl (11), the two half-cystine residues must exist in a disulfide bond.

molecule, since only 50% of the peptides are identical (14). Amino acid sequence heterogeneity was confirmed by determining the N-terminal amino acid sequences of CNBr-3 pilus peptide from three strains of gonococci. Differences are noted in positions 1, 4, 7, 11, 19, 21, and 22 (Fig. 3).

TYPE-SPECIFIC AND COMMON ANTIGENIC DOMAINS

Evidence has been presented that gonococcal pili possess type-specific and common antigenic determinants. Studies were therefore undertaken to ascertain the structural basis for these serological properties. Rabbit antibody was prepared to antigenically distinct pili from two strains of gonococci and to their CNBr-2 and CNBr-3 fragments. Antigen-antibody reactions were detected by an enzyme-linked immunosorbent assay and by Ouchterlony gel diffusion. Anti-CNBr-2 antisera bound the homologous and heterologous CNBr-2 fragment and, of greater significance, also the antigen of homologous and heterologous pili. Thus, the region known by chemical means to be highly conserved and by functional assays to encompass the receptor binding domain also contains an antigenic determinant common to all gonococcal

pili. The common determinant becomes immunodominant only when cleaved from the pilus subunit, and the antibody which it engenders binds gonococcal pili which are otherwise physically, chemically, and serologically diverse.

In contrast, anti-CNBr-3 antibody bound only the pilus antigen from which the CNBr-3 immunogen was prepared. Therefore CNBr-3, which encompasses the region known by chemical means to be unconserved, contains the type-specific antigenic determinant of gonococcal pili. When the intrachain disulfide bond present in CNBr-3 (Fig. 2) is reduced and alkylated, the type-specific antigenic determinant is destroyed. Thus, it is the amino acid sequence variability of this region which is responsible for the serological diversity of these organelles, but it is the intrachain disulfide loop which confers the conformational requirements for antigenicity.

ANTIGENICITY-IMMUNOGENICITY AND THE COMMON DETERMINANT

The antigenic diversity of gonococcal pili implies that the common determinant is normally immunorecessive. Accordingly, antibody to native pili binds poorly the homologous CNBr-2 fragment although anti-CNBr-2 antibody binds heterologous gonococcal pili. The common de-

Strain	Residue Number									
	1	2	3	4	5	6	7	8	9	10
MS11	Leu	Ser	Ser	Gly	Val	Asn	Asn	Glu	Ile	Lys
R10	Ala	Ser	Ser	Asn	Val	Asn	Lys	Glu	Ile	Lys
2686	Ala	Ser	Ser	Asn	Val	Asn	Lys	Glu	Ile	Lys
	11	12	13	14	15	16	17	18	19	20
MS11	Gly	Lys	Lys	Leu	Ser	Leu	Trp	Ala	Arg	Arg
R10	Asp	Lys	Lys	Leu	Ser	Leu	Trp	Ala	Arg	-
2686	Asp	Lys	Lys	Leu	Ser	Leu	Trp	Ala	Lys	Arg
	21	22	23	24	25	26	27	28		
MS11	Glu	Asp	Gly	Ser	Val	Lys	Trp			
R10	Glu	Ala	Gly	Ser	Val	Lys	Trp	Lys		
2686	Gln	Asp	Gly	Ser	Val	Lys	Trp	Lys		

FIG. 3. Amino-terminal amino acid sequences of peptides in CNBr-3 fragments of pili from the isogenic transparent (Tr) and opaque (Op) clones of gonococcal strains MS11, R10, and 2686. Amino acid sequence heterogeneity is noted at positions 1, 4, 7, 11, 19, 21, and 22. No differences were noted in the primary structure of peptides from the isogenic Tr and Op clones of the same strain.

terminant of native pili is therefore antigenic but not strongly immunogenic. It is evident from these observations that the capacity to engender an immune response (immunogenicity) and the capacity to bind antibody (antigenicity) are distinct biological phenomena.

SUMMARY AND CONCLUSIONS

Functional and antigenic domains of the gonococcal pilus subunit can be assigned to peptides

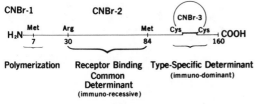

FIG. 4. Functional and antigenic domains of the gonococcal pilus subunit. CNBr-2 mediates receptor binding function and contains an immunorecessive common antigenic determinant. CNBr-3 encompasses a variable region of the pilus subunit which determines type-specific antigenicity. The hydrophobic character of the N-terminal amino acid sequence (8, 14) may stabilize polymeric structure.

prepared by chemical cleavage of methionine residues. CNBr-2 encompasses a highly conserved region which mediates receptor binding, whereas CNBr-3 contains a variable region which determines type-specific antigenicity and therefore the serological diversity of gonococcal pili (Fig. 4). An immunodeterminant common to all pili is proximal to, or co-extensive with, the receptor binding domain, but is normally immunorecessive. It becomes immunodominant when CNBr-2 is cleaved from the pilus subunit, and the antibody it then engenders binds heterologous gonococcal pili.

Although the molecular basis for this phenomenon has not been determined, its relevance for the pathogenesis of gonorrhea may be as follows. Under selective pressure from the host immune system, a mechanism has evolved by which the immunodominant antigenic determinant of gonococcal pili is multiform, whereas the molecular structure responsible for adherence is constant. The constant region is a candidate for the immunoprophylaxis of gonorrhea because the cyanogen bromide fragment which encompasses it is immunogenic, and the resulting antibody binds heterologous gonococcal pili and may block their adherence to host mucosa.

ACKNOWLEDGMENTS

This work was supported by Public Health Service grant AI 10615 from the National Institute of Allergy and Infectious Diseases. G.K.S. is supported in part by a fellowship from the American Social Health Association.

LITERATURE CITED

1. **Brinton, C. C., Jr.** 1965. The structure, function, synthesis and genetic control of bacterial pili and a molecular model for DNA and RNA transport in gram negative bacteria. Trans. N.Y. Acad. Sci. **27**:1003–1054.

2. **Brinton, C. C., J. Bryan, J. A. Dillon, N. Guerina, L. J. Jacobson, S. Kraus, A. Labik, S. Lee, A. Levene, S. Lim, J. McMichael, S. Polen, K. Rogers, A. C. C. To, and S. C. M. To.** 1978. Uses of pili in gonorrhea control: role of pili in disease, purification and properties of gonococcal pili, and progress in the development of a gonococcal pilus vaccine for gonorrhea, p. 145–178. *In* G. F. Brooks, Jr., E. C. Gotschlich, K. K. Holmes, W. D. Sawyer, and F. E. Young (ed.), Immunobiology of *Neisseria gonorrhoeae*. American Society for Microbiology, Washington, D.C.

3. **Buchanan, T. M.** 1975. Antigenic heterogeneity of gonococcal pili. J. Exp. Med. **141**:1470–1475.

4. **Buchanan, T. M., and W. A. Pearce.** 1976. Pili as a mediator of the attachment of gonococci to human erythrocytes. Infect. Immun. **13**:1483–1489.

5. **Buchanan, T. M., J. Swanson, K. K. Holmes, S. J. Kraus, and E. C. Gotschlich.** 1973. Quantitative determination of antibody to gonococcal pili. J. Clin. Invest. **52**:2896–2909.

6. **Fischetti, V. A.** 1978. Streptococcal M protein extracted by nonionic detergent. III. Correlation between immunological cross-reactions and structural similarities with implications for antiphagocytosis. J. Exp. Med. **147**:1771–1778.

7. **Gross, E., and B. Witkop.** 1962. Nonenzymatic cleavage of peptide bonds: the methionine residue in bovine pancreatic ribonuclease. J. Biol. Chem. **237**:1856–1860.

8. **Hermodson, M. A., K. C. S. Chen, and T. M. Buchanan.** 1978. Neisseria pili proteins: amino-terminal amino acid sequences and identification of an unusual amino acid. Biochemistry **17**:442–445.

9. **James-Holmquest, A. N., J. Swanson, T. M. Buchanan, R. D. Wende, and R. P. Williams.** 1974. Differential attachment of piliated and nonpiliated *Neisseria gonorrhoeae* to human sperm. Infect. Immun. **9**:897–902.

10. **Lambden, P. R., J. N. Robertson, and P. J. Watt.** 1980. Biological properties of two distinct pilus types produced by isogenic variants of *Neisseria gonorrhoeae* P9. J. Bacteriol. **141**:393–396.

11. **Oliveira, E. B., E. C. Gotschlich, and L. Teh-yung.** 1979. Primary structure of human C-reactive protein. J. Biol. Chem. **254**:489–502.

12. **Robertson, J. P., P. Vincent, and M. E. Ward.** 1977. The preparation and properties of gonococcal pili. J. Gen. Microbiol. **102**:169–177.

13. **Salit, I. E., M. Blake, and E. C. Gotschlich.** 1980. Intrastrain heterogeneity of gonococcal pili is related to opacity colony variance. J. Exp. Med. **151**:716–725.

14. **Schoolnik, G. K., J. Y. Tai, and E. C. Gotschlich.** 1982. The human erythrocyte binding domain of gonococcal pili, p. 172–180. *In* J. B. Robbins, J. C. Hill, and G. Sadoff (ed.), Bacterial vaccines, vol. 4. Thieme Stratton, New York.

15. **Swanson, J.** 1973. Studies on gonococcus infection. IV. Pili: their role in attachment of gonococci to tissue culture cells. J. Exp. Med. **137**:571–589.

16. **Swanson, J., S. J. Kraus, and E. C. Gotschlich.** 1971. Studies on gonococcus infection. I. Pili and zones of adhesion: their relation to gonococcal growth patterns. J. Exp. Med. **134**:886–906.

17. **Tramont, E. C., and J. Ciak.** 1978. Antigonococcal antibodies in genital secretions, p. 274–278. *In* G. F. Brooks, Jr., E. C. Gotschlich, K. K. Holmes, W. D. Sawyer, and F. E. Young (ed.), Immunobiology of *Neisseria gonorrhoeae*. American Society for Microbiology, Washington, D.C.

18. **Ward, M. E., P. J. Watt, and J. N. Robertson.** 1974. The human fallopian tube: a laboratory model for gonococcal infection. J. Infect. Dis. **129**:650–659.

Specificity of Fimbriae and Fimbrial Receptors

ALF A. LINDBERG

Department of Bacteriology, National Bacteriological Laboratory, S-105 21 Stockholm, Sweden

The ability of microorganisms to adhere to host tissues is thought to be an important factor both for the maintenance of a "normal" flora (18, 25, 59) and for initiation of infection by pathogenic microorganisms (3, 9, 52). With few exceptions pathogenicity is rarely the property of a single determinant of the microorganism but is usually multifactorial (64). Understanding the molecular biology of adhesion requires knowledge of the surface component(s) of the microorganism responsible for adhesion and the receptor structure(s) on the host tissue cells. In general, the adhesion process is poorly understood.

In bacteria, fimbriae (or pili), which are nonflagellar protein filaments, are surface appendages involved in adhering the cells to host tissues. Often no more than 4 to 7 nm in diameter but up to 1,000 nm in length, with several hundred usually arranged peritrichously on the cell envelope, they function as ideal probes for overcoming the repulsive energy barrier between bacteria and host tissue cells (54). The most commonly used strategy in studying the adhesion process has been to examine what different kinds of human and animal erythrocytes were agglutinated by fimbriated bacteria. This undoubtedly has been of value for classification of fimbriae (9). However, the ability of fimbriated bacteria to agglutinate human but not ox erythrocytes does not permit any conclusions to be drawn regarding the nature of the receptor. This is so because our detailed knowledge of membrane structures, although rapidly growing, is still limited (24, 27, 40). It was, however, the observation that fimbriated pyelonephritogenic *Escherichia coli* strains were unable to agglutinate a particular class of human erythrocytes that led to the eventual identification of the receptor structure for P fimbriae (32; also below).

So far, few definitive receptor structures have been identified, but a rapid development is expected in the next few years. The topic has been extensively reviewed recently (3, 6, 9, 28, 52), and the reader is referred to these articles for a complete coverage. This review focuses on recent developments in the field.

The several classifications of fimbriae that exist are mostly based on morphological properties (7, 8, 50). Our present knowledge of the chemical, immunochemical, and functional properties of the various fimbriae is too limited to allow a classification on a molecular or an immunological basis. In the following, the various types of fimbriae will be named in the way they are most commonly referred to in the literature.

TYPE 1 FIMBRIAE—D-MANNOSE SENSITIVE

Type 1 fimbriae are found in most enterobacterial species (9) and are often referred to as "mannose-sensitive" or "common" fimbriae. They are protein filaments 7 nm wide and up to 2 μm long (7). The subunit of type 1 fimbriae isolated from *E. coli* has a molecular weight of 17,000 (7, 56), and the corresponding subunit from *Salmonella typhimurium* has a molecular weight of 21,000 (T. K. Korhonen et al., in preparation). Both are characterized by a high content of hydrophilic amino acids (7, 56; Korhonen et al., in preparation), and the *E. coli* fimbrial subunit has been reported to contain one reducing sugar unit (39). The amino acid sequence of the N-terminal part of the *E. coli* subunit has been established (26) and differs from that of other *E. coli* adhesins such as K88, K99, colonizing factor antigen (CFA) I, and F41 (17).

The receptor binding site on the pilin subunit has not yet been defined. The observation by Brinton (7) that the type 1 fimbriae bind to polystyrene latex particles by their tips does not mean that this represents a specific fimbria-receptor interaction but could merely reflect a hydrophobic interaction. Studies of the binding of type 1 fimbriae to monkey kidney cells by Salit and Gotschlich (57) led them to conclude that binding occurred along the length of the fimbriae. This suggests that the specific binding sites are laterally located, a situation which allows multiple interactions between each fimbrial filament and receptors on the surface. It must be stressed that the observations regarding tip versus lateral binding are not mutually exclusive: a nonspecific hydrophobic binding by the tip of the filament can be supplemented by multiple lateral fimbria-receptor interactions.

Bacteria possessing type 1 fimbriae are subject to phase variation which is under transcriptional control (10). The presence of type 1 fimbriae is associated with D-mannose–sensitive hemagglutination. D-Mannose has been found to be a powerful inhibitor of the adhesion to all types of animal, plant, and fungal cells tested, whether fimbriated bacteria (9) or isolated fimbriae (57) were used. The inhibitory activity of methyl-α-D-mannopyranoside, or D-mannose, was found to be very specific (46). Testing of substances with modified OH groups at C-2, C-3, C-4, or C-6 in the D-mannopyranosyl residue caused loss of inhibitory activity. Of other substances tested, only D-fructose was active, and this was surmised to be a consequence of its conformation, i.e., formation of a β-D-fructopyranosidic ring in which the stereochemistry is very similar to that of D-mannopyranoside. Since type 1 fimbriae mediate adhesion to a wide variety of cells, including erythrocytes from several different vertebrate species (9), epithelial cells (45), phagocytes (5), yeast cells (9, 36), and Tamm-Horsfall protein (40), this would suggest that unsubstituted D-mannopyranosidic groups or residues, or both, preferably α-linked, are present on all these cells and molecular species. Our detailed knowledge of the structures of eucaryotic membrane glycoproteins and glycolipids is still limited, but the presence of terminal α-D-mannopyranosyl groups is common in completed oligomannosidic saccharide chains and α-D-mannose residues are common in cores of several glycoproteins (Table 1) (27, 37, 40). The surface of yeast cells is also covered by D-mannose–containing polymers (Table 1) (4). The Tamm-Horsfall glycoprotein, which is released into the tubular urine, is produced by the terminal cells of the ascending limb of the loop of Henle and of the distal convoluted tubule and has a complex structure (1). Analysis of glycopeptides isolated from pronase digests suggested that Tamm-Horsfall glycoprotein has at least five asparagine residues substituted by complex carbohydrate moieties: three of a type rich in D-galactose, two of another type with more sialic acid but less D-galactose, and a small amount of a third type rich in D-mannose (1). The latter structural entity is thus surmised to contain the active structure responsible for the reported trapping of type 1 fimbriated E. coli, which is D-mannose sensitive (48, 49).

It is striking that so far no attempts have been made to study the interaction between purified type 1 fimbriae and various glycoproteins, or glycopeptide/saccharide fractions thereof. Until such studies have been undertaken, it is impossible to define the receptor(s) for type 1 fimbriae more closely. The simplest explanation of the inhibitory action of D-mannose is that it binds to and blocks the binding sites of the fimbriae, which otherwise would bind to receptors on cells. This is supported by the ability of type 1 fimbriated bacteria to bind α-D-mannopyranosyl groups covalently linked to polyacrylamide beads (S. B. Svenson and T. K. Korhonen, unpublished data).

MANNOSE-RESISTANT FIMBRIAE AND ADHESINS

Besides common type 1 fimbriae many E. coli strains produce fimbriae and adhesins of a type classified as D-mannose resistant, because their agglutinating activity with erythrocytes is resistant to inhibition by D-mannose (9). It is obvious that with such a broad definition several types of adhesins can fit into the group. Some of these are discussed below.

P fimbriae of E. coli. The ability to adhere to epithelial cells is a frequent characteristic of E. coli strains isolated from pyelonephritis as opposed to strains from other types of urinary tract infection or from feces of healthy persons (23, 67). These pyelonephritogenic strains show also a D-mannose–resistant hemagglutination of human erythrocytes (23, 31, 36). At least two different classes of D-mannose–resistant hemagglutination have been identified so far, P and X, based on their binding specificity (68). P fimbriae purified from four E. coli strains were morphologically similar to E. coli type 1 fimbriae but differed from them by (i) showing multiple bands in sodium dodecyl sulfate-polyacrylamide gel electrophoresis with molecular weights between 17,000 and 22,000 and (ii) showing immunochemical nonidentity with type 1 but strong identity reactions with each other in an enzyme-linked immunoassay (T. K. Korhonen, V. Väisänen, H. Saxén, H. Hultberg, and S. B. Svenson, Infect. Immun., in press).

The binding specificity of P fimbriae was established by the use of human erythrocytes of various blood group types (32). The P blood group antigens are present on most human erythrocytes (43); only a few individuals are known to lack them, i.e., to be of p̄ phenotype. Erythrocytes from p̄ individuals were not agglutinated by P-fimbriated bacteria. By using the known structures of the P blood group glycosphingolipid antigenic determinants and synthetic saccharides, the receptor-active structure could be defined as the D-Gal$p$ $1\underset{\alpha}{\rightarrow}4$ D-Gal$p$ $1\underset{\beta}{\rightarrow}$ disaccharide entity (Table 1) (32; Korhonen et

TABLE 1. Structural determinants in receptors for bacterial fimbriae[a]

Type of fimbriae	Generally isolated from	Inferred receptor-active structure	Eucaryotic structures with receptor activity	References
MSHA type 1	E. coli, Shigella, Salmonella, Klebsiella, Serratia, Enterobacter, Citrobacter, Providencia	α-D-Manp 1→	Several glycolipids and glycoproteins	1, 5, 9, 36, 40, 45, 46, 57
MRHA P	E. coli	α-D-Galp 1→4 β-D-Galp 1→	Trihexosylceramide Globoside P₁ glycosphingolipid Forssman antigen	32, 38; Korhonen et al., in press
MRHA CFA/I	E. coli	β-D-GalNAcp 1→4 β-D-Galp 1→4 β-D-Glcp SA α↓2 3	GM₂ ganglioside	14
MRHA K88	E. coli	β-D-Galp α-D-Galp 1→6 α-D-Galp 1→6 α-D-Glcp 1→2 β-D-Fruf	Mucin Intestinal glycolipid Intestinal glycoprotein	2, 19, 33, 55, 61
MRHA K99	E. coli	β-D-GalNAcp 1→4 β-D-Galp 1→4 β-D-Glcp SA α↓2 3	GM₂ ganglioside	14
MRHA	N. gonorrhoeae	β-D-Galp 1→3 β-D-GalNAc 1→4 D-Galp	Glycolipids	52

[a] Abbreviations: MSHA, D-mannose–sensitive hemagglutination; MRHA, D-mannose–resistant hemagglutination; Gal, D-galactose; GalNAc, N-acetyl-D-galactosamine; Glc, D-glucose; Man, D-mannose; SA, sialic acid or N-acetylneuraminic acid.

al., in press). The independent identification of globoside as a receptor of P fimbriae (38) may seem surprising at first. However, the D-Gal$p$ 1$_{\overrightarrow{\alpha}}$4 D-Gal$p$ 1$_{\overrightarrow{\beta}}$ disaccharide is a structural element in the globoside (Table 1), the conformation of which well may make the disaccharide accessible to the P-fimbrial binding site. This theory finds strong support in the fact that coating of p̄ erythrocytes, which are devoid of receptor activity for P fimbriae, with either trihexosylceramide or globoside makes them agglutinable by P-fimbriated E. coli isolates (68). This agglutination is inhibited by the synthetic D-Gal$p$ 1$_{\overrightarrow{\alpha}}$4 D-Gal$p$ 1$_{\overrightarrow{\beta}}$OMe glycoside. Evidence supporting the virulence-enhancing property endowed upon E. coli strains with P fimbriae has recently been obtained in an experimental pyelonephritis model in monkeys, where a P-fimbriated E. coli strain caused more severe renal effects than non-P-fimbriated strains (J. A. Roberts et al., personal communication).

In a study of the frequency of P fimbriae among pyelonephritogenic E. coli strains, 23 (81%) were P fimbriated (68). However, 6 (19%) of these also agglutinated p̄ erythrocytes, an agglutination which could not be inhibited by the disaccharide receptor analog (68). These strains were tentatively classified as being X fimbriated, although it is at present likely that X represents at least two types of fimbriae (68). Types P and X fimbriae can coexist on the same bacterial strain, also together with type 1 (quoted in 68).

Colonizing factor antigens (CFA) I and II from human enterotoxigenic E. coli. The CFA/I and II fimbrial structures have been identified in enterotoxigenic strains of E. coli isolated from humans with diarrhea (11, 12). The fimbriae, which are encoded for on plasmids, are serologically distinct, are heat labile, and cause D-mannose-resistant hemagglutination. The N-terminal sequence of the first 22 amino acids was found to differ from that of K88, E. coli type 1, Neisseria gonorrhoeae, Moraxella nonliquefaciens, and Pseudomonas aeruginosa fimbrial protein (35).

The ability of various glycolipids to inhibit the CFA/I-induced hemagglutination of human erythrocytes was studied (14). Only the GM$_2$ ganglioside was found active (for structure, see Table 1). It is unknown which structural entities of the GM$_2$ ganglioside are involved in the CFA/I receptor. The observation that pronase-treated human erythrocytes were rendered non-agglutinable by CFA/I-positive strains, as were neuraminidase-treated erythrocytes, made the authors speculate that glycoproteins as well as glycolipids might be involved in the receptor (14). Further experimental studies are necessary for verification of the hypothesis.

K88 and K99 adhesins of E. coli. Diarrheal disease caused by enteropathogenic E. coli is a frequent cause of death among young domestic animals. Enteropathogenic E. coli strains are characterized by their ability to proliferate in the upper small intestine of the infected animal by adhering to intestinal mucosa, where they produce one or both of two types of enterotoxin (65). Since adhesion is a prerequisite for the infectious process, studies of the E. coli K88 fimbrial adhesin have been intensive during the past decade. The gene(s) for the K88 adhesin is located on a transmissible plasmid (34, 41, 62). At least three serological variants of the K88 antigen (K88ab, K88ac, K88ad) can be distinguished (22). These differences do not necessarily reflect differences in adhesin receptor specificity.

Interest in identifying the K88 adhesin receptor in piglets was stimulated when it was demonstrated that at least two pig phenotypes occur: one that has K88 receptor(s) in its intestinal mucosa and another that lacks the receptor(s) (55). Inhibition of the hemagglutination between guinea pig erythrocytes and K88 fimbriae was found with mucus glycoproteins (19). Chemical modification of the saccharide part gave results which indicated that terminal β-D-galactopyranosyl groups were part of the K88 receptor(s). No inhibition was found with glycosaminoglycans, glycogen, or any simple sugar or glycoside, which suggested that the receptor should be larger than a monosaccharide residue. Further studies using binding of labeled K88 fimbrial preparations to isolated pig intestinal brush border cells have given results which are only partially in accordance with the above data. (i) A polar glycolipid extracted from pig intestine, and not present in K88-resistant pigs, was implicated as the receptor structure (33). The oligosaccharide was reported to be composed of D-glucose and D-galactose residues (quoted in 61). (ii) Stachyose, which has terminal α-linked D-galactopyranosyl groups and a galactan, reportedly inhibited binding (61). (iii) Asialo ovine submaxillary mucin (in accordance with 19) but also N-acetyl-galactosamine N-acetyl-mannosamine, and N-acetyl-glucosamine (in disagreement with 19) were found inhibitory by other investigators (2). Examining the results of the inhibition experiments (2, 19, 61), one observes that the concentrations needed for inhibition are relatively high. This suggests that the monosaccharides and oligosaccharides used as inhibitors have not had all the structural information required for efficient binding of the K88 fimbrial adhesin. That the receptor-active saccharide chain is found in a glycolipid is most likely (33), but a glycoprotein K88 receptor has not been ruled out (61).

The use of the K88 fimbrial protein-pig intestinal brush border cell binding assay is favorable. The observation that one of the plasmids, pMK066, constructed by Kehoe et al. (34) gave rise to a bacterial phenotype which adhered to brush border cells but not to guinea pig erythrocytes suggests that the reactions involved in adhesion of K88 to the two cell types are not identical. Furthermore, adhesion to the erythrocytes is stable only at 4°C, and K88-positive bacteria or isolated fimbrial protein elutes rapidly at higher temperatures (9), whereas the adhesion to brush border cells is stable also at 37°C.

The plasmid-coded K99 fimbrial adhesin is found on bovine, ovine, and some porcine enterotoxigenic E. coli strains (42). Only a brief, and as yet inconclusive, report links the K99 receptor with the structure of the GM$_2$ ganglioside (14). The absence of inhibition studies with the asialo derivative of GM$_2$ and saccharides thereof makes it impossible to draw any conclusions about receptor-active structures in the GM$_2$ oligosaccharide chain. Furthermore, a high concentration (10 mg/ml) of GM$_2$ was required for the inhibition. Gangliosides have been reported to aggregate fimbriated gonococci although the mechanism was unclear (69).

Fimbriae of N. gonorrhoeae. Fimbria-mediated attachment of N. gonorrhoeae is D-mannose–resistant (53). Monosaccharides and a variety of alditols were also unable to block binding. The chemical nature of the binding reaction between purified fimbriae and buccal mucosal epithelium was studied with the use of a wide variety of inhibitors (52). Several, such as gangliosides, heparin, fetuin, normal human serum, and synovial fluid, were found to be inhibitory although the inhibition occurred only at a relatively high concentration and was only partial. No unifying structural concept could be identified. Purified GM$_1$, GD$_{1a}$, GD$_{1b}$, and GT gangliosides were all inhibitory, but varying the concentrations did not result in a typical dose-response curve: at 0.3 µM concentration, the inhibition ranged between 14 and 33%; at 74 to 230 µM, inhibition ranged between 38 and 63%. A nonspecific effect on the gonococcal fimbriae, as reported by others (69), cannot be ruled out.

Using various purified glycosidases to cleave off saccharides from the buccal cell surface and then study the binding of the fimbriae, the authors gave the following tentative structures for the receptor: α-SA 2→3 β-D-GalNAcp 1→4 D-Gal and β-D-Gal$p$ 1→3 β-D-GalNAc 1→4 D-Gal. It would certainly be interesting to study the ability of these oligosaccharides, and permu-tations thereof, to inhibit the fimbrial binding to the buccal cells. Not until such studies have been done will the receptor structure for gonococcal fimbriae be definitely identified.

Gonococcal fimbriae are distinctly different antigenically. However, they seem to adsorb to identical, or similar, receptors on human cells (51).

Other types of fimbriae or adhesins. There are a number of adhesins not covered here: some because there is no information available about possible receptor structures, others because the morphological characteristics have not been determined. The first category includes fimbrial structures from Bordetella pertussis (58), Proteus mirabilis (63), Pseudomonas aeruginosa (70), Neisseria meningitidis (66), Providencia (47), Haemophilus influenzae and H. parainfluenzae (30, 60), and Bacteroides nodosus (13). In the second are the D-galactose– and D-mannose–specific hemagglutinins of P. aeruginosa (20, 21) and the three adhesins of Vibrio cholerae, of which one can be inhibited by D-mannose, another with L-fucose, and a third with no substance yet identified (15, 16, 29, 44; L. F. Hanne, Ph.D. thesis, University of Texas, Dallas, 1981).

CONCLUDING REMARKS

From the foregoing it is evident that a definitive identification of a receptor structure has been obtained for (i) the type 1 fimbriae of E. coli and S. typhimurium, where terminal α-D-mannopyranosyl residues have been identified, and (ii) type P fimbriae of pyelonephritogenic E. coli, where the receptor is a α-D-galactopyranosyl 1→4 β-D-galactopyranosyl 1→ disaccharide entity in either a terminal or internal chain position. For other fimbrial adhesins the receptor structures are only tentative (Table 1). The intensive research activities within the adhesin field makes this an area where new knowledge is rapidly accumulated. It is my opinion that, to be able to identify fimbrial receptor structures and to study the interaction between fimbriae and receptor on the molecular level, a few prerequisites must be fulfilled: (i) isolated and defined fimbrial proteins devoid of contaminants shall be used; (ii) use of isolated and defined receptor structures from host tissues are preferable, and (iii) the ability of isolated molecular species, such as saccharide structures from glycolipids and glycoproteins, to inhibit in a specific way the binding between fimbrial protein and receptor must be determined.

Based on such information, general models of fimbrial structure-function relationships may eventually emerge. An understanding of these relationships may then be used to suggest ways to interrupt adhesion, thereby interfering with the infectious process at an early stage. It must be remembered, however, that the seemingly simple binding between a microorganism and its receptor is a multistep process influenced by many factors whose importance might have been overlooked in recent years (15).

ACKNOWLEDGMENTS

Work reported herein was supported by the Swedish Medical Research Council (grant no. 16X-656).

I am grateful to S. B. Svenson and G. Källenius for providing unpublished results.

LITERATURE CITED

1. **Afonso, A.-M. M., P. Charlwood, and R. D. Marshall.** 1981. Isolation and characterization of glycopeptides from digests of human Tamm-Horsfall glycoprotein. Carbohydr. Res. **89:**309–319.
2. **Anderson, M. J., J. S. Whitehead, and Y. S. Kim.** 1980. Interaction of *Escherichia coli* K88 antigen with porcine intestinal brush border membranes. Infect. Immun. **29:**897–901.
3. **Arbuthnott, J. P., and C. J. Smyth.** 1979. Bacterial adhesion in host/pathogen interactions in animals, p. 165–198. *In* D. C. Ellwood, J. Melling, and P. Rutter (ed.), Adhesion of microorganisms to surfaces. Academic Press, London.
4. **Ballou, C. E.** 1976. Structure and biosynthesis of the mannan component of the yeast cell envelope. Adv. Microb. Physiol. **14:**93–158.
5. **Bar-Shavit, Z., I. Ofek, R. Goldman, D. Mirelman, and N. Sharon.** 1977. Mannose residues on phagocytes as receptors for the attachment of *Escherichia coli* and *Salmonella typhi.* Biochem. Biophys. Res. Commun. **78:**455–460.
6. **Beachey, E. H.** 1981. Bacterial adherence: adhesin receptor interactions mediating the attachment of bacteria to mucosal surfaces. J. Infect. Dis. **143:**325–345.
7. **Brinton, C. C., Jr.** 1965. The structure, function, synthesis and genetic control of bacterial pili and a molecular mechanism for DNA and RNA transport in Gram negative bacteria. Trans. N.Y. Acad. Sci. **27:**1003–1054.
8. **Duguid, J. P.** 1968. The function of bacterial frimbrial. Arch. Immunol. Ther. Exp. **16:**173–188.
9. **Duguid, J. P., and D. C. Old.** 1980. Adhesive properties of Enterobacteriaceae, p. 185–217. *In* E. H. Beachey (ed.), Bacterial adherence (Receptors and recognition, series B, vol. 6). Chapman and Hall, London.
10. **Eisenstein, B. I.** 1981. Phase variation of type 1 fimbriae in *Escherichia coli* is under transcriptional control. Science **214:**337–339.
11. **Evans, D. G., and D. J. Evans, Jr.** 1978. New surface-associated heat-labile colonization factor antigen (CFA/II) produced by enterotoxigenic *Escherichia coli* of serogroups O6 and O8. Infect. Immun. **21:**638–647.
12. **Evans, D. G., R. P. Silver, D. G. Evans, Jr., D. G. Chase, and S. L. Gorbach.** 1975. Plasmid-controlled colonization factor associated with virulence in *Escherichia coli* enterotoxigenic for humans. Infect. Immun. **12:**656–667.
13. **Every, D.** 1979. Purification of pili from *Bacteroides nodosus* and an examination of their chemical, physical and serological properties. J. Gen. Microbiol. **115:**309–316.
14. **Faris, A., M. Lindahl, and T. Wadström.** 1980. GM₂-like glycoconjugate as possible erythrocyte receptor for the CFA/I and K99 haemagglutinins of enterotoxigenic *Escherichia coli.* FEMS Microbiol. Lett. **7:**265–269.
15. **Freter, R.** 1980. Prospects for preventing the association of harmful bacteria with host mucosal surfaces, p. 439–458. *In* E. H. Beachey (ed.), Bacterial adherence (Receptors and recognition, series B., vol. 6). Chapman and Hall, London.
16. **Freter, R., and G. W. Jones.** 1976. Adhesive properties of *Vibrio cholerae*: nature of the interaction with intact mucosal surfaces. Infect. Immun. **14:**246–256.
17. **Gaastra, W., F. R. Mooi, A. R. Stuitje, and F. K. de Graaf.** 1981. The nucleotide sequence of the gene encoding the K88ab protein subunit of porcine enterotoxigenic *Escherichia coli.* FEMS Microbiol. Lett. **12:**41–46.
18. **Gibbons, R. A.** 1975. Attachment of oral streptococci to mucosal surfaces, p. 127–131. *In* D. Schlessinger (ed.), Microbiology—1975. American Society for Microbiology, Washington, D.C.
19. **Gibbons, R. A., G. W. Jones, and R. Sellwood.** 1975. An attempt to identify the intestinal receptor for the K88 adhesin by means of a hemagglutination inhibition test using glycoproteins and fractions from sow colostrum. J. Gen. Microbiol. **86:**228–240.
20. **Gilboa-Garber, N.** 1972. Inhibition of broad spectrum hemagglutinin from *Pseudomonas aeruginosa* by D-galactose and its derivatives. FEBS Lett. **20:**242–244.
21. **Gilboa-Garber, N., L. Mizrahi, and N. Garber.** 1977. Mannose-binding hemagglutinins in extracts by *Pseudomonas aeruginosa.* Can. J. Biochem. **55:**975–981.
22. **Guinee, P. M., and W. H. Jansen.** 1979. Behavior of *Escherichia coli* K antigens K88ab, K88ac, and K88ad in immunoelectrophoresis, double diffusion, and hemagglutination. Infect. Immun. **23:**700–705.
23. **Hagberg, L., U. Jodal, T. K. Korhonen, G. Lidin-Janson, U. Lindberg and C. Svanborg-Edén.** 1981. Adhesion, hemagglutination, and virulence of *Escherichia coli* causing urinary tract infections. Infect. Immun. **31:**564–570.
24. **Hakomori, S.** 1976. Glycolipids of animal cell membranes, p. 223–249. *In* G. Aspinall (ed.), International review of science series two, vol. 7. Butterworths, London.
25. **Hartley, C. L., C. S. Neumann, and M. H. Richmond.** 1979. Adhesion of commensal bacteria to the large intestine wall in humans. Infect. Immun. **23:**128–132.
26. **Hermodson, M. A., K. C. S. Chen, and T. M. Buchanan.** 1978. *Neisseria* pili proteins: amino-terminal sequence and identification of an unusual amino acid. Biochemistry **17:**442–445.
27. **Hubbard, S. C., and R. J. Ivatt.** 1981. Synthesis and processing of asparagine-linked oligosaccharides. Annu. Rev. Biochem. **50:**555–583.
28. **Jones, G. W.** 1977. The attachment of bacteria to the surface of animal cells, p. 139–176. *In* J. L. Reissig (ed.), Microbial interactions. Chapman and Hall, London.
29. **Jones, G. W., G. D. Abrams, and R. Freter.** 1976. Adhesive properties of *Vibrio cholerae*: adhesion to isolated rabbit brush border membranes and hemagglutinating activity. Infect. Immun. **14:**232–239.
30. **Kahn, M. E., and R. Gromkova.** 1981. Occurrence of pili on and adhesive properties of *Haemophilus parainfluenzae.* J. Bacteriol. **145:**1075–1078.
31. **Källenius, G., and R. Möllby.** 1979. Adhesion of *Escherichia coli* to human periurethral cells correlated to mannose-resistant agglutination of human erythrocytes. FEMS Microbiol. Lett. **5:**295–299.
32. **Källenius, G., R. Möllby, S. B. Svenson, J. Winberg, A. Lundblad, S. Svensson, and B. Cedergren.** 1980. The p^k antigen as receptor for the haemagglutinin of pyelonephritogenic *Escherichia coli.* FEMS Microbiol. Lett. **7:**297–302.
33. **Kearns, M. J., and R. A. Gibbons.** 1979. The possible nature of the pig intestinal receptor for the K88 antigen of *Escherichia coli.* FEMS Microbiol. Lett. **6:**165–168.
34. **Kehoe, M., R. Sellwood, P. Shipley, and G. Dougan.** 1981. Genetic analysis of K88-mediated adhesion of enterotoxigenic *Escherichia coli.* Nature (London) **294:**122–126.

35. **Klemm, P.** 1979. Fimbrial colonization factor CFA/I protein from human enteropathogenic *Escherichia coli* strains. Purification, characterization and N-terminal sequence, FEBS Lett. **108**:107–110.

36. **Korhonen, T.** 1979. Yeast cell agglutination by purified enterobacterial pili. FEMS Microbiol. Lett. **6**:421–425.

37. **Krusius, T., J. Finne, and H. Rauvala.** 1978. The poly(glycosyl) chains of glycoproteins. Characterization of a novel of glycoprotein saccharides from human erythrocyte membrane. Eur. J. Biochem. **92**:289–300.

38. **Leffler, H., and C. Svanborg-Edén.** 1980. Chemical identification of a glycosphingolipid receptor for *Escherichia coli* attaching to human urinary tract epithelial cells and agglutinating erythrocytes. FEMS Microbiol. Lett. **8**:127–134.

39. **McMichael, J. C., and J. T. Ou.** 1979. Structure of common pili from *Escherichia coli*. J. Bacteriol. **138**:969–975.

40. **Montreuil, J.** 1980. Primary structure of glycoprotein glycans. Basis for the molecular biology of glycoproteins. Adv. Carbohydr. Chem. Biochem. **37**:157–222.

41. **Mooi, F. R., N. Harms, D. Bakker, and F. K. de Graaf.** 1981. Organization and expression of genes involved in the production of the K88ab antigen. Infect. Immun. **32**:1155–1163.

42. **Moon, H. W., B. Nagy, R. E. Isaacson, and I. Ørskov.** 1977. Occurrence of K99 antigen on *Escherichia coli* isolated from pigs and colonization of pig ileum by K99⁺ enterotoxigenic *E. coli* from calves and pigs. Infect. Immun. **15**:614–620.

43. **Naiki, M., and D. M. Marcus.** 1975. An immunochemical study of the human blood group P₁, P and pᵏ glycosphingolipid antigens. Biochemistry **14**:4837–4841.

44. **Nelson, E. T., J. D. Clements, and R. A. Finkelstein.** 1976. *Vibrio cholerae* adherence and colonization in experimental cholera: electron microscopic studies. Infect. Immun. **14**:527–547.

45. **Ofek, I., D. Mirelman, and N. Sharon.** 1977. Adherence of *Escherichia coli* to human mucosal cells mediated by mannose receptors. Nature (London) **265**:623–625.

46. **Old, D. C.** 1972. Inhibition of the interaction between fimbrial haemagglutinins and erythrocytes by D-mannose and other carbohydrates. J. Gen. Microbiol. **71**:149–157.

47. **Old, D. C., and S. S. Scott.** 1981. Hemagglutinins and fimbriae of *Providencia* spp. J. Bacteriol. **146**:404–408.

48. **Ørskov, I., A. Ferencz, and F. Ørskov.** 1980. Tamm-Horsfall protein or uromucoid is the normal urinary slime that traps type 1 fimbriated *Escherichia coli*. Lancet i:887.

49. **Ørskov, I., R. Ørskov, and A. Birch-Andersen.** 1980. Comparison of *Escherichia coli* fimbrial antigen F7 with type 1 fimbriae. Infect. Immun. **27**:657–666.

50. **Ottow, J. C. G.** 1975. Ecology, physiology and genetics of fimbriae and pili. Annu. Rev. Microbiol. **29**:79–108.

51. **Pearce, W. A., and T. M Buchanan.** 1978. Attachment role of gonococcal pili. Optimum conditions and quantitation of adherence of isolated pili to human cells *in vitro*. J. Clin. Invest. **61**:931–943.

52. **Pearce, W. A. and T. M. Buchanan.** 1980. Structure and cell membrane-binding properties of bacterial fimbriae, p. 289–343. *In* E. H. Beachey (ed.), Bacterial adherence (Receptors and recognition, series B, vol 6). Chapman and Hall, London.

53. **Punsalang, A. P., Jr., and W. D. Sawyer.** 1973. Role of pili in the virulence of *Neisseria gonorrhoeae*. Infect. Immun. **8**:255–263.

54. **Rogers, H. J.** 1979. Adhesion of microorganisms to surfaces: some general considerations of the role of the envelope, p. 29–55. *In* D. C. Ellwood, J. Melling, and P. Rutter (ed.), Adhesion of microorganisms to surfaces. Academic Press, London.

55. **Rutter, J. M., M. R. Burrows, R. Sellwood, and R. A. Gibbons.** 1975. A genetic basis for resistance to enteric disease caused by *E. coli*. Nature (London) **257**:134–135.

56. **Salit, I. E., and E. C. Gotschlich.** 1977. Hemagglutination by purified type 1 *Escherichia coli* pili. J. Exp. Med. **146**:1169–1181.

57. **Salit, I. E., and E. C. Gotschlich.** 1977b. Type 1 *Escherichia coli* pili: characterization of binding to monkey kidney cells. J. Exp. Med. **146**:1182–1194.

58. **Sato, Y., K. Izumiya, M.-A. Oda, and H. Sato.** 1979. Biological significance of *Bordetella pertussis* fimbriae or hemagglutinin: a possible role of the fimbriae or hemagglutinin for pathogenesis and antibacterial immunity, p. 51–57. *In* C. R. Manclark and J. C. Hill (ed.), Third International Symposium on Pertussis. U.S. Government Printing Office, Washington, D.C.

59. **Savage, D. C.** 1975. Indigenous microorganisms associating with mucosal epithelia in the gastrointestinal ecosystem, p. 120–123. *In* D. Schlessinger (ed.), Microbiology—1975. American Society for Microbiology, Washington, D.C.

60. **Scott, S. S., and D. C. Old.** 1981. Mannose-resistant and eluting (MRE) haemagglutinins, fimbriae and surface structure in strains of *Haemophilus*. FEMS Microbiol. Lett. **10**:235–240.

61. **Sellwood, R.** 1980. The interaction of the K88 antigen with porcine intestinal epithelial cell brush borders. Biochim. Biophys. Acta. **632**:326–335.

62. **Shipley, P. L., G. Dougan, and S. Falkow.** 1981. Identification and cloning of the genetic determinant that encodes for the K88ac adherence antigen. J. Bacteriol. **145**:920–925.

63. **Silverblatt, F., and I. Ofek.** 1978. Influence of pili on the virulence of *Proteus mirabilis* in experimental hematogenous pyelonephritis. J. Infect. Dis. **138**:664–667.

64. **Smith, H.** 1977. Microbial surfaces in relation to pathogenicity. Bacteriol. Rev. **41**:475–500.

65. **Smith, H. W., and M. A. Linggood.** 1971. Observations on the pathogenic properties of the K88, Hly and Ent plasmids of *E. coli* with particular reference to porcine diarrhea. J. Med. Microbiol. **4**:467–485.

66. **Stephens, D. S., and Z. A. McGee.** 1981. Attachment of *Neisseria meningitidis* to human mucosal surfaces: influence of pili and type of receptor cell. J. Infect. Dis. **143**:525–532.

67. **Svanborg-Edén, C., L.-Å. Hansson, U. Jodal, U. Lindberg, and A. Sohl-Åkerlund.** 1976. Variable adherence to normal human urinary tract epithelial cells of *Escherichia coli* strains associated with various forms of urinary tract infections. Lancet ii:490–492.

68. **Väisänen, V., J. Elo, L. G. Tallgren, A. Siitonen, P. H. Mäkelä, C. Svanborg-Edén, G. Källenius, S. B. Svenson, H. Hultberg, and T. K. Korhonen.** 1981. Mannose resistant hemagglutination and P antigen recognition characteristic of *E. coli* causing primary pyelonephritis. Lancet, in press.

69. **Watt, P. J., and M. E. Ward.** 1980. Adherence of *Neisseria gonorrhoeae* and other *Neisseria* species to mammalian cells. p. 251–288. *In* E. H. Beachey (ed.), Bacterial adherence (Receptors and recognition, series B, vol. 6). Chapman and Hall, London.

70. **Woods, D. E., D. C. Straus, W. G. Johanson, Jr., V. K. Berry, and J. A. Bass.** 1980. Role of pili in adherence of *Pseudomonas aeruginosa* to mammalian buccal epithelial cells. Infect. Immun. **29**:1146–1151.

Hemagglutinins (Colonization Factors?) Produced by *Vibrio cholerae*

RICHARD A. FINKELSTEIN AND LARRY F. HANNE[1]

Department of Microbiology, University of Missouri School of Medicine, Columbia, Missouri 65212

Although cholera is the prototype of the enterotoxic enteropathies in which the etiological agents (after passing the gastric barrier) adhere to and colonize the epithelial surface of the small bowel (and there liberate their enterotoxin), relatively little is known about the mechanism(s) of attachment. Suggestive evidence that *Vibrio cholerae* has fimbriae (pili) was presented in 1968 (16), but this isolated report has not been substantiated by subsequent investigations. Observations in our laboratory (4, 11, 12) provided no support for the participation of surface organelles in adherence; rather, the evidence suggested that adherence was the result of a more direct interaction between the surface coat of the vibrios and the tips of the microvilli of the host intestinal epithelial cells.

In 1961, G. L. Bales and C. E. Lankford (Bacteriol. Proc., p. 118, 1961) observed that cholera vibrios could directly agglutinate erythrocytes (RBC) and that broth cultures exhibited high titers of hemagglutinating activity. Finkelstein and Mukerjee (5) in 1963 reported that El Tor, but not classical, biotype vibrios, when grown on solid media, agglutinated chicken RBC. Since that time *V. cholerae* has been shown to produce a variety of hemagglutinins (HAs) which have been proposed as possible mediators of attachment (1–4, 6–8). A partially purified "soluble" HA (called "cholera lectin"), isolated from culture supernatants of a classical biotype strain, inhibited attachment of an El Tor biotype strain to rabbit tissue and thus is a likely candidate as a relevant adhesive factor (4).

The present work examines the distribution of the various HAs among the cholera vibrios and describes the isolation and characterization of the "soluble" HA ("cholera lectin") which is produced by all strains examined.

(This work constitutes a portion of the dissertation of Larry F. Hanne, submitted in partial fulfillment of the requirements for the Ph.D.

degree, University of Texas Health Sciences Center at Dallas.)

Studies with 10 strains, representing both Inaba and Ogawa serotypes and El Tor and classical biotype strains from different epidemics, confirmed that agar-grown El Tor vibrios were hemagglutinative for chicken RBC whereas classical biotypes were not. This cell-associated HA was inhibited by D-mannose (and D-fructose).

Supernatants of late-log-phase tryptic soy broth cultures of both biotypes (and serotypes) were hemagglutinative. This "soluble" HA was active on only a proportion (10 of 18) of RBC tested, from different chickens, and it required Ca^{2+} for maximal activity. "Nonresponder" chicken RBC could be converted to "responder" RBC by treatment with mixed glycosidase (Miles Laboratories, Inc.). The soluble HA was not inhibited by any sugar tested (D-mannose, L-fucose, D-galactose, D-mannitol, D-glucosamine, D-fructose, D-ribose, D-glucose, *N*-acetylgalactosamine, dextran) or by mixed gangliosides, phosphatidyl choline, or dithiothreitol.

A third HA activity, which was cell-associated and was inhibited by L-fucose, was found in early-log-phase, broth-grown cells of some strains of the classical biotype and in spontaneous mutants of the El Tor biotype which lacked the mannose-sensitive HA (MSHA⁻) and which had been selected after co-sedimentation of the MSHA⁺ parents with responder chicken RBC.

Interestingly, cells of a classical *V. cholerae* strain (which do not ordinarily express a cell-associated HA in vitro), harvested from the intestinal fluids of infected infant rabbits, were found to agglutinate responder, but not nonresponder, RBC. This observation suggests that the soluble HA may be expressed in vivo in a cell-associated form.

Because of the previous evidence suggestive of its potential role as a colonization factor (4) and its ubiquity among cholera vibrios, the soluble HA (cholera lectin) was purified to apparent homogeneity, from fermentor-grown tryptic soy broth culture supernatants, by a sequence of

[1] Present address: Department of Microbiology and Immunology, University of Oregon, Portland, OR 97201.

procedures including concentration by membrane ultrafiltration, $(NH_4)_2SO_4$ precipitation, Sephadex gel filtration, and preparative isoelectric focusing in a Sephadex gel matrix (Ultradex, LKB Instruments Inc.). Three pH isotypes, with pIs of pH 6.3, 5.3, and 4.7, were isolated. Of these, the predominant pI 6.3 form was homogeneous in disc gel electrophoresis in sodium dodecyl sulfate, whereas the other products still contained small amounts of contaminating proteins. Sodium dodecyl sulfate-polyacrylamide gel electrophoresis with and without boiling in sodium dodecyl sulfate prior to electrophoresis, revealed that each of the preparations consisted of noncovalently associated oligomers of identically sized (32,000 molecular weight) protein subunits. Reduction, with 2-mercaptoethanol, had no effect, indicating that there were no interchain disulfide bonds.

The HA activity was heat labile: it was totally destroyed by heating for less than 1 h at 60°C, and it lost all activity on incubation for 24 h at 37°C and for 1 week at 25°C, but it was relatively stable at 4°C. Although only fractions with HA activity were pooled for further purification during the isolation procedure, recovery of activity during purification was poor (<0.2%), and the specific activity (HA units per milligram of protein) did not increase during purification. This was despite the fact that the inactive protein which was discarded constituted the vast majority of the starting material. These observations suggested the possibility that the HA activity was diminishing through effects of protease(s).

Consequently, the purified material was examined and found to have protease activity on azoalbumin (Sigma Chemical Co.) and dimethyl casein. Further, when purified HA was subjected to disc electrophoresis, the protease activity comigrated with the HA activity, which corresponded, in position, with the single band observed in a gel run in parallel which was stained for protein.

Protease activity was monitored, in parallel with HA activity, during the purification. As did the HA, the protease also isoelectrically focused at pHs of 6.3 and 5.3 to 4.7. If the protease and the HA are a single molecule, it would be expected that their specific activities should fluctuate in parallel at each step in purification. However, this was not the case: the most purified HA preparation had a lower ratio of HA/protease activity than the starting material.

Transmission electron microscopy, with uranyl acetate staining, revealed that the purified HA appeared as long filaments. It was further observed that, whereas the HA was fully active at 4°C, the protease activity was maximal at 37°C and barely detectable when the assays were performed in the cold.

From the above information, we are led to the tentative operational hypothesis that the HA and protease activities reside on the same molecule and that the spontaneous self-aggregation into filaments may have a more marked effect on the HA activity than on the protease.

Further evidence that the HA molecule has both activities was provided by immunological studies. Antisera were prepared in rabbits immunized with the different pH isotypes of the HA. These antisera gave reactions of identity in Ouchterlony tests with the different preparations. Thus, they are all immunologically identical. Further, antiserum against the pI 6.3 material gave only a single precipitin band (with a reaction of identity to the purified material) with concentrated crude culture supernatants of the parent strain and with all the other strains tested. This antiserum was used, in parallel with preimmune serum from the same rabbit, in the following experiment.

Purified pI 6.3 material was subjected to disc electrophoresis in duplicate. One gel was stained for protein with Coomassie brilliant blue R (Sigma Chemical Co.), and as had been observed previously, only one protein-stained band was obtained. The other gel was embedded in skim milk agar (15) to detect and localize protease activity. Two troughs were cut in the skim milk agar, parallel to and equidistant from the disc gel. Immune serum was placed in one trough and preimmune serum in the other. After overnight incubation at 25°C, zones of proteolysis were observed on both sides of the embedded gel corresponding to the position of the protein band in the stained gel. However, the zone of proteolysis was markedly inhibited by the immune serum.

Fab fragments prepared from this serum significantly ($P < 0.025$) inhibited in vitro attachment of ^{14}C-labeled vibrios to tissue disks of infant rabbit ileum in comparison with Fab fragments from the preimmune control serum.

It should also be mentioned that antiserum against a partially purified V. cholerae protease, isolated independently by Schneider and Parker (13, 14), gave a precipitin reaction of identity with the purified soluble HA and our anti-HA serum.

It should be emphasized that, although this HA has been isolated from culture supernatants and has therefore been called a "soluble HA," production and release of such a soluble adhesin would be disadvantageous to the vibrios unless its purpose was to promote detachment of the vibrios from host intestinal epithelial membrane receptors. The fact that it was isolated from supernatants may be an artifact of in vitro growth. The "soluble HA" may, in fact, be cell-associated in vivo, as indicated by the finding that in vivo-grown vibrios directly agglutinated responder but not nonresponder RBC and by the inhibition-of-binding studies. It may be found in the supernatants of late-log-phase cultures in vitro because of the vibrios' tendency to release outer membrane fragments by "blebbing."

From the present results and those of others, we propose that adherence by *V. cholerae* is a multifactorial process which may involve motility of the vibrios, chemotactic events, and trapping in the mucous gel (as discussed by R. Freter, this volume); the "soluble HA-protease-cholera lectin" described here; and perhaps the mannose- and fucose-sensitive cell-associated HAs in certain circumstances. Different factors may be more important in some experimental models than in others, and it remains to be determined which is/are most important in the natural host, humans. It would be of interest to ascertain whether active (passive) immunization with the purified HA (of the present work) is protective in animal models and whether antibody to this HA contributes to the immunity which has been observed in humans after convalescence from the disease (9) and after oral immunization with the Texas Star-SR A^-B^+ attenuated mutant candidate vaccine strain (10).

ACKNOWLEDGMENTS

This study was supported, in part, by Public Health Service grants AI-08877 and AI-17312 under the U.S.-Japan Cooperative Medical Science Program, from the National Institute of Allergy and Infectious Diseases.

LITERATURE CITED

1. **Bhattacharjee, J. W., and B. S. Srivastava.** 1978. Mannose-sensitive haemagglutinins in adherence of *Vibrio cholerae* El Tor to intestine. J. Gen. Microbiol. **107:**407–410.
2. **Chaicumpa, W., and N. Atthasishtha.** 1977. Study of intestinal immunity against *V. cholerae*: role of antibody to *V. cholerae* haemagglutinin in intestinal immunity. Southeast Asian J. Trop. Med. Public Health **8:**13–18.
3. **Chaicumpa, W., and N. Atthasishtha.** 1979. Study of intestinal immunity against *V. cholerae* El Tor haemagglu-
tinin and the protective role of its antibody in experimental cholera. Southeast Asian J. Trop. Med. Public Health **10:**73–80.
4. **Finkelstein, R. A., M. Arita, J. D. Clements, and E. T. Nelson.** 1978. Isolation and purification of an adhesive factor ("cholera lectin") from *Vibrio cholerae*. Proceedings of the 13th Joint Conference on Cholera, U.S.-Japan Cooperative Medical Science Program, Atlanta, Ga., 19–21 September 1977. Department of Health, Education, and Welfare Publication 78-1590.
5. **Finkelstein, R. A., and S. Mukerjee.** 1963. Hemagglutination: a rapid method for differentiating *Vibrio cholerae* and El Tor vibrios. Proc. Soc. Exp. Biol. Med. **112:**355–359.
6. **Freter, R., and G. W. Jones.** 1976. Adhesive properties of *Vibrio cholerae*: nature of the interaction with intact mucosal surfaces. Infect. Immun. **14:**246–256.
7. **Jones, G. W., G. D. Abrams, and R. Freter.** 1976. Adhesive properties of *Vibrio cholerae*: adhesion to isolated rabbit brush border membranes and hemagglutinating activity. Infect. Immun. **14:**232–239.
8. **Jones, G. W., and R. Freter.** 1976. Adhesive properties of *Vibrio cholerae*: nature of the interaction with isolated rabbit brush border membranes and human erythrocytes. Infect. Immun. **14:**240–245.
9. **Levine, M. M., R. E. Black, M. L. Clements, L. Cisneros, D. R. Nalin, and C. R. Young.** 1981. Duration of infection-derived immunity to cholera. J. Infect. Dis. **143:**818–820.
10. **Levine, M. M., R. E. Black, M. L. Clements, C. R. Young, T. Honda, and R. A. Finkelstein.** 1982. Texas Star-SR: attenuated *Vibrio cholerae* oral vaccine candidate. Proceedings of the 17th Joint Conference on Cholera, U.S.-Japan Cooperative Medical Science Program, Baltimore, Md., 25–28 October 1981, in press.
11. **Nelson, E. T., J. D. Clements, and R. A. Finkelstein.** 1976. *Vibrio cholerae* adherence and colonization in experimental cholera: electron microscopic studies. Infect. Immun. **14:**527–547.
12. **Nelson, E. T., M. Hochli, C. R. Hackenbrock, and R. A. Finkelstein.** 1977. Electron microscopic observations on intestinal colonization by *Vibrio cholerae*: Freeze-etching studies, p. 81–86. *In* H. Fukumi and Y. Zinnaka (ed.), Symposium on Cholera: Sapporo 1976 (Proceedings of the 12th Joint Conference, U.S.-Japan Cooperative Medical Science Program, Cholera Panel).
13. **Schneider, D. R., and C. D. Parker.** 1978. Isolation and characterization of protease-deficient mutants of *Vibrio cholerae*. J. Infect. Dis. **138:**143–151.
14. **Schneider, D. R., and C. D. Parker.** 1982. Purification and characterization of the mucinase of *Vibrio cholerae*. J. Infect. Dis., in press.
15. **Sokol, P. A., D. E. Ohman, and B. H. Iglewski.** 1979. A more sensitive plate assay for detection of protease production by *Pseudomonas aeruginosa*. J. Clin. Microbiol. **9:**538–540.
16. **Tweedy, J. M., and R. W. A. Park.** 1968. Evidence for the presence of fimbriae (pili) on vibrio species. J. Gen. Microbiol. **51:**235–244.

ROLE OF SURFACE POLYSACCHARIDES IN BACTERIAL ADHESION

Pathogenic Role of Surface Polymers of *Streptococcus pyogenes*

EDWIN H. BEACHEY, W. ANDREW SIMPSON, ITZHAK OFEK, DAVID L. HASTY, AND JAMES B. DALE

Veterans Administration Medical Center and The University of Tennessee College of Medicine, Memphis, Tennessee 38104, and Tel Aviv University School of Medicine, Tel Aviv, Israel

At least three polymeric substances on the surfaces of group A streptococci (*Streptococcus pyogenes*) play important roles in the pathogenesis of infections caused by these microorganisms. The lipoteichoic acid (LTA) mediates the adhesion of the streptococcal cells to mucosal epithelial cells (2, 7, 19). The hyaluronate capsule and the M protein prevent the recognition of the organisms by phagocytic cells of the nonimmune host (7, 18, 27). The hyaluronate capsular material lacks immunogenicity (18). LTA and M protein both are immunogenic, but only antibodies directed against the M protein are protective once the organisms invade into the deeper tissues (18). In this paper, we briefly review the evidence that each of these surface polymers is an important determinant in the pathogenesis of group A streptococcal infections.

MEDIATION OF ADHESION OF STREPTOCOCCI TO EPITHELIAL CELLS BY LTA-PROTEIN COMPLEXES

Bartelt and Duncan (1) have demonstrated that the hyaluronate capsule on group A streptococci prevents the attachment of the organisms to epithelial cells. Whitnack et al. recently showed that the capsule also prevents attachment to phagocytic cells (30). We have found that removal of the hyaluronate capsule by hyaluronidase digestion of whole streptococci enhances attachment. If the hyaluronate capsule is allowed to regenerate in fresh culture media for 15 min, adhering ability again is lost (31). Overnight (18 h) cultures of streptococci which lack capsules adhere readily to epithelial cells, and transmission electron microscopy suggests that attachment is mediated by the surface fibrillar structures radiating from the surfaces of streptococcal cells to the epithelial cells (Fig. 1). Of the purified cell wall substances tested, including hyaluronic acid, LTA, M protein, C carbohydrate, or a peptidoglycan sonic extract, only LTA was able to inhibit attachment (7). In agreement, antibody to LTA, but not the other surface components, was inhibitory (2, 7).

By use of radiolabeled LTA, specific binding sites for LTA have been demonstrated on erythrocytes (6), isolated erythrocyte membranes (13), platelets (4), lymphocytes (5), neutrophilic leukocytes (15), and oral epithelial cells (27). Each cell type was found to possess a single population of binding sites, with dissociation constants ranging from a low of 4.5 μm for erythrocytes to a high of 89 μm for lymphocytes (11). The 10-fold greater LTA-binding capacity of right-side-out as compared with inside-out erythrocyte membrane vesicles (13) suggested that the receptor sites for LTA were restricted to the outer surfaces of the cell membranes. The latter findings lent further support to the idea that LTA-binding sites are specific.

LTA-PROTEIN COMPLEXES

Further studies indicated that the binding of LTA to cell membranes is mediated by the glycolipid portion of the molecule (2, 3, 6). The apparent dilemma created by this finding with respect to the proposed orientation of LTA (22, 30, 32) has now been tentatively resolved by the finding that LTA is capable of forming complexes through its polyanionic backbone with streptococcal surface proteins under physiological conditions (20). To demonstrate the phenomenon, we employed a structurally defined polypeptide fragment of streptococcal M protein (8–10) and purified LTA. The complexes formed between M protein and LTA were demonstrated by (i) the increased ethanol solubility of M-protein solutions to which LTA had been added, (ii) the increased electrophoretic mobility of M

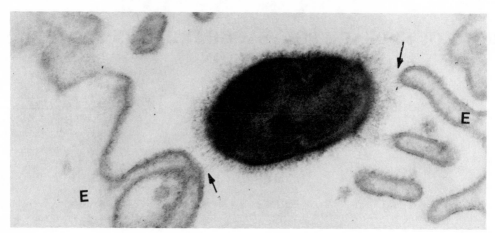

FIG. 1. Fibrillae radiating from the surface of *S. pyogenes* cells to membranes (arrows) of buccal epithelial cell (E). From reference 7.

protein associated with radiolabeled LTA in immunoelectrophoresis agar gels, and (iii) the precipitation of M protein-LTA complexes at low pH levels, with maximal precipitation at pH 3.7 (11, 20). The complexes were formed equally well by LTA and deacylated LTA, indicating that the polyanionic backbone rather than the glycolipid moiety mediated the formation of complexes (20).

Thus, it appeared that clusters of positive charges on the M protein (16, 17) must be important determinants. Having established the primary structure of most of the peptide fragments of type 24 M protein, we have proposed an alignment between M protein and LTA that would permit ionic interaction between the polyanionic backbone of LTA and clusters of positive charges of M protein (20). Our proposed model assumes an α-helical coiled-coiled structures of the M-protein molecule (21). The idea that the interaction was mediated by ionic bonds was supported by studies showing that maleylation of the positively charged lysyl residues of M protein abolished the ability of the protein to form complexes with LTA (20).

The ionic interaction of LTA and surface protein would permit the orientation of the LTA molecule to expose its glycolipid end toward the surface of the bacterial cells. The idea that some of the LTA molecules expose their lipid ends toward the surface of the bacteria is consistent with recent findings that the surfaces of group A streptococci are hydrophobic (23, 29). Moreover, we have recently found that serum albumin, which binds via its fatty acid binding sites to the lipid moieties of LTA (25, 26), inhibits the attachment of the intact streptococci to epithelial cells in a dose-related fashion (11).

Taken together, our data suggest a hypothetical model for the orientation and anchorage of LTA and LTA-binding proteins on the surface of *S. pyogenes* cells (Fig. 2). LTA and M protein may anchor and orient each other on the surfaces of streptococcal cells in such a way that the lipid moieties of LTA may interact with specific receptors on the surfaces of mucosal epithelial cells.

ATTACHMENT OF GROUP A STREPTOCOCCI TO PHAGOCYTIC CELLS

Although it has been shown that *S. pyogenes* cells attach to phagocytic cells in a LTA-sensitive fashion in a serum-free system (15), in the presence of serum or plasma virulent cells of *S. pyogenes* become resistant to phagocytic recognition. It is likely that the serum albumin competitively blocks the binding of the cell surface LTA to membrane receptors on the phagocytic cells. In addition, it has been shown that the M protein in some way prevents the binding of complement via the alternative pathway to the streptococcal cells (12). Preliminary evidence (30a) indicates that the M protein blocks complement binding by binding large amounts of fibrinogen to the surfaces of virulent organisms. The only way the host can recognize M-rich streptococci, therefore, is to elaborate opsonic antibodies directed toward the M protein (18). We have shown that the binding of antibody-coated streptococci to phagocytic cells can be blocked by Fc fragments of immunoglobulin G but not by LTA (15).

The M protein has now been shown to be composed of repeating covalent structures, each of which contains several distinct protective

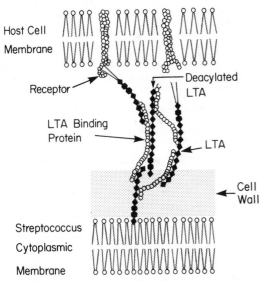

Host Cell Membrane

Receptor

LTA Binding Protein

Deacylated LTA

LTA

Cell Wall

Streptococcus Cytoplasmic Membrane

FIG. 2. Hypothetical model of the interaction between LTA and M protein on the surface of *S. pyogenes* cells (bottom). The interaction of LTA and deacylated LTA with several M-protein molecules (LTA-binding protein) would result in a fibrillar network of LTA and protein, and would permit exposure of the lipid ends of firmly anchored LTA molecules to interact with receptors in host cell membranes (top). From reference 20.

antigenic determinants (10). Indeed, we have shown that antibodies directed against limited regions of the M protein exposed on the surfaces of virulent organisms are protective (10). Recently, a chemically synthesized 35-amino acid fragment (S-CB7) of type 24 M protein was shown to evoke protective immune responses, and one of the protective determinants has been located in a subpeptide fragment of S-CB7 as small as 12 amino acid residues (8).

Since the use of polyclonal antibodies has made it difficult to determine precisely which determinants of the M-protein molecule are exposed on the surface of the intact streptococcal cell, we have recently produced a set of monoclonal antibodies against the isolated type 24 M protein (17a). Each of the monoclonal antibodies showed high titers of anti-M24 antibodies ranging from 1:204,400 to 1:819,200 as determined by enzyme-linked immunosorbent assays in which the isolated M protein was used as the antigen. The ability of some but not all of these antibodies to bind to the intact M protein on the surface of the parent streptococci indicates that the M protein exposes some but not all of its immunodeterminants to the surface of virulent organisms. The monoclonal antibodies directed toward the exposed determinants but not toward

the buried ones were opsonic and protected mice against challenge infections with the homologous serotypes of streptococci (17a).

Preliminary studies suggest that with a set of peptide fragments and a set of monoclonal antibodies one may be able to map the orientation of the protective immunodeterminants of the M-protein molecule on the surface of the intact bacteria. Moreover, a library of monoclonal antibodies against a particular serotype of M protein may be used to determine whether different strains of the same serotype expose different determinants under various epidemiological settings as a result of antigenic drift, as has recently been suggested may occur in group A streptococci (14).

Our studies indicate that on mucosal cell surfaces the major component mediating epithelial cell attachment is the LTA. In deeper tissues the adhesive activity of LTA is probably neutralized by serum albumin, and other mechanisms are required for attachment to phagocytic cells. In virulent organisms such attachment is mediated by antibodies directed against exposed antigenic determinants of M protein. Since the M protein and LTA appear to interact closely with each other, it is quite possible that they influence each other's conformation on the surface of virulent organisms.

Although the mucosal cell receptor for *S. pyogenes* has, as yet, not been isolated, recent studies in our laboratory (W. A. Simpson and E. H. Beachey, unpublished data) suggest that fibronectin on the surfaces of epithelial cells may act as a receptor. The variation in the level of fibronectin on epithelial surfaces may modify the ability of the mucosal surfaces of susceptible individuals (i.e., patients susceptible to rheumatic fever [24]) to bind virulent strains of *S. pyogenes*.

ACKNOWLEDGMENTS

The studies reported herein from our own laboratories were supported by institutional research funds from the U.S. Veterans Administration, by Public Health Service research grants AI-13550 and AI-10085 from the National Institute of Allergy and Infectious Diseases, and by U.S.-Israeli Binational research grant 2138:80. E.H.B. is the recipient of a Medical Investigatorship Award from the U.S. Veterans Administration. W.A.S. and D.L.H. are the recipients of Young Investigatorship Awards (DE-05773 and DE-05062) from the U.S. Public Health Service.

We thank Johnnie Smith for expert secretarial assistance in preparing the manuscript.

LITERATURE CITED

1. **Bartelt, M. A., and J. L. Duncan.** 1978. Adherence of group A streptococci to human epithelial cells. Infect. Immun. **20:**200–208.
2. **Beachey, E. H.** 1975. Binding of group A streptococci to human oral mucosal cells by lipoteichoic acid (LTA). Trans. Assoc. Am. Physicians **88:**285–292.

3. **Beachey, E. H.** 1981. Bacterial adherence: adhesin receptor interactions mediating the attachment of bacteria to mucosal surfaces. J. Infect. Dis. **143:**325–345.

4. **Beachey, E. H., T. M. Chiang, I. Ofek, and A. H. Kang.** 1977. Interaction of lipoteichoic acid of group A streptococci with human platelets. Infect. Immun. **16:**649–654.

5. **Beachey, E. H., J. B. Dale, S. Grebe, A. Ahmed, W. A. Simpson, and I. Ofek.** 1979. Lymphocyte binding and T cell mitogenic properties of Group A streptococcal lipoteichoic acid. J. Immunol. **122:**189–195.

6. **Beachey, E. H., J. B. Dale, W. A. Simpson, J. D. Evans, K. W. Knox, I. Ofek, and A. J. Wicken.** 1979. Erythrocyte binding properties of streptococcal lipoteichoic acids. Infect. Immun. **23:**618–625.

7. **Beachey, E. H., and I. Ofek.** 1976. Epithelial cell-binding of group A streptococci by lipoteichoic acid on fimbriae denuded of M protein. J. Exp. Med. **143:**759–771.

8. **Beachey, E. H., J. M. Seyer, J. B. Dale, W. A. Simpson, and A. H. Kang.** 1981. Type specific protective immunity evoked by a synthetic peptide of *Streptococcus pyogenes* M protein. Nature (London) **292:**457–459.

9. **Beachey, E. H., J. M. Seyer, and A. H. Kang.** 1978. Repeating covalent structure of streptococcal M protein. Proc. Natl. Acad. Sci. U.S.A. **75:**3163–3167.

10. **Beachey, E. H., J. M. Seyer, and A. H. Kang.** 1980. Primary structure of protective antigens of type 24 streptococcal M protein. J. Biol. Chem. **255:**6284–6289.

11. **Beachey, E. H., W. A. Simpson, and I. Ofek.** 1980. Interaction of surface polymers of *Streptococcus pyogenes* with animal cells, p. 389–405. *In* R. C. W. Berkeley, J. M. Lynch, J. Melling, P. R. Rutter, and B. Vincent (ed.), Microbial adhesion. Ellis Horwood, Chichester.

12. **Bisno, A. L.** 1979. Alternate complement pathway activation by group A streptococci: role of M-protein. Infect. Immun. **26:**1172–1176.

13. **Chiang, T. M., M. L. Alkan, and E. H. Beachey.** 1979. Binding of lipoteichoic acid of group A streptococci to isolated human erythrocyte membranes. Infect. Immun. **26:**316–321.

14. **Cleary, P. P., D. Johnson, and L. W. Wannamaker.** 1979. Genetic variation in the M antigen of group A streptococci: reassortment of type-specific markers and possible antigenic drift. J. Infect. Dis. **140:**747–757.

15. **Courtney, H., I. Ofek, W. A. Simpson, and E. H. Beachey.** 1981. Characterization of lipoteichoic acid binding to polymorphonuclear leucocytes of human blood. Infect. Immun. **32:**625–631.

16. **Elbein, A. D.** 1974. Interactions of polynucleotides and other polyelectrolytes with enzymes and other proteins. Adv. Enzymol. **40:**29–64.

17. **Fischer, W., H. U. Koch, P. Rosen, F. Fiedler, and L. Schmuck.** 1980. Structural requirements of lipoteichoic acid carrier for recognition by the poly(ribitol phosphate) polymerase from *Staphylococcus aureus* H. A study of various lipoteichoic acids, derivatives, and related compounds. J. Biol. Chem. **255:**4550–4556.

17a.**Hasty, D. L., E. H. Beachey, W. A. Simpson, and J. B. Dale.** 1982. Hybridoma antibodies against protective and nonprotective antigenic determinants of a structurally defined polypeptide fragment of streptococcal M protein. J. Exp. Med. **155:**1010–1018.

18. **Lancefield, R. C.** 1962. Current knowledge of type-specific M antigens of group A streptococci. J. Immunol. **89:**307–313.

19. **Ofek, I., E. H. Beachey, W. Jefferson, and G. L. Campbell.** 1975. Cell membrane-binding properties of group A streptococcal lipoteichoic acid. J. Exp. Med. **141:**990–1003.

20. **Ofek, I., W. A. Simpson, and E. H. Beachey.** 1982. Formation of molecular complexes between a structurally defined M protein and acylated or deacylated lipoteichoic acid of *Streptococcus pyogenes*. J. Bacteriol. **149:**426–433.

21. **Phillips, G. N., Jr., P. F. Flicker, C. Cohen, B. N. Manjula, and V. A. Fischetti.** 1981. Streptococcal M protein: alpha-helical coiled-coil structure and arrangement on the cell surface. Proc. Natl. Acad. Sci. U.S.A. **78:**4689.

22. **Pieringer, R. A., and M. C. W. Ganfield.** 1975. Phosphatidylkojibiosyl diglyceride: metabolism and function as an anchor in bacterial cell membranes. Lipids **10:**421–426.

23. **Rosenberg, M., D. L. Gutnick, and E. Rosenberg.** 1980. Adherence of bacteria to hydrocarbon: a simple method for measuring cell surface hydrophobicity. FEMS Microbiol. Lett. **9:**29–33.

24. **Selinger, D. S., N. Julie, W. P. Reed, and R. C. Williams.** 1978. Adherence of group A streptococci to pharyngeal cells: a role in the pathogenesis of rheumatic fever. Science **201:**455–457.

25. **Simpson, W. A., I Ofek, and E. H. Beachey.** 1980. Binding of streptococcal lipoteichoic acid to the fatty acid binding sites on serum albumin. J. Biol. Chem. **255:**6092–6097.

26. **Simpson, W. A., I Ofek, and E. H. Beachey.** 1980. Fatty acid binding sites of serum albumin as membrane receptor analogues for streptococcal lipoteichoic acid. Infect. Immun. **29:**119–122.

27. **Simpson, W. A., I Ofek, C. Sarasohn, J. C. Morrison, and E. H. Beachey.** 1980. Characteristics of the binding of streptococcal lipoteichoic acid to human oral epithelial cells. J. Infect. Dis. **141:**457–462.

28. **Swanson, J., K. C. Hsu, and E. C. Gotschlich.** 1969. Electron microscopic studies on streptococci. I. M antigen. J. Exp. Med. **130:**1063–1091.

29. **Tylewska, S., S. Hjerten, and T. Wadstrom.** 1979. Contribution of M protein to the hydrophobic properties of *Streptococcus pyogenes*. FEMS Microbiol. Lett. **6:**249–253.

30. **Van Driel, D., A. J. Wicken, M. R. Dickson, and K. W. Knox.** 1973. Cellular location of the lipoteichoic acids of *Lactobacillus fermenti* NCTC 6991 and *Lactobacillus casei* NCTC 6375. J. Ultrastruct. Res. **43:**483–497.

30a.**Whitnack, E., and E. H. Beachey.** 1982. Antiopsonic activity of fibrinogen bound to M protein on the surface of group A streptococci. J. Clin. Invest. **69:**1042–1045.

31. **Whitnack, E., A. L. Bisno, and E. H. Beachey.** 1981. Hyaluronate capsule prevents attachment of group A streptococci to mouse peritoneal macrophages. Infect. Immun. **31:**985–991.

32. **Wicken, A. J., and K. W. Knox.** 1975. Lipoteichoic acids: a new class of bacterial antigen. Science **187:**1161–1167.

Pathogenic Role of the Exopolysaccharides of Types III and Ia of Group B Streptococci

DENNIS L. KASPER, CAROL J. BAKER, MORVEN S. EDWARDS, HAROLD J. JENNINGS, AND ANNE NICHOLSON-WELLER

Division of Infectious Diseases, Beth Israel Hospital and Channing Laboratory, Department of Rheumatology and Immunology, Brigham and Women's Hospital, Department of Medicine, Harvard Medical School, Boston, Massachusetts 02115; Department of Pediatrics, Baylor College of Medicine, Houston, Texas 77025; and the National Research Council of Canada, Ottawa, Ontario, Canada

Lancefield originally identified group B streptococci as a distinct phenotypic serogroup (20). This is an antigenic classification of bacteria based on the presence of a phenotypic immunodeterminant, the group B antigen, which is present in all strains. Definitive identification requires serological grouping of isolates with antiserum containing antibodies to the group B determinant. Group B streptococci can be divided further into five distinct serotypes, based on the presence of type-specific antigens which are immunologically distinguishable from the common group antigen. Types Ia, Ib, II, and III strains all have distinct polysaccharide capsular determinants (21). Type Ic strains have the type Ia capsular polysaccharide and also another determinant thought to be a protein which it shares with type Ib strains, the Ibc protein (23).

The common structural denominator to the group is the cell wall-specific polysaccharide. When extracted with hot formamide, this polysaccharide is composed of rhamnose, galactose, and glucosamine (6). In contrast, the type-specific polysaccharides have each been found to contain identical constituent monosaccharides: galactose, glucose, 2-acetamido-2-deoxyglucose, and sialic acid (16, 17; H. J. Jennings and D. L. Kasper, unpublished data). When extracted with acid, these antigens are immunologically incomplete and of lower molecular size than native antigens extracted by neutral buffered solutions (16, 17). These acid-extracted or "core" antigens all lack a sialic acid residue which is present as a terminal sugar on the repeating unit of the polysaccharide (16, 17).

In this review, we consider the role that these polysaccharides play in interactions with the host immune system. Two of the five serotypes of group B streptococci will be considered: type III and type Ia. Type III organisms have been of greatest interest because the majority of neonatal infections can be attributed to this single serotype (1, 2). The structure of the native type III polysaccharide has been determined by partial degradation techniques utilizing methylation analysis combined with gas chromatography-mass spectroscopy (16). The molecular configuration of the type III polysaccharide was ascertained from ^{13}C nuclear magnetic resonance spectrum (15). The core antigen, which is extracted with acids, has the same primary structure as the native antigen except that it lacks the terminal sialic acid residue. Therefore, the side chain of the core terminates in a galactopyranose residue. Of interest, the structure of the core antigen is identical to that of the type XIV pneumococcal polysaccharide (15, 16, 18). ^{13}C nuclear magnetic resonance studies demonstrated that the sialic acid is critical in maintaining a conformation of the polysaccharide (14, 15), and this tertiary structure renders antigenic specificity to the polysaccharide. This critical conformation exists most likely because of hydrogen bonding between the carboxyl group of sialic acid and the hydroxyl group at C3 of the 2-acetamido-2-deoxyglucose residue. Reduction of the carboxyl group of the sialic acid to a hydroxymethyl group changes the molecular conformation and resultant immunospecificity in the native antigen to resemble those characteristics of the core antigen.

The presence of sialic acid in the type III polysaccharide appears to be critical in the virulence of these organisms by modulation of complement activation (9). Complement is required for opsonophagocytosis of type III group B streptococci, and this is thought to be the major mechanism of protection against these organisms (5, 9). This effect is regulated by a critical concentration of antibody which promotes opsonophagocytosis (7). The mechanism of regulation is complement fixation and not interaction with the neutrophil Fc receptor (9). Serum which lacks antibody to the native antigen cannot opsonize type III organisms. Low levels of antibody promote opsonophagocytic killing by the classical pathway, but higher levels of antibody are required for alternative pathway activation. Fearon has shown that sialic acid on erythrocyte membranes is a potent modulator of alternative pathway activation (10). His studies demonstrated that sialic acid modulates alternative pathway activation by increasing the affinity of beta-lH relative to B for C3b. This results in blocking the formation of the alternative pathway, C3 convertase, C3bBb. The sialic acid-rich capsule of group B *Streptococcus* similarly acts as a nonactivator of the alternative pathway (9). After neuraminidase digestion of type III organisms, these organisms become alternative pathway activators without the requirement of antibody. The carboxylate group of sialic acid, functioning as a critical component of the sialic acid molecule by rendering structural conformation or charge to type III group B streptococcal antigen, modulates the capacity of these organisms to activate the alternative pathway (8). Formalin-killed organisms which were chemically modified were employed as particles to assess alternative pathway-mediated complement consumption by sera deficient in type-specific antibody. Three such modified organisms were compared: (i) native type III group B streptococci containing one sialic acid residue per antigenic repeating unit; (ii) neuraminidase-cleaved type III group B streptococci; and (iii) type III group B streptococci in which the carboxylate groups of sialic acid were reduced to hydroxymethyl groups, thereby altering the tertiary configuration while retaining 5-acetamido-3,5-dideoxynonulose (reduced form of sialic acid) residues in a terminal position on the molecule. The fully sialated group B streptococci failed to induce consumption of C3 and factor B in C2-deficient serum and in serum with a low specific antibody concentration which was chelated with magnesium–ethylene glycol-bis(β-aminoethyl ether)-*N,N*-tetraacetic acid (MgEGTA) buffer (preventing classical pathway activation). In contrast, neuraminidase-cleaved organisms induce 23% and 45% consumption of C3 and B, respectively, in C2-deficient serum, and 43% and 47% consumption of C3 and B, respectively, in MgEGTA-chelated serum which had a low specific antibody concentration. Consumption of C3 and B by chemically reduced type III organisms quantitatively and kinetically paralleled that observed for neuraminidase-treated organisms. The use of MgEGTA-chelated serum ruled out activation by the C1 bypass mechanism of complement activation. Finally, consumption of C3 and B was induced by neuraminidase-cleaved, chemically reduced particles, but not by control particles in the presence of agam-

maglobulinemic serum, which rules out the participation of non-type-specific antibody in activating the alternative pathway. These data support the concept that tertiary molecular conformation rendered to the capsule of type III group B streptococci by the charge on the carboxylate group of sialic acid could be critical to inhibition of the alternative pathway by serum deficient in a specific antibody. The alternative complement pathway serves as a primary recognition mechanism in the nonimmune host for a variety of microbial polysaccharides (12, 19). Because several virulent microorganisms have capsular polysaccharides which contain terminal sialic acid residues, this mechanism of bypassing normal humoral defense may be the reason that specific antibody is absolutely required for protection against these virulent microorganisms (4, 11). The presence of sialic acid on the bacterial cell surface must be a means of evading an important surveillance mechanism of natural immunity, namely, activation of the alternative complement pathway by the surface of the organism, an evasion mechanism which is overcome by antibody. These studies suggest that activation of this pathway takes place by a conformational arrangement of the inactivator antigen.

Another serotype of group B *Streptococcus* responsible for invasive infection in neonates is type Ia. In contrast to type III strains, however, almost all these infections have their onset in the first few days of life. The structures of the capsular polysaccharide of these two serotypes are quite similar in that terminal sialic acid residues completely mask the underlying galactopyranose groups, although the specific linkages of these two monosaccharides differ (17). Some studies have suggested that low levels of antibody to type Ia polysaccharide in maternal sera are, in a manner analogous to serotype III, a risk factor to neonatal type Ia septicemia (13, 22). However, very few sera from these infants or their mothers have been evaluated to date. Investigations regarding the functional capacity of type Ia-specific antibody have employed the mouse-passed, highly encapsulated type Ia strain (Lancefield O090) exclusively. A study was undertaken to define the relative role of human antibody to the native type Ia polysaccharide and complement in opsonophagocytosis of the type Ia group B streptococcal isolates (3). Opsonophagocytic requirements of human sera containing endogenous complement for a variety of type Ia group B streptococcal strains were defined. Significant reduction in colony-forming units was noted after 40 min of incubation with polymorphonuclear leukocytes and serum for the highly encapsulated mouse-passed prototype

O90 strain by sera containing moderate to high concentrations of antibody to type Ia polysaccharide, whereas bacterial growth occurred in 25 sera with low levels of specific antibody. This absolute requirement for a critical amount of specific antibody is promoting opsonophagocytic killing of strain O90 was not found when 18 fresh type Ia clinical isolates were tested. In antibody-deficient and agammaglobulinemic sera, respectively, mean reductions of colony-forming units of 94% and 95% were seen from fresh clinical isolates, whereas strain O90 was not killed by polymorphonuclear leukocytes in the presence of these sera. All strains required a considerable amount of specific antibody for alternative pathway-mediated opsonophagocytosis. That opsonophagocytic killing of clinical type Ia isolates was mediated by the classical pathway in a non-antibody-dependent fashion was shown when MgEGTA chelation of agammaglobulinemic sera or use of serum deficient in C2 resulted in bacterial growth. Addition of purified C2 to C2-deficient serum restored the bactericidal activity of this serum. Incubation of these sera containing low levels of type-specific antibody with a fresh clinical isolate of type Ia group B *Streptococcus* induced 36% and 54% consumption of C4. This degree of C4 consumption is consistent with activation of the classical complement pathway. Finally, utilizing the C1 transfer test, $C1^{hu}$ was shown to bind readily to a fresh clinical isolate in the absence of specific antibody, whereas binding with strain O90 did not occur (M. M. Eads, A. Nicholson-Weller, C. J. Baker, and D. L. Kasper, in preparation). These data support the concept that antibody-independent activation of the classical pathway of the complement system may play a role in natural immunity to these pathogenic microbes and that a high degree of encapsulation of bacteria may prevent this activating site from being exposed, and therefore define an absolute requirement for the presence of antibody for opsonophagocytic killing of this strain. However, fresh clinical isolates of type Ia group B *Streptococcus* have relatively little capsular antigen and therefore are activators of the classical pathway. This suggests the possibility that neonates developing disease due to type Ia group B *Streptococcus* may have inadequate levels of functional components of the classical pathway of complement.

ACKNOWLEDGMENTS

This work was supported by contract NO1 AI-72538 and Public Health Service grant AI 13249-05 from the National Institute of Allergy and Infectious Diseases. C.J.B. is the recipient of research career development award AI-00323 from the National Institute of Allergy and Infectious Diseases.

LITERATURE CITED

1. Baker, C. J., and F. F. Barrett. 1973. Transmission of group B streptococci among parturient women and their neonates. J. Pediatr. **83**:919–925.
2. Baker, C. J., F. F. Barrett, R. C. Gordon, and M. D. Yow. 1973. Suppurative meningitis due to streptococci of Lancefield group B: a study in 33 infants. J. Pediatr. **82**:724–729.
3. Baker, C. J., M. S. Edwards, B. J. Webb, and D. L. Kasper. 1982. Antibody-independent classical pathway-mediated opsonophagocytosis of Type Ia, group B *Streptococcus*. J. Clin. Invest. **69**:394–404.
4. Baker, C. J., and D. L. Kasper. 1976. Correlation of maternal antibody deficiency with susceptibility to neonatal group B streptococcal infection. N. Engl. J. Med. **294**:752–756.
5. Baltimore, R. S., D. L. Kasper, C. J. Baker, and D. K. Goroff. 1977. Antigenic specificity of opsonophagocytic antibodies in rabbit antisera to group B streptococci. J. Immunol. **118**:673–678.
6. Curtis, S. N., and R. M. Krause. 1964. Antigenic relationships between groups B and G streptococci. J. Exp. Med. **120**:629–637.
7. Edwards, M. S., C. J. Baker, and D. L. Kasper. 1979. Opsonic specificity of human antibody to type III polysaccharide of group B *Streptococcus*. J. Infect. Dis. **140**:1004–1008.
8. Edwards, M. S., D. L. Kasper, H. J. Jennings, C. J. Baker, and A. Nicholson-Weller. 1982. Capsular sialic acid prevents activation of the alternative complement pathway by type III, group B streptococci. J. Immunol. **128**:1278–1283.
9. Edwards, M. S., A. Nicholson-Weller, C. J. Baker, and D. L. Kasper. 1980. The role of specific antibody in alternative complement pathway-mediated opsonophagocytosis of type III, group B *Streptococcus*. J. Exp. Med. **151**:1275–1287.
10. Fearon, D. T. 1978. Regulation by membrane sialic acid of Beta-1H-dependent decay dissociation of ampliferation C3 convertase of alternative complement pathway. Proc. Natl. Acad. Sci. U.S.A. **75**:1971–1977.
11. Goldschneider, I., E. C. Gotschlich, and M. S. Artenstein. 1969. Human immunity to the meningococcus. II. Development of natural immunity. J. Exp. Med. **129**:1327–1348.
12. Gotschlich, E. C., T. Y. Liu, and M. S. Artenstein. 1969. Human immunity to the meningococcus. III. Preparation and immunochemical properties of the group A, group B and group C meningococcal polysaccharides. J. Exp. Med. **129**:1349–1365, 1969.
13. Hemming, V. G., R. T. Hall, P. G. Rhodes, A. O. Shigeoka, and H. R. Hill. 1976. Assessment of group B streptococcal opsonins in human and rabbit serum by neutrophil chemiluminescence. J. Clin. Invest. **58**:1379–1387.
14. Jennings, H. J., D. L. Kasper, C. Lugowski, and K.-G. Rosell. 1981. The structure and conformation of the capsular polysaccharides of group B *Streptococcus*, p. 161–172. American Chemical Society Symposium Series 150.
15. Jennings, H. J., C. Logowski, and D. L. Kasper. 1981. Conformational aspects critical to the immunospecificity of the type III group B streptococcal polysaccharide. Biochemistry **20**:4511–4518.
16. Jennings, H. J., K.-G. Rosell, and D. L. Kasper. 1980. Structural determination and serology of the native polysaccharide antigen of type III group B *Streptococcus*. Can. J. Biochem. **58**:112–120.
17. Jennings, H. J., K.-G. Rosell, and D. L. Kasper. 1980. Structure and serology of the native polysaccharide antigen of type Ia group B *Streptococcus*. Proc. Natl. Acad. Sci. U.S.A. **77**:2931–2935.
18. Kasper, D. L., C. J. Baker, R. S. Baltimore, J. H. Crabb, G. Schiffman, and H. J. Jennings. 1979. Immunodetermi-

nant specificity of human immunity to type III, group B *Streptococcus*. J. Exp. Med. **149**:327–339.

19. **Kasper, D. L., J. L. Winkelhake, W. Zollinger, B. L. Brandt, and M. S. Artenstein.** 1973. Immunochemical similarity between polysaccharide antigens of *Escherichia coli* 07:K1(L):NM and group B *Neisseria meningitidis*. J. Immunol. **110**:262–268.

20. **Lancefield, R. C.** 1934. A serologic differentiation of specific types of bovine hemolytic streptococci (group B). J. Exp. Med. **59**:441–458.

21. **Lancefield, R. C.** 1938. Two serological types of group B hemolytic streptococci with related, but not identical, type-specific substances. J. Exp. Med. **67**:25–40.

22. **Mathews, J. H., P. H. Klesius, and R. A. Zimmerman.** 1974. Opsonin system of the group B *Streptococcus*. Infect. Immun. **10**:1315–1320.

23. **Wilkinson, H. W., and R. G. Eagon.** 1971. Type-specific antigens of group B type Ic streptococci. Infect. Immun. **4**:596–604.

Role of the Capsular Polysaccharide of *Bacteroides fragilis* in Pathogenicity

A. B. ONDERDONK, D. L. KASPER, M. E. SHAPIRO, AND R. W. FINBERG

Infectious Disease Research Laboratory, Tufts University School of Veterinary Medicine; The Channing Laboratory, Harvard Medical School; Department of Surgery, Beth Israel Hospital; and Department of Medicine, Brigham and Womens' Hospitals, Boston, Massachusetts 02130

Organisms of the genus *Bacteroides* represent the major group of obligate anaerobes involved in human infections. Of the numerous species of *Bacteroides*, *B. fragilis* is the single most frequent clinical isolate and is most often encountered in cultures of blood or abscess contents. *B. fragilis* has a chemically incomplete lipopolysaccharide as compared with the lipopolysaccharide (endotoxins) of the facultative gram-negative species, and the lipopolysaccharide of *B. fragilis* lacks the biological potency characteristic of endotoxin. However, strains of *B. fragilis* have an immunologically common capsular polysaccharide which has been shown to provoke abscess development in an animal model for intra-abdominal sepsis. Antibody against this capsular polysaccharide is protective against bacteremia due to *B. fragilis*, but does not prevent abscess development. Recent experimentation in two animal species indicates that protection against abscess development is a T cell-mediated response.

Additional studies have also shown that the capsular polysaccharide is an important factor in the adherence of *B. fragilis* to peritoneal mesothelium and that this adherence can be blocked by pretreatment of host mesothelium with purified *B. fragilis* capsular polysaccharide.

Among the obligately anaerobic bacterial species, *B. fragilis* is the most frequently encountered in intra-abdominal sepsis or bacteremia. Members of the genus *Bacteroides* were second only to *Escherichia coli* as a cause of gram-negative septicemia in patients at the Mayo Clinic (Rochester, Minn.), and 78% of the *Bacteroides* isolates were identified as *B. fragilis* (14). Studies of intra-abdominal sepsis and infection of the female genital tract indicated that *B. fragilis* is the most common cause of bacteremia in these clinical settings (12, 13).

The distribution of the *B. fragilis* group is markedly different in normal flora and infected sites. In the colon, the usual source of *B. fragilis* in septic processes, the numerically dominant species are *B. distasonis, B. vulgatus,* and *B.*

thetaiotaomicron; B. fragilis accounts for only about 0.5% of the colonic microflora (6). Thus, when compared with its numerical concentrations in normal flora, *B. fragilis* is present in a disproportionately large number of clinical infections (1, 11); its predominance in exudate and blood strongly suggests that this species has unique virulence factors.

The outer membrane in gram-negative bacteria contains protein, lipopolysaccharide, and loosely bound lipids. Capsular polysaccharide is also present in some bacteria, including *B. fragilis* (2). The lipopolysaccharide component is regarded as a major virulence factor of gram-negative bacteria. However, the lipopolysaccharide of *B. fragilis* is biologically distinct from that of aerobic gram-negative bacteria (3). Although, chemically, it is a lipopolysaccharide, it does not function as an endotoxin.

Another possible virulence factor, the bacterial capsule, is exemplified by the polysaccharide of *Streptococcus pneumoniae.* Strains of *B. fragilis* possess a capsular polysaccharide of large molecular size. Partial immunochemical purification can be achieved by gentle separation of the polysaccharide from the outer membrane (2). Capsules can be demonstrated by several techniques including electron microscopy (4), and a possible explanation for the higher rates of recovery associated with *B. fragilis* as compared with other *Bacteroides* species found in clinical specimens may be apparent from these studies.

DEVELOPMENT OF AN ANIMAL MODEL FOR INTRA-ABDOMINAL SEPSIS

Initial experiments for development of an animal model were designed to simulate the septic consequence of colonic perforation in human beings (10, 15). Gelatin capsules containing an inoculum that included obligate anaerobes (*Eubacterium, Clostridium, Bacteroides, Peptococcus,* and *Fusobacterium*) and aerobes (*E. coli,* enterococcus) in a ratio of 100:1 (anaerobes to aerobes) were implanted into the peritoneal cavity of Wistar rats. The natural course of this experimental infection was biphasic. The early phase (less than 5 days) was characterized by acute peritonitis with free-flowing exudate; the mortality was 43%. In the second phase all animals that survived for 7 days after challenge developed intra-abdominal abscesses. Quantitative bacteriological studies of both phases of disease resulted in isolation of an average of 6.2 bacterial species per specimen. The four most common organisms isolated were *E. coli*, enterococci, *Bacteroides*, and *Fusobacterium*. The two aerobic species outnumbered the anaerobic species in the peritoneal exudates, whereas the opposite was true for abscess contents. Blood cultures were predictably positive for *E. coli* during the early (peritonitis) phase and were seldom positive for this microbe in cultures obtained after the third postoperative day.

In another series of experiments, the animals were challenged with various bacterial species instead of with the complex fecal inoculum. These studies showed that *E. coli* was required to produce mortality, whereas abscesses occurred only when an anaerobe and an aerobe were combined (7). However, the strain of *Bacteroides* used in this experiment was subsequently shown to be unencapsulated, and further studies showed that the aerobe was unnecessary as an adjunct for abscess development when encapsulated *B. fragilis* was used as the anaerobe for infection of animals (8). Subsequent experiments have shown that heat-killed *B. fragilis* produced abscesses indistinguishable from those resulting from infection with viable organisms. Finally, when purified capsular material from *B. fragilis* was implanted, abscesses again resulted. Control studies, including the implantation of capsular polysaccharide of *E. coli* and heat-killed type III *S. pneumoniae*, failed to produce detectable disease.

PROTECTION AFFORDED BY IMMUNIZATION

The protective efficacy afforded by immunization with the capsular antigen of *B. fragilis* against abscess formation and bacteremia due to this organism was studied in an experimental rat model of intra-abdominal sepsis (5). More than 90% of unimmunized animals, animals immunized with methylated bovine serum albumin and complete Freund adjuvant, and animals immunized with lipopolysaccharide of *B. thetaiotaomicron* developed abscesses when challenged intraperitoneally with strains of *B. fragilis* or *B. distasonis* (implanted with enterococci) or with the cecal contents of meat-fed rats. In contrast, animals immunized with *B. fragilis* capsular polysaccharide, administered with or

without methylated bovine serum albumin and complete Freund adjuvant, and animals immunized with the outer membrane of *B. fragilis* strain 23745 were protected to a significant degree from abscesses caused by intraperitoneal challenge with *B. fragilis* or *B. distasonis*. Such immunization had no overall effect on the development of abscesses in animals challenged with the entire cecal contents of meat-fed rats; however, *B. fragilis* was eliminated from the abscesses of these animals. Animals immunized with the capsular polysaccharide were also protected from early *B. fragilis* bacteremia.

Studies were next conducted to determine the mechanism of this immunity. Challenge of animals passively receiving immune rat globulin prior to implantation with *B. fragilis* did not result in any decrease in abscess incidence as compared with nonimmunized controls, despite the persistence of transferred antibody in the serum of recipients for 72 h or more. Despite the appearance of abscesses in passively immunized animals receiving hyperimmune sera, the early bacteremia with *B. fragilis* noted in nonimmunized animals was qualitatively and quantitatively reduced by passive transfer in these animals.

To assess host immune factors other than antibody which were responsible for immunity to abscesses, spleen cells were transferred from actively immunized rats to recipients who were subsequently challenged with *B. fragilis*. These animals were protected from intra-abdominal abscess formation. Nonimmune spleen cells were not protective, and the protection afforded by immune spleen cells was specific for *B. fragilis* challenge and did not protect against abscesses resulting from implantation of *Fusobacterium varium* and enterococcus. The recipient animals did not develop serum antibody after immune spleen cell transfer; therefore, transfer of B cells producing specific antibody was not the protective mechanism.

To confirm the role of cell-mediated immunity afforded by the capsular antigen, inbred congenitally athymic RNU-Ola rats and their phenotypically normal littermate controls were actively immunized. Despite the development of antibody during immunization, 100% of the immunized athymic rats developed abscesses after challenge with *B. fragilis*, as did 100% of unimmunized athymic control rats. However, no phenotypically normal littermate control rats that were actively immunized developed abscesses when challenged with *B. fragilis*, whereas 100% of phenotypically normal unimmunized rats developed abscesses. The data suggest that the immune mechanism is a T cell-dependent response.

These studies have been confirmed and refined by using a modification of the abscess model in C57/B10 mice. In addition, the mouse offers a well-studied genetic background in which specific markers of immune cells can be used to identify active immune cell participation.

ADHERENCE OF B. FRAGILIS

The ability of encapsulated *B. fragilis* strains to adhere to rat peritoneal mesothelium has been compared with that of other *Bacteroides* species (*B. distasonis, B. vulgatus, B. thetaiotaomicron, B. ovatus*). It was shown that *B. fragilis* adhered to peritoneal mesothelium significantly better than other *Bacteroides* species. Neither active immunization nor pretreatment of tissue with antibody to *B. fragilis* capsular polysaccharide decreased the ability of *B. fragilis* to adhere to mesothelial tissue. In contrast, preincubation of peritoneal mesothelium with purified capsular polysaccharide decreased the number of adherent *B. fragilis* cells. These results indicated that *B. fragilis* adheres better to rat peritoneal mesothelium than do nonencapsulated species and further suggested that the capsular polysaccharide of *B. fragilis* is an important factor in bacterial adhesion. Studies are currently in progress to determine the specificity of this adherence phenomenon and to determine which portion of the capsular polysaccharide is the active determinant.

LITERATURE CITED

1. **Jones, R. N., and P. C. Fuchs.** 1976. Identification and antimicrobial susceptibility of 250 *Bacteroides fragilis* subspecies by broth dilution methods. Antimicrob. Agents Chemother.**9:**719–721.
2. **Kasper, D. L.** 1976. The polysaccharide capsule of *Bacteroides fragilis* subspecies *fragilis*: immunochemical and morphologic definition. J. Infect. Dis. **133:**79–87.
3. **Kasper, D. L.** 1982. Chemical and biological characterization of the lipopolysaccharide of *Bacteroides fragilis* subspecies *fragilis*. J. Infect. Dis., in press.
4. **Kasper, D. L., M. E. Hayes, B. G. Reinap, F. O. Craft, A. B. Onderdonk, and B. F. Polk.** 1977. Isolation and identification of encapsulated strains of *Bacteroides fragilis*. J. Infect. Dis. **136:**75–81.
5. **Kasper, D. L. A. B. Onderdonk, J. H. Crabb, and J. G. Bartlett.** 1979. Protective efficacy of immunization with capsular antigen against experimental infection with *Bacteroides fragilis*. J. Infect. Dis. **140:**724–731.
6. **Moore, W. E. C.** 1977. Anaerobes as normal flora: gastrointestinal tract, p. 222–228. *In* S. M. Finegold (ed.), Proceedings of the International Metronidazole Conference, Montreal, Quebec, Canada. Excerpta Medica, Princeton, N.J.
7. **Onderdonk, A. B. J. G. Bartlett, T. J. Louie, N. Sullivan-Siegler, and S. L. Gorbach.** 1976. Microbial synergy in experimental intra-abdominal abscess. Infect. Immun. **13:**22–26.
8. **Onderdonk, A. B. D. L. Kasper, R. L. Cisneros, and J. G. Bartlett.** 1977. The capsular polysaccharide of *B. fragilis* as a virulence factor: comparison of the pathogenic potential of encapsulated and unencapsulated strains. J. Infect. Dis. **136:**82–89.
9. **Onderdonk, A. B., N. E. Moon, D. L. Kasper, and J. G. Bartlett.** 1978. Adherence of *Bacteroides fragilis* in vivo. Infect. Immun. **19:**1083–1087.
10. **Onderdonk, A. B., W. M. Weinstein, N. M. Sullivan, J. G. Bartlett, and S. L. Gorbach.** 1974. Experimental intra-abdominal abscesses in rats. II. Quantitative bacteriology of infected animals. Infect. Immun. **10:**1256–1259.
11. **Polk, B. F., and D. L. Kasper.** 1977. Bacteroides fragilis subspecies in clinical isolates. Ann. Intern. Med. **86:**569–571.
12. **Thadepalli, H., S. L. Gorbach, and P. N. Broido.** 1973. Abdominal trauma, anaerobes and antibiotics. Surg. Gynecol. Obstet. **137:**270–276.
13. **Thadepalli, H., S. L. Gorbach, and L. Keith.** 1973. Anaerobic infection of the female genital tract: bacteriologic and therapeutic aspects. Am. J. Obstet. Gynecol. **117:**1034–1040.
14. **Washington, J. A., II.** 1971. Comparison to two commercially available media for detection of bacteremia. Appl. Microbiol. **22:**604–607.
15. **Weinstein, W. M., A. B. Onderdonk, J. G. Bartlett, and S. L. Gorbach.** 1974. Experimental intra-abdominal abscesses in rats. I. Development of an experimental mode. Infect. Immun. **10:**1250–1255.

Contributions of Lipoteichoic Acids to Dental Adhesion and Pathogenesis of Oral Diseases

ROBERT E. KESSLER

The Dental Research Institute, The University of Michigan, Ann Arbor, Michigan 48109

The current perception of the mechanisms of adhesion of oral bacteria to teeth, which should be distinguished from accumulation and retention via extracellular polysaccharides, has been divided into two basic points of view. Both viewpoints have been argued to take into account the highly selective adhesion of different bacterial species to different sites within the oral cavity (9). The first viewpoint, as discussed in detail elsewhere (7, 8; R. J. Gibbons, this volume), is based upon "lock and key" receptor mechanisms, that is, one or more of lectin-carbohydrate, enzyme-substrate, or antigen-antibody types of binding. Evidence that lipoteichoic acids (LTAs) are involved in the binding of *Streptococcus mutans* (21, 23, 24), which is thought to be the primary etiological agent of caries, has been used to form an alternative mechanism that accounts for selective aggregation or adhesion on the basis of differences in surface potential. Principles of colloid chemistry, which have been adapted to describe the attraction and stabilization of adhesion of one bacterial cell to another or to a surface (6, 26), have been applied in support of this concept (24). Theoretically, selective aggregation or adhesion based upon differences in surface potential, i.e., the sum of the van der Waals attraction potential and the repulsion potential from the diffuse electrical double layers (6, 26), is well within the limits of sensitivity required (6). Although it is clear that a mechanism based upon surface potentials alone does not account for the adhesion of oral bacteria, the influence of surface potential on the free energy of interaction at different distances may play an important role in determining which species get close enough for additional adhesion mechanisms to operate, especially if the latter are surface bound rather than on an appendage. Thus, the question of selectivity and of binding strength may ultimately be found to depend upon a delicate interplay of several surface characteristics, including surface potential, ligands, hydrophobicity and discrete ionic or hydrophobic domains, as well as extracellular bridging mechanisms involving excreted polymers such as LTA, all of which may

vary between strains or with cultural and environmental conditions.

After the following brief digression to some pertinent points about the surfaces involved, the potential roles of LTAs in dental adhesion and oral diseases will be described. The tooth surface and most oral bacterial surfaces possess a net negative charge under physiological conditions. The net negative charge of the tooth surface is due to a greater exposure of phosphate ions than calcium ions on the outer surface of the hydroxyapatite matrix (16, 22). However, the tooth surface is also amphoteric in that it binds basic proteins via the phosphate groups as well as acidic proteins via the calcium ions in the hydration layer (20, 22). The acquired pellicle formed by these adsorbed proteins (summarized in 8, 20, 22) is not only complex and heterogeneous in composition but may also be heterogeneous with respect to charge. It may also vary greatly in thickness within very short distances along the tooth surface, especially in early stages of formation (5, 17, 18, 20).

The bacterial cell surface is generally considered to consist of all structures external to and including the cytoplasmic membrane. Diagrammatic representations often depict these major structures in discrete, uniform layers and thus fail to convey several important features: the complexity of the functional, structural, and spatial relationships of one component to another; the dynamic nature of the surface as a cell grows and divides; and the relationship of substances that are released from or assembled on the membrane and which may be transiently associated with or firmly bound to surface components (27). Although information about cell surface composition and topological differences between oral species or within a single strain under different growth conditions is slowly accumulating, the influence of these differences on adherence remains to be determined. That differences do occur under different growth conditions (27) indicates that in vitro comparisons of relative adherence between strains or species may not reflect either optimal conditions for a given strain or in vivo conditions, especially those of the microenvironment of a site that later becomes a carious lesion or those in the oral cavity of a caries-prone individual. LTAs have chemical properties and biological features including diversities of structure and differences in excretion patterns which make them attractive for consideration in promoting adhesion to the tooth surface via mechanisms accessory to their major influence on surface potential.

LTAs AND THEIR INVOLVEMENT IN ADHESION

LTAs are amphiphilic polymers which consist of a poly(glycerol phosphate) chain (20 to 30 units in length) covalently bound to a lipid moiety (29). The glycerol phosphate "backbone" may be substituted at the second hydroxyls of the glycerols with various types and amounts of carbohydrate as well as D-alanine. The very high density of charge provided by the phosphate groups can thus be modulated to some extent by the degree of substitution of D-alanine or carbohydrate. Differences in carbohydrate substitution are found between strains, species, and genera (29). Apparent differences in D-alanine substitution may be the result of losses during extraction as well as interstrain differences (3, 29). LTAs appear to be located over the surface of the membrane in most species (28, 30), and significant quantities of LTA may be found extracellularly (14, 19). In some *S. mutans* strains, e.g., strain BHT, the latter may exceed the amount found associated with the cell (10, 12, 29). LTA may be isolated from both locations as a high-molecular-weight acylated micellar aggregate (LTA) and as a low-molecular-weight deacylated monomer (dLTA). The relative amounts of each in the two locations as well as the relative proportions of acylated, micellar form to deacylated monomer vary with species, strain, and growth conditions (14, 15, 19). The documented and proposed relationships of LTAs to the cell wall-membrane complex are shown diagrammatically in Fig. 1. The LTA exposed at the edge of the cell wall, as shown by immunoelectron microscopy with *Lactobacillus casei* and *L. fermentum* (28), could either be anchored LTA of sufficient chain length to reach through the wall, or LTA/dLTA in transit through the cell wall (30).

LTA will bind to surfaces and to other soluble molecules. Most of the data available strongly support the view that binding to erythrocytes and other eucaryotic cells is mediated by the fatty acid substituents of LTA (30). LTA also adsorbs rapidly, and apparently strongly, to hydroxyapatite (25). This is considered to be an ionic interaction mediated through binding of

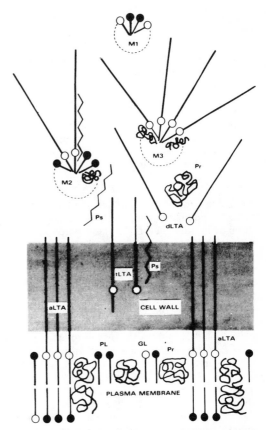

FIG. 1. Diagrammatic representation of a generalized cell wall-membrane complex. The cell (plasma) membrane is depicted as being composed of protein (Pr), phospholipid (PL), glycolipid (GL), and, in the upper leaflet of the bilayer, acylated LTAs (aLTA). The hydrophilic poly(glycerol phosphate) chains of the latter extend through the cell wall matrix and may reach the cell surface. LTA molecules in transit out of the cell are shown in both acylated and deacylated forms (tLTA). Wall polysaccharide (Ps) is also shown in transit and extracellularly. The extracellular milieu is shown as being composed of excreted protein, polysaccharide, deacylated LTA monomers (dLTA), and micellar complexes of: excreted membrane lipids (M1); acylated LTAs, protein, phospholipid, and polysaccharide (M2); and acylated LTA and protein (M3). (Figure reproduced and legend adapted from reference 30 with the kind permission of the authors and publisher.)

calcium ions in the hydration layer of hydroxyapatite to ionized phosphate groups on LTA. The binding appears to be quite strong since a concentration of less than 1 μM LTA will bind in the presence of 1 mM phosphate (2). Complete desorption of bound LTA with 100 mM phosphate and inhibition of binding in the presence of fluoride indicate the importance of the calcium and phosphate interaction (2). Pertinent to this is the enhancement in adhesion of whole bacteria to hydroxyapatite in the presence of calcium ions but reduction in adhesion in high phosphate buffer (25). Binding of LTA is inhibited only minimally by precoating the hydroxyapatite with saliva (2). However, saliva does inhibit binding of whole bacteria to hydroxyapatite (25), indicating that factors other than LTA may also influence adhesion. LTA, and teichoic acids in general, also bind to proteins and polysaccharides (4, 23), including the extracellular glucans produced by sucrose-grown *S. mutans* (4).

The different ways in which LTA could be mediating binding to the tooth, in addition to an influence on the minimum distance of separation through its influence on surface potential, and the range of reactive groups that may be involved are shown in Fig. 2. Three basic possibilities, binding to the pellicle, binding via LTA-calcium bridges across the pellicle, and direct binding to the hydroxyapatite surface, are shown. The last is less likely to be an initial event but may occur in "mature" plaque. Selectivity would be influenced by the following:

(i) The degree and type of substitution, e.g., carbohydrate or D-alanine, or both, along the glycerol phosphate backbone. D-Alanine has a much greater effect in reducing the net negative charge since it is in ester linkage.

(ii) The relative amount of LTA released by the cell and thus the relative amount available for bridging.

(iii) The relative degree of exposure of LTA at the cell wall margin (which may be related to ii). Comparison of *L. casei* and *L. fermenti*, for example, by immunoelectron microscopy, revealed a uniform distribution of exposed LTA in the case of the latter, whereas the distribution was patchy in the case of the former.

(iv) Whether the LTA is surface bound or part of an appendage or fuzzy coat. As discussed by Jones (13), a decreased radius of curvature, as would occur with a surface projection, would facilitate approach of two surfaces as a result of reduction in forces of repulsion. This would influence the kinetics of adhesion as well as specificity.

(v) The interaction of other surface molecules with LTA. This includes the influence of other molecules on LTA as well as the influence of LTA on other molecules. For example, LTA binds readily to dextrans (4); in fact, insoluble and soluble glucans from *S. mutans* contain or bind LTA (24). The sucrose-induced plaque formed on teeth, the adhesiveness of which has long been attributed to the glucan, also contains higher amounts of LTA than other plaques (23). Thus, the meshwork of extracellular dextran may be providing a scaffold from which binding through LTA can be strengthened.

Besides increasing the adhesive ability of *S. mutans*, it has been hypothesized that a layer of LTA could also act as an ionic diffusion barrier and may cause accumulation of acid within the plaque (2). Saturation of the negatively charged

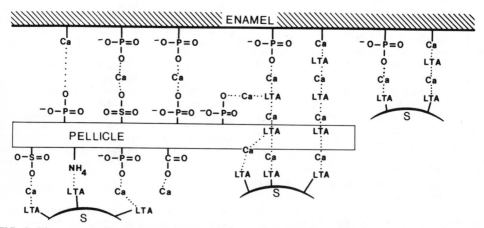

FIG. 2. Diagrammatic illustration of the possible interactions of LTA with various chemical groups on the enamel or acquired pellicle of a tooth. The suggested mechanisms of binding for the streptococcus (S) at the left are adapted from Rolla (23, 24). The streptococcus at the center is shown to be bound through calcium (Ca) and LTA (either acylated or deacylated) bridges in which LTA may be part of the acquired pellicle. The streptococcus at the right is shown bound directly to the enamel in the absence of pellicle, although this is considered by most investigators to be an unlikely occurrence. The LTA at the cell surface may be in transit or "trapped" in the extracellular glucan, or both.

phosphate groups of LTA with calcium ions from saliva or dimineralization of the tooth enamel, or both, would result in a positively charged barrier which would hinder further diffusion of positive (i.e., hydrogen) ions surrounding the tooth surface (2), resulting in increased acid demineralization. By the same reasoning, however, a layer of LTA bound to the hydration layer of hydroxyapatite might prevent diffusion of hydrogen ions *toward* the hydroxyapatite, thus affording some protection. In relation to the other major area of oral diseases, the periodontal diseases, LTA may contribute to pathogenesis through stimulation of bone resorption (11), and through interactions with the immune system, such as macrophage stimulation (30) and mitogenicity (1, 30). In general, these areas of study are in early stages of investigation, and specific conclusions await fuller development of research on these proposed effects of LTA.

LITERATURE CITED

1. **Beachey, E. A., J. B. Dale, S. Grebe, A. Ahmed, W. A. Simpson, and I. Ofek.** 1979. Lymphocyte binding and T-cell mitogenic properties of group A streptococcal lipoteichoic acid. J. Immunol. **122:**189–195.

2. **Ciardi, J. E., G. Rolla, W. H. Bowen, and J. A. Reilly.** 1977. Adsorption of *Streptococcus mutans* lipoteichoic acid. Scand. J. Dent. Res. **85:**387–391.

3. **Coley, J., J. Duckworth, and J. Baddiley.** 1975. Extraction and purification of lipoteichoic acids from Gram-positive bacteria. Carbohydr. Res. **40:**41–52.

4. **Doyle, R. J., A. N. Chatterjee, U. M. Streips, and F. E. Young.** 1975. Soluble macromolecular complexes involving bacterial teichoic acids. J. Bacteriol. **124:**341–347.

5. **Frank, R. M., and A. Brendel.** 1966. Ultrastructure of the approximal dental plaque and the underlying normal and carious enamel. Arch. Oral Biol. **11:**883–912.

6. **Friberg, S.** 1977. Colloid phenomena encountered in the bacterial adhesion to the tooth surface. Swed. Dent. J. **1:**207–214.

7. **Gibbons, R. J.** 1977. Adherence of bacteria to host tissue, p. 395–406. *In* D. Schlessinger (ed.), Microbiology—1977. American Society for Microbiology, Washington, D.C.

8. **Gibbons, R. J.** 1980. Adhesion of bacteria to the surfaces of the mouth, p. 79–82. *In* R. C .W. Berkley, J. M. Lynch, J. Melling, P. R. Rutter, and B. Vincent (ed.), Microbial adhesion to surfaces. Ellis Horwood, Ltd., Chicester, England.

9. **Gibbons, R. J., and J. van Houte.** 1975. Bacterial adherence in oral microbial ecology. Annu. Rev. Microbiol. **29:**19–44.

10. **Hardy, L., N. A. Jacques, H. Forester, L. K. Campbell, K. W. Knox, and A. J. Wicken.** 1981. Effect of fructose and other carbohydrates on the surface properties, lipoteichoic acid production and extracellular proteins of *Streptococcus mutans* Ingbritt grown in continuous culture. Infect. Immun. **31:**78–87.

11. **Hausmann, E., O. Luderitz, K. Knox, and N. Weinfeld.** 1975. Structural requirements for bone resorption by endotoxin and lipoteichoic acid. J. Dent. Res. **54:**B94–99.

12. **Jacques, N. A., L. Hardy, K. W. Knox, and A. J. Wicken.** 1979. Effect of growth conditions on the formation of extracellular lipoteichoic acid by *Streptococcus mutans* BHT. Infect. Immun. **25:**75–84.

13. **Jones, G. W.** 1977. The attachment of bacteria to the surfaces of animal cells, p. 139–176. *In* J. L. Reissig (ed.), Microbial interactions (Receptors and recognition, series B, vol. 3). Chapman and Hall, London.

14. **Joseph, R. J., and G. D. Shockman.** 1975. Synthesis and excretion of glycerol teichoic acid during growth of two streptococcal species. Infect. Immun. **12:**333–338.

15. **Kessler, R. E., and G. D. Shockman.** 1979. Precursor-product relationship of intracellular and extracellular lipoteichoic acids of *Streptococcus faecium.* J. Bacteriol. **137:**869–877.

16. **Kibby, C. L., and K. W. Hall.** 1972. Surface properties of calcium phosphates, p. 663–724. *In* M. L. Hair (ed.), The chemistry of biosurfaces, vol. 2. Marcel Dekker, New York.

17. **Leach, S. A., and C. A. Saxton.** 1966. An electron microscopic study of the acquired pellicle and plaque formed on the enamel of human incisors. Arch. Oral Biol. **11:**1081–1094.

18. **Lie, T.** 1975. Pellicle formation on hydroxyapatite splints attached to the human dentition: morphologic confirmation of the concept of adsorption. Arch. Oral Biol. **20:**739–742.

19. **Markham, J. L., K. W. Knox, A. J. Wicken, and M. J. Hewett.** 1975. Formation of extracellular lipoteichoic acid by oral streptococci and lactobacilli. Infect. Immun. **12:**378–386.

20. **Orstravik, D.** 1980. Salivary factors in initial plaque formation, p. 408–423. *In* R. C. W. Berkley, J. M. Lynch, J. Melling, P. R. Rutter, and B. Vincent (ed.), Microbial adhesion to surfaces. Ellis Horwood, Ltd., Chicester, England.

21. **Rolla, G.** 1976. Inhibition of adsorption—general considerations, p. 309–324. *In* H. Stiles, T. O'Brien, and W. Loesche (ed.), Proceedings: Microbial Aspects of Dental Caries (a special supplement to Microbiology Abstracts), vol. 2. Information Retrieval Inc., Washington, D.C.

22. **Rolla, G.** 1977. Formation of dental integuments—some basic chemical considerations. Swed. Dent. J. **1:**241–251.

23. **Rolla, G.** 1980. On the chemistry of the matrix of dental plaque, p. 425–438. *In* R. C. W. Berkley, J. M. Lynch, J. Melling, P. R. Rutter, and B. Vincent (ed.), Microbial adhesion to surfaces. Ellis Horwood, Ltd., Chicester, England.

24. **Rolla, G., P. Bonesvall, and R. V. Opermann.** 1979. Interactions between oral streptococci and salivary proteins, p. 227–244. *In* I. Kleinberg, S. Ellison, and I. Mandel (ed.), Saliva and dental caries. Information Retrieval Inc., Washington, D.C.

25. **Rolla, G., S. A. Robrish, and W. H. Bowen.** 1977. Interaction of hydroxyapatite and protein-coated hydroxyapatite with *Streptococcus mutans* and *Streptococcus sanguis.* Acta Pathol. Microbiol. Scand. Sect. B **85:**311–346.

26. **Rutter, P. R., and B. Vincent.** The adhesion of microorganisms to surfaces: physico-chemical aspects, p. 79–92. *In* R. C. W. Berkley, J. M. Lynch, J. Melling, P. R. Rutter, and B. Vincent (ed.), Microbial adhesion to surfaces. Ellis Horwood, Ltd., Chicester, England.

27. **Shockman, G. D., R. Kessler, J. B. Cornett, and M. Mychajlonka.** 1978. Turnover and excretion of streptococcal surface components, p. 803–814. *In* J. R. McGhee, J. Mestecky, and J. L. Bass (ed.), Secretory immunity and infection. Plenum Press, New York.

28. **Van Driel, D., A. J. Wicken, M. R. Dickson, and K. W. Knox.** Cellular locations of the lipoteichoic acids of *Lactobacillus fermenti* NCTC 6991 and *Lactobacillus casei* NCTC 6375. J. Ultrastruct. Res. **4:**483–497.

29. **Wicken, A. J., and K. W. Knox.** 1974. Lipoteichoic acids: a new class of bacterial antigen. Science **187:**1161–1167.

30. **Wicken, A. J., and K. W. Knox.** 1980. Bacterial cell surface amphiphiles. Biochim. Biophys. Acta **604:**1–26.

Surface Receptors of Selected Oral Streptococci and Their Role in Adhesion to Hydroxyapatite

BURTON ROSAN AND BENJAMIN APPELBAUM

University of Pennsylvania School of Dental Medicine, Philadelphia, Pennsylvania 19104

The differences in ecology of oral streptococci constitute an exquisite example of the specificity of bacterial adhesion (7). *Streptococcus salivarius*, the most abundant streptococcus in saliva, resides predominantly on the tongue; as tongue epithelial cells are desquamated, the bacteria appear in saliva. In contrast, *S. sanguis* and *S. mutans* appear to be adherent to teeth, a non-shedding surface, and consequently are not as numerous in saliva. *S. mitis* has been associated with both teeth and mucous membranes, but this ambiguity may be related more to improper taxonomy of this species than to differences in its ecological distribution (2, 12). Once this taxonomic problem is corrected, we may find the organism does have a rather specific ecological niche. The differences in their ecological distribution are a function of the differences in cell surface structure (14). At the ultrastructural level, *S. salivarius* can be shown to possess an enriched network of fimbriae ("fuzz"), whereas these appendages are very much reduced or absent in *S. sanguis*, *S. mitis*, and *S. mutans*. The differences in fimbriae are probably a superficial manifestation of differences in the composition of the surfaces of oral streptococci; it is these differences in molecular composition and the interaction of these bacterial molecules with specific components of host cells or secretions which govern their ecological distribution in the mouth.

The importance of saliva in the adherence of *S. sanguis* was dramatically shown by Orstavik et al. (11), who found that these organisms did not adhere to enamel surfaces in the absence of saliva. Similar interactions can be shown by using hydroxyapatite (HA) beads as a model for tooth surfaces (1, 4). The advantage of the HA substrate is that it provides a relatively reproducible surface area large enough to allow for quantitation by using radioactively labeled bacteria. Enamel slabs, though theoretically the ideal substrate, cannot be procured in sufficient quantity, reproducible size, or quality of enamel to serve as a constant substrate for adhesion assays (16). HA and enamel powders, which have also been used to study adhesion, have so

large a surface area that artifacts due to the large adsorptive capacities are introduced into the system (10). Studies in several laboratories have now shown that adhesion to the HA beads is essentially similar to adhesion to enamel slabs (1, 4, 5). *S. sanguis* was chosen as a model organism for our studies of adhesion because it has been shown to be among the earliest bacteria to colonize tooth surfaces; it is also a major component of mature dental plaque (7). The questions we posed were: (i) what is the nature of the surface adhesin(s) of *S. sanguis* which interacts with the saliva-coated HA (SHA), and (ii) what are the effects of environment on the production of these adhesins?

A flow chart of the assay used in these studies is shown in Fig. 1. The adsorption assay was originally described by Clark et al. (4) and consists of adding increasing concentrations of [³H]thymidine-labeled bacteria to a fixed quantity of SHA. The number of cells adhering and the number of free cells can be estimated by scintillation spectrometry. In Fig. 2A the curve of the experimental data of free cells at equilibrium is plotted against bound cells. Although this curve for *S. sanguis* strain G9B demonstrates saturation kinetics, occasionally some strains or changes in environmental conditions show different types of kinetics. The saturation kinetics can be fitted to the Langmuir adsorption isotherm (3)

$$c/q = K_d/N + (1/N)^c$$

where c is free cells; q is bound cells; K_d is a dissociation constant; and N is the maximum number of binding sites on the beads. A plot of c/q versus c allows estimation of the dissociation constant (K_d) and its reciprocal, the affinity constant (K_a), from the x intercept. The theoretical number of binding sites (N) on the HA can be estimated from the slope. These numbers should not be taken as absolute, since there is a relatively high coefficient of variation in these assays (1). Indeed, we have done a number of replicate assays with a similar strain (G9B), and even with modifications in procedures which have reduced technical errors, the coefficient of

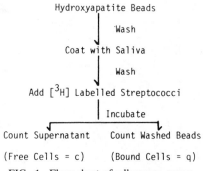

FIG. 1. Flow chart of adherence assay.

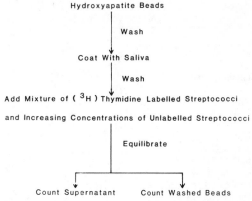

FIG. 3. Flow chart of adherence competition assay.

variation is still ±25%. One of the major influences on the values of K_a and N is that small differences in values at saturating concentrations have very large influences on the x intercept and the slope. The Langmuir isotherm was developed to describe adsorption equilibria in very simple molecular systems (8), and thus even though the equation seems to describe the kinetics of microbial adsorption, caution must be observed in attributing the same qualities to the constants that one does in more defined molecular systems (15). Indeed, recent studies (10a), using a Scatchard plot rather than the Langmuir isotherm, suggest that there are at least three distinct binding sites for *S. mutans* which show a positive cooperativity for binding.

We have employed the Langmuir isotherm to rank the relative adherence of oral streptococci to SHA. Since adhesion would be related to both the affinity and the number of binding sites, the product, K_aN, was employed (1). The data confirm the clinical observation that *S. sanguis* adheres more readily to teeth than do other oral streptococci (7). This result would not have been apparent if only the affinity or number of binding sites had been used to rank these organisms.

To define these molecules, we performed a competition assay (Fig. 3). Each assay contained positive controls in which labeled and

unlabeled cells were used; these controls show the expected competition for binding sites (Fig. 4). A variety of extracts, from whole cells, shown in Table 1 were tested for competing activity. Although mutanolysin (a muramidase) extracts were active, it was difficult to remove the enzyme, whose activity interfered with the assay. Guanidine and urea extracts tended to aggregate on purification; extracellular components were active, but control sterile broth also exhibited activity. The procedure which appeared most useful was cell disruption achieved in a pressure cell. (Sonic treatment of cells also resulted in release of activity but appeared to be less efficient than did cell disruption.) Trypsin

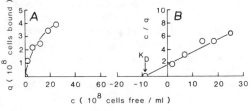

FIG. 2. (A) Experimental plot of free cells at equilibrium (c) versus bound cells (q). (B) Linear transformation of experimental plot c/q versus c. (See text for equation.)

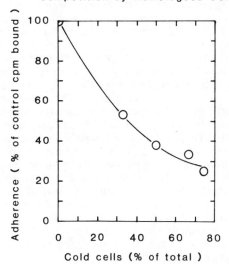

FIG. 4. Competition assay of inhibition of [³H]thymidine-labeled G9B with homologous unlabeled cells.

TABLE 1. Procedures used to extract adhesin from whole cells

Method	Activity[a]
Mutanolysin lysis	+
Urea	+
Guanidine HCl	+
Extracellular	+
Ribi press, 50,000 psi	+
5 M NaCl	−
5 M LiCl	−
8 M LiCl	−
3 M KSCN	−
0.02 M Tris	−
0.25 M disodium EDTA	−
0.01 M HCl	−
5% Trichloroacetic acid	−
0.01 M NaOH	−
5% CETAB	−
1% Triton X-100	−
1% Deoxycholate	−
0.1 M acetate, pH 6.0	−
45% Phenol, 68°C	−
Buffer, 121°C, 15 min	−

[a] Activity: +, strong (>50%) inhibition of adhesion; −, no inhibition of adhesion.

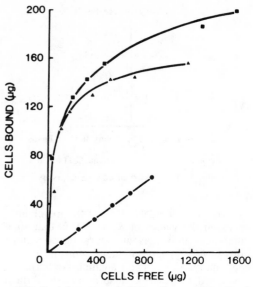

FIG. 5. Adherence of G9B cells to SHA. Batch cells (■). Continuous culture cells: $D = 0.5$ h^{-1} (generation time, 1.4 h) (▲); $D = 0.1$ h^{-1} (generation time, 7 h) (●). (From reference 13. Published with permission of American Society for Microbiology.)

treatment of whole cells resulted in a loss of activity, as did heating above 60°C. These results suggested the possibility that a surface protein was involved in adhesion.

To isolate and characterize this protein, the supernatant resulting from cell disruption was treated with DNase and RNase and was dialyzed. The nondialyzable fraction was centrifuged at 100,000 × g to remove membrane and other insoluble components. A column of SHA was used to further purify the adherence competing components; the column was eluted with increasing concentrations of phosphate buffer, pH 6.8. The highest inhibition activity relative to the number of bands found in sodium dodecyl sulfate gels was eluted with 0.2 M phosphate buffer. The sodium dodecyl sulfate gel pattern of this fraction was compared with the gel pattern of trypsin-treated whole cells. These studies suggest that SHA fractionation does result in a limited spectrum of proteins. The proteins sensitive to trypsin had molecular weights of 160,000, 92,000, and 86,000. Liljemark and Bloomquist (9) have recently suggested that proteins in a similar molecular weight range also inhibited attachment of another strain of *S. sanguis*. Recent studies of the surface proteins of streptococci and staphylococci which bind to serum protein suggest that limited numbers of these components in the 70,000 to 90,000 molecular weight range (3) are present.

We have recently found that cells grown in a chemostat under different environmental condi-

tions also vary in their adhesion to SHA (13); the most dramatic change was observed between cells grown at a generation time of 1.4 h and cells grown at a generation time of 7 h. The results shown in Fig. 5 indicate that the slow-growing cells no longer show saturation kinetics but exhibit direct proportionality between the free and the bound cells. Moreover, competition studies indicate that these slowly grown cells do not compete for the same binding sites as the batch-grown cells; the more rapidly grown cells compete as well as or better than batch-grown control cells. These studies suggest some profound alterations in these streptococcal surfaces. It is hoped that the resolution obtained with an extrinsic radioactive label will provide a potent tool for determining the molecular basis of adhesion of *S. sanguis* to tooth surfaces.

In summary, our studies suggest that the adhesion of *S. sanguis* to SHA involves one or more high-molecular-weight streptococcal surface proteins. Profound changes in adhesion are associated with changes in growth rate and other environmental alterations. These environmentally altered cells can be used as probes to characterize the surface components of *S. sanguis* responsible for adhesion to SHA.

ACKNOWLEDGMENTS

This work was supported by Public Health Service grants DE-03180, DE-02623 (to B.R.), and 1-F32-DE-05164 from the National Institute of Dental Research to B.A.

LITERATURE CITED

1. **Appelbaum, B., E. Golub, S. C. Holt, and B. Rosan.** 1979. *In vitro* studies of dental plaque formation: Adsorption of oral streptococci to hydroxyapatite. Infect. Immun. **25**:717–728.

2. **Bouvet, A., I. de Rijn, and M. McCarty.** 1981. Nutritionally variant streptococci from patients with endocarditis. Growth parameters in a semisynthetic medium and demonstration of a chromophore. J. Bacteriol. **46**:1075–1082.

3. **Bjorek, L., and G. Kronvall.** 1981. Analysis of bacterial cell wall proteins and human serum proteins bound to bacterial cell surfaces. Acta. Path. Microbiol. Scand. **89**:1–6.

4. **Clark, W. B., L. L. Bamman, and R. J. Gibbons.** 1977. Comparative estimates of bacterial affinities and adsorption sites on hydroxyapatite surfaces. Infect. Immun. **19**:846–853.

5. **Clark, W. B., E. L. Webb, T. T. Wheeler, W. Fischlschweiger, D. C. Birdsell, and B. J. Mansheim.** 1981. Role of surface fimbriae (fibrils) in the adsorption of *Actinomyces* species to saliva-treated hydroxyapatite surfaces. Infect. Immun. **33**:908–917.

6. **Gibbons, R. J., E. C. Moreno, and D. M. Spinell.** 1976. Model delineating the effects of a salivary pellicle on the adsorption of *Streptococcus miteor* on hydroxyapatite. Infect. Immun. **14**:1109–1112.

7. **Gibbons, R. J., and J. van Houte.** 1975. Bacterial adherence in oral microbial ecology. Annu. Rev. Microbiol. **29**:19–44.

8. **Langmuir, I.** 1918. The adsorption of gases on plane surfaces of glass, mica and platinum. J. Am. Chem. Soc. **40**:1361–1402.

9. **Liljemark, W. F., and C. G. Bloomquist.** 1981. Isolation of a protein-containing cell surface component from *Streptococcus sanguis* which affects its adherence to saliva coated hydroxyapatite. Infect. Immun. **34**:428–434.

10. **Liljemark, W. F., and S. V. Schauer.** 1975. Studies on the bacterial components which bind *Streptococcus sanguis* and *Streptococcus mutans* to hydroxyapatite. Arch. Oral Biol. **20**:609–615.

10a. **Nesbitt, W. E., R. J. Doyle, K. G. Taylor, R. H. Staat, and S. D. Langley.** 1982. Positive cooperativity in the binding of *Streptococcus sanguis* to hydoxyapatite. Infect. Immun. **35**:157–165.

11. **Orstavik, D., F. W. Kraus, and L. C. Henshaw.** 1974. *In vitro* attachment of streptococci to the tooth surface. Infect. Immun. **9**:794–211.

12. **Rosan, B.** 1978. Absence of glycerol teichoic acids in certain oral streptococci. Science **201**:918–920.

13. **Rosan, B., B. Appelbaum, L. K. Campbell, K. W. Knox, and A. J. Wicken.** 1982. Chemostat studies of the effect of environmental control on *Streptococcus sanguis* adherence to hydroxyapatite. Infect. Immun. **35**:64–70.

14. **Rosan, B., C. H. Lai, and M. A. Listgarten.** 1976. *Streptococcus sanguis*: a model in the application of immunochemical analysis for the *in situ* localization of bacteria in dental plaque. J. Dent. Res. **55**:A124–141.

15. **Rutter, P. R., and B. Vincent.** 1980. The adhesion of micro-organisms to surface physiochemical aspects, p. 79–92. *In* R. C. W. Berkeley, T. M. Lynch, J. Melling, P. R. Rutter, and B. Vincent (ed.), Microbial adhesion to surfaces. Ellis Horwood, Chichester, England.

16. **Slade, H.** 1976. *In vitro* models for the study of adherence of oral streptococci, p. 21–38. *In* W. A. Bowen, R. J. Genco, and T. C. O'Brien (ed.), Proceedings: Immunologic Aspects of Dental Caries (a special supplement to Immunological Abstracts). Information Retrieval Inc., Arlington, Va.

Fibronectin—a Modulator of the Oropharyngeal Bacterial Flora

W. ANDREW SIMPSON, HARRY COURTNEY, AND EDWIN H. BEACHEY

Veterans Administration Medical Center and the University of Tennessee College of Medicine, Memphis, Tennessee 38104

Fibronectin is a large (molecular weight of $\approx 440,000$) glycoprotein that has been demonstrated in animal and human sera, in connective tissue, and as a component of the extracellular matrix of tissue culture cells (see 5 for a recent review). Serum fibronectin acts as a nonimmune opsonin against a variety of foreign particles, including denatured collagen (3), gelatin-coated colloidal carbon (6), and gelatin-coated latex beads (2). Certain clinical evidence suggests that serum fibronectin may play a protective role against serious bacterial infections in patients who have suffered extensive burns, undergone major surgery, or suffered other forms of serious trauma (7). It has been shown, for example, that the administration of serum cryoprecipitates which are rich in fibronectin markedly reduced the incidence and duration of bacterial septicemias in victims of trauma (7). Purified fibronectin binds to and agglutinates *Staphylococcus aureus* (4, 5) and *Streptococcus pyogenes* (W. A. Simpson, E. D. Pinals, D. L. Hasty, J. M. Mason, and E. H. Beachey, Abstr. Annu. Meet. Am. Soc. Microbiol. 1981, B97, p. 30) but not *Escherichia coli* (4), *Pseudomonas aeruginosa*, or *Klebsiella pneumoniae* (W. A. Simpson et al., submitted for publication).

Preliminary studies suggest that fibronectin may promote the ingestion of *S. aureus* cells by phagocytic cells (R. A. Proctor, E. Prendergast, and D. F. Mosher, Clin. Res. **27**:650A, 1979) and the attachment of certain strains of *S. pyogenes* to human polymorphonuclear leukocytes (Simpson et al., Abstr. Annu. Meet. Am. Soc. Microbiol. 1981, B97; Simpson et al., submitted for publication); however, the role of fibronectin as an efficient opsonin for *S. aureus* (8) and *S. pyogenes* (Simpson et al., submitted for publication) has recently been challenged.

An alternative explanation for the clinical significance of fibronectin was suggested by the recent work of Woods et al., who have shown that *P. aeruginosa* cells adhere in high numbers to oral epithelial cells from seriously ill patients in intensive care units (9) and that this increased adherence is correlated with a greatly reduced level of fibronectin on the epithelial cell surface. In this regard we have recently presented evidence to suggest that fibronectin on the surface of oral epithelial cells may be a receptor for *S. pyogenes* (W. A. Simpson and E. H. Beachey, Meeting of the Lancefield Society, Chicago, Ill., 1981; W. A. Simpson and E. H Beachey, submitted for publication). Confirmation of these findings would lead to the interesting situation in which fibronectin on the surface of oral epithelial cells would allow the adherence of a gram-positive organism and the lack of fibronectin on oral epithelial cells would allow the adherence of a gram-negative organism.

In the oral cavity, fibronectin can be detected only on the superficial epithelial cells distal from the connective tissue (10). No fibronectin is detected in the intercellular spaces of the epithelium or within the cytoplasm of the epithelial cells (10). The origin of cell surface fibronectin is unknown. However, the presence of fibronectin only on cells exposed to the oral cavity suggested that cell surface fibronectin on oral epithelial cells might be derived from saliva.

To determine whether fibronectin is present in saliva, whole stimulated saliva was collected from normal volunteers, clarified by centrifugation, first at $10,000 \times g$ and then at $100,000 \times g$, and concentrated 25-fold by ultrafiltration. A line of identity was formed between purified fibronectin and the concentrated saliva when diffused against antisera specific for serum fibronectin (Fig. 1), suggesting that whole saliva contained a protein immunologically identical to serum fibronectin. To confirm these results, whole stimulated saliva was clarified and passed over a column of gelatin immobilized on cyanogen bromide-activated agarose (1). The column was washed thoroughly with phosphate-buffered saline, and the protein was eluted with 8.0 M urea. The eluted protein was dialyzed, boiled in a sodium dodecyl sulfate-containing sample buffer, and applied to an 8% polyacrylamide gel. The protein bands were then transferred to nitrocellulose and processed for autoradiography with antifibronectin. The pattern of migra-

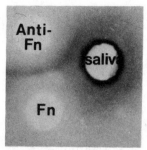

FIG. 1. Immunodiffusion pattern formed when antifibronectin was diffused against purified serum fibronectin and whole, concentrated saliva, showing a line of identity. The contents were diffused overnight, thoroughly washed in buffered saline, and stained with Coomassie blue before being photographed.

tion was consistent with purified serum fibronectin. Thus, it appears that saliva contains a protein that binds to gelatin and is immunologically identical with serum fibronectin.

It is possible that the salivary fibronectin is derived from fibronectin shed from the oral epithelial cells. However, the demonstration by Zetter et al. (10) that only the exposed surface of the most superficial layer of epithelial cells contains fibronectin and the recent finding in our laboratory that the level of fibronectin is the same in both stimulated and whole saliva (Simpson et al., in preparation) suggest that fibronectin is a secreted salivary component.

On the basis of our findings and those of Wood et al. (9), one might speculate that the level of salivary fibronectin, which may be influenced by the relative concentrations of proteolytic enzymes, or the level of serum fibronectin, determines the amount of fibronectin on the epithelial cells of the oral cavity and the upper respiratory tract. Changes in the amount of fibronectin coating the epithelial cells may result in changing populations of bacteria such that increased amounts of fibronectin would favor the colonization by gram-positive bacteria whereas decreased amounts would favor the colonization by gram-negative bacteria. Whether fibronectin plays such a modulatory role in the colonization of the upper respiratory tract remains to be proved.

ACKNOWLEDGMENTS

We thank Ella Pinals for technical assistance and Johnnie Smith for secretarial assistance.

These studies were supported by program directed research funds from the U.S. Veterans Administration and by Public Health Service research grants AI-10085 and AI-13550 from the National Institute of Allergy and Infectious Diseases. E.H.B. is the recipient of a Medical Investigatorship Award from the U.S Veterans Administration and W.A.S. is the recipient of a Young Investigator Award (DE-05773) from the U.S. Public Health Service.

LITERATURE CITED

1. **Cuatrecasas, P.** 1970. Protein purification by affinity chromatography. J. Biol. Chem. **245:**3059–3065.
2. **Doran, J. E., A. R. Mansberger, H. T. Edmondson, and A. C. Reese.** 1981. Cold insoluble globulin and heparin interactions in phagocytosis by macrophage monolayers: lack of heparin requirement. RES J. Reticuloendothel. Soc. **29:**275–283.
3. **Hopper K. E., B. C. Adelmann, G. Gentner, and S. Gay.** 1976. Recognition by guinea-pig peritoneal exudate cells of conformationally different states of the collagen molecule. Immunology **30:**249–259.
4. **Kuusela, P.** 1978. Fibronectin binds to *Staphylococcus aureus.* Nature (London) **276:**718–720.
5. **Mosher, D. F.** 1980. Fibronectin. Prog. Hemostasis Thromb. **5:**111–151.
6. **Pardy, B. J., R. C. Spencer, and H. A. F. Dudley.** 1977. Hepatic reticuloendothelial protection against bacteremia in experimental hemorrhagic shock. Surgery **81:**193–197.
7. **Saba, T. M., F. A. Blumenstock, W. A. Scovill, and H. Bernard.** 1978. Cryoprecipitate reversal of opsonic α_2-surface binding glycoprotein deficiency in septic surgical and trauma patients. Science **201:**622–624.
8. **Verbrugh, H. A., P. K. Peterson, D. E. Smith, B. T. Nguyen, J. R. Hoidal, B. J. Wilkinson, J. Verhoef, and L. T. Fwrcht.** 1981. Human fibronectin binding to staphylococcal surface protein and its relative inefficiency in promoting phagocytosis by human polymorphonuclear leukocytes, monocytes, and alveolar macrophages. Infect. Immun. **33:**811–819.
9. **Woods, D. E., D. C. Straus, W. G. Johanson, and J. A. Bass.** 1981. Role of fibronectin in the prevention of adherence of *Pseudomonas aeruginosa* to buccal cells. J. Infect. Dis. **143:**784–790.
10. **Zetter, B. R., T. E. Daniels, C. Quadra-White, and J. S. Greenspan.** 1979. LETS protein in normal and pathological human oral epithelium. J. Dent. Res. **58:**484–488.

VARIABLE SURFACE FACTORS IN BACTERIAL ADHESION

Host and Bacterial Factors in the Colonization of the Respiratory Tract

DONALD E. WOODS, BARBARA H. IGLEWSKI, AND W. G. JOHANSON, JR.

Department of Microbiology and Immunology, Oregon Health Sciences University, Portland, Oregon 97201, and Department of Medicine, University of Texas Health Science Center, San Antonio, Texas 78284

The respiratory tracts of healthy individuals are rarely populated with *Pseudomonas aeruginosa* (9, 11). In contrast, *P. aeruginosa* can frequently be isolated from the respiratory tracts of seriously ill patients. We have recently demonstrated that the ability of *P. aeruginosa* to persist in the respiratory tract is correlated with the organism's ability to adhere to upper respiratory epithelium (8, 9, 12).

Colonization of the respiratory tract by *P. aeruginosa* is accompanied by the adherence of *P. aeruginosa* to epithelial cells of the upper respiratory tract in vivo. When studied in vitro, greater numbers of *P. aeruginosa* adhere to cells of colonized subjects than to cells of noncolonized subjects. These data imply that there may be specific in vivo alterations in the epithelial cell surface which permit the adherence of *P. aeruginosa*. The objectives of our studies have been to define these epithelial cell alterations which lead to increased *P. aeruginosa* adherence and to define the structure(s) on the bacterial surface important in the adherence process.

IN VITRO STUDIES

Initial attempts to alter the cell surface to promote *P. aeruginosa* adherence involved the use of *Vibrio cholerae* neuraminidase. It was found that removal of sialic acid from the cell surface by use of neuraminidase failed to promote *P. aeruginosa* adherence to cells from colonized patients or noncolonized controls (Table 1). Much more sialic acid, however, was removed from the cells of normal individuals than from those of colonized patients, as measured by the thiobarbituric acid assay (2). Since sialic acid residues are normally anchored to protein present on the cell surface (3), and sialic acid removal alone did not lead to increased *P. aeruginosa* adherence, it was thought that perhaps an alteration in cell surface protein might

be responsible for increased adherence of these organisms to cells from colonized subjects.

This hypothesis was tested by exposing buccal cells to trypsin at a concentration of 2.5 µg/ ml for 10 min at 37°C prior to testing them for in vitro adherence of *P. aeruginosa*. A significant increase in adherence was noted after trypsin treatment of normal cells (3.1 ± 0.9 versus 26.1 ± 4.8, $P < 0.01$), whereas only a slight increase of *P. aeruginosa* adherence occurred after trypsinization of cells from colonized patients (Table 2).

To examine more closely the effects of trypsinization on cell surface proteins, membrane preparations of normal and trypsinized cells, prepared by the method of Brunette and Till (4), were examined by sodium dodecyl sulfate (SDS)-polyacrylamide gel electrophoresis. Figure 1 represents a densitometry scan of a 5% SDS-polyacrylamide gel stained with Coomassie blue after electrophoresis of membrane preparations of control and trypsinized buccal epithelial cells obtained from a noncolonized control. The principal difference between the two preparations is the loss from the trypsinized cells of a high-molecular-weight (200,000 to 220,000) protein. One of the trypsin-sensitive proteins in this molecular weight range that has been reported to be present on a number of different cell types is fibronectin. This is a 200,000- to 220,000-molecular-weight protein present on the surface of fibroblasts, endothelial cells, and some epithelial cells. It is immunologically identical to a plasma protein known as cold insoluble globulin (16). Employing an indirect fluorescent-antibody procedure, we were able to demonstrate that fibronectin was indeed present on the surface of normal buccal epithelial cells and that it was, in fact, removed by the brief trypsinization required to promote *P. aeruginosa* adherence (13). Thus, *P. aeruginosa* adherence to buccal cells in vitro coincided with the loss of fibronectin from

TABLE 1. Effect of *V. cholerae* neuraminidase (VCN) treatment on adherence of *P. aeruginosa* to buccal cells obtained from 12 colonized patients and 11 noncolonized controls[a]

Source of buccal cells	*P. aeruginosa* adherence		Sialic acid released (nmol/min)
	Pre-VCN	Post-VCN	
Colonized subjects	29.8 ± 3.1^b	30.1 ± 3.7^b	23.1 ± 17.3^b
Noncolonized controls	3.9 ± 1.1	3.4 ± 1.0	143.6 ± 83.6

[a] Colonization was defined as the presence of any colonies of *P. aeruginosa* in cultures of specimens from the respiratory tracts of patients. Data are given as mean ± the standard error.

[b] Significantly different from the value of the noncolonized controls ($P < 0.01$) by Student's *t* test.

the cell surface and appeared to be protease induced.

IN VIVO STUDIES

Having established these in vitro correlates, we focused our studies on the in vivo situation, asking the questions: (i) is there a decrease in, or absence of, fibronectin on the cell surface of buccal cells from colonized patients, and (ii) do these patients have increased amounts of protease activity in their secretions relative to controls? Utilizing a radioimmunoassay employing purified antibody to fibronectin (^{125}I labeled), we have demonstrated that there is in fact a decreased amount of fibronectin present on the surface of buccal cells from colonized patients relative to controls (12). Additionally, using an ^{125}I-labeled fibrin plate assay, we have demonstrated increased protease levels in the secretions from colonized patients over controls (12). These results are summarized in Table 3, in

TABLE 2. Effect of brief trypsinization on adherence of *P. aeruginosa* to buccal cells obtained from 12 colonized patients and 11 noncolonized controls[a]

Source of buccal cells	*P. aeruginosa* adherence	
	Untreated	Trypsin treated
Colonized subjects	39.5 ± 2.7	43.4 ± 4.1
Noncolonized controls	3.1 ± 0.9	26.1 ± 4.8^b

[a] Colonization was defined as the presence of any colonies of *P. aeruginosa* in cultures of specimens from the respiratory tracts of patients. Data are given as mean number of bacteria attached per epithelial cell ± the standard error.

[b] Significantly different from the value for the untreated controls ($P < 0.01$) by Student's *t* test.

200,000

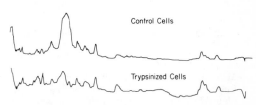

FIG. 1. Densitometry scan of a 5% SDS-polyacrylamide gel stained with Coomassie blue after electrophoresis of membrane preparations of control and trypsinized buccal epithelial cells.

which an absolute correlation can be demonstrated between increased *P. aeruginosa* adherence, decreased cell surface fibronectin, and increased protease levels in secretions.

Although the loss of fibronectin may not be the only in vivo alteration which leads to increased *P. aeruginosa* adherence, the correlation of fibronectin loss with increased adherence and increased salivary protease levels makes this hypothesis an attractive one. Further support for this was obtained from the results of a prospective study of patients undergoing elective coronary artery bypass surgery (14). The

TABLE 3. *P. aeruginosa* adherence, buccal cell surface fibronectin, and protease activity in secretions in 12 colonized subjects and 11 noncolonized controls[a]

Group	*P. aeruginosa* adherence[b]	Cell surface fibronectin[c]	Protease activity[d]
Colonized subjects	18.3 ± 2.1^e	710 ± 18^e	$74,306 \pm 2,119^e$
Noncolonized controls	2.3 ± 0.9	$3,081 \pm 39$	$21,012 \pm 1,006$

[a] Colonization was defined as the presence of any colonies of *P. aeruginosa* in cultures of specimens from the respiratory tracts of patients.

[b] Measured by radiolabel adherence assay. Data are given as mean number of bacteria attached per epithelial cell ± the standard error.

[c] Measured by radioimmunoassay; values represent mean counts per minute of ^{125}I-antifibronectin bound to 10^4 buccal cells ± the standard error.

[d] Values represent mean counts per minute of ^{125}I released from insoluble ^{125}I-fibrin matrix exposed to 1.0 ml of secretions for 20 h at 37°C ± the standard error.

[e] Significantly different from the value for the noncolonized controls ($P < 0.01$) by Student's *t* test.

TABLE 4. Effect of purified ethanol-precipitable slime on adherence of *P. aeruginosa* to buccal epithelial cells

Epithelial cells[a]	Bacteria per cell[b]
Control	30.6 ± 2.8
Preincubated with slime[c]	34.2 ± 1.6

[a] Buccal epithelial cells obtained from a single patient colonized with *P. aeruginosa*.

[b] Mean ± standard error for five determinations.

[c] Epithelial cells preincubated with 250 µg of slime for 1 h at 37°C, washed, and then placed in adherence assay.

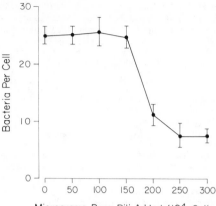

FIG. 2. Dose-response curve reflecting the ability of purified pili to block the adherence of intact *P. aeruginosa*. Buccal epithelial cells were exposed to increasing amounts (0 to 250 µg/ml) of purified pili for 1 h at 37°C prior to being tested for intact *P. aeruginosa* adherence.

status of these patients shifts suddenly from relatively good health, to seriously ill, and back again to a healthy state in a relatively short time span averaging 5 days. In coronary artery bypass patients we have demonstrated a sequential departure from and return to normal values for *P. aeruginosa* adherence, buccal cell surface fibronectin, and salivary protease levels. *P. aeruginosa* adherence in these patients varied directly with salivary protease levels, whereas cell surface fibronectin varied indirectly with adherence and protease levels (14).

P. AERUGINOSA ADHESINS

The interactions leading to bacterial adherence to mucosal surfaces involve both host and microbial factors. For a number of gram-negative bacteria, attention has been directed to surface appendages as mediators of adherence. To determine the nature of the adhesin in *P. aeruginosa*, we utilized purified surface slime layer antigens (1) in an attempt to block the adherence of intact organisms to buccal cells. As can be seen in Table 4, incubation of epithelial cells with *P. aeruginosa* slime had no effect on the adherence of the intact organism.

The effects of preincubation of epithelial cells with purified pili on the adherence of intact *P. aeruginosa* cells are presented in Table 5. The

TABLE 5. Effect of purified pili on adherence of *P. aeruginosa* to buccal epithelial cells

Epithelial cells[a]	Bacteria per cell[b]
Control	31.4 ± 2.9
Preincubated with pili[c]	5.7 ± 1.9[d]

[a] Buccal epithelial cells obtained from a single patient colonized with *P. aeruginosa*.

[b] Mean ± standard error for five determinations.

[c] Epithelial cells incubated with 250 µg of a preparation of pili for 1 h at 37°C, washed, and then placed in adherence assay.

[d] Significantly different from control (P < 0.01) by Student's t test.

purity of pili obtained from *P. aeruginosa* strain DG1 at various stages of the purification procedure was monitored by means of electron microscopy and SDS-discontinuous gel electrophoresis (7, 15). The purified pili migrated as a single band on 12.5% SDS-disc gels with an apparent molecular weight of 17,500 and appeared homogeneous when examined by transmission electron microscopy. A significant (P < 0.001) decrease in the adherence of intact organisms from 30.6 ± 2.8 to 5.7 ± 1.9 was noted after preincubation of epithelial cells with purified pili (Table 5). The ability of purified pili to block the adherence of *P. aeruginosa* was found to be a dose-related phenomenon (Fig. 2), as maximal blocking activity was found to occur with pili present at levels of 250 µg and above.

Antisera to purified pili were tested for their ability to prevent the adherence of organisms of both homologous and heterologous strains of *P. aeruginosa* to buccal epithelial cells. Samples (1 ml) of suspensions of five different strains (J3, J7, PRA, DG1, and PSE) containing 10^6 organisms per ml were incubated separately for 1 h at 37°C with 1 ml of a 1:2,048 dilution of antiserum of purified pili prepared from each of the five strains, washed, and placed in the in vitro assay for measurement of adherence (13). Table 6 represents the effect of antisera to pili from each of the five strains on the adherence of strain J3 to buccal epithelial cells. Antiserum to J3 pili resulted in 94.9% inhibition of adherence of the homologous J3 strain. When heterologous antisera to pili from strains J7, PRA, DG1, and PSE

TABLE 6. Effect of antisera to purified pili on adherence of *P. aeruginosa* strain J3 to buccal cells[a]

Source of antisera[b]	In vitro adherence[c]	% Inhibition
—	25.6 ± 1.9	0
J3	1.3 ± 0.1	94.9
J7	13.1 ± 1.2	48.8
PRA	14.6 ± 1.4	42.9
DG1	15.6 ± 1.3	39.1
PSE	16.7 ± 1.5	34.8

[a] Buccal cells previously treated with trypsin as previously described (15).

[b] Organisms (10^6) incubated for 1 h at 37°C with normal rabbit serum (—) or antibody to pili, washed, and placed in an in vitro assay.

[c] Measured as previously described (15).

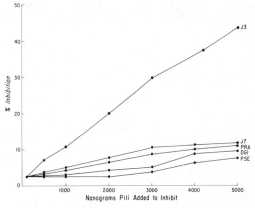

FIG. 3. Radioimmunoassay of pili with ^{125}I-labeled strain J3 pili and antiserum to J3 pili. Inhibition with purified pili from strains J3, J7, PRA, DG1, and PSE.

were employed, considerably less inhibition of *P. aeruginosa* J3 adherence was noted (Table 6). Similar adherence inhibition data were obtained regardless of which strain was employed in the in vitro adherence assay (data not shown).

A radioimmune competitive binding assay was developed to clarify the distribution of antigenic types of pili among *P. aeruginosa* strains colonizing the upper respiratory tract. The radioimmunoassay procedure developed employed purified pili radiolabeled by the procedure of Fraker and Speck (6). Approximately 100 ng of ^{125}I-labeled purified *P. aeruginosa* pili was allowed to react with a quantity of antiserum that produces approximately 65% binding of the radiolabeled pili. To this constant amount of radiolabeled pili and antiserum in a series of microfuge tubes were added incremental amounts of purified pili from a homologous or heterologous *P. aeruginosa* strain. The inhibition of binding of radiolabeled pili was calculated by the formula:

$$\%I = 100\left(\frac{B_W - B_I}{B_W}\right)$$

where I is inhibition, B_W is binding without inhibitor, and B_I is binding in the presence of inhibitor (5). Preparations of heterologous pili were tested for degree of cross-reactivity by comparing the percent inhibition produced in the radioimmunoassay with that of the preparations of homologous pili employed.

Figure 3 compares the inhibiting ability of purified pili from strains J3, J7, PRA, DG1, and PSE in a binding system utilizing ^{125}I-labeled J3 pili and antibody to J3 pili. Nonlabeled pili from strain J3 progressively inhibited the assay, with increments of 500 to 5,000 ng of pili. Little inhibition of the assay was produced with equal amounts of purified pili from strain J7, PRA, DG1, or PSE. Based upon the inhibition data, a percentage of shared antigenicity to strain J3 was calculated for each of the strains tested: strain J3, 100%; strain J7, 11.5%; strain PRA, 10.8%; strain DG1, 9.5%; strain PSE, 8.0%.

CONCLUSIONS

A correlation has previously been demonstrated between the in vitro adherence of *P. aeruginosa* to upper respiratory epithelium of seriously ill patients and subsequent colonization of the respiratory tract by this opportunistic pathogen. We have demonstrated that *P. aeruginosa* adherence can be correlated with the loss of a protease-sensitive glycoprotein, fibronectin, from the cell surface. Adherence of radiolabeled *P. aeruginosa* is directly related to decreased cell surface fibronectin and increased salivary protease levels.

The data reported here for *P. aeruginosa* adhesins are similar to those reported by Buchanan (5) for gonococcal pili; i.e., *P. aeruginosa* pili are antigenically heterogeneous. Certainly, there is some shared antigenicity as demonstrated by the ability of preparations of heterologous pili to inhibit binding of a preparation of pili to its homologous antiserum. The ability of antisera to heterologous pili to inhibit adherence of intact *P. aeruginosa* strains to buccal cells also supports this view. Whether the level of shared antigenicity is sufficient to prevent infection is unknown and warrants further study.

ACKNOWLEDGMENTS

This study was supported by Public Health Service grant AI 14671 from the National Institute of Allergy and Infectious

Diseases. D.E.W. was supported by a Postdoctoral Research Fellowship from the Cystic Fibrosis Foundation.

LITERATURE CITED

1. **Alms, T. H., and J. A. Bass.** 1967. Immunization against *Pseudomonas aeruginosa*. I. Induction of protection by an alcohol-precipitated fraction from the slime layer. J. Infect. Dis. **117**:249–256.
2. **Aminoff, D.** 1961. Methods for the quantitative estimation of N-acetyl neuraminic acid and their application to hydrolysates of sialomucoids. Biochem. J. **81**:384–392.
3. **Blix, F. G., A. Gottschalk, and E. Klenk.** 1957. Proposed nomenclature in the field of neuraminic acid and sialic acid. Nature (London) **179**:1088–1090.
4. **Brunette, D. M., and J. E. Till.** 1971. A rapid method for the isolation of L-cell surface membranes using an aqueous two-phase polymer system. J. Membr. Biol. **5**:215–224.
5. **Buchanan, T. M.** 1975. Antigenic heterogeneity of gonococcal pili. J. Exp. Med. **141**:1470–1475.
6. **Fraker, P. J., and J. C. Speck, Jr.** 1978. Protein and cell membrane iodinations with a sparingly soluble chloroamide, 1, 3, R, 6-tetrachloro-3A, 6A-diphenylglycoluril. Biochem. Biophys. Res. Commun. **80**:849–857.
7. **Frost, L. S., and W. Paranchych.** 1977. Composition and molecular weight of pili purified from *Pseudomonas aeruginosa* K. J. Bacteriol. **131**:259–269.
8. **Johanson, W. G., Jr., J. J. Higuchi, T. R. Chaudburi, and D. E. Woods.** 1980. Bacterial adherence to epithelial cells in bacillary colonization of the respiratory tract. Am. Rev. Resp. Dis. **121**:55–63.
9. **Johanson, W. G., Jr., A. K. Pierce, and J. P. Sanford.** 1969. Changing pharyngeal bacterial flora of hospitalized patients. Emergence of gram-negative bacilli. N. Engl. J. Med. **281**:1137–1140.
10. **Johanson, W. G., Jr., D. E. Woods, and T. R. Chaudburi.** 1979. Association of respiratory tract colonization with adherence of gram-negative bacilli to epithelial cells. J. Infect. Dis. **139**:667–673.
11. **Rahal, J. J., Jr., R. H. Meade III, C. M. Bump, and A. J. Reinauer.** 1970. Upper respiratory tract carriage of gram-negative enteric bacilli by hospital personnel. J. Am. Med. Assoc. **214**:754–756.
12. **Woods, D. E., J. A. Bass, W. G. Johanson, Jr., and D. C. Straus.** 1980. Role of adherence in the pathogenesis of *Pseudomonas aeruginosa* lung infection in cystic fibrosis patients. Infect. Immun. **30**:694–699.
13. **Woods, D. E., D. C. Straus, W. G. Johanson, Jr., and J. A. Bass.** 1981. Role of fibronectin in the prevention of adherence of *Pseudomonas aeruginosa* to buccal cells. J. Infect. Dis. **143**:784–790.
14. **Woods, D. E., D. C. Straus, W. G. Johanson, Jr., and J. A. Bass.** 1981. Role of salivary protease activity in adherence of gram-negative bacilli to mammalian buccal epithelial cells *in vivo*. J. Clin. Invest. **68**:1435–1440.
15. **Woods, D. E., D. C. Straus, W. G. Johanson, Jr., V. K. Berry, and J. A. Bass.** 1980. Role of pili in adherence of *Pseudomonas aeruginosa* to mammalian buccal epithelial cells. Infect. Immun. **29**:1146–1151.
16. **Yamada, K. M., and K. Olden.** 1978. Fibronectins-adhesive glycoproteins of cell surface and blood. Nature (London) **275**:179–184.

Protein II Variants of Gonococci

JOHN SWANSON

National Institute of Allergy and Infectious Diseases, Laboratory of Microbial Structure and Function, Rocky Mountain Laboratories, Hamilton, Montana 59840

Previous studies of mine and from other groups have correlated opacity of gonococcal colonies with the presence of one or more heat-modifiable proteins in the outer membranes (OMs) of the organisms comprising these colonies (7, 10, 11). In general, transparent or non-opaque (O^-) colonies contain gonococci whose OMs lack these heat-modifiable proteins that are lumped together in the protein II family. Opaque colonies contain gonococci that exhibit one or more protein II constituents. A number of recent studies have compared transparent-colony versus opaque-colony gonococci in a variety of ways including their susceptibilities to killing by pooled normal human sera (2), liabilities to growth inhibition by exogenously added proteases (1), and adherence propensities on incubation with tissue culture or organ culture cells (4, 8, 12). The results of those studies suggest that OM protein II constituents significantly alter or affect some biological reactivities of gonococci. These results, along with demonstration that transparent versus opaque colonies differ in their occurrences in clinical specimens depending on the sex of the patient, the site cultured, the phase of the female patient's menstrual cycle when the culture is taken, etc. (3, 5, 6), suggest that the phenomena of colony opacity phenotype and OM protein II constituents are related to the interactions between host components and gonococci and, hence, to the virulence or pathogenicity, or both, of these bacteria. In the past few months, I have been reexamining the colony opacity phenomena and OM protein II species to better understand these facets of the gonococcus' life.

OCCURRENCE OF COLONY OPACITY/ PROTEIN II VARIANTS

The solid medium used for detection and selection of opacity variants is quite critical since most commercial media for gonococcal cultivation do not sustain very opaque colony growth. Within any given strain, one can usually select a range of opacity variants by simply streaking out a single transparent colony such that individual colonies will be found the next day when the progeny are screened with a dissecting microscope for opacity variants. Either piliated (P^+, P^{++}) or nonpiliated (P^-) gonococcal colonies can be used, but the latter are

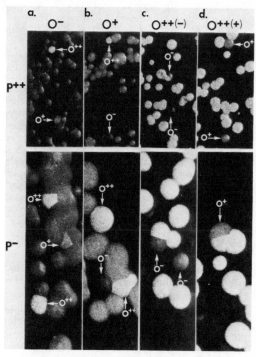

FIG. 1. Dissecting microscopic appearances of opacity variants from piliated (P^{++}) and nonpiliated (P^-) cultures of *Neisseria gonorrhoeae*. Single colonies with O^+ or O^{++} phenotypes were occasionally found within cultures derived through passage of single, transparent O^- colonies (a). On subpassage, most progeny from the selected O^+ colony had the same opacity, but both O^- and $O^{++(+)}$ variants could be found (b). Progeny from O^{++} colonies were mainly of the same phenotype, but O^- forms were also occasionally present (c). On subpassage, the $O^{++(+)}$ forms were sometimes "contaminated" with O^+, but not O^-, variants (d). It should be noted that these photographed fields were selected because they contained the occasional variants occurring within the otherwise homogeneous culture whose opacity phenotypes were identical to those of the parent colonies.

353

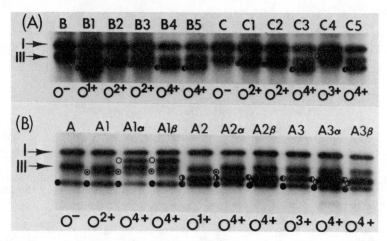

FIG. 2. (A) Protein II compositions of opacity variants selected from two transparent colonies. Two colonies that had transparent (O⁻) phenotype were passaged, and opaque variants were selected from among the progeny. Subculture of each selected variant and parental colony forms was followed by ^{125}I labeling of these preparations and SDS-PAGE. The central portion of an autoradiogram from the SDS-PAGE gel is shown. Lanes B and C represent the two original O⁻ colony preparations, and lanes B1–B5 and C1–C5 represent preparations from the opacity variants derived from each parental colony (B and C). Note that several degrees of opacity (O^{1+} to O^{4+}) were found among the variants, as noted beneath the autoradiogram. Note also that each variant displays a single protein II and that these differ in their apparent molecular weights. These preparations were solubilized for SDS-PAGE by boiling in the presence of 2-mercaptoethanol. Four different protein II species (each identified by a different symbol) were identified in this typical experiment. (B) Acquisition of additional protein II constituents by gonococci bearing one protein II. A single colony from a gonococcal population (lane A) which possessed a single protein II (●) but no discernible opacity (O⁻) was passaged, and opaque variants were selected from its progeny. At this first passage, three colonies (A1, A2, and A3) were selected, and single colonies of each were again passaged. At this second passage step, two very opaque variants (A1α, A1β, A2α, A2β, A3α, and A3β) were selected from each intermediate opacity colony (A1, A2, and A3). These were all radioiodinated and subjected to SDS-PAGE. Note the stepwise acquisition of a single protein II at each step in this selection of increasingly more opaque variants.

preferable since subtle variations in opacity are more easily appreciated in P⁻ colonies. On careful examination, most cultures have two or more kinds of opacity variants (Fig. 1), each of which comprises about 0.1% of the colonies present. These can be selected for passage, and the next day's cultures should yield almost pure cultures of the selected opacity phenotype which can be used for analysis of their OM protein II compositions by sodium dodecyl sulfate-polyacrylamide gel electrophoresis (SDS-PAGE). I have usually labeled the organisms with ^{125}I by the IodoGen method to enhance visualization of protein II bands by autoradiography on the slab gel since some protein II bands are poorly differentiated by Coomassie blue staining. Whether by staining or by autoradiography, one can easily compare the SDS-PAGE profiles of opacity variants and their transparent colony progenitors. Figure 2A depicts a typical experiment using the approach noted above. Each of the variants that is more opaque than its parental colony will have one protein II not

found in the latter's SDS-PAGE profile. Some opacity variants are only slightly opaque. Within subcultures of some of those colonies, more opaque variants that contain a second protein II can be selected (Fig. 2B).

In one strain I have studied, five different heat-modifiable protein II species have been identified by the methods described above. Each of these protein II species seems to be correlated with a different degree of opacity in this strain. In fact, one of the protein II constituents has no discernible influence on opacity either when present as the sole protein II or in combination with others and was discovered accidentally. The different protein II constituents of this strain exhibit several differing properties as follows: (i) different migration characteristics and apparent subunit size, (ii) different temperatures at which they display their heat modifiability, and (iii) differences in their susceptibilities to 2-mercaptoethanol regarding their electrophoretic mobilities (Table 1). Within this one strain, these five protein II species are distinctly different in their

TABLE 1. Characteristics of protein II constituents

Constituent	Apparent mol wt		Colony opacity phenotype	Modification of apparent mol wt	
	Fast, unmodified	Slow, modified		By 2-ME[a]	Temp[b] (°C)
IIa	26,000	29,000	O^-	−	<25, 60
IIb	26,800	30,250	$O^{-/+}$ (O^{1+})	+ +	100, 100
IIc	27,000	30,500	O^{++} (O^{4+})	+	100, 100
IId	26,500	31,000	O^+ (O^{2+})	+	100, >100
IIe	28,500	33,000	$O^{+/++}$ (O^{3+})	−/+	60, 100

[a] 2-Mercaptoethanol.

[b] Two temperatures are given. The first denotes the lowest temperature at which conversion to the slower migrating form is seen, and the second gives the temperature at which this conversion seems complete.

antigenicities/immunogenicities as discerned by radioimmunoprecipitation assays (Fig. 3).

Of particular interest are the findings that protein II constituents are immunogenic in rab-

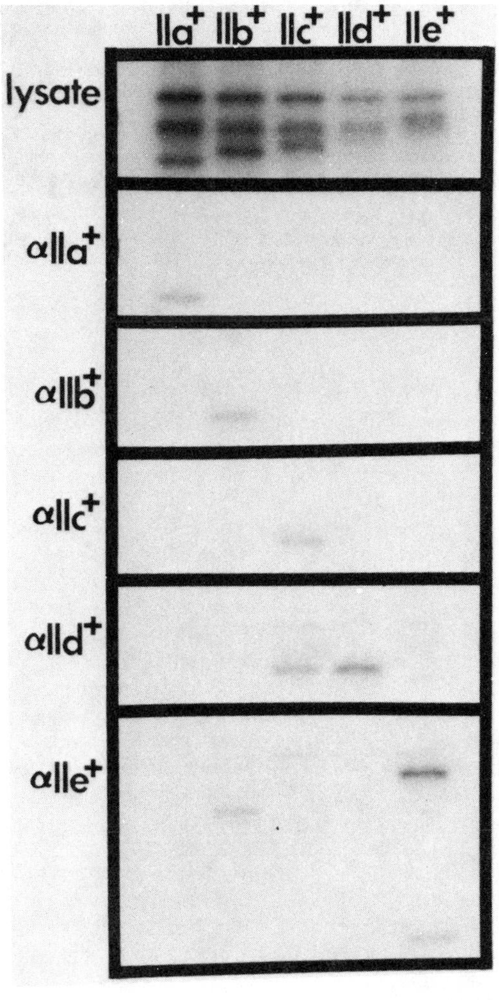

FIG. 3. Radioimmunoprecipitation reactions of gonococci possessing different protein II constituents. Gonococci from a single strain that had been selected for having different protein II constituents were used to immunize rabbits whose sera were used in this experiment. These five variants were also used for immunoprecipitation by radioiodinating the organisms, incubating them with rabbit sera, lysing the organisms with detergent, and immunoprecipitating immunoglobulin G with Sepharose-conjugated protein A (from *Staphylococcus aureus*). Those radioiodinated constituents of gonococci to which immunoglobulin G was complexed were also immunoprecipitated and are displayed in these autoradiograms. In each reaction, all five variants (IIa⁺, IIb⁺, IIc⁺, IId⁺, and IIe⁺) were incubated with a single antiserum (anti-IIa⁺, anti-IIb⁺, etc., as indicated). The top panel displays the central portion of the autoradiogram obtained with lysates of the antigens used and provides a reference for the immunoprecipitation gels. Note that only protein IIa is precipitated by the anti-IIa⁺ serum. Antisera raised against IIb⁺ and IIc⁺ organisms show little or no heterologous reactivities. A clear-cut cross-reaction of anti-IIe⁺ serum is seen with protein IIb along with the homologous reaction. Anti-IId⁺ serum also seems to react with both homologous (protein IId) and heterologous (protein IIc) constituents. Minor reactivities of two antisera (anti-IIb, anti-IId) with protein IIe are also present, but are difficult or impossible to appreciate in this figure. Note the relative lack of protein I in these immunoprecipitates; greater homologous reactivity to protein I species has been found in antisera against organisms of different strains, but is consistently weak with the particular strain shown (JS3).

bits and that the antigenic reactivities of different protein II species in the same strain are quite distinct. Regarding the immunogenicities of these OM constituents, sera raised in rabbits against whole, viable gonococci often show dominant immunoglobulin G reactivities directed toward protein II with little reactivity against protein I, for example. It is not known whether patients with gonorrheal infections develop antibodies toward these OM proteins, but it seems likely that they do. The antigenic distinctiveness of most protein II species may have relevance in concert with the observation that gain and loss of protein II occurs at a high frequency as deduced from the rates of opaque to transparent (and the reverse) transitions (9). It seems probable that gonococcal populations can almost continuously change their protein II compositions and provide a "moving antigenic target" to the immunological surveillance system of the human host. This possibility plus previously demonstrated modifications of adhesiveness and aggregability for gonococci bearing or lacking protein II constituents make these OM proteins quite interesting for studying the behavior of gonococci.

LITERATURE CITED

1. **Blake, M. S., E. C. Gotschlich, and J. Swanson.** 1981. Effects of proteolytic enzymes on the outer membrane proteins of *Neisseria gonorrhoeae*. Infect. Immun. **33:**212–222.
2. **Brooks, G. F., C. J. Lammel, E. Z. Burns, and J. F. James.** 1980. Confounding factors affecting normal serum killing of *N. gonorrhoeae* colony phenotype variants, p. 251–254. *In* D. Danielsson and S. Normark (ed.), Genetics and immunobiology of pathogenic neisseria. University of Umea, Umea, Sweden.
3. **Draper, D. L., J. F. James, G. F. Brooks, and R. L. Sweet.** 1980. Comparison of virulence markers of peritoneal and fallopian tube isolates with endocervical *Neisseria gonorrhoeae* isolates from women with acute salpingitis. Infect. Immun. **27:**882–888.
4. **James, J. F., C. J. Lammel, D. L. Draper, and G. F. Brooks.** 1980. Attachment of *N. gonorrhoeae* colony phenotype variants to eukaryotic cells and tissues, p. 213–216. *In* D. Danielsson and S. Normark (ed.), Genetics and immunobiology of pathogenic neisseria. University of Umea, Umea, Sweden.
5. **James, J. F., and J. Swanson.** 1978. Color/opacity colonial variants of *Neisseria gonorrhoeae* and their relationship to the menstrual cycle, p. 338–343. *In* G. F. Brooks, E. C. Gotschlich, K. K. Holmes, W. D. Sawyer, and F. E. Young (ed.), Immunobiology of *Neisseria gonorrhoeae*. American Society for Microbiology, Washington, D.C.
6. **James, J. F., and J. Swanson.** 1978. Studies on gonococcus infection. XIII. Occurrence of color/opacity colonial variants in clinical cultures. Infect. Immun. **19:**332–340.
7. **Lambden, P. R., and J. E. Heckels.** 1979. Outer membrane protein composition and colonial morphology of *Neisseria gonorrhoeae* strain P9. FEMS Microbiol. Lett. **5:**263–265.
8. **Lambden, P. R., J. E. Heckels, L. T. James, and P. J. Watt.** 1979. Variation in surface protein composition associated with virulence properties in opacity types of *Neisseria gonorrhoeae*. J. Gen. Microbiol. **114:**305–312.
9. **Mayer, L. W.** 1980. Colony opacity changes in *N. gonorrhoeae*, p. 135–137. *In* D. Danielsson and S. Normark (ed.), Genetics and immunobiology of pathogenic neisseria. University of Umea, Umea, Sweden.
10. **Swanson, J.** 1978. Studies on gonococcus infection. XII. Colony color and opacity variants of gonococci. Infect. Immun. **19:**320–331.
11. **Swanson, J.** 1978. Studies on gonococcus infection. XIV. Cell wall protein differences among color/opacity colony variants of *Neisseria gonorrhoeae*. Infect. Immun. **21:**292–302.
12. **Virji, M., and J. S. Everson.** 1981. Comparative virulence of opacity variants of *Neisseria gonorrhoeae* strain P9. Infect. Immun. **31:**965–970.

Mucosal (Immunoglobulin A) Immune Response to Noninvasive Bacteria in the Gut

DAVID F. KEREN

Department of Pathology, The University of Michigan, Ann Arbor, Michigan 48109

It is well known that the mucosa of the gastrointestinal tract contains a large number of immunoglobulin A (IgA)-secreting cells and their precursors (1, 14). The IgA response of the gastrointestinal tract is usually best stimulated by oral immunization with either soluble or particulate antigens. The exact mechanisms for optimally stimulating the mucosal immune response are still poorly understood.

To better define the optimal regimen for stimulating the mucosal immune response, my colleagues and I have developed a chronically isolated intestinal loop model system in rabbits (8–11). In the present communication I describe our method for preparing chronically isolated ileal loops in rabbits and the application of this model in studying the IgA memory response to both invasive and noninvasive bacteria.

CONSTRUCTION OF CHRONICALLY ISOLATED ILEAL LOOPS

Our previously described method (9) was used to construct chronically isolated segments of ileum, 20 cm long, in 3-kg New Zealand white rabbits. Briefly, while the animals were anesthetized with a combination of xylazine and ketamine, a midline abdominal incision was made and the terminal ileum was identified. A 20-cm segment containing a single, grossly identifiable Peyer's patch was isolated with its vascular supply intact. Continuity was restored to the ileum by an end-to-end anastomosis. Silastic tubing was then sewn into each end of the 20-cm segment of ileum. The silastic tubing was brought out through the midline abdominal incision. The isolated loop, however, was allowed to remain in the peritoneal cavity. The silastic tubing was then dissected subcutaneously to the nape of the rabbit's neck, where it was exteriorized and secured.

Secretions from the isolated loops were collected daily by injecting air into the silastic tubing, thereby expelling loop fluid from the other silastic tube. Approximately 2 to 4 ml of fluid would be obtained daily from each loop. This material was centrifuged to clarify it and was stored at −20°C until time of assay.

ENZYME-LINKED IMMUNOSORBENT ASSAY

An enzyme-linked immunosorbent assay for IgA and IgG activity to *Shigella flexneri* lipopolysaccharide (LPS) was performed as described previously (7). All reactions were performed in duplicate. This technique allows detection of as little as 1.3 ng of specific antibody per ml, with coefficients of variation on replicate samples of IgG and IgA of 3.6 and 9.0%, respectively.

BACTERIAL PREPARATIONS

Three live *Shigella* strains, one acetone-killed strain, and one Westphal LPS preparation containing *S. flexneri* 2a somatic antigens were used in these studies. Strain M4243 has been shown to invade the epithelium of guinea pig intestine and to persist, with the formation of focal ulcerations (2). *Shigella* X16 is a hybrid of *S. flexneri-Escherichia coli* which will invade locally and may form ulcers, but does not thrive (persist) in guinea pig intestine (3). Strain 2457-0 is noninvasive (4). The preparations of acetone-killed M4243 and *Shigella* LPS have been described previously (4, 5).

RESPONSE TO DIRECT MUCOSAL IMMUNIZATION WITH BACTERIAL PREPARATIONS

As previous studies had shown that multiple doses of bacteria result in an optimal mucosal immune response (11), the animals were given 10^8 bacteria, or 2.5 mg of acetone-killed M4243 per ml, or 200 μg of the Westphal preparation of *Shigella* LPS per ml directly intraloop on days 1, 8, and 15 after surgical creation of the isolated loops. The results shown in Fig. 1 demonstrate that an IgA response to *S. flexneri* LPS was found in all but the group given LPS only. Although I initially predicted that the M4243 and X16 strains would have a significantly stronger response by virtue of their ability to invade the surface epithelium, no significant difference was found between the response to these two locally

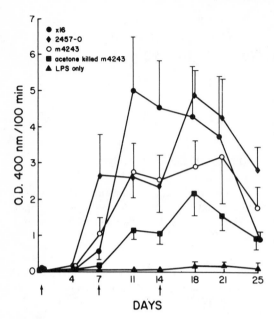

FIG. 1. Mean IgA anti-*Shigella* LPS response in secretions from chronically isolated ileal loops directly immunized with the indicated preparations (see text). Results from an enzyme-linked immunosorbent assay for IgA activity to *Shigella* LPS are expressed on the vertical axis. Days after initial antigen administration are expressed on the horizontal axis. Arrows indicate days when antigen was administered. Standard errors of means are indicated. From reference 8, used with permission.

invasive strains and the 2457-0 noninvasive strain. Furthermore, the acetone-killed M4243 was also able to elicit effective mucosal IgA responses.

Only trivial IgA or IgG anti-*S. flexneri* LPS activity was detected occasionally in sera of animals given intraluminal antigen. IgG against the *Shigella* LPS was not found in the intestinal secretions. We know that the latter is not due to the lack of stability of IgG in these isolated loop fluids (12). Rather, it is due to the lack of effective stimulation of IgG in this model system by applying antigens directly to the mucosal surface.

It has been difficult to study mucosal memory responses with this model of mucosal immunity. In the first place, it is technically difficult to maintain the chronically isolated ileal loops for long periods of time in these animals. Secondly, the direct stimulation of the isolated loops is highly artificial. By doing so, the effects of gastric acid, bile, digestive enzymes, normal intestinal flora, and food products are bypassed. All of these substances might be able to alter the

mucosal immune response to orally administered bacteria.

Therefore, in the next series of studies, rather than directly stimulating the isolated ileal loops, I immunized the animals orally. The mucosal IgA response to invasive and noninvasive bacteria was followed by studying the secretions from the isolated ileal loops (that had never received antigen directly) for their specific IgA activity.

The ability to use this approach is a logical extension of studies involving antigen stimulation of mucosal immunity and leukocyte trafficking in the bowel. It has been shown by several laboratories that precursor B lymphocytes and regulatory T lymphocytes in Peyer's patches and other gut-associated lymphoid tissue will migrate to mesenteric lymph nodes, the thoracic duct, the systemic circulation, and, lastly, to several mucosal surfaces, including other areas of the gut where antigen was not directly applied after giving oral antigenic stimulation (1). This has been called the common mucosal immune system. If such a system exists as hypothesized, then it should be possible to give an oral dose of antigen and follow the response in the chronically isolated ileal loops.

Figure 2 shows the results of such an experiment when the rabbits were given oral doses of live, locally invasive *Shigella* X16 the day after surgical creation of the isolated ileal loop. Al-

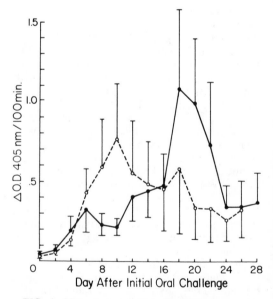

FIG. 2. Mean IgA anti-*Shigella* LPS response in secretions from isolated loops of animals given a single (○) or three weekly (●) oral doses of 10^{10} live *Shigella* X16 cells on day 0. Standard errors of the means are indicated. From reference 11, used with permission.

TABLE 1. IgA anti-*Shigella* in loop secretions

Day after challenge[a]	Not primed[b]	Primed[c]
0	0.061 ± 0.17[a]	0.387 ± 0.267
1	0.146 ± 0.88	0.216 ± 0.109
2	0.109 ± 0.039	0.276 ± 0.126
3	0.176 ± 0.070	0.571 ± 0.232
4	0.423 ± 0.153	2.030 ± 0.400
5	0.894 ± 0.242	2.434 ± 0.493
6	1.580 ± 1.398	2.671 ± 0.498

[a] Day 0 is the day of final challenge.

[b] Unprimed animals were given 10^{10} *S. flexneri* 2457-0 cells on day 0 ($n = 16$).

[c] Rabbits were primed orally with 10^{10} *S. flexneri* 2457-0 cells on days −75, −68, and −61 prior to oral challenge on day 0 ($n = 10$).

[d] Results expressed as mean absorbance at 405 nm/ 100 min ± standard error of the mean.

though the magnitude of the mucosal immune response is less than when bacteria were directly applied into the isolated loops, the kinetics of the response are the same.

In Table 1 are shown results from animals given noninvasive *S. flexneri* strain 2457-0 orally 1 day after surgical creation of their isolated ileal loops. Again, it is clear that the kinetics of the development of secretory IgA locally against the orally administered *S. flexneri* strain 2457-0 are the same as when the antigen is applied directly to the mucosal surface. This reaffirms my impression from the direct immunization studies that noninvasive bacteria do elicit mucosal immune responses.

Recent studies have already shown that a mucosal memory response to the locally invasive *Shigella* X16 can be achieved (11a).

In Table 1, the preliminary data are shown from animals given three oral doses of live *S. flexneri* strain 2457-0 60 days prior to creation of their isolated ileal loops. On the first day after creation of their isolated ileal loops, these animals were given a single oral challenge with the same live antigens. A memory response was seen in most of the animals in this group. The responses on days 2, 3, and 4 are significantly greater than when animals were given only a single oral dose of *S. flexneri* strain 2457-0 but not a previous priming. These data indicate that a mucosal IgA memory response can be achieved by immunization with noninvasive bacteria. Our previous studies have already shown that a mucosal memory response to the locally invasive *Shigella* X16 can be achieved.

This demonstration of a local IgA response to noninvasive bacteria is consistent with some earlier clinical trials. At least two such studies have indicated that oral immunization to *Shigella* can be achieved with killed preparations (6, 13).

In summary, the kinetics of development of the mucosal immune response to locally administered live invasive *S. flexneri* antigens was the same as that to noninvasive *S. flexneri* strain 2457-0. A similar local IgA response could be achieved whether the antigen was directly applied to the mucosa of chronically isolated ileal loops or was given orally.

ACKNOWLEDGMENTS

This work was supported in part by U.S. Army Medical Research and Development contract no. DAMD 17-80-C-0113.

LITERATURE CITED

1. **Cebra, J. J., R. Kamat, P. Gearhart, S. Robertson, and J. Tseng.** 1977. The secretory IgA system of the gut. Ciba Found. Symp. **46:**5–12.
2. **Formal, S. B., T. H. Kent, S. Austin, and E. H. LaBrec.** 1966. Fluorescent antibody and histological study of vaccinated and control monkeys challenged with *Shigella flexneri.* J. Bacteriol. **19:**2368–2376.
3. **Formal, S. B., E. H. LaBrec, T. H. Kent, and S. Falkow.** 1965. Abortive intestinal infection with an Escherichia coli-*Shigella flexneri* hybrid strain. J. Bacteriol. **89:**1374–1382.
4. **Formal, S. B., E. H. LaBrec, A. Palmer, and S. Falkow.** 1965. Protection of monkeys against experimental shigellosis with attenuated vaccines. J. Bacteriol. **90:**63–68.
5. **Formal, S. B., R. M. Maenza, S. Austin, and E. H. LaBrec.** 1967. Failure of parenteral vaccines to protect monkeys against experimental shigellosis. Proc. Soc. Biol. **125:**347–349.
6. **Grahneis, H.** 1974. Successful field trials with oral killed *Shigella sonnei* vaccine. Acta Microbiol. Acad. Sci. Hung. **21:**75–80.
7. **Keren, D. F.** 1979. Enzyme-linked immunosorbent assay for immunoglobulin G and immunoglobulin A antibodies to *Shigella flexneri* antigens. Infect. Immun. **24:**441–448.
8. **Keren, D. F., H. H. Collins, P. Gemski, P. S. Holt, and S. B. Formal** 1981. Role of antigen form in development of mucosal immunoglobulin A response to *Shigella flexneri* antigens. Infect. Immun. **31:**1193–1202.
9. **Keren, D. F., H. L. Elliott, G. D. Brown, and J. H. Yardley.** 1975. Atrophy of villi with hypertrophy and hyperplasia of Paneth cells in isolated (Thiry-Vella) ileal loops in rabbits. Gastroenterology **68:**83–93.
10. **Keren, D. F., P. S. Holt, H. H. Collins, P. Gemski, and S. B. Formal.** 1978. The role of Peyer's patches in the local immune response of rabbit ileum to live bacteria. J. Immunol. **120:**1892–1896.
11. **Keren, D. F., P. S. Holt, H. H. Collins, P. Gemski, and S. B. Formal.** 1980. Variables affecting the local immune response in Thiry-Vella loops. I. Role of immunization schedule, bacterial flora, and postsurgical inflammation. Infect. Immun. **28:**950–956.
11a. **Keren, D. F., S. E. Kern, D. H. Bauer, P. J. Scott, and P. Porter.** 1982. Direct demonstration in intestinal secretions of an IgA memory response to orally administered *Shigella flexneri* antigens. J. Immunol. **128:**475–479.
12. **Keren, D. F., P. J. Scott, and D. Bauer.** 1980. Variables affecting the local immune response in Thiry-Vella loops.

II. Stability of antigen-specific IgG and secretory IgA in acute and chronic Thiry-Vella loops. J. Immunol. **124**:2620–2624.

13. **Ketyi, I., K. Rauss, and A. Vertenyi.** 1974. Oral immunization against dysentery. Acta Microbiol. Acad. Sci. Hung.

21:81–85.

14. **Tomasi, T. B., E. M. Tan, A. Solomon, and R. A. Prendergast.** 1965. Characteristics of an immune response common to certain external secretions. J. Exp. Med. **121**:101–111.

IV. THE MACROPHAGE IN HOST DEFENSE

(from a Symposium at the 21st International Conference on Antimicrobial Agents and Chemotherapy, held 4–6 November 1981 in Chicago, Illinois)

Introduction

RICHARD K. ROOT

Infectious Disease Section, Yale University School of Medicine, New Haven, Connecticut 06510

Macrophages and their precursor circulating cells, blood monocytes, are phagocytic cells which play a unique dual role in the afferent and efferent limbs of the immune response. Although they may be defined by morphological criteria and thus easily separated from other phagocytic cell classes, it is their functional heterogeneity and capacity for long life in the host which make them the center of intense investigation by students of microbiology and immunology alike. Macrophages play an important role in the initial processing of many foreign antigens, in particular proteins. The presentation of these antigens together with immune recognition antigens on the macrophage plasma membrane to T lymphocytes are central events in initiating T-dependent immune responses. This will not be the focus of the symposium presented below. Rather, recognizing the microbiological orientation of the audience, the emphasis will be on macrophages as effector cells in anti-infectious host defense. The presentation of papers will begin with a description of the development of macrophages from their precursor monocytes, followed by a discussion of mechanisms involved in the phenomenon known as macrophage "activation." A summary of the general role of activated macrophages in host defense will initiate more detailed discussions of macrophage functional mechanisms against bacterial protozoans and fungi. The presentations will emphasize both the state of the art and contributions to the field from the laboratories of the participants.

Development of the Macrophage

STANTON G. AXLINE

Veterans Administration Medical Center and University of Arizona Health Sciences Center, Tucson, Arizona 85724

The macrophage is functionally and quantitatively the most important member of a series of cells identified collectively as the mononuclear phagocytic system. The concept of the mononuclear phagocytic system was first put forward in 1969 by Langevoort (6) and was subsequently elaborated upon by van Furth (12) and others. It is now generally accepted that this system is composed of a spectrum of cells that all have a common origin in the bone marrow. Various constituents of the mononuclear phagocytic system differ markedly in morphology, functional characteristics, and metabolic patterns. Although differences exist among the members of the system, their biological significance is, in large measure, a reflection of their special ability to engage in extensive heterophagic activity.

CHARACTERIZATION OF MONONUCLEAR PHAGOCYTES

Multiple properties are used for identification of cells as mononuclear phagocytes. These involve morphological as well as biochemical and functional characteristics. The morphology of cells of the mononuclear phagocytic system varies and depends upon the stage of cellular development. In the mouse the freshly explanted peritoneal monocyte closely resembles the circulating blood monocyte. Cells maintained in vitro as monolayers differentiate into macrophages, become well spread, and possess numerous pseudopodia extending radially from the cell body. The centrosphere region contains abundant large, phase-dense, secondary lysosomes which are well demarcated from more peripheral cell regions. Peripheral to the centrosphere region are phase-dense mitochondria as well as pinocytic vesicles. The nucleus is slightly indented and contains prominent nucleoli. Ultrastructural differences among members of the mononuclear phagocytic system include increases in cytoplasm-to-nucleus ratio as the cell matures from monoblast to macrophage. Similarly, microvillous projections increase with maturation. Mitochondrial mass is not reliably different in mature as compared with immature members of the series. However, substantial changes in mitochondrial mass and mitochondri-

al enzyme activity can occur in response to environmental stimuli. Polyribosomes are more abundant in the monoblast, whereas rough endoplasmic reticulum is increased in the macrophage. The Golgi apparatus is larger and more prominent in the macrophage than in the monoblast. These findings are in keeping with the increase in number of lysosomal granules present in the more mature cells.

Other principal features used to specify cells belonging to the mononuclear phagocytic series are outlined in Table 1 (10). A reliable histochemical marker for identification of mononuclear phagocytes is the nonspecific esterase which is localized diffusely in the cytoplasm (8). Nearly all monocytes and macrophages are positive when α-naphthyl butyrate or acetate is used as the substrate. Lysozyme is another good marker which can be demonstrated with immunofluorescence or by immunoperoxidase methods using species-specific anti-lysozyme antibody. Peroxidase is also a useful marker. Cytochemical methods useful for light microscopy show the presence of peroxidase-positive granules in the monoblast, promonocyte, monocyte, and exudate macrophage. In contrast, resident macrophages are peroxidase negative. By electron microscopy peroxidase activity can be localized to endoplasmic reticulum, nuclear envelope, and Golgi apparatus.

Ectoenzymes that are useful in characterizing mononuclear phagocytes are 5'-nucleotidase, leucine aminopeptidase, and alkaline phosphodiesterase I. For the latter two enzymes, activity increases with differentiation or activation of the macrophage. In contrast 5'-nucleotidase activity is much greater in normal resident macrophages than in activated macrophages.

Receptors for the Fc portion of immunoglobulin G and the C3 component of complement are cell surface markers useful in identifying mononuclear phagocytes (3). Both Fc and C3 receptors are present in all stages of development of the macrophage although quantitative differences are observed. Mature macrophages are receptor positive less often than are immature monocytes.

All cells of the mononuclear phagocytic series

TABLE 1. Outline for the identification of
mononuclear phagocytes

Feature	Characteristics
Structure	Features in light, phase-contrast, and electron microscopy
Cytoplasmic and lysosomal enzymes	Nonspecific esterase, lysozyme, peroxidase
Ectoenzymes	5'-Nucleotidase, leucine aminopeptidase, alkaline phosphodiesterase I
Membrane characteristics	Fc and complement receptors, specific antigens
Function	Immune phagocytosis, pinocytosis
Cell proliferation	[^{3}H]thymidine incorporation, DNA content of nucleus, survival or multiplication in culture

exhibit the ability to engage actively in endocytosis. The ability to ingest particles by immune phagocytosis such as the ingestion of opsonized bacteria or immunoglobulin G-coated erythrocytes is an essential requirement for a cell to be regarded as part of the mononuclear phagocytic series. Mononuclear phagocytes also exhibit extensive pinocytic activity. Macropinocytosis, uptake involving formation of large vesicles (0.1 to 1 μm in diameter), predominates in the macrophage and accounts for nearly all solute uptake and membrane interiorization.

The ability to proliferate is an important characteristic of mononuclear phagocytic cells which helps to distinguish immature from the more mature members of the series. The immature monoblast and promonocyte are able to divide readily, whereas the monocyte and macrophage are normally unable to divide.

ORIGIN AND TURNOVER OF CELLS IN THE MONONUCLEAR PHAGOCYTIC SERIES

The most immature cell of the monocyte series, the monoblast, is found only in the bone marrow. Division of the monoblast gives rise to the promonocyte which, in turn, is the direct precursor of the monocyte. Kinetic studies using radioactive labeling techniques have shown that monocytes remain in the bone marrow for only a short period of time and then enter the circulation. From that site they migrate by poorly

understood mechanisms to various tissues to become macrophages (11). Quantitative studies of the distribution of circulating murine blood monocytes have shown that 56% become liver macrophages, 15% become lung macrophages, 8% become peritoneal macrophages, and 21% are found in all other tissues.

Macrophages and tissue histiocytes are identified by a variety of different names, depending upon their location. Macrophages normally found in tissues are identified as resident macrophages, whereas mononuclear phagocytes that accumulate in exudates in response to an inflammatory stimulus are termed exudate macrophages.

Epithelioid cells represent another form of differentiation of cells of the mononuclear phagocytic series and are usually found in granulomata. Epithelioid cells possess Fc and C3 receptors and are less active in phagocytosis than are macrophages.

Multinucleated giant cells are formed by fusion of exudate macrophages. The Langhans multinucleated giant cells have relatively few nuclei arranged peripherally in the cytoplasm, whereas the foreign body giant cell has many nuclei dispersed throughout the cytoplasm. Transitional forms can be found, and it is likely that the Langhans and foreign body type represent different stages of development of the same cell.

The ultimate fate of tissue macrophages is poorly understood. Macrophages, however, can migrate to local lymph nodes and die there. Alternatively, they may migrate to the free air space of the lung or to other tissues. There is evidence for only minimal recirculation by way of peripheral blood.

Kinetic studies have shown that the liver macrophage constitutes by far the largest pool of cells in the mononuclear phagocytic system. The cell cycle time for the murine monoblast is 12 h and for the promonocyte is 16 h. The half-life of the circulating monocyte is short, being approximately 17 h in mice and 71 h in humans.

DIFFERENTIATION OF MONONUCLEAR PHAGOCYTES

As early as 1939, it was observed that monocytes differentiated into macrophages continuously and that such changes became particularly prominent at sites of inflammation. Differentiation was shown to be of functional significance to the host by conferring enhanced nonspecific resistance to infection, increased endocytic capacity, and increased antimicrobial activity.

The much more recent observations that differentiation of monocytes could be duplicated in

TABLE 2. Pyruvate kinase[a] and cytochrome oxidase[b] specific activities for mouse macrophages cultivated under anaerobic conditions

Enzyme	Serum concn (%)	Incubation time			
		1 h	24 h	48 h	72 h
Pyruvate kinase	30	133 ± 11[c]	509 ± 56	721 ± 61	585 ± 51
	2	133 ± 20	346 ± 38	331 ± 24	307 ± 30
Cytochrome oxidase	30	12.0 ± 0.6	11.7 ± 0.9	10.3 ± 1.0	7.7 ± 0.8
	2	11.6 ± 0.4	11.1 ± 0.4	9.9 ± 0.6	7.8 ± 1.0

[a] Expressed as micromoles of phosphoenolpyruvate converted to pyruvate per minute per milligram of protein.

[b] Expressed as micromoles of cytochrome c oxidized per minute per milligram of protein.

[c] Mean ± standard error of the mean for six to eight experiments.

vitro permitted detailed morphological and biochemical investigations of the process by use of homogeneous cell populations. Landmark studies in this field have been conducted by Cohn et al. over the past 15 years (4, 5). Freshly explanted mouse peritoneal macrophages were shown to resemble the circulating blood monocyte. Striking morphological changes which occurred with prolonged incubation included increased number and size of lysosomes, increased number of mitochondria, increased number of lipid droplets, and progressive elevation of lysosomal enzyme activity (acid phosphatase, β-glucuronidase, and cathepsin D among others). These data and autoradiographic evidence of accumulation of newly formed protein in lysosomes suggested that new formation of hydrolytic enzymes accompanied differentiation.

Further studies showed that the morphological and biochemical properties of the cultivated macrophage are profoundly affected by the concentration of soluble macromolecules in the medium. At low serum concentrations, the cells develop a few small lysosomes and there is little or no increase in lysosomal enzymes. As the serum concentration is increased, larger granules are formed at a more rapid rate and the lysosomal enzyme activity increases. The process is readily reversible.

The rate of pinocytic activity was also shown to be directly correlated with concentration of serum components including fetuin, albumin, and certain macroglobulins. In addition, mucopolysaccharides, nucleosides, nucleotides, and macroanions including poly-L-glutamic acid, DNA, and RNA were potent pinocytic inducers. Inducers of pinocytosis led to increased lysosome formation. Phagocytosis was also shown to induce increased activity of lysosomal enzymes in the macrophage (1).

In studies of the range of substrates that could induce lysosomal enzymes, I found that phagocytic uptake of digestible particles led to increased lysosomal enzyme activity that was dependent on continued protein synthesis, whereas nondigestible particles were ineffective inducers. These studies established a clear functional link between endocytosis and lysosome formation that accompanies differentiation in vitro.

REGULATION OF GLYCOLYSIS AND OXIDATIVE METABOLISM IN THE PERITONEAL MACROPHAGE

Cellular changes that accompany differentiation are not limited to the lysosomal system. Among the more striking changes are those in metabolic patterns (7). My colleagues and I have conducted a number of studies designed to investigate possible control mechanisms that might account for the differences (9). Pyruvate kinase and cytochrome oxidase activities of cultivated mouse peritoneal macrophages were examined. These enzymes were selected because prior studies had shown that they provide accurate indices for glycolytic capacity and mitochondrial oxygen utilization, respectively.

A continuous increase in pyruvate kinase and cytochrome oxidase activities was observed during in vitro differentiation of mouse peritoneal macrophages cultivated under aerobic conditions ($pO_2 \sim 140$ torr).

The effects of ambient oxygen tension on the energy metabolism of the cultivated macrophage were investigated. As shown in Table 2, both the rate and the magnitude of increase in pyruvate kinase activity were markedly greater in cells cultivated anaerobically ($pO_2 \sim 15$ torr) than in cells cultivated under aerobic conditions. By 48 h of anaerobiosis, peak enzyme specific activity

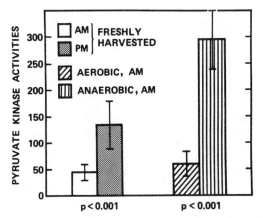

FIG. 1. Pyruvate kinase activity (micromoles of phosphoenolpyruvate converted to pyruvate per minute) in freshly explanted mouse alveolar and peritoneal macrophages and in alveolar macrophages cultivated aerobically and anaerobically. Values are means ± standard deviations.

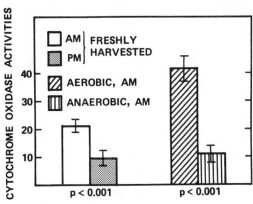

FIG. 2. Cytochrome oxidase activity (micromoles of cytochrome c oxidized per minute) in freshly explanted mouse alveolar and peritoneal macrophages and in alveolar macrophages cultivated aerobically and anaerobically. Values are means ± standard deviations.

was fivefold higher than that found in freshly explanted macrophages.

The pattern of cytochrome oxidase response for anaerobically cultivated cells differed markedly from that seen in aerobically maintained cells. Cytochrome oxidase activity for cells cultivated in 30% normal bovine serum increased by 40% under aerobic conditions and dropped by 40% under anaerobic conditions during 72 h of incubation.

To determine whether protein synthesis was required, the effect of cycloheximide on pyruvate kinase activity of cells cultured under aerobic and anaerobic conditions was studied. Cycloheximide (1.8×10^{-4} M) inhibited by 95% the increase in pyruvate kinase activity of cells cultured under aerobic or anaerobic conditions. Cycloheximide at the dosage employed reduced protein synthesis by 90% but did not reduce cell numbers.

ALVEOLAR MACROPHAGE ENERGY METABOLISM

Studies of macrophage energy metabolism were extended to include alveolar macrophages from the mouse (2). Freshly explanted alveolar macrophages showed a lesser dependence on glycolysis and a greater dependence on oxygen metabolism than did peritoneal macrophages. Pyruvate kinase activity of alveolar cells was 29% of that for peritoneal macrophages (Fig. 1). During aerobic cultivation of alveolar macrophages for 96 h, pyruvate kinase activity did not change significantly, whereas cytochrome oxi-

dase activity more than doubled (Fig. 2). In contrast, during anaerobic cultivation for 96 h, pyruvate kinase activity increased by 650% and cytochrome oxidase activity decreased by 50%.

During in vitro cultivation in an anaerobic environment, alveolar macrophages exhibited adaptive changes in response to environmental pO_2. During exposure to pO_2 of 15 torr, cytochrome oxidase activity decreased to values seen in freshly explanted peritoneal macrophages (Fig. 2). Phosphofructokinase activity increased to values that were not significantly different from those for peritoneal macrophages, and pyruvate kinase activities of chronically anaerobic alveolar macrophages were even higher than those found in peritoneal cells (2). Thus, during exposure to low oxygen tension the alveolar macrophages exhibited metabolic patterns more characteristic of peritoneal macrophages.

EFFECT OF ANAEROBIOSIS ON ENDOCYTIC ACTIVITY

The endocytic activity of macrophages cultivated aerobically and anaerobically was examined to determine whether oxygen availability in part regulated the functional correlate of differentiation. Phagocytosis of PVT particles by mouse alveolar macrophages increased threefold (under conditions producing maximal linear particle uptake) during 96 h of aerobic cultivation. Phagocytosis was also shown to be oxygen independent in freshly explanted cells. After aerobic cultivation of alveolar macrophages, however, uptake of particles was oxygen dependent. Uptake of particles under acutely anaerobic conditions for alveolar macrophages cultivated for 96 h in air was less than 50% of the uptake under aerobic conditions. Studies of the effect of anaerobiosis on phagocytosis showed that uptake of PVT particles by cells maintained in an environment with a pO_2 of ~15 torr increased to values virtually identical to those obtained with cells cultivated in air. In contrast, particle uptake for cells maintained under chronic anaerobiosis was not dependent upon oxygen availability as shown by identical rates of phagocytosis under acutely anaerobic or aerobic conditions.

It was of interest to examine the effects of oxygen availability on pinocytosis since phagocytosis and pinocytosis are variants of the more general process of endocytosis but have differing metabolic requirements. Pinocytosis by freshly explanted peritoneal macrophages, assessed by determining the rates of cellular uptake of [^{3}H]sucrose, was inhibited by anaerobiosis and inhibitors of oxygen phosphorylation. However, phagocytosis by these cells was oxygen independent. During in vitro cultivation for 96 h under aerobic conditions, pinocytosis increased by four- to fivefold. Comparative studies of pinocytic activity of alveolar macrophages maintained in chronic aerobic or anaerobic conditions were also performed. Pinocytosis increased significantly in cells maintained under chronic anaerobiosis (96 h) but was approximately half the maximal value achieved by cells cultivated aerobically. Additional studies showed that inhibition of pinocytosis produced by chronic hypoxia could be reversed by cultivating cells under aerobic conditions.

Evidence supporting the role of molecular oxygen as a metabolic regulator is provided by the finding that glycolytic capacity, as assessed by pyruvate kinase and phosphofructokinase activities, and mitochondrial oxygen utilization, as reflected by cytochrome oxidase activity, exhibited marked reciprocal changes in response to changes in oxygen concentration in the media. In aerobic culture conditions of 48- to 96-h duration, cytochrome oxidase activity increased 40 to 90%, whereas under anaerobic conditions, it decreased by nearly 40%. Conversely, in anaerobic culture conditions, pyruvate kinase and phosphofructokinase increased to levels three- to sixfold higher than those found in cells cultured aerobically.

These studies showed that alveolar macrophages are not end-stage cells but rather are capable of further functional and metabolic changes in response to environmental stimuli. With regard to sources of energy provision,

alveolar macrophages maintained under conditions of chronic hypoxia were converted to cells more closely resembling peritoneal macrophages.

The adaptive response of the macrophage to environmental oxygen may help to explain the metabolic differences observed in cells of the mononuclear phagocytic series at different body sites. By extrapolation from the in vitro findings to the situation in vivo, differentiation of macrophages in the relatively anaerobic environment of the peritoneal cavity would be expected to lead to a dependence on glycolysis for energy provision. Similarly, alveolar macrophages residing in an oxygen-rich environment would become more dependent on oxidative pathways for energy provision.

My observations have pathophysiological implications for understanding alveolar macrophage function in respiratory disease processes resulting in reduced alveolar pO_2. Acute hypoxia could depress oxygen-dependent energy provision and, thus, its energy-dependent functions, including phagocytosis and pinocytosis. With more chronic hypoxia, decreased molecular oxygen could alter alveolar macrophage energy metabolism enzymes, resulting in a more favorable pattern for energy provision in the diseased lung.

LITERATURE CITED

1. **Axline, S. G.** 1970. Functional biochemistry of the macrophage. Semin. Hematol. **7**:142–159.
2. **Axline, S. G., L. M. Simon, E. D. Robin, and E. L. Pesanti.** 1980. Effects of oxygen on metabolic patterns and endocytosis of macrophages, p. 1247–1269, *In* R. van Furth (ed.), Functional aspects of mononuclear phagocytes. Martinus Nijhoff, Boston.
3. **Bianco, D., F. M. Griffin, and S. C. Silverstein.** 1975. Studies of the macrophage complement receptor: alteration of receptor function upon macrophage activation. J. Exp. Med. **141**:1278–1290.
4. **Cohn, Z. A.** 1965. The metabolism and physiology of the mononuclear phagocytes, p. 323–353. *In* B. W. Zweifach, L. Grant, and R. T. McCluskey (ed.), The inflammatory process. Academic Press, Inc., New York.
5. **Cohn, Z. A., M. E. Fedorko, and J. G. Hirsch.** 1966. The in vitro differentiation of mononuclear phagocytes. V. The formation of macrophage lysosomes. J. Exp. Med. **123**:757–770.
6. **Langevoort, H. L., Z. A. Cohn, J. G. Hirsch, W. G. Spector, and R. van Furth.** 1970. The nomenclature of mononuclear phagocytic cells: proposal for a new classification, p. 1–18. *In* R. van Furth (ed.), Mononuclear phagocytes. Blackwell Scientific Publications, London.
7. **Oren, R. A., A. E. Farnham, K. Saito, E. Milofsky, and M. L. Karnovsky.** 1963. Metabolic patterns in three types of phagocytizing cells. J. Cell Biol. **17**:487–501.
8. **Osbaldiston, G. W., and R. J. Sullivan.** 1978. Cytochemical demonstration of esterases in peripheral blood leukocytes. Am. J. Vet. Res. **39**:683–685.
9. **Simon, L. M., E. D. Robin, J. R. Phillips, J. Acevedo, S. G. Axline, and J. Theodore.** 1977. Enzymatic basis for bioenergetic differences of alveolar versus peritoneal mac-

rophages and enzyme regulation by molecular O_2. J. Clin. Invest. **59:**443–448.

10. **van Furth, R.** 1980. Cells of the mononuclear phagocyte system: nomenclature in terms of sites and conditions, p. 1–40. *In* R. van Furth (ed.), Functional aspects of mononuclear phagocytes. Martinus Nijhoff, Boston.

11. **van Furth, R., and Z. A. Cohn.** 1968. The origin and kinetics of mononuclear phagocytes. J. Exp. Med. **128:**415–435.

12. **van Furth, R., Z. A. Cohn, J. G. Hirsch, J. H. Humphrey, W. G. Spector, and H. L. Langevoort.** 1972. The mononuclear phagocyte system. A new classification of macrophages, monocytes and their precursor cells. Bull. WHO **46:**845–851.

Activation of Macrophages

JOHN L. RYAN AND RICHARD K. ROOT

Infectious Disease Section, Yale University School of Medicine, New Haven, Connecticut 06510

The preceding paper described the events which characterize macrophage development, progressing from their origin in the bone marrow from a committed stem cell population, through their circulation as monocytes, their arrival at various tissue sites, and their further modification at these sites by the relative aerobic or anaerobic nature of the environment. The thrust of this presentation will be to describe some of the biochemical phenomena and mechanisms involved in the transition of these resident macrophages to cells capable of killing microbes or other foreign cells, i.e., the process known as macrophage activation. This transition of relatively quiescent resident phagocytes to activated cells is a complex event associated with multiple biochemical and biophysical changes in the cells themselves. An elegant series of experiments by Mackaness established the immunological basis of macrophage activation. He demonstrated that a specific antigenic stimulus triggers lymphocytes to release factors that transform the macrophage into a cell endowed with increased microbicidal capabilities (12). This dependence on immunological mechanisms partially distinguishes activated macrophages from other cells whose phagocytic function is increased above that of the resident population. These cells which are induced by the injection of an inflammatory stimulus such as thioglycolate or casein into the peritoneal cavity of animals have been termed elicited macrophages. Although similar to activated macrophages in some respects, elicited macrophages generally lack their augmented microbicidal and cytocidal properties (3).

Since the observations of Mackaness, the morphological and biochemical changes associated with macrophage activation have been worked out in considerable detail by Karnovsky, Cohn, and many others (4, 8). Details of the mechanism of the transition of the resident macrophage to an "angry" macrophage are still poorly understood despite these multiple investigations. Selected aspects of the activation process, with particular emphasis on what is known at the molecular level, will be reviewed here. Studies involving the lipids of macrophages will be emphasized, as this has become an area of particular interest for us. It is now clear that the transition of the resident macrophage to an activated macrophage is a multistep process with recognizable intermediate stages (15). This process has been reviewed in a series of concise, but thorough, essays (3, 7, 16).

MACROPHAGE LIPIDS

The ability of activated macrophages to function as microbe killers is in large part regulated by changes in the plasma membrane; this is the most dynamic of the organelles of the cell and undergoes rapid turnover even in the absence of a phagocytic stimulus. Alterations on the lipid content of macrophages have been associated with changes in functional activity. In fact, these changes in membrane lipids may represent some of the basic biochemical events associated with macrophage activation.

Hibbs and his co-workers have convincingly demonstrated that serum lipids may play a central role in modulating macrophage functions (1). Specific serum fractions were shown to modulate the tumoricidal capacity of *Mycobacterium bovis* BCG-activated macrophages. The specific lipid component of serum was not identified, but was associated with low-density lipoproteins. In experiments employing liposomes, it was demonstrated that enrichment of macrophage membranes with cholesterol resulted in inhibition of cytotoxic effects. Since cholesterol content is directly associated with decreased fluidity of the lipid bilayer, these experiments suggested that the fluid status of the membrane may be a critical parameter with respect to functional ability. This suggestion has been supported by a variety of experiments. For example, Lucas et al. assessed fluidity by the technique of fluorescence photobleaching and measured the diffusion coefficient of lipid in both resident and elicited macrophages (11). Lipid mobility was significantly enhanced in the elicited cells compared with the resident cells. Other studies have demonstrated that addition of unsaturated fatty acids to elicited macrophages enhanced their ability to ingest *Shigella* (21). More direct evidence for the critical importance of the lipid composition of the macrophage has been derived from the recent data of Schlager and

Meltzer (20). In this study, lymphokines were used to enhance macrophage cytotoxicity, and a detailed analysis of the lipid composition of the macrophage was correlated with their cytotoxic function at various times. Maximal unsaturated fatty acid content correlated with maximal cytotoxicity. Total cholesterol (free plus esterified) was decreased at the same time compared with a control. These data are consistent with the hypothesis that the fluid status of the plasma membrane may be altered by activating stimuli and determine functional ability.

We have investigated the potential role of glycosphingolipids as modulators of macrophage activation. Gangliosides were employed because of their ubiquitous presence as components of eucaryotic plasma membranes and their documented ability to serve as receptors for bacterial toxins, polypeptide hormones, and interferons (5). In addition, gangliosides have been found to regulate cellular proliferation in diverse systems. Gangliosides are amphipathic compounds and are characterized by the presence of sialic acid. Considerable variation exists with respect to the fatty acid and sugar composition of gangliosides from various sources. We have employed murine brain gangliosides and studied their effects on macrophage metabolism and enzyme secretion induced by bacterial lipopolysaccharides (LPS) and lymphocytes. These gangliosides are able to inhibit arginase production by cultured resident macrophages which have been stimulated with LPS (Fig. 1). Specific gangliosides are also able to inhibit lymphocyte-induced changes in use of glucose by the macrophage. When nonadherent spleen cells, composed of both B and T cells, are co-incubated with elicited macrophages, a striking increase in the rate of glucose metabolism is noted (19). This increase is blocked by co-cultivation with disialoganglioside and trisialoganglioside (Fig. 2). It is not yet clear from our studies whether the gangliosides are active because of their ability to alter the fluid state of the plasma membrane or whether they interfere with the binding of LPS to specific receptors. We do know that the gangliosides do not affect macrophage viability as assayed by trypan blue exclusion. Furthermore, it appears that the adherence properties of the macrophages are adversely affected by the presence of gangliosides. In earlier experiments we demonstrated that the ability of the macrophage to produce superoxide anion and hydrogen peroxide could be dependent on its physical state. Macrophages in monolayer could readily be triggered to release these products of oxidative metabolism whereas the same cells in suspension were much less active (2). Thus, the inhibi-

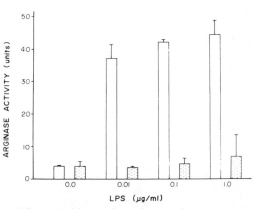

FIG. 1. Resident peritoneal macrophages were cultured for 72 h in medium containing 1% fetal calf serum and stimulated by various concentrations of LPS in both the presence (hatched bars) and absence (open bars) of 50 μg of murine brain disialoganglioside per ml. Each bar represents the mean ± standard deviation for triplicate cultures for arginase activity in the supernatant expressed as urea per minute per 10^6 cells.

tion of macrophage adherence by gangliosides may be correlated with the decrease in LPS and lymphocyte-stimulated events referred to above. This is an area of active investigation for us.

ROLE OF LYMPHOKINES

Lymphocyte products have been shown to be critically important for the development of bactericidal and cytocidal competence in the macrophage. Few of these lymphokines have been defined on a biochemical basis. Different molecules may stimulate different functions in macrophages, as was shown in a recent report from Meltzer's laboratory, where rickettsiacidal activity and tumoricidal activity were present in different molecular weight classes (13). The 45,000-molecular-weight peak which contained both activities corresponds to the molecular weight range found in many laboratories for the lymphokine MAF (macrophage-activating factor). This lymphokine confers upon the macrophages the ability to differentiate into a fully functional killer cell. A major problem in the biochemical analysis of MAF has been the difficulty in separating it from MIF (migration inhibitory factor), the lymphokine which has been the subject of elegant investigations in John David's laboratory for the past 15 years. Recently, however, these two important lymphokines have been separated by using isoelectric focusing in the presence of 4 M urea (6). This procedure has been used to prepare highly pure MAF, free

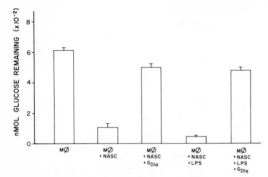

FIG. 2. Elicited (thioglycolate) mouse peritoneal macrophages were cultured ± nonadherent spleen cells (NASC), disialoganglioside (G_{Dia}), and LPS (*Escherichia coli* K235, phenol extracted). After 4 days, the amount of glucose consumed was assessed. Each bar represents the mean ± standard deviation for triplicate cultures of 10^5 macrophages. The NASC alone used negligible amounts of glucose (19).

from MIF activity. When this material was injected into mice by the intraperitoneal route, cytotoxic macrophages could be recovered (9).

The molecular basis for the interaction of these lymphokines with macrophages has also been partially elucidated. Sepharose beads with coupled gangliosides have been shown to absorb both MIF and MAF activity from lymphocyte supernatants (18). Both neuroaminidase and fucosidase have the ability to abrogate MIF activity. Thus, it appears that a fucose-containing ganglioside may be a critical receptor for certain lymphokines (10, 17).

SUMMARY

A complex series of events must occur to produce a functionally active killer cell from a circulating monocyte. Changes in the plasma membrane lipids may represent early steps in the activation process which are critical for the development of a fully functional state. The activation process results in the production of cells capable of ingesting vast quantities of material and of secreting hundreds of biologically active products. The cell has a characteristic appearance with a ruffled membrane and is capable of adhering tightly and spreading on surfaces. Its biochemical armamentarium includes hydrolytic and proteolytic enzymes as well as increased metabolic capacity and production of active products of oxygen reduction. This armamentarium endows the cell with microbicidal and cytocidal abilities so that it may function as a highly effective component of the host defense system. The complex nature of the process of macrophage activation and the criti-

cal interdependency of macrophages and lymphocytes in this process were underscored in a recent review by Nathan et al. (14). "Well over 50 sustained structural and functional alterations have been found to occur in mononuclear phagocytes in response to lymphocyte mediators. . . . only lymphocyte mediators have been shown to induce the full spectrum of changes associated with macrophage activation." Inroads to an understanding of this process on a molecular basis have been made, but it is evident that we have far to go before a complete understanding is achieved.

ACKNOWLEDGMENTS

The original research presented here was supported by the Veterans Administration.

We thank Carl Nathan for helpful discussions, Laurice Gobran for technical assistance, and Katherine Barrett for preparing the manuscript.

LITERATURE CITED

1. **Chapman, H. A., Jr., and J. B. Hibbs, Jr.** 1977. Modulation of macrophage tumoricidal capability by components of normal serum: a central role for lipid. Science **197:**282–285.
2. **Cohen, M. S., J. L. Ryan, and R. K. Root.** 1981. The oxidative metabolism of thioglycollate-elicited mouse peritoneal macrophages: the relationship between oxygen, superoxide and hydrogen peroxide and the effect of monolayer formation. J. Immunol. **127:**1007–1011.
3. **Cohn, Z.** 1978. The activation of mononuclear phagocytes: fact, fancy, and future. J. Immunol. **121:**813–816.
4. **Cohn, Z., and B. Benson.** 1965. The differentiation of mononuclear phagocytes. Morphology, cytochemistry, and biochemistry. J. Exp. Med. **121:**153–169.
5. **Fishman, P. H., and R. O. Brady.** 1976. Biosynthesis and function of gangliosides. Science **194:**906–915.
6. **Hubner, L., E. M. Kneip, H. Laukel, C. Sorg, H. Fischer, W. D. Gassel, K. Havemann, B. Kickhofen, M.-L. Lohmann-Mathes, A. Schimpl, and E. Wecker.** 1980. Chemical characterization of macrophage cytotoxicity factor, macrophage migration inhibiting factor, T-helper cell replacing factor, and colony stimulating factor from culture supernatants of conconvalin A stimulated murine spleen cells. Immunobiology **157:**169–178.
7. **Karnovsky, M. L., and J. K. Lazdins.** 1978. Biochemical criteria for activated macrophages. J. Immunol. **121:**809–813.
8. **Karnovsky, M. L., J. Lazdins, D. Drath, and A. Harper.** 1975. Biochemical characteristics of activated macrophages. Ann. N.Y. Acad. Sci. **256:**266–274.
9. **Lang, H., D. M. Sun, and M. L. Lohmann-Mathes.** 1981. In vivo activation of macrophages by the macrophage cytotoxicity factor (MCF, MAF). Immunobiology **159:**105.
10. **Liu, D. Y., K. D. Petschek, H. G. Remold, and J. R. David.** 1980. Role of sialic acid in the macrophage glycolipid receptor for MIF. J. Immunol. **124:**2042–2047.
11. **Lucas, D. L., P. Dragsten, D. M. Robinson, and C. A. Bowles.** 1981. Increased lateral diffusion of a lipid probe in the plasma membranes of elicited macrophages. RES J. Reticuloendothel. Soc. **30:**107–114.
12. **Mackaness, G. B.** 1964. The immunological basis of acquired cellular resistance. J. Exp. Med. **120:**105–120.
13. **Nacy, C. A., E. J. Leonard, and M. S. Meltzer.** 1981. Macrophages in resistance to rickettsial infections: char-

acterization of lymphokines that induce rickettsiacidal activity in macrophages. J. Immunol. **126**:204–207.

14. **Nathan, C. F., H. W. Murray, and Z. A. Cohn.** 1980. The macrophage as an effector cell. N. Engl. J. Med. **303**:622–626.

15. **Nathan, C. F., and R. K. Root.** 1977. Hydrogen peroxide release from mouse peritoneal macrophages. Dependence on sequential activation and triggering. J. Exp. Med. **146**:1648–1662.

16. **North, R. J.** 1978. The concept of the activated macrophage. J. Immunol. **121**:806–809.

17. **Poste, G., H. Allen, and K. L. Matta.** 1979. Cell surface receptors for lymphokines. II. Studies on the carbohydrate composition of the MIF receptor on macrophages using synthetic saccharides and plant lectins. Cell. Immunol. **44**:89–98.

18. **Poste, G., R. Kirsh, and I. J. Fidler.** 1979. Cell surface receptors for lymphokines. I. The possible role of glycolipids as receptors for macrophage migration inhibitory factor (MIF) and macrophage activation factor (MAF). Cell. Immunol. **44**:71–88.

19. **Ryan, J. L., and W. B. Yohe.** 1981. Lymphocyte mediation of lipopolysaccharide-stimulated macrophage metabolism. J. Immunol. **127**:912–916.

20. **Schlager, S. I., and M. S. Meltzer.** 1981. Macrophage activation for tumor cytotoxicity: analysis of cellular lipid and fatty acid content during lymphokine activation. RES J. Reticuloendothel. Soc. **29**:227–240.

21. **Schroitt, A. J., and R. Gallily.** 1979. Macrophage fatty acid composition and phagocytosis: effect of unsaturation on cellular phagocyte activity. Immunology **36**:199–205.

Role of the Activated Macrophage in Resistance to Infection

JACK S. REMINGTON

Department of Immunology and Infectious Diseases, Research Institute, Palo Alto Medical Foundation, Palo Alto, California 94301, and Division of Infectious Diseases, Department of Medicine, Stanford University School of Medicine, Stanford, California 94305

My discussion will focus on the importance of the macrophage in resistance to infection. Since the large volume of literature on this subject precludes an attempt at a review of this subject, I shall focus on certain qualitative aspects and rely heavily on results obtained with a number of different models in my laboratory.

The concept of cross-resistance to infection is seminal to the subject of my presentation. No discussion of this subject can be placed into proper perspective without referring to the stellar works of Mackaness and his colleagues (14). In their model, mice infected with a sublethal dose of *Listeria monocytogenes* resist subsequent challenge with a dose of *Listeria* which kills 100% of normal mice. Remarkably, they are also resistant to challenge with unrelated "intracellular" bacteria, such as *Salmonella typhimurium*. Peritoneal macrophages from the *Listeria*-infected mice were discovered to be the effector cells responsible for the observed resistance to *Listeria* and cross-resistance to *Salmonella*. Whereas normal macrophages support the intracellular multiplication of *Listeria* and *Salmonella*, macrophages from the *Listeria*-infected mice are activated to kill the bacteria. Interestingly, although the microbicidal effector function of the activated macrophage is nonspecific, the activation process is specific and is mediated by T lymphocytes. The observed resistance to infection and the activation of macrophages to kill persist only so long as the immunogenic stimulus is present—in this case, viable *Listeria* cells. Thereafter, resistance dissipates and is only recalled after challenge of the mice with specific antigen.

In 1967, I set out to determine whether the cross-resistance observed against unrelated bacterial species might reflect a common mechanism of resistance against all "intracellular" pathogens. The work stemmed from the fact that I had been working with the intracellular protozoan *Toxoplasma gondii*, against which cell-mediated immunity had been shown to be of paramount importance in both primary infection and subsequent homologous challenge (7). To test the hypothesis, Ruskin and I challenged mice chronically infected with *T. gondii* with a 75 to 100% lethal dose of *Listeria* or *Salmonella*. The percent survival in *T. gondii*-infected mice was significant when compared with controls (22). In another experiment, 80% of normal mice challenged with *Cryptococcus neoformans* died within 24 days, whereas less than 10% of mice with chronic *T. gondii* infection died (8). This was the first demonstration of resistance conferred by one organism against phylogenetically unrelated organisms. In Table 1 is a partial list of the intracellular pathogens (bacteria, fungi, viruses, and protozoa) against which infection with *T. gondii* confers resistance. Because infection with this protozoan provides an immunogenic stimulus virtually for the life of the infected mouse (organisms persist in the tissues), nonspecific resistance conferred by *T. gondii* is long-lived when compared with that conferred by *Listeria* (Table 2).

In seeking an explanation for the remarkable resistance to unrelated organisms observed in the *T. gondii*-infected mice, we discovered that their peritoneal macrophages were activated to inhibit or kill a variety of unrelated organisms (bacteria, fungi, and protozoa) (8, 21, 23) and tumor target cells (10, 11). We were unable to demonstrate any specificity in the microbicidal effector function of the activated macrophages (15).

T. gondii has proved to be a remarkable organism for the study of macrophage activation and killing; it is easily visualized in its intracellular habitat, and it multiplies readily within normal macrophages but is inhibited or killed by activated macrophages (3, 12, 13). When coated with specific antibodies, *T. gondii* is killed by normal macrophages (1, 3). The ponderous counting of intracellular organisms was overcome when McLeod found that radiolabeled uracil is preferentially taken up by multiplying intracellular *T. gondii*, but not by macrophages (Fig. 1) (16, 18). This has allowed for rapid quantitative studies of other organisms (e.g., *Nocardia*) within macrophages.

In 1970, Cline described the methodology for culture of human monocyte-derived macrophages (4). Anderson in our group employed Cline's method to study the intracellular fate of *T. gondii* within human macrophages (3). Normal human macrophages support multiplication of *T. gondii* but can be activated by lymphokines to inhibit or kill this organism (2). Thus, the observation in mouse macrophages was reproducible in their human counterpart. What remained an enigma were the observations that *T. gondii* is able to multiply within normal mouse and human macrophages which readily kill many other organisms, whereas human monocytes

readily kill *T. gondii* (17, 26). Wilson in our group found that, whereas human monocytes exhibit the normal oxidative burst during phagocytosis of *Candida albicans* or *T. gondii*, normal macrophages do so after phagocytosis of *Candida* but not of *Toxoplasma* (Fig. 2) (26). The fact that toxic oxygen radicals are produced by monocytes but not by macrophages phagocytizing *T. gondii* provides at least one explanation for the observation that these organisms (and probably other organisms as well) survive within

TABLE 1. Spectrum of nonspecific resistance to infection in protozoa-infected mice

Group	Pathogen
Bacteria	*Listeria monocytogenes*
	Salmonella typhimurium
	Brucella abortus
	Mycobacterium leprae
	Nocardia asteroides
Fungi	*Cryptococcus*
	Aspergillus
Protozoa	*Toxoplasma* or *Besnoitia*
	Trypanosoma cruzi
Viruses	Mengovirus
	Lactic dehydrogenase virus

TABLE 2. Results of mengovirus challenge in mice infected with *Toxoplasma*

Organism	Duration of infection (mo)	% Survival
Toxoplasma	1	90
	6	80
	16	80
Controls		7

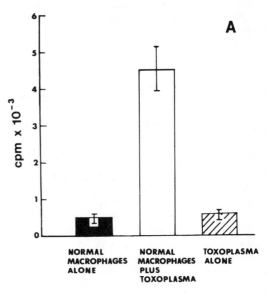

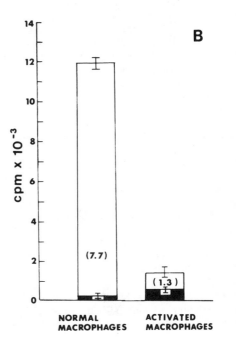

FIG. 1. (A) Incorporation of [5,6-³H]uracil into normal macrophages cultured alone, macrophages challenged with *Toxoplasma*, and *Toxoplasma* incubated alone. The same number of *Toxoplasma* cells from the same inoculum was employed for each culture. From McLeod et al. (18). (B) Effect of normal and activated mouse macrophages on nucleic acid synthesis of intracellular *Toxoplasma*. Solid bars, uninfected cultures; open bars, infected cultures. Counts per minute were determined 18 to 24 h after cultures were infected with *Toxoplasma*. Percent infected cells at 24 h was 6% for normal macrophages and 3% for activated macrophages. Numbers in parentheses are mean number of *Toxoplasma* cells per vacuole at 24 h in Giemsa-stained preparations. From McLeod et al. (18).

normal mouse and human macrophages. Of interest in this regard are our findings with *N. asteroides*. This bacterium rapidly destroys normal mouse macrophage monolayers but is inhibited and killed by activated mouse macrophages (5, 6). Interestingly, human monocytes and neutrophils phagocytize *Nocardia* but are unable to kill the bacterium in significant numbers. These studies, performed by Filice, were extended to determine whether the failure of killing by monocytes might be associated with a lack of the oxidative burst during phagocytosis of *Nocardia*. Chemiluminescence during phagocytosis of *Nocardia* was observed to be normal (5). Thus, survival of *Nocardia* intracellularly within monocytes is not due to failure of this organism to stimulate the oxidative burst but to as yet undefined mechanisms.

We and others (19, 20, 26) have accumulated sufficient data to suggest that in addition to toxic oxygen radicals (H_2O_2, hydroxyl radical, superoxide, singlet oxygen) nonoxidative mechanisms are involved in killing of a variety of organisms. This subject as it relates to the killing of *Candida* species is discussed by R. I. Lehrer and J. Fleischmann (this volume). In the case of *T. gondii*, this occurs in cells of patients with chronic granulomatous disease (26) and in a macrophage cell line which resembles chronic granulomatous disease cells (S. Sharma et al., manuscript in preparation).

Two additional concepts which place activated macrophages into proper perspective in relation to resistance of the host to infection are that the degree of activation varies depending on the anatomical location of the macrophages and that activated macrophages may differ in their functional characteristics. Ryning found that, at a time during which peritoneal macrophages of *T. gondii*-infected mice were activated to kill intracellular organisms, pulmonary macrophages were not (24). The pulmonary macrophages were found to be activated for only a relatively brief period (during a period when there was a remarkable inflammatory process in the lungs as a result of the host response to the infection). Thus, one cannot necessarily extrapolate data obtained from one anatomical site to another to define the state of activation of macrophages. This observation may explain the puzzling observation that mice injected with *Corynebacterium parvum* had peritoneal macrophages which were activated to kill *T. gondii* in vitro, yet the mice were not resistant to challenge with *T. gondii* in vivo (25).

In 1971, Hibbs in our group first reported that infection with *T. gondii* confers upon mice a remarkable resistance to autochthonous and

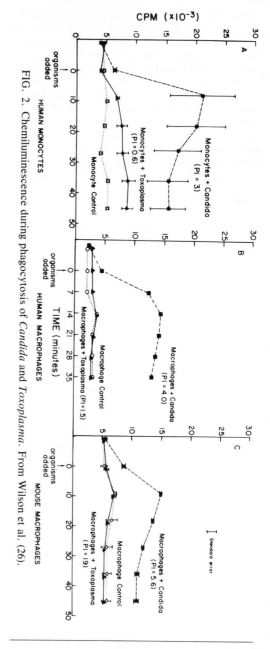

FIG. 2. Chemiluminescence during phagocytosis of *Candida* and *Toxoplasma*. From Wilson et al. (26).

transplantable tumors (9) and that "nonspecifically activated" (in contrast to specifically "armed") macrophages could kill tumor target cells (10, 11). This model was used to study and define what we found to be a dissociation of the effector function of activated macrophages obtained from a single source. For example, whereas activated macrophages from *T. gondii*-infected mice are both tumoricidal and microbicidal, macrophages from mice infected with *Trichina* are tumoricidal but are not microbicidal (for *T. gondii*). *C. parvum*-activated peritoneal macrophages act similarly to those of *T. gondii*-infected mice. There are a number of possible explanations for these observations, including different degrees of activation of macrophage populations from mice infected with different pathogens (different degrees of stimulus) as well as differences in the actual numbers of activated macrophages present in a given population of peritoneal macrophages. Thus, different subpopulations of effector macrophages with different functional capacities may exist. Macrophages which inhibit tumor cell DNA synthesis may be distinct from those which inhibit intracellular multiplication of organisms. The complete separation of functions which we observed may be more consistent with the existence of different functional populations of activated macrophages.

Finally, although activated macrophages may confer upon the host a remarkable degree of nonspecific resistance to infection and cancer, they rarely operate alone. Antibody (and monocytes and neutrophils) acting in concert with macrophages is important in resistance against most pathogens. Unfortunately, this fact is frequently omitted from discussion on this subject and has led to the erroneous concept that the presence of activated macrophages alone is sufficient for protection against intracellular pathogens per se. Perhaps this is true in a few in vivo models of infection, but in humans with intact specific and nonspecific immune mechanisms, resistance against intracellular pathogens is multifactorial.

ACKNOWLEDGMENT

This work was supported in part by Public Health Service grant AI04717 from the National Institute of Allergy and Infectious Diseases.

LITERATURE CITED

1. **Anderson, S. E., Jr., S. C. Bautista, and J. S. Remington.** 1976. Specific antibody-dependent killing of *Toxoplasma gondii* by normal macrophages. Clin. Exp. Immunol. **26**:375–380.
2. **Anderson, S. E., Jr., S. C. Bautista, and J. S. Remington.** 1976. Induction of resistance to *Toxoplasma gondii* in human macrophages by soluble lymphocyte products. J. Immunol. **117**:381–387.
3. **Anderson, S. E., Jr., and J. S. Remington.** 1974. Effect of normal and activated human macrophages on *Toxoplasma gondii*. J. Exp. Med. **139**:1154–1174.
4. **Cline, M. J.** 1970. Bactericidal activity of human macrophages: analysis of factors influencing the killing of *Listeria monocytogenes*. Infect. Immun. **2**:156–161.
5. **Filice, G. A., B. L. Beaman, J. A. Krick, and J. S. Remington.** 1980. Effects of human neutrophils and monocytes on *Nocardia asteroides*: failure of killing despite occur-

rence of the oxidative metabolic burst. J. Infect. Dis. **142**:432–438.
6. **Filice, G. A., B. L. Beaman, and J. S. Remington.** 1980. Effects of activated macrophages on *Nocardia asteroides*. Infect. Immun. **27**:643–649.
7. **Frenkel, J. K.** 1967. Adoptive immunity to intracellular infection. J. Immunol. **98**:1309–1319.
8. **Gentry, L. O., and J. S. Remington.** 1971. Resistance against *Cryptococcus* conferred by intracellular bacteria and protozoa. J. Infect. Dis. **123**:22–31.
9. **Hibbs, J. B., Jr., L. H. Lambert, Jr., and J. S. Remington.** 1971. Resistance to murine tumors conferred by chronic infection with intracellular protozoa, *Toxoplasma gondii* and *Besnoitia jellisoni*. J. Infect. Dis. **124**:587–592.
10. **Hibbs, J. B., Jr., L. H. Lambert, Jr., and J. S. Remington.** 1972. Possible role of macrophage mediated nonspecific cytotoxicity in tumor resistance. Nature (London) New Biol. **235**:48–50.
11. **Hibbs, J. B., Jr., L. H. Lambert, Jr., and J. S. Remington.** 1972. Control of carcinogenesis: a possible role for the activated macrophage. Science **177**:998–1000.
12. **Jones, T. C., and J. G. Hirsch.** 1972. The interaction between *Toxoplasma gondii* and mammalian cells. J. Exp. Med. **136**:1173–1194.
13. **Jones, T. C., L. Len, and J. G. Hirsch.** 1975. Assessment in vitro of immunity against *Toxoplasma gondii*. J. Exp. Med. **141**:466–482.
14. **Mackaness, G. B., and R. V. Blanden.** 1967. Cellular immunity. Prog. Allergy **11**:89–140.
15. **McLeod, R., and J. S. Remington.** 1977. Studies on the specificity of killing of intracellular pathogens by macrophages. Cell. Immunol. **34**:156–174.
16. **McLeod, R., and J. S. Remington.** 1977. A new method for evaluation of intracellular inhibition of multiplication or killing by mononuclear phagocytes. J. Immunol. **119**:1894–1897.
17. **McLeod, R., and J. S. Remington.** 1977. Influence of infection with Toxoplasma on macrophage function, and role of macrophages in resistance to Toxoplasma. Am. J. Trop. Med. Hyg. **26**:170–186.
18. **McLeod, R., and J. S. Remington.** 1979. A method to evaluate the capacity of monocytes and macrophages to inhibit multiplication of an intracellular pathogen. J. Immunol. Methods **27**:19–29.
19. **Murray, H. W., and Z. A. Cohn.** 1979. Macrophage oxygen-dependent antimicrobial activity. J. Exp. Med. **150**:938–949.
20. **Murray, H. W., C. W. Juangbhanich, C. F. Nathan, and Z. A. Cohn.** 1979. Macrophage oxygen-dependent antimicrobial activity. J. Exp. Med. **150**:950–964.
21. **Ruskin, J., J. McIntosh, and J. S. Remington.** 1969. Studies on the mechanisms of resistance to phylogenetically diverse intracellular organisms. J. Immunol. **103**:252–259.
22. **Ruskin, J., and J. S. Remington.** 1968. Immunity and intracellular infection: resistance to bacteria in mice infected with a protozoan. Science **160**:72–74.
23. **Ruskin, J., and J. S. Remington.** 1968. Role for the macrophage in acquired immunity to phylogenetically unrelated intracellular organisms. Antimicrob. Agents Chemother. **8**:474–477.
24. **Ryning, F. W., and J. S. Remington.** 1977. Effect of alveolar macrophages on *Toxoplasma gondii*. Infect. Immun. **18**:746–753.
25. **Swartzberg, J. E., J. L. Krahenbuhl, and J. S. Remington.** 1975. Dichotomy between macrophage activation and degree of protection against *Listeria monocytogenes* and *Toxoplasma gondii* in mice stimulated with *Corynebacterium parvum*. Infect. Immun. **12**:1037–1043.
26. **Wilson, C. B., V. Tsai, and J. S. Remington.** 1980. Failure to trigger the oxidative metabolic burst by normal macrophages: possible mechanism for survival of intracellular pathogens. J. Exp. Med. **151**:328–346.

Macrophage Antibacterial Defense

MARCUS A. HORWITZ

Laboratory of Cellular Physiology and Immunology, The Rockefeller University, New York, New York 10021

ROLES OF CELL-MEDIATED AND HUMORAL IMMUNITY IN HOST DEFENSE AGAINST INTRACELLULAR AND EXTRACELLULAR BACTERIA

Mononuclear phagocytes, activated by cellular immune mechanisms, are central to host defense against intracellular bacterial pathogens (*Mycobacterium tuberculosis, M. leprae, Listeria monocytogenes, Brucella* sp., *Salmonella* sp., *Francisella tularensis, Legionella pneumophila*), whereas polymorphonuclear leukocytes, in conjunction with antibody and complement, are central to host defense against extracellular bacterial pathogens. In vivo, mononuclear cells often dominate sites of infection with intracellular pathogens, whereas polymorphonuclear leukocytes often dominate the sites of infection with extracellular pathogens. In vitro, polymorphonuclear leukocytes phagocytize extracellular bacteria more efficiently than do monocytes (3). Humoral immunity is important for host defense against extracellular bacterial pathogens because most of these pathogens are encapsulated, and phagocytes cannot ingest and kill encapsulated extracellular bacteria unless these bacteria are coated with antibody and complement (2, 3).

MILESTONES IN UNDERSTANDING ACQUIRED CELL-MEDIATED IMMUNITY TO INFECTION

Many of the major milestones in understanding the role of cell-mediated immunity and macrophage activation in host defense were made by investigators studying bacterial pathogens, particularly *M. tuberculosis*. These investigations followed upon Koch's discovery of the etiological agent of tuberculosis in 1882, 100 years ago (8). In 1884, Metchnikoff pointed out the importance of mononuclear phagocytes in chronic infection (13). In 1891, Koch described cutaneous delayed-type hypersensitivity to tuberculin (9). A half century later, in 1945, Chase demonstrated that cutaneous delayed-type hypersensitivity to tuberculin was transferable by specifically sensitized lymphoid cells and not by serum (1). About the same time, in 1942, Lurie demonstrated the importance of the macrophage in immunity by demonstrating that macrophages harvested from vaccinated animals display an enhanced capacity to inhibit the multiplication of tubercle bacilli in vitro (11). Following Lurie's discovery, others showed that macrophages harvested from animals immunized with other intracellular pathogens, specifically *Brucella, Salmonella,* and *L. monocytogenes,* were similarly capable of expressing increased antimicrobial activity in vitro. Finally, Mackaness, in the 1960s, explained the functional link between Lurie's and Chase's results. He demonstrated that immunity to *L. monocytogenes* could be passively transferred to mice with sensitized lymphoid cells and that these cells, in the presence of the sensitizing organism or its antigens, conferred on macrophages the capacity to inhibit the multiplication of intracellular bacteria nonspecifically (12).

Soon after, in 1971, Simon and Sheagren reproduced Mackaness's result in vitro by demonstrating that sensitized lymphocytes in cell culture, in the presence of specific antigen, conferred on mononuclear phagocytes the capacity to inhibit intracellular bacteria nonspecifically (15). About this time, Lane and Unanue (10) and North (14) showed that the lymphoid cells responsible for transferring immunity to listeriosis and tuberculosis were T cells. Other investigators demonstrated that lymphocyte alteration of macrophage function is mediated by molecules called lymphokines.

L. PNEUMOPHILA MULTIPLIES INTRACELLULARLY IN MONOCYTES

I have studied the interaction of *L. pneumophila,* the agent of Legionnaires disease, with human leukocytes, and the roles of humoral and cell-mediated immunity in host defense against *L. pneumophila* (4–7). These studies have demonstrated that *L. pneumophila* is an intracellular bacterial pathogen (4). Virulent egg yolk-grown *L. pneumophila,* Philadelphia 1 strain, multiplies intracellularly in human blood monocytes and only intracellularly under tissue culture conditions. Neither polymorphonuclear leukocytes nor lymphocytes support *L. pneumophila* multiplication. Since the bacterium can multiply extracellularly on complex medium, *L. pneumophila* is a facultative intracellular parasite.

378

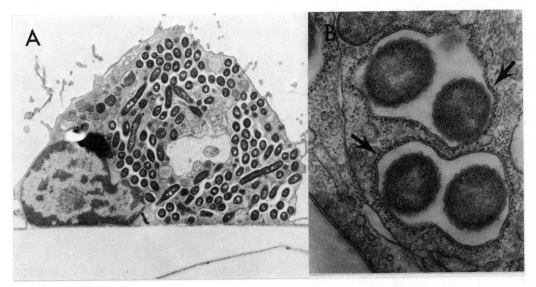

FIG. 1. Electron micrographs of human monocytes infected with *L. pneumophila*. (A) Monocyte heavily infected with *L. pneumophila*. ×5,400. (B) *L. pneumophila* inside a monocyte in membrane-bound vacuoles studded with ribosome-like structures. Each vacuole contains two bacilli. The ribosome-like structures (arrows) appear to be separated from the cytoplasmic face of the vacuolar membrane by a gap of ~10 nm. ×32,400. (Reprinted from reference 4.)

L. pneumophila multiplies in monocytes with a mid-log-phase doubling time of 2 h, a rate of growth that is faster than that observed in specialized media used to grow the organism. In monocyte cultures, the bacteria multiply until all the monocytes are destroyed.

Inside monocytes, all bacteria are found in membrane-bound cytoplasmic vacuoles (Fig. 1). Strikingly, the cytoplasmic sides of the membrane-bound vacuoles surrounding the *L. pneumophila* are studded with structures resembling monocyte ribosomes (Fig. 1B). This morphological feature has also been observed in infected alveolar macrophages in human lung tissue specimens obtained from patients with Legionnaires disease. *L. pneumophila* is evidently unique among bacterial pathogens in promoting the formation of these vacuoles, the origin and role of which are unknown.

ROLE OF HUMORAL IMMUNITY IN HOST DEFENSE AGAINST *L. PNEUMOPHILA*

Patients with Legionnaires disease respond to the infection by producing antibody against *L. pneumophila*. To assess the role of humoral immunity in host defense against *L. pneumophila*, I have studied the influence of antibody on the interactions between virulent *L. pneumophila* and human polymorphonuclear leukocytes, monocytes, and complement, in vitro, under antibiotic-free conditions (5, 6).

L. pneumophila in concentrations ranging from 10^3 to 10^6 colony-forming units per ml is completely resistant to the bactericidal effects of 0 to 50% fresh normal human serum, even in the presence of high concentrations of rabbit or human anti-*L. pneumophila* antibody. The resistance to complement is not due to a failure of the bacteria to fix complement. In the presence of antibody, the bacteria fix complement to their surface, but this does not result in the death of the bacteria.

Polymorphonuclear leukocytes efficiently phagocytize *L. pneumophila* only in the presence of both antibody and complement. Polymorphonuclear leukocytes also require both antibody and complement to kill any *L. pneumophila*; even then, polymorphonuclear leukocytes reduce colony-forming units of *L. pneumophila* by only 0.5 log under conditions in which they reduce colony-forming units of a serum-resistant strain of *Escherichia coli* by 2.5 logs.

Monocytes also require both antibody and complement to efficiently phagocytize *L. pneumophila* and to kill any *L. pneumophila* cells; even then, monocytes kill only a limited proportion (0.25 to 0.5 log) of an inoculum (6). The surviving bacteria multiply several logs in the monocytes and multiply as rapidly as when the bacteria enter monocytes in the absence of antibody.

These findings suggest that humoral immunity

may not be an effective host defense against *L. pneumophila*. Consequently, a vaccine that resulted only in antibody production against *L. pneumophila* may not be efficacious.

ROLE OF CELL-MEDIATED IMMUNITY IN HOST DEFENSE AGAINST *L. PNEUMOPHILA*

To investigate the role of cell-mediated immunity in host defense against *L. pneumophila*, I have examined the interaction between in vitro-activated human monocytes and virulent egg yolk-grown *L. pneumophila* (7).

Freshly explanted human monocytes activated by incubation with concanavalin A and human lymphocytes inhibit the intracellular multiplication of *L. pneumophila* (Fig. 2). Both concanavalin A and lymphocytes are required for activation. Concanavalin A is consistently maximally effective at ≥ 4 μg/ml.

Monocytes activated by incubation with cell-free filtered supernatant from concanavalin A-sensitized mononuclear cell cultures also inhibit the intracellular multiplication of *L. pneumophila*. The most potent supernatant is obtained from mononuclear cell cultures incubated with ≥ 15 μg of concanavalin A per ml for 48 h. The degree of monocyte inhibition of *L. pneumophila* multiplication is proportional to the length of time monocytes are preincubated with supernatant (48 h > 24 h > 12 h) and to the concentration of supernatant added (40% > 20% > 10% > 5%). Monocytes treated with supernatant daily are more inhibitory than monocytes treated initially only. With time in culture, monocytes progressively lose a limited degree of spontaneous inhibitory capacity and also their capacity to respond to supernatant with inhibition of *L. pneumophila* multiplication.

Supernatant-activated monocytes inhibit *L. pneumophila* multiplication in two ways. They phagocytize fewer bacteria, and they slow the rate of intracellular multiplication of bacteria that are internalized. As was the case with nonactivated monocytes, antibody has no effect on the rate of intracellular multiplication in supernatant-activated monocytes.

These findings show that human monocytes can be activated to inhibit the multiplication of *L. pneumophila*. Thus, inhibition of *L. pneumophila* multiplication is accomplished by activating the monocytes and not by coating the bacteria with antibody and complement. This indicates that cell-mediated immunity likely plays a major role in host defense against *L. pneumophila*, as it does against other intracellular pathogens.

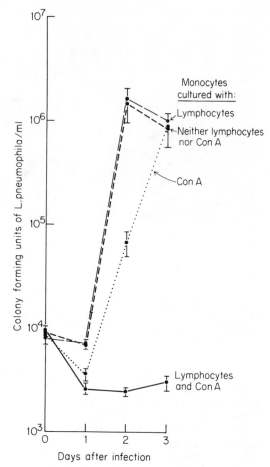

FIG. 2. Inhibition of the intracellular multiplication of *L. pneumophila* by monocytes activated by incubation with concanavalin A (ConA) and by human lymphocytes. Monocytes were cultured with lymphocytes only, ConA only, neither lymphocytes nor ConA, and both lymphocytes and ConA for 24 h, and were then infected with *L. pneumophila*. *L. pneumophila* multiplied, as determined by assaying colony-forming units in cultures daily after infection, in all monocyte cultures except those containing both ConA and lymphocytes, where multiplication was inhibited. (Reprinted from reference 7.)

UNANSWERED QUESTIONS

Much remains to be learned about the interactions between macrophages and intracellular bacteria. Here are but a few of the unanswered questions. First, since antibody and complement are not required, what ligands on the bacteria mediate their ingestion by phagocytes? Second, what are the special features of the phagosome that render it a hospitable environment for bacterial multiplication? Third, how do intracellular bacteria resist monocyte microbicidal activities? The answer to this question may vary among bacterial species, depending upon, for example, whether the organisms inhibit phagosome-lysosome fusion or can survive within the normally inhospitable milieu of the phagolysosome, or whether the organisms contain such protective enzymes as catalase and superoxide dismutase. Fourth, how do activated mononuclear phagocytes inhibit the multiplication of intracellular bacteria? Fifth, how do lymphokines activate mononuclear phagocytes?

ACKNOWLEDGMENTS

I am supported by the John A. Hartford Foundation, the American Cancer Society, the National Institutes of Health (Public Health Service grant AI-17254), and the Heiser Foundation for Research in Leprosy.

LITERATURE CITED

1. Chase, M. W. 1945. The cellular transfer of cutaneous hypersensitivity to tuberculin. Proc. Soc. Exp. Biol. Med. 59:134–135.

2. Horwitz, M. A. 1982. Phagocytosis of microorganisms. Rev. Infect. Dis. 4:104–123.

3. Horwitz, M. A., and S. C. Silverstein. 1980. Influence of the *Escherichia coli* capsule on complement fixation and on phagocytosis and killing by human phagocytes. J. Clin. Invest. 65:82–94.

4. Horwitz, M. A., and S. C. Silverstein. 1980. The Legionnaires' disease bacterium (*Legionella pneumophila*) multiplies intracellularly in human monocytes. J. Clin. Invest. 66:441–450.

5. Horwitz, M. A., and S. C. Silverstein. 1980. Interaction of the Legionnaires' disease bacterium (*Legionella pneumophila*) with human phagocytes. I. *L. pneumophila* resists killing by polymorphonuclear leukocytes, antibody, and complement. J. Exp. Med. 153:386–397.

6. Horwitz, M. A., and S. C. Silverstein. 1980. Interaction of the Legionnaires' disease bacterium (*Legionella pneumophila*) with human phagocytes. II. Antibody promotes binding of *L. pneumophila* to monocytes but does not inhibit intracellular multiplication. J. Exp. Med. 153:398–406.

7. Horwitz, M. A., and S. C. Silverstein. 1981. Activated human monocytes inhibit the intracellular multiplication of Legionnaires' disease bacteria. J. Exp. Med. 154:1618–1635.

8. Koch, R. 1882. The etiology of tuberculosis. Berl. Klin. Wochenschr. no. 15 (April 10, 1882), p. 221–230. (Reprinted in English *in* T. Brock [ed.], Milestones in microbiology [1975], p. 109–115. American Society for Microbiology, Washington, D.C.)

9. Koch, R. 1891. Forsetzung der mittheilung uber ein heilmittel gegen tuberkulose. Dtsch. Med. Wochenschr. 17:101.

10. Lane, F. C., and E. R. Unanue. 1972. Requirement of thymus (T) lymphocytes for resistance to listeriosis. J. Exp. Med. 135:1104–1112.

11. Lurie, M. B. 1942. Studies on the mechanisms of immunity in tuberculosis. The fate of tubercle bacilli ingested by mononuclear phagocytes derived from normal and immunized animals. J. Exp. Med. 75:247–268.

12. Mackaness, G. B. 1969. The influence of immunologically committed lymphoid cells on macrophage activity in vivo. J. Exp. Med. 129:973–992.

13. Metchnikoff, E. 1884. A disease of Daphnia caused by a yeast. A contribution to the theory of phagocytes as agents for attack on disease-causing organisms. Arch. Pathol. Anat. Physiol. Klin. Med. 96:177–195. (Reprinted in English *in* T. Brock [ed.], Milestones in microbiology [1975], p. 132–138. American Society for Microbiology, Washington, D.C.)

14. North, R. J. 1973. Importance of thymus-derived lymphocytes in cell-mediated immunity to infection. Cell. Immunol. 7:166–176.

15. Simon, H. B., and J. N. Sheagren. 1972. Enhancement of macrophage bactericidal capacity by antigenically stimulated immune lymphocytes. Cell. Immunol. 4:163–174.

Macrophage Activity Against Intracellular Protozoa

HENRY W. MURRAY

Division of International Medicine, The Cornell University Medical College, New York, New York 10021

By virtue of their broad phagocytic capacity, monocytes and macrophages are called upon to act against a wide spectrum of ingested microbial pathogens ranging from bacteria to fungi to protozoa. Among the latter microorganisms, interest has long been focused on a diverse group comprised of *Toxoplasma gondii*, *Leishmania*, and *Trypanosoma cruzi*, because of their ability to enter and replicate within host mononuclear phagocytes. In the initial stages of mammalian infection, unstimulated macrophages appear to provide a protective environment for the growth of these parasites; however, during the subsequent cell-mediated immune response, these same phagocytes become sufficiently activated to participate as key effector cells in their destruction (2). This paradoxical activity of macrophages has stimulated examination not only of how these protozoa initially evade the antimicrobial responses of certain macrophage populations, but also of what mechanisms activated macrophages utilize to successfully inhibit or kill intracellular parasites. This report briefly reviews experimental work which has been directed at these two key questions and summarizes recent data derived from the mouse peritoneal macrophage model which suggests an important role for oxygen-dependent mechanisms in macrophage antiprotozoal activity.

IN VITRO MODELS OF MACROPHAGE-PROTOZOAN INTERACTION

Unstimulated resident peritoneal macrophages from normal mice fail to display any activity against ingested *T. gondii* trophozoites, *T. cruzi* trypomastigotes, or *L. donovani* amastigotes, and 24 to 48 h after infection, toxoplasmas and *T. cruzi* freely replicate while *L. donovani* persists unharmed (7, 8, 10). The bulk (80 to 95%) of *T. cruzi* epimastigotes and *L. donovani* promastigotes, however, are readily destroyed by normal cells within 24 h (3, 10) (Table 1). In contrast, peritoneal cells from mice previously infected or immunized with viable or dead microbial agents, including *Mycobacterium bovis* BCG, *T. gondii, T. cruzi*, or *Corynebacterium parvum*, demonstrate enhanced antiprotozoal activity toward *T. cruzi* trypomastigotes and toxoplasmas (6, 7, 9). The most effective (micro-bicidal) cells appear to be those from mice immunized and later boosted intraperitoneally with specific antigen before cell harvest. Thus, macrophages from *T. gondii*-immune animals display in vitro toxoplasmastatic activity, whereas boosting induces a striking toxoplasmacidal capacity (7). Similarly, macrophages from *T. cruzi*- or BCG-infected and boosted mice kill 60 to 75% of ingested *T. cruzi* trypomastigotes within 24 h (9, 10). Paradoxically, however, macrophages from mice immunized and boosted with *T. gondii*, BCG, or *C. parvum* display no microbicidal activity against the intracellular amastigote form of *L. donovani* (8).

The complexities of macrophage-protozoan interaction are perhaps even better illustrated by normal cells activated in culture by exposure to soluble products of sensitized T lymphocytes (lymphokines). Resident macrophages pretreated with antigen- or mitogen-stimulated lymphokines readily destroy ingested *T. cruzi* trypomastigotes and *L. donovani* amastigotes and promastigotes (3, 8, 9), but exert no activity toward *T. gondii* (6) (Table 1). If an inflammatory agent such as heart infusion broth (a presumed source of endotoxin) is included with lymphokine, however, normal cells can be induced to display toxoplasmastatic activity (6).

Thus, despite the variations within each of these experimental systems, different macrophage populations can nevertheless be distinguished on the basis of their in vitro antiprotozoal activity. These include (i) macrophages which support parasite replication or persistence, (ii) those which display microbistatic activity, and (iii) cells which readily kill the majority of ingested organisms.

MACROPHAGE ANTIPROTOZOAL MECHANISMS

To begin to unravel the complex interaction of various macrophages with *T. gondii*, *Leishmania*, and *T. cruzi*, I and others have examined the role of oxygen-dependent antimicrobial mechanisms from the standpoint of both the parasite target and the effector macrophage. We sought to ascertain whether there was a correlation between protozoan intracellular fate and three particulate characteristics: (i) protozoan suscep-

TABLE 1. Macrophage in vitro antiprotozoal activity 24 to 48 h after infection[a]

Protozoan	Intracellular antiprotozoal activity		
	Normal resident	Lymphokine activated	In vivo activated[b]
T. gondii trophozoites	None	None	Cidal
T. cruzi trypomastigotes	None	Cidal	Cidal
T. cruzi epimastigotes	Cidal	—	—
L. donovani promastigotes	Cidal	Cidal	Cidal
L. donovani amastigotes	None	Cidal	None

[a] From references 3, 4, 6–10.

[b] Macrophages from mice immunized and boosted with T. gondii, T. cruzi, BCG, C. parvum, or L. donovani.

tibility to H_2O_2, (ii) the ability of parasites to evade triggering the macrophage oxidative burst during ingestion, and (iii) the magnitude of the macrophage respiratory burst.

Protozoan susceptibility to H_2O_2. Although T. gondii, T. cruzi, and L. donovani display strikingly different susceptibilities to enzymatically generated H_2O_2 (3, 9, 11; Y. Tanaka et al., Fed. Proc. **40**:760, 1981) (Table 1), resistance to H_2O_2 appears to correlate with their fate within normal resident macrophages. At first glance, the differences between the 50% lethal dose of H_2O_2 for T. cruzi epimastigotes versus trypomastigotes and for L. donovani amastigotes versus promastigotes do not appear to be impressive; however, at low fluxes of H_2O_2, 80 to 100% of epimastigotes and promastigotes are lysed while trypomastigotes and amastigotes remain virtually unaffected (3, 5, 9). It should also be noted that T. gondii contains abundant endogenous levels of the H_2O_2 scavengers, catalase and glutathione peroxidase, which may explain toxoplasma resistance to H_2O_2 (3). Leishmania and T. cruzi, however, possess little or no activity of either enzyme (3, 5).

Macrophage oxidative capacity. The intrinsic capacity of the various macrophage populations to generate oxygen intermediates has been assessed after triggering with the soluble surface-active agent phorbol myristate acetate or ingestible stimuli such as opsonized zymosan. Cells activated in vivo by immunological microbial agents display a marked enhancement of oxidative activity and release 10 to 20 times more O_2^- and H_2O_2 than normal resident macrophages (1, 6, 7, 9). Lymphokine-treated cells also release more O_2^- and H_2O_2 than normal macrophages (6, 9). Thus, macrophage microbicidal activity against T. gondii, T. cruzi, and L. donovani appears to be paralleled by an enhanced capacity to generate oxygen intermediates.

Triggering of the macrophage oxidative burst. As judged by the qualitative reduction of nitroblue tetrazolium, a reaction which is mostly O_2^- dependent, there also seems to be a correlation between the capacity of a protozoan to evade stimulating the macrophage oxidative burst during ingestion and its ability to successfully parasitize the susceptible macrophage (3–6, 11) (Tables 2 and 3). An exception appears to be in the interaction of L. donovani amastigotes with normal cells (Table 2), 50% of which respond to amastigote ingestion but do not kill amastigotes (5, 8) (Table 1). However, it should be noted that in quantitative assays, these normal macrophages generate only scant amounts of O_2^- and H_2O_2 (7, 9). The data in Table 3 also indicate that L. donovani amastigotes, but not T. gondii

TABLE 2. Correlates of protozoan intracellular fate within normal and oxidatively deficient macrophages[a]

Protozoan	LD50 of H_2O_2 (nmol/min)[b]	Normal macrophages		J774G8 cells	
		% Cells NBT +	Intracellular fate	% Cells NBT +	Intracellular fate
T. gondii	20	16	Replicates	8	Replicates
L. donovani					
Promastigotes	1.5	91	Killed	12	Replicates
Amastigotes	8.0	49	Persists	9	Replicates
T. cruzi					
Epimastigotes	6.5–7.7	84	Killed	21	Persists
Trypomastigotes	9.4–14.7	—	Replicates	—	—

[a] From references 3–5, 8–10, and Tanaka et al. (Fed. Proc. **40**:760, 1981).

[b] Fluxes of H_2O_2-generated enzymatically by glucose oxidase.

TABLE 3. Protozoan interaction with activated (microbicidal) macrophages which generate high levels of O_2^- and H_2O_2[a]

Protozoan	Lymphokine-activated		In vivo activated	
	% Cells NBT +	Fate	% Cells NBT +	Fate
T. gondii	21	Replicates	88	Killed
L. donovani amastigotes	90	Killed	24	Persists
L. donovani promastigotes	91	Killed	89	Killed

[a] From references 5–8. NBT+, Qualitative nitro-blue tetrazolium reduction.

or *L. donovani* promastigotes, readily evade triggering the oxidative burst of in vivo-activated macrophages—cells which are primed to generate high levels of microbicidal intermediates (3, 5–7) and, hence, are likely to destroy them.

Role of oxygen intermediates in macrophage antiprotozoal activity. To provide evidence that toxic oxygen intermediates participate in intracellular killing, the ability of macrophages to generate O_2^- and H_2O_2 was impaired by pretreating microbicidal cells before infection with (i) soluble scavengers of O_2^- and H_2O_2 (e.g., superoxide dismutase and catalase), (ii) medium free from glucose, or (iii) phorbol myristate acetate. All three manipulations render macrophages oxidatively hyporesponsive to subsequent phagocytic stimuli and inhibit nitroblue tetrazolium reduction and O_2^- and H_2O_2 generation (3–7). In parallel, these treatments significantly decrease or abolish the killing of *T. cruzi* epimastigotes and *L. donovani* promastigotes by normal macrophages, the inhibition of *T. gondii* replication and the killing of *L. donovani* amastigotes by lymphokine-activated cells, and the killing of toxoplasmas by in vivo-activated macrophages (3–7).

We have also examined protozoan fate within phagocytes derived from the J774 macrophage cell line which are inherently deficient in the production of O_2^- and H_2O_2 (4). As shown in Table 2, these J774G8 cells (which release 10-fold less H_2O_2 than normal peritoneal macrophages [4]) fail to respond to parasite ingestion with nitroblue tetrazolium reduction and display considerably less or no antiprotozoal activity when compared with that of oxidatively intact normal macrophages (4, 5).

IMPLICATIONS

Although these studies reemphasize the complexities and heterogeneity of the macrophage antiprotozoal response, observations derived

from each of the models also suggest a key role for oxygen-dependent mechanisms in those cells capable of inhibiting or killing intracellular parasites. In addition, these findings reemphasize the need to focus attention on both the microbial target and the effector macrophage when considering the outcome of phagocyte-protozoan interaction. Thus, from the standpoint of oxidative microbicidal mechanisms, there appear to be at least three key determinants of parasite intracellular fate: susceptibility to H_2O_2, the ability to evade triggering the macrophage oxidative burst, and the intrinsic capacity of various macrophages to generate toxic oxygen intermediates.

ACKNOWLEDGMENTS

This work was supported by Public Health Service research grant AI-16963 from the National Institute of Allergy and Infectious Diseases and by grant RF-78021 from the Rockefeller Foundation. I am recipient of a Career Development Award in Geographic Medicine from the Rockefeller Foundation.

LITERATURE CITED

1. **Badwey, J. A., and M. L. Karnovsky.** 1980. Active oxygen species and the functions of phagocytic leukocytes. Annu. Rev. Biochem. **49:**695–719.
2. **Jones, T. C.** 1981. Interactions between murine macrophages and obligate intracellular protozoa. Am. J. Pathol. **102:**127–139.
3. **Murray, H. W.** 1981. Susceptibility of *Leishmania* to oxygen intermediates and killing by normal macrophages. J. Exp. Med. **153:**1302–1315.
4. **Murray, H. W.** 1981. Interaction of *Leishmania* with a macrophage cell line. Correlation between intracellular killing and the generation of oxygen intermediates. J. Exp. Med. **153:**1690–1695.
5. **Murray, H. W.** 1982. Cell-mediated immune response in experimental visceral leishmeniasis. II. Oxidative killing of *Leishmania donovani* amastigotes. J. Immunol., in press.
6. **Murray, H. W., and Z. A. Cohn.** 1980. Macrophage oxygen-dependent antimicrobial activity. II. Enhanced oxidative metabolism as an expression of macrophage activation. J. Exp. Med. **152:**1596–1609.
7. **Murray, H. W., C. W. Juangbhanich, C. F. Nathan, and Z. A. Cohn.** 1979. Macrophage oxygen-dependent antimicrobial activity. II. The role of oxygen intermediates. J. Exp. Med. **150:**950–964.
8. **Murray, H. W., H. Masur, and J. S. Keithly.** 1982. Cell-mediated immune response in experimental visceral leishmaniasis. I. Correlation between resistance to *Leishmania donovani* and lymphokine-generating capacity. J. Immunol., in press.
9. **Nathan, C. F., N. Nogueira, C. Juangbhanich, J. Ellis, and Z. A. Cohn.** 1979. Activation of macrophages in vivo and in vitro. Correlation between hydrogen peroxide release and killing of *Trypanosoma cruzi*. J. Exp. Med. **149:**1056–1069.
10. **Nogueira, N., S. Gordon, and Z. Cohn.** 1977. *Trypanosoma cruzi*: modification of macrophage function during infection. J. Exp. Med. **146:**157–171.
11. **Wilson, C. B., V. Tsai, and J. S. Remington.** 1980. Failure to trigger the oxidative burst by normal macrophages. Possible mechanism for survival of intracellular pathogens. J. Exp. Med. **151:**328–344.

Antifungal Defense by Macrophages[1]

ROBERT I. LEHRER AND JACOB FLEISCHMANN

Divisions of Hematology/Oncology and Infectious Diseases, Department of Medicine, UCLA School of Medicine, The Center for the Health Sciences, Los Angeles, California 90024

Mononcuclear phagocytes are equipped to play a significant role in antifungal defenses. Some, such as alveolar macrophages, are among the first phagocytic leukocytes to encounter fungal cells or spores that infect the host via the respiratory tract. Others, such as hepatic Kupffer cells or other components of the reticuloendothelial system may play significant roles in the clearance and containment of fungemia. Moreover, circulating blood monocytes constitute a constantly renewed pool of juvenile mononuclear phagocytes that can emigrate to tissue sites of fungal infection, guided by chemoattractants emitted by the organism or generated by interactions of serum components with the infecting fungi.

For several years our laboratory has studied the fungicidal mechanisms of various types of phagocytes, especially those effective against various *Candida* species. In this paper we briefly review these studies and some related work from other laboratories. A more extensive review of this topic will appear in the near future (R. I. Lehrer and J. Fleischmann, in preparation).

ANTIFUNGAL PROPERTIES OF BLOOD MONOCYTES

Human beings have provided the chief source of blood for the study of monocyte function, a fact probably attributable to their large size, relative to mice, and agreeable nature, relative to bears. Since there may be significant intraspecies differences in the biochemical composition of neutrophils or monocytes (16), this is probably a fortunate circumstance for students of human infection. Like their neutrophil "cousins," normal human monocytes possess myeloperoxidase, lysozyme (muramidase), and the ability to generate O_2^- (superoxide anion), H_2O_2, and other reactive species derived from oxygen. They appear to lack cathepsin G (un-

published data), a chymotrypsin-like cationic protein that may contribute to the microbicidal performance of neutrophils (4, 12).

Human monocytes can ingest and kill yeast-phase *C. albicans*, requiring both myeloperoxidase and hydrogen peroxide to accomplish the task effectively (7). Other *Candida* species, such as *C. parapsilosis* and *C. pseudotropicalis* are killed quite effectively by monocytes that lack myeloperoxidase, indicating that some *Candida* species are susceptible to myeloperoxidase-independent mechanisms (7). These alternative candidacidal mechanisms appear to be dependent on reactive oxygen derivatives, for monocytes from children with chronic granulomatous disease, deficient in their ability to generate these reactants, kill *C. parapsilosis* and *C. pseudotropicalis* poorly (7).

Lysozyme, a prominent constituent of monocytes and macrophages, can itself adversely affect the structural integrity and viability of *Coccidioides immitis* (3). Whether its limited antifungal properties are enhanced by H_2O_2 and ascorbate (11), or other radical-generating systems, as was reported in studies with gram-negative bacteria, is unknown.

SOME PROPERTIES OF TISSUE MACROPHAGES

Although peritoneal and alveolar macrophage populations may derive from a common stem cell (19), the two types of macrophages show substantial differences in their energy metabolism and biochemical composition. For example, alveolar macrophages typically contain much higher concentrations of lysozyme and certain other hydrolytic enzymes than do peritoneal macrophages (2). Moreover, whereas peritoneal macrophages derive their energy for phagocytosis primarily from glycolytic metabolism, alveolar macrophages are more dependent on oxidative phosphorylation (6). Alveolar and peritoneal macrophages are both able to generate O_2^-, H_2O_2, and other active molecular species derived from oxygen (1), but myeloperoxidase is typically lacking from these cells (8).

[1] Publication no. 38 of the Collaborative California Universities-Mycology Research Unit.

ANTIFUNGAL ACTIVITY OF TISSUE MACROPHAGES

Sasada and Johnston examined the ability of murine peritoneal macrophages to kill *C. albicans* and *C. parapsilosis* and reported that resident (unstimulated) macrophages exerted less candidacidal activity than did *Mycobacterium bovis* BCG- or lipopolysaccharide-elicited cells (17). *C. albicans* was less susceptible than *C. parapsilosis* (15 to 30% versus 70 to 90% killed in 3 h). Candidacidal activity by resident or elicited macrophages was partially inhibited by scavengers of oxygen radicals such as O_2^- (superoxide anion) and OH· (hydroxyl radical), suggesting that candidacidal activity was dependent on the generation of such oxygen metabolites by the macrophages. *C. parapsilosis* elicited a greater oxidative metabolic response from macrophages than did *C. albicans*, possibly contributing to the relative susceptibility of the former species to intracellular destruction by peritoneal macrophages.

Although earlier investigators had failed to observe killing of various *Candida* species by resident murine peritoneal macrophages, possibly this was attributable to the use of less sensitive analytic methods (13, 18).

Other published reports (5) suggested that cultured murine peritoneal macrophages have little ability to restrict the intracellular or extracellular multiplication of *Blastomyces dermatitidis*, *Cryptococcus neoformans*, *Histoplasma capsulatum*, and *Saccharomyces cerevisiae*. In contrast, some isolates of *C. pseudotropicalis*, *C. parapsilosis*, *T. glabrata*, *C. guilliermondii*, and *C. krusei* have been reported to be killed or significantly restrained by such macrophages.

We recently reported that resident rabbit alveolar macrophages killed *C. albicans* (approximately 30% in 2.5 h) more effectively than did resident peritoneal macrophages (approximately 15% in 2.5 h) and that peritoneal and alveolar macrophages from animals pretreated with an intravenous injection of complete Freund adjuvant manifested enhanced and relatively equal candidacidal activity (9). Fractionated rabbit alveolar macrophages were found to contain two unusual, low-molecular-weight peptides that we called MCP 1 and MCP 2, names derived from the phrase "macrophage cationic peptide" (14). Highly cationic, each peptide was unusually rich in arginine (MCP 1, 25.5 mol%; MCP 2, 14.9 mol%) and cysteine (MCP 1, 18.7 mol%; MCP 2, 9.8 mol%) (15). Recent studies, to be reported in detail elsewhere (M. E. Selsted and R. I. Lehrer, submitted for publication), demonstrated that each peptide consisted of 32 amino acids, with molecular weights approximately 3,400.

Both peptides lacked carbohydrate, free sulfhydryl groups, and any aromatic amino acids. Abundant in rabbit lung macrophages, the peptides constituted 1.8% of the total protein content of Freund adjuvant-elicited cells (10). Little or no MCP 1 or MCP 2 has been detected in peritoneal resident or complete Freund adjuvant-elicited rabbit peritoneal macrophages.

Under defined in vitro conditions, MCP 1 and MCP 2 killed many microorganisms, being especially active against fungi such as *C. albicans*, *C. parapsilosis*, and *C. neoformans*. They killed certain gram-positive organisms, including *Listeria monocytogenes*, *Streptococcus faecalis*, and *Bacillus subtilis*, although higher peptide concentrations (approximately 20 μg/ml) were required. The peptides were relatively ineffective against gram-negative organisms, including *Escherichia coli* and *Salmonella typhimurium*.

Our exploration of the functional significance of MCP 1 and MCP 2 in host-defense mechanisms against fungi is still incomplete, and we cannot yet assign definite roles for them in macrophage and pulmonary defense mechanisms. The ability of these peptides to kill various bacteria and fungi suggests that they may play a significant role. Further studies, including attempts to determine whether analogous natural peptide antibiotics exist in macrophages of humans or other species, might prove rewarding.

ACKNOWLEDGMENTS

This work was supported by Public Health Service grants AI 16005 and AI 16252 from the National Institute of Allergy and Infectious Diseases.

LITERATURE CITED

1. **Badwey, J. A., and M. L. Karnovsky.** 1980. Active oxygen species and the functions of phagocytic leukocytes. Annu. Rev. Biochem. **49**:695–726.
2. **Cohn, Z. A., and E. Wiener.** 1963. The comparative hydrolases of macrophages. I. Comparative enzymology, isolation and properties. J. Exp. Med. **118**:991–1008.
3. **Collins, M. S., and D. Pappagianis.** 1974. Inhibition by lysozyme of growth of the spherule phase of *Coccidioides immitis* in vitro. Infect. Immun. **10**:616–623.
4. **Drazin, R. E., and R. I. Lehrer.** 1977. Fungicidal properties of a chymotrypsin-like cationic protein from human neutrophils: adsorption to *Candida parapsilosis*. Infect. Immun. **17**:382–388.
5. **Howard, D. H.** 1981. Mechanisms of resistance in the systemic mycoses, p. 475–494. In A. J. Nahmias and R. O'Reilly (ed.), Immunology of human infection (part I). Plenum Publishing Corp., New York.
6. **Karnovsky, M. L.** 1962. Metabolic basis of phagocytic activity. Physiol. Rev. **42**:143–168.
7. **Lehrer, R. I.** 1975. The fungicidal mechanisms of human monocytes. I. Evidence for myeloperoxidase-linked and myeloperoxidase-independent candidacidal mechanisms. J. Clin. Invest. **55**:338–346.
8. **Lehrer, R. I.** 1978. Metabolism and microbicidal function,

p. 79–82. *In* M. J. Cline (moderator), Monocytes and macrophages: function and diseases. Ann. Intern. Med. **88**:78–88.

9. **Lehrer, R. I., L. G. Ferrari, J. Patterson-Delafield, and T. Sorrell.** 1980. Fungicidal activity of rabbit alveolar and peritoneal macrophages against *Candida albicans*. Infect. Immun. **28**:1001–1008.

10. **Lehrer, R. I., D. Szklarek, M. E. Selsted, and J. Fleischmann.** 1981. Increased content of microbicidal cationic peptides in rabbit alveolar macrophages elicited by complete Freund adjuvant. Infect. Immun. **33**:775–778.

11. **Miller, T. E.** 1969. Killing and lysis of gram-negative bacteria through the synergistic effect of hydrogen peroxide, ascorbic acid and lysozyme. J. Bacteriol. **98**:949–955.

12. **Odeberg, H., and I. Olsson.** 1975. Antibacterial activity of cationic proteins from human granulocytes. J. Clin. Invest. **56**:1118–1124.

13. **Ozato, K., and I. Uesaka.** 1974. The role of macrophages in *Candida albicans* infection *in vitro*. Jpn. J. Microbiol. **18**:29–35.

14. **Patterson-Delafield, J., R. J. Martinez, and R. I. Lehrer.**

1980. Microbicidal cationic proteins in rabbit alveolar macrophages: a potential host-defense mechanism. Infect. Immun. **30**:180–192.

15. **Patterson-Delafield, J., D. Szklarek, R. J. Martinez, and R. I. Lehrer.** 1980. Microbicidal cationic proteins of rabbit alveolar macrophages: amino acid composition and functional attributes. Infect. Immun. **31**:723–731.

16. **Rausch, P. G., and T. G. Moore.** 1975. Granule enzymes of polymorphonuclear neutrophils: a phylogenetic comparison. Blood **46**:913–919.

17. **Sasada, M., and R. B. Johnston, Jr.** 1980. Macrophage microbicidal activity. Correlation between phagocytosis-associated oxidative metabolism and the killing of *Candida* by macrophages. J. Exp. Med. **152**:85–98.

18. **Stanley, V. C., and R. Hurley.** 1969. The growth of *Candida* species in cultures of mouse peritoneal macrophages. J. Pathol. **97**:357–366.

19. **Van Furth, R.** 1975. Modulation of monocyte production, p. 161–172. *In* R. Van Furth (ed.), Mononuclear phagocytes in immunity, infection and pathology. Blackwell Scientific Publications, Oxford.

V. CELL SURFACE RECEPTORS INVOLVED IN THE IMMUNE SYSTEM

(from a Symposium at the 81st Annual Meeting of the American Society for Microbiology, held 1–6 March 1981 in Dallas, Texas)

Introduction

EDGAR E. HANNA

Laboratory of Molecular Genetics, National Institute of Child Health and Human Development, Bethesda, Maryland 20205

A prevalent hypothesis among immunobiologists and cell biologists in general is that cells communicate with each other and their environment by way of cell surface receptors. In the case of the immunocyte, it is a prerequisite that receptors be highly specific for their ligands. This appears to be true whether the immunocyte synthesizes the particular receptor or acquires it semipassively. (The term immunocyte is used here to represent any cell type known to be involved in the immune system, e.g., B lymphocytes, T lymphocytes, and macrophages.)

B-CELL RECEPTOR

A long-standing hypothesis about which there is much consensus is that the precursor antibody-synthesizing cell (B cell) makes and uses, as its receptor for antigen, a molecule which is very similar if not identical to the antigen-binding site or variable region (V region) of immunoglobulins.

T-CELL RECEPTOR

It was, unfortunately, premature to include a presentation relevant to the T-cell receptor(s) in this symposium. Because of this and its high relevancy, I am compelled to comment in a minimal way about the concepts on the very interesting but very elusive T-cell receptor. Our understanding of the nature of the receptor(s) of thymus-derived regulatory cells and effector, or cytotoxic, cells (T cells) is much more deficient than it is for B cells and macrophages. The hypotheses, thoughts, and, indeed, requirements are that the T-cell receptor(s) be similar to its B-cell companion. That is, because T-cell responses are at least as highly specific for ligand as are B-cell products, the T-cell receptor should be similar to the V-region gene product of B cells. There are at least two prominent and immediate ideas with some support in this respect. The most comfortable and rational hypothesis is that the T-cell receptor is a V-region gene product of the T cell. An alternative hypothesis, which cannot be excluded until the former is ascertained, is that the T cell makes a receptor (Fc receptor) which binds immunoglobulin at the rear (Fc region), thus acquiring its working receptor. Because of this dilemma and other associated observations, the approach in many laboratories (1–9) has been to construct or to isolate monoclonal T-cell lines that grow and function perpetually in immune cell culture. Together with Misfeldt (2, 3), I have recently constructed a library of T-cell lines by use of the hybridoma technology. Among the lines studied so far, representatives of both helper and suppressor phenotypes have been identified. Interestingly, we have observed that some of our cloned T-cell lines express an Fc receptor for immunoglobulin and some do not. All lines tested to date express a V_H-region gene product at their cell surfaces. Thus, these approaches (1–9) should facilitate a clearer understanding of the T-cell receptor at both the genotypic and the phenotypic levels very soon.

MACROPHAGE RECEPTORS

Macrophages are known to possess Fc and complement (C3b) receptors. The availability of macrophage cell lines and monoclonal antibodies have facilitated progress in the isolation and chemical characterization of these receptors. Moreover, our understanding of the regulatory mechanisms involving the macrophage receptors has improved.

ACKNOWLEDGMENTS

I am grateful to Rose Mage for co-convening this symposium with me and to her and all the other contributors for their participation. I thank Terri Broderick for secretarial assistance during the organization of the symposium, and Natalie Hanna, my daughter, for typing this section.

LITERATURE CITED

1. **Kappler, J. W., B. Skidmore, J. White, and P. Marrack.** 1981. Antigen-inducible, H-2-restricted, interleukin-2-producing T-cell hybridomas. J. Exp. Med. **153:**1198–1214.
2. **Misfeldt, M. L., and E. E. Hanna.** 1981. Complementation of the plaque-forming cell responses of T-cell-deficient *nude* mice by a T-cell hybridoma. Proc. Natl. Acad. Sci. U.S.A. **78:**1813–1817.
3. **Misfeldt, M. L., and E. E. Hanna.** 1982. Suppressor T-cell hybridomas that exhibit various capacities to negatively regulate PFC responses in a T-cell dependent mouse model. Cell. Immunol. **66:**180–189.
4. **Nabel, G., L. R. Bucalo, J. Allard, H. Wigzell, and H.**

Cantor. 1981. Multiple activities of a cloned cell line mediating natural killer cell function. J. Exp. Med. **153:**1582–1591.

5. **Pacifico, A., and J. D. Capra.** 1980. T-cell hybrids with arsonate specificity. I. Initial characterization of antigen-specific T-cell products that bear a cross-reactive idiotype and determinants encoded by the murine major histocompatibility complex. J. Exp. Med. **152:**1289–1301.

6. **Ruddle, N. H.** 1978. T-cell hybrids with specificity for individual antigens. Curr. Top. Microbiol. Immunol. **81:**203–211.

7. **Ruddle, N. H., B. B. Beezley, and D. D. Eardley.** 1980. Regulation of self recognition by T-cell hybrids. Cell. Immunol. **55:**42–55.

8. **Swain, S. L., G. Dennert, S. Wormsley, and R. W. Dutton.** 1981. The Lyt phenotype of a long-term allospecific T-cell line. Both helper and killer activities to IA are mediated by Ly-1 cells. Eur. J. Immunol. **11:**175–180.

9. **Taniguchi, M., and J. F. A. P. Miller.** 1978. Specific suppressive factors produced by hybridomas derived from the fusion of enriched suppressor T-cells and T-lymphoma cell line. J. Exp. Med. **148:**373–382.

Cell Surface Receptors Involved in the Immune System

ROSE G. MAGE

Laboratory of Immunology, National Institute of Allergy and Infectious Diseases, Bethesda, Maryland 20205

RECEPTORS AND REGULATED IMMUNE RESPONSES

The immune system provides many striking examples of biological regulation. A complex, yet oversimplified, diagram of some of the interactions that occur during normal regulated immune responses is presented in Fig. 1. Antigens interact with each of the major cell categories depicted as well as with some of the factors and immunoglobulins produced by the B and T cells. In addition, complexes of antigen, antibody, and complement may bind to C3 receptors of B cells and accessory cells and affect their subsequent reactivities and functions (F. M. Griffin, Jr., J. A. Griffin, and P. J. Mullinax, this volume; D. T. Fearon, this volume). The immunoglobulins of particular classes and subclasses or isotypes, possibly in the form of complexes, bind to and affect those subsets of cells of each type that bear the appropriate Fc receptors (J. C. Unkeless and I. S. Mellman, this volume). Some of the functional complexes may be formed between immunoglobulins and anti-immunoglobulins or between immunoglobulin idiotypes and anti-idiotypes rather than between the introduced antigens and antibodies formed in response to them.

Out of these interactions, which involve cell-to-cell contacts, cell-to-antigen binding, and releases of soluble factors, come the positive and negative effects upon the differentiation, clonal expansion, and development of effector functions (including T cell-mediated immunity detectable, for example, as delayed-type hypersensitivity, graft-versus-host reactions, and cytotoxic killing) and upon differentiation of B cells into antibody-producing cells secreting various immunoglobulin classes and subclasses. The immunoglobulins bear isotypic, allotypic, and idiotypic structures. Some of these structures appear to be recognized by autoregulatory antibodies or T-cell receptors and factors and thus affect certain regulatory circuits.

Although some B-cell responses are referred to as "T independent," modulating effects of T lymphocytes upon B-cell responses can be demonstrated in most systems. T-cell help and suppression also function within the T-cell compartment to modulate the production of helpers and suppressors and the generation of T effector cells.

Other receptors with important roles in immune responses undoubtedly await discovery, and many that we are aware of will not be considered in this symposium. These include receptors for (i) polyclonal B-cell activators, such as bacterial lipopolysaccharides (18), and (ii) lectins on both B and T cells (30). In addition, the structures on cell surfaces encoded by genes in the major histocompatibility complex (such as H2 and Ia antigens in mice) either are themselves receptors or are recognized by receptors (11). They thus appear to be important in cell-to-cell interactions, antigen recognition phenomena, triggering of factor production, and factor binding. A number of other specialized surface components, such as those termed "differentiation antigens," may have receptor functions during ontogeny, but relatively little is now known about the postulated differentiation signals or functions of such receptors (17).

IMMUNOGLOBULIN GENES AND LYMPHOCYTE DIFFERENTIATION

The precursor of immunoglobulin-producing cells, the B cell with surface immunoglobulin (sIg), is a key target upon which major regulatory and selective events operate. In this volume E. S. Vitetta et al. discuss the roles that the sIg's of B lymphocytes play in triggering further differentiation into antibody-secreting cells. Antigenic, tolerogenic, and anti-idiotypic regulatory signals require the presence of sIg receptors with specific antigen binding and idiotypic sites. These receptors display a particular pair of variable regions of light chain (V_L) and heavy chain (V_H). The genetic information coding for both V_L and V_H is generated by DNA rearrangements. The diversity of antibody-combining sites and of idiotypic determinants displayed on the surface of B cells results from the DNA rearrangements, from the V_L to V_H pairing, and from additional somatic mutational events.

A great deal of differentiation occurs before even the earliest of these cells with sIg appears in the bone marrow. In the past 3 years, the

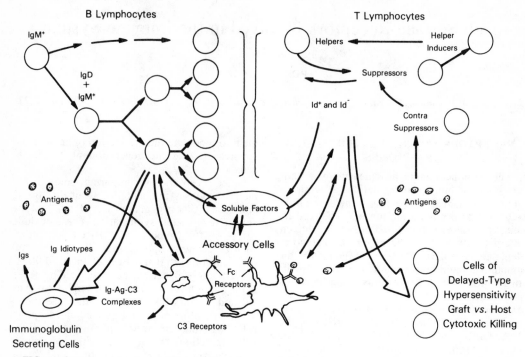

FIG. 1. Complex yet oversimplified diagram of some of the interactions that occur during normal regulated immune responses.

techniques of molecular biology and recombinant DNA technology have elucidated the remarkable series of gene rearrangements that occur during differentiation of cells of the B lineage (reviewed in 1 and 27). Comparable rearrangements are predicted to be involved in the expression of specific receptors of T cells, but there is little experimental documentation of this at present.

The studies of Nisonoff and his collaborators (20, 34) are giving us new insights into the genetics of idiotype expression and are revealing

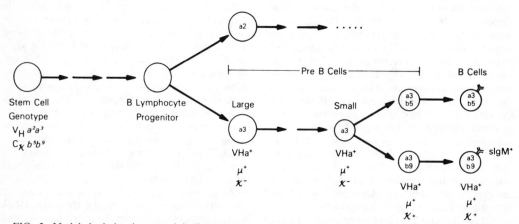

FIG. 2. Model depicting immunoglobulin gene expression in cells of the B lineage from a heterozygous $a^2a^3b^5b^9$ rabbit. Large, surface μ-negative, cytoplasmic μ-positive pre-B cells have detectable V_H allotypes a2 or a3, but not both. Small pre-B cells of the same phenotype are also found. A small proportion (10 to 20%) of the pre-B cells express κ allotypes b5 or b9, but not both. B cells with allelically excluded V_Ha and C_κ allotypes are thought to be derived from these small transitional μ^+, κ^+ pre-B cells.

some of the mechanisms through which T lymphocytes regulate the immune system. The expression of certain idiotypes and anti-idiotype receptors on T cells or T-cell factors is controlled by genes linked to the genetic region on mouse chromosome 12, known to carry the genes for variable (V), diversity (D), joining (J), and constant (C) regions of the immunoglobulin heavy chains produced by B cells (14, 20, 31, 34). In addition, some characteristic cellular alloantigens associated with T-cell receptors for idiotype and T cell-inducer functions (23) map to chromosome 12 but are separable from the genes for C regions of B-cell products by recombination events (22). It appears from work in several laboratories that T-cell products may be encoded in part by genes analogous to those for immunoglobulin C_{HS}. There is some evidence that they are located farther away from the V regions (3′ to the Igh locus for B-cell C-region products). Any description of the nature of the genetic information for the antigen or idiotype-specific structural parts of such receptors must be highly speculative. Current investigations at the DNA level may reveal whether there are separate V, D, and J genes coding for T cell-recognition structures and whether some V (or D) regions found coding for B-cell immunoglobulins also code for the T-cell products. One possibility is that a common set of V-region (and perhaps D) genes undergoes rearrangements to a T cell-specific set or sets of J structural genes (12, 29).

RNA TRANSCRIPTION AND PROCESSING

Differential primary RNA transcription and processing play an important role in the differentiation of B cells to express alternative forms of μ and δ heavy chains. The details of these RNA transcription and processing events are under active investigation in several laboratories (2, 5, 6, 15, 19, 28). We must integrate our understanding of these molecular events with the picture that is developing of the differentiation of cells of the B lineage and their subsequent responsiveness to triggering signals. In the pre-B cell, the earliest cell of the B lineage in which an immunoglobulin protein product has been detected, the μ heavy chain protein and mRNA resemble, but are not necessarily identical to, the μ-secreted form (13, 24, 25, 32 33). The development of a B cell with sIgM from such a pre-B cell must be accompanied by production of mRNA and protein translated from it bearing the hydrophobic μM form. Subsequently, daughter cells from such a B-cell clone may express both membrane IgM and IgD. This may result from the processing of an extremely long primary transcript with VDJ, μ, and δ genes, but this has not yet been proved (6, 15, 19, 35). Daughter cells may also be triggered to produce the secreted form of IgM (2, 5, 16, 28). Still later, cells of this clonal lineage may switch to production of another class of immunoglobulin. This heavy-chain switch involves yet another DNA-level recombinational event which leads to the same VDJ information located adjacent to another C-region gene (4, 9, 10).

EXPRESSION OF IMMUNOGLOBULIN GENES IN CELLS OF THE B LINEAGE

The earliest cells of the B lineage in which immunoglobulin protein products are detected are the pre-B cells that are found in fetal liver and newborn and adult bone marrow (21). The large sIg-negative cells contain intracytoplasmic μ heavy chains. My colleagues and I have been able to use allotype-defined rabbits with genetic traits associated with the V_H and with the C region of the κ light chains to analyze the early differentiation events in cells of the B lineage (7, 8). Cells of heterozygous rabbits with genotypes for V_{HS}, a^2a^3, and κ C regions, b^5b^9, were studied by use of fluorescein- and rhodamine-labeled anti-allotype reagents. The model depicted in Fig. 2 was developed after extensive studies of the staining of cells in bone marrow of neonatal heterozygous rabbits (7, 8) and previous investigations of pre-B cells in mice, rabbits, and humans (3, 26). Most of the pre-B cells that stained for intracytoplasmic μ heavy chains also stained for the V-region marker a2 or a3, but not both (7). This is evidence that early differentiation events lead to expression of the products of one parental chromosome but not the other (allelic exclusion). Pre-B cells of smaller size that have cytoplasmic μ chains and are V-region allotype positive are also observed (7). A small proportion of the total pre-B cells (10 to 20%) in rabbits tend to be small (~6 to 11 μm) and still lack sIg but are found to contain also κ-type light chains with allotypes of one or the other parental type (8). I believe that these are cells in transition to becoming sIg^+ B cells. In heterozygotes, we find b5 or b9, but not both (8). This differentiation pathway allows the pairing of a particular heavy chain, VDJ, with different light chains and thus the display of different antibody sites and idiotypes by different daughter cells.

In adult heterozygous rabbits, there is a so-called pecking order of allotype expression: more B lymphocytes and plasma cells are found that express the b5 type than the b9 allotype, and serum immunoglobulin of the b5 type predominates over b9. This pecking order appears to result from regulatory effects upon the cells after the appearance of sIg on the early B cells. In the bone marrow of newborn heterozygous b^5b^9 rabbits, the sIgM-positive B cells of the b5 and b9 types are found in equal proportions. Even the small percentage of pre-B cells in which κ light chains can be found express equal proportions of the two parental κ types. Similar observations have been made concerning the relative expression of the V_H genes a2 and a3. Again, adults produce more a3 than a2, but the pre-B cells exhibit balanced expression of these two parental forms (7). It thus appears that events occurring after the appearance of sIg lead to the preferential expansion of clones of cells expressing one parental type compared with the other.

This leads us back to our overview of interacting regulatory circuits in the immune system (Fig. 1). Antigens, regulatory anti-idiotypic, anti-allotypic, and anti-isotypic cells and factors, and accessory cells and their products may all contribute to the finally observed proportions of immune effector cells. Some of the many receptors involved in the interactions which regulate immune cell functions are described and discussed in the papers that follow.

LITERATURE CITED

1. Adams, J. M. 1980. The organization and expression of immunoglobulin genes. Immunol. Today 1:10–17.

2. Alt, F. W., A. L. M. Bothwell, M. Knapp, E. Siden, E. Mather, M. Koshland, and D. Baltimore. 1980. Synthesis of secreted and membrane-bound immunoglobulin μ heavy chains is directed by mRNAs that differ at their 3' ends. Cell 20:293–301.

3. Cooper, M. D., J. F. Kearney, W. E. Gathings, and A. R. Lawton. 1980. Effects of anti-Ig antibodies on the development and differentiation of B cells. Immunol. Rev. 52:29–53.

4. Davis, M. M., S. K. Kim, and L. Hood. 1980. Immunoglobulin class switching: developmentally regulated DNA rearrangements during differentiation. Cell 22:1–2.

5. Early, P., J. Rogers, M. Davis, K. Calame, M. Bond, R. Wall, and L. Hood. 1980. Two mRNAs can be produced from a single immunoglobulin μ gene by alternative RNA processing pathways. Cell 20:313–319.

6. Fitzmaurice, L., J. Owens, H. L. Cheng, P. W. Tucker, C. P. Liu, A. L. Shen, F. R. Blattner, and F. Mushinski. 1981. Transcription of δ chain genes in mouse myeloma cells and normal spleen, p. 263–269. In C. A. Janeway, E. Sercarz, H. Wigzell, and C. F. Fox (ed.), Immunoglobulin idiotypes and their expression. Proceedings of the ICN-UCLA Symposium, vol. 20. Academic Press, Inc., New York.

7. Gathings, W. E., R. G. Mage, M. D. Cooper, A. R. Lawton, and G. O. Young-Cooper. 1981. Immunofluorescent studies of the expression of V_Ha allotypes by pre-B and B cells of homozygous and heterozygous rabbits. Eur. J. Immunol. 11:200–206.

8. Gathings, W. E., R. G. Mage, M. D. Cooper, and G. O. Young-Cooper. 1982. A subpopulation of small pre-B cells from rabbit bone marrow expresses κ light chains and exhibits allelic exclusion of b locus allotypes. Eur. J. Immunol. 12:76–81.

9. Honjo, T., Y. Nishida, A. Shimizu, N. Takahashi, T. Kataoka, M. Obata, Y. Yamawaki-Kataoka, T. Nikaido, S. Nakai, T. Yaoita, and N. Ishida. 1982. Organization of immunoglobulin heavy chain genes and genetic mechanism for class switch. In L. A. Hanson, K. W. Sell, and W. Strober (ed.), Recent advances in mucosal immunity, in press. Raven Press, New York.

10. Kataoka, T., T. Miyata, and T. Honjo. 1981. Repetitive sequences in class-switch recombination regions of immunoglobulin heavy chain genes. Cell 23:357–368.

11. Klein, J. 1975. Biology of the mouse histocompatibility-2 complex. Springer-Verlag, New York.

12. Kurosawa, Y., H. von Boehmer, W. Haas, H. Sakano, A. Trauneker, and S. Tonegawa. 1981. Identification of D segments of immunoglobulin heavy-chain genes and their rearrangement in T lymphocytes. Nature (London) 290:565–570.

13. Levitt, D., and M. D. Cooper. 1981. Mouse pre-B cells synthesize and secrete μ heavy chains but not light chains. Cell 19:617–625.

14. Liu, C. P., P. W. Tucker, J. F. Mushinski, and F. R. Blattner. 1980. Mapping of heavy chain genes for mouse immunoglobulins M and D. Science 209:1348–1353.

15. Maki, R., W. Roeder, A. Traunecker, C. Sidman, M. Wabl, W. Raschke, and S. Tonegawa. 1981. The role of DNA rearrangement and alternative processing in the expression of immunoglobulin delta genes. Cell 24:353–365.

16. Mather, E. L., F. W. Alt, A. L. Bothwell, D. Baltimore, and M. E. Koshland. 1981. Expression of J chain RNA in cell lines representing different stages of B lymphocyte differentiation. Cell 23:369–378.

17. Moller, G. (ed.). 1977. Immunology and differentiation. Immunol. Rev. 33:3–145.

18. Moller, G. 1980. Non-antigen specific receptors, theme 4 summary, p. 279–281. In M. Fougereau and J. Dausset (ed.), Progress in immunology IV. Academic Press, London.

19. Moore, K. W., J. Rogers, T. Hunkapiller, P. Early, C. Nottenburg, I. Weissman, H. Bazin, R. Wall, and L. E. Hood. 1981. Expression of IgD may use both DNA rearrangement and RNA splicing mechanisms. Proc. Natl. Acad. Sci. U.S.A. 78:1800–1804.

20. Nisonoff, A., and M. I. Greene. 1980. Regulation through idiotype determinants of the immune response to the p-azophenylarsonate hapten in strain A mice, p. 57–80. In M. Fougereau and J. Dausset (ed.), Progress in immunology IV. Academic Press, London.

21. Owen, J. J. T. 1980. B cell development, p. 303–314. In M. Fougereau and J. Dausset (ed.), Progress in immunology IV. Academic Press, London.

22. Owen, F. L., R. Riblet, and B. A. Taylor. 1981. The T suppressor cell alloantigen Tsu^d maps near immunoglobulin allotype genes and may be a heavy chain constant region marker on a T cell receptor. J. Exp. Med. 153:801–810.

23. Owen, F. L., and G. M. Spurll. 1981. Evidence for a T cell constant region gene family: characterization of cell surface antigens by immunoprecipitation with alloantisera and monoclonal antibodies, p. 419–428. In C. A. Janeway, E. Sercarz, H. Wigzell, and C. F. Fox (ed.), Immunoglobulin idiotypes and their expression. Proceedings of the ICN-UCLA Symposium, vol. 20. Academic Press, Inc., New York.

24. Perry, R. P., and D. E. Kelley. 1979. Immunoglobulin messenger RNAs in murine cell lines that have characteristics of immature B lymphocytes. Cell 18:1333–1339.

25. Perry, R. P., D. E. Kelley, C. Coleclough, and J. F. Kearney. 1981. Organization and expression of immunoglobulin genes in fetal liver hybridomas. Proc. Natl. Acad. Sci. U.S.A. 78:247–251.

26. Riley, S. C., E. J. Brock, and W. M. Kuehl. 1981. Induction of light chain expression in a pre-B cell line by fusion to myeloma cells. Nature (London) 289:804–806.

27. **Robertson, M.** 1981. Genes of lymphocytes I: diverse means to antibody diversity. Nature (London) **290**:625–627.

28. **Rogers, J., P. Early, C. Carter, K. Calame, M. Bond, L. Hood, and R. Wall.** 1980. Two mRNAs with different 3′ ends encode membrane-bound and secreted forms of immunoglobulin μ chain. Cell **20**:303–312.

29. **Sakano, H., Y. Kurosawa, M. Weigert, and S. Tonegawa.** 1981. Identification and nucleotide sequence of a diversity DNA segment (D) of immunoglobulin heavy-chain genes. Nature (London) **290**:562–565.

30. **Sharon, N.** 1980. Cell surface receptors for lectins: markers of murine and human lymphocyte subpopulations, p. 254–278. *In* M. Fourgereau and J. Dausset (ed.), Progress in immunology IV. Academic Press, London.

31. **Shimizu, A., N. Takahashi, Y. Tamawaki-Kataoka, Y. Nishida, T. Kataoka, and T. Honjo.** 1981. Ordering of mouse immunoglobulin heavy chain genes by molecular cloning. Nature (London) **289**:149–153.

32. **Siden, E., F. W. Alt, L. Shinefeld, V. Sato, and D. Baltimore.** 1981. Synthesis of immunoglobulin μ chain gene products precedes synthesis of light chains during B-lymphocyte development. Proc. Natl. Acad. Sci. U.S.A. **78**:1823–1827.

33. **Sidman, C.** 1981. B lymphocyte differentiation and the control of IgM μ chain expression. Cell **23**:379–389.

34. **Sy, M.-S., A. Brown, B. A. Bach, B. Benacerraf, P. D. Gottlieb, A. Nisonoff, and M. I. Greene.** 1981. Genetic and serological analysis of the expression of crossreactive idiotypic determinants on anti-p-azobenzenearsonate antibodies and p-azobenzenearsonate-specific suppressor T cell factors. Proc. Natl. Acad. Sci. U.S.A. **78**:1143–1147.

35. **Tucker, P. W., C. P. Liu, J. F. Mushinski, and F. R. Blattner.** 1980. Mouse immunoglobulin D: messenger RNA and genomic DNA sequences. Science **209**:1353–1360.

Receptor-Mediated Activation of Murine B Cells

ELLEN S. VITETTA, ELLEN PURÉ, PETER ISAKSON, and JONATHAN W. UHR

Department of Microbiology and the Immunology Graduate Program, University of Texas Health Science Center, Dallas, Texas 75235

The B cell is unique among immunocytes because its antigen-specific receptors, secreted products, and pathways of differentiation have been characterized. However, the steps involved in inducing tolerance in B cells or in triggering B cells to differentiate into either plasma cells or memory cells remain obscure.

One of the major themes of our research has been to elucidate the function of the antigen-specific receptors on B cells in delivering tolerogenic versus immunogenic signals. In particular, we want to understand the differential functions of the two major immunoglobulin receptors, IgM and IgD, in signaling the virgin B cell.

INDUCTION OF POLYCLONAL PROLIFERATION BY ANTI-μ AND ANTI-δ

A direct approach to determining whether a particular molecule on the surface of a B cell can transmit a signal to that cell is to demonstrate that specific antibody to that molecule can induce a change in the rate of proliferation, differentiation, or another parameter of cell activation. This approach has two advantages over conventional activation by antigen. First, anti-immunoglobulin can potentially stimulate a much larger percentage of the total B-cell population. Second, antigens can bind specifically to both surface IgM (sIgM) and sIgD, and therefore the particular role played by each of these two types of antigen receptors cannot be analyzed. By employing isotype-specific antibodies (anti-μ or anti-δ) the capacity of each of the two receptors to transmit a signal to the B cell can be separately evaluated.

We have recently shown that F(ab')$_2$ fragments of anti-δ and intact anti-δ coupled to an insoluble matrix (Sepharose) are as effective as anti-μ in transmitting a proliferative signal to the B cells in vitro (5, 8). Thus, as shown in Fig. 1 and 2, F(ab')$_2$ fragments or Sepharose-coupled affinity-purified anti-μ induce proliferation of adult spleen cells. In contrast, the intact soluble antibody inhibited background [^{3}H]thymidine incorporation (Fig. 1). These results confirm previous reports on the mitogenicity of anti-μ antibodies (9, 10, 12). The F(ab')$_2$ fragment of anti-δ (Fig. 1) antibodies and the Sepharose-

coupled anti-δ (Fig. 2) antibodies also clearly stimulated proliferation although somewhat less effectively than the anti-μ; the intact soluble anti-δ antibody had no effect. More importantly, two preparations of anti-δ-Sepharose (affinity-purified rabbit anti-δ and the allotype-specific hybridoma anti-δ^a, H10-4.22) are as effective as anti-μ-Sepharose in inducing a proliferative response; proliferation was not observed with normal rabbit immunoglobulin-Sepharose or with Sepharose coupled to mouse IgG2A (RPC-5) (Fig. 2). These results indicate that IgD as well as IgM can transmit a proliferative signal to B cells after surface IgD is effectively cross-linked by specific antibody.

ROLE OF IgM AND IgD IN ACTIVATION OF B CELLS BY ANTIGEN

Although these experiments demonstrate that receptor cross-linking with anti-immunoglobulins activates B cells in a polyclonal fashion, they do not address the question of whether one or both receptors are required for antigen-dependent differentiation into specific antibody-secreting cells. To answer this question, we performed a series of "blocking" experiments in which either IgM or IgD was removed from cells prior to stimulation with antigen. We chose trinitrophenylated polyacrylamide beads (TNP-PAB) as the experimental system to investigate the role of the antigen in determining the requirement for IgD on the B cell. The advantages of the system are that the carrier portion of the antigen is inert (i.e., neither antigenic nor mitogenic) and the epitope density on the carrier can be easily manipulated. This system was initially described by Dintzis et al. (2) and was further evaluated by Mond et al. (6). This antigen can be rendered thymus independent or thymus dependent by derivatizing the carrier with different numbers of TNP determinants. Moreover, it has been shown that activation of B cells is directly related to the number of epitopes on the carrier (1–3, 13). Using a radioimmunoassay to evaluate our antigen preparations (7), we prepared two types of antigens, a high-epitope-density TNP-PAB and a low-epitope-density TNP-PAB, which differed in the number of epitopes present

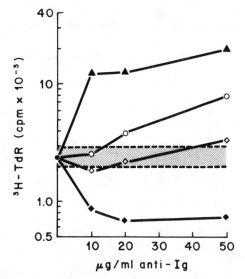

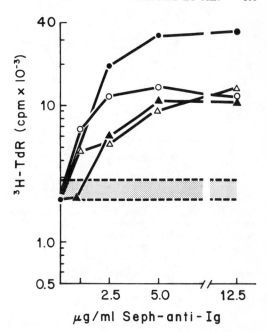

FIG. 1. Effect of anti-immunoglobulins on proliferation of BALB/c spleen cells. Cells were cultured at 10^6/ml in microtiter plates for 24 h, pulsed with 1 μCi of [^{3}H]thymidine, and harvested 16 h later on glass-fiber filters. Results shown are the mean of triplicate cultures. Affinity-purified rabbit antibodies added at the start of culture were: ◆, anti-μ; ◇, anti-δ; △, F(ab')$_2$-anti-μ; ○, F(ab')$_2$-anti-δ. The shaded region represents the range of control responses [normal rabbit immunoglobulin and F(ab')$_2$ rabbit immunoglobulin].

FIG. 2. Effect of Sepharose-coupled anti-immunoglobulins on proliferation of BALB/c spleen cells. Cells were cultured as described in Fig. 1. Results shown are the mean of triplicate cultures. Affinity-purified rabbit or murine hybridoma antibodies were: ●, RAMIg; ▲, R$\alpha\mu$; ○, R$\alpha\delta$; △, $\alpha\delta^a$ (H10.4.22). The shaded area represents the range of control responses [normal rabbit immunoglobulin; RPC-5 (γ_2aκ); α-TNP; α-OVA and α-γ] (8).

on the surface of the beads by 10-fold. When spleen cells from normal mice were cultured with 10^4 to 10^6 beads, the resulting direct anti-TNP plaque-forming cell responses were similar. In contrast, underivatized beads elicited no anti-TNP response. Moreover, none of the preparations induced responses to either sheep erythrocytes or horse erythrocytes. These results confirmed earlier reports that the carrier is not a polyclonal activator for murine B cells (4, 6, 11).

To determine the thymus dependency of the response to TNP-PAB, spleen cells were treated with complement and a hybridoma anti-Thy-1.2 antibody to delete T cells. This treatment effectively eliminated 30 to 40% of the spleen cells and, as shown in Fig. 3, abrogated the response to the low-epitope-density TNP-PAB. The response to the high-epitope-density TNP-PAB was reduced by an average of 50 to 60% after similar treatment. These results indicate that there is a correlation between the thymus dependency of the anti-TNP response and the epitope density of the antigen. The partial inhibition of the response to the high-epitope-density antigen could be due to heterogeneity either in the antigen preparation or in the responding B cells.

Whatever the explanation, the results clearly indicate that at least a portion of the in vitro response to the high-epitope-density antigen is thymus independent.

Having established the thymus dependency of the response to TNP-PAB, we next determined the sIg requirement for activation of the responding B cells. This was accomplished by adding anti-μ or anti-δ to antigen-containing cultures. As can be seen in Fig. 4, the response to the low-epitope-density TNP-PAB was abrogated by treatment of cells with *either* anti-μ or anti-δ. In contrast, the response to the high-epitope-density TNP-PAB was completely blocked by anti-μ but only partially (30 to 70%) inhibited by anti-δ. These results suggest that when the epitope density of the antigen is high, IgD is not required on all the responding B cells. To explore this relationship in greater depth, we designed experiments to determine whether the thymus-independent portion of the response to the high-epitope-density TNP-PAB required IgD on the responding B cells. Thus, one portion of a spleen cell suspension was treated with anti-

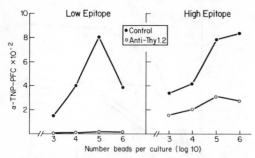

FIG. 3. Anti-TNP plaque-forming cell (PFC) responses to low- and high-epitope TNP-PAB in the absence of T cells. Spleen cells were treated with monoclonal anti-Thy-1.2 and complement or complement alone and washed extensively. Cells were then cultured with various doses of either low-epitope-density (left panel) or high-epitope-density (right panel) TNP-PAB. After 4 days in culture, cells were assayed for anti-TNP PFC. Data are presented as PFC per 10^6 viable input cells prior to T-cell depletion.

Thy-1.2 plus complement, a second with anti-δ, and a third with both anti-Thy-1.2 plus complement and anti-δ. As shown in Table 1, the combined treatment reduced the response to the same extent as either deleting the T cells or blocking with anti-δ. It was therefore concluded that the thymus-independent portion of the response could be triggered in the absence of IgD receptors and, by deduction, that the thymus-dependent responses to TNP-PAB requires IgD as well as IgM to activate the responding B cells.

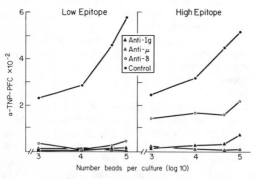

FIG. 4. Effect of anti-immunoglobulin, anti-μ, and anti-δ on the anti-TNP plaque-forming cell (PFC) response to TNP-PAB. Cells were cultured with normal rabbit immunoglobulin or affinity-purified anti-immunoglobulin, anti-μ, or anti-Ig5[b] antibodies for 1 h under capping conditions. Cells were washed, and 5 μg of the appropriate antibody per ml and various doses of low- (left panel) or high- (right panel) epitope-density TNP-PAB were added. After 4 days of culture, cells were assayed for anti-TNP PFC.

TABLE 1. Effect of anti-δ on the thymus-independent portion of response to high-epitope TNP-PAB

Prepn	% Inhibition of response after:		
	Anti-Thy + complement	Anti-δ	Both treatments
Rabbit anti-δ^a	59	57	64
Hybridoma anti-δ (H11.6.3)^b	53	47	61

^{a} With 5×10^5 TNP-PAB; average of two experiments.

^{b} With 10^5 TNP-PAB; average for four experiments.

The ability of high-epitope-density antigens to trigger B cells in the absence of IgD suggests that such antigens can effectively cross-link the IgM receptors. In contrast, antigens of lower epitope density may be incapable of accomplishing the required cross-linking without interacting with surface IgD. This explanation implies a major difference between the two isotypes in their ability to be cross-linked by antigen. The difference could reside in density, valency, or mobility of membrane IgM compared with membrane IgD.

The relationship between the thymus dependency of the response and the requirement for IgD on B cells is not clear; one possibility is that the ability of B-cell receptors to be cross-linked by antigen affects the capacity of B cells to accept T-cell help. Another possibility is that IgD molecules may bind the T-cell factor directly.

LITERATURE CITED

1. **Desaymard, C., and M. Feldmann.** 1975. Role of epitope density in the induction of immunity and tolerance with thymus independent antigens. Eur. J. Immunol. 5:537–547.
2. **Dintzis, H. M., R. Z. Dintzis, and B. Vogelstein.** 1976. Molecular determinants of immunogenicity: the immunon model of immune response. Proc. Natl. Acad. Sci. U.S.A. 73:3671–3675.
3. **Feldmann, M.** 1972. Induction of immunity and tolerance *in vitro* by hapten protein conjugates. J. Exp. Med. 135:735–745.
4. **Feldmann, M., M. F. Greaves, D. C. Parker, and M. B. Rittenburg.** 1974. Direct triggering of B lymphocytes by insolubilized antigen. Eur. J. Immunol. 4:591–601.
5. **Isakson, P. C., K. A. Krolick, J. W. Uhr, and E. S. Vitetta.** 1980. The effect of anti-immunoglobulin antibodies on the *in vitro* proliferation and differentiation of normal and neoplastic murine B cells. J. Immunol. 125:886.
6. **Mond, J. J., K. E. Stein, B. Subbarao, and W. E. Paul.** 1979. Analysis of B cell activation requirements with TNP-conjugated polyacrylamide beads. J. Immunol. 123:239–245.
7. **Puré, E., and E. S. Vitetta.** 1980. The murine B cell response to TNP-polyacrylamide beads: the relationship between the epitope density of the antigen and the re-

quirements for T cell help and surface IgD. J. Immunol. **125:**420–427.

8. **Puré, E. and E. S. Vitetta.** 1980. Induction of murine B cell proliferation by insolubilized anti-immunoglobulins. J. Immunol. **125:**1240–1242.

9. **Sidman, C. L., and E. R. Unanue.** 1978. Control of proliferation and differentiation in B lymphocytes by anti-Ig antibodies and a serum derived factor. Proc. Natl. Acad. Sci. U.S.A. **75:**2401–2405.

10. **Sieckmann, D. G., R. Asofksy, D. E. Mosier, I. A. Zitron, and W. E. Paul.** 1978. Activation of mouse lymphocytes by anti-immunoglobulin. I. Parameters of the proliferative response. J. Exp. Med. **147:**814–829.

11. **Trump, G.** 1976. Cellular requirements for the *in vitro* response to moderately haptenated forms of the solid phase immunogen DNP-O-Biogel-P. J. Immunol. Methods **20:**241–246.

12. **Weiner, H. L., J. W. Moorhead, and H. N. Claman.** 1976. Anti-immunoglobulin stimulation of murine lymphocytes. I. Age dependency of the proliferative response. J. Immunol. **116:**1656–1661.

13. **Yasuda, T., G. F. Dancey, and S. C. Kinsky.** 1977. Immunogenic properties of liposomal model membranes in mice. J. Immunol. **119:**1863–1867.

Phagocytosis Mediated by the Macrophage Receptor for C3b: Requirement for Receptor Activation by a Unique Lymphokine

FRANK M. GRIFFIN, JR., JOHANNA A. GRIFFIN, AND PEGGY J. MULLINAX

Division of Infectious Diseases, Department of Medicine, University of Alabama in Birmingham, Birmingham, Alabama 35294

ACTIVATION OF THE MACROPHAGE COMPLEMENT RECEPTOR

Engagement by particle-bound immunoglobulin G (IgG) of Fc receptors of either polymorphonuclear or mononuclear phagocytes virtually always leads to ingestion of IgG-coated particles (4, 6, 11, 17). In contrast, engagement by particle-bound C3b of complement receptors of neutrophils, monocytes, and "resting" tissue macrophages always promotes efficient particle binding but uniformly fails to promote ingestion of C3b-coated particles (1, 4, 6–8, 11, 17). Several years ago, we found that peritoneal macrophages from mice that had been injected intraperitoneally with Brewer thioglycolate medium several days before macrophage harvest were able to phagocytize via their complement receptors (1). Thioglycolate medium, which induces an intense inflammatory response, either strikingly modified the resident macrophage population or induced the influx of a physiologically different population of mononuclear phagocytes. Since thioglycolate-elicited macrophages resemble in some respects macrophages acted upon by lymphokines such as macrophage activating factor (MAF) (1, 10, 13, 16, 18), we hypothesized that lymphokine-activated macrophages would also be able to phagocytize via their complement receptors.

In our initial experiments, therefore, we infected mice with *Mycobacterium bovis* BCG and, at times up to several months thereafter, harvested their splenic lymphocytes and incubated them with BCG antigens. This technique is commonly used to induce T lymphocytes to elaborate a variety of lymphokines, including MAF and interferon (18). We then incubated freshly harvested resident mouse peritoneal macrophages with the lymphocyte culture supernatants and assessed the macrophages' interaction with complement-coated erythrocytes [E(IgM)C]. [E(IgM)C were prepared by coating sheep erythrocytes first with anti-erythrocyte immunoglobulin M (IgM) and then incubating the E(IgM) with C5-deficient mouse serum, a source of the first four complement components. The macrophage does not recognize the erythrocyte itself, the IgM molecule, or C1, C4, or C2. It recognizes only C3b, so E(IgM)C are functionally EC3b.] We were surprized to find that these supernatants had no effect on macrophage complement receptor function.

Certain T-lymphocyte functions can be enhanced by treatment with monokines, products elaborated by mononuclear phagocytes (2, 20, 21). In some cases, the elaboration of monokines by macrophages is triggered by phagocytosis (2, 20). We fed macrophages an ingestible particle, co-cultivated these macrophages with splenic lymphocytes, and then tested the ability of the lymphocyte-macrophage culture supernatants to enhance the complement receptor function of freshly harvested mouse peritoneal macrophages. Macrophages treated with these supernatants avidly phagocytized via their complement receptors (8). Our tentative interpretation of these results was that phagocytosis triggered macrophages to elaborate a monokine that triggered T lymphocytes to elaborate a lymphokine that enabled freshly harvested macrophages to phagocytize via their complement receptors. Subsequent experiments proved that this interpretation was, in general, correct.

GENERATION OF THE LYMPHOKINE

The particles we had fed macrophages in our initial experiments were sheep erythrocytes coated with anti-erythrocyte IgG [E(IgG)]. Our next experiments were designed to determine whether phagocytosis of any particle or only phagocytosis of selected particles could trigger the macrophage's participation in the generation of supernatant activity. We fed macrophages a variety of ingestible particles (Table 1). Group I included particles that are ingested by nonimmunological means; group II, particles whose ingestion is mediated by the C3b receptors of thioglycolate-elicited macrophages, the macro-

TABLE 1. Effect of phagocytosis via different receptors upon the macrophage's ability to participate in the generation of supernatant activity

Group	Particle incubated with macrophages in supernatant generation cultures	PI[a] of test particle by macrophages in supernatant generation cultures	PI[a] of E(IgM)C by freshly harvested macrophages
I	*Escherichia coli*	1,400	11
	Latex beads	1,400	12
	Zymosan	750	18
II	E(IgM)C	1,200	8
	Complement-coated zymosan	900	24
III	E(IgG)	1,300	360
	Ox E(IgG)	1,250	351
	IgG-coated pneumococci	1,400	158
	Aggregated IgG	+[b]	350
	HSA-anti-HSA[c] complexes	+	340

[a] Phagocytic index, the number of particles ingested by 100 macrophages.
[b] The soluble complexes, when tagged with a fluorochrome, were found in abundance within the macrophage.
[c] HSA, Human serum albumin.

phages used in this portion of the experiments; and group III, particulate and soluble immune complexes whose ingestion is mediated by the cell's Fc receptors. All particles were avidly ingested. The macrophages were then co-cultivated with splenic lymphocytes, and the culture supernatants were assayed for their ability to enhance the complement receptor function of freshly harvested resident peritoneal macrophages. Supernatants from cultures containing macrophages that had phagocytized either by nonimmunological means or via their complement receptors were inactive, whereas all supernatants from cultures containing macrophages that had phagocytized via their Fc receptors were active (Table 1). These results indicated that it is not phagocytosis per se but rather

TABLE 2. Identification of the cellular source of the molecule that augments macrophage complement receptor function and characterization of the mechanism by which it is elaborated

Lymphocytes used to generate supernatants	% of standard PI[a]
Whole spleen	100
T cell enriched	93
B cell enriched	10
Treated with effector macrophage supernatants	14
Separated from effector macrophages by filter	10

[a] Percentage of the phagocytic index (PI) of E(IgM)C by macrophages treated with supernatants prepared as described in the text, with a mixture of T and B cells from normal mouse spleen used as the source of lymphocytes.

engagement of its Fc receptors that triggers the macrophage's participation in the generation of supernatant activity.

By using lymphocyte populations enriched in or depleted of either B or T cells, we found that the T cell performed the necessary and sufficient lymphocyte function in the generation of supernatant activity (Table 2, lines 2 and 3). In addition, by first culturing T lymphocytes with Fc receptor-triggered macrophages and then culturing the two cell types separately and testing the macrophage and lymphocyte supernatants independently, we found that the T cell, and not the macrophage, elaborated the active product (data not shown). Thus, the molecule that augments macrophage complement receptor function is a lymphokine.

Results of the following experiments defined the role of the macrophage in the generation of the lymphokine. Fc receptor-triggered macrophages were cultured alone for several hours; the culture supernatants were harvested and added to T lymphocytes. Lymphocytes were cultured in these supernatants for several hours, after which the final supernatants were harvested and their effect on macrophage complement receptor function was assessed. These supernatants were inactive (Table 2, line 4), suggesting that the macrophage may signal T lymphocytes to elaborate the lymphokine by a cell contact-dependent mechanism rather than by a monokine. This suggestion was confirmed by our finding co-cultivation of T lymphocytes with Fc receptor-triggered macrophages in the same dish, but separated by a membrane filter (Millipore Corp.), failed to generate the lymphokine (Table 2, line 5).

TABLE 3. Effect of the lymphokine on the phagocytic capabilities of macrophages

Particle incubated with macrophages	PI[a] by macrophages that were	
	Nontreated	Lymphokine treated
Concanavalin A-coated sheep erythrocytes	18	17
Zymosan	529	504
E(IgG)	1,114	1,148

[a] Phagocytic index.

TABLE 4. Effect of the lymphokine on macrophage complement receptor topography

Treatment of cultures	Attachment index[a] of E(IgM)C
None	668
Lymphokine	21
Lymphokine, then C3b inactivator	721

[a] Number of E(IgM)C attached by 100 macrophages.

The results presented indicate that the lymphokine is generated by a unique mechanism. Macrophages are triggered by engagement of their Fc receptors to signal T lymphocytes, via a cell contact-dependent mechanism, to elaborate a lymphokine that enables freshly harvested mouse peritoneal macrophages to phagocytize via their complement receptors. The molecule itself appears to be different from any previously described lymphokine, as judged by some of its physical characteristics, including its apparent molecular weight of 1,000 to 10,000 (7). As discussed below, the mechanism by which the lymphokine acts on macrophages appears to be novel as well.

MECHANISM OF ACTION OF THE LYMPHOKINE

We considered several means by which the lymphokine might augment macrophage complement receptor function. The first possibility, that it might nonspecifically activate the macrophage plasma membrane so that the macrophage indiscriminately ingested anything attached to its surface, was excluded by our finding that, like their nontreated counterparts, lymphokine-treated macrophages failed to ingest sheep erythrocytes bound to their surfaces by cross-linking with the lectin concanavalin A (Table 3, line 1). The second possibility, that the lymphokine may enhance the function of all phagocytic receptors, was excluded by our finding that lymphokine-treated macrophages were no better able then their nontreated counterparts to ingest either zymosan particles (Table 3, line 2) or E(IgG) (Table 3, line 3). These results indicated that the effect of the lymphokine on the phagocytic capabilities of macrophages was selective and specific for the cell's complement receptors.

We also found that inhibition of macrophage protein synthesis failed to diminish the effect of the lymphokine on macrophage complement receptor function (data not shown), indicating that the lymphokine does not act by triggering the synthesis of new or additional complement receptors or other proteins, but rather that it exerts its effect upon existing cellular components.

Recent studies (7a) have defined more precisely how the lymphokine enhances macrophage complement receptor function. In these studies, we used immobilized immune complexes to study the influence of the lymphokine on macrophage complement receptor topography.

Complement-containing immobilized immune complexes were prepared by binding bovine serum albumin (BSA) to glass cover slips with poly-L-lysine used as a cross-linker, treating the cover slips with antibody to BSA, and then treating the BSA–anti-BSA complexes with fresh mouse serum. We found, as had Michl et al. (12), that when resident mouse peritoneal macrophages were plated on these BSA–anti-BSA-C-coated cover slips, they retained the ability to bind E(IgM)C (Table 4, line 1). Resident macrophages plated on the complexes and treated with the lymphokine for periods as short as 5 min, however, were no longer able to bind complement-coated particles (Table 4, line 2). Loss of complement receptor activity from the nonadherent macrophage surface was a consequence of receptor migration to and sequestration on the immobilized C3b ligands, for cleaving the C3b ligand with C3b inactivator enabled complement receptor activity to return promptly to the nonadherent surface of lymphokine-treated macrophages (Table 4, line 3).

These findings strongly suggest that the complement receptors of resident mouse peritoneal macrophages are normally fixed and immobile within the macrophage plasma membrane and that lymphokine treatment frees the receptors from their plasma membrane anchors, enabling them to wander randomly within the plane of the plasma membrane. As they encounter immobilized C3b ligands on the immune complex substrate, they are trapped on the adherent macrophage surface.

Results of several studies (3, 5, 7a, 9, 12, 14, 15) demonstrate a precise correlation between the ability of receptors to redistribute on the macrophage surface and their ability to promote phagocytosis. Engagement of macrophage complement receptors does not normally result in phagocytosis, probably because the receptors cannot move. Receptor mobility appears to be required to convert ligand-receptor binding at the cell surface into the intracellular phagocytic response; that is, receptor mobility appears to be an essential component of the phagocytic signal. Treatment of macrophages with the lymphokine enables their complement receptors to diffuse within the plane of the plasma membrane. When engaged by particle-bound C3b, these receptors can then either aggregate among themselves or perhaps become associated with an intramembrane second messenger, thereby initiating the phagocytic signal and linking the cell surface binding event with the intracellular phagocytic machinery, actin and its regulatory proteins (19, 22). Changes in the physical state of actin then provide the motive force for ingestion of the ligand-coated particle.

ACKNOWLEDGMENTS

This work was supported by grant IM-173 from the American Cancer Society, Inc., and Research Career Development Award AI-00135 from the National Institutes of Health to F.M.G.

LITERATURE CITED

1. **Bianco, C., F. M. Griffin, Jr., and S. C. Silverstein.** 1975. Studies of the macrophage complement receptor. Alteration of receptor function upon macrophage activation. J. Exp. Med. **141:**1278–1290.
2. **Calderon, J., J.-M. Kiely, J. L. Lefko, and E. R. Unanue.** 1975. The modulation of lymphocyte functions by molecules secreted by macrophages. I. Description and partial biochemical characterization. J. Exp. Med. **142:**151–164.
3. **Douglas, S. D.** 1976. Human monocyte spreading in vitro—inducers and effects on Fc and C3 receptors. Cell. Immunol. **21:**344–349.
4. **Ehlenberger, A. G., and V. Nussenzweig.** 1977. The role of membrane receptors for C3b and C3d in phagocytosis. J. Exp. Med. **145:**357–371.
5. **Griffin, F. M., Jr.** 1981. Roles of macrophage Fc and C3b receptors in phagocytosis of immunologically coated Cryptococcus neoformans. Proc. Natl. Acad. Sci. U.S.A. **78:**3853-3857.
6. **Griffin, F. M., Jr., C. Bianco, and S. C. Silverstein.** 1975. Characterization of the macrophage receptor for complement and demonstration of its functional independence from the receptor for the Fc portion of immunoglobulin G. J. Exp. Med. **141:**1269–1277.
7. **Griffin, F. M., Jr., and J. A. Griffin.** 1980. Augmentation of macrophage complement receptor function in vitro. II. Characterization of the effects of a unique lymphokine upon the phagocytic capabilities of macrophages. J. Immunol. **125:**844–849.
7a.**Griffin, F. M., Jr., and P. J. Mullinax.** 1981. Augmentation of macrophage complement receptor function in vitro. III. C3b receptors that promote phagocytosis migrate within the plane of the macrophage plasma membrane. J. Exp. Med. **154:**291–305.
8. **Griffin, J. A., and F. M. Griffin, Jr.** 1979. Augmentation of macrophage complement receptor function in vitro. I. Characterization of the cellular interactions required for the generation of a T-lymphocyte product that enhances macrophage complement receptor function. J. Exp. Med. **150:**653–675.
9. **Kaplan, G., T. Eskeland, and R. Seljelid.** 1978. Difference in the effect of immobilized ligands on the Fc and C3 receptors of mouse peritoneal macrophages in vitro. Scand. J. Immunol. **7:**19–24.
10. **Mackaness, G.** 1964. The immunological basis of acquired cellular resistance. J. Exp. Med. **120:**105–120.
11. **Mantovani, B., M. Rabinovitch, and V. Nussenzweig.** 1972. Phagocytosis of immune complexes by macrophages. Different roles of the macrophage receptor sites for complement (C3) and for immunoglobulin (IgG). J. Exp. Med. **135:**780–792.
12. **Michl, J., M. Pieczonka, J. C. Unkeless, and S. C. Silverstein.** 1979. Effects of immobilized immune complexes on Fc- and complement receptor function in resident and thioglycollate-elicited mouse peritoneal macrophages. J. Exp. Med. **150:**607–621.
13. **Nathan, C. F., M. L. Karnovsky, and J. R. David.** 1971. Alterations of macrophage functions by mediators from lymphocytes. J. Exp. Med. **133:**1356–1376.
14. **Rabinovitch, M., R. E. Manejias, and V. Nussenzweig.** 1975. Selective phagocytic paralysis induced by immobilized immune complexes. J. Exp. Med. **142:**827–838.
15. **Ragsdale, C. G., and W. P. Arend.** 1980. Loss of Fc receptor activity after culture of human monocytes on surface-bound immune complexes. Mediation by cyclic nucleotides. J. Exp. Med. **151:**32–44.
16. **Rocklin, R. E., C. T. Winston, and J. R. David.** 1974. Activation of human blood monocytes by products of sensitized lymphocytes. J. Clin. Invest. **53:**559–564.
17. **Shaw, D. R., and F. M. Griffin, Jr.** 1981. Phagocytosis requires repeated triggering of macrophage receptors during particle ingestion. Nature (London) **289:**409–411.
18. **Simon, H. B., and J. N. Sheagren.** 1972. Enhancement of macrophage bactericidal capacity by antigenically stimulated lymphocytes. Cell. Immunol. **4:**163–174.
19. **Stossel, T. P., and J. H. Hartwig.** 1976. Interactions of actin, myosin, and a new actin-binding protein of rabbit pulmonary macrophages. II. Role in cytoplasmic movement and phagocytosis. J. Cell. Biol. **68:**602–619.
20. **Unanue, E. R., J.-M. Kiely, and J. Calderone.** 1976. The modulation of lymphocyte functions by molecules secreted by macrophages. II. Conditions leading to increased secretion. J. Exp. Med. **144:**155–166.
21. **Wahl, S. M., M. Wilton, D. L. Rosenstreich, and J. J. Oppenheim.** 1975. The role of macrophages in the production of lymphokines by T and B lymphocytes. J. Immunol. **114:**1296–1301.
22. **Yin, H. L., and T. P. Stossel.** 1979. Control of cytoplasmic actin gel-sol transformation by gelsolin, a calcium-dependent regulatory protein. Nature (London) **281:**583–586.

Purification and Characterization of a Mouse Immunoglobulin Fc Receptor

JAY C. UNKELESS AND IRA S. MELLMAN[1]

Department of Cellular Physiology and Immunology, The Rockefeller University, New York, New York 10021

The analysis of plasma membrane proteins has been greatly facilitated by the new technique for the preparation of monoclonal antibodies (8). These reagents make feasible the efficient identification and purification of minor cell proteins which bear a common and unique antigenic determinant, although they may be heterogeneous with respect to isoelectric point and M_r. Monoclonal antibodies also permit the unambiguous detection of antigenic determinants which may be present on a variety of cell types. In addition, it is now possible to separate cell populations with defined antigens by fluorescence-activated cell sorting or by "panning."

We have used a monoclonal antibody directed against a mouse Fc receptor (FcR) for immunoglobulin G (IgG) to study receptor specificity and to purify the protein. The FcRs for IgG on macrophages, neutrophils, B cells, and some subclasses of T cells are membrane proteins of great interest because, together with the receptors for complement components, they provide a key recognition system which "informs" effector cells such as macrophages and neutrophils of the presence of foreign antigens to which IgG molecules are directed (4, 18). Furthermore, the binding of immune complexes to macrophages triggers not only phagocytosis of sensitized particles but also the release of potent mediators of inflammation such as elastase, plasminogen activator, activated oxygen intermediates, leukotrienes, and prostaglandins (5, 7, 15, 16, 22). Because of the discrepant results which have been reported when FcRs for IgG have been isolated by affinity chromatography on immobilized IgG columns, we were particularly interested in obtaining monoclonal anti-FcR reagents.

MOUSE FcRγ HETEROGENEITY

Analysis of mouse macrophage FcR is complicated by the presence of three FcR binding sites with specificity for IgG2a, IgG2b/IgG1, and IgG3 mouse IgG subclasses. The experiments were based on inhibition by aggregated mouse myeloma proteins of the binding of erythrocytes sensitized with monoclonal antibodies to mouse macrophages (1–3). Furthermore, variant macrophage cell lines have been isolated which lack $FcR_{\gamma 2b/\gamma 1}$ (21) and $FcR_{\gamma 3}$ (3) or which fail to ingest via $FcR_{\gamma 2a}$ (1). This evidence, together with the trypsin sensitivity of the IgG2a binding site (20), supports the thesis that there exist independent FcR sites for the different IgG subclasses. However, it should be noted that monomeric IgG subclasses are reported to compete for binding (6, 17). Interestingly, although the binding of IgG2a- and IgG2b-sensitized erythrocytes can be differentiated by the sensitivity of the former to low temperature and cytochalasin B (1), the different mouse IgG subclasses apparently all promote phagocytosis and mediate antibody-dependent cellular cytotoxicity (14).

ISOLATION AND SPECIFICITY OF AN ANTI-FcRγ2b/γ1 MONOCLONAL ANTIBODY

In our experiments spleen cells from a rat immunized with mouse macrophage cell lines $P338D_1$ and J774 were fused with the P3U1 myeloma line. The conditioned media from the hybrid clones were screened for ability to inhibit rosetting of the J774 cell line with IgG2b-coated erythrocytes. The rationale behind this experiment was that an antibody would have to be directed against a determinant on the receptor to block rosetting effectively. Indeed, although we have isolated many hybridoma antibodies directed against macrophage determinants (10), only one (2.4G2 IgG) inhibited FcR function (19). After purification of 2.4G2 IgG from ascites, the antibody was digested with papain to generate the Fab fragment. Preincubation of macrophages with the Fab fragment, which can interact with macrophages only through its antigenic binding site, inhibited rosettes formed with IgG2b- and IgG1-sensitized erythrocytes; there was no effect on the binding of IgG2a or IgG3.

The binding of ^{125}I-labeled 2.4G2Fab to cell lines was then correlated with the ability of the cells to form rosettes with IgG-sensitized erythrocytes. In addition, we examined the effects of

[1] Present address: Section on Cell Biology, Yale University School of Medicine, New Haven, CT 06520.

TABLE 1. Purification of FcR from J774 tumors by affinity chromatography with 2.4G2Fab-Sepharose

Fraction[a]	Protein (mg)	[^{35}S]methionine (cpm)	FcR recovered (U)[b]	Specific activity (U/mg of protein)
Nonidet P-40 homogenate	1,337.7	3.36 × 10^7	139	0.1
Column eluate	0.149	1.38 × 10^4	79	530
Recovery (%)	0.011	0.041	57	

[a] The initial homogenate was centrifuged to remove nuclei; the resulting supernatant was designated the Nonidet P-40 homogenate.

[b] A unit was defined as the amount of FcR which resulted in binding of 1 μg of ^{125}I-labeled 2.4G2Fab to concanavalin A-Sepharose.

preincubation of macrophages with 2.4G2 IgG on FcR activity. Only the cell lines that formed rosettes with IgG-sensitized erythrocytes bound labeled 2.4G2 IgG, and IgG rosettes were blocked by preincubation of the cells with 2.4G2 IgG. These observations suggest that the antigen to which 2.4G2 IgG binds may be the principal FcR detected by conventional rosette formation with rabbit IgG-sensitized cells. In addition to macrophage-like cell lines, spleen cells, the B cell line WEHI-231, the T cell line S49.1, and null lymphocytic cell lines P388 and PU5.1 bound ^{125}I-labeled 2.4G2Fab. The antigen was largely (>95%) absent from a set of J774 variant which lacked the ability to bind IgG2b-sensitized erythrocytes but still bound IgG2a normally (21). Unfortunately, 2.4G2 IgG neither bound to nor inhibited receptors on macrophages from other species, including rat, rabbit, hamster, and human. However, the potential usefulness of this reagent in studies of mouse antibody-mediated events is demonstrated in two recent reports which study blockage by 2.4G2 IgG of antibody-dependent cellular cytotoxicity (12) and antibody-mediated enhancement of West Nile virus infectivity for macrophages (13), a model for Dengue virus hemorrhagic disease.

CHARACTERIZATION OF FcR$_{\gamma 2b/\gamma 1}$

The receptor was purified (11) from Nonidet P-40 detergent lysates of J774 tumors by batch adsorption of the antigen onto 2.4G2Fab-Sepharose. The immunoadsorbent was then repeatedly washed with a sodium dodecyl sulfate–Nonidet P-40 mixture before the bound receptor was eluted by a pH 11.5 deoxycholate-triethylamine buffer. The eluate was then rapidly neutralized with Tris-hydrochloride. To assess recovery of the glycosylated receptor, we took advantage of the binding of ^{125}I-labeled 2.4G2Fab-receptor complexes to small concanavalin A-Sepharose columns, which do not retain the ^{125}I-labeled Fab fragment. The purification procedure (Table 1) resulted in a 60% recovery of antigen with overall 5,000-fold purification. This is roughly consistent with the theoretical amount of antigen present on the J774 cell line, which has 500,000 2.4G2 Fab binding sites per cell.

The purified receptor from J774 cells displayed two very broad and poorly resolved peptides of 47,000 and 60,000 M_r. Tentative results based on two-dimensional thin-layer peptide mapping of trypsin and chymotrypsin digests of the large and small peptides cut from polyacrylamide gels indicated that the two proteins are related and that the larger protein has some peptides which are absent from the smaller one. This suggests that a proteolytic event was responsible for the generation of the two peptides. This is substantiated by the observation that trypsinization of J774 cells, which does not destroy either the activity of FcR$_{\gamma 2b/\gamma 1}$ or the binding of 2.4G2Fab to cells, converted the 60,000 M_r protein to the 47,000 M_r species. However, FcR immunoprecipitated from a variety of cell types after surface iodination showed considerable variability in M_r. The antigen isolated from thioglycolate-elicited macrophages had only one broad peptide of 47,000 M_r, whereas the receptor from WEHI-231, a B cell line, had an M_r of 70,000. These differences may relate to the more active secretion of neutral hydrolases by thioglycolate-elicited macrophages compared with the B cell line.

FcR$_{\gamma 2b/\gamma 1}$ is an integral membrane protein, which can be solubilized from isolated membranes only by detergent. As commonly observed for integral viral membrane proteins, in the absence of detergent, the purified receptor forms large aggregates. These aggregates still retain receptor activity, as is evident from the hyperagglutination that the purified detergent-free FcR induces when added to IgG-coated erythrocytes. Controls of F(ab')$_2$-sensitized erythrocytes showed no effect. The agglutination of IgG-sensitized erythrocytes mediated by FcR preparations was particularly dramatic when monoclonal antibodies, which do not hem-

TABLE 2. Binding of ^{125}I-labeled FcR to Sephadex or erythrocytes coated with IgG

Prepn	Binding (% of input ^{125}I-FcR)
DNP^a-Sephadex–rabbit anti-DNP (Fab')$_2$	0.21
DNP-Sephadex–rabbit anti-DNP IgG	29
DNP-Sephadex–anti-DNP IgG2b	28
DNP-Sephadex–anti-DNP IgG1	7.6
DNP-Sephadex–anti-DNP IgG3	0.46
IgG2a Sephadex	25
Erythrocytes.........................	0.43
IgG2b erythrocytes	49
IgG1 erythrocytes	18
IgG2a erythrocytes	28

^{a} DNP, Dinitrophenol.

agglutinate efficiently, were used as sensitizing agents. However, the specificity of the detergent-free FcR for IgG subclasses was broader than previous results on the inhibition of binding of subclasses by the 2.4G2Fab fragment would indicate. IgG2a-sensitized erythrocytes were agglutinated in addition to IgG2b- and IgG1-sensitized cells. Similar results were found when the binding of ^{125}I-labeled FcR to IgG-coated Sephadex beads was measured directly (Table 2).

However, tentative results from this laboratory suggest that the apparent IgG2a specificity of isolated FcR$_{\gamma2b/\gamma1}$ in the absence of detergent is an artifact. Although the iodinated FcR binds to IgG2b in the presence of Nonidet P-40, and to a lesser extent to IgG1-coated surfaces, it did not bind to IgG2a. In addition, purified receptor from a cell line which does not bind IgG2a, S49.1, will also bind to IgG2a in the absence of detergent. It is possible that the FcR$_{\gamma2a}$ is formed by aggregation of the FcR$_{\gamma2b/\gamma1}$ receptor and that such aggregation cannot occur on the plasma membrane of S49.1 cells. Alternatively, S49.1 may lack ancillary proteins which may be sensitive to trypsinization, thus accounting for the trypsin sensitivity of FcR$_{\gamma2a}$. Obviously, our understanding of the relation of FcR$_{\gamma2a}$ and FcR$_{\gamma2b/\gamma1}$ is incomplete. A recent report (9) claims that the 60,000 M_r protein is the FcR$_{\gamma2a}$ and a 52,000 M_r protein is FcR$_{\gamma2b/\gamma1}$. If confirmed, the structural comparison of these two proteins should be quite interesting.

We have recently prepared a monospecific rabbit anti-FcR serum by immunizing with purified FcR. This serum blocks FcR activity on J774 cells at high dilution and immunoprecipitates the same two peptides as 2.4G2 IgG. Tentative results show that the antiserum will precipitate a 46,000 M_r peptide from a wheat germ translation system primed with S49.1 mRNA, thus identifying the primary translation product. This is a crucial step in our current attempt to isolate an FcR cDNA clone. Such a probe, in addition to furthering the obvious goal of obtaining sequence information, would enable us to map the gene and possibly to study closely related receptors as well. The monoclonal antibody we have made has enormously simplified the task of purification of the receptor, and we hope that new antibodies we are currently making against purified receptor will be of value in defining receptor domains and in facilitating our understanding of the mechanisms of receptor function.

ACKNOWLEDGMENTS

The work reported here was supported by Public Health Service grant AI-14603 from the National Institute of Allergy and Infectious Diseases. J.C.U. is an Andrew W. Mellon Foundation fellow and recipient of a Faculty Research Award (FRA-205) from the American Cancer Society. I.S.M. is recipient of a Junior Faculty Research Award (JFRA-26) from the American Cancer Society.

LITERATURE CITED

1. Diamond, B., B. R. Bloom, and M. D. Scharff. 1978. The Fc receptors of primary and cultured phagocytic cells studies with homogenous antibodies. J. Immunol. 121:1329–1333.
2. Diamond, B., and M. D. Scharff. 1980. IgG1 and IgG2b share the Fc receptor on mouse macrophages. J. Immunol. 125:631–633.
3. Diamond, B., and D. E. Yelton. 1981. A new Fc receptor on mouse macrophages binding IgG3. J. Exp. Med. 153:514–519.
4. Dickler, H. B. 1976. Lymphocyte receptors for immunoglobulin. Adv. Immunol. 24:167–214.
5. Gordon, S., J. Unkeless, and Z. A. Cohn. 1974. Induction of macrophage plasminogen activator by endotoxin stimulation and phagocytosis. J. Exp. Med. 140:995–1010.
6. Haeffner-Cavaillon, N., M. Klein, and K. J. Dorrington. 1979. Studies on the Fc$_\gamma$ receptor of the murine macrophage-like cell line Pe88D$_1$. I. The binding of homologous and heterologous immunoglobulin G. J. Immunol. 123:1905–1913.
7. Johnston, R. B., Jr., J. E. Lehmeyer, and L. A. Guthrie. 1976. Generation of superoxide anion and chemiluminescence by human monocytes during phagocytosis and on contact with surface bound immunoglobulin G. J. Exp. Med. 143:1551–1556.
8. Kohler, G., and C. Milstein. 1975. Continuous cultures of fused cells secreting antibody of predefined specificity. Nature (London) 256:495–497.
9. Lane, B. C., J. Kan-Mitchell, M. S. Mitchell, and S. M. Cooper. 1980. Structural evidence for distinct IgG subclass-specific Fc receptors on mouse peritoneal macrophages. J. Exp. Med. 152:1147–1161.
10. Mellman, I. S., R. M. Steinman, J. C. Unkeless, and Z. A. Cohn. 1980. Selective iodination and polypeptide composition of pinocytic vesicles. J. Cell Biol. 86:712–722.
11. Mellman, I. S., and J. C. Unkeless. 1980. Purification of a functional mouse Fc receptor through the use of a monoclonal antibody. J. Exp. Med. 152:1048–1069.
12. Nathan, C., L. Brukner, G. Kaplan, J. Unkeless, and Z. A. Cohn. 1980. Role of activated macrophages in antibody-dependent lysis of tumor cells. J. Exp. Med. 152:183–197.
13. Peiris, J. S. M., S. Gordon, J. C. Unkeless, and J. S.

Porterfield. 1981. Monoclonal anti-Fc receptor IgG blocks antibody enhancement of viral replication in macrophages. Nature (London) 289:189–191.

14. Ralph, P., I. Nakoinz, B. Diamond, and D. Yelton. 1980. All classes of murine IgG antibody mediate macrophage phagocytosis and lysis of erythrocytes. J. Immunol. 125:1885–1888.

15. Rouzer, C. A., W. A. Scott, A. L. Hamill, and Z. A. Cohn. 1980. Dynamics of leukotriene C production by macrophages. J. Exp. Med. 152:1236–1247.

16. Rouzer, C. A., W. A. Scott, J. Kempe, and Z. A. Cohn. 1980. Prostaglandin synthesis by macrophages requires a specific receptor-ligand interaction. Proc. Natl. Acad. Sci. U.S.A. 77:4279–4282.

17. Segal, D. M., and J. A. Titus. 1978. The subclass specificity for the binding of murine myeloma proteins to macrophage and lymphocyte cell lines and to normal spleen cells. J. Immunol. 120:1395–1403.

18. Silverstein, S. C., R. M. Steinman, and Z. A. Cohn. 1977. Endocytosis. Annu. Rev. Biochem. 46:669–722.

19. Unkeless, J. C. 1979. Characterization of a monoclonal antibody directed against mouse macrophage and lymphocyte Fc receptors. J. Exp. Med. 150:580–596.

20. Unkeless, J. C., and H. Eisen. 1975. Binding of monomeric immunoglobulins to Fc receptors of mouse macrophages. J. Exp. Med. 142:1520–1533.

21. Unkeless, J. C., G. Kaplan, H. Plutner, and Z. A. Cohn. 1979. Fc-receptor variants of a mouse macrophage cell line. Proc. Natl. Acad. Sci. U.S.A. 76:1400–1404.

22. Werb, Z., and S. Gordon. 1975. Elastase secretion by stimulated macrophages. Characterization and regulation. J. Exp. Med. 142:361–377.

Topography and Function of C3b Receptors on Human Peripheral Blood Cells

DOUGLAS T. FEARON

Departments of Medicine, Brigham and Women's Hospital and Harvard Medical School, Boston, Massachusetts 02115

Cells and immune complexes that have activated the complement system acquire the capacity to adhere to primate erythrocytes, podocytes of the glomerulus, and immunological effector cells such as polymorphonuclear leukocytes (PMN), monocyte/macrophages, B lymphocytes, and mast cells. The adherence is mediated by C3b, or its degradation products, C3bi and C3d, which are affixed to the complement-activating material, and by specific receptors for each of these fragments of C3 that are present on the plasma membranes of these cell types (Table 1). These adherence reactions facilitate phagocytic responses of neutrophils and monocyte/macrophages, and may have roles in the immune response of B lymphocytes. Recently, the C3b receptor (5, 6) and the C3d receptor (11) of human cells have been purified to homogeneity, and monospecific antisera to these membrane proteins have been prepared. This report reviews some of the findings that have evolved from purification of the C3b receptor.

The function of C3b receptors is related to the dual binding sites of its ligand, C3b, which is the major cleavage fragment of the third component of complement. During the conversion of C3 to C3b by proteolytic cleavage of C3a from the parent molecule, an internal thiol ester between cysteine and glutamic acid residues of the α polypeptide chain (20) apparently breaks to yield a reactive carbonyl. For a brief time, the carbonyl may form an ester, and possibly an amide, linkage with constituents of the activating complex to result in firm, covalent attachment of the C3b molecule (12). A separate site on the C3b then can reversibly bind to C3b receptors to mediate uptake of the complement-activating material by cells expressing this membrane structure. Thus, C3b can be considered as having two binding sites: a site for relatively nonspecific, covalent attachment to soluble or particulate complexes, and a site for the highly specific, reversible interaction with C3b receptors.

IDENTIFICATION OF THE MEMBRANE GLYCOPROTEIN THAT IS THE C3b RECEPTOR

A glycoprotein of human erythrocyte membranes with an apparent molecular weight of 205,000 (gp 205), as estimated by sodium dodecyl sulfate-polyacrylamide gel electrophoresis, was purified to homogeneity based on its capacity to inhibit the alternative complement pathway (5). The glycoprotein accelerated decay of the amplification C3 convertase of this pathway and promoted cleavage-inactivation of C3b by C3b inactivator. As these inhibitory activities, and the reversible adsorption of the glycoprotein by Sepharose-C3, indicated that the gp 205 had an affinity for C3b, its possible identity as the C3b receptor was examined.

Rabbit antibody to gp 205 was prepared and assessed for its capacity to inhibit the adherence of sheep erythrocytes bearing C3b (EC3b) to human erythrocytes. Human erythrocytes were pretreated with buffer or with increasing concentrations of pre-immunization rabbit immunoglobulin G (IgG) or with IgG anti-gp 205, washed, and then incubated with sheep EC3b in microtiter wells. A positive immune adherence reaction, which was seen as a blanket of cells on the bottom of the wells (Fig. 1), was not impaired by any dose of pre-immunization IgG, whereas anti-gp 205 inhibited the adherence of sheep EC3b to human erythrocytes in doses ranging from 640 to 10 μg of IgG/10^8 human erythrocytes (Fig. 1). Since anti-gp 205 impaired the function of C3b receptors of human erythrocytes, gp 205 was considered to be the C3b receptor of these cells.

To determine whether the C3b receptor of other cells was related to gp 205, PMN, monocytes, partially purified B lymphocytes, and erythrocytes were incubated with sheep EC3b in buffer alone or buffer containing increasing concentrations of F(ab')$_2$ anti-gp 205, and the percentage of cells forming rosettes with EC3b was

TABLE 1. Human cells expressing receptors for C3b, C3bi, and C3d

Cell type	Receptor			References
	C3b	C3bi	C3d	
Erythrocyte	+	?	−	16
Neutrophil	+	+	−	9[a]
Monocyte/macrophage	+	+	−	3, 10[a]
B lymphocyte	+	+	+	3, 13, 19
Glomerular podocyte	+	?	?	8

[a] G. D. Ross and E. M. Rabellino, Fed. Proc. 33:1467a.

quantitated. Anti-gp 205 inhibited in a dose-response manner the capacity of each cell type to bind sheep EC3b; 50% inhibition was achieved with concentrations of 0.1, 0.9, 1.2, and 1.2 µg/ml for reactions involving erythrocytes, B lymphocytes, PMN, and monocytes, respectively (6). Although this experiment demonstrated that C3b receptors of nucleated cells antigenically resembled gp 205, approximately 10-fold higher concentrations of anti-gp 205 were required for 50% inhibition of their rosette reactions than was necessary for comparable impairment of C3b receptor function on human erythrocytes. This difference reflected the presence of more C3b receptors on the nucleated cells than on erythrocytes, since the former had 20,000 to 60,000 specific ^{125}I-labeled F(ab')$_2$ anti-gp 205 binding sites per cell and the latter expressed only 1,000 sites per cell (6).

More direct evidence for the identity of gp 205 of erythrocytes as the C3b receptor also of peripheral blood nucleated cells was provided by immunoprecipitation of the antigen recognized by anti-gp 205 from these cells. Membrane proteins of erythrocytes, PMN, B lymphocytes, and monocytes were radiolabeled by lactoperox-

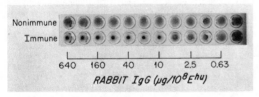

FIG. 1. Inhibition of adherence of human erythrocytes and sheep EC3b by anti-gp 205. Human erythrocytes were pretreated with increasing concentrations of pre-immunization rabbit IgG or with IgG anti-gp 205, washed, and incubated with sheep EC3b in microtiter wells. Adherence with sheep EC3b mediated by C3b receptors on human erythrocytes appears as a diffuse layer of cells on the bottom of the wells, whereas absence of adherence results in all cells forming a button.

idase-catalyzed iodination, after which they were solubilized with nonionic detergent and immunoprecipitated with anti-gp 205. Analysis of the immunoprecipitates by sodium dodecyl sulfate-polyacrylamide gel electrophoresis demonstrated that a single labeled antigen was derived from each cell type which exhibited an apparent molecular weight of 205,000. Thus, gp 205 is the human C3b receptor (6).

ADSORPTIVE PINOCYTOSIS BY C3b RECEPTORS

Functions of membrane receptors may be related to their topographic distribution on cell surfaces. C3b receptors on PMN, monocytes, and B lymphocytes were found to be distributed in small clusters on the plasma membranes of these cells when examined by indirect immunofluorescence after incubation at 0°C with Fab' or F(ab')$_2$ anti-C3b receptor (Fig. 2) (7, 18). This nonrandom distribution was observed even if the cells had been fixed with paraformaldehyde prior to uptake of anti-receptor antibody. This topographic pattern of the C3b receptor suggested that the mobility of the glycoprotein within the plane of the plasma membrane of these cells was restricted. The rate of lateral diffusion of C3b receptors on PMN and monocytes labeled with fluorescein-conjugated Fab' anti-C3b receptor was measured directly by the fluorescent photobleaching recovery method. No measurable lateral diffusion of C3b receptors on PMN or monocytes was observed, indicating a diffusive rate of less than 10^{-11} cm^2/s, which contrasted with a rate of 1.5×10^{-10} cm^2/s for another membrane protein, HLA (18).

The absence of diffusion and the clustered distribution of C3b receptors suggested the possibility of physical interaction with subplasmalemmal elements of the cells and prompted the consideration of specialized functions for the receptor in addition to the binding of C3b-bearing material. Among the biological consequences of this receptor-ligand interaction, those relating to the role of the C3b receptor in phagocytic reactions of PMN and monocytes have been most extensively investigated. C3b receptors are considered to synergistically enhance phagocytosis of C3b-coated particles by these cells, but not to directly mediate internalization of the targets (14, 15); the endocytic process is stimulated by other membrane constituents of the phagocytes, such as Fc receptors which interact with IgG on the targets and trypsin-sensitive receptors on monocytes which recognize particles whose surfaces lack sialic acid (4). Two exceptions to this role of the C3b receptor that is limited to the attachment phase

FIG. 2. Clustered distribution of C3b receptors on PMN. C3b receptors were stained at 0°C by indirect immunofluorescence with F(ab')₂ anti-C3b receptor and examined with the plane of focus at the tops of the cells.

of phagocytosis have been found; mouse peritoneal macrophages (1) that have been functionally altered by a product of T lymphocytes (F. M. Griffin, Jr., J. A. Griffin, and P. J. Mullinax, this volume) and human peripheral blood monocytes that have been held in culture (17) can bind and ingest sheep EC3b.

In contrast to their usual inability to mediate phagocytosis, or the uptake of particles, C3b receptors on PMN have recently been shown to pinocytize F(ab')₂ anti-C3b receptor and C3b that has been cross-linked with F(ab')₂ anti-C3 (7). Neither Fab' anti-receptor nor monomeric C3b was internalized despite binding specifically to C3b receptors. Adsorptive pinocytosis was temperature dependent; cell-bound ligand remained on the plasma membrane when cells were held at 0°C and was internalized within 7 to 10 min on bringing the cells to 37°C. Cytochalasin B, which interacts with cellular actin and blocks many phagocytic reactions, did not impair endocytosis of F(ab')₂ anti-C3b receptor. Therefore, cross-linking C3b receptors with soluble multivalent ligands induces an endocytic response of the receptor, indicating that they may function in clearance of soluble C3b-bearing complexes.

The capacity of the receptor to mediate adsorptive pinocytosis but not phagocytosis probably indicates that the cytoskeletal proteins involved in the two types of endocytic reactions differ. Normal function of microfilaments is essential for phagocytosis, but may not be necessary for receptor-mediated uptake of soluble ligand. The mechanism by which C3b receptors internalize ligand may be related to clathrin-coated regions of the plasma membrane since other receptors that mediate adsorptive pinocytosis have been observed to be internalized via coated pits and coated vesicles (2). Indeed, in

recent studies, visualization by electron microscopy of ferritin-conjugated F(ab')₂ anti-C3b receptor being internalized by PMN and monocytes has localized the receptor-ligand complexes within these structures (D. Abrahamson and D. T. Fearon, unpublished data).

LITERATURE CITED

1. **Bianco, C., F. M. Griffin, Jr., and S. C. Silverstein.** 1975. Studies of the macrophage's complement receptor. Alteration of receptor function upon macrophage activation. J. Exp. Med. **141**:1269–1285.

2. **Brown, M. S., and J. L. Goldstein.** 1979. Receptor-mediated endocytosis: insights from the lipoprotein receptor system. Proc. Natl. Acad. Sci. U.S.A. **76**:3330–3334.

3. **Carlo, J. R., S. Ruddy, E. J. Streuler, and D. H. Conrad.** 1979. Complement receptor binding of C3b-coated cells treated with C3b inactivator, β1H and trypsin. J. Immunol. **123**:523–528.

4. **Czop, J K., D. T. Fearon, and K. F. Austen.** 1978. Membrane sialic acid on target particles modulates their phagocytosis by a trypsin-sensitive mechanism on human monocytes. Proc. Natl. Acad. Sci. U.S.A. **75**:3831–3835.

5. **Fearon, D. T.** 1979. Regulation of the amplification C3 convertase of human complement by an inhibitory protein isolated from human erythrocyte membranes. Proc. Natl. Acad. Sci. U.S.A. **76**:5867–5871.

6. **Fearon, D. T.** 1980. Identificaton of the membrane glycoprotein that is the C3b receptor of the human erythrocyte, polymorphonuclear leukocyte, β lymphocyte, and monocyte. J. Exp. Med. **152**:20–30.

7. **Fearon, D. T., I. Kaneko, and G. G. Thomson.** 1981. Membrane distribution and adsorptive endocytosis by C3b receptors on human polymorphonuclear leukocytes. J. Exp. Med. **153**:1615–1628.

8. **Gelfand, M., M. M. Frank, and I. Green.** 1975. A receptor for the third component of complement in the human renal glomerulus. J. Exp. Med. **142**:1029–1035.

9. **Gigli, I., and R. A. Nelson, Jr.** 1968. Complement-dependent immune phagocytosis. I. Requirements for C'1, C'4, C'3. Exp. Cell Res. **51**:45–53.

10. **Huber, R., J. J. Polley, W. D. Linscott, H. H. Fudenberg, and H. J. Müller-Eberhard.** 1968. Human monocytes. Distinct receptor sites for the third component of complement and for immunoglobulin G. Science **162**:1281–1284.

11. **Lambris, J. D., N. J. Dobson, and G. D. Ross.** 1981. Isolation of lymphocyte membrane complement receptor type two (the C3d receptor) and preparation of receptor-specific antibody. Proc. Natl. Acad. Sci. U.S.A. **78**:1828–1832.

12. **Law, S. K., and R. P. Levine.** 1977. Interaction between third complement protein and cell surface macromolecules. Proc. Natl. Acad. Sci. U.S.A. **74**:2701–2705.

13. **Lay, W. H., and V. Nussenzweig.** 1968. Receptors for complement on leukocytes. J. Exp. Med. **128**:991–1008.

14. **Mantovani, B.** 1975. Different roles of IgG and complement receptors in phagocytosis by polymorphonuclear leukocytes. J. Immunol. **115**:15–20.

15. **Mantovani, B., M. Rabinovitch, and V. Nussenzweig.** 1972. Phagocytosis of immune complexes by macrophages. Different roles of the macrophage receptor sites for complement (C3) and for immunoglobulin. J. Exp. Med. **135**:780–794.

16. **Nelson, D. S.** 1963. Immune adherence. Adv. Immunol. **3**:131–180.

17. **Newman, S. L., R. A. Musson, and P. M. Henson.** 1980. Development of functional complement receptors during *in vitro* maturation of human monocytes into macrophages. J. Immunol. **125**:2236–2244.

18. **Petty, H. R., L. M. Smith, D. T. Fearon, and H. M. McConnell.** 1980. Lateral distribution and diffusion of the

C3b receptor of complement, HLA antigens and lipid probes in peripheral blood leukocytes. Proc. Natl. Acad. Sci. U.S.A. **77:**6587–6591.

19. **Ross, G. D., M. J. Polley, E. M. Rabellino, and H. M. Grey.** 1973. Two different complement receptors on human lymphocytes: one specific for C3b and one specific for C3b inactivator-cleaved C3b. J. Exp. Med. **138:**798–814.

20. **Tack, B. F., R. A. Harrison, J. Janatova, M. L. Thomas, and J. W. Prahl.** 1980. Evidence for the presence of an internal thiolester bond in third component of human complement. Proc. Natl. Acad. Sci. U.S.A. **77:**5764–5768.

AUTHOR INDEX

Subject Index

Adhesion, bacterial
  colonization of intestine by autochthonous bacteria, 274
  colonization of respiratory tract by *P. aeruginosa*, 348
  contributions of lipoteichoic acids in dental disease, 338
  genetic control of type I fimbriae in *E. coli*, 308
  influence of saliva on, 282
  of autochthonous bacteria to tissue surfaces, 266
  of *E. coli* to uroepithelia, 286
  of streptococci to hydroxyapatite, 342
  pathogenic mechanisms mediated by pili, 305
  role in disease caused by neisseriae, 292
  role in pathogenesis, 261
  role of capsular polysaccharide in, 335
  role of mucus gel system of the gut, 278
  role of *N. gonorrhoeae* surface proteins, 301
  role of streptococcal exopolysaccharides, 331
  role of surface polymers of *S. pyogenes*, 327
  specificity of fimbriae and fimbrial receptors, 317
  surface structures involved in, 296
Aggregation, induction by sex pheromones, 101
Amino acid sequence conservation in MLS resistance determinants, 159
Aminoglycoside-aminocyclitol antibiotics, resistance of streptococci to, 162
α-Amylases, regulation of production and molecular cloning, 8
Antibiotic resistance
  conjugative transfer in beta-hemolytic streptococci, 105
  in hemolytic streptococci, 147
  in *S. pneumoniae*, 177
  in *S. pyogenes*, 151
  transduction within and between streptococcal groups, 112
Antifungal defense by macrophages, 385
Antimicrobial synergism, enterococcal response to, 195
Aphidicolin, effect on *Bacillus* small phages, 45
Attachment (*see* Adhesion, bacterial)
Autochthonous bacteria
  colonization of the intestine, 274
  colonization of tissue surfaces, 266

B-cell receptors, 391, 393
B cells, receptor-mediated activation of, 398
Bacilli, site-specific restriction endodeoxyribonucleases in, 66
Bacillus small phages, DNA replication, 45
Bacillus subtilis
  functions of RNA polymerase core-associated polypeptides, 58
  heterospecific gene expression in, 22
  initiation of chromosome replication in, 47
  molecular cloning in, 15
  molecular events during transformation in, 62
  physical map of rRNA genes, 28

  recombination between phage and plasmid vectors in, 5
  RNA processing in, 32
Bacillus subtilis α-amylases, regulation of production and molecular cloning, 8
Bacillus subtilis chromosome
  novel promoters of, 51
Bacillus subtilis genes, isolation from Charon libraries, 3
Bacillus subtilis plasmid, construction of, 15
Bacillus subtilis restriction endonucleases, genetic study of, 71
Bacillus subtilis ribosomal genes, comparison with *E. coli*, 19
Bacillus subtilis transduction, dependence on transformation competence, 12
Bacteriocins
  of lactic streptococci, 225
  production and transfer in streptococci, 221
Bacteroides fragilis, role of capsular polysaccharide in pathogenicity, 335
Beta-hemolytic streptococci, conjugative transfer of antibiotic resistance in, 105

Capsular polysaccharide, role in *B. fragilis* pathogenicity, 335
Carbohydrate metabolism in streptococci, 232
Cell surface
  complement receptors on human peripheral blood cells, 410
  Fc receptors on, 406
Cell surface proteins of *S. mutans*, synthesis and function in *E. coli*, 253
Cell surface receptors, 391, 393
Charon libraries, isolation of *B. subtilis* genes from, 3
Chromosomal resistance determinants
  conjugative transfer of, 88
  of *S. agalactiae*, 170
Chromosome replication, initiation in *B. subtilis*, 47
Cloned donor DNA from *B. subtilis*, 62
Cloned genes of *B. subtilis*, 3
Cloning in streptococci, 234
Cloning of the replication origin, 41
Colonization by autochthonous bacteria
  intestine, 274
  tissue surfaces, 266
Colonization of the respiratory tract, host and bacterial factors in, 348
Competence for transformation in *S. pneumoniae*, 136
Complement receptors
  on human peripheral blood cells, 410
  phagocytosis mediated by, 402
Conjugative properties of plasmid variants, 97
Conjugative R determinants, evidence for transposition in *S. agalactiae*, 109
Conjugative transfer
  of antibiotic resistance in beta-hemolytic streptococci, 105
  of chromosomal resistance determinants, 88
Core-associated polypeptides, functions of, 58

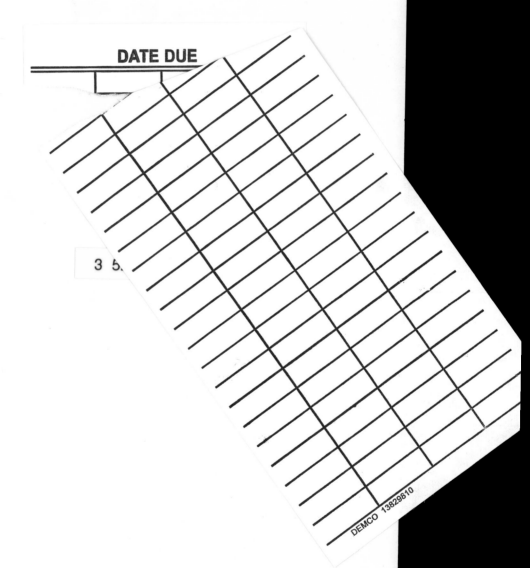

DATE DUE

3 5

DEMCO 13829810